THIS BLESSED PLOT

THIS
BLESSED PLOT

Britain and Europe from Churchill to Blair

HUGO YOUNG

THE OVERLOOK PRESS
Woodstock · New York

First published in the United States in 1999 by
The Overlook Press, Peter Mayer Publishers, Inc.
Lewis Hollow Road
Woodstock, New York 12498

ISBN: 0-87951-939-8

3 5 7 9 8 6 4 2

A CIP catalog record for this book is available from
The Library of Congress.

Typeset by SetSystems Ltd, Saffron Walden, Essex

To L, of course

Contents

Acknowledgements

I WOULD LIKE to thank, first of all, my sources for this history, beyond the published works cited in the Bibliography. In the nature of things, many of them were quite old when I spoke to them, and a number have since died. Those whom I can only posthumously acknowledge, but from whom I captured moments of their fugitive wisdom early in my inquiry, include: Lord Amery (formerly Julian Amery), George Ball, Lord Gladwyn (formerly Gladwyn Jebb), Emile van Lennep, Emile Noël, Sir Frank Roberts, John Robinson, Maurice Schumann, Lord Sherfield (formerly Roger Makins), Dirk Spierenburg and Lord Thorneycroft (formerly Peter Thorneycroft).

Of living participants, whom I saw for the purposes of constructing the story, and who are mostly cited in the text, I would like to thank particularly: Lord Armstrong of Ilminster (formerly Robert Armstrong), Jean-René Bernard, Georges Berthoin, Jean-Pierre Brunet, Sir Michael Butler, William Cash, Lord Chalfont, Maurice Couve de Murville, Lord Croham (formerly Douglas Allen), Sir Roy Denman, Lord Hailsham, Sir David Hannay, Sir Edward Heath, Lord Hunt of Tanworth (formerly John Hunt), Sir Curtis Keeble, Sir Donald Maitland, Sir Michael Palliser, Lord Rodgers of Quarry Bank (formerly William Rodgers), Lord Roll of Ipsden (formerly Eric Roll), Sir Crispin Tickell, Ernst van der Beugel and Edmund Wellenstein.

There are a number of other public people with whom I have talked, in some cases often, about the themes and history the book addresses. They include: Antonio Armellini, Paddy Ashdown, Tony Benn, Lord Biffen (formerly John Biffen), Tony Blair, Sir Leon Brittan, Gordon Brown, Charles Clarke, Kenneth Clarke, Lord Cockfield, Robin Cook, Tam Dalyell, Jacques Delors, Andrew Duff, Lord Garel-Jones (formerly Tristan Garel-Jones), Lord Gilmour of Craigmillar (formerly Ian Gilmour), Lord Hattersley (formerly Roy Hattersley), Lord Healey (formerly Denis Healey), Sir Nicholas Henderson, Michael Heseltine, Lord Howe of Aberavon (formerly Geoffrey Howe), Lord Hurd (formerly Douglas Hurd), Lord Jenkins of Hillhead (formerly Roy Jenkins), Sir John Kerr, Neil Kinnock, Helmut Kohl, Norman Lamont, Ruud Lubbers, John Major, Peter Mandelson, Geoffrey Martin, Denis McShane, Sir Christopher Meyer, Lord Owen (formerly David Owen), Chris Patten, Michael Portillo, Sir Charles Powell, Giles Radice, Lord Renwick of

Clifton (formerly Robin Renwick), Sir Malcolm Rifkind, Lord Ryder of Wensum (formerly Richard Ryder), Robert Schaetzel, Richard Shepherd, Lord Shore of Stepney (formerly Peter Shore), Lady Thatcher (formerly Margaret Thatcher), Sir Roger Tomkys, Lord Tugendhat, William Waldegrave, Karel Van Miert, Lode Willems and Robert Worcester. I am more grateful to them than perhaps they, or I, knew at the time.

Among professional friends and colleagues in the same category are John Newhouse, Anthony Sampson and William Wallace.

I have some particular personal debts: to Anthony Teasdale, who instructed me a great deal in contemporary Euro-politics; to Phillip Whitehead, with whom I made a series of films for Channel Four TV, *The Last Europeans*, that provided substantial momentum for the book I had already begun; to Sir Christopher Audland, also a first-hand source, who read and helpfully commented on the early chapters; and especially to John Pinder, one of the great scholars of contemporary Euro-British history, who read the entire text, saved me from numerous errors of fact and nuance, and is at fault for none that remain.

As my agents, I am fortunate to have Graham Greene and Ed Victor, both of whom kept pushing this project on its way. At Macmillan's, I want to thank Ian Chapman, for his encouraging personal enthusiasm for the book as it emerged; Tanya Stobbs, for overseeing its transmission into print; and Josine Meijer, for her inventive picture research. A little beyond Macmillan's, Peter James again applied his unsurpassed punctilio as an editor, and Sarah Ereira compiled with her usual creativity what is an essential reader-service in this kind of book, the index.

Behind all these people, however, there is the most indispensable source of material for any history: other texts and papers. For their assistance and sometimes their tolerance with my delayed returns, I thank the staff of the London Library, the Chatham House Library and the Research Department at the *Guardian*. Still more vital is the Public Record Office at Kew: a luxuriant secret outpost of the public sector, where there is so much to discover, and the staff are very helpful. Of the many books listed in the bibliography, I feel a particular weight of gratitude to two, constantly consulted: Michael Charlton's irreplaceable work, *The Price of Victory*, and *The Penguin Companion to European Union*, by Timothy Bainbridge with Anthony Teasdale.

Closer to home, Dominic Young again helped generously to teach me how to use my systems, his tolerance for my computer-dumbness putting to shame the impatience I used to show when trying to teach him Latin. Most of all, though, my debt is to Lucy Waring Young, whose affectionate enthusiasm, sustained over several years, has been my strongest influence. It was strange to discover the ways in which a maker of things seen is in the same line of creative business as a documentary writer, and can teach him a lot about how to tell a story. I owe her, in the largest sense, everything.

That said, this is my book. Nobody else is responsible for any part of it. It was finished, by chance, on the day in May when the terms and membership of the European single currency were formally agreed by the European Council, led by Tony Blair, in Brussels. There will be developments beyond that, to incorporate in another edition. There will also certainly be errors to correct and gaps to fill: and many readers, I am sure, could help improve the record. If they feel inclined, they could write to me, c/o Ed Victor Ltd, 6 Bayley St, Bedford Square, London WC1B 3HB.

HUGO YOUNG

Hampstead
3 May 1998

List of Illustrations

This royal throne of kings, this scepter'd isle,
This earth of majesty, this seat of Mars,
This other Eden, demi-paradise,
This fortress built by Nature for herself
Against infection and the hand of war,
This happy breed of men, this little world,
This precious stone set in the silver sea,
Which serves it in the office of a wall,
Or as a moat defensive to a house,
Against the envy of less happier lands,
This blessed plot, this earth, this realm, this England.

William Shakespeare, *Richard II*, Act 2, scene 1

A day will come when you, France; you, Italy; you, England; you, Germany; all you nations of the continent, without losing your distinct qualities and glorious individuality, will merge into a higher unity and found the European brotherhood.

Victor Hugo, 1849

Introduction: The Plot

THIS IS THE STORY of fifty years in which Britain struggled to reconcile the past she could not forget with the future she could not avoid. It is the history of an attitude to history itself. It is a record not of triumph, but rather of bewilderment concerning a question which lay in wait, throughout the period, to trouble successive leaders of the nation, and which latterly tested some of them to destruction. Could Britain, the question ran, truly accept that her modern destiny was to be a European country?

At the beginning of the half-century, with a world war barely over, Winston Churchill first placed on record the outline of a new, united Europe. At the end of it, an agreement was signed, under the collaborative eye of Prime Minister Blair, who was at the time the chairman of what we mean by 'Europe', to create a single currency for the European Union. There was an uneasy continuity between these two moments of creative apotheosis. Both Mr Churchill and Mr Blair, at their different times and from their own vantage-points, were spectators rather than actors in a continental drama from which Britain, the island nation, chose to exclude herself.

Plots of several kinds run through the saga.

The first is certainly blessed. The mythology of the scepter'd isle, the demi-paradise, bit deep into the consciousness of many who addressed the question, beginning with Churchill himself. The sacredness of England, whether or not corrupted into Britain, became a quality setting it, in some minds, for ever apart from Europe. Tampering with this blessed plot was seen for decades as a kind of sacrilege which, even if the sophisticates among the political class could accept it, the people would never tolerate.

The island people were not only different but, mercifully, separate, housed behind their moat. They were also inestimably superior, as was shown by history both ancient and modern: by the resonance of the Empire on which the sun never set, but equally by the immediate circumstances out of which the new Europe was born, the war itself. In that war, there had been only one unambiguous victor among European peoples, and she was not to be found on the mainland. The defence of historic uniqueness, against contamination from across the silver sea, was one powerful explanation for the course the British took during these fifty years.

But the plot was also tortuous. Little in the story was very straight. The nation's thinking about itself lurched between different destinies. Hanging on to the past, in the form of the post-imperial Commonwealth, seemed for a time to be the answer. Remaining constant to the Anglo-American relationship, the most powerful bond in the English-speaking world, was apparently another necessity, which would be fatally compromised by the lure of something called the European Community. The idea that these amounted to alternative choices, the one necessarily imperilling the other, afflicted the decision of all leaders from Churchill to Margaret Thatcher, if not beyond.

Such convolutions, however, were also personal as much as collective. Every individual story, as well as the national story, had its complexities. On no question of this period did more people in British public life change their minds than on Europe. There were conversions from one side to the other, and sometimes back again, each position often being held with a passion summoned from the realm of faith more than reason, where there are secret uncertainties that only the loudest voice can mask. Many, who first opposed British entry, later decided they had been wrong. Many others, who helped take Britain in, became virulent critics of their own handiwork. This made for a serpentine plot on several levels.

On top of that, though, the story was also, in many eyes, devious: not just a plot but a conspiracy. The making of Britain into a European country was accomplished, according to a sceptical reading of events, only by deception. The *de jure* transformation brought about by the British signature on the Treaty of Rome was not, we learned, a true conversion. The full-hearted consent of the people was never obtained, for the simple reason that the true nature of the contract was never put to them. This was subterfuge most foul.

Such were the plots which history has to disentangle. Beside them stand two less complicated truths, that help make sense of the historian's task.

The first is that Britain's resolution of her destiny, while it grew out of many strands quite different from those that influenced the continental states, was dominated by one – above all others. For the makers of the original 'Europe', beginning to fulfil Victor Hugo's dream, their creation was a triumph. Out of defeat they produced a new kind of victory. For Britain, by contrast, the entry into Europe was a defeat: a fate she had resisted, a necessity reluctantly accepted, the last resort of a once great power, never for one moment a climactic or triumphant engagement with the construction of Europe. This has been integral in the national psyche, perhaps only half articulated, since 1973. The sense of the Community as a place of British failure – proof of Britain's failed independence, site of her failed domination – is deep in the undertow of the tides and whirlpools this book attempts to chart.

The second narrative truth here implied is more contentious. Hindsight may be an unrespectable tool, but there are times when its application is inescapable. High political misjudgement is the thread running through this history. This is not an opinion, but a surely incontestable fact. It is proved by the outcome, Britain's presence inside the European apparatus. Since this is what did finally come to pass, one is entitled to cast a jaundiced eye on the record of those who resisted its happening, believed it would not happen, asserted it did not need to happen, pretended to themselves and the country that alternative destinies would happen instead. These turned out to be misperceptions of the truth. The people who made the error had their reasons, but subsequent events show that, for too long, their attachment to Britain's cultural and historic differences got the better of their political judgement. Ultimately, Britain did choose the fate her leaders long resisted or failed fully to embrace – but only after a period in which much opportunity was, by sheer lapse of time, wasted.

One does not need to carry either of the labels pejoratively invented in this time – Euro-phile or Euro-phobe – to accept the force of that. If objectivity can, for once, be brought to a question long drenched in opinionated emotion, it might be commonly agreed. As an exercise in leadership, the extended episode of Britain in and out of the European Community reveals a mismatch between political judgement and eventual, irresistible fact.

This book is an account and study of leadership, up to and just over the threshold into the present era when its quality seems likely, at last, to be less conflicted. It is a history of the great question, and of why a nation found it so difficult to answer: and of how the blessed plot became, instead, the graveyard, where the reputations of a large political class lie buried.

1

WINSTON CHURCHILL

Rule Britannia

IN MAY 1945, when the second German war ended, British self-esteem was higher than it had been in living memory. The little island nation had played a decisive part in liberating the continent from the abominations of Hitler. Britain was Europe's rescuer, the only power in the land mass and archipelago that could be so described. The United States and the Soviet Union may have had greater armies, and taken most of the military pain. But Britain was unique, indisputably the chief among European equals. Directly from that fact – that exquisite sense of national selfhood, and the experience of vindication going with it – stemmed all the large decisions of British foreign policy for the next fifteen years. These were the formative years, of crucial choices and chances. The influence of this history did not stop in 1960, but reached decades further forward. It was the defining experience, at different levels of consciousness, of every British leader for half a century.

Bestriding the fifty-year story is the man who set it on course. Three months after winning the war, Winston Churchill lost the election and surrendered his post as Prime Minister. But the people who flung him from office were unable to remove him from their minds. He was the leader round whom the entire nation from left to right had gathered, and his political defeat in no way diminished the hold he exerted over the British imagination. This effect, too, reached far beyond his own time. When Margaret Thatcher placed herself in direct descent from 'Winston', as she often called him, she knew what she was doing. He was the hero from whom the British weakness for nostalgia gained its richest nourishment. The belief that Britain, under Churchill, had won the war in 1945 retained its grip, twitching the nerve-ends and coursing through the bloodstream of Euro-sceptics in the 1990s.

Anyone wishing to explore the puzzle of Britain's relations with continental Europe in the twentieth century's second part must begin with Churchill, and not just because he came first. In the history, Churchill's record plays as important a part as the aura that came after him. The last begetter of British greatness, he was also the prime exponent of British ambiguity. In him the two strains mingling in Britain's post-war presentation of herself – illusion and uncertainty – had their most potent source. He epitomized the characteristic consistently displayed by almost every politician, irrespective of party, who came after him: an absence of steady vision on the greatest question concerning the future of Britain in the last fifty years. But he also spoke, none louder, for the reasons why such unsteadiness did not matter: why the issue of Europe could always be the plaything of fickle British politicians, because there always existed other possibilities for Britain, growing out of imperial history and military triumph.

Churchill was called the father of 'Europe', and he said much to justify that label. But he was also the father of misunderstandings about Britain's part in this Europe. He encouraged Europe to misunderstand Britain, and Britain to misunderstand herself.

Nobody stood closer to history than Churchill. He had studied it, written it, made it. But Harold Macmillan once said that his real greatness lay in 'his extraordinary power always to look forward, never back'.[1] This prophetic quality was his chief claim to public trust. The people believed what he said and promised. He was the last British leader whose reputation for sagacity was incontestable. Such a man might have been expected to rise above some of the comfortable illusions that gripped the British in the aftermath of war. Instead, he was the first in a long line of leaders who shared them. Indeed, his very presence, as Leader of the Opposition, did an enormous amount to endorse the general sense that Britain, after the war, did not have too much to worry about.

This was, after all, a united as well as a triumphant nation. War had been a unifying experience. National unity, wrote Sir William Beveridge in 1943, was the great moral achievement of the Second World War. It rested not on temporary deals or party coalitions but on 'the mutual understanding between Government and people', and expressed 'the determination of the British democracy to look beyond victory to the uses of victory'.[2] Common sacrifices had produced a common sense of the future, in which even the class system, among other divisive British traditions, seemed to have liquefied. When a Labour government was elected in July to replace Churchill's wartime coalition, the peaceful transfer of power to a party of the left, summarily despatching the hero, registered a country apparently at ease with its capacity for renovation.

This country also appeared to be strong. It possessed not only the army but many elements of the economy of a great power, on course for post-war recovery. Despite heavy German bombing of many significant centres, Britain's industrial capacity was higher in 1945 than it had been in 1939. Although exports had fallen during the war, they recovered swiftly under a determined government and a stoically purposeful workforce, in which almost nobody was unemployed. In 1947, British exports were five times those of France, as large, in fact, as those of France, Germany, Italy, Belgium, the Netherlands, Luxembourg, Norway and Denmark combined.

The most devastated war powers – Germany, France, Italy, the Netherlands – ran huge and persistent deficits, whereas Britain was a creditor with the whole of Europe. Whereas Britain was in every respect a giant, Germany was a devastated country, her industrial power dismantled, her housing stock decimated. Germany's national income in 1946 was less than one-third of what it had been in 1938, and France's only one-half, with the franc an all but valueless international currency. In Italy, the national output in 1945 was at the level it had been in 1911, down by nearly half since 1938. Britain, by contrast, was galvanized by war to new levels of output, based on a sense of national endeavour that victory did not dissipate.

On the contrary, victory confirmed a good many things that the country wanted to know about itself. The expression of it – of the assurance it supplied to an idea of nation that long preceded it – reached beyond economists, generals and politicians. If you look at what British writers were saying about England before and after the war, you read for the most part a seamless paean to the virtues of the nation's strength and identity. It occurred to hardly anyone, whether in 1935 or 1945, to doubt the value of being British (for which 'English' was then a synonym the Scots and the Welsh tamely put up with). In both decades, plenty of argument raged around the British national interest in rearmament or disarmament, central planning or market economics. The value and purpose of Britain's contribution to the world was the natural sub-text of a lot of these debates. But the greatness of its scale, like the history behind it, was not a matter over which many of the British yet agonized; and the war confirmed them in their complacency. Almost all writers, from left to right, believed in the qualities of their country. It never occurred to them to do otherwise. The notion that Britain/England might reconsider her role in the world, relinquishing her status as a global power or doubting her contribution to the welfare of mankind, did not arise. Nor was this confined to little Englanders, or celebrators of narrowly English cultural virtues in the mould of J. B. Priestley. It was a 'European', Herbert Read, a high-flown prophet of the continental avant-garde, who in the mid-1930s caught a note that the defeat of Germany did nothing to diminish. Introducing his anthology, *The English Vision*, the dangerous anarchist sounded like a man with indestructible pride in the special qualities of his country. 'What I wish to emphasise most is the universal validity of this our vision,' Read wrote. 'Alone of national ideals, the English ideal transcends nationality.'[3]

This unquestioning sense of nation persisted through and after the war. There was a striking contrast with the national attitude after the First World War, with its powerful aura of hope betrayed. 'I feel a doom over the country, and a shadow of despair over the hearts of men, which leaves me no rest,' wrote D. H. Lawrence at that time.[4] The 1940s satires of Evelyn Waugh derided the English middle classes. But they stopped well short of apocalypse in their prediction for the future of England. Nobody in any walk of life imagined that this was a country whose future might have been rendered more rather than less problematic by military victory.

George Orwell's odyssey through the England of the war maps the typical experience. Orwell was an honest, unposturing man, whom the right wing disliked because he was a socialist and the left wing disliked because he told the truth.[5] His writings trace the evolution of a nation's feeling about itself.

Back from Spain, after fighting for the republicans in the civil war, Orwell rediscovers a country offering wonderful reassurance in the places of his childhood – but he also senses the imminence of some kind of explosion. The year is 1938, in 'the huge peaceful wilderness of outer London', with 'the barges on the miry river, the familiar streets, the posters telling of cricket matches and Royal weddings, the men in bowler hats, the pigeons in Trafalgar Square, the red buses, the blue policemen – all sleeping the deep, deep sleep of England, from which I sometimes fear that we shall never wake till we are jerked out of it by the roar of bombs'.[6]

When the bombs fall, however, Orwell's ambivalence vanishes. Mockery is overcome by patriotism, and the man of the people emerges to castigate the intelligentsia whose love of country he does not always trust. He still calls England 'the most class-ridden country under the sun', but is adamant about his belief in the virtues of simple national pride. 'We must add to our heritage or lose it, we must grow greater or grow less, we must go forward or backward,' he writes at the height of the Blitz. 'I believe in England, and I believe that we shall go forward.'[7]

When it is all over, this belief is shaken only slightly, if at all. Orwell expresses the sober, but ultimately sure, conviction that Britain could claim a role in the world sufficient unto itself. His conviction fell on receptive ears. The war was a period when the people especially revelled in their past. Huge commercial success, for example, attended G. M. Trevelyan's triumphalist *English Social History*, published in 1944. Orwell's version of how Britain could expect to perform after 1945 was no less gratifying than Trevelyan's account of the past.

He caught a glimpse of the problem that might beckon. If global conflict continued, he said, there might be room for only two or three great powers, and he conceded that 'in the long run Britain will not be one of them'. She was just too small. But she had great things to give the world, one of them 'the highly original quality of the English ... their habit of not killing one another'. There was now a decent chance of this imposing itself on others, as Britain/England defined a new kind of domination. 'If the English took the trouble to make their own democracy work, they would become the political leaders of western Europe,' he concluded, 'and probably of some other parts of the world as well. They would provide the much-needed alternative to Russian authoritarianism on the one hand and American materialism on the other.'[8]

Leadership, of course, was the point. Although a mere essayist, Orwell was quite influential at the time – far more so than any such writer in the 1990s – and his description was consistent with Britain's objective position vis-à-vis the mainland countries. If there was to be a leader, she was it. Her democracy, meanwhile, had in Orwell's terms worked. A few months after he set down these sentiments, the ordinary English did, as he advocated, 'get their hands on power' through the agency of a people's government led by Clement Attlee. They had demonstrated the proof of what the war was about, the capacity of men to choose and defend the peaceful transfer of democratic power.

Churchill's part in that, his humble acceptance of an almost incomprehensible result, served to increase his prophetic stature. Although he was rejected by the voters, who decided that the fruits of victory would be better distributed by the people's party, his was still the voice that

resounded loudest through the opening discussion about the future of
Europe, after Europe had been saved.

*

WINSTON CHURCHILL had no objection, emotional or political, to the
idea of the unification of Europe. Compared with the defenders of
sovereignty who took control of his party in the 1990s, he was
untroubled by its impact on the sovereign nation. His attitude was
pragmatic, and it had an instructive history.

As early as 1930, he came out straight. Writing in an American
magazine, he argued the case for creating a United States of Europe. He
understood better than many contemporaries the failure of the Treaty of
Versailles, after the 1914–18 war, to produce a secure settlement of the
historic enmity of France and Germany. 'The conception of a United
States of Europe is right,' he wrote. 'Every step taken to that end which
appeases the obsolete hatreds and vanished oppressions, which makes
easier the traffic and reciprocal services of Europe, which encourages
nations to lay aside their precautionary panoply, is good in itself.'[9] So he
believed in a USE for political reasons. But he also saw 'Europe' in
economic terms. He noted the underlying dynamism of the American
economy, especially its respect for 'science and organisation', and pon-
dered how the Old World might emulate the New. He proposed, as the
model for his United States of Europe, the single market and unified
governing principle of the United States of America.

This was not the utterance of a serving statesman, nor even of a
representative party politician. Churchill at the time was parading round
the political wilderness, earning what he could by his pen. His piece was
sufficient to the moment and its market. Besides, as anyone quickly
learns who ventures beyond the bare facts of political history, judgements
on matters that don't require an immediate answer are always open to
shifts of nuance, if not outright reversal. Politicians do not expect to be
held to all their visions. The discussion of foreign affairs is a paradise for
musing soothsayers whose ideas at any given time seldom have to pass
exacting tests of consistency. They can drift from one interesting proposition to its opposite in the reassuring knowledge that disproof by
events is unlikely. On the future of Britain in the world – more exactly,
the future of the world as it revolved around Britain – there was room
in the middle decades of the century for incessant adjustment of the
point of view.

Above all other questions, in fact, Europe has been the prime example of such uncertainty among modern British politicians. The habit of constant revision, with violent contradictions sometimes emanating from a single mind, is an unvarying feature of the history. The sole consistent pattern to be found, from the moment debate began in earnest, is the inconsistency – casual or tormented, selfless or self-indulgent – that almost every protagonist has brought to it. Fittingly, it is Churchill, Britain's last geo-strategist of world significance, who established the pattern.

Nonetheless, what he wrote in 1930 has to be taken seriously. It indicated a willingness to think irregular thoughts. A man of large horizons was casting about to meet a crisis he believed the nation-state might not be able to avert. And when war happened, he continued to think adventurously about the future of the continent whose freedoms he was fighting to preserve.

Wartime diaries and papers, his own and those of others, reveal the constructive restlessness of a mind not content with the shape of things as they had been. It was moved by the horrors of the fighting to explore possibilities which, at the time, seemed to the colleagues who heard them inexplicably bold. For example, in December 1940, only six months after becoming Prime Minister, Churchill discussed with some intimates a version of the future that bore resemblance to the model of European unity that in fact came to evolve by the end of the 1980s. He saw a Europe of five single powers – England, France, Italy, Spain and what he called Prussia – along with four confederations covering the rest of the continent: 'These nine powers would meet in a Council of Europe which would have a supreme judiciary and a Supreme Economic Council to settle currency questions etc.'[10] The Council, moreover, would take the power to deal with any breach of the peace. This foreshadowed the court, council and commission of the European Community.

Two years later, he was still musing about a Council of Europe, which would also interest itself in a common continental market. In a minute to Anthony Eden, the Foreign Secretary, he identified 'Russian barbarism' as the future enemy and a united Europe as the necessary bulwark against it. 'Hard as it is to say now, I trust that the European family may act unitedly as one, under a Council of Europe in which the barriers between nations will be greatly minimised and unrestricted travel will be possible.' He also hoped to see 'the economy of Europe studied as a whole'.

He continued to amplify this line of thinking. At the beginning of

1943, in a paper dictated from his bed on an Orient Express wagon-lit in the middle of Turkey, where he had gone to consult about the dangers of Soviet influence when the war was over, Churchill reiterated the need for a Council of Europe. He called these 'Morning Thoughts', to mark the informality of their composition. But the paper had a perennial influence, if only on debate inside a sceptical Foreign Office.[11] An 'instrument of European government' was at the heart of it, to be distinguished from the project of world government so ineffectually expressed by the pre-war League of Nations. He followed this, in March, with one of his grander wartime broadcasts, publicly explaining the need to start thinking now about 'the largest common measure of the integrated life of Europe that is possible, without destroying the individual characteristics and traditions of its many ancient and historic races'.[12] A little later, in May the same year, a mixture of these half-formed thoughts appeared in a conversation Churchill had with a group of Americans at lunch in the Washington embassy. The European 'instrument', consisting of twelve states and confederations, had now evolved in his mind into one of three regional bodies covering the globe, which would be answerable to a World Council.[13]

So Churchill was fertile in his wartime thinking. The constraints of national politics did not inhibit his creative reach. Frontiers did not trouble him, as he cast forward from the terrible time through which he was living. Indeed, within a month of taking office he had put his name to the most ambitious plan for the voluntary subsuming and remaking of two great nations that had ever been conceived, when, in response to the fall of France, he took up the embryonic proposal for an Anglo-French Union. The way to sustain France, it was felt by leaders from both sides of the Channel, was to sublimate these two nations into an 'indissoluble union'. They would 'no longer be two nations, but one Franco-British Union', and every citizen of each would immediately become a citizen of the other. There would be a single cabinet and a single parliament.

This project never came to pass. Dreamed up by senior British officials working together with some of the leading Frenchmen in temporary exile in London, it briefly attracted the interest of the French Government. But the Government fell before the extravagant idea, some of whose progenitors would later become very important in the grander post-war European project, could be put to the test. Churchill's interest in it cannot be read as indicating any more than the extremes to which he was prepared to go to sustain the war effort and defeat Hitler. It was plainly not intended to form a template for the Europe he might be expected to favour when hostilities were over. Nonetheless, it showed a supple approach to nationhood. It suggested that a national interest, in Churchill's conception, might in certain circumstances transcend the boundaries of national sovereignty as usually understood. It is one of the early bases – there were more important ones to come – of the claim by later 'Europeans' in British debates that Churchill was one of them.

Even at this stage, however, such a claim was seriously flawed. And the fault in this version of Churchillism is relevant to the argument that came after him. It doesn't amount to anything so crude as the notion that Churchill was in reality a serious anti-European: the greatest Conservative icon made available, on further inspection, for retrospective recruitment by the Euro-sceptic camp. This, at times, was how 'Winston' was later claimed. But the claim was empty. On the contrary, he remained always a European of highly romantic disposition. His idea of Europe was benign and passionate, informed by the prescience of the historian as well as of the public man. The flaw lay in his description of what Europe was, where its limits lay. Although in the east these had generous scope, encompassing his Danubian and Balkan confederations, to the west they stopped at the English Channel. In short, Britain did not belong inside the Churchillian concept of 'Europe'.

At times this appeared to be a product of mere muddle and oversight. In the grand sweep of mid-war speculation about how the tectonic plates of the global system might ultimately be redesigned, confusion about Britain's exact place in it was perhaps a trivial detail. When Churchill propounded his first big scheme in December 1940, he assigned England both to the great new Council of Europe, with its new supreme judiciary and economic union, yet also to some place beyond it. Britain would belong, and yet not belong. For 'the English-speaking world', he wrote, 'would be apart from this', while at the same time being in some unspecified way 'closely connected'.

Most of Churchill's blueprints, however, placed Britain/England outside the European construct. Even his 1930 account, untouched by the triumphalism of victory in the war, put the country above and beyond the continent. 'We have our own dream and our own task,' he wrote. 'We are *with* Europe but not *of* it. We are linked but not comprised.'[14] Thirteen years later, in his notion of three Regional Councils responsible to a World Council, he instinctively distanced Britain from the role of equal partner in any European enterprise. Britain would be a kind of godmother or broker, her relationship to Europe very similar to that of the US. America was more like Britain's equal partner than Europe could ever be. Together the two Anglo-Saxon peoples, Churchill opined, would share the common problem of maintaining 'large numbers of men indefinitely on guard', to keep the continental peace.

For the visionary had other dreams, and the historian other romantic attachments. These coexisted with his ideas about Europe and, though he seldom discussed the contradiction, in practice overshadowed them.

The war-winner could in no way surrender his belief that the British purpose must be to sustain the status of a great power, as near as possible equal in political weight with the US and the Soviet Union: a belief in which Churchill was unexceptional in either the public world where national prestige could never be compromised or the private circles in which he moved. Hardly anywhere, on the left or the right, in the journalistic or literary or political milieus, was the concept of Britain's solitary greatness, uniquely positioned at the hub of several global groupings, subjected to serious reassessment. At the same time, the strategist could never forget the concept of the English-speaking world. He had written a four-volume history of it. Empire, and then Commonwealth, formed bonds that were a part of many British families' inheritance and every British leader's responsibility. They had helped to win the war. Here were truly indissoluble unions, and they were in conflict with any simple idea of European Britain.

Churchill's failure to resolve this conflict, or come anywhere near doing so, was not surprising. Most of his successors – in differing measures and with varying commitment, some addressing the same conflict, others discovering new fields of difference – failed in the same way.

The contradiction, however, did not inhibit Churchill from making the unity of post-war Europe the great cause of his years as Leader of the Opposition. He proposed himself as the intellectual prophet of the European idea, investing in it a large portion of such emotional reserves as were left over from political defeat. In doing so, moreover, he was not a lonely eccentric, but was speaking to a country already to some extent acquainted with the grand notions for which he appeared to be speaking: the idea that there might be a worthwhile entity larger than the nation-state, and a way of organizing Europe that might better guarantee the avoidance of war.

Federalism, a word which by 1995 epitomized all that was alien in the project of 'Europe', possessed a different aura fifty years earlier. It had a certain purchase on parts of the British consciousness. So did the concept of union, as applied to Europe.

Federalism had blossomed before the war. By June 1940, when the flame of Anglo-French Union briefly lit the scene, the British federalist movement, called Federal Union, had more than 10,000 members in over 200 branches. The failure of the League of Nations and the shock of Munich had spurred more support, sometimes from names that were widely known, for a federation of free peoples, a union of sovereign states, or whatever similar arrangement might lower the possibility of conflict. Adherents came from the usual cadre of pious dreamers. 'The whole scheme of Federal Union has made a staggeringly effective appeal to the British mind,' the Archbishop of York enthused in 1939.[15] The abandonment of sovereignty made a natural appeal to the parsonical tendency, hoping to avoid war at a stroke. But serious men of affairs also put themselves behind the cause. William Beveridge was a federalist, and so was Harold Laski. The *Manchester Guardian* and the *New Statesman* came out for the federal idea, as did a former editor of *The Times*, Wickham Steed. Lord Lothian, former Cabinet minister and later ambassador to Washington, was a federalist of long standing. Richard Law MP, son of Bonar Law, the Conservative Prime Minister, wrote a pamphlet on the subject. There was also heavy academic support. The historian Arnold Toynbee, the constitutional jurist Ivor Jennings and the two most illustrious economists of the day, Lionel Robbins and Friedrich von Hayek, all did serious work on the practicalities of a federal constitution and its implications for defence, economic policy, tax, justice and the rest of state activity.

So federalism at this time was not the obsession of some irrelevant cranks' corner of British public life. Important people had begun to see it as perhaps the only solid guarantor of peaceful coexistence between peoples. There was a sizeable British literature on the subject, with roots in the thinking of John Locke, and extended by such varied political thinkers as Lord Acton, James Bryce and Ernest Barker. A famous continental federalist, Altiero Spinelli, prime author of a 1944 manifesto for federalism, and a man of deep conceptual influence on the post-war idea of Europe, when reflecting on his own intellectual formation, attributed much to 'the clean, precise thinking of these English federalists'.[16]

This was part of the context into which Churchill projected himself in 1945. By then, admittedly, the federal idea had suffered some degradation. Strong at the beginning of the war, it lost support when the fact

of battle, especially of victorious battle, exalted the loyalties attaching to
the nation-state. Federal Union closed down many branches. The European dimension, moreover, was overtaken in many minds by the
necessity for something much wider. Among British federalists, disputes
broke out between those still mainly interested in a federation of Western
Europe and those who thought that a world potentially at ransom to
nuclear super-powers required nothing less than a complete World
Federation. Crankdom beckoned. The limited project of a federal
Europe, itself requiring enough massive adjustments in the thinking of
several ancient nations, tended to become engulfed by the case for world
government, which had the early effect of returning such credibility as
federation had to parsonical irrelevance.

Churchill was never seduced by world government. But he had ideas
for Europe that, while eschewing federalism, made the case for a
European Union. He set about promoting them in irresistible style.
Three great meetings, of which the highlight in each case was a
Churchillian oration, have become benchmarks of his career as a hero of
the European peace.

The first was in Zurich on 19 September 1946. One must remember
the mantle of inextinguishable gallantry in which he was arrayed by his
collaborators in the war. Nobody regarded him as less than the greatest
man in Europe, even though his own people had rejected him. He came
to the University of Zurich, in a country at the confluence of the peoples
and languages that had almost destroyed the continent, to deliver a
judgement which, he said, would 'astonish' his audience. What he called
the United States of Europe, an idea then only vestigially dreamed of,
was a project on which 'we must begin now'. And at the heart of it –
this was the astonishing bit – there had to be a partnership between
France and Germany. 'In this way only can France recover the moral
and cultural leadership of Europe,' he insisted. 'There can be no revival
of Europe without a spiritually great Germany,' he added. 'We must re-
create the European family in a regional structure called, as it may be,
the United States of Europe.'

The Zurich speech made a very great impact. It is less commonly
remembered now than the speech Churchill gave earlier that year in
Fulton, Missouri, when he publicized the phrase and fashioned the
thinking about the Iron Curtain which the Soviet Union had brought
down between the free and unfree worlds. But Zurich was a beacon. It
inspired many continental politicians, then struggling to remake their
ruined countries. It roused enthusiasts for a united Europe to ecstatic

excitement. They really seemed to think it meant that Churchill, for Britain, was making a choice. Leo Amery MP, Churchill's Tory comrade, who along with his son Julian was one of the few politicians who saw no conflict between strong attachment to the British Empire and a commitment to European Union, marked his leader's card. 'The French are startled, as they were bound to be, but the idea will sink in all the same,' he wrote. 'As for the Germans, your speech may have been just in time to save them from going Bolshevist. You have done few bigger things, even in the great years behind us.'[17]

The Zurich speech, however, was once again 'European' only in a sense that placed Britain outside Europe. It was the speech of a grandiloquent map-maker who wanted to dissolve the emotional frontiers between warring continental countries, but was rooted in a system that cast Britain as facilitator, even mere spectator, of the process. It does not seem to have entered Churchill's mind that the destiny he envisaged for Europe, as the only way to prevent a repetition of the war, was something his own country should embrace. Far from plotting a clear course forward, Churchill's spumes of oratory proposed a feel-good world in which just about every country was involved. Britain and the Commonwealth and 'mighty America', he said at Zurich, 'and I trust Soviet Russia, for then all would be well', must be 'friends and sponsors of the new Europe, and must champion its right to live and shine'.

Britain, in other words, was separate from Europe. Her sense of national independence, enhanced by her unique empire, absorbed by all creeds and classes and spoken for by virtually every analyst, could not be fractured. Churchill urged Europe to become united, and set about creating a movement with this as its purpose. But to be achieved by what means, exactly? His only practical proposal involved a quite limited form of unity. He reiterated what he had said in private, and sometimes in public, during the war: that the first step should be the formation of a Council of Europe, which would not be some grandiose agent of European governance, still less a federalist super-state, but a forum for association between sovereign governments. The extravagances that he sometimes gave voice to – 'supreme judiciary ... supreme economic council' – were by now abandoned.

As a blueprint, Zurich was therefore quite a modest affair. It dripped with symbolism, and in its time and place, less than eighteen months after the slaughter had ended, was a bold response to popular alarms. Its particular genius, perhaps, lay in launching the idea of Franco-German partnership, allied to the concept, for these other countries, of a United

States of Europe. It was attacked in *The Times*, by a young leader-writer who later became a famous European, Con O'Neill,[18] on the ground that it was anti-Russian, when the world needed unity more than it needed some divisive new European institution. It was a grand idea, and gave birth in Britain to a United Europe Movement to which Churchill offered himself as chairman, and some excited old-style federalists immediately pledged their support. But it was never intended to be federalist.

For Churchill certainly wasn't a federalist, and nor was his chief lieutenant in these matters, Duncan Sandys, his son-in-law. Sandys, having lost his parliamentary seat in the Attlee landslide, became the main functionary of United Europe, a potent behind-the-scenes figure in the evolution of the Great European that Churchill gave such a large impression of being. Sandys's talents were not for the arts of persuasion. He was more the scheming manager. His energy helped shape the vaporous effusions of his father-in-law in a direction that was at once strongly European and quite unspecific as to what this might really mean. 'Duncan was an organizer and intriguer with a great capacity to manipulate people,' Lord Hailsham told me in 1993. 'I was at Eton with him, and he was a manipulator of great skill even as a schoolboy. I expect he manipulated Churchill.'[19]

Sandys locked United Europe into a non-federalist platform, but above all was anxious to ensure that Churchill got fully and publicly committed. This is what places Sandys among the most significant of the early British Europeans. At this stage, the movement stood for a loose and cautious association of governments, and the old man used his next great opportunity to rally support for the missionary undertaking. 'Let Europe Arise' was the title of his address to the Primrose League on 18 April 1947. The Albert Hall in London heard another Zurichean summons to European destiny. But, again, the inconveniences were glossed over. United Europe was the expansive theme, but Churchill's tone also reflected a message Sandys sent him the day before, warning that Conservative back-bench MPs felt out of touch with his European ideas, and urging him to do more to secure their support for 'our movement'. So the speech insisted on giving a higher place in the scheme of things to people who did not speak French, German or any other of the alien mainland tongues. 'We shall allow no wedge', the great voice intoned, 'to be driven between Great Britain and the United States of America, or be led into any course which would mar the growing unity in thought and action, in ideals and purpose, of the English-speaking nations, spread so widely about the globe, but joined together by history and by destiny.'

This was no more than an oratorical hors d'oeuvre. The movement expanded, and made links with similar groupings, more copious and still more passionately committed, across the Channel. With Duncan Sandys active in the back room, the idea was conceived for a great international congress to give continent-wide impetus to a European Union. The first Congress of Europe met in The Hague on 7 May 1948, with Churchill as the keynote speaker.

It was an extraordinary assembly. The big names gathered from all over West Europe. From France came Léon Blum, Paul Reynaud and Jean Monnet, from Italy Alcide De Gasperi, from Belgium Paul-Henri Spaak and Paul van Zeeland. From all over came many others who make prominent appearances later in this story. Altogether there were eight former prime ministers and twenty-eight former foreign ministers. No fewer than 140 British participants turned up, out of some 800 delegates all told, including Harold Macmillan and twenty-three of his party colleagues. Adrian Boult, the orchestral conductor, and John Masefield, the Poet Laureate, were among those whose presence showed that this was a movement appealing to instincts much deeper than the merely political. Among younger attenders, later to be leaders of their own political generation, were François Mitterrand and Christopher Soames. Soames, whom Churchill designated his personal assistant at The Hague, was another of his sons-in-law, thus a second lifelong 'European' in the family.

The assembly, however, was shot through with ambivalence. Its main promoters were federalists, of whom there were many more in high places in Europe than there ever were in Britain. Though Churchill was not a federalist, his presence at The Hague again blurred the truth about where he stood. His eminence persuaded continentals they had to have him, and his rhetoric gave small indication that he did not in his heart belong on their side. The occasion was the high point of Churchill's ambiguity, arrived at not by any calculating deviousness, but as the natural emanation of a man immersed in certainty that history entitled Britain to ordain the best of all worlds for herself.

The United Europe movement, Churchill told the Congress, was not of parties but of peoples. His speech was rich in the highest-flown rhetoric, and this style was more than decorative. It was meant to rouse and dramatize. Read half a century later, it still summons up the horror of war, and recalls the idly forgotten fact that fear of war and thirst for

peace, above all else, were the sources for the extraordinary idea that
national frontiers might be lowered. For many of those present at the
Hague assembly, their project was a matter of life or death. Churchill
appeared to speak to and for them. 'We shall only save ourselves from
the perils which draw near', he said, 'by forgetting the hatreds of the
past, by letting national rancours and revenges die, by progressively
effacing frontiers and barriers which aggravate and congeal our divisions,
and by rejoicing together in that glorious treasure of literature, of
romance, of ethics, of thought and toleration belonging to us all, which
is the inheritance of Europe.'

Political unity, he went on, must 'inevitably' accompany economic
and military collaboration, a process, as he explained, that did not
necessarily damage a nation. What he said about that might have had a
special resonance down the years. It touched on the issue that raised the
most enduring anxieties among the British, and was an occasion where
Churchill got closer than he often did to a practical description of what
he meant. 'It is said with truth that this involves some sacrifice or merger
of national sovereignty,' he began. But then he added that 'it is also
possible and not less agreeable to regard it as the gradual assumption, by
all nations concerned, of that larger sovereignty which can also protect
their diverse and distinctive customs and characteristics, and their
national traditions'.

These words could have served as a text for the proponents of British
entry into the European Community in the 1960s and 1970s. The
'pooling' of sovereignty, with its implication that all participants drew
greater sustenance from a pond bigger than their own, became a
favourite way of describing what happened inside the Community. But
the national sovereignties Churchill contemplated curtailing again did
not include Britain's. That appears to have been an idea beyond the
reach of his imagination. As a result, his speech at The Hague, which
was regarded at the time as an historic address, could in due course be
more exactly seen as a source-book for the confusion he created,
simultaneously giving succour to the federalists while intending to do no
such thing.

What happened as a result of the Hague Congress was also, in the
end, ambivalent. Churchill made a concrete proposal, building on his
frequent allusions to a future Council of Europe. He now suggested that
it was time for a new institution 'in one form or another', which he
specified as a quasi-parliamentary annexe to the Council, some kind of
European Assembly, to enable the voice of United Europe 'to make itself

continuously heard'. Three months later, France formally proposed that the Assembly should be created, and within a year the statute of the Council was agreed and the inaugural meeting of the Assembly arranged, at Strasbourg. The first institution of 'Europe' was in place, divided between a Council of Ministers and a Consultative Assembly.

In its beginnings, moreover, the Council fulfilled both the federalist and the Churchillian ideals. They were apparently conjoined within it. Paul-Henri Spaak, the Belgian federalist, was its first president, and Churchill its first hero. On the evening it opened, 10 August 1949, Churchill addressed a rally of 20,000 people crammed into the Place Kléber. Every corner was filled with people from the city closest to the heart of Franco-German Europe, to hear the great man address them, which he did in better French than usual. Then, as the Assembly debates began, he threw himself into its proceedings with a verve that impressed a fellow delegate. 'This extraordinary man', Harold Macmillan wrote in a letter home, 'seemed to come down almost too rapidly to the level of normal political agitation.' His early interventions were calculated 'to reveal him as a parliamentarian, rather than as a great international figure. He certainly took more trouble to listen to the debates than I have ever known him to do in the House of Commons. He walked about, chatted to each representative, went into the smoking room, and generally took a lot of trouble to win the sympathetic affection of his new parliamentary colleagues.'[20]

He also made another speech. Again it had a grand, uplifting effect. He saw the Council of Europe as 'a European unit' in the United Nations, which had lately been formed. He regretted the absence of the countries of Eastern Europe, now suffering under the tyrannies of communism, and asked that empty chairs be left for their representatives to fill in good time. He also inquired, dramatically, 'Where are the Germans?', and demanded that the Government of West Germany should be invited into the Council, alongside France, Belgium, Italy, Holland and the rest, without delay. He had never lost the sense he expressed at Zurich three years before, that, if European harmony was to endure, Germany must be in the concert.

At the same time, Churchill never intended the Council to break the nation-state. Having apparently scorned the narrow view of sovereignty just a year before, he was now unwilling to investigate the ways in which it might be modified, even for countries other than Britain. What interested him was the development of mood and feeling. 'I hope we shall not put our trust in formulae or in machinery,' he told the

Assembly. It was by 'the growth and gathering of the united sentiment of Europeanism, vocal here and listened to all over the world, that we shall succeed in taking, not executive decision, but ... a leading and active part in the revival of the greatest of continents which has fallen into the worst of misery'.

The Europeans didn't see the limits this implied. They allowed themselves to be deceived. And Churchill allowed himself to sound terribly confused. Many years later, Macmillan wrote in his memoirs that Churchill had 'had no clear or well-defined plan'. He wasn't interested in details. He merely wanted to 'give an impetus towards movements already at work'.[21] But that wasn't quite how European leaders, desperate to be led out of the ante-chamber of another war, saw the matter. They exulted in Churchill's compelling rhetoric, without thinking very hard about the realities that underlay it. And the price of their deception was going to be quite great, both for them and for Britain.

*

THERE WAS, besides, another kind of deception. This wasn't so much in Churchill's rhetoric as in the British mind, and it concerned the state of Britain herself. The Churchillian view, against which there was very little argument, took for granted Britain's capacity for independent decision-making in any area her leaders chose. This rested on imperial sentiment and national pride and the other outgrowths of the victory that saved Europe. But it also made assumptions about Britain's enduring economic strength that did not entirely stand up to examination. Anglo-Saxon triumphalism blinded even as it exulted. The figures of comparative growth and production immediately after the war told the truth but not the whole truth. They said what was true in 1945, and even in 1948, but they ignored the trends that told what might well be true by, say, 1955.

Behind the superficial encouragement of selected statistics was another kind of reality. While Britain was by some measures strong, by others she was weak. The struggle against Germany had been immensely costly. During the war, a quarter of the national wealth, £7,000 million, was lost: twice as much as in the First World War and more, proportionately, than in any other combatant country. The exports of this trading nation had not just declined but plummeted: in 1944 they were only 31 per cent of their level in 1938. The gold and dollar reserves were seriously run down, and in November 1945 it was necessary, with great difficulty, to arrange an American loan of £3.75 billion. In a famous memorandum, the man who negotiated it, John Maynard Keynes, warned the Attlee Government of the scale of the crisis which was being masked by public euphoria. 'The financial problems of the war', he wrote in August 1945, 'have been surmounted so easily and silently that the average man sees no reason to suppose that the financial problems of the peace will be any more difficult.' But Britain, he judged, was facing 'a financial Dunkirk'.[22]

This ominous phrase remained in the private realm, for the eyes of ministers alone. In any case, the US cavalry arrived in the shape of the loan. In 1945, Keynes's meaning, reinforced by his warning that 'a greater degree of austerity would be necessary than we have experienced at any time during the war', did not seriously impress itself on the politicians of any party. They agreed the loan, but did not draw the conclusion, or even register the question, that Britain might no longer be able to afford her imperial role, stretched round the globe, while building a welfare state at home.

Other truths were also disguised. Although the speed of the post-war economic recovery was impressive, especially on the exports side, it was less impressive than that of other countries. The important figures were comparative. In isolation they might look reasonably encouraging, but in fact the competitive decline that was to continue for the next half-century started now. Growth among the defeated or ravaged powers was consistently faster than it was in Britain. An assortment of reasons contributed to this. With no unemployment and hardly any immigration, Britain had no surplus labour to cope with expansion: the continentals had a surfeit. Britain had huge overseas obligations, not least the cost of policing the defeated countries: Germany and Italy had no such costs. Britain under a Labour government was preoccupied with wealth redistribution, and operated a top tax rate of over 90 per cent: on the continent there was far greater concern to create the incentives that would remake ruined economies.

Victory, in other words, produced decidedly less dynamic energy than did defeat. As a result, between 1947 and 1951, while British industrial production rose by a gratifying 30 per cent, France and Italy achieved 50 per cent, and Germany 300 per cent. By the end of 1950, German production, after the devastation of the infrastructure, not to mention the controls imposed by the occupying powers, was back at pre-war levels. It is true that in that year the British economy, measured by gross national product per head of the population, remained the second strongest in the world, with only the US ahead of it. But Germany and even France were closing steadily.

This was knowable at the time. The trends and statistics were no secret. But it wasn't commonly apprehended, least of all in the quarters where it might have been most expected that the details would be closely studied, and the lessons honestly drawn. In government circles where, Keynes excepted, victory in the war had done more to fortify the conceptions of the past than provoke new ones for the future, the evidence was received, as it were, blindfold. Anyone who saw behind it to the truth tended to be ostracized.

One man who did was Sir Henry Tizard, chief scientific adviser at the Ministry of Defence. In 1949, he composed a telling minute, contesting the wisdom of the age. 'We persist in regarding ourselves as a Great Power,' Tizard wrote, 'capable of everything and only temporarily handicapped by economic difficulties. We are not a Great Power and never will be again. We are a great nation, but if we continue to behave like a Great Power we shall soon cease to be a great nation.'

This fine and prescient distinction gave an answer to Orwell's question. It did not go down well. Whitehall received Tizard's warning 'with the kind of horror one would expect if one made a disrespectful remark about the King'.[23]

So an imposing consensus presented itself. On the question of Britain's place in the world, most pillars of the society took a similar attitude. The spirit of the times said that Britain's destiny had been determined by her military victory, and nourished the illusion that war had increased the country's inherent strength, not sapped it. This strength was imperial and global, another source, almost everyone believed, of advantage rather than burden. 'Our empire illustrated co-operation without domination for the whole of the world – co-operation between countries without the domination of one over the other,' the Dean of St Paul's preached on Empire Day, 1945. 'It was probably the greatest creation of British political genius.'[24] The Dean spoke in the past tense, no doubt, because the Empire was in process of being converted into the Commonwealth. But this remained the British Commonwealth, run by one nation, to which others still owed fealty. As the historian of Empire has written of the British at the end of the 1940s, 'They believed in their hearts that things British were necessarily things best. They believed that they, above all their Allies, had won the war. They saw themselves still, like their grandfathers, as a senior and superior race.'[25]

This was the *Zeitgeist* with which British political leadership after the war had its ambivalent relationship. Churchill spoke for part of it. He continued to assure the Americans that 'only the English-speaking peoples count; that together they can rule the world'.[26] Although out of office, he carried the weight of ages with him. This massive iconic figure, absolved from bothering with details or structures, set the tone that many on the continent desired to hear. His oracular pronouncements were as ambivalent as those of the goddess-seer at Delphi, but with less cunning intent. They were as devoid of clarity about European institutions as they were of rigour about Britain's economic prospects. They had enormous force. But they addressed less than half the picture.

On the one hand, there was Churchill's world. Proud nation. Inventive people. Stubborn, stoical, self-confident people. Future stretching indefinitely ahead. Second great power of the Western world watching with sympathy, seldom with alarm, the efforts of its neighbours across the Channel to remake themselves. Europe a place to which the British felt ineffable superiority. Little Attlee, no less than Churchill, was fated to personify this national pride, which it had become impossible for most Englishmen to question.

On the other hand, there was the world as seen by Henry Tizard. To this world, Churchill was absolutely blind. So, as we shall discover, were most of the people who, unlike Churchill, had to deal with it as responsible ministers. The consensus in favour of being a great power was impossible to challenge. On the left as well as the right, it was a given of national politics. After all, 'greatness' expresses the commonest of all ideas that, in one form or another, democratic politicians promise their electors. 'If we continue to behave like a Great Power, we shall soon cease to be a great nation.' Such a possibility of loss was unimaginable to British leaders in the post-war world – as it has been to most of their successors.

2

ERNEST BEVIN

Great Brit

WHILE ONE MAN controlled the emotional tone of post-war Britain's self-regard, somebody else was in charge of what actually happened. Ernest Bevin was the only man in the Attlee Cabinet who faintly resembled Winston Churchill. They had in common a capacity for domination. Each deserved the overworked description of a force of nature. Each addressed events from a basis of conviction that carried almost all before it – against colleagues, against enemies, sometimes against their closest allies. But Bevin had the advantage. He held cabinet office for a continuous period of nearly eleven years, as Minister of Labour during the war and Foreign Secretary immediately after it, whereas Churchill was cut out of power after five. He was also present at the making of the post-war world. Churchill could write and speak about it, and enjoyed the uniquely lustred admiration of audiences everywhere. Bevin made decisions.

With the United States and the Soviet Union, Britain still belonged to what were called, awesomely, the Big Three. At this, the topmost table of global leadership, Ernest Bevin was the British representative. Over the future of Europe, in particular, this gave him great influence. Europe was the cockpit in which the new struggle for mastery was joined. In the years between 1945 and 1950, the key alliances of Western power were shaped, and the debate about what 'Europe' meant reached its first conclusion. It is with decisions Bevin made and defended in those years that a British attitude which has endured for fifty years was first defined.

In particular, he embodied the paradox that was to repeat itself in different guises for decades ahead. He speaks with almost the same eloquence as Churchill for the elusive nature of the European idea. But his position, like Churchill's, declined to address an inherent contradiction. On the one hand, he conveys a sense of European unity mattering intensely to him. On the other, he seems to regard the concept of 'Europe' as forever hostile to the British interest.

Bevin was an improbable figure to have become the arbiter of these matters. Before 1945, there had never been a Foreign Secretary who remotely resembled him. Having left school at eleven, he was uninstructed in the niceties of the French Revolution, the Franco-Prussian War or any of the other half-remembered intellectual baggage his predecessors brought to the office, and in particular to their consideration of European politics. But he is commonly judged a great Foreign Secretary, and, in respect of the scale of the decisions he made, the verdict is not disputable.

Attlee gave him the job because he was the largest man among the colleagues who took over power. The original plan had been to send Bevin to the Treasury and Hugh Dalton, an Old Etonian and bonhomous intellectual, socially a more much congruent choice, to the Foreign Office. But over a lunch-time the Prime Minister reversed himself. 'I thought a heavy tank was what was required, rather than a light sniper,' he subsequently explained.[1]

Born in 1881, Bevin had risen from the humblest origins, through service as a trade unionist organizing draymen and carters in the West Country, to become the most powerful trade union leader in the country before he was forty-five. By the middle of the 1920s, he had created his own union, the Transport and General Workers, which, when the Second World War began, was the largest trade union in the world. He was a union man through and through, personified the 'industrial' side of the Labour movement, for most of his life had a wary relationship with the 'political' side, and distrusted all politicians who might be categorized as intellectuals. He was always interested in politics, and the power to which politics gave access. But, in the beginning, he was not easily bonded to the Labour Party. He greeted the first Labour administration in history, Ramsay MacDonald's Government of 1924, with a national dock strike a month after it came to office. 'Governments may come and governments may go,' he wrote with bluff self-regard, echoes of which were later transposed to the international scene, 'but the workers' fight for betterment of conditions must go on all the time.'

For most of his life, Bevin was not a politician at all. Only after Churchill brought him into the wartime coalition as Minister of Labour did he become a Member of Parliament. In the 1930s, after the disaster of the National Government, he devoted much time to rebuilding the Labour Party as the political wing of the trade union movement. The singleness of his purpose, backed by the size of his union, made him the crucial influence in pre-war party conferences. He was the very prototype of union baron that was later feared, derided and ultimately legislated out of political existence. But orthodox parliamentary politics was not the natural arena of a man who nevertheless became, after Churchill, the British politician most celebrated in the chancelleries of Europe and the world. He was in no way *soigné*. His considerable bulk burst out from ill-fitting suits. He had little patience with the niceties of debate, and was given to malapropisms that sent the educated Foreign Office smoothies around him into transports of patronising admiration. For many of them, he was the first man of toil with whom they had ever had contact as an equal, let alone as their master. When he entered the world stage, it could never have been as a diplomatic technician. Roy Jenkins observed of Bevin as Foreign Secretary: 'There was no other position in the Foreign Office, unless it was that of a rather truculent lift-man on the verge of retirement, which it would have been possible to imagine his filling.'[2]

He had, however, given thought to foreign affairs in earlier stages of his life. As an important union leader, he was caught up in the crises of the inter-war years. In 1927, he persuaded the Trades Union Congress to pass a resolution in favour of the same 'United States of Europe' that Churchill advocated three years later. He, too, likened it to the USA and urged its merits 'at least on an economic basis, even if we cannot on a totally political basis'. Such a great free trade area, it was argued later, might even have precluded the war, by sustaining the Weimar Republic and forestalling Hitler. And federation of a kind spoke to the left's ever seductive dream of world government. When war broke out, the Labour leader himself subscribed to it. 'In the common interest,' Clement Attlee wrote in December 1939, 'there must be recognition of an international authority superior to the individual states and endowed not only with rights over them, but with power to make them effective, operating not only in the political but in the economic sphere. Europe must federate or perish.'[3] It was a classic statement of the British federal idea as espoused by many leading figures at different times: pious, trenchant – and of only passing seriousness.

A species of it survived when Bevin became Foreign Secretary. Labour feeling replicated what ebbed and surged in other intellectual quarters, after as well as before the war. Coinciding with the Americans' nuclear bombing of Japan, the union baron's arrival in Whitehall was accompanied by a grand resurgence of the case for inventing not merely regional but worldwide organizations for peace. Stafford Cripps, the new Chancellor of the Exchequer, made the case for world federation. Attlee wanted 'the rule of law to be established throughout the world'. Bevin himself, in the first speech on foreign affairs that secured him the universal approval of his own side, overflowed with lyricism for a power beyond that of the nation-state. He was ready, he told the Commons on 23 November 1945, to merge the power of the British Parliament 'into the greater power of a directly elected world assembly'. There would be 'a world law with a world judiciary to interpret it, with a world police to enforce it'. The assembly would be 'the world sovereign elected authority which would hold in its care the destinies of the peoples of the world'.

There was a more down-to-earth way of putting this, and a few days later Bevin found it, in what became the most famous single remark he made on international affairs. 'Someone once asked me when I became Foreign Secretary', he told delegates to the preparatory commission then meeting in London to create the United Nations, 'what my policy really was. I said I have only one: it is to go down to Victoria Station here, take a ticket and go where the hell I like without anybody pulling me up with a passport.'[4]

His conduct of British diplomacy, however, was based on more exigent realities. Whatever Bevin's emotional preferences might have been, he could not escape the world of frontiers and control, of great forces that were fully capable of unleashing another war, which would be far worse than the war the Germans had just lost. It is hard to exaggerate the domination that fear of war had over the minds of all statesmen at this time. The bombing of Hiroshima in 1945 exposed the horrendous potential of the nuclear age. The outbreak of the Korean War in 1951 fulfilled the worst anticipations of a world living on the edge of permanent hostilities. Between those two events, Bevin was preoccupied with the creation of a new order to stabilize not just Europe but the international arena, which was now dominated by the two greatest powers, the United States and the Soviet Union. Vacuous oratory aside, Britain, the third occupant of a seat at the top table, took the idea of 'Europe' into account only as a residual consideration, out of much larger forebodings.

When Bevin entered the Foreign Office, it was committed to a strategy that might have been expected to be congenial to the Labour Party. This was the end-of-war, merging into post-war, policy of collaboration with the Soviet Union. Such was the orthodoxy of the moment, shared equally by the Americans, who themselves lost no time in packing up and starting to go home from Europe. The notion of a kind of global peace best guaranteed by equalities of allegiance between the victorious powers was what the Foreign Office was devoting itself to advance. Gladwyn Jebb, one of its architects, summarized its essence: 'All our own papers were then based on the assumption that there should in no circumstances be any Anglo-US line-up against the USSR or indeed against Communism, until such time at any rate as the Soviets should have made it abundantly clear that they did not intend to co-operate with the West.'[5]

With the advent of the Labour Government, Jebb recalled, 'a fresh and determined effort was made to secure this vital co-operation'. It was a stance, however, with which Labour as a party was happier than the new Foreign Secretary. It spoke to Labour's socialist internationalism, but was soon exposed as a denial of any tenable reality. By March 1946, Churchill, who had also been bewitched by its possibilities, repudiated it with his Iron Curtain speech. Not much later, Bevin too began to move towards the conclusion that collaboration was no longer a possibility. He reached this opinion sooner than most of the civil servants with whom he now found himself consorting. His life's education – 'plucked from the 'edgerows of experience', as he once told King George VI – prepared him better than them for hard-headed scepticism. 'Ernie was one of the very few British ministers who'd read Karl Marx and who knew about Communism,' one of his senior officials later recalled.[6] He stood out from the mandarins whose enchantment with their own fine formulae and optimistic constructs sometimes failed to engage with the facts that a democratic politician could not overlook.

From this basis, Bevin fashioned a position that both enhanced the integrity of Western Europe and diminished the possibility of Britain allying herself, in any institutional manner, with the continental urge for a closer form of union. Russia's behaviour in the post-war years, culminating in the occupation of Czechoslovakia in 1948, removed the last illusions that she could be a partner in peace. The need for an American alliance became paramount. This, the return of American military power to Europe, finally expressed in the creation of the North Atlantic Treaty Organization, became Bevin's overarching objective. Without Bevin, to whom Attlee sub-contracted Labour foreign policy as an almost independent fiefdom, it is doubtful whether either Washington or the Labour Party would have seen Nato through to its consummation by treaty in April 1949.

Bevin was equally essential to the process of implanting the American economic programme, which preceded Nato as a vital prop to the uncertain European peace. His biographer Alan Bullock reckons this 'his most decisive personal contribution' as Foreign Secretary.[7] On 5 June 1947, General George Marshall, the US Secretary of State, with little warning to anyone, proposed an American aid programme for European recovery, which eventually became the fuel for the remaking of France, Germany and Britain in particular. The first Bevin heard of the Marshall Plan was when he was lying in bed listening to the radio. But his instincts were impeccable. He went into the Foreign Office next day and got to work to assemble a response. Unencumbered by mandarin caution, he thought the Secretary of State had made 'one of the greatest speeches in world history'. Marshall laid down a challenge to Europe. It had to decide what it needed. 'The initiative, I think, must come from Europe,' Marshall said. Bevin seized on this with a kind of visceral recognition. Whereas the Foreign Office was initially cool, and the State Department was unsure what its leader meant, Bevin determined to take him at his word and help him fulfil it. 'It was like a lifeline to sinking men,' he later told the National Press Club in Washington.

So Nato and the Marshall Plan were at the heart of Bevin's achievement. He was, in his way, as central to their architecture as were the Americans. They implemented a world view that was global, strategic and conscious of imminent apocalypse. In this sense, Bevin was Britain's first peacetime Atlanticist, the man who saw less ambiguously than anyone that Washington should be taken up on its offer to guide and protect the evolution of post-war Europe. He carried the bulk of his party with him on a painful journey, beginning with the discovery that Moscow was as great an enemy of British socialism as it was of Western capitalism. He maintained the stance of a great power despite his awareness that Britain's economic strength had been sapped by the war. 'If only I had 50 million tons of coal to export, what a difference it would make to my foreign policy,' he was fond of saying. But this didn't induce him to behave like the leader of a fundamentally weakened country. He saw the immediate problem but, in common with almost everybody else, got nowhere near understanding, if he ever heard, the prophetic quality of Tizard's warning that Britain stood in danger of ceasing to be a great nation.

These strands – the Atlantic priority, the British self-image – came together in Bevin's attitude to the idea of 'Europe'. In effect, he carried out, against the background of Churchill's periodic forays into the uplifting language of European pseudo-federalism, a policy that betrayed the same ambiguity. That is to say, it was confused if not duplicitous. The impression of certainty concealed a refusal to recognize hard choices. The promises of solidarity with the ravaged nations of the continent were qualified by Bevin's total hostility to any real 'Europe' that presumed to include Britain.

At the core of this was an analysis that Churchill famously made, and Bevin did not dissent from. Represented as the essence of wisdom, it could equally well be described as a biblical text for the justification of strategic indecision. Always remember, Churchill would pronounce, that the British interest lies in remaining at the intersection of three circles, representing the United States, the Commonwealth and Europe. Never, he said, permit Britain to escape from any of them. It was a diplomatic philosophy, reverently repeated and hardly ever challenged, that now made an enduring impact on the shape of the European circle in particular.

Bevin's personal attitude began with disdain for the sheer weakness of all continental countries, which was probably shared by most of the British. They were entities in which Britain could repose neither hope nor reliance. Bevin spoke of them with despair, echoing the image sometimes to be found in the Foreign Office documents of the period, which refer to the danger of Britain 'chaining itself to a corpse'. It was one of the things that made him so committed to reawakening Americans' belief that Europe was one of their own most vital national interests.

His definitive speech on the subject, one of what he called his 'tours de reason', was made to the House of Commons on 22 January 1948. It was as spacious as it was ambiguous, and in both respects deserved to be called Churchillian.

On the one hand, this was the moment when Bevin announced that any complicit alliance with the Soviet Union had finally been rendered impossible by Soviet tactics in Central Europe. To mark a new turn in history, he proposed what he called a Western Union. The Russians, he remarked, had prevented Eastern Europe from joining any collective enjoyment of the fruits of the Marshall Plan, and were doing their best through the activities of communist parties in the West to impede the economic recovery of Europe. This meant that the free nations of Western Europe must draw together. 'I believe the time is ripe for consolidation,' Bevin said. Moreover, it must involve as many nations as possible in 'the spirit and the machinery of co-operation', not excluding Britain. 'Britain', the Foreign Secretary said, 'cannot stand outside

Europe and regard her problems as quite separate from those of her European neighbours.'

This speech had a deep formative influence. It led directly to the Treaty of Brussels, which united Britain to the continent in a defence pact with France and the Benelux countries – Belgium, the Netherlands, Luxembourg – which in turn led on to the making of Nato. On the other hand, the speech gustily emulated Churchill's own rhetoric of imprecision, and was made by a man whose vision was quite sceptical of European, as distinct from Western, Union. It did not define what Western Union was – deliberately, says Bullock – because Bevin didn't know where his call to unite 'trade, social, cultural and all other contacts' among all available nations would lead. He saw a vast world beyond Europe, in which somehow all Britain's interests could be reconciled under one umbrella. There would be the 'closest possible collaboration with the Commonwealth and with overseas territories, not only with British but French, Dutch, Belgian and Portuguese', and between these and Europe there was no necessary conflict. But the role of Britain, especially in the defence of Western Europe, was left vague. In an earlier Cabinet paper, Bevin appeared to be groping for a distinctive European part in the scheme of things. We should, he suggested, 'show clearly that we are not subservient to the United States or the Soviet Union'. But at the same time, he said his aim was to achieve 'what I called a spiritual union of the West'.[8] There was, in short, a lot of unexamined woolliness about Bevin's world view. He acted on the presumption that Britain was, and would remain, a world power, while at the same time occasionally being prepared to recognize that economic weakness might undermine such a claim. He wanted the West to unite, but was quite unsure how this might best be brought about or who the candidates for union might be. He saw Britain, correctly, as the prime mover among the European powers, yet at every relevant moment, as we shall see, he directed a foreign policy that weakened the 'European' option.

In all these positions, he was supported by the Foreign Office. There was a community of attitude between the unlettered union leader, a man who had the greatest difficulty in writing down, in his almost illegible hand, the thoughts to which he usually gave rather meandering verbal expression, and the officials who called him, without knowing conde-scension, Uncle Ernie. Instinct, allied to reasoning that turned out to be less than prophetic, led minister and mandarins in the same direction.

Instinct, surprisingly, was as decisive in the processes of the officials as it was in the gut of the typical politician. Until 1949, they had no such thing as a planning staff to assist their policy-making. The notion that rational foresight, meditated carefully and subjected to collective debate, might assist the making of foreign policy was one that took some time to gain acceptance in the British Foreign Office. Lord Halifax said before the Second World War: 'I distrust anyone who foresees consequences and advocates remedies to avert them.'[9] Halifax, admittedly, was a politician. But the condition was departmental. When one senior official recommended to another, in June 1944, the case for a two-year foreign policy statement updated every six months, the recipient, Sir Alexander Cadogan, the permanent secretary, replied: 'That way lies Bedlam.'[10] When Christopher Mayhew, on becoming a junior minister at the Foreign Office in 1946, asked for a document outlining foreign policy, he was told 'not merely that no such document existed' but 'that it was really rather doubtful whether we had a foreign policy in the proper sense at all'.[11]

There followed from this lordly amateurism not only a bias against the making of hard choices, but a reluctance sometimes to obey the logic of an analysis that was at least half discerned. To try to maintain a central position in all three of the intersecting circles defined by Churchill was a sensible, indeed elementary, objective. But to ignore some of the facts that might soon make this an illusory proposition was less defensible. Yet that was the regular tendency of the Foreign Office in the post-war half-decade and beyond.

At least some officials understood well enough that the British claim to great-power ranking was already compromised by the facts of economic life. Their words may not have had the vivid finality of Henry Tizard's, but they knew the score even before the war was over. A paper written in March 1945 spoke of Britain's enormous external debts, and cautioned against making 'commitments which our economic strength will not bear' and 'another series of humiliations' comparable with the events of the 1930s to which these would give rise. If Britain did not make clear that it would overcome its difficulties, 'other countries will say the lion is in his dotage and try to divide up his skin'. The man who wrote this, Sir Orme Sargent, deputy under-secretary, did have the prudence to note that Britain was 'the weakest and geographically the smallest' of the great powers. She was like 'Lepidus in the triumvirate with Mark Antony and Augustus'. But no sense of restraint followed from these observations. On the contrary, said Sargent before the Cold War with the Soviet Union declared itself, it was 'essential to increase our strength', by taking on more responsibilities. Sargent's clarity of analysis was matched only by the utter perversity of the conclusion he drew. Leadership of the Dominions, and of France and Western Europe, would be 'the only way to compel our two big partners to treat us as an equal'.[12] The Foreign Office saw Britain as a global player for the foreseeable future.

In 1945, the apparent contradiction between economy and politics was mitigated by a large amount of hope. At that time, the formal position of the Foreign Office was that economic strain was a temporary phenomenon. 'This country possesses all the skill and resources required to recover a dominating place in the economic world,' it wrote. By 1947, however, such optimism should have been banished from its councils. The dollar drain was incessant, Palestine and India were in turmoil, the cost of the vast German garrison, by which Britain paid to protect the rebuilding of her defeated enemy, was crippling. 'We shall be on the rocks in two years unless we can redress our balance of payments,' Hugh Dalton minuted Attlee in December 1945.[13] Yet the Foreign Office view of Britain's place in the world went defiantly, perhaps routinely, unrevised. The official view did allow that 'we do not seem to have any economic resources available for political purposes' – which limited what Britain could do for European economic recovery. But the case for an independent British foreign policy was 'still valid'.[14] And the necessity for choice between competing interests in the three circles was almost nowhere recognized as a problem meriting serious thought.

In the European circle, moreover, challenges now presented themselves whose outcome was preordained. While Churchill, however deceptively, was emitting a stream of pan-European rhetoric and starting to organize a European Movement, the Foreign Office was closing down each practical opportunity to make of 'Europe' something more than a collection of rival governments. In this ruthless exercise there was nothing to choose between the adamancy of the minister and the limpid certainty of his officials, who included some of the most influential policy-makers in the history of the British civil service.

The three exemplary moments in the process need not detain us for long. They are mere preliminaries to the decisive event that occurred in 1950, when Britain, under Bevin's ailing but determined hand, excluded herself from what became known as the Schuman Plan. But the justifications for what happened in each case are resonant. They sound the authentic note of their time. They can also be heard echoing through much that happened from first to last, right down to the 1990s.

The Treaty of Brussels, following Bevin's big speech on Western

Union, might have been a great leap forward. Its early devisers were infected with federalist possibilities: a parliament, a mechanism for economic co-operation, as well as a mutual defence agreement between Britain, France and Benelux. The idea of supra-nationalism was appearing between the draft lines, a development which Attlee himself at one stage did not reject, averring that in Western Union 'we are prepared, with other powers, to pool some degree of authority'.[15]

In the event, the outcome was more modest. Economic co-operation was mentioned, and a Permanent Consultative Council was created. But nobody could pretend this was a parliament, and that was as the British wanted it. Britain's destructive role was later regretted by one of the officials who performed it as Bevin's agent. Other officials invariably defended their part in British negativism towards Europe, on the many occasions they were approached by historians in later years. But Gladwyn Jebb, Poo-Bah of post-war construction and intellectual butler to the ministers who shaped many of its institutions, did concede that he had made a tactical mistake. The Foreign Office, he recalled in the 1980s, had been right in 1948 to rule out Britain entering a supra-national organization 'because it wouldn't have gone through Parliament'.[16] All the same, the FO could have been cleverer. It could have gone to the Europeans, who were more federalist inclined, and told them to be patient. Britain would come round, Jebb reckoned he should have told them. This embryonic European parliament might come to something: that is what the British might have said from their position of influence as Europe's strongest nation. 'Even though it won't have many supranational powers, it could have more as time goes on,' is the way Jebb could have allayed continental fears. But the British declined to offer that kind of hope. 'I blame myself for not having done that,' Jebb said.

This was of a piece with the second development, which started before the drafting of the Brussels Treaty and cast a long shadow beyond it. In 1947, talks began on the formation of a customs union in Western Europe, essentially an American idea. Lowering barriers and equalizing tariffs was a way of freeing up European trade. Freer trade within Europe would be the necessary prelude to the strengthening of both the European and American economies. But this initiative the British vowed from an early stage to obstruct and, if possible, prevent.

It summoned up another great spectre that alarmed British leaders about the idea of 'Europe'. First the Brussels Treaty – heaven forfend! – looked as though it might set up a body bearing the same name as the Westminster Parliament and perhaps challenging its power. Then a

European customs union, if completed, would compromise, perhaps ultimately destroy, the British Commonwealth – and the sterling area, which mainly consisted of the Commonwealth countries' monetary resources kept in London.

The case for a customs union, making Europe into a single market without barriers, was the classic free trader's argument, arising from the crippled circumstances in which war had left the world. The US had a vast trade surplus, but the European economies were so decimated that there was a danger of world trade drying catastrophically. This consideration was the moving spirit of self-interest behind General Marshall and his generous Plan. European free trade was pressed as a precondition of the Plan. But the terms on which it began to happen were, in the end, the minimalist British terms.

This was the last time Britain succeeded in stopping a European development she did not desire – and even then the success was only temporary. It is not too much to say that the customs union that didn't happen in 1948 became the Common Market that did happen, without Britain, in 1958.

Bevin himself wanted a customs union to happen, for political reasons – and yet, for different political reasons, did not want it in the form desired by other countries. We see the embryo of a dilemma that was to continue for fifty years. The politics of *economy* pushed Bevin one way. As late as November 1947, he was minuting the economic policy sub-committee of the Cabinet on the desirability of Western Europe attaining a measure of economic union 'if it was to maintain its independence'.[17] But the politics of *politics* pushed him in the opposite direction. Any union, in Bevin's view, had to be between sovereign governments, with no power ceded to a supra-national body.

Between these prongs of Morton's Fork, the Foreign Office decided early where it was likely to finish up. Whereas later, when economic and monetary union became a pressing issue in the 1990s, Britain faced a terrible choice between losing sovereignty through EMU and losing world influence by staying out of EMU, in the late 1940s the decision was seen as obvious, at least by the officials in charge of it. The most powerful of these, Sir Roger Makins, assistant under-secretary at the Foreign Office, wrote in August 1947 that any customs union implied 'social and political' association. For Britain, this could happen only at the expense of links with the Commonwealth, the weakening of which would lead in turn to 'the disintegration of the sterling area and spell the end of Britain as a world power'. The anti-European position, in other words, was then the opposite of what it became. It was credibly consistent with Britain's global aspirations. In fact, officials thought, it was the only way to sustain them. Supported by the Whitehall economic departments, the Foreign Office therefore set about undermining the proposed union. There was a 'general decision to go slow on the whole matter', Makins wrote. Reflecting on this later, he exhibited nothing resembling the conversion experience of his contemporary-in-influence, Gladwyn Jebb. 'We were fighting a rearguard action,' he said in the early 1980s. The Americans 'pushed us far too hard', were 'not sympathetic to our colonial obligations' and 'never understood the sterling area'.[18] Makins played a vital part in resisting what he termed the 'blackmail' of Washington, which implied that the Marshall Plan might not be launched if the customs union succumbed to British resistance.

The Cabinet decision against the union was prepared with care, with Bevin in the lead. The British had the power to dictate the outcome, and at this stage in history were able more or less to satisfy both sides of their contradictory position. The Marshall Plan did get launched, and the body that oversaw it did not exercise the supra-national powers which the Americans at first envisaged and most other European countries would have been content to surrender. The Organization for European Economic Co-operation (OEEC) was a truly inter-governmental body. The Americans, and the French, wanted this to have its own secretariat, capable of taking initiatives, with the ultimate objective, as Marshall himself described it, of 'closer integration of Western Europe'. Not only did the British reject that, they vetoed the man the integrationists named to run it, Paul-Henri Spaak, the dynamic Belgian leader, whom they saw as far too strong. 'We had absolutely nothing against Spaak, who we regarded as being an absolutely first-rate fellow,' Makins later recalled. 'We resisted because we felt that there should not be an individual of that kind standing between the governments.'[19]

These were palmy days for British influence. Having evicted Spaak, London secured control for its own man, the third in this trio of civil servants who mattered so much more than any of their successors in later decades. Alongside Jebb and Makins, Oliver Franks exercised an influence on the Labour Government seldom matched by any official at any other time. With Franks as chairman of the executive of OEEC, Britain had established what Makins called 'a matter of principle': that European integration, although espoused in numerous vague orations by Ernest Bevin, should remove not one particle of power from individual governments. And Franks, like Makins, later offered an unrepentant explanation for the British attitude. Britain was always interested in co-operation, he told Michael Charlton, but objected to the *institutions* of co-operation.

He thought that being in at the beginning of a new European institution wouldn't necessarily be enough to guarantee the national interest. 'If', Franks said on the radio in 1982, 'you are part of, and subject to, an institution which in some degree has a life of its own, initiative, spontaneity, ability to formulate policy, then you are no longer as free as you were before. And this is the point. Even though you can help mould the institution, the facts about the institution remain even when you've had your influence. The problem has been that we have been very reluctant to submit ourselves, if you like, to the rulings of an institution.'[20] There could hardly be a more unbending statement of hostility to the notion at any time of entering the European Community.

So the British got their way. But it was not a painless victory. Nor was there universal agreement that the right course had been taken. The tide of Europeanism, which Churchill among others was accelerating in 1948, did not stop at Foreign Office command. The Hague Congress, great climax of quasi-federalist effusion, took place in May. But, before we come to that, the accuracy of rival prophecies about the future of Britain, a question that crops up time and again, needs to be touched on.

The Foreign Office position, defended in particular by Makins and Franks, rested on a prediction about the future state of British power, most notably economic power. The sterling area, they thought, was Britain's lifeline, and the Commonwealth a source of both raw materials and industrial markets that had no discernible end. 'People did not foresee then that the sterling area would one day break up, that the countries of the Commonwealth wouldn't all want to hold their reserves in sterling,' Franks said later. It actually began to happen in less than a decade. But 'none of this was foreseen at the time'.[21]

That wasn't quite true. Henry Tizard wasn't alone in his more sceptical apprehensions. Bridging the Foreign Office and the Treasury was a man called Edmund Hall-Patch, Bevin's economic adviser. Hall-Patch regarded the choice identified by Makins and Franks as a false one. In August 1947, he minuted Bevin that this claim of an either/or choice between Europe and the Commonwealth had 'successfully blocked for two years our efforts to look at these proposals objectively'.[22] We should be more imaginative, he suggested. The integration of the United States had its lessons. 'If some such integration does not take place, Europe will gradually decline in the face of pressure from the United States on the one hand and the Soviet Union on the other.'

Hall-Patch was an atypical mandarin. In early life, he had earned his living as a busker on the streets of Paris, and had served abroad, Oliver Franks remarked, in such out-of-the-way places as Bangkok. Talking later, Franks conceded that Hall-Patch was a prescient man. 'He was seeing ahead with very considerable accuracy.' But his views at the time did not carry weight. They weren't congruent with 'the structure of thinking in government departments', which was the thinking Makins, Franks and Jebb, to name its three most influential designers, did nothing whatever to question. Therefore Hall-Patch wasn't heard.

Nor, however, were mildly integrationist views consistent with majority desires in the Labour Party. The party was the other great engine of Bevin's foreign policy, alongside the Foreign Office. The Labour Party has much to say in this whole story. It was a vital player at all the critical junctures of Britain's engagement with the continent. But the Labour thinking as it bore upon Bevin had a special relevance to the moment at which he, who is almost classifiable as the leading Euro-sceptic of his day, came under most baleful pressure from the supposed 'European', Winston Churchill: the Hague Congress and its aftermath.

Bevin, as we have seen, had not been hostile to federalist tendencies in his younger days. Like Attlee, he put his name to motions and resolutions that carried the stamp of desperate men desiring almost any expedient that might avoid a European war. After the war, a federalist tendency subsisted among Labour politicians, as it did among Conservatives. Indeed, on the very brink of the Hague meeting, 5 May 1948, when a Labour motion was debated suggesting that MPs from all European countries should assemble to work out a federal constitution, Attlee, the Prime Minister himself, was not averse. Maybe this reflects the vaporous manner in which the idea was then contemplated. Perhaps Attlee did not intend to be taken as making any very meaningful commitment. Nonetheless, the *Hansard* record shows him saying: 'Ultimately I believe we must come to federation of Europe. I have often spoken against the continuance of some sort of sovereignty.' The question was how to work towards 'some sort of federation' by dealing with 'practical matters'.

As aspirational rhetoric, this wasn't something Bevin especially disagreed with. On the other hand, the faction in the party which most warmly espoused the cause was one that, for other reasons, he most heartily abominated. Federation, in those days, was the ambition of the left. In May 1947, the Keep Left group of MPs published a manifesto urging a federation of Europe as far as the Soviet frontier, starting with the 'less spectacular' collaboration of France and Britain, and leading, as they hoped, to the eventual raising of the Iron Curtain.[23] A minor feature of this was the evidence it offered that shameless personal inconsistency, a feature of Labour politics no less than Conservative, began early. Composed by Ian Mikardo, the pro-federal tract was signed by fourteen MPs, among them two later scions of the anti-European cause, Richard Crossman and Michael Foot. Its major political effect, however, was to rouse Bevin's fury. For the purpose of the left was blatantly anti-American. At the very moment when Bevin had determined there was no longer any alternative to enlisting the US in the defence of Europe, this not insignificant faction in his party, containing around 100 MPs, was canvassing for a 'Third Force' to stand between the US and the USSR and supposedly heal the breach between them.

Federalism's Labour friends, in short, constituted one reason for Bevin to view with chilly disapproval Churchill's venture at The Hague. But they were not the main cause of it. Other party pressures exerted themselves on Bevin which he was, for the most part, content to experience. The party man coexisted with the international statesman. Europe, after all, was hardly a socialist paradise. Here was a Labour government, at the head of what appeared to be the most powerful country, surrounded by enfeebled nations run by anti-socialists. Adenauer in Germany, Robert Schuman in France, De Gasperi in Italy headed Catholic parties running would-be capitalist economic policies. Labour politicians were instructed in the language of unambiguous party politics not to attend the Hague Congress. 'The National Executive Committee', wrote the general secretary, Morgan Phillips, 'is unconditionally opposed to any action which might appear to associate the prestige of the governing majority party in Great Britain, however indirectly, with an organisation calculated to serve the interests of the British Conservative Party.'[24]

All the same, twenty-six Labour MPs did attend at The Hague. This did not please Bevin any more than did the resolution passed there, which was to lead to the Council of Europe, and the creation of its Assembly in Strasbourg. Bevin by now detested the European Movement as much as he disliked the Keep Left group. On returning from The Hague, Churchill had even had the impertinence, as Harold Macmillan recalls in his diaries, to lead a march from Parliament to 10 Downing Street to insist on the Assembly being created. There had been 'trouble from this so-called European movement, not always in the open', Bevin later complained in a Commons debate, 'and it had been extremely difficult to carry on negotiations with this kind of semi-sabotage going on behind the scenes.' (To which Churchill replied: 'You are the arch-saboteur).'[25]

Like it or not, however, the Government was driven along the road towards creating the Assembly. In the second most quoted line he ever uttered, Bevin had bestowed upon it an image straight from the 'edgerows of experience. 'If you open that Pandora's Box,' he once said, 'you never know what Trojan 'orses will jump out.' But in November one thing led to another and the tame little Consultative Council, which was all that remained of the 'parliament' the Brussels Treaty was once intended to provide, met in Paris in order to consider a proposal for a proper parliamentary European Assembly.

Britain could not avoid attending. In fact she sent a high-level delegation, led by Hugh Dalton, the Old Etonian intellectual who thought he should have had Bevin's job, and staffed among others by the ubiquitous Gladwyn Jebb. It worked hard to prevaricate. Instead of an assembly, it suggested a non-parliamentary consultative body with limited terms of reference, to be controlled by the governments. An impasse beckoned, assisted not least by another strand in Labour anti-Europeanism which Dalton personified. Dalton was almost uncontrollably anti-German. He regarded Churchill's efforts to bring the recent enemy into the concert of nations as a betrayal. 'We'll gouge out their eyes! We'll stamp on their bellies! We'll tear out their livers!' he once sang to a friend on the way to a function where Germans were to be present.[26] Although Bevin took a more statesmanlike view, he agreed with Dalton's opinion that, if the Council had to happen, it should be minimalist in conception.

For the most part, it was. 'We'll give them this talking shop,' Bevin eventually conceded.[27] During the negotiations, he wriggled and writhed. He wanted delegations appointed by governments not parliaments, and voting done in blocs, controllable by governments, rather than individually. In the end, a compromise was again achieved, as a result of which the Council of Europe had no power and rather little influence, a condition for which the British Labour Government was responsible.

As well as Churchill, with his grand inaugural speech, many large figures attended the first meeting of the Strasbourg Assembly. The Conservative delegation included Harold Macmillan, Duncan Sandys, David Eccles and Robert Boothby. None was a federalist, but all were by their own lights passionate 'Europeans'. They wanted the idea of Europe to succeed, and thought Britain should consider herself a leader among partners. The Labour team was also talented. Led by Dalton, it included James Callaghan, Fred Lee, Aidan Crawley and the young international secretary of the party, Denis Healey. But the Labour prejudice, following Bevin's, was different – or at least more explicit and, as some might say, more honest. 'We could not approve any policy that took us further away from the Commonwealth,' Dalton wrote at the time.[28]

The Strasbourg federalists didn't give up hope. Although the Council's statute had been written, ideas were still in the melting-pot. That was the spirit of the time. Enthusiasm and uncertainty abounded. Not everything seemed to be fixed. No sooner had they gathered than the continentals were pressing forward, pushing at the first meeting for 'a political authority of a supra-national character' to be created without delay. The Assembly passed a resolution to this effect, enjoining the Council to develop such an authority 'with limited functions but real powers', words coined by the Labour MP Kim Mackay, and every British Conservative voted for it. Paul-Henri Spaak personified the atmosphere of optimistic rejoicing. 'I came to Strasbourg', he said, 'convinced of the need for a United States of Europe. I am leaving with the certitude that union is possible.'[29]

But this underrated the opposition. Led by the Labour Government, the Council's committee of ministers simply killed off the Assembly's initiatives. They refused to surrender the veto which Bevin and the Foreign Office had made sure they kept, ignored the demand for a political authority and even tried to prevent the Assembly discussing any matter that fell within the functions of any other international body such as OEEC or the United Nations. Of Strasbourg's grand aspirations, only a Commission and Court of Human Rights, enforcing a European Convention, were eventually permitted to have an existence that endured.

By early 1950, therefore, the scene appeared to be set, and it accorded more closely with the priorities of establishment Britain – the Britain of Ernest Bevin, the Foreign Office, the Treasury, the whole of Whitehall, almost the whole of the governing Labour Party – than it did with the rhetorical clouds put out with such captivating power by Winston Churchill. These clouds, moreover, proved on inspection to be little more than hot air. They enveloped what was actually a consensus, shared by an entire political class, indeed by most of the arbiters of an entire culture. This consensus agreed, all in all, that the island nation belonged not to the continent but to the world, and could better maintain its global importance by spurning every inducement to reconsider the continent. It saw such lures, whether from the United States or from Europe, as a trick. And it was able until this date to impose its own terms on these allies, who were either too distant or too feeble to count. It was the captain of its fate, or so it thought, and the dominant force among the countries it had to deal with: the leader, in a word, of a Europe congenial to it.

This, however, was the last time such a sweet picture could be conjured up. The claim to leadership, hitherto unchallengeable, raised a question that could not be answered for ever by reference to intersecting circles, or any other image that obscured the necessity for choice. The luxury of calm disdain for 'Europe' was a pose with a limited life. The first great moment of truth was about to present itself.

*

ON 9 MAY 1950, at six o'clock in the evening, the French Foreign Minister, Robert Schuman, held a press conference that he hoped would change the world. This hope was less than well illuminated by some of the circumstances of the occasion. Schuman's modest presence and hesitant voice did not convey a sense of history in the making. Moreover, there were 200 journalists present but no movie cameras. To make sure something was recorded for posterity, Schuman was obliged to re-enact the scene some months later. Nonetheless, 9 May 1950 was the day that established Europe as being more serious about 'Europe' than the British could believe.[30]

To Ernest Bevin, it was a day mingling fury with regret. These emotions, moreover, were suffused by illness. Bevin was by now a sick man. He had returned to work only the day before Schuman's press conference, after a month in the London Clinic following an operation to ease his respiratory system. He sometimes said himself that he was 'only half alive'. He retained control of foreign policy, and the power of his pre-fixed positions concerning the future of Europe remained the dominant influence over what now happened. It is worth remembering, though, that this was now a man who by his own confession had difficulty staying awake and, according to his subordinate, Kenneth Younger, chaired meetings at which 'he could barely read out the agenda, let alone take charge'.[31]

The reason for Bevin's professional fury was obvious. The announcement Schuman made had been cooked up without his knowledge, and partly as an act of deception against him. But Bevin got over that. What he couldn't overlook was the regrettable possibility that Britain had lost control of events. In the five years since the end of the war, she had been able to forestall questions that embarrassed her or ensure they were answered in her favour. The Schuman Plan was something else again.

It proposed the boldest fusing of the resources and interests of two great nations that modern Europe had ever seen. Coal and steel, the base materials of industrial economies, would cease to be controlled and sold by the respective governments of France and Germany, and would be subject to shared decisions. These decisions would be made not by national governments acting as sovereign powers, but by a new organization – a high authority – which they would agree to create, and to which they would, over these particular resources, surrender sovereignty. French and German citizens would run the Authority. But their role would transcend nation. They would be the functionaries of a new and formal community.

There was no model for a coal and steel community in European or any other history. And the creative mind that lay behind it, which was entirely French, was inspired in part by economic necessity. The French were alarmed by Germany's post-war industrial recovery. Steel, in particular, had always been cheaper there than in France, and the pattern continued. Victor and vanquished were already exchanging the economic as well as psychological advantages that 1945 might have been expected to bring them. Though German production levels were controlled by the occupying powers, France knew the Americans would always sympathize with German demands for more. Indeed, it was because the Americans and British, who controlled the Ruhr, were on the verge of raising the ceiling for German production that the French were forced to act fast. For France, there were immediate attractions to a scheme over which she would share control. For Germany, collaboration as an equal partner with France, five years after the war, offered an irresistible opportunity.

But economics was not the largest consideration. The most relevant propensity of coal and steel was their use in the tools of war. Above and beyond the likely economic consequences of German domination – dumping, protectionism, cartels and the stifling of free trade – were the political attractions of a new way of peace. Removing these elements of the war machine from national control would reduce the risk of a mainland war recurring. This would be the earnest of a new political intention: Franco-German reconciliation, the prize that would change future history.

The three men who made the Schuman Plan – the patron, the architect and the grateful supplicant – were men of mettle. They knew what they wanted. This did not discount or exclude Britain. But neither did it contemplate submission to Britain's superiority. With Bevin and with Britain, each had a complex relationship. These were Europeans it was not given to a Briton thoroughly, intuitively, easily to understand.

Robert Schuman, the patron, uniquely personified what the Franco-German problem was about. His home territory was Lorraine, borderland between Germany and France, for ever in pawn to the warring continent. In childhood, Schuman, though French by descent, was categorized German, spoke French with a Rhineland accent, and was conscripted into German uniform in the First World War. He became a Frenchman only at thirty-two. But as a Lorraine politician he understood about coal and steel. They were produced there, fuelling the wars that were fought there. This was a place where the Légion d'Honneur and the Iron Cross could sometimes sit on the same mantelpiece. Georges Berthoin, a young Schuman aide and later the influential EEC ambassador in London, told me he saw such juxtapositions. There are still memorials to both French and German soldiers in the same squares of the same towns of Alsace-Lorraine.

According to Berthoin, it was partly as a way of freeing his home territory from 'historical schizophrenia' that Schuman saw his famous Plan. He was an improbable vehicle for such a grand scheme. The inaudible voice issued from a thin, ascetic figure, who had characteristics seldom found among politicians of the time, let alone forty years later. He lived in monastic chastity, a bachelor and scholar, expert in philosophy and theology, his bookshelves bearing copiously annotated editions of Hegel and André Gide. But he was also a public man of iron, who clung with determination to the carousel of the Fourth Republic. In an earlier turn of the wheel, before he took charge of the Foreign Ministry at the Quai d'Orsay, he had been Prime Minister. As a serious Catholic, he knew how to forgive, but did not indulge in the disgrace of forgetting. Above all, he never forgot the causes of the war. 'As regards the Coal and Steel Community,' said Georges Berthoin, 'Schuman was a man absolutely aware he was fulfilling a historic mission.'[32]

He was not, however, the Plan's inventor. Jean Monnet, the architect, was the chief creative mind. And since Monnet was the godfather, if not father, of this 'Europe' that has caused the British so much trouble, he should detain us a little longer.

History sometimes reallocates the credit for great events, as time goes on. But, for the idea and fact of 'Europe', Monnet has never lost the credit or the blame. Among all who came to favour the idea, sometimes years late, he enjoys an admiration verging on sanctity, just as for its enemies he is the devil incarnate. In Britain, as much as anywhere, Monnet was duly infamous. I once heard Kenneth Baker, a senior Cabinet minister in the 1990s, refer from a public platform to 'Jean' Monnet, as if he thought he was talking about a woman.[33] Perhaps this was a calculated insult from a politician keen to stress his anti-European credentials in the debate then raging in the Conservative Party. But from the 1950s to the 1970s there was no member of the British establishment whose hand Monnet had not in all probability shaken.

He was an internationalist in a rare sense, contact man supreme, originally a brandy salesman born in Cognac, banker, tireless factotum to the diplomatic gentry. Arranging a loan for Poland in 1927, for example, he made the lifelong acquaintance of John Foster Dulles, the US Secretary of State two decades later. He had a formative period in London, where he learned about British ways. But America was his first base. Years before 'Europe' was thought of, Dean Acheson, John McCloy, Henry Stimson, Averell Harriman and other East Coast paladins were Monnet's friends. He gave early meaning to the label 'international civil servant', being on the payroll of the British Government in the First World War and the American in the Second, as well as, for a while, deputy secretary-general of the League of Nations.

Monnet wasn't elected. He was never more than an official at any time, and often not even that, flitting through the underworld of unpublicized influence in the capitals of the West. Elbow-gripper, shoulder-tapper, a wanderer with a fat address-book, he was also a man of action, determined to harness a vision, which anyone might have, to the means of advancing it in the real world, which the average visionary tended to neglect. Contemplating why it was that Monnet was thought both by admirers and detractors to be so extraordinarily effective, François Duchêne suggests in his biography, a marvellous work of scholarship and insight: 'His secret, if he had one, came from a combination of creative and critical faculties. He appealed to the romantic in people through the idealism of his goals, and to the expert in them through the realism of his means.' Making 'Europe' was Monnet's richest dream. What drove him was the experienced fact of war. He thought the

reason the First World War lasted longer than necessary was that the
allies had fought 'side by side and not as a single organised force'. He is
that rare specimen, a public man with one driving idea, able over half a
century to see this idea, the weakening of the nation-state, begin to come
to pass. The Schuman Plan was the largest stride he took towards it.

It connected seamlessly with his past. He had been the fertile brain
behind the plan for Anglo-French Union in the dark days of 1940. He it
was who mainly persuaded both Churchill and General de Gaulle of its
merits. But after the war he wanted to go much further than Churchill.
He was a committed federalist, and could see that the ambitions of the
European Movement, for all the exalted vapourings of the Hague
Conference (which he did not attend), led no further than the Council
of Europe, which was carefully limited to collaboration between states.
What Monnet wanted was not mere co-operation, but the creation
within Europe of a common interest, formally constructed and legally
ratified.

In its final form, the Coal and Steel Community did not conform
exactly to the Monnet blueprint. There were significant dilutions. He
was, however, its undisputed originator, and has identified the moment
when it took specific shape. In the middle of March 1950, he repaired to
the Swiss Alps, as was his habit, for a walking tour to clear his head. We
may picture this stocky figure, accompanied only by a guide, as his
memoirs describe, for two weeks striding across the mountains from one
overnight lodge to another, physically on holiday but emotionally and
intellectually preoccupied with what he saw as an essential idea. Five
years after the last war, how best could the next one be prevented?
Actually, he wrote, 'we are at war already'. The Cold War, now burgeoning, was 'the first phase of real war', and the danger for Europe still lay
in Germany – not because Germany was in a position to start war again,
but because she was in danger of becoming the stake in a struggle to the
death between Washington and Moscow. The Berlin blockade was less
than two years in the past. What Germany needed was some dramatic
readmission to the Western system.

This was what Monnet sold to Schuman, and what he had no
difficulty, of course, in inducing the West German leader, Konrad
Adenauer, the third founder of this 'Europe', gladly to accept. West
Germany was less than a year past its rebirth as an independent country.
The new Federal Republic still lived under the shadow of defeat and
moral ostracism, and was still divided into four zones of foreign
occupation, the symbol of its mistrusted and inferior status. Chancellor

Adenauer, fiercely rejecting neutralism, was always likely to be receptive to Monnet's design, once it was put to him. When Schuman's message came, he says in his memoirs, 'I agreed to his proposal with all my heart.' To Monnet he said, 'I regard the implementation of the French proposal as my most important task. If I succeed, I believe that my life will not have been wasted.'

Before these men put anything on the table, they represented, it has to be said, a problem for the British. There were certain anterior difficulties. If this was to be a project that enlisted Britain's support, as it was certainly intended to be, it had to overcome preliminary obstacles and prejudices. Even a great tide of history, if that is what was about to be launched, might be set back or somewhat diverted by quotidian flesh and blood.

Robert Schuman, for one thing, was Germanic not only by territorial origin but by cultural sympathy. He understood English but did not speak it well, knew little English history, had consorted no more than he had to with British leaders. 'He did not understand Britain,' Georges Berthoin recalled. Forcibly thrown together, Schuman and Bevin actually got on quite well. They shared a somewhat austere attitude to the extravagances of life, and prided themselves on their connection with ordinary people. But between the Cartesian intellectual and the uneducated West Country yokel the mutual cultural understanding that might have overcome their political differences did not exist.

In the case of Adenauer, there was no natural lack of empathy with Britain, but there had been an unfortunate event. After the First World War, when he was a rising leader in the Rhineland, the British had helped him to recover part of a pension that had been removed from him. So he was originally never anti-British. But he had a bad experience in 1945 when he was ousted from his post as Lord Mayor of Cologne on the orders of a British brigadier, and expelled into the countryside. This was an action grimly symbolic of the persistent British failure after the war to build a constructive relationship with Germany. Had a German alliance been foreseen as a crucial ingredient of foreign policy in any of the post-war decades, the entire history of Britain and the European idea might have followed a different course. But, in any case, there was something deeper with Adenauer which, as with Schuman, voided him of pro-British predilections. He simply thought other countries understood Germany's problems better. As one of his advisers testified: 'He did not see in Britain the same partner, with the same kind of antennae for European thinking, as he did in France with people like Monnet and de Gaulle, or in America with people like John Foster Dulles, John McCloy and Dean Acheson.'[34]

Schuman and Adenauer composed a Germanic alliance, culturally speaking. Adding his part to it was the Italian Prime Minister, Alcide De Gasperi who – further to the endless fluidity of continental politics – had been a young politician in Vienna during the last days of the Austro-Hungarian Empire. De Gasperi was another German-speaker. Berthoin watched the *arrières-pensées* comfortably shared between them. But more significant was the religious affiliation of all three. They were more than routine Roman Catholics. Church was important to their project: a church the British never warmed to.

For the British, the Catholic nature of 'Europe' was a generous source of prejudice against it, adding to the others. Britain in 1950 was still an emphatically Protestant country, in which Catholicism was something foreign and therefore suspect. As a child at a Catholic prep school at the time, I was taught to see myself as a member of God's elect, whose earthly fate was to be excluded from the mainstream by the ignorant, anti-Catholic majority. My heavenly destiny, however, would be to look down upon these heathens paying for their errors in hell. In the senior reaches of public life, where there were almost no Catholics, this attitude was reversed. The Protestants were the chosen ones. Anti-Catholic prejudice was instinctive, and Ernest Bevin was one who exhibited it. Gladwyn Jebb records a scene on a journey with Mr and Mrs Bevin to a trade union conference in Southport: 'The train was rather full and people often went by in the corridor, including from time to time a Catholic priest in a soutane. Whenever this happened Mr and Mrs Bevin became uneasy and Mr Bevin muttered "black crows". I understood that he believed that Catholic priests brought bad luck, and nothing that I could say had any effect.'[35]

These feelings were not limited to superstition. They acquired a strong political formulation among people who saw in the Schuman Plan the beginnings of a Vatican conspiracy or, even more luridly, an attempt to recreate the Holy Roman Empire. And such speculations were not confined to fusty old imperialists and Little Englanders. Kenneth Younger, Bevin's astute and educated junior, was one of the few politicians or officials sympathetic to the Schuman Plan. But his suspicions on this account were evidently important to him. Schuman, he noted in his diary in May 1950, was 'a bachelor and a very devout Catholic who is said to be very much under the influence of the priests'. The Plan, Younger felt obliged to admit to himself, 'may be just a step in the consolidation of the Catholic "black international", which I have always thought to be a big driving force behind the Council of Europe'.[36]

The post-war continental Church, moreover, was known to be anti-socialist. Denis Healey, as international secretary of the Labour Party, found alarming proof of this in Holland. 'The Dutch Social Democratic Party had completely reconstructed itself after the war and turned itself into a Labour Party with no Marxist dogma at all,' Healey remembered. 'Yet, in the first election after the war in Holland, the Dutch Catholic hierarchy excommunicated people who voted Labour.'[37]

Such was the background beyond politics to the case of Schuman and the British. There was a mountain of suspicion to overcome. But this was as nothing to the foreground, where Britain, instead of playing her accustomed role as orchestrator of weaker nations, found herself artfully outmanoeuvred. The sequence of events that now unfolded might have been calculated to enrage Britain and her Foreign Secretary. Were they so calculated? It is hard to be sure. What cannot be disputed is that the British Government, placing the worst interpretation on events, adopted a position calculated, with malice aforethought, to frustrate what the continentals wanted and, come what may, to exclude Britain from it. At this watershed, Britain decided that there would be no confluence.

The deception was clumsy, and perhaps unnecessary. Schuman was due anyway to meet Bevin and Dean Acheson, the American Secretary of State, in London in early May, to talk about Nato and other large matters. A serious argument beckoned. France wanted to curtail the effects of Germany's menacing industrial recovery, without incurring the hostility of the Americans, who wanted to encourage it. Schuman needed something to propose. There was thus a timely vacuum into which Monnet, with characteristic deftness, launched the idea of a coal and steel community.

The largest steel and coal producer in Europe, however, was not admitted to the secret before it was announced. Nor were many other people. It required what Monnet joyously called a 'conspiracy'. Having accepted the idea, Schuman took it over as his own, without informing the foreign policy officials at the Quai d'Orsay. But what was worse than Britain's exclusion from the cabal was the incorporation within it of the Americans. Dean Acheson appeared to be a co-conspirator. This Bevin could not forgive.

Acheson was passing through Paris, prior to the London meeting of the Big Three, and Schuman went personally to the American embassy to tell him of the Plan before it was announced. It came as a great surprise. 'I have just had a most startling statement made to me,' Acheson told an associate after the meeting.[38] And his first reaction was to sniff the beginnings of a giant European cartel that would damage the American steel industry. So Acheson was not, in the first instance, entranced by Schuman's Plan. He knew it would enrage the British, who saw him as one of the few men in Washington sharing some of their scepticism about the integration of Europe. But it didn't take long for him to be converted to the political and security benefits that might flow from the Monnet–Schuman concept. Almost overnight, he switched his allegiance. The scene was set for sulphuric encounters in London.

The first of these was with Bevin. Acheson arrived on the morning the Cabinets in both Paris and Bonn were reaching the conclusion Monnet and Schuman had conspired to produce. He was sworn to secrecy, a pledge it seemed possible for him to sustain during lunch that day with Bevin, but the duplicity of which became apparent earlier than he might have hoped, when the French ambassador, René Massigli, turned up unannounced in the Foreign Secretary's ante-room with an 'important message' to deliver. 'My embarrassment grew as the company speculated about this mystery,' Acheson later recalled.[39] When he returned to the Foreign Office that afternoon, after Bevin had found out what was going on, he knew what to expect. 'I kept a four o'clock appointment ... with dragging feet,' he wrote. 'Bevin asked me to see him alone. He was in a towering rage, and at once charged that I had known of Schuman's plan and had kept it from him. This, of course, was true and I said so.'[40]

Acheson later regretted what happened. He said Schuman had committed a 'stupid' mistake by appearing to conspire against Bevin, and so had he by going along with it. But, if this was a mistake, it was not, on the part of Monnet or Schuman, accidental. It was based on an appreciation of the obstructive power of British diplomacy if given forewarning of initiatives it did not like.

Monnet was pretty open about this. He said later that he always knew the British would reject the Plan, and he was determined that this attitude, coming from the major European power, should not be allowed to frustrate the Franco-German idea. Schuman was less candid, and also less certain that Britain could not be persuaded to go along. When the Big Three had their meeting, on 11 May, he insisted there was no question of the French seeking to create a *fait accompli*. The minutes make him sound like a bad newspaper editor, insincerely apologizing to fend off a libel action. Schuman, they record, offered 'personal regrets for any embarrassment that might have been caused'. The French, he said, were merely putting up a proposal.

But they had certainly wanted to break the diplomatic rules that normally obtained between allies. Both for Germans and for Europeans, Schuman explained to Bevin and Acheson, the French desired 'to produce a psychological shock'. And this purpose they achieved, to which could be added the equal shock to the Americans, who were not accustomed to being taken so violently by surprise by anything the French Government chose to do.

By this time, two days after the thunderbolt, Ernest Bevin, though still dozy from the effects of sedative drugs, had recovered some of his sang-froid. The disarray in Britain's immediate response to the Plan had, in any case, been worsened by other little accidents. On top of Bevin's own serious disability, Attlee and Cripps were on holiday in France when the shock arrived. But now they were back at the Cabinet table, where Bevin showed that his indignation had passed, and the Foreign Office was back in pragmatic business.

There followed, according to the minutes, a discussion that foretold in outline the hundreds, indeed thousands, of similar discussions that would take place at the same table, covering the very ground and raising the same anxieties that preoccupied other British governments over the next forty-five years. On and on these debates would go, through the governments of Eden and Macmillan, and that of Harold Wilson, here present on this day as a youthful President of the Board of Trade. Past Wilson in the 1960s, into the years of Edward Heath, then in turn through the time of James Callaghan, Margaret Thatcher and John Major, the same musings and fears would incessantly recur.

There is a temptation, reaching for the cliché, to describe this similarity between 11 May 1950 and a hundred other later dates as uncanny. But of course it is not. For, whether in 1950 or in 1995, the problems that bothered the British about European integration, so long as it was considered a contingent possibility open to infinite debate, were unlikely to differ very much. There was nothing strange about them. They have always been the essence of the matter.

Part of the British response to Schuman's proposition was peculiar to its time. Was this a French plot, someone asked (Cabinet minutes rarely say who), to save money on defence by creating a European Third Force that would do business with the Russians? This was a question which in due course ceased to have any significance. Mostly, the debate exuded suspicion on grounds that became exceedingly familiar through subsequent decades. The scheme threatened disaster for the British steel industry, the ministers felt. It would produce a protectionist cartel which Britain might feel obliged to join. Yet inside a cartel of private steel-makers the public ownership of British coal and steel, one of Labour's proudest achievements, might be compromised, and the iron and steel industry might be 'seriously reduced in size'.

So the proposed community, as they thought, was in every way an economic threat, and an intrusion on the sovereign decision of a Labour government to nationalize basic industries. But it compromised political sovereignty in other senses too. Once Britain entered the scheme, 'it could not easily retrace its steps if it disliked the effects'. (The same would be said forty years later about the continental ambition to create a single European currency. The fearful irreversibility of 'Europe' has always been an aspect the British were most aware of.) Moreover, if there was to be a coal and steel community of the kind Schuman described, the ministers concluded that 'political federation might be an essential pre-requisite'.

The Cabinet vowed to find out more. Jean Monnet, they knew, was the designated contact man. He would be approached with a view to answering the question that has continued to puzzle so many successors to this, the first generation of the British political class to be faced with a hard choice in Europe which they might not be able to bury. Their quandary was simple, but of epic proportion. They needed to determine, the men round the table are drily reported as agreeing, if the continental proposal 'represented an economic scheme which had been put forward at this juncture for political reasons, or whether the project was primarily political in character'.

Similarly prophetic in their tone were the first responses of the Foreign Office and the Treasury, each prepared with swift professional-ism for the Cabinet committee. Both their May 1950 submissions reveal the first stirrings of awareness of the dilemma that became so familiar. They could see pros and cons to a coal and steel community. But they also contemplated the hitherto unthinkable possibility that something serious was about to happen on the continent which might curtail Britain's own freedom of choice.

The Foreign Office, through Sir Ivone Kirkpatrick, a peppery little Ulsterman, noted that it had been the declared policy of the Government 'to incorporate Germany into the Western comity of nations', a policy against which France had always raised more serious objections than any other nation. Here, therefore, was a device which might overcome an insoluble post-war problem. Kirkpatrick produced a substantial list of other ways in which the Schuman Plan would also be a triumph of diplomatic progress.

On the other hand he indicated that there were the difficulties. These benefits were highly desirable – as long as Britain didn't actually have to join. All the British needed was 'consultative association', he suggested. Anything fuller was 'likely to involve us in Europe beyond the point of no return', an implicitly undesirable condition. So Kirkpatrick was ready with his thoughts about damage-limitation, should the continentals decide to go ahead. Britain, he said, should not 'take the lead' in criticizing the Plan, because it was already proving quite popular. He advised a stress on the positive benefits of the Atlantic community, rather than on 'our reluctance to become excessively involved in Europe'. The Foreign Office began to prepare the defences. But the Treasury's paper was even more wary. In the short term, it said, the British coal and steel industries could hold their own whether outside or inside the Franco-German Plan. But the long term might be disastrous either way. If Britain stayed out, the integrated continental steel producers could 'attack our export and probably even our domestic markets'. Yet, if Britain went in, the High Authority might well see the economic logic in concentrating all steel production outside Britain, in Schuman's own territory near the Ruhr. Likewise with coal, the British market-share, already sliding in Europe, would diminish further. There was also the danger that the Authority would insist on equalizing wages and conditions, a 'social chapter'-in-embryo of the kind that divided European opinion in the 1990s.

This was a dismal picture, apparently inviting Britain to do all she could to crush the Plan by any means available. According to these officials, it had no real advantage of any kind. Moreover, the Treasury peered with the same incredulity as the Foreign Office at the implications for national independence. It thought a 'political federation' the likely consequence of a community for coal and steel, remarking that 'no national government could give up sovereignty over such essential elements in its economic structure without prejudice to its power of action in almost every other field' – another apprehension that was to echo down the years with respect to other commodities, including the very stuff of ultimate economic union, money itself.

These, then, were the first reactions: deeply suspicious, presumptively hostile, initial bemusement already crystallizing into a purposeful discussion of how the Schuman Plan might be frustrated. That should not be done openly. The aim should be to find out more without showing too much interest. 'A close interest in the technical aspect might give the impression that we were prepared to commit ourselves further than we actually wished,' murmured the committee of officials set up to handle the Plan.

Such was the climate when the arch-begetter, following Schuman's own visit, arrived to explain himself to the British. This encounter was not as sulphurous as Bevin's with Acheson. But it exhaled the noxious fumes of a disagreement reaching close to the bowels of two nations – or at least of the two political classes that represented them.

Jean Monnet had reason to be pleased with the first wave of responses to his brainchild. For this most committed of integrationists, they were encouraging. German enthusiasm was not very surprising, for the Plan was a way back towards international respectability. But the reception in France had been almost as keen. Collaboration with the Germans apparently did not horrify the nation. 'Considering recent history and the personal experiences of practically every living French-man,' the man at the British embassy reported, 'this is, to say the least, remarkable.' What France wanted, however, was British participation. The same embassy man found a wave of feeling in Paris that 'unless Britain comes in, the scheme cannot succeed'. His counterpart in the Bonn embassy stressed the judgement of the German Government, too, that without Britain all such schemes of European co-operation 'were bound to fail'. But this was not Monnet's opinion. Nor was it a consideration that moved the British Government – except perhaps to optimism.

When Monnet reached London, his first meeting gave unexpected reason for hope. Stafford Cripps, the Chancellor of the Exchequer, told him that in his opinion negotiations should begin at once. Cripps evidently wasn't bothered by the precondition that a high authority, Schuman's unique creation, should be accepted from the start. He wanted to go ahead with talks, mainly because he didn't think Britain 'would ever be able to come in later on a scheme which had been worked out by France, Germany and Benelux'. This opinion of Cripps is worth dwelling on. He was, of course, a former federalist – but then so were many others, and in any case the post-war Cripps was a different man from the pre-war anti-warrior who had spoken out in favour of world government. His reaction to Monnet now is interesting not as some cryptic integrationist gesture to satisfy the Chancellor's personal agenda. That wasn't the point. What the Cripps–Monnet conversation did mark, however, was both the first and the last moment of conditional enthusiasm for the Schuman Plan to be voiced by a senior British minister. Cripps may not have wanted to join, but he did want to talk. And it was talking – the sucking-in effect of formal negotiation – that the entire British political establishment now turned itself, in effect, to resisting.

Most appalled by Cripps's amiable reception of Monnet were the officials who witnessed it. Edwin Plowden and Monnet had known and respected each other during the war. Plowden now had the further connection of being the nearest thing to Monnet's equivalent in London: the industrialist-turned-planner whom the Labour Government had recruited to be Stafford Cripps's senior adviser on economic regeneration. (Monnet's formal job in Paris was as head of the commissariat for Le Plan, France's post-war blueprint for economic recovery.) As a young businessman, Plowden had slipped easily into Whitehall life during the war and remained there, to be burdened with every kind of establishment task and clothed with every honour, for thirty years beyond it. He wasn't clever, in the formal Whitehall way. 'He only got a poor third,' a subordinate noted of his university career. But he became a formidable in-fighter. 'He was very good at arguing with ministers,' his private secretary of the period, Douglas Allen, later head of the Treasury, told me. 'They had to listen to him because they'd made such a fuss about appointing him.'[41]

Allied with Plowden at this critical moment was the more bruising figure of Roger Makins from the Foreign Office, already established as a rabid Euro-sceptic. He took the official note of Cripps's meeting with Monnet, a record dripping with mandarin horror. So anxious and yet confident was Plowden that he felt quite free to intervene dismissively in the ministerial conversation he was witnessing. He did not hesitate to explain to Monnet, according to Makins, that 'these were just the Chancellor's personal views which he had not discussed with colleagues'. And on leaving the meeting, Makins immediately went away and minuted his Foreign Office boss on the urgent need for a Bevin corrective: 'This plunge of the Chancellor took Edwin completely by surprise. Edwin agreed that the S. of S. must be told, the question is when and how. R.M.'

It didn't take long. Bevin saw the Makins note that day, and Attlee saw it soon after. But these politicians were not the significant players during Monnet's visit. That distinction undoubtedly went to Plowden and Makins, who now met the Frenchman on their own, at breakfast next day in the Hyde Park Hotel, for one of the more crucial engagements of the early days of Britain's reluctant flirtation. The story of Britain and Europe is, among other things, a story of many meals. Seldom does a moment of history fail to be accompanied by some kind of banquet. This was an early meal that became famous in the annals of the courtship.

Unlike the French opinion sampled by the British embassy in Paris, Monnet did not regard British involvement in the Schuman Plan as essential to its success, and neither in the end did Schuman. Monnet, indeed, subsequently made this opinion crystal-clear with his claim to have understood all along that Britain would always wait to see how any European institution worked, and apply to join only when satisfied that it did. Certainly the set-up at the time, beginning with the shock announcement by Schuman and continuing with a meeting that the British officials found wholly lacking in reassurance, did not seem designed to increase the chances of collaboration. In fact it could have been programmed to repel.

For Monnet had few answers to their questions. The British record of the meeting exudes grim pleasure in the long list of issues the French had evidently failed to think about: how coal and steel would be priced, how sold abroad, where produced at home, how governed by wage equalization and so on and so forth. From their note, Makins and Plowden sound weary and disdainful – but also shocked. For on one point Monnet was unalterably plain. The treaty would have to be agreed and signed as a matter of principle, before all these pettifogging minutiae were decided. And the principle in question was the independence of the High Authority. It would, said Monnet, mean 'the surrender of national sovereignty over a wide strategic and economic field': a point the potential signatories would have to concede before negotiations began.

This was a severe requirement for the representatives of a country already reluctant to comprehend the smallest revision of sovereignty in any particular. 'It was, so to speak, sprung on us,' Makins later told me. 'Well, Jean, what's all this about?' he remembered asking, in a formula he grew used to delivering to any historian who turned up on his doorstep. 'Oh, I've got it all here,' Monnet replied. Whereupon 'he fished a piece of paper out of his pocket, and gave it to us to read. We said, "But it says here that the objective is to set up a European federal structure. You know the British Government is not in favour of that." And he just said, "Yes".'[42]

Interestingly, the official British record of the meeting makes no reference to the Schuman Plan portending a federal Europe. That apocalyptic interpretation came a little later. Even though the High Authority, within the bounds of coal and steel, was indeed a body that might have federalizing tendencies, and the Community itself had been announced as 'the realization of the first concrete foundations of a European federation', that was not yet anywhere in evidence. The High Authority involved merely ceding sovereignty to a supra-national body for a limited purpose. The achievement of wholesale federation was an enormous inference to draw, entirely dependent on what the members eventually did to bring it about, far down the road.

All the same, the 'federal' spectre has been prominent in all subsequent recollection of what happened in May 1950. It is because federalism seemed imminent that the British said they were suspicious of the Schuman Plan, hoped it would not work and did their best, behind a fair amount of diplomatic camouflage, to prevent it working. This is how Makins, in particular, has always recalled it.

Early in this inquiry I called on Makins at his Kensington flat. By then he was ninety, long ago ennobled as Lord Sherfield, imposingly tall, still with a vigorous manner and booming voice, and entirely unrepentant about his role in the history whose direction he did much to determine. His fine collection of pre-Raphaelite paintings, though acquired with the help of a wealthy American wife, somehow testified to that distant era when a civil servant might be grand enough to own such things. The mind was still confident that he had had no option but to advise against what he often referred to at the time as the 'institutional adventures' proposed by Monnet and Schuman.

Throughout his time in the Foreign Office, Makins was the epitome of the post-war Atlanticist. He devoted the serious part of his professional life to nurturing the American connection, protecting Britain's special relationship with Washington, and therefore – a logical consequence, as he saw it – seeing 'Europe' as an idea to be regarded with gravest scepticism. He had consistently taken the view that even if 'Europe' worked, which he doubted, Britain's future would always lie elsewhere. This judgement, of course, he had to revise, and he found a brisk way of doing it which deflected the blame to forces beyond his control. It was all due to the unpredictable failure of British industry in the 1960s, he told me with a gesture that swept away the intervening years, during which time he had had to change his mind – about the economy, if not about his advice on the chances of 'Europe'.

But another judgement was harder to explain. The British *idée fixe*, that the Schuman Plan would lead to a European federation, did not materialize. That analysis turned out to be premature, if not something of a hallucination. The Coal and Steel Community came into being, but it did not in reality diminish the economic powers of governments over vital resources. In later decades, certain species of federalistic power did develop. The European Economic Community took away individual governments' sovereignty over external trade, and the Single European Act their sole control over external trade. There was a momentum. But it did not attain a recognizable federation. The full grandeur of the Coal and Steel Community's aspiration proved to be rather empty.

This was the first large judgement falsified by later events. But at the time it dominated all that flowed from Monnet's visit to explain the Plan to London.

Stafford Cripps, after his own talk with Monnet, paid little attention to Plowden's anxieties. Next day he pressed the Economic Policy Committee of the Cabinet to set in hand a detailed study of the Schuman Plan with a view to ensuring 'a practical scheme. . . . not inconsistent with our essential interests'. But these essential interests imposed great caution. Care would have to be taken, the committee concluded, 'to prevent this plan from becoming involved with proposals for federalism in Europe'.

The work began.[43] Makins and Plowden were in charge of it. Their premise was not to rule out the possibility of a high authority being set up, nor British participation in some form. 'If the proposals are successful, the United Kingdom should be associated with them,' their committee agreed at an early meeting. The diplomacy of inclusiveness, however sceptical its purpose, gathered pace. In a couple of days, Makins was ready with his preliminary advice to Bevin, which again was conciliatory. Her Majesty's Government should encourage the French and Germans to start talks immediately, 'and should express a strong desire to take part in them from the start'.

But this desire was in fact so conditional as to be unreal. It was a fine example of diplo-speak. Monnet had ruled out any discussion about the precondition – the supra-national High Authority. The Makins advice therefore covered all the bases. On the one hand, we should take part from the start (paragraph 3). On the other, there was 'no justification' for taking part (paragraph 10), unless ministers were prepared 'to abrogate certain sovereign rights'. This impenetrable contradiction was resolved, however, by the informal footnote Makins attached to brief

Bevin for a meeting with Schuman. Here he was unambiguous about the follies of the French and the Germans: 'We shall have to do what we can to get them out of the mess into which they have landed themselves.'

When his comrade, Plowden, appeared to induce Monnet to soften his position, Makins was equally caustic. The files include the record of a telephone conversation between Plowden and Monnet in which the latter concedes that once negotiations opened 'each of the points put forward in the communiqué as bases for negotiation would itself have to be the subject of negotiation'. Did this foretell a willingness to talk about the High Authority, after all? 'I think this is rather a pity,' Makins comments. 'It would have been better to leave M. Monnet alone.'

An elaborate minuet now begins between London and Paris, ostensibly about the terms and conditions on which the Schuman Plan should be advanced. In fact it seems more like an exercise in preparing allocation of the blame for failure. Did France really want Britain to get involved? Was Britain in any circumstances ready to negotiate? Were any imaginable talks, from the British point of view, a step beyond the point of no return? Whatever – the stately dance accelerated through the last week in May.

On 25 May, a message from London to Paris crossed with one going the other way. Bevin formally told Schuman that the French and Germans should start talking. This should be a bilateral not an international conference, though Britain 'would like to participate' in order to get 'a clearer picture'. Meanwhile, though, France formally told London that the British Government 'must commit themselves to acceptance of the principles of the scheme before discussing it in detail'.

This seemed to be an impasse. But the diplomats scurried to open it. Schuman's top official, Alexandre Parodi, saw an opportunity for some soothing casuistry. Surely, he told the British ambassador, expressing a wish to participate 'meant acceptance by His Majesty's Government of the principle involved'? Accepting the invitation to talk 'would in no way bind us to accept the eventual treaty', the ambassador reported Parodi as saying. To which seduction, the ambassador, Sir Oliver Harvey, whose papers show that he was keener than most officials that Britain should get involved, faithfully came back with his master's voice. The British 'could not engage themselves at this point to accept the principle of pooling'.

In parallel there was further casuistry on the subject of what *kind* of British attendance might theoretically be appropriate. In one and the same telegram to Harvey, Bevin instructed him to deny the rumour that

Britain planned to attend as an observer, and urged him to make the case for all interested governments to 'sit in on' the Franco-German talks when they started. He told Harvey to be 'realistic', which apparently did not encompass a warm reception for another Schuman suggestion about how, with a little diplomatic finesse, Britain could participate without commitment. Another Schuman aide proposed that by accepting the 'principles' of the Plan a government did not commit itself to accepting the decisions of the High Authority. That could only be done in the eventual treaty: 'and if in the course of negotiations any Government did not like the terms of the treaty, then it would always be open to that Government to decline to become party to it'.

So there was evidence that the French desired to be helpful. They wanted to make things seem easier, find language that reflected this, lure the British in. And this tendency wasn't confined to officials. On 30 May, Schuman himself sent for the British ambassador to discuss further linguistic refinements. It had occurred to him, he said, that there was some confusion between the words 'engagement' and 'commitment' in the French and English languages. This, he thought, had perhaps made London think that the precondition was more binding than it was intended to be. All London had to agree was the final desired objective, but the negotiations always had the chance of failing, in which case the British would have lost nothing. They might engage to negotiate without committing to the outcome. Speaking for himself, Schuman sincerely hoped Britain would take part in the coal and steel pool. Couldn't Britain at least say it would *like* to belong?

Now it was Britain's turn to be Delphic. Harvey said the British had 'a completely open mind', but it was a question of 'honesty' and 'not encouraging false hopes'. Upon that basis, next day, London nonetheless agreed to amend the British position with its own new language. Britain could not enter a 'precise commitment', but would participate 'in a constructive spirit', hoping to produce a scheme the Government wanted to be a part of.

On the face of it, this went a fair distance to meet what Schuman said he wanted – but not, it turned out, far enough. Studying the British documents that chart the course of this critical week, one has a strong sense of minds that were never destined to meet. Each apparent gesture of good intention is followed soon enough by an agonized restatement of position that somehow effaces it. The British expression of desire to participate and the French attempt to make this seem possible turn out each to be misleading, within and perhaps beyond the normal canons of diplomatic manoeuvring. For now Schuman, having first sought words with which to square the circle, turns round and claims to have misunderstood the British line all along. While fully seeing that they couldn't commit all their coal and all their steel into the common pool before an agreement was reached, what he *hadn't* understood, he claimed, was the demand that the High Authority itself must be negotiable. This he could not stomach. He could delay no longer. The British would have to decide, yes or no, within twenty-four hours. Or, as Monnet later wrote, 'we had to make an end of it'.

Even then, there was one more attempt by Schuman apparently to make things easier for the British. Issuing his ultimatum to Harvey, he proposed a face-saving new formula. A new text was produced in which the participants were saying not that they had 'decided' to establish the pool and set up the Authority, but that they 'had the immediate aim' of doing so. Harvey reported that Schuman believed this 'would meet us since it did not involve any commitment'.

Whether or not this was sincerely meant, it did not impress itself on London. There the question had advanced from the primitive perception in which Makins had framed it, as a matter of bringing the French to their senses, or 'helping them out of the mess'. It now merited the Foreign Office's most solemn judgement. The rest of inner Europe beyond France and Germany were assembling behind the Schuman Plan. The Dutch were interested, and the Italians keenly pressuring London to stop quibbling over detail. The Italian Foreign Minister, Count Sforza, used a phrase redolent of what was often to divide the continent from its off-shore neighbours in future years. It was, he said, 'the music and not the words that counted'.

At the Foreign Office, the duty of advising the Cabinet passed from Makins to the topmost official, Sir William Strang, the permanent under-secretary. His opinion came like an organ-blast. 'We are called upon to take a decision of foreign policy of a fundamental character which will have far-reaching consequences,' he began. It could not be based on tactical considerations alone. Nor, it seemed, should the Quai d'Orsay's seductive wordplay be taken for more than that. 'The decision which the French are now summoning us to take is, in fact, the decision whether or not we are to bind ourselves irrevocably to the European community,' Strang wrote. This was something 'I cannot bring myself to recommend.' What was at risk from saying no was mere 'temporary embarrassment', a condition that could not compare with the virtue of 'a cool appraisement of the national interest in all its aspects'.

The Treasury made the same assessment, recoiling with horror from the French suggestion. 'It has been our settled policy hitherto', wrote its chief, Sir Edward Bridges, 'that in view of our world position and interests, we should not commit ourselves irrevocably to Europe either in the political or the economic sphere unless we could measure the extent and effects of the commitment.' Britain wanted, in other words, to know exactly where she was going. By not going into Schuman, moreover, the British were risking nothing. It wouldn't stop them 'participating in European discussions in some manner later on', the Bridges committee said. Even the direct consequences for the coal and steel industries were now seen with less alarm than in the Treasury paper just a couple of weeks before, which anticipated dire effects whether Britain was in or out. Now, apparently, 'there need be no cause for alarm if at this stage the French decided to proceed without us'.

Thus was the Cabinet advised. And thus did it agree. But the circumstances in which it took the advice were, in the eye of history, bathetic. They rather muted the trumpets from Whitehall.

By 2 June, when Schuman's ultimatum expired, the principal British ministers were absent from the scene. Bevin was again in hospital, his duties assumed by Kenneth Younger. Both Attlee and Cripps were back on holiday in France, from which they felt no need to return. Herbert Morrison, in charge on the evening the message from Paris arrived, had to be rooted out of London's theatreland to respond to it – which he did with a phrase that became famous for epitomizing the hearts-of-oak mentality so important to British disdain for what 'Europe' is supposed to mean.

It fell to Plowden to track him down, at the Ivy restaurant. 'We retired to a sort of passage at the back of the restaurant where spare tables and chairs are stored,' Plowden recalled. Whereupon Morrison apparently stated: 'It's no good. We can't do it. The Durham miners will never wear it.'[44]

Next day, he presided over what was left of the Cabinet, which had heard the message of the Strang and Bridges papers. Bevin was consulted in hospital, and delivered the predictable blast. No one present dissented, which shows that too much shouldn't be made of the depleted attendance. A full turn-out would have decided no differently. Far from promising to watch benignly from the sidelines as Schuman and Adenauer went ahead, the Cabinet took a harder position, ruling that there should be a further attempt 'to dissuade the French from going forward ... without our participation'. Plowden and Makins were speaking for an official British mind that gathered almost the whole governing class under its sway.

The very act of talking was what the British Government balked at. It wasn't simply the precondition about the High Authority, which Schuman had in any case found ways of softening, but the terror felt in Whitehall that misleading signals might be given out. 'Nothing would be more likely to exacerbate Anglo-French relations than for us to join in the discussions with mental reservations and withdraw from partici- pation at a later stage' was the pious thought with which the Cabinet excused itself.

*

THIS WAS NOT a marginal call. At the level where it counted, Britain decided that to negotiate as a signed-up partner in the Schuman Plan would be an absolute error. Makins and Strang and Bridges and Attlee and Bevin all thought that. But it was not an unthinkable thing to do. There were other voices that made sense of the idea. What told against it were not axioms about Britain's world role, but mere opinions about the nature of reality.

One voice, or at any rate opinion, was in the Government. Kenneth Younger was a relatively young man to be thrust, thanks to Bevin's incapacity, into the role of proxy Foreign Secretary. On the night the ultimatum arrived he set down privately on paper the pros and cons of Schuman's formula, and placed much weight on the dangers of rejecting it.

He listed the consequences of the Plan not succeeding: French humiliation, American displeasure, British culpability for the failure of this extraordinary act of Franco-German reconciliation. He also counted the costs of the Plan being successfully put in place without Britain belonging to it. The coal and steel industries would face fearsome competition. But there would be something worse. The case for procras- tinating, which was the fall-back position in the unlikely event that the Plan succeeded, would be seen to have a heavy cost. 'While we might be able to join in the Plan before it reached finality,' Younger wrote, 'we should, by failing to participate at the start, greatly reduce our chance of getting a scheme worked out on lines proposed by ourselves.'

Standing in for Bevin at the Cabinet, Younger did not make these points. He kept his prescience to himself. But later he wrote that the Schuman proposals were 'handled in a curiously offhand way' in

London, and 'largely by officials'. Quite soon he decided that this combination of hauteur and neglect had produced the biggest foreign policy failure since the war.

Parliament held a big debate before the end of June, and here pro-Plan voices did make an explicit counterpoint to the heavy official drumbeats. Anthony Eden, the shadow Foreign Secretary, said the Plan 'must not be allowed to fail'. It was in Britain's interest it should succeed and in her capacity, by talking, to see it did so. This wasn't, he said, an assault on sovereignty but 'a fusion of sovereignty or, if you will, its merger or extension'. Eden's driving passion was for peace in Europe. He saw the Plan as a way of thwarting both German and, ultimately, Soviet propensities to disturb it. He insisted that any project must be Atlanticist as well as European, keeping the Americans in Europe – which was a universal British obsession. But on the politics of British independence he sounded only slightly ambivalent. 'The acceptance of European federation was no part of the political declaration just signed,' he noted. The Dutch had agreed it on the explicit condition that they might not, in the end, accept the High Authority. They insisted this be negotiated. 'Would we be prepared to enter discussions as a result of which a high authority would be set up whose decisions would be binding upon the nations who were parties to the agreement?' Eden asked. 'My answer to that question would be yes, provided [Hon. Members: 'Ahhh,' *Hansard* reports] that we were satisfied with the conditions and safeguards.'[45]

Winston Churchill's line was more stratospheric. He couldn't imagine any significant strategic discussion anywhere taking place without Britain. But younger Tories addressed the particulars. David Eccles, later a Cabinet minister, deplored the 'smug self-satisfaction' he saw around him, and thought the British refusal to talk would be 'utterly incomprehensible' to the millions all over Europe who feared another war. He ridiculed inter-governmental agencies where the members were 'nothing more than delegates of national policies', and urged that under the Schuman Plan 'we must arrange matters so that they speak and act not as Frenchmen and Germans but as Europeans'.

Julian Amery, bearer of a family loyalty to colonies and Commonwealth, said, 'I look at this question primarily as an imperialist.' Imperial interests, far from debarring engagement, 'dictate our participation in the talks'. The young Quintin Hogg came in on the same side. He thought the Commonwealth would survive only if Britain joined Europe. Adopting 'constructive attitudes' or 'friendly poses', he said, was not an alternative to 'adopting the principle of pooling resources or the institution of a High Authority'. A certain supra-nationalism was desirable, irrespective of the short-term shock it might cause a proud people. Hogg's memory, when I talked to him forty years later, was that 'all the people whose reputation has endured, the brains of the younger generation, were on one side'. In which *galère* he included not only himself and Eccles, but Peter Thorneycroft and another young man who was later to make the deepest mark, Edward Heath. Given future events, it is fitting that the Schuman Plan debate was the occasion for Heath's maiden parliamentary speech. Late of the Heavy Anti-Aircraft Regiment, Lieutenant-Colonel Heath had just been visiting Germany, where he had seen an economy already recovering, and an interest in the Schuman Plan 'governed entirely by political considerations'. The Plan, he wrote at the time, was 'a great chance, perhaps the greatest in twenty years' for Britain to influence the shape of things. It was being thrown away. In the House, he said that the supra-national aspect was not a 'principle' but an 'objective', and should not be feared. But his particular foreboding related to the economy. 'By standing aside from any discussions,' Heath predicted, 'we may be taking a very great risk with our economy – a very great risk indeed.'

These speeches had no influence. A few days later, the Cabinet committee deliberated as though Eccles, Hogg and Heath had not spoken. There was 'general opposition on both sides of the House', ministers comforted themselves in recording, both to a supra-national body wielding powers over British coal and steel and to participation in 'any federal system limited to Europe'. Such reassuring 'unanimity' meant that the issue could be closed.

Did this decision cost Britain the leadership of Europe? It is often said so,[46] but there may be something politically incorrect about the question. The Coal and Steel Community, which evolved into the Common Market and the European Union, was not primarily about 'leadership'. It was an exercise in collaboration by which countries sank some of the aspirations that keep the competitive quest for leadership going. Who is going to be top dog in Europe was, after all, the question that started most of the wars. Nostalgia for that missed moment when leadership could have been seized, which is the way many British 'Europeans' have tended to think of it, perhaps exposes a congenital inability to see what 'Europe' is all about, one reason why the British mind and the European mind had such difficulty in meeting.

It is also possible to argue that, if Britain had jumped the other way,

'Europe' might not have happened. Britain had many reasons to hope
the Schuman Plan would fail. Bevin's desire to oversee Franco-German
reconciliation, and strengthen the Western Union against the Soviet
Union, didn't extend to seeing Britain's own heavy industries, which
were bigger than the continentals', compromised by some kind of
multilateral control, nor to presiding over the violation of national
sovereignty. Sovereignty mattered most of all to a nation that had
triumphantly exercised it in war, and still saw it reaching wherever the
map was painted red. If Britain had entered the talks in order to destroy
Monnet's vision, she might have done so – at least for the moment.
Britain, in other words, might indeed have enjoyed old-fashioned 'leadership', but over a 'Europe' she had prevented from coming to pass.

Neither of these hypothetical talk-outs for what happened strikes me
as convincing. The Europe of the Coal and Steel Community was going
to happen. The strength of feeling behind something of the kind was
enormous, and if Britain had entered only to destroy, she would have
hastened her exclusion not only from the European but from the
American intersecting circle of influence and interest. Nor did Europe,
in truth, occupy such a Utopian level of unreality as to exclude the
concept of leadership from its vocabulary. In both the Community and
the Union, there has been a spirit of collaboration and even of national
self-sacrifice. But both economy and geography impose the possibilities
of leadership, just as history shows that the struggle for ascendancy can
never be entirely extinguished. Power does not permit the existence of a
vacuum. Some dog is top, as Germany has found to her advantage. The
verdict of one of the men most influential in cultivating the atmosphere
of British non-participation, the mood and reading that infected just
about the entire senior political class, is the right one. 'The decision',
Oliver Franks wrote, 'cost us the leadership of Europe which we had
enjoyed from the end of the war until May 1950.'

In the end, three aspects of the decision and its making are washed
up on the shore for critical scrutiny, after the tide of history has moved
on.

The first is a double-whammy of misjudgement. Britain hoped the
Plan would not succeed, and did not think it would do so. The hoping
was shot through with ambiguity: not even Roger Makins could actually
have desired that a scheme for Franco-German reconciliation would
come to nothing. Disclosing one side of his schizoid calculations, Franks
said that bringing France and Germany together 'as Schuman described
it to me "in an embrace so close that neither could draw back far enough

to hit the other" was worth everything for the peace of Europe'. Nobody in London wanted to be charged with responsibility for making it fail, as most of the participants thought it would unless Britain went along. But the Public Record Office files are littered with sceptical judgements about the ability of France and Germany to make the necessary compromises over the future of their coal and steel industries. Well into 1951, British ambassadors round Europe are filing accounts of the widespread fear of German domination of coal as well as steel, and emphasizing the improbability of a deal being done. They plainly underestimated the political will to make progress, but they also could not believe what they were being invited to think about. Con O'Neill, a young diplomat in Bonn at the time, said years later: 'I'm ashamed to say that I did not realise its enormous importance.' He also said: 'The idea that there should be a body with real authority over the decisions of national governments was something we felt was grotesque and absurd.'

Second, the collective judgement in London seems to have been extraordinarily pessimistic about the possibilities of an advantageous negotiation. This, perhaps, is the best evidence that at bottom there was a mysteriously visceral hostility great enough to transcend any amount of cool calculation. It began with the belief that the French did not want Britain as a full member of the Plan: true, perhaps, of Monnet, at least until the supra-national institutions had become a 'fact', but not so obviously true of Schuman, whose conduct gives plenty of evidence to the contrary. Springing the Plan as a big surprise wasn't the best way of securing agreement, and was openly designed to forestall a British veto. The existence of something called a high authority was never going to be wished away. But the scope of this body, its relationship to governments, the measure of its supra-nationalism, and its federalist implications: all this was open for discussion. The other member states all found ways of accommodating the French coup and shaping the Authority into a body they could live with, which violated their sovereignty only in a specific and limited way. Britain was in a stronger position than any of them to exercise this kind of negotiating muscle, for Great Britain was the most desired of all allies. The Dutch, the Belgians and Luxembourg faced the need to join but also the discomfort of being caught between overbearing continental neighbours. On 15 May, the British ambassador in Bonn reported a talk with the German Vice-Chancellor as follows: 'During the whole conversation, Bluecher returned again and again to one theme, the necessity for British participation. Without Britain, schemes for West European co-operation were bound to fail.'

The third striking feature of Britain's blindness to this desire is how little credit it did the British governing system, in which it may be ministers who decide but officials are supposed to bring their matchless wisdom to bear, in a spirit of detachment, on the evidence their political masters consider. What happened in 1950, under the ailing ministeriat of Clement Attlee, was rather like what happened in the 1980s under the overmighty hand of Margaret Thatcher. That, too, was a period when the civil service, with detachment drained out of it, did a poor job for the country. The condition then was a bit different: of weak officials finding it easier to succumb to the unsupported certainties of the governing ideology rather than challenge them. In the 1950s, nobody would have dared call Makins, Bridges and the rest weak. They were at least equal partners in defining the orthodoxy as regards Europe. Only at the lower levels and in occasional outposts were there people who challenged the advice ministers were getting, and these were seldom heard. In the balance of intellectual power, Whitehall was in this era more than a match for a cadre of Westminster leaders who were in many cases exhausted, and in some, like Bevin's, getting ready to die. One incontrovertible message of hindsight, to put it no higher, surely is that the official advice on this occasion was laughably erroneous.

It was, however, Bevin's to take or to refuse. The officials knew what he wanted, and he knew how they thought. It was he, with their smooth assistance in the drafting, who defined the line epitomized at the end of the Commons debate by Stafford Cripps, who said on the Government's behalf: 'It seems to us that, even if desirable, such a scheme could hardly prove to be workable . . . unless it were preceded by complete political federation.'[47]

Nine months later Bevin was out of office, and a month after that he was dead. The European Coal and Steel Community came into being on 18 April 1951, with Jean Monnet at its head, and it survives to this day.

3

RUSSELL BRETHERTON

The Sacrificial Agent

EUROPE WAS MORE THAN coal and steel. One community did not finish the job. In the 1950s, the idea, for those who believed in it, was a force with irresistible momentum. Its logic, the logic of alliance against war, reached into all corners. When next this logic presented itself at the door of the British Government, the response did not differ very much, save in one respect. But this difference told a story. The man positioned to stand against the European Idea – the capital letters that Foreign Office papers now accorded the Idea suggest it was beginning to engender mockery – was no longer a titan but a cipher. Not only was Bevin long dead, but Bevinishness, the loud, certain, confident, unignorable voice that ruled the roost on Britain's behalf, had gone as well. The Conservatives, by 1955, could produce nothing to match it. In place of a world figure, the public official they sent to deal with 'Europe' was a figure no one in the world had heard of.

Russell Bretherton was flesh and blood. He did what he was told, though as it happens he didn't like it. He was an obscure middle-ranking official, and that was the point. His presence at the scene of combat was designed not to intimidate but to insult. This already said something about Britain's altering place in the world, even though few of the citizens saw it that way. Mulish domination was subtly making way for something more like disdain, but a disdain edged with the beginnings of alarm, and Bretherton was its symbol. By showing that Europe mattered so little to Britain, perhaps Europe would be persuaded that 'Europe' ought not to matter so much to itself.

This was the meaning of Bretherton. He was the nominee, void of power or status or the faintest resemblance to the roaring British lion, whom the politicians sent to register their continuing absence from the integration of Europe. But, before his moment came, several matters had occurred.

The decision to reject participation in the Schuman Plan caused barely a tremor in the British body politic. It was thinly reported, and criticized by only one organ of opinion, the *Economist*. It played no part in the election campaign leading up to the defeat of the Labour Government in October 1951. Nor was interest in it revived by the reappearance in power of the party that had supposedly favoured Britain's involvement, and of the leader whose magnetism and grandiloquence had persuaded many European leaders that he was one of them. Winston Churchill's return to office, in plenty of time to reverse Labour's rejection of Schuman, produced no such outcome. The moment, if it ever was a real moment and not the indulgence of mere oppositionism, had passed. Once back at the helm, Churchill gave little thought to 'Europe', his ancient gaze being trained around the globe, where the Korean War had begun, and where there were American presidents to parley with and a Soviet menace to be confronted. Besides, Churchill was no longer energetic. At seventy-four, he was old and half exhausted.

The voice that spoke for Conservatism in the Schuman Plan debate, though plainly oppositionist, was also steeped in irony. Although Anthony Eden, at that moment, came on with passionate contempt for Labour's isolationism from Europe, his personal disposition was, in practical terms, similar. It was part of his complexity. Eden was a sensitive, erratic, romantic, anxious internationalist. These qualities were ominously appropriate for the first Conservative leader who had the opportunity to align Britain with the integration of Europe and failed to take it.

His parliamentary attitude in June 1950 was more than posturing. He did seem to want Britain to join the Schuman negotiations. The proposed self-exclusion aroused his apocalyptic sensitivities. Strolling in his garden, he told a friend at the time: 'I think this is so serious, our refusal to go into this and see what it's all about, and show willing – I think it could be the beginning of World War Three.'[1] Despite its evasiveness – 'aaaah' said the House – over the High Authority, his Commons speech gave the continentals every reason to anticipate a change in the British position once Eden became Foreign Secretary. The Churchill syndrome of false expectation extended well beyond the voice of the master.

Eden, however, had never been a Churchill in this matter. Like the Foreign Office, he had looked on the old man's grand, post-war forays with some disdain. He refused to go to the Hague conference, and was absent from Strasbourg. 'There was an element of distaste in Eden for this whole *emotional* approach,' one of his staff recalled. He was therefore outside the Tory mainstream, which in opposition was dominated by the Churchillians, who made their presence felt at all these assemblies in the persons of Sandys and Soames and Amery, as well as the rival whom Eden most apprehended, Harold Macmillan. For Eden, Europe, let alone 'Europe', would never engage the deepest feelings of the British people. 'What you've got to remember', he told his private secretary, Evelyn Shuckburgh, 'is that if you looked at the post-bag of any English village and examined the letters coming in from abroad, ninety per cent would come from way beyond Europe.'

During Eden's tenure as Foreign Secretary, from October 1951 to April 1955, such personal attitudes – prejudices, biases, atavistic passions, the instincts reason had to start from – made their way into the arrangement of his professional priorities. But these, in turn, were naturally influenced by facts of power and geography that nobody in that job could ignore. What happened to British foreign policy in the early 1950s was fruit of the reality that Britain did not have the option to overlook: the historic inheritance that continued, *pro tem*, to assign her the responsibilities if not the entire arsenal of a great power. There were 15,000 British troops fighting in the Korean War. The imperial sun had not entirely ceased to set. In these years, Eden, the spokesman for a country whose foreign policy was still rooted in a reddened map, was a decisive arbitrator in Indo-China, in Persia, in Cyprus, in Egypt, in India.

He was the obverse of a Little Englander. Unlike later Euro-sceptics, he was a man of European culture, spoke French and a little German, would never have dreamed of carrying a supply of corn-flakes on the Channel ferry. He simply did not think that 'Europe', on the model of Schuman and Monnet, would ever work. All his knowledge of history told him that nationalisms were for ever. They could not be abandoned. They were, at best, the raw material with which foreign secretaries did their work. Above all, British nationalism, generously present around the world, could never be buried in some alien construct. Somewhere between his apparent enthusiasm for the coal and steel idea and his resumption of power in the Foreign Office, his real opinion forced itself upon him. In a famous speech at Columbia University, in January 1952, he told the Americans what it was. There had been suggestions, he said, that Britain should join 'a federation on the continent of Europe'. This was something 'we know in our bones we cannot do'. It violated 'the unalterable marrow' of the British nation.

Later in life, when he was often named as one of the culprits for Britain's late entry into Europe, Eden detested the accusation. It was entirely wrong, he said, and his friends came to his defence, saying that 'he just had a totally different concept of what a united Europe should be about'.[2] It's interesting, all the same, to see how little space 'Europe' gets in Eden's memoirs. He evidently did not reckon the subject merited a place at the centre of the history he was concerned with.

He did, however, have one important part in its evolution. This was a backdrop to what was about to happen of more epic moment. It is, in its way, the perfect little microcosm of the troubled Anglo-Euro relationship as it failed to develop in these early, formative days. Foreshadowing the Common Market Britain didn't join was the Defence Community which she had, first, apparently advocated, then second, helped destroy by refusing to join, then third, thanks to Eden himself, retrieved from oblivion by a device that seemed blithely to ignore most of the objections she had raised against it in the second stage.

Churchill, it must be recalled, had included the idea of a European army among his pan-Europe effusions. He saw it as the apotheosis of what he was talking about, Germans included. As midwife at the birth of the Strasbourg Assembly, in August 1950 he caused an early post-natal sensation by declaring that such an army would be a message 'from the House of Europe to the whole world'. Warrior nations would now put their armies under unified command to defend the cause of peace against all aggressors. And Britain, it seemed, was not excluded. 'We should all play a worthy and honourable part,' Churchill said.

No sooner was the Coal and Steel Community on the way to being an accomplished fact than this Churchillian vision arrived on the agenda of practical Europeans. The rhetoric of the old man, by now in office, was put sharply to the question, and the main agents of this interrogation were his old and closest allies, the Americans. For believing and committed Europeans, too, it was a natural development. For the ending of war, one community was plainly only a start. America, however, had special reasons and, one would have thought, also had in Britain an ally whose special agonies in all these European speculations would have made her susceptible to American influence.

There was surely a benign kind of syllogism at work. First, British policy under both Bevin and Eden was driven by the desire to maintain special links with the US, keep America in Europe and strengthen the transatlantic alliance against Moscow. Second, US policy, under Presidents Truman and Eisenhower, plus Secretaries Acheson and John Foster Dulles, was to encourage the integration of Europe under the political leadership of Britain, Washington's special ally and nuclear friend. Given these two premises, logic dictated that Britain would incline positively towards the negotiation of a proper 'European' role as a way, not least, of sustaining her American influence. Instead of which, the opposite occurred. Throughout the Foreign Office files of the period, if one argument runs deeper than any other against these Community entanglements it is the dually destructive consequence that was seen to flow from them. First, by getting into 'Europe', Britain would lose her unique position in Washington, and second, by assisting at such integration, Britain would be an accomplice at what she least desired and the Americans then most wanted, some disengagement of US troops from Europe – 'letting them off the hook', as Roger Makins called it.

In Washington there was a further consideration. Superficially, again, it met a Churchillian point. Having assumed the global burden, America pressed Europe to take on a more substantial part of its own defence, something that could not be contemplated without raising the issue of the country at Europe's geographic heart. The Berlin blockade and the communist coup in Czechoslovakia, both in 1948, greatly reinforced America's will to rearm Germany. With French troops heavily engaged in Indo-China, and the British defence budget under acute strain, Germany, as Churchill had said, could not be left out of the picture. Yet how could France, in particular, tolerate German rearmament in any form? Only by means of the same principles that had guided Schuman and his Plan. Following the Schuman Plan, therefore, came the Pleven Plan, a scheme put together, again in Paris, and with strong American support, for a European army in European uniform under European command, to be assembled for an indefinite period as proof of solidarity and a bulwark against enemies both within and without.

Ultimately, the Pleven Plan did not succeed. The Benelux countries and, naturally, Germany were quick to ratify it, but it failed because the French Assembly declined to do the same. The idea of one branch of the French political class was vetoed, several governments later, by another. The prior accessory to failure, however, was Britain, whose conduct was a lugubrious foretaste of future episodes, and whose leader drew from his closest ally a verdict that sounded a tocsin. Britain, wrote President Eisenhower in his diary, in December 1951 just after his own first election, 'was living in the past'. As for Churchill, he refused 'to think in terms of today'. 'My regretful opinion', Ike concluded, 'is that he no longer absorbs new ideas.'

The new idea of the European Defence Community proved unabsorbable, notwithstanding the fact that Churchill was virtually its first begetter. And that was the prime sense in which it can be seen as establishing the British style. It contradicted promise. The new military protector of 'the House of Europe' quickly acquired another label. 'European Army! European Army! It won't be an army, it'll be a sludgy amalgam,' the old man muttered to himself in Paris in 1952. 'What soldiers want to sing are their own marching songs.'[3]

There were other harbingers of future politics. One was the abysmal confusion the EDC provoked inside the Tory Cabinet, and the reputation for evasion and duplicity that thereby received another lift among the continentals. The mixture of incompetence and bad faith was exquisitely prophetic. One minister, David Maxwell Fyfe, went solemnly to Strasbourg to let the Assembly know that Britain supported the EDC, and promised 'our determination that no genuine method shall fail through lack of thorough examination'. Construing his own words much later, he insisted that his message had been that Britain 'agreed to the principle of joining the European Army'. Mere hours later on the very same day, 28 November 1951, Anthony Eden told a press conference in Rome that 'no British military formations would be made available'. Maxwell Fyfe, a strong European, was furious. In his memoirs, he wrote that 'this, more than any other single act, destroyed Britain's good name on the continent'. But Eden was unrepentant. And it was Eden's position that held firm, to decisive effect. Britain's refusal to place sufficient soldiers in the sludgy amalgam under European command was, effectively, what drove French parliamentarians to kill the EDC.[4]

That wasn't the end of British perversity, however. At this stage, Britain was still just about as capable of rescuing a version of 'Europe' as destroying it, and Eden now did so. When the Pleven Plan collapsed, no one was more horrified than he. For little though he was convinced by its military quality, and hard though he fought to keep the British out, he knew better than anyone what Washington thought, and was appalled to hear that, as a result, Dulles might be on the brink of conducting what he was calling, in a famous phrase, 'an agonizing reappraisal' of American foreign policy.

So Eden now acted with speed and brilliance – and, as it seemed, bewildering volatility. Spurred by the threat from Washington, he built a framework for German rearmament within a few weeks. This involved cajoling the French and, in major substance, reversing the stubbornness with which Britain had assisted at the abortion of the EDC. The Western European Union, the invention that did this, had the crucial quality of retaining national rights. It was inter-governmental. British troops would not be sent to battle under a French or German general. But the numbers that were offered for assignment on the continent would have amply satisfied the French, had they been offered to the EDC. Germany was readmitted to the company of fighting nations. More important for Eden, Britain agreed to keep an army on permanent standby in Europe, the price he was prepared to pay, having previously rejected it, for guarantees of a continuing American presence as well. From 1955 to 2025, the British military presence would not be removed except by agreement with the WEU allies.

The WEU was Eden's contribution to 'Europe' and, like Nato, a notable despatch of some portion of the King's own sovereignty into the hands of other powers beyond the sea. Serious federalists were not best pleased: the collapse of the EDC was seen by the more missionary continentals as the prelude, quite possibly, to the end of the entire Community venture. But WEU, as a second-best necessity, was a deal that satisfied almost everyone. It was done – further strand of consistency both before and after – with little serious debate in government and none, until after the relevant hour, in Parliament. Even when Eden came for approval of his final plan, the full Cabinet did not assemble to consider it. This was surprising, given the seventy-year military commitment the deal involved. Yet it was not so surprising, when considered in a pedigree line which shows that every positive development that has eventually succeeded in positioning Britain inside a European venture has been characterized, by its proponents, as doing nothing terribly significant.

The rule of thumb is roughly as follows. On those occasions when an agreement finally becomes expeditious, or impossible to avoid, let the world be informed of its banality, its minimal implications for the constitution, the utter impossibility of its changing reality in ways that anyone would notice. When, on the other hand, a proposition beckons which the politicians, for any or all of a host of reasons, do not like, or fear to try and sell, let it be stigmatized as an insupportable assault on the British way of life.

And let Mr Russell Bretherton or his heirs be sent to deliver the message.

*

MESSINA, A SMALL town on the north-east point of Sicily, is an improbable site for the birth-place of a great idea. In a country of immortal cultural repositories, it is notably lacking in grandeur. Discriminating visitors have always tended to stay at Taormina, down the coast. But the reason Messina occupies an indelible place among the benchmarks of modern history is unusually apt. It is famous as the fount of the European Economic Community – once the Common Market, later the European Community, now the European Union – owing to a pressing circumstance of strictly national politics. Ministers of the Coal and Steel Community were due to meet in Italy at the beginning of June 1955. But Gaetano Martino, the Italian Foreign Minister, had a problem. His power-base was Sicily, and an election was imminent there. He was not prepared to hold the conference in Rome. His colleagues, the foreign ministers of France, Germany, Belgium, the Netherlands and Luxembourg, were obliged, a little frostily, to accommodate him.

They thereby registered from the start a truth that would never subsequently be erased. The EEC, the culminating creation of the 'European Idea', was born in the way it would continue: as a dream of supra-national union modified, for every leader who has ever taken part in it, by the mundane accidents and irresistible demands of survival as a national politician. Martino, incidentally, won his election.

Messina, for the British, was the next European challenge: further proof, bewildering and enraging by turns, that after the failure of the Defence Community to happen in the way the continental integrationists wanted it, there was still life in the Big Idea. At the time Messina precisely took place, that first weekend in June, it meant virtually nothing. Not being a member of the Coal and Steel Community, Britain was not present at the meeting, and nor were British correspondents. Had the word Messina entered the columns of British newspapers, the resonance it drew would have been far from the world of high diplomacy. For the meeting coincided with the Old Bailey trial of the brothers Messina, charged with pimping and racketeering. It was the biggest tabloid story of the time. For most of the British, mention of Messina inspired only thoughts of prostitution and extortion by oily Italians running a corner of London gang-land. Indeed, exchange 'Messina' for

'Brussels', in the modern era, and you have a fair evocation of what the most extreme of British phobes and sceptics continue to think about the entire project that Messina began.

Less than two months before Messina, Anthony Eden succeeded Churchill as Prime Minister. Less than a week before, he was confirmed in office at a general election. The British had other things on their mind than the evolution of 'Europe'. But once again they were drawn, ineluctably, in. They were outside 'Europe', but were still a great European power. They could not be avoided. They had acquired associate status – country member, no voting rights – with the Coal and Steel Community. It was second nature in Europe once again to invite them to negotiate the new project, but this time without preconditions. After Messina, there began another minuet resembling what occurred in May 1950, which had similarities to, but also a difference from, the earlier experience.

The difference was simple. What took about a week in 1950 took six months in 1955. The similarities are more jarring. The passage of years had not rendered any clearer Britain's view of herself and her destiny. The pattern turns out to be very much the same. Confronted with an invitation to talk, the political class shudders and prevaricates, half-heartedly inches forward and then passionately withdraws. The same language of disbelief courses through the Foreign Office files in 1955 as five years before. A new generation of officials gives different ministers the same advice they want to hear. Ministers accept, still less questioningly, the old assumptions on which this advice is based. The one significant evolution is towards a hardening of both advice and response. Whereas Schuman, though widely predicted to fail, was regarded with pragmatic affability in London once it had come to pass, Messina was designated, almost from the start and certainly by the end, for destruction with extreme prejudice. The shift is a measure of Britain's sharpening vanity – but also of her fear-filled diminishment.

The change of cast occurred not only in London. New figures were taking centre stage in Europe. First on the agenda at Messina, curiously, was the fate of Jean Monnet, who had announced his resignation as head of the Coal and Steel Community with a view to resuming his role as manipulative activist on behalf of 'Europe', following the collapse of the EDC. At this beginning of what became the Common Market, its visionary begetter returned to the shadows where he had always been more at home and perhaps more influential. But Monnet had his proxies, none more important than the Belgian Foreign Minister, Paul-Henri

Spaak, a name to remember. Spaak stepped forward as the new, presumptive father of 'Europe', a role for which he had, among other things, the usual British credentials. He had spent most of the war in London, passionately desired British involvement in Europe, believed in Winston Churchill.

Spaak was one of the two facilitators of what happened at Messina. He wasn't, in fact, the original begetter of the idea of a customs union, which is what 'Messina' became and which he began by opposing. That credit did not even belong to Jean Monnet, who was also at first sceptical of its possibilities, and had to be persuaded. The true fount and origin was a man seldom heard of since, named J. W. Beyen, the Dutch Foreign Minister. It was Beyen who persuaded Spaak, who then incontestably became the politician chiefly responsible for what happened afterwards.

After disposing of the Monnet problem, the foreign ministers got down to serious, ambitious work. They had before them a proposal jointly fashioned by the small members – Belgium, the Netherlands, Luxembourg, collectively known as Benelux – which, to begin with, disturbed and rather horrified the larger ones. This, in the words of the preamble to the document they all eventually agreed to discuss, committed them to the belief 'that it is necessary to work for the establishment of a united Europe by the development of common institutions, the gradual fusion of national economies, the creation of a common market and the gradual harmonisation of . . . social policies'.

This might, the proposal stated, be approached in different ways. It was for discussion. Possibly the right way – this was at first Spaak's own preference – was through the creation of several new communities to deal with different functions. After coal and steel, we give you land transport, air transport, conventional energy, nuclear energy, whatever. An alternative or perhaps parallel way – favoured and prepared by Beyen – would be through a customs union yoking these six national markets into one. Two days were spent by the Sicilian seaside discussing each of these ideas, and not deciding between them. In the end, the discussion would go on, the Messina Six decided, across the whole field. There would be joint studies made by experts, some of them about 'functional' possibilities – improved canals, better railways and roads, exchange of gas and electric power, pooling atomic know-how – some of them about a 'common market', which would involve a common customs barrier with the outside world as well as common tariffs within, and the possible harmonization of social laws and monetary policy.

This, if meant seriously, was a bold agenda. Spaak's memoirs describe the end of the Messina conference as an apotheosis almost resembling the dramatic exhaustion described by Gibbon on completing *The Decline and Fall of the Roman Empire*. 'Each morning,' he writes, 'we prepared the day's agenda in the hotel gardens, surrounded by flowers ... On the last day of the conference we had to work through the night, drafting the final communiqué. The sun was rising over Mount Etna as we returned to our rooms, tired but happy. Far-reaching decisions had been taken.'[5] To others, however, the very spaciousness of the communiqué suggested that nothing had been decided and nothing, therefore, was likely to happen. *Il Tempo* described the communiqué as 'another unnecessary document'. The British ambassador in Rome reported his Dutch colleague as saying that the meeting was never intended to achieve anything, 'but all the foreign ministers enjoyed their holiday in Taormina'.[6] The Luxembourg representative, Joseph Bech, said on his return that the most significant thing about Messina was its omission of any smell of a high authority, Schuman-style, to ruffle the sovereignties of the French, or the British. Messina, he wrote, 'had not made the mistake that had bedevilled European politics during the last few years of trying to steal a march on time'. Monnet himself deemed it a 'timid step towards the making of Europe', all too likely to end in mere co-operation between nations.

There was, however, plenty to play for. The studies would now begin, and Spaak, the most dynamic man at Messina, would be their chairman. An amazingly short deadline, 1 October, four months hence, had been set for their completion. Even Monnet, a sceptic about other people's efforts in this field, opined that 'they could hardly end just in smoke'.

From the beginning of the process, Britain, as if by automatic right, was given special treatment accorded no other non-member of the ECSC, nor to any collective grouping of nations who might think they had a right to be kept informed. Spaak showed the Benelux draft to the British before he ever got to Messina, and before he showed it to the Germans, the French or the Italians. His first priority, he told the British ambassador to Belgium, was not to be seen doing anything behind Britain's back. For this favour, Spaak was most grudgingly rewarded.

The Foreign Office, despite experience with the Schuman Plan, at first approached the document he had considerately handed them as if it were a novel exercise in mystification. It was 'woolly', 'a hotch-potch', 'intangible', but clearly to be resisted. Two weeks before Messina, the relevant desk officer minuted that Britain should 'continue to deprecate, if asked, any further measures of economic integration at this stage'. The day before the meeting began, judgement came from higher up the hierarchy. 'There can of course be no question', wrote John Coulson, the senior line official, 'of our entering any organisation of a supra-national character.' But, in any case, it was far from clear that anything would emerge. Messina would be designed mainly to give 'an impression of activity'. If there was any question of her attending post-Messina meetings, Britain should 'think very carefully before accepting'.[7]

These, in fact, became the two preliminary issues to test the judgement of London. On neither was the official performance very acute.

Most officials thought nothing at all would happen. Coulson, taking the temperature at a meeting of the OEEC, found nobody that mattered who was interested in hastening the pace of supra-nationalism. Gladwyn Jebb, now the ambassador in Paris, cut through the subtleties of French ambivalence with a fine flourish. The Foreign Minister, Antoine Pinay, he judged to be anxious to keep European unity alive without making commitments. Pinay was 'thinking of organisations which had the power of decision (and were therefore supra-national) but whose decisions would be reached unanimously (and were therefore inter-govern-mental)'. 'This sort of double-talk does seem to keep the Europeans quiet,' the ambassador noted scornfully, before offering the opinion that no spectacular developments out of Messina were likely, and that progress in coming months 'will be purely verbal'.[8]

The collective Whitehall view, in short, was that what Spaak and the others had launched at Messina was almost certainly going to be a mess. The practical question on this occasion, unlike with Schuman, was not whether Britain should be present at the working out of this mess, but in what guise and on what assumptions her presence should be offered. Although the formal invitation had yet to arrive, it was made known through several embassies, immediately after Messina, that London's presence would be unanimously welcome.

Here, however, the ambivalences in London began. Something called the Mutual Aid Committee first expressed them. This, a White-hall power-centre controlled by the Treasury not the Foreign Office, was charged with matters of European integration, as if to emphasize the exclusively economic, indeed eleemosynary, tests by which the project might be thought to have measurable relevance to Britain. Mutual Aid has the antique feel of post-war recovery, as far away as possible from the futuristic adventure of European integration. The MAC agreed that it would be 'politically embarrassing' to refuse to attend, and that it would be as well to send 'something rather more than a mere observer'. On the other hand, watch it. The British should make clear they were not taking part 'as a seventh member of the group', and did not necessarily accept the Messina objectives of a merger between economies and a harmonization of social policies. Now, also, the politicians came into the picture. This part of Messina was Schuman all over again. Preoccupied with the election, no Cabinet minister features in any of the relevant files for May 1955 as having an opinion about Messina, or even being sent a paper advising him what to think. Early attitudes are all struck between officials. No need to trouble the great men with so trivial a distraction. But, as June begins, the silence starts to be broken.

The first to speak was R. A. Butler, Chancellor of the Exchequer. Chairing an OEEC dinner a few days after Messina, he was loftiness personified. This was a time, as he reminded a later inquirer, when Britain was 'the normal chairman of Europe'.[9] From this elevated seat he remarked that he had heard of 'some archaeological excavations' at an old Sicilian town, in which Britain had not taken part. This did not go down well. It sounded as though Britain regarded the venture as digging up a past that would better remain buried. Either that, or he was offering a superior classical reference, the kind of Delphic little joke with which he often loved to tease. Butler, as we shall see, never was a 'European'. In June 1955, his tone did not misrepresent British establishment opinion.

The decision on whether to get involved in the post-Messina process was, initially, Butler's call. Not only was the MAC, the superintending committee, run from his department, but the new Foreign Secretary, Harold Macmillan, was abroad.

Butler was extraordinarily disengaged. 'Very weak and uninteresting', he scribbled in the margin of the first Treasury paper he saw, setting out the Messina communiqué.[10] Additionally, he suffered a visit from Beyen, Spaak's co-visionary from Holland, who arrived in London to press the case for British involvement. Beyen was a silky operator, exotically sophisticated by Dutch standards. He put himself about, stressing his Anglophile tendencies and waxing about our two 'sea-faring countries' which would never want to exclude 'the other world'. In private, he began to sharpen up Messina, conceding that the British were against supra-nationalism, but filling out the possible shape of the new 'Community' he wanted them to get involved in talking about. Butler couldn't stand Beyen. 'He was a very pushing man . . . always telling you what to do,' he later said.[11] Despite it all, Butler recalled that he had manfully 'overcome my personal repugnance to him'. But the visit did not send him rushing to Brussels, where the post-Messina studies were supposed to start in early July. His department by now had got closer to a considered assessment.[12] Mutual Aid notwithstanding, the Treasury view was that Messina was 'inspired as much by political as economic motives', and was a way of 'binding Germany into western Europe'. But the economic plans were highly suspect. A common market was an unacceptable objective 'for ourselves', though if others wanted one 'among themselves', we could not object. As for taking part in talks, we didn't like being asked the question just yet. We would have preferred 'a pause for thought'. We didn't like Beyen's ideas, but 'this may be an argument for joining the discussions'. By joining the Six at the table, we might 'guide their thoughts towards suggestions for forms of co-operation in which we might be willing to join'. We should do so, however, only as observers, and should open proceedings with a statement making clear we fundamentally objected to the supra-national basis of the enterprise.

It was some time before Macmillan, the Foreign Secretary and real opposite number of Spaak and Beyen, could get involved in this. He was away in San Francisco celebrating the tenth anniversary of the United Nations, and these were days when news travelled slowly. He read of Beyen's visit only in the press. The fax did not exist, telephone and telegraph appear to have been sparingly used. Even within Europe itself, many of the messages cited here took days to arrive. But Macmillan did send a message, after reading his newspaper, that he wanted the Messina decision postponed until he got back. When he did so, however, it was with no immediate countermand to Butler. 'Europe' apparently featured no higher in his mind than in anyone else's. Since taking over from Eden, he had made one foreign policy speech, in which Messina was not mentioned. His department had reached the same view as the Treasury, that an 'observer' only should be sent to Brussels.

But Macmillan's antennae did begin to twitch. A Cabinet meeting to decide the matter was due on 30 June. Europe was still not at the top of the agenda. This was a Britain much more preoccupied with imperial and domestic problems. The Kenyan Mau Mau guerrillas competed for quality political time with incessant dock strikes, and, challenged by traffic congestion in Park Lane, the Cabinet solemnly decided to consider the novel remedy of something called a 'dual carriageway'. But it also decided about Messina, and meanwhile Macmillan had slightly changed the Foreign Office mind.

Instead of an 'observer', he told his top mandarins the day before the Cabinet, Britain should send a proper participant. He positively enthused about a new 'relaunch' of Europe, and if this was to be a version in which the British could join, they had to be there to shape it.[13] Supra-nationalism was to be avoided, and perhaps it could be. To the Cabinet he said, 'We might be able to exercise greater influence in the forthcoming discussions if we were to enter them on the same footing as the other countries and not in the capacity as an observer.'[14]

The Cabinet didn't have much of a discussion, if the minutes are to be believed – which is not always the case, though this time it is quite believable that the Park Lane dual carriageway might have seemed more absorbing. Insofar as the minutes reveal anything, it is the reek of anxiety and doubt. But the ministers agree that Britain should go to Brussels. And Butler and Macmillan are sent away to settle the details, which they do after a telling little interchange.

Butler was the first to compose a draft. It accepted Beyen's invitation, but proposed to make something clear. 'There are, as you are no doubt aware,' Butler wrote, 'special reasons which preclude this country from joining a European common market.' A categoric assertion, it seemed, that 'Europe' should understand there would always be a distance between them and us. 'Preclude' sounds adamantine. A sense of the axiomatic breathes from the Butler formula, and Macmillan noticed it. He made a subtle adjustment, of which the carbon copy in the Public Record Office bears the mark. A handwritten amendment deletes 'preclude'. Instead of 'special reasons which preclude', there are 'special difficulties for this country in any proposal for "a European common market".'

The Macmillan version, softening the sense of absolute negative inevitability, was the one that was sent to Europe. It might have been received in a spirit of some optimism. After all, it had seemingly found the language of negotiation. 'Difficulties' could always be ironed out, if the goodwill was there, which the further promise, to examine all problems 'without prior commitment and on their merits', suggested would be so. There was a lot of room for creative diplomacy in the fashioning of what this common market might eventually add up to.

Britain, moreover, would send no mere observer – though the designation arrived at was still perhaps a little opaque. She would, the

Foreign Secretary announced, 'appoint a representative to take part in these discussions'.

*

A POLITICIAN pressed hard to be that representative. He was Anthony Nutting, Minister of State at the Foreign Office, Eden's protégé and admirer, and one of very few out-and-out 'Europeans' anywhere near relevant office in the Government. Bevin had his Younger, Eden his Nutting, and each was treated with identical scorn by his master. 'I begged Anthony to let me go as an observer, just to sit there, just to show some presence,' Nutting said many years later. 'But he turned against *any* participation once he got into office.'[15]

To send a minister would at least have ensured a certain equality of representation. 'Europe', for the most part, ensured that the game now beginning in Brussels was played by its First Eleven. Paul-Henri Spaak, the dominating presence, was a foreign minister, and so was the chief German representative, Dr Walter Hallstein. The French team was made up of senior énarques from the Quai d'Orsay. But that degree of distinction, favouring 'Europe' with its brightest stars, was precisely not what Whitehall wanted. At two days' notice, a name had to be selected, and the one that presented itself was Russell Bretherton.

Bureaucratically, Bretherton had the right credentials, which were professional yet insignificant. He was an economist connected not to the Treasury or the Foreign Office but, well down-table, to the Board of Trade. He was already much involved with European trade issues, having been his department's representative on OEEC for the past year. Before that, he had been at the conference that set up the Marshall Plan in 1947, and then again on the economic side of the discussions that led to the formation of Nato. He had now attained the princely rank of under-secretary, but his experience was entirely relevant to the task of keeping an eye on what Spaak and his burgeoning committees might get up to, insofar as it affected trade. Trade was what Bretherton was about, and trade was the level of discourse at which London had decided to pitch its contributions to a process which, for the most part, it would have deeply preferred not to be having.

Quite soon, however, it became apparent to Bretherton that trade was an inadequate description of the issues on which he, the senior and effectively solitary British representative at the table, would be required to intervene.

He was, in fact, a man whose character spilled beyond the confines of his arid curriculum vitae. There was more to him than the grey template of a trade economist. For one thing, he wasn't just a career civil servant, but had spent time teaching economics at Oxford, where he was a fellow of Wadham for seventeen years, before he got into the Board of Trade. For another, one of his students there was Harold Wilson, a statistician-economist who went into politics – a happening that later produced a career-intersection unusual even in the tight little world of the British political class. In 1947, when Wilson became President of the Board of Trade, at thirty-one barely out of college, who should he find toiling on the lower corridors but the tutor, ten years older than himself, who taught him much of what he knew about economics.

Bretherton had admirers before and after his work on the Spaak committee. He made a personal mark, even in obscurity. A short, spare man, easily missed in a crowd, he was very clever. 'He didn't put you at your ease,' Roy Denman, a young BoT entrant in Bretherton's time, told me. 'He worked on the basis of intellect. His meetings used to be called audiences, because when Mr Bretherton spoke, nobody dissented.'[16]

His political boss at the time of Messina was also fulsome. Peter Thorneycroft, President of the Board 1951–7, told Michael Charlton that Bretherton 'was one of the most brilliant officials I've ever had the privilege of working with'. That was in 1982. When I went to see Thorneycroft in 1993, not long before he died, the glow of memory was more refulgent still. I didn't entirely trust Thorneycroft's recollection. Depicting himself as one of the Eden Cabinet's only real Europeans, he cast Bretherton as an indispensable aide. Thorneycroft's memory of himself was a shade romanticized. Although it is perfectly true he opposed imperial preference – the trade system that gave all Commonwealth countries big advantages – and faced down the Conservative Party conference to press the point, it is less clear what risks he took to push a sceptical Cabinet towards Europe in 1955. Nevertheless, remembering Bretherton, he thought the world of him, especially over Europe. His words are part of the record. 'You need a minister, like me, who has a view. But he needs some prophet, some man of real enthusiasm who in moments of weakness will help him struggle on. Bretherton was superb, a marvellous man. A real believer in the European cause.'

Bretherton's own beliefs are not yet relevant. Later they become so. The last reason he was sent to Brussels was because of any known enthusiasm for what the Messina powers were trying to put together. If anything, the opposite. But the matter did become an issue, when history

casually demonized the British representative as the man who walked
Britain out of the Common Market.

Arriving in Brussels, his first reaction was one of amazement at being
treated on the same level as the German Foreign Minister. 'Never before
or since have I been called Your Excellency,' he remembered a long time
later.[17] He did not, however, so far lose his sense of balance that he
could not almost immediately see what was going on: or, as much to the
point, see how it diverged from what London thought was likely to
happen.

The Whitehall position was, in the broad, to wait and see. But even
before their man was installed in Brussels, a series of studies had been
set in train to examine the implications. Although these tracked the
Brussels agenda, examining case by case the different functional integra-
tions – electricity, canals, air transport and so on – these were, with one
exception, never taken as seriously as the studies of the Common Market
itself. The exception, naturally, was atomic energy, a field in which
Britain had all to give and almost nothing to gain in any new community, being the only atomic power between Washington and Moscow.
But it was the idea of a common market, with its consequences for
industry, for agriculture, for the Commonwealth, for almost every aspect
of the gross domestic product, which attracted the highest level of British
concern. That is what engaged the Whitehall combatants, and gave rise
to the bedrock objection which became the tactical, if not quite the
strategic, base of Britain's attitude. The strategic case concerned sovereignty, supra-nationalism and high politics. The tactical argument to
support it, which contained substance as well as stratagem, was that any
new institution was essentially unnecessary. It could only duplicate
OEEC, the multi-national, inter-governmental body Britain already
chaired. This was the position that Britain was endlessly to repeat.

It was accompanied, at this early moment, by another, which was
more covert but of seminal importance. Whitehall continued to believe
that the Messina process was not, ultimately, serious. It would not lead
anywhere. The conflicts of national interest were too great. The proposed
Customs Union would find the parties violently disagreeing about tariff
levels. Protectionist France, in particular, would find it no easier to
surrender high tariff barriers than to liquidate any part of her sovereignty. Even the trading aspects of the plan would founder. As for the
political entity people like Johan Beyen spoke of, it would not get off
the ground.

Bretherton's first report from Brussels was painfully disabusive. He did not tell his superiors what they wanted to hear. The first meeting of the Spaak committee, he wrote, had shown 'firm determination to implement the Messina proposals'. The project was indeed 'predominantly political'. On his first trip back to London for face-to-face talking, he told colleagues that his brief, which was to 'steer Spaak Britain's way', was unlikely to be achieved. So much for the 'purely verbal' progress predicted by Gladwyn Jebb. The Customs Union was already almost agreed in principle. An atomic energy committee had been set up over his objections. Bretherton was already, it seemed, more observer than achiever. 'I still see his face in front of me,' said one of his European interlocutors, remembering the scene. 'He usually had a rather cynical and amused smile on his face, and he looked at us like naughty children, not really mischievous, but enjoying themselves by playing a game which had no relevance and no future.'[18]

It sounds as though Bretherton was playing the part he had been instructed to play, more than halfway outside the enterprise. But this was to some extent a masquerade. In less than a month he became well aware that Messina had more relevance and more future than anyone in London dared imagine.

He was also acutely sensitive to what was soon happening to his own position. It should be remembered that he was on his own, unhooked from ministerial or Whitehall control. In 1955, communications were far too slow to permit him to be briefed on his response to every turn in the discussion. The diplomatic bag took four days to reach Brussels. Bretherton saw himself getting drawn in. 'Influence' and 'steering' were, he began to realize, chimerical delusions. 'If we take an active part in trying to guide the final propositions', he wrote to a colleague on 4 August, 'it will be difficult to avoid later on the presumption that we are, in some sense, committed to the result.' How could Britain insist on such-and-such a point, get it accepted into the conclusions, and then renege on the whole deal? 'On the other hand, if we sit back and say nothing, it's pretty certain that many more things will get into the report which would be unpleasant from the UK point of view whether we in the end took part in the Common Market or not.'[19]

Between 1955 and 1995, the British dilemma, in a sense, never changed. Although it is true that the 1990s opt-out from economic and monetary union, EMU, preserved Britain's right to take part in all the preliminaries without obligation, the 'sucking-in' effect of involvement in any talks on any subject was what the latter-day enemies of 'Europe' regarded as the lesson of history, which they were determined not to see repeated. In exactly the same way, the ins and the outs constituted an axis of tension: choosing to be 'out', in the 1990s as in the 1950s, by no means disposed of any problem caused by the 'ins'.

Bretherton had to pass the ball back to London. He did not have plenipotentiary powers. And the thinness of London's commitment to the process did not take long to show itself. Before the end of August, the Mutual Aid Committee instructed him '*not* to imply, in saying that certain features of the proposals would make it very difficult for the UK to join, that we would join if our points were met'.[20] In plainer language, even if Bretherton won every point Whitehall wanted, Britain wouldn't necessarily accept the bargain.

Actually, and surprisingly, one school of thought had by now developed in London which considered that the case for joining what Brussels might give birth to was strong. Treasury economists had been studying the consequences of some kind of European customs union for several years, and concluded that the benefits it brought Britain would exceed any loss of preference in Commonwealth markets. They repeated this work now, and reached the same conclusion. Although other Treasury divisions had a different gloss, the majority judgement was that, in economic terms, Britain would be better advised to join than to stay out of a common market if it was put together. Looking at trade, taxation, commercial policy, labour and capital movement, the economists concluded that, although short-term calculation favoured abstention, in the long term its disadvantages would become clear.

Economics, however, wasn't the name of the real game, and the Treasury at this stage was not a place of decisive influence over major questions of external policy. What mattered was the high political judgement. And here, as autumn beckons, one begins to sense from the documents the gulf widening between the Whitehall panjandrums and the functionary they had sent to handle the case in Brussels.

Bretherton, on the spot, was beginning to be aware of how much there might be to gain. In his August letter, he had already written: 'We have, in fact, the power to guide the conclusions of this conference in almost any direction we like, but beyond a certain point we cannot exercise that power without ourselves becoming, in some measure, responsible for the results.' Within his brief he was doing his best. At one point, Spaak openly thanked him for his co-operative attitude. A Frenchman noted that his manner had become collaborative: 'You really could not make a distinction between Britain and the rest.' And speaking at a distance, much later, Bretherton revealed himself, at least by now, to be the man Peter Thorneycroft fondly imagined him to have been all along. The process, he said, changed him. 'Did you yourself begin to change your mind while this conference was going on?' Michael Charlton asked him. 'Oh yes,' he insouciantly replied.[21] In particular, he recollected, France was determined that British entry was a precondition of her own, and was prepared to pay a British price for that. Again in recollection: 'If we had been able to say that we agreed in principle, we could have got whatever kind of Common Market we wanted. I have no doubt of that at all.'

This, then, was Bretherton's position. He thought the Common Market was on the way to happening. He believed Britain could shape it. He put this advice on paper more than once. But, he said, 'I don't think anybody took any notice.'

He was right about that. The big guns were turning in the opposite direction.[22] The Treasury man who headed the MAC, William Strath, said mid-September would be 'a convenient moment to disengage'. Edward Bridges, still the head of the Treasury, now told Butler it had been 'a great pity' anyone had been sent to work with Spaak. He was firmly convinced Britain should have no part in this 'mysticism', which 'appeals to European Catholic federalists and occasionally, I fear, to our Foreign Secretary'. But the Foreign Office, in truth, was just as sceptical. Whereas the Treasury at least thought the Common Market might happen, the FO still believed there was almost no chance. It criticized the 'highly doubtful assumptions' of Treasury papers. What both departments agreed on was that the failure of the project should be encouraged to happen. Burke Trend, a rising star in mandarin Whitehall who later became Cabinet secretary, was the drafter of the final advice to ministers. They should be told, he wrote, that it would 'on balance be to the real and ultimate interest of the UK that the Common Market should collapse, with the result that there would be no need for the UK to face the embarrassing choice of joining it or abstaining from joining it'.

Trend also discussed tactics. Outright withdrawal would be 'a quite considerable gamble'. The Six '*might* go ahead without us, and they *might* pull it off'. Equally, they might fail, in which case we might be accused of sabotage, the implications of which 'are not pleasant'. But playing for time had its risks too, because the British were likely to find it harder to withdraw the longer they stayed in the talks. Nor was the idea of steering the Six towards OEEC very persuasive either. It would either be seen as another form of sabotage, or perhaps lead to the Six eclipsing OEEC and destroying it from within.

We see, all in all, what a damnable nuisance the idea of 'Europe' had now become, what a no-win situation it was beginning to present to the power that had grown accustomed over many years to securing what it could call victory, in all three of the intersecting world circles that uniquely defined Britain's range and role. The best advice that Trend could think of was to try and find some 'bribe', as he put it, which would lure the Six towards a free trade area rather than a customs union. Special tariff benefits, and a bit of British generosity on the nuclear front, he wrote, might be enough to do the trick.

Even if every policy carried risks, and no tactic could conceal them, however, there was never any doubt what the final Whitehall advice would be. On 27 October, the MAC, mindful of its audience and banishing the counter-views which at least one body of economists had submitted, loaded its assessment on the entirely negative side. There were, it said, four 'decisive considerations' against British membership. One, it would weaken Britain's relationship with Commonwealth and colonies. Two, Britain was a world power, and the Common Market would run against world free trade. Three, membership would lead to further integration, and perhaps federation, which the public would not accept. Four, British industry would no longer be protected against European competition.

There remained the end-game. It had to be accomplished with as much finesse as possible. In the various accounts of what happened next, we witness the usual distortions of memory and desires for self-vindication, of countries and politicians and officials who do not want to be blamed for the terminal event that now occurred. At this distance of time, the details may be of rather modest relevance – by comparison with the outcome. But Russell Bretherton, inevitably, is at the centre of them.

The extreme and most remembered version is also, naturally, the most alluring: the one that seems to reflect a due momentousness. Spaak, it is not disputed, had called a meeting for 7 November which was designed to bring matters to a head. This was a piece of blatantly aggressive chairmanship. In place of the sub-committees working on different aspects of the putative 'Europe', he proposed that all the work should now be subsumed into a single report, produced under his hand, coming to firm conclusions that would implement the Messina communiqué. Suddenly confronted with this coup, Bretherton is supposed to have summoned up a burst of Disraelian grandeur, expressed with Macaulayesque symmetry. Before rising from the table, he is alleged to have declared: 'Gentlemen, you are trying to negotiate something you will never be able to negotiate. But if negotiated, it will not be ratified. And if ratified, it will not work.'[23] To anyone who might doubt the probability of a trade economist, however clever, coming up with this impromptu formulation, the further word comes, from some sources, that Bretherton's text was drafted in Anthony Eden's own hand.

There is no documentary evidence that anything so exciting occurred. Marginal support might seem to emanate from the reaction of Spaak to Bretherton's intervention. 'Spaak just blew up at that point,' Bretherton himself said.[24] But such a response might as easily have been provoked, at this sensitive moment, by the rather more mundane expressions which there is some evidence the British representative did use. 'I had what amounted to almost a written instruction,' he remembered. It is in the PRO file. 'Following for Bretherton,' says a ciphered message sent, with rare speed, by bag to Brussels on 5 November. Therein he is given the words he must read out, which, for the first time, is what he does. They pour cold water, above all, on the duplication which this idea of a common market will entail. 'The main point I wish to make', the draft says for him, 'is that, to an important extent, the studies undertaken by these committees relate in varying degrees to matters within the competence of existing and broader institutions, and in particular to OEEC.'[25]

This was certainly enough to enrage Spaak. Bretherton's memory of what the Belgian said is unlikely to be precise, but the sense of it is surely faithful. 'Spaak just said, "Well, I am astonished and very hurt at this. You are just sticking to your guns. England has not moved at all, and I am not going to move either."'

Further evidence that Bretherton did not, in fact, make the spectacular exit legend attributes to him is supplied by the fact that his bosses in London never gave this meeting, either before or after it, quite the decisive importance which in retrospect it came to deserve. They told Bretherton to say what he said, but saw it as a form of prevarication, a delaying mechanism until they had worked out exactly when and how to achieve the same result, namely Britain's formal withdrawal from the Spaak committee. Later in November, Whitehall is still seething with disagreement about exactly what should be done. Ambassadors bombard London with questions. What exactly is going on, they ask? Our man at the ECSC complains at being 'left in the dark as to what HMG's policy really is'. Our man in Bonn says that, from what he has heard, we are taking the economic issue too narrowly. His superior at the FO messages back that yes, some Treasury economists favoured Britain joining, but it was for the Foreign Office 'to supply the spectacles of political reality as to how much of "Messina" will come to pass and, if it does, how it will fit in with our interests'.[26]

Plainly nothing had been decided exactly on 7 November. No doubt it is this that produced the lengthy argument, which zealots have conducted over decades, as to whether Britain withdrew from the Spaak committee, or was thrown out of it. Bretherton always insisted he did not withdraw. And that is technically quite true. He did not leave the room, and Britain did not there and then announce that she would take no further part. It does not even seem as though Spaak, for all his hair-trigger bombast, was on that very date laying down terms and conditions that banned Britain from taking further part.

On the other hand, that was Bretherton's last meeting. He never did return. The moment had presented itself, to both Spaak and the man who was chiefly in charge of the end-game in London, R. A. Butler, when Britain's pretence to any further allegiance to the project had to stop. Spaak's final report could be completed only by people who were committed to its recommendations. London, collective London, had decided it could not comply. At the edge of this Anglo-Europe consensus, London's part of the decision was the more definitive. Such was Spaak's keenness for Britain to come in – and his certainty, like Monnet's, that if the Six got their project together Britain would want to join it – that he would have been perfectly prepared for Bretherton to remain as a presence until the final proposition was agreed, which it was in early 1956. But then Bretherton would have had to be well and truly an 'observer', occupying the limbo between compliance and dissent, free to bark but not to bite, semi-acquiescent spectator at an event which Britain had decided to refrain from trying to control.

Against that alternative, absence was no doubt a more convincing option. But it committed Britain to the objective Whitehall had always put at the head of its wish-list, while desiring not to be seen to do so: assisting the Common Market, in Burke Trend's clinical judgement, 'to collapse'.

Mountains of words have issued forth about this sequence of events since it unfolded forty years ago. To a subsequent inquirer, curious to map the pathology of the political class most influential in shaping it, and to ask about the weight of countervailing wisdom at the time, two contributions cut the sharpest across any tendency to lie down tolerantly in front of the immutable facts of history.

The first is R. A. Butler's. Butler's relationship to 'Europe' was influenced by a considerable accumulation of interests and memories, some perhaps more admirable than others. For one thing, as a farmer who represented farming interests in Parliament, he was always likely to be wary of a project that might upset his personal and constituency arrangements. For another, he was among those Conservative politicians who were usually more sensitive to what the party might not like than to what it ought to be persuaded, against its instincts, to accept. Although a reformer, he seldom went about the business of social change by means of explicit challenge to the past. He did not, in that sense, have a brave political imagination.

Infusing this muted, oblique, crabwise character was a complicated past, especially as it had been touched by Europe. He was not at ease with all parts of his record. As an under-secretary at the Foreign Office, he had been closely associated with Neville Chamberlain, the Prime Minister who famously went to Bad Godesberg as an emissary seeking appeasement with Hitler. Butler was embarrassed by this connection with a man whose name for ever summoned up the image of two appurtenances: the famous 'piece of paper' he brought back ensuring peace in our time, and the furled umbrella that was his trademark. Later, Butler was always in a hurry to explain that he had had nothing to do with the formulation of Chamberlain's policy. It had just been his bad luck, so he said, to be the spokesman for it in the Commons, since the Foreign Secretary was in the Lords. But, as he knew, this didn't entirely wash. He had been in the appeasement camp, something he went to such lengths to obliterate as would intrigue any psychiatrist specializing in the behaviour of public men. The extent of it was revealed suddenly, when he himself visited Bad Godesberg many years later, as Chancellor. His memory was triggered. Out walking beside the Rhine with his private secretary, Robert Armstrong, he flourished the silver-headed cane that he invariably favoured, and, recalling his time with Chamberlain, said: 'Since then, I have never carried an umbrella.'[27]

So Butler lacked natural affinity with the Europe question, other than as the guilt-ridden veteran of a past that made it harder than usual for him to think straight. What should one make, nonetheless, of his apologia many years later?

When he was an old man, he looked back at the past with a candour that might disarm criticism, if it did not also carry an aura almost of complacency about it: shoulder-shrugging before whatever fate might bring. There was, he told Michael Charlton, 'a definite lack of foresight on the part of myself, and a much bigger lack of foresight on the part of the Treasury, and a very big lack of foresight on the part of the Foreign Office'.[28] But it was really all down to the advice the politicians were getting, especially about whether Messina would come to something. 'That is how the bad start, the late start for Europe, really started.' The withdrawal of Bretherton, Butler thought, had come about more than anything 'through boredom'. 'Anthony Eden was bored by this. Frankly he was even more bored than I was.' It was certainly 'a mistake', Butler said. But there was a consolation. 'I wasn't blamed at the time at all. And I have not been blamed very much in history.'

It may be a bit of a rarity to come across so open a confession of error. And perhaps the faintly comical world-weariness, the air of plangent and inexplicable non-sequitur, comes straight from the style-book of a notorious *flaneur*. But, conveying as he does London's fundamental lack of serious or constructive interest, Butler rather under-mines any defence there might be for the manifest error of judgement that occurred in the second half of 1955. If 'history' has any part in allocating 'blame', the exoneration of the Chancellor of the Exchequer, or the other ministers who would have said very much the same as he did, cannot be guaranteed in perpetuity.

Their lack of awareness, even, one might say, of intelligence, becomes the more painful when set beside the evidence of what some other minds were saying. This was long before 'Europe' had become a fractious political subject, on which all factual assessments became hopelessly contaminated by attitude-striking. Measured, cold-eyed calculation could still be made without prejudice.

In February 1956, the Federation of British Industries, forerunner of today's CBI, sent its international affairs man for a round of talks in Brussels and The Hague. His name was Peter Tennant, and he had been recently recruited from the Foreign Office. After a distinguished wartime career serving MI6 from the British embassy in Stockholm, Tennant moved, via Paris, to be Deputy Commandant in the British Sector of Berlin. Perhaps his provenance imposes the need to give some small recognition, after all, to the prophetic capacity of at least part of the public service. Tennant, now private industry's top adviser, returned from Europe with a very different verdict from the sonorous vacuities of the Foreign Office.

The Messina process, he judged, was far from being 'purely idealistic, impractical Europeanism'. He found the urgency surrounding it greater than at the start of either OEEC or the ECSC. Nor were the participants doctrinaire about supra-nationalism of the Monnet variety. The UK attitude, which Tennant characterized as lurching between belligerence and indifference, he found extremely puzzling.

He saw the political dilemma. Protectionism, sheltering behind imperial preference, was a hard nut to crack. But Tennant criticized the thinking about the emerging Common Market, which 'seems to have resulted in the advantages and disadvantages appearing to cancel out and thereby producing inactivity'. Inactivity, he went on, might be justified 'if one were not dealing with a reality'. Messina might produce a mess, and probably would do unless it had the benefit of British advice and experience. But the mess 'would for us be just as serious as a successful outcome from which we were excluded'. Imperial trade might presently account for almost 50 per cent of Britain's market, but this would inevitably shrink under pressure of more competition. Britain couldn't afford 'to be excluded from 20 per cent of our trade by the formation of a common market between six European countries, which might be joined by others and which, as a unit, would inevitably represent increased competition and bargaining power against us in third markets'.

What Tennant saw was an opportunity sliding away. Instead of identifying ourselves with Europe 'on our own terms', we were 'leaving events to proceed outside our control'. Unless this policy was somehow reversed, the result would cause far more disruption to the economy than any inconveniences that had to be dealt with now. 'We will be faced some 10 or 15 years hence with a decision to join the club on its terms and at a high entrance fee.'[29]

Russell Bretherton appears to have known that as well. Such was his own account of his judgement when he was released from the inhibitions of professional neutrality. But it also fits in with what he plainly thought at the time. Late in my inquiry, I came across a letter he wrote to Frank Lee, his permanent secretary at the Board of Trade. Dated 17 November 1955, on his return from Brussels, this already reflects on the crisis to come. 'I only wish that I felt happier about the line we are taking,' Bretherton said. 'I think that we underestimate the amount of steam, both political and economic, which is still behind the Messina ideas, and also the dangers for the UK in a purely negative attitude on our part.' The message about Bretherton's differences with his masters emerges at a later moment too. The last time we come across him in the official documents of this period, he has returned to his role as a Board of Trade civil servant. Eden is preparing for a visit to President Eisenhower, in the course of which he knows he will need to explain Britain's negative attitude to the integration that Washington had always been keen to foster. Peter Thorneycroft is asked to produce a paper, and Bretherton, who drafts it for him, dutifully assembles a measured case explaining why the Customs Union would be against the British interest. It is a professional piece of work, reflecting the stance to which the Government was now committed.

His official superiors, however, scrutinizing it before it was sent up to Thorneycroft, didn't like it. The draft, wrote Sir Edgar Cohen, second secretary at the BoT, was 'too reasonable'. What was required, to make the British position unmistakably clear to the Americans, was 'to sound a note of hysteria'.[30] Wiping out Bretherton's cool words, Cohen rewrote Eden's brief, in the kind of language that did proper justice to the mentality these esteemed masters of the universe were beginning to depend on.

4

HAROLD MACMILLAN

Agonizing for Britain

THE TREATY OF ROME, providing for a common market and an ever closer union of the peoples whose leaders invented it, was signed on 25 March 1957.[1] British hysteria, whether applied directly to the Messina Six or mediated via Washington, did not succeed in impeding the creation of a customs union, together with the apparatus of court, commission and council that was needed to make it work.

Hysteria of a different kind was adjacent to the scene. Here the word didn't describe a Foreign Office aspiration, a tactical ploy to fend off the future. It was the right word for the feeling that was engendered, behind the usual front of British sang-froid, by the diplomatic disaster, military humiliation and psychic catastrophe known forever after under a generic name: Suez.

'Suez' and 'Europe', concepts that billow beyond the words that represent them, are the two motifs twined round Britain's definition of herself in the second half of the century. That the Suez disaster and the Rome Treaty occurred almost simultaneously – November 1956, March 1957 – was an accidental fact. But their repercussions one upon the other were, from the British standpoint, intimate. They shaped the British political realm as it has subsequently existed. Together they raised the question of national identity as a predicament that has perhaps been experienced more acutely in Britain than in any other European nation. Suez, the terminal calamity of Empire, infused the British mind at the moment when the European dilemma, which has tormented it ever since, was already beginning to assume massive importance.

Britain's self-exclusion from the Treaty presented itself, to the small coterie of people who were even aware that it was happening, as a deliberative act. The official papers abound with rational arguments. In fact, it had much more to do with inchoate feelings about where Britain belonged in the world: visceral sentiments of grandeur that Suez, eventually, made untenable. But such awareness of the limits of instinct took time to dawn. Meanwhile, the stirrings of something new in the official mind were beginning very slightly to make themselves felt.

In one respect, the Foreign Office attitude to the Common Market – that it would never happen – was perfectly intelligible. It revolved around France, and France did not come smoothly to the party. The French attitude to nation and sovereignty resembled Britain's, with a preference for putting country before continent, and a measure of protection for traditional markets before the internal free trade the Market aspired to. French ratification was at times in doubt, and in any case had to be carried through by a government other than the one which had negotiated and signed the Treaty. It was at all times a risky venture, upon whose failure British diplomats rested their faith. But it happened. France surmounted her doubts and difficulties. She negotiated terms for her colonies, the equivalent of the British Commonwealth – for which Mother Britain found it inconceivable that a negotiation should even be attempted. Deploying their considerable negotiating panache, the French political class came round to falsifying the predictions and smashing the hopes of almost all their British counterparts.

Almost all, but not quite. In London there were the beginnings of dissent from the ideology that gripped upper Whitehall. The presence of these murmurings now needs to be registered. In the Whitehall of the middle 1950s, they did not get a hearing, but they did exist. The dominant culture belonged to Sir Roger Makins, but not everybody in it had drawn the same lessons from the war as he had done. These new men knew well enough that Atlanticism, the American relationship, the god before which Makins and his generation worshipped, was at the heart of the British national interest. The war and the victory had proved it. But theirs was a different kind of war, far from the armchair generalship that had imparted to older men a single-minded obsession with the Pax Americana. For them, the shot and shell of the front line were what they could never forget. Their war gave them a different perspective. And since they were the men of the future, many of whom rose high in the Foreign Office by the time the prejudices of their elders proved to have been misdirected, they are a cadre of some interest.

Consider Donald Maitland, born in 1922, whose diplomatic career crested as ambassador to the European Communities, 1975–9. In 1955, Maitland wasn't involved with Europe. What was quaintly known in the Office as an orientalist, he had learned Arabic and served, in his early career, in Baghdad and Lebanon. He spent his war not in Europe but in Asia and the Middle East. But the experience left him sceptical of the British orthodoxies. 'I came back from the war absolutely persuaded that the imperial idea – the idea of us ruling other countries – was finished,' he told me in the 1990s. 'We had to decolonize, and if we were going to do that we had to have another kind of foreign policy.'[2] The only basis for this, he thought as a young man, was Europe. He didn't pretend to know how it might happen, but he regarded as elementary the need for structures and treaties that were likely to stop Europe ever going to war again.

To anyone who thought like that, Messina was obviously a missed opportunity. But the official policy said otherwise. As the files voluminously show, from the moment Bretherton got to Brussels, the discussion in London centred not on how he might constructively use his seat but how he might gracefully vacate it. Quite a lot of Maitland's generation believed as he did. To me he named, among others, Oliver Wright (b. 1921), Brooks Richards (b. 1918), James Murray (b. 1919), Anthony Montague Browne (b. 1923), a varied group of distinguished career diplomats. There were others of similar age. But they never officially discussed Europe. Strong convictions produced no debate, a silence that reflected the lack of excitement, or even argument, in the wider world. 'We all worked terribly long hours,' Maitland remembered. 'There was no opportunity to talk except in the canteen or the gents.'

Some of them, occasionally, had opportunities which they took to extremes. The first posting of Christopher Audland (b. 1926) was to the UK high commissioner's office near Bonn, where the capital of the new-born German Federal Republic had just been established. There, at the age of twenty-three, he was the British negotiator of one of the Bonn Conventions, which were to lead to the full independence of West Germany. In this work, he took part in meetings with Konrad Adenauer once a week. Not surprisingly, he became immersed in Germany, and saw at close quarters the need for German integration into the European system. His next posting was to Strasbourg and the Council of Europe, where he decided that the Monnet approach to European unity, via a community, was much preferable to the inter-governmental approach favoured by Britain. 'In this I was thought very eccentric,' Audland later said. 'I was seen as having gone native.' But such Europeanism permeated all the advice he gave to his superiors when he returned to the Foreign Office to spend much of a decade involved in the great question, and then set the seal on his commitment by becoming a full-blooded

Eurocrat, working for the Commission in Brussels from 1973 until retirement. Thus Audland can be seen from the early 1950s as part of a new generation, unheard but significantly aberrant, which presaged a Foreign Office that sooner or later would be ready to revise its Euro-scepticism.

Among this youthful crowd was a figure who could be called, in retrospect, its leader. Personally, he collected more Euro-credentials than anyone else. Professionally, his career turned out to track with metronomic regularity Britain's European policy throughout the thirty-five years it took him to rise to the senior post in the Foreign Office.

Michael Palliser (b. 1922) spent his war in Europe, in the Coldstream Guards. He was part of a tank brigade, and what he remembered when I talked to him forty years later was not so much the war itself as the scenes it left behind, the towns that even tanks could not traverse for rubble. 'Simply taking a train journey from Berlin through the Ruhr and up to the Hook of Holland, you saw a place that was absolutely flattened,' Palliser said. It made a powerful impression on him. 'I came out feeling that this was something one simply can't allow to happen again. It hit you like a kick in the stomach.' In his chosen profession of diplomacy, that kind of youthful memory can have a potent afterlife. 'If you go into the international field,' Palliser said, 'the gut feeling perhaps continues in a way it does less in other jobs. Your view of the world can be formed by instinct as much as reason.'[3]

Like Audland, Palliser chose to live at first hand through Germany's post-war experience, remaining in the army for eighteen months, watching 'the deliquescence of a society'. He found himself poised between despair for what Germany had done and great personal sympathy for individual Germans. 'Here were people who were basic human beings, who had been appallingly knocked about. At nightfall, all you could see were piles of rubble, but then at daybreak people climbed out of the cellars and went to work.' In the Foreign Office, Palliser's first job was as secretary of the allied powers' committee that settled output levels for the German steel industry. Not long after, at the birth of the Schuman Plan, he spent three years dealing with Germany in all her aspects.

It was a formation that never left him. He could still recall in 1993 his disgust at watching the senior Foreign Office mandarins disposing of questions raised by Herbert Morrison, who succeeded Bevin as Foreign Secretary, concerning coal and steel policy and its relationship to the Schuman Plan. Makins was the lordly agent of the Labour politician's correction. His scornful minute, repelling all temptations to make common cause with 'Europe', was circulated 'in the print', a category of despatch that made sure the entire foreign service would see it. 'I remember being immensely discouraged by that,' said Palliser, 'and thinking, for God's sake, these people are living in the wrong world.' But, being near the bottom of the pecking-order, he could do nothing about it.

Palliser qualifies to be called the archetypal British 'man of Europe'. Although in the early days he was professionally frustrated, he secured some compensation by marrying, in 1948, the daughter of none other than Paul-Henri Spaak. The young diplomat was received into the European purple, at some cost to the political reputation of the Belgian Foreign Minister. For Palliser was a Catholic and Spaak was not, and Spaak had to tell his anti-Catholic socialist party to go to hell when Michael and Marie were married at the Papal Nunciature in Brussels. But that was only the beginning of Palliser's declaration for Europe. His later career was lived there. He was in Paris when the Rome Treaty was signed, in Downing Street when Britain made her second attempt to accede to it, in Paris again when the third and last attempt was made, in Brussels as ambassador when Britain finally limped into the Community, and in London as permanent under-secretary when the last undone piece of business relating to British membership was on the verge of being completed.

But in the middle 1950s, he was a man before his time. So were they all. They were no match for the great men of the Foreign Office, who had not only the rights bestowed on superior status but the belief that their wisdom was as incontestable as their position. If Makins was the high priest of Atlanticism, our man at the Paris embassy when the Treaty of Rome was signed was a Poo-Bah of still more eclectic range.

Sir Gladwyn Jebb (b. 1900) is, in his way, as emblematic of his time and class as was his subordinate, Michael Palliser. Jebb it was who, writing to London from Paris, reassured his department on numerous occasions that what had happened at Messina would come to nothing. He exposed occasional crevices of doubt about the advisability of London taking *quite* such an openly hostile attitude to all matters European, but he did not challenge the essential orthodoxy. Yet – and here is where he is typical of his time as well – this didn't remain his position. Quite the reverse. Jebb was the most eminent official whose trajectory on the Europe question follows the tortuous path taken by almost all the politicians whose lives it touched: from scepticism to enthusiasm – and sometimes back again. Jebb himself eschewed the last of these manoeuvres. He, who had called the Hague conference of the European Movement an 'ill-considered and emotional hullabaloo' and pursued an official career which had seldom challenged that premise, changed his mind for ever. On retiring from the Foreign Office in 1960 after thirty years' service, he began an opposite line of service that lasted another thirty years. Lord Gladwyn, as he was soon entitled, became a missionary European. The filling-out of Europe, with Britain at the heart of it, became his later life's work. When I saw him in 1993, he was still struggling through the consequences of a stroke to preach the cause in the House of Lords in speeches which the shorthand writers were hard put to decipher into an accurate note. But I couldn't help being more struck by the fact that, in his middle nineties, Gladwyn Jebb was far more interested in the likely results of the Treaty of Maastricht than in details of the history of Messina.

To listen to such prophetic concern was an impressive experience. But in the days when he counted for a great deal Jebb was no more prescient than any of his colleagues. He was a clever, arrogant man, a bully, whose flamboyance, Donald Maitland recalled, spread itself through the Foreign Office wherever he was posted. 'He was good with ministers. With their similar background, he could take on Eden on equal terms. And he got on very well with Bevin.'

He was, in a word, an official who counted more than any official could expect to in the 1990s. He belonged to a lost breed. And lest there be doubt about that, it is necessary to refer only to his memoirs, where the recitation of the author's achievements conjures up a forgotten world of British greatness, epitomized by none more spaciously than himself. 'The European Advisory Commission was, in varying forms, first advocated by me,' he writes. 'The famous "Four Power Plan" (which ended up with the United Nations) was originated by myself. It was I who first prepared a draft for an "Atlantic Treaty", which blossomed out eventually into Nato. The German Occupation Zones (which, for good or evil, largely shaped the whole post-war development of Europe) were at any rate prepared in the committee of which I was chairman. And, above all perhaps, suggestions for some kind of Western European Union (which ended up in the Brussels Treaty Organisation and in the WEU) were, so far as I know, first formulated in that dark back room [the room Jebb occupied at the Foreign Office, 1935–7, 1942–4].'⁴ Gladwyn was not troubled by modesty. The list speaks for a breathtaking intellectual aggrandizement. But it is not complete. The memoirist says something else that reveals a certain inflation of memory. 'If there has been any idea to which I have been exceptionally faithful over the years,' he writes, 'it has been "Europe" ... This is something I feel I really do know something about.'

What he knew in the middle 1950s, however, proved to be false. It reflected rather than challenged the mind of middle England. Jebb was a Euro-sceptic in every sense except the one most necessary, namely the capacity to apply a doubting mind to the orthodoxy that had taken Bretherton away from Spaak's table, or an anxious one to the economic prognosis which supported that political gesture.

For this was also an economic question. In the Foreign Office, the economic issue tended to be swept aside as if it barely needed addressing. Could Britain survive unscathed the creation of an economic zone across the Channel of which she wasn't part? Was the British economy, rooted in trading patterns far beyond Europe, strong enough to be indifferent to what happened there? These were always pressing questions, but had invariably been spared rigorous examination. In the run-up both to the Schuman Plan and to Messina, official analyses were sufficiently agnostic to give succour to the many people whose strong preference was for persuading themselves that the politics of 'Europe' required Britain, whatever the economic facts, to keep out.

By the middle 1950s, however, such a stance was beginning to be taken with somewhat less confidence. Some economists in the Treasury saw reasons for worry. Self-excluded from Messina, Britain embarked, as we shall see, on a defensive strategy which revealed a certain anxiety. The truth was becoming available, for those who could count.

The illusion of Britain's economic strength received plenty of rein-forcement, not all of it mendacious. Both 1953 and 1954 were years of success. In 1953, there was a surplus on the balance of payments, which reflected an increase in output and exports. Stability was seemingly being followed by expansion. This remained, moreover, the enterprise of a great power that believed in its historic role. In 1955, befitting her history and status, Britain still spent 9 per cent of her gross national product on defence, financing massive troop encampments in the Middle and Far East. The military budget dominated both the shipbuilding and engin-eering industries. The island people continued to give a passable per-formance as a warrior nation of which the entire world had to take note.

Other trends, however, were more ominous, and they are not all the evidence of hindsight. Between 1954 and 1959, unit labour costs in manufacturing industry rose by 25 per cent in Britain, twice as fast as in other industrial countries. In 1958, the relentless trend line of German growth produced the cross-over between the economies of the war winners and losers: that was the year the German economy grew bigger than the British, and German exports first exceeded British exports. It was the climax of a period, 1950–8, in which the annual percentage growth rates for manufactured exports were as follows: West Germany 15.0, Netherlands 9.8, Italy 8.9, Britain 1.8.[5] Annual average growth rates overall, 1950–60, were: West Germany 7.8 per cent, Italy 5.8, France 4.6, Britain 2.7. Of course, the continentals had started from a lower base. But this was the seed-bed of the pattern of which the economist Peter Oppenheimer was obliged to write in 1970: 'It was estimated that all the other countries of north-western Europe [except Ireland] had surpassed Britain in output per head by the time the Conservatives left office' in 1964.[6]

There was, retrospect shows, a dire match between economic trends, on the one hand, and the political judgements that ignored them. The very year of Messina, 1955, was actually the moment when the balance of payments, the crucial residue of these trends, began to falter. The balance returned to deficit, the sterling reserves took a downward turn and there was no quick recovery from either development. The complacency of the Chancellor, R. A. Butler, based on the 1953–4 performance, began to be overtaken by a sense of depression, especially at the state of manufacturing industry.

This depression, however, was as yet far from terminal. It wasn't deep enough to prompt a serious re-examination of what government might do to give manufacturing a higher priority, and address the competitiveness problem. This was a nation whose thinking was hard to shake. In official circles, the conventional wisdom had never cared much about manufacturing anyway. Compared with the continentals, the Conservative governments of the 1950s were mistrustful of anything like an industrial policy, and pursued trading and commercial priorities which grew out of geo-strategic attitudes rather than any committed idea of the interests of Great Britain Ltd. International finance and the role of sterling continued to be the determinants of most British official thinking. Relationships with the Commonwealth retained a much tighter grip on the Tory, and for that matter the Labour, mind than the awkward realities of a trading bloc of expanding economies across the Channel. The politicians persuaded themselves, in the teeth of the trends, that they could survive and perhaps defeat the economic power of 'Europe' anyway. They were able to pretend that the world had not changed for ever, still believing, for example, that the main reason for

German and French success was the wartime destruction those countries had suffered. Therefore, they assumed, it would not last.

When I talked to Roger Makins in the 1990s, and asked him to explain why, in his rejection of 'Europe' in the mid-1950s, he had been so spectacularly wrong, his answer acknowledged the error but deflected the blame. After Messina, he had been transferred from the Foreign Office to the Treasury, where he was permanent secretary from 1956 to 1959. What he said to me conveyed the amateurish puzzlement that was often a convenient bolt-hole, an ironic escape, for the tigerish certainties of the post-war mandarinate. 'What I didn't foresee,' Makins told me, 'and what many people didn't foresee, was the total failure of British industry in the 1960s and 1970s. It was not to be foreseen. I agree that, if I'd read the statistics, I should have known we were bound to go downwards. But as permanent head of the Treasury, you weren't allowed to deal with anything under ten million pounds. As for reading obscure statistics, that was for somebody else.'[7]

But not all mandarins were so flippant. If one is looking for a beginning to the slow, stuttering reversal of Whitehall opinion about the proper relationship Britain had to have with the European Common Market, it can perhaps be located at a critical moment of decision in the career of Roger Makins's successor at the Treasury, Sir Frank Lee. If the worm was turning, the manoeuvre could never be accomplished by Michael Palliser and the other committed young Europeans at the Foreign Office, but it might be assisted by a fearless mind of suitable seniority. Frank Lee became that mind.

Lee had shown counter-cultural tendencies on occasions in his past. Seldom has a British civil servant combined intellectual independence, career success and collegial admiration to the extent that he did. He was a small, ugly man with a large spirit and a rasping voice. His Whitehall experience was wide beyond the dreams of any modern successor. He began in the Colonial Office, went to the Treasury, thence to Supply, more than once to Washington. He was a compleat mandarin of the meritocratic breed, becoming top man at Food, then top man at Trade, and finally the topmost of men, permanent secretary at the Treasury. But he remained, throughout, a leader in tight control of all that happened. One of his successors, Douglas Allen (Lord Croham), told me that, however high Lee rose, he would never delegate the main task of an official. 'He drafted everything himself. He was a brilliant draftsman, and an excellent chairman. He was one of my heroes.'[8]

Roy Denman is another witness to the impression Lee made. 'His appearance', writes Denman, 'suggested a more than usually dilapidated, second-hand suit which had spent the night in a hedgerow. His voice was like the creaking of a rusty gate. But he spoke with force and fire and with an intellectual clarity few could match. To hear him laying down the law to a minister was an experience not easily forgotten.'[9]

Along the line, Lee had challenged some sacred cows. When at Trade, he was the force behind Peter Thorneycroft's desertion of imperial preference. Given the Tory Party's imperial preferences, this was as defiant an attitude for Lee as it was a risky one for his minister. But still more significant was the choice he made in November 1955 to decouple from the Whitehall wisdom that decreed Bretherton's withdrawal from the Messina process. When the official paper went forward to the politicians, the name of the permanent secretary at the Board of Trade was among those appended to it, but he had in fact dissented, as the files record.[10] Being in a minority of one, he chose not to press his case. While acknowledging that ministers were taking a political decision, he told his colleagues that in his opinion the economic argument for entering the Messina project with a view to joining the Common Market was persuasive.

It was to be some years before Lee saw this opinion bear fruit. But he had made plain that it existed. For the first time, it was heard at a high level. It could be a catalyst, when the time came. It was lying in wait, as it were, for the moment when ministers themselves, and a larger handful of politicians, and a growing segment of the business community, and even a few flexible intellects near the top of the Foreign Office became ready to embrace the recognition that the world had changed.

In fact, it already had. By the time Britain's decision to exclude herself was set in metal in the Treaty of Rome signed by the Messina Six, Suez had knocked aside the main assumptions on which this withholding was based. That wasn't fully perceived in November 1956 when the fiasco occurred. Suez was too profound an event for its implications to be immediately understood, still less gathered into clear enough shape to prompt a change of policy towards Europe. But it was the death-blow for Britain's fading belief in her imperial reach, and should have told the governing class to re-examine their ideas about British independence.

Actually, the link between Suez and Europe emerged as a creative possibility before the disaster occurred. There were those who hoped for a synergy. The war-planning process brought France and Britain close.

Both countries saw their interests at stake when the Egyptian President, Colonel Nasser, seized the Suez Canal. Their leaders were deeply embroiled together in the middle months of 1956. The French Prime Minister of the time, Guy Mollet, a socialist and Anglophile, saw an opportunity, in preparing the conspiracy by which the Canal would be retaken with Israel's assistance, for the more durable involvement of Britain in the European system. He was still interested in readmitting Britain to the Messina process, advanced though that then was. 'There was a real spirit of confidence between the British and French leaders,' said one who witnessed it.[11]

The man who told me this was Mollet's secretary, Emile Noël, later the first secretary-general of the European Commission. Of the many old men I talked to during this inquiry, none had a more energetic memory than Noël. The mental habits of the old, their reliability on points of history, and their interest in reviewing their versions of it, could be a capacious sub-plot of any work that relies at all on oral reminiscence. Old men with an important past, I have learned, cover the gamut of truth between self-vindication and self-knowledge, vagueness and precision. But Noël, even at seventy-three, had the best-stocked recollection of detail of anyone I met. The formal histories seldom, if ever, contradicted it. Noël seemed to have an exact memory of every European Council meeting he ever attended. On the events of 1956, he confirms what was only to be expected. In the four months of meetings that led up to Suez, Selwyn Lloyd, the British Foreign Secretary, Harold Macmillan, by now the Chancellor, and Anthony Eden, Prime Minister, met their French equivalents Pineau, Bourges-Manoury and Mollet many times. 'In the margins of those meetings,' Noël recalled, 'Guy Mollet tried to convince his counterparts to make a move into the European Community, and said that France would make it easier for them. But there was no answer.'[12]

Nor could there have been. The leap of imagination required for such a move had been considered and definitively rejected, as we have seen, a year before. It never occurred to any of the British leaders that the enterprise they were now plotting might reopen the matter. And when it ended in disaster, after a single week's abortive engagement with Nasser, it had driven the French and British perspectives on Europe far apart.

To France, Suez greatly reinforced the case for concluding a treaty of European union. Negotiations were far advanced, but still incomplete. Before Suez, there was a substantial chance that French politics, moved by many similar considerations to the British, would not permit the Economic Community, as it was coming to be called, to be created. After the event, opinion swung round, and saw Europe more as a boost than a threat to French influence. 'The Suez fiasco had generated a new wave of "Europeanism",' writes one analyst, 'and had visibly strengthened the feeling in France that only through European unity could France regain a position of power and independence in the world.'[13] And without, if necessary, the British. It was, after all, the British who called a halt to the Suez operation, under pressure from their American friends. To any Frenchman still inclined to hesitate before sinking the nation's destiny into a construct among neighbours, Suez could only erode his scepticism. So France, after Suez, moved decisively to push her version of a union to the front of the agenda. She got her colonial empire included, and insisted on provisions for agricultural support that did not sell the birthright of French farmers.

Suez thus helped bring the European treaty to a constructive climax. But on Britain the immediate effect was very different. A lesson reveals itself, concerning the durability of British prejudices. For it was indisputably true that the American connection had shown how little it could be worth. The operation ended because Washington declined to help sustain it. What brought Britain to her knees wasn't military but economic weakness. In the run-up to hostilities, the sterling reserves fell by £20 million in September and £30 million in October. After two days of battle round Port Said, Macmillan felt obliged to warn his colleagues that maybe another £100 million had left the British vaults in the first week in November. He begged them to surrender. As the flight from sterling accelerated, national ruin loomed, and the Americans refused all requests for a bail-out. Eisenhower and his advisers decided to let Britain swing impotently in the wind. Yet, despite this lack of comradeship in the country's hour of need, the British leadership reacted to Suez first and above all by seeking to remake the Washington relationship. The Europeans had hoped for a different outcome. From Paris, Gladwyn Jebb, unconsciously prefiguring later alarms about the magnetic attraction of the Pacific Rim to the American mind, wrote: 'Some Frenchmen are comforting themselves with the thought that American policy favouring the Asiatic races will drive the United Kingdom further in the direction of Europe.'[14] But America, not Europe, was still Britain's uncontested priority. Preserving the sterling area, where Commonwealth countries kept their funds, continued to eclipse any thought of European solidarity. Keith Kyle has put it aptly: 'The sterling area gave some lingering substance to the notion that Britain was still a World Power. It was to uphold that notion that Britain was at Suez. One aspect of fading greatness was sacrificed to save another.'[15]

In some fields of policy, this greatness was soon seen to have been compromised fatally. In defence matters, for example, the imperial lion sacrificed her pretensions with extraordinary speed. Less than a year after Suez, the Government set in train a huge military shift by ending conscription, and reducing the British presence east of Suez, which was the border-line of Empire, and even to some extent in Europe. It was a seminal moment, which did further European damage by apparently reneging on the pledges France understood to have been given about Britain's commitment to the Western European Union. Simultaneously, Suez was a watershed for British colonialism. Although decolonization had begun with India in the previous decade, India is where it had stopped. It was no coincidence that it should resume in 1957, after a decade when the Conservative Party's strong colonial prejudices had continued to be just about sustainable. After Suez, resistance to independent nationhood for Nigeria, Tanganyika, Cyprus, Uganda and the rest evaporated. The fight, perhaps the romance, had gone out of the nation. It had been taught no end of a lesson.

What took longer to follow was the quest for an alternative, a new matrix within which to fit Britain's strategic objectives. The Empire was fraying at the edges and softening at the centre. The writing was on the wall for those prepared to read it, and to study with detachment the financial data that underpinned its meaning. A number of important people were beginning to examine it, finally moved by some apprehension at what they could see of both the political and economic future. But they needed a leader who was prepared to grasp the nettle of the past: someone who came from the past and understood it, and gave the reassuring impression of being steeped in its wonderful, heroic qualities, but who seriously suspected its time had come.

*

SUEZ WAS THE END, of course, of Eden. The pressures, of duplicity and failure alike, were too much for his health, which at the best of times was not robust. His successor as Prime Minister had no more honourable a record in the crisis than he did. Of all the ministers around Eden, Harold Macmillan played the most ignominious role, being among the first into the breach and the first to leave it. As Chancellor, he was the man who felt most directly the cold American withdrawal of financial support. But his response, which was to tell the Foreign Secretary, Selwyn Lloyd, that 'in view of the financial and economic pressures, we must stop', was singularly shameless. 'Considering the role he had played so far, his talk of "all or nothing", of "selling Britain's last securities", of "dying in the last ditch",' Keith Kyle writes, 'this was a sensational loss of nerve.'[16] But it was one for which the Conservatives did not punish him.

As was the practice of those days, Macmillan 'emerged' as their chosen leader. Had there been a leadership election, it is possible he wouldn't have done so. The favourite candidate, in the sense of the man most widely expected to win, was Butler, who deputized when Eden fell ill and was seen, especially by the press, as his senior heir apparent. But, when soundings were taken across the party, Macmillan was clearly preferred.

The choice had its European aspect. By contrast with the 1990s, Conservatism in the 1950s did not make 'Europe' the test of a politician's standing. In keeping with the absence of public debate throughout the Messina process, not even the faintest question about their continental attitudes affected the party's assessment of what kind of a Conservative Macmillan, on the one hand, or Butler, on the other, might be. Butler, however, was blackballed by significant numbers of Tory MPs and peers because of his record as a pre-war appeaser: which was one sort of European credential. And, by preferring Macmillan, the party was choosing the man who had already distinguished himself from his rival by desiring at least to send Bretherton to the Spaak committee. Unlike Butler, Macmillan declined to associate himself with statements of incredulity at the notion of Britain being an active partner in the development of 'Europe'.

Insofar as Europe did intrude on this leader's background, it seemed not to be an idea he resisted. Personal attitudes and instinctive attachments always matter in politics, and Macmillan had given plenty of thought to Europe, most of it comradely.

It began a long time before. When Harold Macmillan referred, as he often did, to 'the war' the allusion was usually not to Hitler's conflict but to the First World War, in which he had fought and had seen many friends, the flower of England, die. Throughout Macmillan's life, memories of the Somme appeared regularly in his discourse, and deeply penetrated his attitude to foreign relations. He was an internationalist, as beguiled as Eden by the fascination of foreign affairs, though he spent

Winston Churchill, Strasbourg, 1949: Europe, your Europe.

Ernest Bevin, Foreign Secretary 1945–51: the first Euro-sceptic.

Sir Henry Tizard,
Chief Scientific
Adviser, Ministry
of Defence: the
first realist.

Edward Heath MP:
smoothly against
the grain.

Robert Schuman and Jean Monnet, 1951: beginning with coal and steel.

The Messina Six; from the left, foreign ministers
Johan Beyen (Holland), Gaetano Martino (Italy), Joseph Bech (Luxembourg),
Antoine Pinay (France), Walter Hallstein (Federal Republic of Germany)
and Paul-Henri Spaak (Belgium).

Russell Bretherton, under-secretary, Board of Trade, 1955: the sacrificial agent.

Sir Anthony Eden and R.A. Butler, 1955: these excavations do not concern us.

Harold Macmillan, prime minister, Conservative Party Conference, 1962:
let us face the future – and the past.

President de Gaulle and Macmillan, 1961: old men don't forget.

Macmillan and R. A. Butler: a definite lack of foresight.

De Gaulle, 14 January 1963: what could be more obvious than '*Non*'?

much less time involved with them professionally. One reason Eden removed him from the Foreign Office after barely six months, in 1955, was his dislike of Macmillan's creative independence in the field Eden regarded as his personal domain. Nor was Eden the only Prime Minister who preferred an unthreatening subordinate in the job. Macmillan himself, when the time came, retained there Selwyn Lloyd, an incorrigible second-rater, and then appointed Alec Douglas-Home, shrewd and fearless but, as a disfranchised peer, a man who knew his place.

By pedigree, Macmillan was a Churchillian. Before the Second World War, he echoed the great man's vision of a single continent, with the off-shore island apparently included, brought together for the survival of the species. 'If western civilisation is to survive,' he wrote in 1939, 'we must look forward to an organisation, economic, cultural and perhaps even political, comprising all the countries of Western Europe.' When the war was over, and a version of this dream, minus the island, was being preached from the rostrums and grandstands of continental capitals, Macmillan was again of the company. In the Tory divide over the Council of Europe, he was unambiguously with Churchill, unlike Eden and Butler who were always disdainful.[17] He favoured the European Army, declaring to the Strasbourg Assembly that 'Britain's frontier is not on the Channel; it is not even on the Rhine; it is at least on the Elbe.' As the European Movement developed in the first few years, he consistently supported it.

Unlike Churchill, moreover, Macmillan carried this position into office. At the time of the Schuman Plan, his feelings had contrasted with the routine oppositionism of the party line. His critique of the Attlee Government's refusal to join it rested on a desire, within limits, for it to succeed. When the Tories took over, and Macmillan became Minister of Housing and Local Government, he infuriated more senior colleagues by circulating a disrespectful attack on the conventional wisdom that favoured Britain's aloofness. His line was a mixture of contradictions, of the kind that were still richly present in political argument in the 1990s. He wanted 'to attach Germany permanently to Western Europe'. Yet he also feared 'a German-dominated Continental Community' that might one day side with the Russians. But his driving belief was that Britain should get intimately involved. In March 1952, he wrote privately to Churchill after a Cabinet meeting that had poured cold water on the idea of European unity, flaying the 'continued opposition of the Foreign Office, in big and small things alike', to the whole European movement, and reminding the old man of the inconsistency between what he had said for years after the war and what he was now saying in government. The Foreign Office had produced 'a quite dreadful paper' on Europe, Macmillan wrote. According to his biographer, Alistair Horne, he now came closer to resigning than on any other occasion in his career.[18]

So this was a European. That designation wasn't as definitive in the mid-1950s as it became forty years later. Like every Conservative of the period, Macmillan was also a man of Empire. For the country that found it hard to contemplate the thought of no longer being a big player in the world, Empire was a timeless seduction. As the Foreign Office discarded Europe, Macmillan easily ruminated on alternative visions. A club-land diarist, Jock Colville, wrote of him in May 1952: 'Harold Macmillan said to me at the Turf yesterday that he thought development of the Empire into an economic unit as powerful as the U.S.A. and the U.S.S.R. was the only possibility . . .'[19] But his sense of both history and geography kept him nagging away at the prime option, which he saw Churchill and Eden neglecting at the country's peril.

Europe, however, wasn't by any means a fixed objective. Macmillan's disagreements with Eden went only so far. The moment of truth, Messina, occurred on his watch as Foreign Secretary, and he didn't grasp its importance. That short span, from April to December 1955, enclosed the whole evolution of British decision-making on Messina and the Spaak committee, and the 'European' at the Foreign Office presided over it with notable indifference. When, for example, the foreign ministers of the Six met to review progress, at Nordwijk in September 1955, Macmillan was invited, but said he was otherwise engaged. 'If they ask me, tell them I'm busy with Cyprus' is how he instructed his staff to deal with the matter.[20] He also swallowed Gladwyn Jebb's prediction that the Spaak operation would get nowhere. 'The French will never go into the "common market" – the German industrialists and economists equally dislike it,' he wrote in his diary, when visiting Jebb in Paris in December. And although it was Macmillan who got Bretherton to Spaak's table, he appears not to have lifted a finger to keep him there.

He was, therefore, a European only of his time and place, which is to say a tormented and indecisive one. He had a more open mind than Butler, but the idea that Britain might join or lead the continental venture as defined by the heirs and allies of Jean Monnet was still beyond the reach of Macmillan's imagination. When Eden moved him, against his will, from the Foreign Office to the Treasury – 'from geography to arithmetic', he mordantly reflected – he became the prime orchestrator of Britain's attempt to outflank if not wreck the great idea, because that rather suddenly became an essential British interest.

For, contrary to so many expert prophecies, the European Idea did move, within months, from fancy to reality. Although not signed until March 1957, the embryonic Treaty of Rome became a hypothesis to reckon with much sooner than that. Driven by Spaak, and led by France and Germany, the continentals were not giving up. Within three months of Bretherton leaving the table, they reached outline agreement on the principles of a common market, thus confronting Britain with a prospect that galvanized the political class out of the vacillating torpor in which their negative prognosis had allowed them to indulge. They now had to act, and Macmillan, sitting in the Treasury, was their agent. He devised a plan, saw it through the corridors of British power, and all the time exhibited a kind of helpless ambivalence, a lurching between the cool and the warm, that revealed him at this stage to be less a disciple of Jean Monnet than a seamless successor to the post-war Winston Churchill.

Plan G, as it was known, was plucked from an alphabetic list of Treasury options, and consisted of a proposal for a European Free Trade Area: all the trade and none of the politics. Although the Six were far advanced, their project had not reached its final shape before Plan G emerged, and it was the British ambition to supplant their fierce and narrow concept with a softer, broader one. The Six would be at the core of the EFTA, but the membership would be wider and there would be no common customs barrier: this would not, in other words, aspire to be a single unit, trading globally, with all the apparatus for negotiation and adjudication that converted it into a semi-political body, but would exist essentially for free trading within its own frontiers. The members would continue to have their separate tariffs against the outside world, thus disturbing none of Britain's historic buying-and-selling links with the Commonwealth. Moreover, EFTA wouldn't include agriculture at all. All the old preferential deals for food would stay. This would be a purely industrial arrangement. It was an entirely different concept from the one the continentals had already expended massive political resources on trying to achieve.

Macmillan saw this as 'European', but also as British, which was only appropriate for the people who regarded themselves as the senior European nation. His troubled mind expressed itself over many months. In February 1956, a hitherto unimaginable spectre was beginning to take shape there. 'I do not like the prospect of a world divided into the

Russian sphere, the American sphere and a united Europe of which we are not a member,' Macmillan wrote to his permanent secretary, Sir Edward Bridges.[21] The evolution of Plan G was propelled alongside the final, painful phases of negotiating the Rome Treaty: an irritant to the continentals, a delusion to the British. In January 1957, Foreign Secretary Lloyd produced a wrecking blueprint for a so-called "Grand Design", to unify all existing institutions in and out of the Six into a "General Assembly for Europe". It did nothing but open people's eyes to Britain's increasingly desperate antagonism to the Six. But in April 1957, by now Prime Minister, Macmillan was even more panicky. 'What I chiefly fear, and what we must at all costs avoid,' he wrote, 'is the Common Market coming into being and the Free Trade Area never following.' This would lead to German domination and 'put us in a very bad position'.[22] By July, with the Treaty signed, the matter had become one of open contest between the ins and the outs. 'We must not be bullied by the activities of the Six,' Macmillan told a colleague. 'We could, if we were driven to it, fight their movement ... We must take the lead, either in widening their project, or, if they will not co-operate with us, in opposing it.'[23]

Macmillan understood, in short, that 'Europe' was an abiding and central interest to Britain, for which the idea of 'Empire' was not a serious alternative. He might flirt with that around the club fireplace, but he was beginning to concede its unreality. And yet, at the same time, addressing a 'Europe' that was now becoming real was a task which exposed all kinds of hideous difficulties.

On 1 January 1958, 'Europe' finally happened. The European Economic Community of the Six came into being, and the balance of power as between the makers and the supplicants dramatically shifted. Their differences became more prominent than the interest in compromise between them. Britain, a free-trading nation with a low-tariff tradition sustained by its worldwide Commonwealth, faced a Europe largely shaped by France, a protectionist nation, jealous of Britain, determined to protect the agriculture Britain wanted to leave out. After the *fait accompli*, the drive was accelerated for a Free Trade Association, a Europe of the Seventeen, as it was conceived, but it was doomed by a series of inherent conflicts of national interest. That would probably have been so even if General de Gaulle had not been summoned to power in France following the fall of the Fourth Republic in May 1958. As it was, late that year, de Gaulle brought negotiations to an abrupt and final close.

This, de Gaulle's first crucial intervention, recalls, incidentally, how copious are the accidents of history, how decisive the comings and goings of personalities who might have shaped the story differently. The General spent the formative years, when 'Europe' was being put together, distanced in his village of Colombey-les-Deux Eglises, from where he opposed the sacrifices of national sovereignty it entailed. Had he come to power mere months before he did, he might have been able to prevent French accession to the Treaty of Rome. But when he did attain the presidency, he was clear and ruthless in advancing the French interest in a project it was too late to change. Similar fortuitous chances, with large results for the Europe project, can be readily picked out in the careers of both Edward Heath and Margaret Thatcher: in the whole later history of British Conservatism, in fact. Like so much else, the shaping of post-war Europe came about through a delicate interlacing of the strands of geo-politics, on the one hand, and half-chance arrivals and departures on the other.

Macmillan's first reaction to de Gaulle's return was to make a radical proposal. The two men went back a long way. During the war, Macmillan had spent time along with de Gaulle in Algiers, where he was sometimes known as "Viceroy of the Mediterranean", and had been embroiled with the Free French forces that de Gaulle was orchestrating from exile in London. Macmillan, indeed, had been responsible on more than one occasion for saving de Gaulle's political life, when it was threatened with termination by Roosevelt and Churchill. So these two leaders, now thrown together at the peak of their careers, were steeped in the history of the century and, if international affairs had anything to do with sentiment, the one was owed a debt of gratitude by the other. Macmillan thought he saw his chance to put Anglo-French relations back on a proper course when he visited Paris soon after the General was installed there. De Gaulle's memoirs recount an embarrassing scene. Macmillan, he writes, suddenly 'declared to me with great feeling: "The Common Market is the Continental System all over again. Britain cannot accept it. I beg you to give it up. Otherwise we shall be embarking on a war which will doubtless be economic at first but which runs the risk of gradually spreading into other fields!" '24

This became a familiar British plaint, amounting almost to a threat. The greater union of Europe, designed to avoid war, contained within it, so they claimed, the seeds of war itself. An almost identical analysis was being proposed forty years later by British opponents of the greater European Union, who saw in the single currency the likely source not of unity but of quite possibly bloody division. It was an unsubtle way of attacking an enterprise which, for all kinds of other reasons, Britain did not desire to see to go ahead. De Gaulle in 1958, like Helmut Kohl in 1997, rejected the destructive invitation.

And, quite soon, Macmillan had no alternative but to withdraw his suggestion. An EFTA of Seven came into being: Austria, Denmark, Norway, Portugal, Sweden and Switzerland, alongside the prime economy among them, Britain. It was a trading organization, supposedly defending these countries against the might of the Six. But there was no 'permanent and comprehensive settlement' of the kind Britain had been seeking. Though the Germans had been receptive, de Gaulle had stopped it. The merger of interests having failed, Macmillan was obliged to embrace the reality which, in June 1958, he was still hoping to suffocate, and of which he said, at a small meeting of colleagues not long afterwards, that 'there were three elements who wanted supra-nationalism and who were playing no small part on the Commission ... the Jews, the Planners and the old cosmopolitan élite'.[25]

In December 1959, he put the awful truth into words, in a message to his Foreign Secretary. 'For the first time since the Napoleonic era,' he wrote, 'the major continental powers are united in a positive economic grouping, with considerable political aspects, which, though not specifically directed against the United Kingdom, may have the effect of excluding us both from European markets and from consultation in European policy.' The Common Market, it had to be admitted, was here to stay 'at least for the foreseeable future'. Trying to disrupt it would upset the Americans, play into the hands of the Russians and 'unite against us all the Europeans who have felt humiliated during the past decade by the weakness of Europe'.

The question had at last apparently defined itself. It was, Macmillan wrote, 'how to live with the Common Market economically, and turn its political effects into channels harmless to us'.

*

THE START WAS TENTATIVE. Actual membership was still not easily imaginable. But economic realism began to exert a mighty power. It was economics that effected the beginning of conversion. The argument economics made coexisted with political attitudes that were still almost completely hostile to its logic: that were, indeed, more often by-passed than addressed. The political vision, the dream, the ideal, the grand shining project, of European union were but spectral notions, discernible only by a privileged few Englishmen, and they always have been. From the start, a divide set into the British mind between economic necessity and political resistance which continued as a live and present force, in different degrees at different times, for the rest of the century.

The change of perceptions in this great matter began with the people whose concern with politics was smallest: officials, not politicians. Two months after de Gaulle closed down the prospect of an EFTA–EEC union, a despatch to London from the embassy in Bonn made the kind of points from which no sentient politician, and certainly not Harold Macmillan, could avert his gaze.

James Marjoribanks, minister (economics) at the embassy, wrote as follows. Unless the Free Trade Area, covering a population of 90 million, was able to reach a practical understanding with the Economic Community, an industrialized and rapidly growing bloc of 160 million, Britain faced 'disaster'. Our exports would fall, our economic power diminish. 'Our position would be changed from the biggest market, and the second largest exporter of manufactured goods to Europe, to a member of what would be very much a second eleven scattered round the fringe of an increasingly powerful and rapidly growing United States of Europe.' We were, added Marjoribanks, living under a misapprehension if we believed the Six were prepared to make a lot of concessions to let us into their industrial market while permitting our agriculture, and our Commonwealth food, freedom from their rules. 'I think it is vitally important for us all to rid ourselves of the feeling that the Six cannot do without us ... The consequences for them of the United Kingdom being excluded are far less than the consequences for the United Kingdom of being shut out of Europe.'

This was an early voice. Like others, it hastened to reassure the audience that nothing so impractical as British *membership* of the Common Market was being proposed. But it was part of a gathering chorus of reassessment that began to be heard that year and next. In Paris, the false prophet Jebb, for one, announced his conversion from disdain to optimism. 'I believe that we rather tend to exaggerate the horror of our one day actually joining the Common Market,' he wrote to Macmillan in May 1960. 'For instance, if we ever did, we should be no more committed to the prospect of an actual federation than the government of General de Gaulle, that celebrated nationalist.'[26]

More influential than these comments from the outposts was a voice from the heart of government, the Treasury. We rediscover the rasping tones of Sir Frank Lee. By 1960, the discreet opponent of Bretherton's removal from the negotiations had become a positive exponent of the case for the closest possible association of the Seven with the Six: so close, in fact, that it was hardly distinguishable from membership itself.

Lee was interested in economic realities, and during the summer of 1960 did his best to acquaint a reluctant Cabinet with them. On 23 May, he described, to a special sub-committee Macmillan had established, what was now going on. Officials were working, in effect, on a scheme under which EFTA (for which, in the circumstances, one could read 'Britain') would accept most of the conditions the Six insisted on. They were looking at a common external tariff with modestly special treatment for the Commonwealth: at concessions to the European model for agriculture and horticulture: at harmonized social charges: at majority decisions on trade, rather than a national veto.

A few days later, the forceful official delivered the paper he had masterminded, of which his report to the sub-committee was merely a taste. This made an emphatic case that membership of the Seven was not enough: 'It cannot be compatible with either our political or our economic interests to let the situation drift on indefinitely on the basis of a divided Europe, with the United Kingdom linked to the weaker group.' A wider grouping, said Lee, was inescapable, and an Atlantic Free Trade Area – that distracting jade so often summoned up by critics of European integration – was 'not a practicable objective'. Nor was the Commonwealth a realistic alternative. The Commonwealth, Lee noted, depended essentially on the economic well-being of Britain and the strength of sterling. If Britain was shut out of growing European markets, the Commonwealth 'is not likely to flourish'.[27]

The paper despatched any number of illusions. Since the Common Market was already a success, if we wanted a deal we must be 'prepared to go much further than we have hitherto contemplated'. We must 'put out of our minds' the idea that we could 'secure our objective on the cheap'. Industrial free trade, without a price that recognized the political and economic strength of continental farmers, was simply out of the question. Realism demanded 'difficult and unpalatable decisions', including the contemplation of some surrender of sovereignty.

Lee conjured up a word for what all this meant. It came fresh out of the lexicon of a Whitehall that was sensitive to the implications of what the Treasury was proposing. The idea of *membership*, of course, still had to be eschewed. So crude a proposition would have fallen victim to the fit of vapours it would instantly have induced among the politicians. But, equally, Lee wished to make it plain that the time was past for a status so unreal as mere association. The concept he therefore coined may not have had much ring to it, but it perfectly caught the mood of tentative boldness, of fantastically daring half-heartedness, that now seemed to be called for. Britain and the Seven, he suggested, should seek *'near-identification'* with the Common Market.

Macmillan received this proposition with considerable pain. It was not what he wanted to hear. On the other hand, he wasn't very clear what he did want to hear. The record of the Prime Minister's response, in discussion of the Lee memorandum on 27 May, suggests a man at war with himself. Could there not be some other solution, he is saying? 'Was it necessary for the United Kingdom to give up all hope, even as a long term objective, of an industrial free trade area?' he asked. Trying to secure a large single market is all very well, but consider what Britain would have to give up: control over tariffs, the cohesion of the Commonwealth, her own kind of agricultural support, some of her sovereignty and all the rest of it.

Something else, however, emerges from these ministerial deliberations. By the end of the discussion, which the minutes record with unusual fullness, it is articulated by Macmillan himself. Near-identification was fraught with problems. It would require big changes. So big, in fact, that perhaps it might make more sense 'to go into Europe fully', which might bring scarcely larger problems but carried more possibilities. The two policies, the Prime Minister concluded, were 'so similar that one might lead to the other, and if we were prepared to accept near-identification it might be preferable to contemplate full membership'. The time had possibly come to end 'our traditional policy of remaining aloof from Europe'. Further study was therefore set in train, under Frank Lee's direction.

In the evolution of Macmillan's attitude, one catches the anguished reluctance of the nation he led. Part of him, as we have seen, knew that a sundering from Europe would be fatal. As a student of history, he was as sensitive to the continental interests of his country as to its global reach, and he knew the latter was in retreat. Four months before, he had gone to Cape Town and given the most famous speech he ever made, on the winds of change that were blowing through once imperial Africa. He had always resisted both the low politics and the inflated grandeur – the farmers and the fantasists – that treated opposition to a European venture as axiomatic. And yet even now, with the writing etched ever more insistently on the wall, he was slow to move. The duty of leadership came upon him uncomfortably. It wasn't, yet, the political risks that deterred him, but something deeper. Although the Tory Party would have to be faced in due course, that wasn't the immediate problem What still gripped Macmillan were the tectonic plates of history, no slight matter to shift.

History, however, bore down on him at this moment in another way as well. For a man of private moods, who felt the power of public events moving in his bones, May 1960 had been a bad month. On the 16th, a great-power summit meeting in Paris, which he had done much to promote, ended in futile and dangerous disarray, when Nikita Khrushchev took the downing of an American U2 spy plane over the Soviet Union as the pretext to abandon all progress towards international *détente*. 'It is impossible to describe this day,' Macmillan wrote in his diary, 'I am too tired.' In his memoirs, he called the day 'one of the most agonising as well as exhausting which I have ever been through except, perhaps, in battle'. The fiasco produced in him a 'disappointment amounting almost to despair – so much attempted, so little achieved'. Reflecting in old age, he termed it 'the most tragic moment in my life'.

This trauma occurred a week before the EEC–EFTA debate in Cabinet committee started to get serious. Nothing so coarse as a direct connection between the collapse of the Paris summit and the mounting of an application to join the Common Market can be inferred. But the bleakness it engendered affected the mood. Thrown into the already crumbling certainties about Britain's role in the world, it made its contribution, not least to Macmillan's deepening gloom. His diary entries continued to sweep around the forces of history with a broad, puzzled brush. 'Shall we be caught between a hostile (or at least less and less friendly) America,' he wrote in July, 'and a boastful, powerful "Empire of Charlemagne" – now under French but later bound to come under German control? Is this the real reason for "joining" the Common Market (if we are acceptable) and for abandoning a) the Seven, b) British agriculture, c) the Commonwealth? It's a grim choice.'

Very, very slowly, however, the choice was beginning to disclose itself. Lee's next paper was more pressing.[28] He had proposed to Macmillan that it should be produced in the form of answers to questions: Will the Six develop into a powerful unit? How would Britain's influence from outside compare with her influence from inside? To what extent would entry put Commonwealth preference at risk? And so forth. There were twenty-three such questions, framed by Macmillan under Lee's advice and answered by a team of officials under Lee's control. The answers were getting less ambiguous, though they still clung respectfully to old household gods, opining, for example, that if the Commonwealth connection were weakened 'our standing in the world would suffer'. But the analysis of an entry-scenario now emphasized the advantages slightly more than the problems, in language whose sense of the positive sometimes looks quite startling four decades later. To concede, as it did, that membership of a successful EEC 'might change our concept of what were vital UK interests' revealed a largeness of spirit and intellect that had been entirely banished by the 1980s. Talking about 'our participation in majority voting in the Council of Ministers' as a guarantee rather than a destroyer of British influence was not something widely heard thirty years later. The full Cabinet, which was having its first discussion of the subject, received the Lee questionnaire with the usual agonizings, but also with a certain open-minded equanimity. Ministers' conclusions talked about the unripeness of time but also the need for choice, about fear of federalism but also about confidence in 'a loose confederal arrangement', about loss but also gain. Momentum for change was discernible. The plates were beginning to rumble.

We should note again how this had come about. It was without benefit of the usual ministerial initiative. Although Macmillan blessed it, this was an officials' operation. What happened on 13 July 1960 was a Cabinet decision that launched the process that concluded with Britain's application to join the Common Market, yet no ministerial paper preceded it. According to Roy Denman, for many years a senior official dealing with international trade problems, never before had a major new direction in foreign policy been opened on the basis merely of an official submission. And yet that was profoundly symbolic. It was consistent with the history. Both the Schuman Plan and Messina had been approached under much the same rubric of political detachment. It reflected a state of mind. In 1960, as in 1950, there was a sense in which the politicians were so paralysed by the awesome nature of necessary decisions that they preferred to delegate rather than lead. None was prepared to commit himself full-bloodedly to a single course of action. It was left to others to map the ground. And the officials, who had obliged in one direction in the earlier phase, now saw their duty as the opposite.

Proceeding crabwise, however, Macmillan himself did now get a little more political. He didn't commit himself to applying for entry, but began to prepare the ground for what such an epic decision would entail. He knew he would get nowhere unless he had the right people in place, and a Cabinet reshuffle on 27 July put them there. Nowhere, at the time, was it noticed that this was a 'European' reshuffle, although Edward Heath was appointed Lord Privy Seal, inside the Foreign Office, with responsibilities for what was thereby admitted publicly to be the major issue of relations with the Common Market. Christopher Soames and Duncan Sandys, two champions with a pedigree going back to Churchill's long march round Zurich, Strasbourg and the other shrines, were put in charge of the likely enemy camps of Agriculture and Commonwealth Relations.

Not that this was the signal for anything precipitate. What happened over the next few months was a continuation of the old mud-wrestling, as Macmillan's Cabinet grappled with its own anxieties, on the one hand, and with the continentals, above all France, on the other. Much time and argument had to pass before the leader finally forced himself to accept the unpleasant conclusion his country had spent a decade resisting.

What the British still wanted was a trading arrangement. Macmillan's own contributions between July 1960 and July 1961 are dominated by a kind of elegiac longing for the unattainable. 'If it were impossible to obtain true intimacy in the Councils of the Six without serious disruption of our relations, both economic and political, with the Commonwealth then we are better off outside . . .', he wrote in a minute on the Lee questionnaire. In August 1960, he met the German Chancellor, Adenauer, from whom he drew some apparent comfort that such painless involvement might be available. Adenauer suggested a process that examined the strictly economic difficulties, with a view to economic association, to be followed by unspecified moves towards an 'acceptable political relationship with the Six'. So the economics, in this phase, were the focus of attention. The Commonwealth bulked very large. There are reams of papers from the Treasury and the Board of Trade exploring different outcomes for tropical foodstuffs and temperate foodstuffs, woodpulp and aluminium, Rhodesian tobacco and New Zealand butter. Through the autumn, it is the Commonwealth that starts being squared, or not, as the case may be. With enough derogations and special concessions, the match might be made. London persists in the belief that 'the economic advantages of full membership of the European Economic Community' could be obtained by an association 'with no manifest political content'. The Germans, along with the Benelux countries and the Italians, were sufficiently eager for Britain's involvement to give some grounds for belief, to those with misty eyes, that she might indeed be able to have it both ways.

This was, however, a fantasy, and the people who made that clearest were the French. The old mistrust expressed itself in a new and obvious realism. Britain could not be permitted special treatment for her Commonwealth preferences, nor could she expect to sustain the cheap food policy that went with them. Through the winter of 1960–1, Ted Heath, under Macmillan's direction, pursued the fantasy down many avenues. France was the clearest of the Six in rejecting it, during numerous talks that took place at many different levels from de Gaulle downwards. The leading French official on the case, Olivier Wormser, told Heath that there could be no *modus vivendi* between 'the two regional economic systems – the Commonwealth and the EEC'. There were, of course, other French demons at work, springing out of a Gaullist view of destiny and history and the like. But hard practicalities, rooted in measurable money and countable votes, were France's fixed preoccupation. As late as May 1961, nevertheless, Macmillan was still telling the Commons that there was no question of entering the EEC without giving both the farmers and the Commonwealth what they wanted.

An interesting aspect of the 1961 deliberations is the increasing dominance they gave to these two issues, food and Empire. Time and again, as the pace of ministerial meetings increases, we hear Macmillan reciting his anxieties about Commonwealth reactions to any change in the relationship. The farmers, for their part, had R. A. Butler, now Home Secretary, on their side. The old sceptic had not changed his mind. At a Cabinet meeting in April he was talking as he had always talked, about the 'insuperable difficulties' of joining the Common Market, and the 'very grave political difficulties' of antagonizing British agriculture. This was Butler's song. Years later, as a rather late entrant to the ranks of politicians who felt obliged to concede that they had once got 'Europe' wrong, he tried to explain himself. He had taken his line, he said, because he had always had an agricultural seat. He knew the British farmer. But, he confessed, 'I now think I ought to have been more far-sighted.' He had an excuse, he ventured, in the fact that there had been no pressure to think differently. 'So it was not, so to speak, my fault. But I think that, being a prominent citizen and having a brain, I ought to have looked further ahead.'[29]

What plays rather slight part in the discussion is the matter of national sovereignty. It is present, and yet not present. It underlies, inevitably, the feelings that have made the British so resistant to throwing in their lot with countries that come from the same continent but from what has often seemed a different world. Yet the appearance of this consideration, which had been decisive at the time of the Schuman Plan and resumed a venomous place in the argument forty years later, is in 1961 no more than episodic. A strange combination of forces seems to be at work. On the one hand, sovereignty is just a far less urgent pressure than the baying of farmers and the affronted roars of Robert Menzies (Australia), John Diefenbaker (Canada) and other guardians of the white imperial inheritance. Diminished national sovereignty did not press itself as a real and present danger, at a time when in any case neither the institutions nor the ambitions of the Common Market were fully formed, and de Gaulle was busy frustrating their development. On the other hand, its power to get the project off on the wrong foot was great. It lurked, as something that might better not be mentioned. Looked at in a certain way, it might be too hot to handle.

Macmillan was not ignorant of the size of it. In November 1960, he caused Heath to seek the opinion of the Cabinet's leading lawyer, Viscount Kilmuir, the Lord Chancellor. For this was essentially a legal matter. Kilmuir, a veteran of Strasbourg, a post-war Macmillanite and Churchillite, was a European. But he did not pull his punches. His reply to Heath laid out each of the major constitutional aspects of 'Europe' that have since been treated, by the Euro-sceptic faction, as catastrophic encroachments of which the British knew nothing at the time.

Kilmuir was clinically clear.[30] To sign the Treaty of Rome would be to legislate for a loss of national sovereignty in three respects. First, Parliament would surrender some of its functions to a Council of Ministers which could, by majority vote, make regulations that became the law of the land. Second, the Crown's treaty-making power would in part be transferred to an international organization. Third, British courts would sacrifice some of their independence by becoming subordinate in some respects to the European Court of Justice. These were, he said, serious matters. 'It will not be easy to persuade Parliament or the public to accept them.' There would be objections. But, Kilmuir urged, they should be 'brought out into the open now', because otherwise 'those who are opposed to the whole idea of joining the Community will certainly seize on them with more damaging effect later on'. A prophetic warning, as to which, after many years of relatively acquiescent silence, there grew up some of the most bitter arguments in the whole of this history.

The subject, however, featured little in the April Cabinet meeting. The voices were heard, but their doubts were mainly about other matters. Macmillan placed the matter in the Cold War context, indulging his usual gloom about Britain being squeezed between larger powers and groups. He had begun the year by circulating to his colleagues some apocalyptic ruminations about the state of the world, which concluded, among other things, that the rise of Soviet blackmail and Asian neutralism might well indicate that 'the long predominance of European culture, civilisation, wealth and power may be drawing to a close'.[31] It was against this take that he looked on the Common Market. The Cabinet went round the old, old cycle of pros and cons, except that this time the bias was different, the balance of least-worst options weighted grudgingly towards the positive more than the negative. The future of British influence was more copiously cited, alongside the forecast that, when Adenauer and de Gaulle were gone, Britain's task might be to save Europe from itself. Grandiosity died hard.

It was as if the Cabinet, preparing to face the economic necessity of membership, needed to pump up its belief that it would be negotiating from strength not weakness. At another meeting, on 4 July, it talked about the prize of a large expanding market for Britain's goods, and about the danger of industrial decline if she stayed outside any longer. But there was political consolation for national pride. It was expressed in a sentence that showed how slender was the appreciation of what had been happening during the British absence. 'It tended to be overlooked', ministers agreed, 'that if we entered we might be the most powerful member, and be able to exercise a strong and sometimes a decisive influence upon [the Community's] policies.' Macmillan himself put this in the vernacular, with words which showed that British thinking had made no decisive break with its post-war pedigree. Challenged one night on the dance-floor about the rumours that Britain wanted to join the Common Market, he replied, holding his partner tight, 'Well, my dear, don't worry, we shall embrace them *destructively*.'[32]

This unrealism was part of a pattern, induced by the visceral uncertainties that attended Macmillan's entire approach to Europe. There was much whistling in the wind. France's repeated insistence, for example, that neither the Commonwealth nor agriculture would attract any more than the most minor concessions if Britain did apply was simply, it would seem, buried in the sands of disbelief. The British were angling, in effect, to change the Rome Treaty, and M. Wormser told them it was impossible. Reginald Maudling, the most Euro-sceptic

Cabinet minister, drew from this the conclusion that it was 'pointless talking about any negotiations with them', and criticized a strategy that depended on 'trying to entice an unwilling France to the conference table by successive concessions on our side'. But Maudling was the only minister in the inner group, as a decision neared, to oppose making an application for entry. Macmillan and Heath were determined to press on – but in the most defensive spirit. The Cabinet decision to make the application, taken at meetings in the last week of July, was as niggardly as it could be: not a decision to join, but a decision to establish whether satisfactory terms for joining could be negotiated – after which Britain might or might not decide to accept them.

When, after a good lunch, Macmillan went to the House on 31 July to announce this, he was, he says in his diary, nervous. This was not a man about to announce a glorious new departure for the British nation. The leader could hardly fail to be affected by the moroseness of the Cabinet debates, which seemed to revert, as the moment approached, to the old, neurotic negativism. He had to strike a 'delicate balance', he noted to himself, between giving the impression that Britain had decided to accept membership whatever the terms and 'suggesting to members of the Community that we had no real will to join'. He was sensitive, also, to the fact that none of this was mentioned in the 1959 election manifesto. Above all, he was caught by a quite insidious contradiction.

It is obvious that his own motive for engineering the Conservative Government's change of heart was political. His grand disquisitions on the state of the world meant something. He saw European civilization under threat, and Britain's place within it in danger of being marginalized. He had received telling signals from the new American President, John F. Kennedy, of Washington's undeviating commitment to European integration, and diminishing sympathy in that quarter for British hesitation. Americans never did have much time for the imperial so-called Commonwealth. The economic danger posed by a strong Six mattered a lot, but Macmillan placed this first and foremost in a geo-political context. Safeguarding British power was what, in Macmillan's mind, it was all about: a large, resonant purpose.

But he did not have the nerve to present it in that way. His opening statement was fuller of negatives than positives, of doubt than exhilaration. He emphasized all 'the most delicate and difficult matters' that had to be negotiated, and the many consultations, even permissions, that would be sought thereafter. After the opening announcement, eight months passed before Macmillan made another speech of any significance on the subject. Nowhere did he allow his public discourse to reflect what seemed to be his private feelings, for, if he had, he would have conceded that his geo-political apprehensions about Britain's future in the world might need to be met by something more profound than a commercial deal – which is how it suited him, for the most part, to represent the Common Market negotiations. No sooner had he led the Cabinet to take the plunge than he did almost everything to pretend, to the world outside, that the water was tepid and its depths were shallow.

Thus the political formula was established which has laid its hand on the British approach to Europe ever since this first effort was undertaken. It could sit aptly as an epitaph. It dictated the way every subsequent leader presented every move towards Europe. It speaks loud and clear from the record of Harold Wilson, of Margaret Thatcher, of John Major, and even to some extent of Edward Heath. It was, in essence, a lie. It said, on the one hand, that this move, whatever it was, was absolutely essential for the British national interest. But at the same time, it asserted, nothing whatever would change in the British way of life and government.

In Macmillan's version of his case, for example, the sovereignty issue barely featured. He gave no prominence to the contents of Kilmuir's letter to Heath. His entire tone was weary, pessimistic and above all, on this central point, silently evasive. The implications for Parliament were not mentioned, nor were those for the legal system. He told the Commons on 2 August that 'this problem of sovereignty . . . is, in the end, perhaps a matter of degree', and he addressed only the grandest, most extreme hypothesis: that the EEC might develop into some kind of federation. Naturally, he resisted that, and spoke for 'a confederation, a commonwealth if Hon. Members would like to call it that', as the 'only practical concept'. There is no reason to doubt that he meant it. It was just that he preferred not to think through, and certainly not to pronounce upon, the fact that this was, in two senses, primarily a political venture. It had a political object, to make Britain part of 'Europe'. And it had a huge political result: to reduce the independence of both Parliament and the courts.

This minimalism, it was often said, was a negotiating tactic. The most authoritative history of the time endorses the claim by ministers that, if they became missionaries for Common Market membership, the continentals would harden their terms.[33] In fact, their pinched, apologetic stance had the opposite effect. In the absence of a lead, British public opinion drifted from wary approval to a level of scepticism that was quite unhelpful. Support for the policy peaked in December 1961 at 53 per cent, but by May 1962 Gallup showed it had fallen to 47 per cent (with 32 per cent undecided), dropping to 36 per cent a month later. There were many causes for the failure of the negotiation, but it was certainly not helped by the inflexibility imposed upon the British position by a public opinion which nobody had prepared, still less won over, for a visionary leap into the Common Market.

Besides, the ambivalence was not a tactic. It registered the state of the heart of Harold Macmillan.

*

THE NEGOTIATIONS were always going to be difficult. Here was a project, in existence for less than four years, still forming itself, not ready for the easy accession of a country that had variously spurned and tried to spoil it. It hadn't yet shaped the modalities of its system of agricultural support, a vital matter for its largest members. It was in the middle of discussions about the kind of political union it might now embrace, on top of the economic community. It was, moreover, already coming to be disproportionately influenced by France, the member state with most to lose from British entry, and therefore always likely to be the most sceptical. This was itself a turnaround, poignant proof of the penalties of delay. Was it not France that had, at the time of Messina, most desired Britain to join in, and had even at times made Britain's entry a condition of her own? Now the balance was entirely different. France had got the Treaty of Rome written to suit her more than any other member, and in so doing, Miriam Camps wrote, 'had exploited to the full the advantages of negotiating from weakness, an art the British seem not to have mastered'.[34] Now under de Gaulle, who paraded French nationalism on a continental plane, she negotiated from strength.

The state of supplicancy was central to this British weakness. For all the hauteur that seemed to be implied by Macmillan's posture – that she was negotiating not for membership, but to discover whether satisfactory terms might be available should she graciously decide to accept them – Britain was essentially the beggar. And that wasn't the only problem. The British leader was also faced with several competing audiences. The Commonwealth, the farmers, the Tory Party, the public at large all required reassurance and even (if he were bold) visionary encouragement. The European Community, on the other hand, needed to be told that Britain would be a serious European but also to be alarmed by the possibility that she might not become one. Strategically, Macmillan had to show he was serious, to negotiate in credible good faith, and to rally maximum support for this truly historic enterprise. But his perception of tactics required of him an absence of zeal, a dignified coolness, and the assertion that 'Europe' might never be more than one among the several spheres of British interest.

A man of subtlety as well as history, Macmillan did his best to straddle these competing requirements. He undoubtedly wanted the negotiation to lead to British entry; its failure brought an end, in effect, to his political career. He was very well aware, none better, of the strategic reverberations of what he was attempting. But, looking overall at his performance, one can't help concluding that, in this war for the British soul, caution triumphed over boldness, tactics over strategy. Macmillan knew that accession could be achieved only by the sacrifice of Tory shibboleths, yet this perception was one he shrank from fully addressing.

Once the decision to negotiate had been taken, the British put their best feet forward, in the form of a team whose personal calibre nobody on either side ever doubted. They were the cream of the talent available in Whitehall, under the leadership of a politician, Edward Heath, who was close to Macmillan and whose zeal for the cause of European union had been apparent from the moment of his maiden speech in the Commons urging British participation in the Schuman Plan. Between autumn 1961 and January 1963, a detailed negotiation unfolded. Under Heath's direction, the intricacies of farm support, of Commonwealth imports of every kind from New Zealand butter and Indian tea to aluminium and woodpulp and lead and zinc, of the arrangements that needed to be made for other EFTA countries, of tariff quotas and non-tariff barriers and preferential entry and 'comparable outlets' for this or that commodity, were carried, in some cases, towards points of laborious agreement. Mercifully, the nooks and crannies of all this need not be investigated here. A shrewd and lengthy account of the negotiations was published, with a speed that did not compromise its thoroughness, within a year of the breakdown. Miriam Camps's excellent book has since been supplemented by any number of monographs and papers, as well as biographical studies, drawing on the cornucopia of official documents that began to be released in the early 1990s.

There were oddities and difficulties about the way the British went about this great historic venture. Below Heath, the leadership of the official team was handed to Sir Pierson Dixon, who succeeded in insisting that he would accept the task only if he was allowed to retain his other job as British ambassador in Paris. Heath complied, and the British delegation felt broken-backed as a result. Even though Macmillan wrote in his diary that Dixon 'has the most subtle mind in Whitehall', the choice seemed to confirm the half-heartedness which the confusing mode of the British application already implied. Moreover, it was arguable that the negotiation was allowed to get quite excessively bogged down in detail – a natural consequence, perhaps, of the intense reluctance of the British mind to look at the matter on the grand scale rather than as another complicated trade deal.

But the larger story is so well known that it has acquired the status of folklore. Virtually all accounts agree on the shape of it: the negotiation began in good faith, it was carried on toughly but fairly by Heath's team, they enlisted the support of the Five, they even got pretty far down the road with the French: after laborious if over-extended discussions a complete deal was close to being on the cards, it required only a couple more long sessions – until the whole endeavour was wrecked, on 14 January 1963, by the iron whim of General de Gaulle, President of France, killing off any further talks by exercising his veto on the very principle of British membership of the Common Market.

This familiar account is not false. De Gaulle did stop the whole process in its tracks, against the wishes of all five of the partner states. It was a brutal display of the deformities for which he was best known: unapologetic grandeur, the pursuit of the French interest, the association of the French interest completely with himself. But the story begs some questions. It exonerates Macmillan from any blame for this outcome, and at the time that was probably the only conclusion a reasonable observer could reach. Given what happened later, however, it is less easy to sustain. Whereas, in his own time, Macmillan seemed to be the statesmanlike victim of a malign and unreasonable opponent, subsequent events suggest that his own analysis was fundamentally at fault.

Hindsight, it may be replied, is a fine thing. But, on this question, the judgement of hindsight should at least be exposed, even if the verdict allows a plea in mitigation. And hindsight homes in on a simple fact. The only future for Britain, it soon turned out, was the one Macmillan sought to bring about. His problem was that he did not try hard enough to achieve it. Even as he plunged towards the future, he was besotted and ensnared by the past.

De Gaulle was certainly a bloody-minded antagonist, and there is no better vantage-point from which to watch the unfolding of his bloodiness than the post closest to it, the British embassy in Paris. After the veto, Pierson Dixon, from his double-duty perspective as ambassador and negotiator, wrote a blow-by-blow account that focused with bitter bemusement on the puzzle of the General.[35] Dixon's subtleties of interpretation prove to be well suited to the deviousness, the apparent contradictions, the indecipherable layers of meaning that lay behind a style that was well epitomized by another British diplomat, Sir Evelyn Shuckburgh. De Gaulle, Shuckburgh once wrote, 'does not exactly "conceal" his intentions; he mystifies his adversaries so that they do not quite believe what they suspect to be his motives'.

The mystery, here, was whether the General really did, or really did not, desire Britain to be admitted to 'Europe'. The ambiguity began at the beginning. When Macmillan visited him in January 1961, to sound the waters, de Gaulle was both positive and negative. Dixon reports him saying that he wanted Anglo-French relations to be 'very close', that he had no desire to 'upset' the United Kingdom, and that he certainly didn't envisage the Common Market always being limited to its present Six members, but also that the UK's 'island position and Commonwealth naturally made her look outwards across the oceans', and that he 'wondered how long it would be possible for the United Kingdom to pursue both a European and an American policy simultaneously'.

This set the style for two years of fencing. It had to be remembered, of course, that de Gaulle was involved in a great deal else besides the European Community, principally Algeria, from which he was in the midst of attempting to extricate France for ever. But when told in late July of Britain's intention to apply, he expressed, says Dixon, 'no pleasure at the news, in contrast to the other Heads of Government who received similar messages'. 'He looked distinctly vexed as he read the Prime Minister's letter.' And when, in November, he came at his own suggestion to Macmillan's country house, Birch Grove, he began by being no happier. As Macmillan pleaded the case, based, in this version, on the political need to unite Europe in face of the Soviet menace, his interlocutor agreed – but also said 'he had difficulty in seeing how the United Kingdom would fit into this beginning of Europe'. He was bothered by all the historical baggage. 'He admitted that the British were Europeans in our own special way and said that he and the French wanted the British in Europe. But the French did not want the British to bring their great escort in with them. India and African countries had no part in Europe.' Opaqueness, however, ruled. It was, indeed, part of the discourse of both these men, though it was the British who were constantly the more mystified. For example, the General also said that 'Europe had everything to gain from letting serious-minded people like the British in. British entry was certainly in the common interest; it would hold Europe together and it would add enormously to its influence in the world.'

That was perhaps the high point of Britain's reading of de Gaulle. Never again did his loftiness appear to be directed in Britain's favour. Actually, his driving motives were always pretty familiar. He did not like the Common Market. When Britain applied, he was in the middle of trying to impose on it a form of political union which would in fact have deconstructed it, supplanting its community institutions with mere inter-governmentalism. But, if the Community survived, he wanted France to dominate it, and feared the British would threaten this. A metaphor gained wide currency, both in secret papers and in newspaper cartoons: 'There cannot be two cocks on the dung-hill.' For most of 1962, de Gaulle was making ever clearer who would rule the farm-yard.

On 16 May, the Paris embassy gave it as their considered opinion, in a despatch to the Foreign Secretary, that the General wanted the negotiations to fail. This was signed by Dixon himself, though drafted by a young man, Michael Butler, another of the Euro-diplomats from the Palliser cohort who subsequently trod every step up the ladder in support of a policy they passionately believed in. (In 1997, Sir Michael, whose last FO job was as British ambassador to the European Communities, 1979–85, showed the durability of the truly dedicated believer by becoming personal adviser on Europe to the new Foreign Secretary, Robin Cook.) A few days later, de Gaulle gave direct support to Butler's judgement in a conversation with Dixon. 'He said it was too early for us to enter the Common Market, and spoke a great deal about the difficulties for the Commonwealth.' While denying that he was formally opposed to British entry, he said he thought it would be difficult 'at the present time'.

Successive summit meetings confirmed this. At the Château de Champs, in early June, the two old lions once again surveyed the world. Both were far more interested in politics than economics, and they spent none of their time talking about levies on pig-meat. Great sweeping discourses about the shape of alliances, and the role of the Russians and Americans, were exchanged between them. Macmillan felt that 'after Europe had been created there must be discussions about the political and defence aspects and an attempt made to create a European world position'. The nuclear question was raised again, a subject of the greatest sensitivity to de Gaulle, and one on which subsequent papers and studies teem with argument as to whether or not Macmillan offered nuclear collaboration, whether he was in a position to do so, whether de Gaulle would have been open to seduction by such an offer which, according to some, was never actually made anyway. 'We were all rather baffled by the Champs meeting,' writes Dixon. But the thread of it did not lead anywhere new. The picture one collects is of Macmillan pleading for recognition of 'an important and decisive moment in history', and de Gaulle toying with Britain's historic unsuitability to meet it. 'It would have been possible', as Dixon wearily summarizes, 'to produce evidence in support of almost any interpretation of General de Gaulle's attitude.'

Even then, the British did not regard the situation as doomed. They still believed that the issue in the real world was the negotiations, not the principle: in other words, that de Gaulle wanted the negotiations to fail, but did not want France to take responsibility for the collapse of the enterprise. On this point, Dixon is self-flagellating. Having correctly divined the General's attitude, the embassy had underestimated his capacity to see it through. 'I and my staff were too categorical about General de Gaulle's unwillingness to take the blame for a breakdown,' Dixon reflects. Even by the time of the final summit, at Rambouillet in December, the message has not fully penetrated. The General 'was as negative as he could be', and was, in addition, 'furious' at having been, in Dixon's loyal opinion, out-argued by Macmillan both in private and then more publicly in front of his ministers. Confronted by Macmillan, for once, with the direct charge that he was raising objections in principle to Britain's application, de Gaulle still felt forced to deny it and to say that 'France desired Britain's entry.' Despite the assessment Michael Butler had sent in May, some elements in the Paris embassy were still, amazingly, prepared to take a morsel of succour from such ritualistic statements.

It was perhaps only after the General had applied his political veto, on 14 January 1963, that Dixon got the measure of what he was dealing with. Why had the General done it? 'It is when one attempts to answer a question like this that one finds oneself in a Kafka world,' Dixon writes. 'Hypotheses form and dissolve. There are morasses and mirages everywhere.' The farm-yard returns, as an analytical safe haven. 'There was never room for more than the Gaullist cock of the European roost.' The bewildered envoy concludes on a note that reflected the almost universal opinion of the time. The history of de Gaulle's conversations with Macmillan 'demonstrates, I am afraid, that he is not open to rational discussion'.

From France's viewpoint, de Gaulle's stance, at least to some people, looked different. It arguably had rationality about it. But, even if it didn't, the question of Macmillan's response to the menacing titan across the Channel can't be treated with such sympathy as it has received from many biographers and historians. Could his preparations have been different? Was his strategy flawed? Did he misjudge the weaknesses and strengths of his position? Was the failure of this historic venture absolutely inevitable? It had such immense consequences that the questions are worth posing.

The main case made against Macmillan concerns timing, and the way timing interacted with a decision to contest, for many months, every refined last detail of any deal, especially over agriculture and the Commonwealth. The negotiations dragged on past the summer of 1962. Just when the Europeans were expecting Heath to return with a comprehensive *démarche* in the autumn, they found the British preoccupied with a Commonwealth conference. There followed some unhelpful developments. In November, elections for the French National Assembly produced a Gaullist majority. From a position of perilous weakness, about to lose a referendum on the revision of the constitution, de Gaulle squeaked home on the referendum and swept aside all internal opposition at the polls. He could dig himself in deeper against the British. Moreover, the continuing impasse in Brussels led to an unfortunate coincidence. When Macmillan went to Rambouillet, he was obliged to confirm to de Gaulle, which he did with some airiness, that he was about to attend a summit meeting with President Kennedy at which he hoped to negotiate the supply of a new generation of intercontinental missiles to carry British nuclear warheads: confirmation, if the General required it, of Britain's indissoluble bondage to Washington.

The Rambouillet discussions, which took place in the shadow of the Cuban missile crisis, naturally dwelt on the state of the world on a wider plane than Europe. De Gaulle admired the way Kennedy had handled the crisis, but that didn't weaken his perception that Britain must, in a sense, make a choice between Europe and the Atlantic if she wanted to be taken seriously as an EEC applicant. Macmillan, arguing the opposite, was at one point reduced to tears by the General's unwillingness to share his own sentiments about the common interests of the great powers, among whom he counted France. De Gaulle recounted the occasion, with lordly derision, at a Cabinet meeting a few days later. 'This poor man,' he said, 'to whom I had nothing to give, seemed so sad, so beaten that I wanted to put my hand on his shoulder and say to him, as in the Edith Piaf song, *"Ne pleurez pas, milord."* [36]

Had everything moved faster, which was within British power to achieve in alliance with the Five, de Gaulle might have had smaller opportunity to deploy what was plainly his settled prejudice. Even he had to pay some attention to his political base, and it would have been more vulnerable. Arguably, Macmillan should have been sensitive to the weakness behind Gaullist bluster in the early stages, the better to pre-empt the General's later strengthening.

This matter has been endlessly discussed, in the copious outpourings of scholarship that have long been part of the Britain-in-Europe indus-try.[37] It even has its own term of art: the 'summer' argument, meaning that Britain should have worked harder to close the deal before the autumn. Edward Heath, the chief negotiator, has always resisted this. 'I've never thought that,' he told me in 1994. 'I'm sure there were some people in the Foreign Office who were fed up with a negotiation going on and on. But I don't think it affected the French. You see, they all expected it at that time to be successful. They didn't know what de Gaulle was going to do. I don't think the summer argument has ever held water. It's just people who want to find some other excuse, and somebody to blame.'[38]

In any case, it is at best a subsidiary point. The altogether larger question concerns the nature of the approach: a conditional and tentative venture, creeping in a state of high suspicion towards this moment of historic destiny, declining to make a commitment until the Europeans had shown what ground they were prepared to surrender, and reserving even then the option of a British veto. This was formulated, remember, against a background of enthusiasm on the continent. The Five were well disposed towards British entry into their half-formed project. Even France, at the beginning and in all formal statements, said the same. Yet the British were not prepared to do more than negotiate and hesitate. They were not, actually, applying. They made it clear that they wanted the Treaty of Rome, which they had declined to participate in drafting, unpicked in certain parts, and weren't willing necessarily to accept the *acquis communautaire* – the patrimony of principles, policies and laws already agreed by the Community – that were the basis of the great project.

They had some reason for concern about the details of what membership would require. Plainly the differences between the British

way of subsidizing farmers, and the Common Agricultural Policy the
EEC had just with agonizing difficulty agreed, posed a great problem.
How temperate foodstuffs like butter, on the export of which New
Zealand wholly depended, could go on being admitted tariff-free to the
British market was an issue that obviously foreshadowed long nights of
haggling. But the chosen method magnified the difficulties. It opened
the door to every vested interest to start lobbying intensively. It invited
the Commonwealth countries to make as many objections as they could:
a context which New Zealand handled reasonably, but in which the old
white bastions, like Robert Menzies of Australia and John Diefenbaker
of Canada, deployed massive hostile pressures. It also intensified such
opposition as there was in Europe. The Europeans did not want all their
acquis dismantled, by negotiators who in any case promised nothing in
return. They were driven into highly defensive mode. The momentum
that might have been established by a new status quo, namely the
unalterable new fact of a British decision to which other members had
to accommodate, was lost. This was the most grandly half-hearted
gesture on which any leader ever rested the fate of himself, his government and his country.

The reason lay partly in his political judgement of what was possible,
but also in his vision of what was historically desirable. In the first of
these, Macmillan lacked courage, in the second he failed to rise above
Britain's national disease: aversion to realism.

Macmillan's view of history continued to bestow a specious aura
of reality on the British Commonwealth. Although the very notion of
possibly joining the EEC implied a distancing from the old impedimenta
of Empire, the lure remained strong. This wasn't merely a feeling to
which the Conservative Party was still vulnerable but one that Macmillan
plainly experienced himself. When he said in the first Commons debate
on the application, in August 1961, that the Commonwealth 'has real life
and unity . . . [and] is something precious and unique', he was speaking
of an entity which, although it would now be invited to coexist with the
Common Market, remained in his view central to Britain's own future
interests as a world power. The protection of Commonwealth trade and
the maintaining of Commonwealth links were an essential part of the
negotiations, and became a point of maximal pressure, whether from
distant leaders or local Tories, against their succeeding. For more than a
year, the parading of the timeless Commonwealth connection, and all
the emotional baggage that went with it, was allowed free rein. Fired up
by the Beaverbrook press, something called Empire loyalism made its

way into popular consciousness, ranging white British stock against the sinister continental losers of the last war. Never did Macmillan find the words entirely to repudiate this sentiment, or to scotch with the necessary brutality the notion that the Commonwealth offered any kind of matrix for the economic future of Britain.

Even on the evidence available at the time, the potency of the Commonwealth myth was a rebuke to politicians who allowed themselves to be seduced by it. Suez, surely, had put an end to the political dream into which the Commonwealth fitted, that of Britain as world power. The enlargement of the Commonwealth that followed Suez – with independence for Ghana and Malaya in 1957, for Nigeria in 1960, with a steady stream of African and Asian countries following in the next few years – brought the opposite of greater power: far less coherence. Trading patterns had long since begun to work against the British connection, because that suited the old Commonwealth countries. Well before the 1960s, Canada was becoming more dependent on the United States, and Australia was starting to recognize her Asian destiny. They were plainly not good bets as the basis for British trade. The Commonwealth's own interests, member by member, diverged sufficiently from the British, and from each other, to drain most of the meaning out of any such thing as a Commonwealth bloc.

The bonds of history and culture, however, were stronger than the facts of economic life. They were white bonds, heavily connected to the old rather than the new Commonwealth, and they gripped hard on the British mind. In the 1961 debate, Member after Member rose from the Tory benches to laud the Commonwealth connection, yearning for the vanished, English-speaking world. 'We have since the war devised every sort and kind of scheme for economic co-operation in Europe,' moaned Lord Hinchingbrooke, 'but we have practically nothing comparable in the Commonwealth.'

In retrospect, the blinding emptiness of this suggests that Macmillan's willingness to submit to any part of the Commonwealth argument was more culpable than it seemed at the time. At the time, indeed, hardly anyone looked upon it that way. But here is a moment at which hindsight may be instructively, and not unfairly, consulted. Insofar as the Commonwealth was seen, in any scenario, as an alternative basis for Britain's economic future, this vision was pitifully false. The trade figures indicated it then, the subsequent history proved it afterwards. One may accord a deal of sympathy to the errors of politicians at any given time, but less so when the source of the error is a reluctance, through

sentiment or pain or misbegotten pressure or sheer intellectual feebleness, to acknowledge the harshness of facts that palpably will not change:
facts, moreover, that were well documented by Whitehall departments
which had shed their own illusions before 1961.

The Commonwealth argument was not, admittedly, the only pressure bearing down on Macmillan. Perhaps it wasn't the strongest. The
case of the domestic farmers, who were then so influential in the Tory
Party, was more insistent, and was represented in the Cabinet by the
tocsin-voice of R. A. Butler. But, together, these questions impressed
themselves as a mighty force on Macmillan's mind, contributing to the
dank uncertainty that surrounded the entire enterprise. Although he had
come to the conclusion that Britain *ought* to belong to the European
Economic Community, Macmillan was not prepared, until very late in
the day, to elevate this cause to a rank meriting his full-blooded
leadership of party and public opinion.

A year passed before he began to sell it at all. Only on 13 September
1962 did the Cabinet decide that public opinion was getting dangerously
sceptical and needed correction. Until then, it took the view that any
degree of enthusiasm shown by British leaders might work against their
negotiating position. If Britain got too keen, tactics might harden against
her. But, on the contrary, the failure to prepare and educate opinion at
home produced a scepticism which made it ever harder to risk the kind
of concessions that might have accelerated the negotiation. In the depths
of the impasse, in autumn 1962, heroic failures tended to be politically
more attractive than calculated concessions. As a way of appeasing
opinion, this dismal pattern was often repeated after Britain had got in,
reaching its apogee during the sterile years when John Major (1990–7)
was presiding over the near-disintegration of Anglo-European relations.
Now, in 1961–3, it played its part in dragging out the negotiations,
justifying a counter-scepticism on the part of the Five as well as the
Sixth.

Behind this was Macmillan's pessimistic reading of the Tory Party.
He felt its breath down his neck even when, with a majority of 100 in
the Commons, he had less to fear than any modern Conservative leader
except, twenty-five years later, Margaret Thatcher.

From the beginning, the measure of party scepticism was unimpressive. At its first test, after the August 1961 debate, the Government won
a vote by 313 votes to 5, with twenty abstentions and only one Tory,
Anthony Fell, deeming the leader 'a national disaster'. At that year's
party conference, 40 votes out of 4,000 were cast against the platform.[39]

In March and July 1962, back-bench motions insisting that there should be no deal without special terms for the Commonwealth showed the core figure of Tory Euro-dissenters in the Commons to be between thirty and forty. But they hung heavy over the proceedings. 'One cannot think that when the chips go down people like this will count for much,' Macmillan's press secretary, Harold Evans, noted in his diary. But Macmillan could never lose sight of them. He seemed to fear the vocal minority more than he relied on the majority that was deferential to his wishes. And it was only quite near the end of the road, in autumn 1962, that he began to come out fighting.

When he did so, it was to try and meet head-on the banked-up arguments the sceptics had been assembling, and he was, at last, quite forthright. His language, in a propaganda pamphlet he finally decided to produce, found some urgency. By negotiating for entry, the Government had taken what was 'perhaps the most fateful and forward-looking policy decision in our peace-time history . . .' 'The economic opportunities . . . greatly outweigh the risks involved.' 'A Britain detached from Europe would mean inflicting permanent injury on our common cause.' 'In the past, as a great maritime power, we might give way to insular feelings of superiority over foreign breeds,' but now 'we have to consider the state of the world as it is today and will be tomorrow, and not in outdated terms of a vanished past'.[40]

To modern readers, what Macmillan had to say about sovereignty, at this late stage, is particularly interesting. Up to now, he had not been very explicit. There had been little demand for it: sovereignty was much lower among public anxieties than it became by the 1990s. Others, however, had addressed it. The facts were on the record. Lord Home, the Foreign Secretary, told the Lords in August 1961: 'Let me admit at once that the Treaty of Rome would involve considerable derogation of sovereignty.' Nor would this be confined to the economic area. The consequences would be 'different in kind from any contract into which we have entered before'.

Now, Macmillan himself remained a little more cryptic. He openly acknowledged that political unity was the central aim of the Six, and said, 'we would naturally accept that ultimate goal'. The case for being inside, to influence this process, made its hallowed appearance: the case that Macmillan, in 1957, when offered the chance of belated entry to the Messina process, hardly looked at. 'As a member of the Community,' he wrote, 'Britain would have a strong voice in deciding the nature and the timing of political unity.' By remaining outside, she risked decisions being made 'which we could do nothing to influence'. Besides, under the Rome Treaty, 'in renouncing some of our own sovereignty, we would receive in return a share of the sovereignty renounced by other members'. This he called 'pooling', the term of art already formulated that would be much heard in later years. The obligations that flowed from it wouldn't alter the position of the Crown, he declared, 'nor rob our Parliament of its essential powers, nor deprive our Law Courts of their authority in our domestic life'.[41]

Thus the plainer depictions of Lord Chancellor Kilmuir were watered down for public consumption, and a repetition of Lord Home's crystal clarity was not attempted. But at least Macmillan's pamphlet addressed the anxieties of a public opinion that was doing nothing to help Heath and his colleagues in Brussels, as they struggled to keep the negotiation alive.

A prolific sub-division of the academic discipline that goes by the name of European Studies is devoted to the question of why General de Gaulle brought the negotiation to an end. Was the veto premeditated? Was it precipitated by British errors? Was it always on the cards? Who deceived whom? How these questions are answered seems almost a matter of personal taste. Since the General never gave an *ex cathedra* explanation, there is freedom to speculate.

In my inquiry, I heard many versions, all uttered with conviction. Michael Butler still says it was clear for weeks if not months what would happen. 'The veto certainly shouldn't have come as a shock,' he said, looking back in 1993. 'De Gaulle was absolutely consistent and really very predictable.'[42] Sir Edward Heath doesn't think so. 'The talks weren't always doomed to break down, and there's a lot of evidence to support that,' he said in 1995. Two days before the veto, he was in Paris having a delightful lunch with the French Foreign Minister, Maurice Couve de Murville, exchanging views about the differences between French and British literature and doing some last-minute political business. As Heath remembered, 'Couve said, absolutely clearly, "Nothing can now stop these negotiations from being a success." '[43] As for Couve himself, a serpentine figure even in his near-dotage, he told me in 1994 that there had never, in fact, been a veto. Couve admitted that he had thought de Gaulle's press conference speech unnecessarily irritating to his allies, and advised him to tone it down. 'I think the end of the negotiation should have been announced in a softer way,' he said. 'The press conference is the basis for what is universally called de Gaulle's veto. Which is the wrong way to describe it. Everyone agreed that Britain wasn't ready, though only France said that she should wait. The right way to describe what happened is that the negotiations did not succeed.'[44]

To me, the persuasive evidence derives from the pattern of de Gaulle's behaviour over many years. The odds were long against him ever welcoming Britain into the EEC, if he could find a way of keeping her out that was congruent with his political power at the given moment. Unwilling to take a risk with British opinion, Macmillan gave him the opening he needed. Certainly by the time of the Rambouillet summit, it was clear beyond doubt that the General's intentions were unalterable, and Heath, for one, deluded himself in supposing otherwise. The long delay, culminating with the trip to Bermuda to negotiate Polaris missiles out of President Kennedy for the next generation of British nuclear defence, gave de Gaulle both the opportunity and the ammunition he needed. Even Heath, in general a defender of all that happened, says Macmillan made a mistake there. Being filmed with Kennedy, insouciantly inspecting the troops on parade in Bermuda, was a way of showing the priority de Gaulle most detested. 'He was terrified we might be left without any nuclear weapon,' Heath told me. 'It would leave him in a very weak position with Parliament, and was going to do him enormous damage with the party. So that was what was on his mind. The other aspects just didn't make an impact on him.'

This is, to some extent, an academic discussion. What happened, happened. De Gaulle, without doubt, treated Macmillan monstrously, whichever way you look at it. Either he was going through an elaborate charade, holding summit meetings which he knew would lead nowhere, dragging out an enormous expenditure of effort in Brussels which he always intended to fail. Or, almost quixotically, he decided at the last moment to intervene against the wishes not only of his old antagonist but of all his continental partners – save Chancellor Adenauer, who was giving Macmillan a hard time for almost as long.

What wasn't academic was the consequence. Britain had embarked on a venture that did not succeed. Despite its tentative, conditional nature, the quest to join the Common Market was Britain's only shot. She was not prepared for it to fail, and had no contingency plan ready when it did so. For Macmillan, therefore, the event was catastrophic. He did his best to keep a stiff upper lip, falling into pettiness only once or twice with gestures he regretted, like withdrawing permission for Princess Margaret to visit Paris. In public, he remained dignified and didactic, resuming his global stance. 'A great opportunity has been missed,' he said, in a broadcast to the nation. 'It is no good trying to disguise or minimize that fact ... France and her government are looking backwards. They seem to think that one nation can dominate Europe and, equally wrong, that Europe can or ought to stand alone. Europe cannot stand alone. She must co-operate with the rest of the Free World, with the Commonwealth, with the United States in an equal and honourable partnership.'

But the private man was in a state of greater turbulence. 'I do not remember going through a worse time since Suez,' he wrote to Lady Waverley. In his diary he said, 'French duplicity has defeated us all,' and that Couve had 'behaved with a rudeness which was unbelievable'. But so what? 'All our policies at home and abroad are in ruins.' 'I had terrible difficulties with Macmillan afterwards,' Ted Heath told me. 'He wouldn't do anything, wouldn't concentrate on anything. This was the end of the world.'

In less than a year, he was gone. Other political problems beset his government, including a concatenation of events that would, in a later time, have been categorized as serial sleaze. Scandals of sex and espionage overwhelmed him. But the failure of his European venture removed from him his *raison d'être* in high politics. In October, pleading prostate cancer, he left the leadership of party and country. This proved to be a wrong diagnosis, but he didn't wait for the best specialist who might have told him he had a decent chance of living another quarter-century, which is what he did, dying only in 1986. Instead, Harold Macmillan became the first in a long line of Conservative politicians whose careers were broken on the wheel of Europe.

After the veto, his private office tried to prepare him for the next stage. The Public Record Office files contain an exchange between officials, who note that a good deal of speech-writing would be necessary in the next few weeks, and offer a selection of quotations for possible use. 'I began composing a little anthology,' writes G. H. Andrew to A. W. France. For example, from Laurence Sterne: 'Strange! Quoth I, debating the matter with myself, that one and twenty miles sailing, for 'tis absolutely no further from Dover to Calais, should give a man these rights.' Or Napoleon's: 'Du sublime au ridicule il n'y a qu'un pas.' Or from Thomas Moore: 'How shall we rank there on glory's page / Thou more than soldier and just less than sage.' Or how about *The Merchant of Venice*? 'What? Woulds't thou have a serpent sting thee twice?'[45]

Several other amusing little piquancies suggested themselves to well-stocked mandarin minds. But on reflection, Herbert Andrew confessed, none of them would do. Imagining them in the mouth of Macmillan, he realized they wouldn't sound right. 'It is surprising', he concludes, 'how easy it is to strike a false note, and I have ended up with an anthology of false notes. It may at any rate remind you of a few things to avoid.'

5

HUGH GAITSKELL

Progressively Backwards

HAROLD MACMILLAN was not alone in his embroilment with the past. As the leader of the nation, he reflected a national condition. The British could hardly be said to be thirsting for a new kind of world which threatened to dislocate the allegiances they understood. In fact, by the standards of his time, Macmillan, tentative though he was, and neuroti-cally respectful of the forces around him, was the boldest man alive. He was surrounded by people even more cautious than he was. Though he acted, and, by action, challenged the cycle of conservative contentment, he belonged to a kind of national consensus that regarded such action as almost impossibly risky – and perhaps, as his enemies said, quite unnecessary.

Just as important in this *histoire* as Macmillan's attempt at action was the certain belief, in several quarters, that his chosen line of action was an error. There was a lot of opposition, all of it from one direction. Usually, the political leader finds himself picking a way between one lot of people who say he is going too far and another saying that he isn't going far enough. But this did not describe Macmillan's position when applying for a British place in the Common Market. He had no opponents, as it were, to the left of him. There was no body of opinion, in fact not a single public voice that I have traced, which said that the British approach should be more vigorous: that the conditional basis of the application was too defensive, or a bolder plunge was demanded by Britain's parlous situation. Such criticisms were often heard later. But, at the time, there were no Tory federalists to speak of, and no force in Parliament demanding more urgency rather than more caution. What Macmillan faced was a small army of opponents, in all parties, who found different reasons for saying that the whole idea of British mem-bership of the European Economic Community was a mistake.

This opposition mattered. It played its part in creating the climate in which the consideration, such as it was, of Britain's historic destiny took place. De Gaulle was the agent of failure, but the ground had been prepared at home. Opposition entailed a kind of full-throated roar in favour of the status quo, offered regardless of the fact that those who exhaled it were sometimes also critics of the status quo in other ways: alarmed by lagging competitiveness, hostile to imperial illusions, generally craving for modernity. But the critics were, for the most part, blind to this contradiction. Addressing a choice between past and future, they were conflicted. The tone they set was to resonate for decades.

The opposition was not devoid of reason. A large amount of abstruse ratiocination can be found in the archives concerning the pros and cons of entry as it would affect economic output, the balance of trade, the cost of food, the outlook for invisibles, the future of the Atlantic alliance and so on. The economic case was far from open-and-shut. Treasury and Foreign Office reworked the ground that previous officials had pored over in 1951 and 1955. Publicly also, there is no doubting the earnestness of the debates Macmillan's decision unleashed. In their combination of honest conviction and courteous disagreement, the 1962 debates were without doubt the best of the series that erupted, in the landmark years, with steadily more violent climaxes: 1967, 1971, 1975, 1984, 1992, 1993, 1997.

But overshadowing reason was the mighty power of sentiment: sentiment about the past, on which was based an incorrigible complacency about the present and the future. These attitudes grew one upon the other. They were righteously, unchallengeably, intertwined. Reading, in the 1990s, the arguments against Macmillan which held him half in thrall, one is struck by its marriage of the soft with the hard. There was some hard disagreement, as there was bound to be: contention about the facts, argument about the economic prospects in or out of the Common Market. Going into Europe, whichever way you looked at it, was a life-changing decision for a nation. But the overall timbre of the case made against Macmillan was irredeemably soft- rather than hard-headed.

It did not acknowledge the need for a truly sceptical, realistic look at the future economic prospects for Britain outside Europe, and it rested heavily, instead, on the ultimate recourse of many soft-headed British politicians of that time: the Commonwealth. Concern about the Commonwealth was marked by a double self-indulgence: an unrealistic assessment of what the Commonwealth could do for the British economy, coupled with a fanciful concern for what Britain owed the

Commonwealth. This attitude met with no shred of gratitude from those whose interests the mother country thought she was defending alongside her own.

So the nature of the debate reflected the frightening scale of the decision. Just as history rendered decisiveness impossible, so it produced a debate that was less than open-eyed. The shadow of the past reached forward to darken the British mind, making it reluctant to look too directly into a future whose discomforts were better left unexamined.

The main opposition player in this argument was Hugh Gaitskell, the leader of the Labour Party. For him, one must immediately acknowledge, it did not begin as an argument about national destiny. In its earliest manifestation, the Europe decision did not touch Gaitskell's ample store of passion. It took time to attain a status that would place it near the top of his political concerns. The subject was 'a bore and a nuisance and it has always been so', he once told a friend, and he expressed versions of this sentiment often. It was his preferred posture, about something that caused him much trouble. But even in those days, before Europe had destroyed a single British politician, calling it a bore and a nuisance scarcely met the case. This was an attitude that a good many Labour politicians found themselves falling into in later years. Combined with the sense that Europe 'didn't really matter', it supplied useful cover for a politician who could not make up his mind what he thought about it: a common frailty, later brought to a unique pitch of sophistication by Gaitskell's ally, Denis Healey.

Gaitskell would have liked to remain indifferent to Europe. When it unavoidably presented itself, he was still surviving the after-burn of two great arguments that had already wracked his party, and he could have done without another. At the 1959 party conference, he had fought, but failed, to secure the rewriting of Clause Four of the party constitution, the commitment to public ownership: an article of faith that survived another thirty-six years before Tony Blair succeeded in extinguishing it. In 1960, the party was further torn apart by an attempt to commit it to unilateral nuclear disarmament. This was enough for Gaitskell, as it would have been for any leader. Compared with these great questions of principle, Europe could be presented as speculative, almost otiose, which is how the leader originally preferred to see it.

The political context mattered in another way, which also had the effect of lowering Europe from the heights of grand principle. Parliament was halfway through its term, and a general election couldn't be far away. For Gaitskell, as for Macmillan, political survival infiltrated its way into the matter. That is often forgotten, in the endless dissections of what might have been. High politics cannot exist without considerations of the low. It was the Labour Party's opinion that the main reason Macmillan had embarked on the venture was because he needed a grand gesture of this kind to distract attention from the sense of party failure and national decline that surrounded his government. R. H. S. Crossman, the propagandist and senior leftist MP, told an American audience at the time that applying to get into the Common Market was 'an attempt by a most adroit and ingenious politician to extricate himself from his domestic difficulties and manoeuvre himself into a situation where, having successfully negotiated terms of entry, he could appeal to the country posing as the greatest statesman since Disraeli'.[1] Crossman might have added that the imminence of the election was intended as a bludgeon to keep Conservative MPs in line behind a policy which some of them fiercely disagreed with.

So the politics of party bulked large for Gaitskell – necessarily so. He had been leader since December 1955, and had already failed in the first shot at his appointed task, the winning of an election in 1959. Nothing could matter much more than winning next time. His party was divided over nationalization, divided over nuclear weapons and, as any student of the history could not fail to know, divided over Europe. The divisions of the 1950s lived on: federalists against Bevinites, Europeanists against globalists, left against right – although the cast of characters had sometimes changed sides. It is not hard to see why part of Gaitskell's response to the reappearance of Europe at the heart of British politics was to wish that it would go away.

Nor can one be surprised that this condition gave birth to a certain vacillation in the Leader of the Opposition. If the issue was a bore, and didn't really matter, and if it had to be considered primarily as a matter of manoeuvring towards a species of party unity, then it was to be expected that the Gaitskell record should show, at one level, and over quite a short period, the lurching inconsistency of line that has characterized so many politicians.

He gave many different impressions at different times. During 1960, when the issue first seriously began to surface, he was taken, according to his official biographer, to be a cautious supporter of entry.[2] After Macmillan's application, he maintained an elaborate public agnosticism, which he insisted should be the position of the party as well. It all depended, he said, on the terms the Government could secure. The question was 'tricky and complicated', he wrote to his daughter at

Oxford, and it would be 'absurd' to decide the Labour line too soon. As a party manager, he was determined, above all, to take no line at all until he had to, but on the issues of principle he was, in the beginning, dismissive of the common phobias. These, the political objections, he rejected for fully two years. In the summer of 1961, he strongly criticized a paper from Transport House, the party headquarters, which, he thought, much exaggerated the political drawbacks of British entry. In October, he expressed revulsion from the alliance between Little Eng- lander rightists and pro-Soviet leftists who made up most of the numbers in the hard anti-Market position. He thought they by no means spoke for mainstream public opinion. In early 1962, he wrote: 'provided the terms are satisfactory, I doubt if the country is going to be very anti'. In May, in a broadcast to the nation, he sounded about as far as Macmillan was from believing this would be the end of Britain as we know it. He said: 'You hear people speaking as though if we go into the Common Market . . . this is the end as far as an independent Britain is concerned. That we're finished, we are going to be sucked up in a tunnel of giant capitalist, Catholic conspiracy, our lives dominated by Adenauer and de Gaulle, unable to conduct any independent foreign policy at all. Now frankly, this is rubbish, on the basis of the Treaty of Rome.'

He also said, in a memorandum around that time, that many of the fears, whether about competition from cheap labour or about a federal European super-state, were groundless. 'French or German votes could not decide British foreign policy.' But the Market existed. 'If we stay out of it,' he wrote, in terms that might have been taken from Macmillan's own lexicon, 'we run the risk of becoming nothing more than a little island off Europe. We shall be dwarfed politically by the Six.'

Thus, in half of himself, as he addressed the issue Macmillan had laid on the table, Gaitskell was drawn beyond agnosticism to a position echoing that of his chief political friends. For Europe divided the parties within themselves more emphatically than it separated Labour from the Tories, and in that divide Gaitskell's allies, on the right of the party, were for the most part pro-European. The 'Frognal Set', labelled after the location of the Gaitskell home in Hampstead where his friends often met, contained, among others, the most committed pro-European poli- ticians, in either party, among the post-war generation, chief among them Roy Jenkins but also, if waxing and waning, Anthony Crosland, Patrick Gordon Walker and John Harris. They had been central to his positioning on both unilateralism and Clause Four. They wanted him to be a European, and he gave them grounds to think he was.

But then he said other things as well. Some of this was on the economic side, where he argued – it was one of his more consistent lines – that the benefits to Britain couldn't be assessed at better than fifty–fifty. He ridiculed the flighty prophets departing from what he saw as his own impeccable economic rationalism. But he was hostile to other sorts of irrationalism as well. In April 1962, Roy Jenkins brought Jean Monnet, the founding father, to speak to a dining club they both belonged to and administer a dose of faith. He hoped Monnet would dispel Gaitskell's doubts. But Gaitskell, at his most sceptical, pressed Monnet with an hour's relentless questioning, at the end of which the little Frenchman was pleading for mercy. 'Well, one must have faith' was his despairing curtain line. 'I don't believe in faith,' Gaitskell replied, 'I believe in reason, and there is little reason in anything you have been saying tonight.' Jenkins wrote in his memoirs: 'I have never seen less of a meeting of minds.'[3]

This, then, was a fickle and troubled leader. No more than many other people did he know exactly where he stood on Europe. Though pushed by his friends, he listened almost as attentively to his enemies, the left of the party, Harold Wilson to the fore. While explicitly rejecting their main argument, that the EEC was a capitalist cartel that would be the death of socialism, he shared their generally sceptical, suspicious, very *British* attitude. And it was his enemies rather than his friends he finished up by pleasing.

*

FOUR DECADES ON, now that we have been pounded for many years by the orthodoxy of Euro-scepticism, the seminal moment of the creed holds one particular fascination.

When the political opposition to British entry into the Common Market was first compelled, by Macmillan's overture, to express itself, what case did it make for another way of being an off-shore island? Confronted with a proposition to do one thing, what did it have to say about an alternative? Gaitskell did not like being challenged thus. 'Nothing annoyed him so much as the question, "But what is the alternative?"', his daughter Julia told his biographer. Too bad. It is a question that every generation of Euro-sceptics has found different ways of imperfectly addressing.

In August 1961, after the opening decision, Gaitskell did not lead for the opposition. He was committed to waiting-and-seeing, and, by comparison with the right wing of the Conservative Party, was a model of disinterested investigation. However, a fiery inquisition did immediately begin. It is of special interest to modern readers, not least because it was of very little interest to people at the time. It did not answer the question about an alternative, but that very void is itself illuminating: it shone down the decades, issuing as vacantly from the mouth of William Cash, a Tory Euro-sceptic MP of the 1990s, as it did from that of Sir Derek Walker-Smith, his more winning predecessor of the 1960s. To them, essentially, the emptiness did not need filling. They thought that what mattered above all else was not what the future held for Britain if she did not belong to the Community, but the manifold horrors, the treacheries on history, the depletions of national sovereignty that were the certain, intolerable consequences of belonging.

In his presentation, Macmillan made little of the sovereignty question, as we have seen, and, throughout his engagement with the issue, was seldom pressed to address it. It remained in the margins of his discourse, being considered far less important than the price of food or the future of the Commonwealth. Macmillan invariably got away with a few well-wafted allusions to sovereignty being 'perhaps a matter of degree', and the Treaty of Rome not involving 'any kind of federalist solution'.[4] Hardly anyone contradicted him. Gaitskell began by similarly down-playing the alarms. These moved a few people to distraction, but in 1961–3 they were not the main source of anxiety: and in any case de Gaulle was surely a safeguard against them.

It is worth recalling, however, that quite a lot was said. The constitutional consequences of entry into the Common Market were not concealed. At the same time as Macmillan was making his statement, a parallel debate took place in the House of Lords, in which the Lord Chancellor, Lord Kilmuir, described what would happen. Both the courts and Parliament would be living in a new environment. The UK courts would have to defer, in the final analysis, to the European Court on matters in the Treaty, and British citizens would be obliged to pay European penalties, if imposed. 'I am quite prepared to face that,' said Kilmuir. 'There is this limitation to the interpretation and the carrying out of the Treaty.' Sovereignty would be lost in a different, more contractual way from previous such poolings, through Nato or the OEEC or the United Nations, and this would be 'an unprecedented step'.

This account, it has to be conceded, was less graphic than it might have been. Earlier in the preparations, in a private letter to Ted Heath, Kilmuir had remarked: 'I find the constitutional objections serious.' That didn't mean he found them 'conclusive'. But signing up for membership meant, in practice, transferring to the Council of Ministers Parliament's 'substantive powers of legislating over the whole of a very important field'. His words, already alluded to in the last chapter, bear repeating. 'I am sure it would be a great mistake', he went on, 'to under-estimate the force of the objections . . . But these objections ought to be brought out into the open now because, if we attempt to gloss over them at this stage, those who are opposed to the whole idea of joining the Community will certainly seize on them with more damaging effect later on.'[5]

This proved to be a prophetic statement. As late as the 1997 election, the Referendum Party exhumed Kilmuir's letter from the files, displaying it as evidence of the establishment conspiracy of secrecy which Sir James Goldsmith and other RP zealots believed to have been at the core of Britain's entry into the EEC. And it is true that perceptions of what membership meant for sovereignty were more luridly understood in 1997 than thirty-five years earlier. But that was not, I think, primarily owing to the calculated neglect of the politicians of the day. Kilmuir did tell the House of Lords the essence of the matter, albeit without excitement. The Bow Group, under the direction of a young Tory politician by the name of Geoffrey Howe, produced a legal study in July 1962 which foreshadows with great exactitude the effect the Treaty of Rome has had on British law.[6] In August 1962, Kilmuir's successor, Lord Dilhorne, again went over the ground in a Lords debate, explaining in laborious detail how both judges and politicians would fall under the sway of the European system.

So there was no secret about any of this, for those who wished to know. To the extent that the British could ever justly claim to have been taken by surprise, the culprits were not the ministers who wished to start the entry process in 1962 so much as the nation itself, at the time. The trends and facts and probabilities were, for the most part, exposed. But they were seen through a haze of uncertainty. They achieved no real focus. They simply did not concern the political class in the way they came to do a few decades later.

Whether this reflected people's excessive confidence in British power, their lack of serious interest in the detail, or merely the embryonic evolutionary stage the Common Market had attained, is a question to be answered differently in different cases. In the most important case, that of Macmillan, the power relationship was dominant. Although sensitive to the fuss some people might make about sovereignty, he plainly did not believe it was a real issue. He could not imagine this move except as a way of reinventing British greatness. Time after time, in the documents and in his speeches, he rests his case on the Community as a theatre in which British power will be enhanced, not diminished: a place where Britain will lead, not one where there was intended to be no leader. Macmillan, steeped in great-power thinking, never did really understand this essential aspect of the Monnet–Schuman creation.

Not that the matter was left entirely undiscussed. For one school of Conservatives, the issue of Britain's survival as a sovereign nation was the inextinguishable heart of the matter. Derek Walker-Smith MP was one of them. A capable planning lawyer, Walker-Smith was at one time a man on the rise. He got as far as being Minister of Health, but in 1960 he was sacked, with only a baronetcy to console him. It was no doubt accidental that he should be the very first back-bencher who was called to speak in the debate on the Macmillan announcement, and at the time it didn't signify much. Although he made a brilliant speech, he wasn't talking about the issue that concerned most MPs. As a harbinger of history, however, no one could have been better chosen. He put into words the problem which, in due time, would tear the Conservative Party apart. The central argument he made, while having little impact on the politics of the moment, said what none put better in the years to come.

Unlike many of his successors, who later made Euro-phobia into an instrument for the wrecking of their party, Walker-Smith was a gentleman. His stance towards the Community was exquisitely polite. 'I would associate myself with no derogatory observations that might be made at this or any other time about the Community or the six nations that compose it,' he told the House with palpable sincerity. 'I salute, and all should seek to share, the sense of Christian purpose which animates their aims and aspirations.'

But he was unforgiving on the matter of sovereignty, dissecting with care the ways in which the Treaty took power from the nations, whether on trade relations or labour laws, or through its explicitly political aspirations. The question, he said, was not whether sovereignty was being sacrificed for good purpose, but whether it needed to be sacrificed at all. Could trading not be as favourably governed by inter-national as by supra-national agreements? Did we really need to join up, in order to achieve economic growth? 'I find something humiliating', he said, 'in the proposition that the only way to bring economic realism to a great industrial people is to join the Common Market.' For its component nations were different from Britain. Sovereignty came late to most of them, the detritus of the Holy Roman Empire. 'Their evolution has been continental and collective, ours has been insular and imperial.' They looked to share their practices with each other, 'but not with us'. To forget all this, 'as a sort of postscript to an economic arrangement', was deeply wrong, Walker-Smith thought. 'There are considerations here which go beyond the considerations of the counting house.'

He went on: 'If we adhere to the Economic Community now and the Six proceed, as they are entitled to proceed, to the next stage of political union, what then is the position? If we do not want to go along with them on the political side, could we stay in on the economic side, or could we get out at that stage if we wanted to? Or is the real position this, that if the decision is taken now, we forfeit the power of political decision? ... If we tried to come out of the Community in those circumstances, would not the Six be justified in saying to us, "But you knew all along of our enthusiasm for the next political step. If you did not share it, why did you join us in the first place?" '[7]

This was quite a prescient accounting. Long after Britain joined, these questions began to reappear in the minds of Walker-Smith's successors, gaining an almost violent urgency from the fact that, by the 1990s, they had become impossible to answer by a simple assertion of British independence. What should Britain do?, Walker-Smith asked himself rhetorically. The answer was simple. Tell the Six Britain wishes them well, she desires to co-operate, but she seeks no more than to associate with them, never to belong: exactly what Mr Cash and his friends, with a kind of hopeless longing, wanted to do thirty years later.

This was not, however, the line that Gaitskell took in the beginning, though he later drew potently on the emotional charge it generated. 'I have never been much impressed with the argument about loss of sovereignty,' he told the Commons in June 1962. His first concern, as he often said, was with the economic reckoning. And his parallel compulsion was with the matter of honour: with kith and kin, with our island's global story, with our historic obligations: in short, with the Commonwealth. It was here that he made common cause with politicians he otherwise despised, on the right of the Conservative Party, and with instincts he was not prepared to question, in the heart of the British people.

By both birth and formation, Gaitskell had some of these instincts within him. He was infused with the imperial connection that found its way into the lives of so many of the British professional classes. His father Arthur joined the Indian Civil Service, and spent all his

professional life in Burma, though Hugh was born in Kensington. His
elder brother, Arthur Jr, the founder of a peasant co-operative in the
Sudan, spoke for the same dutiful attachment to public service on the
global scale, and Hugh absorbed the family tradition. He was always, for
example, especially involved with India, and had many close Indian
friends, one of whom, K. B. Lall, India's ambassador in Brussels, is
credited with turning him, finally, against the Common Market. He was
also strongly pro-American. But just as, with a future generation of
British leaders, the nuances of their speeches are examined for clues to
where they really stand as between Europe and America, in Gaitskell's
time the dichotomy was with the Commonwealth, and in his own
utterance it was the Commonwealth connection that invariably came
through strongest. The need to 'carry the Commonwealth' became one
of the earliest tests he determined to apply to the European venture.

The Commonwealth, moreover, had become the acme of political
correctness in the wider Labour Party. The anti-imperialists had made
their mark by granting India independence in 1947, and watched the
evolution from Empire into Commonwealth with unqualified approval.
When Macmillan talked about the Commonwealth problem, he was
referring invariably to the 'old', therefore white, Commonwealth,
whereas for Labour it was a multi-racial entity – 'one of the great
progressive manifestations of the history of mankind', said Maurice
Edelman MP[8] – in which the tropical produce of Ghana mattered as
much as New Zealand butter, and the flourishing of Asian rather than
Canadian manufactures would be the crucial test case for the Community's good faith.

It is hard, as the century closes, to re-create the sway which these
considerations held over the British political class in the 1950s and 1960s.
Any 'weakening of Commonwealth links' was spoken of as if it constituted the death-knell for Britain's honour as well as her self-interest. 'We
shall be sacrificing so much that I am proud of and value in this
country,' said a Tory MP, R. H. Turton, in arguing that negotiations
should not even begin. 'The future of the world will depend a great
deal', he thought, 'on how far by this multi-racial partnership we can
bring the continents together.' The instant alarm expressed by every
Commonwealth government at the prospect of changing trade patterns
impressed him and many of his colleagues direly. Not a few Labour MPs
were similarly struck. In the August 1961 debate, the most emotional
speech came from Lynn Ungoed-Thomas, a senior Labour man, who

bemoaned a proposal 'which is alien to the mind of this country [and] is ruinous to our Commonwealth connection'. He went on: 'Right from its earliest days – the days of Wellesley, of Cornwallis, of Warren Hastings – there has been as a continuous thread amongst the best of our people the conception of the Empire as being a trust to develop into a Commonwealth of all our peoples, including the coloured peoples.' 'If there has to be a choice,' said Harold Wilson, 'we are not entitled to sell our friends and kinsmen down the river for a problematical and marginal advantage in selling washing machines in Düsseldorf.'

The betrayal of the past wasn't the only argument the emotionalists made. They had to do better than talk in terms of Armistice Day parades. Recognizing the need for something more concrete, they constructed some elaborate economic fantasies. The Commonwealth, they persuaded themselves, could be made into a viable economic partner, a growing force, if only London set its mind to the task. For there was certainly an economic downside to entry, in the form of higher food prices. Once Britain was in an arrangement that provided for open frontiers and nil tariffs between members, while abandoning the preferential arrangements to anyone outside the frontiers, New Zealand butter, cheap though it was, wouldn't stand a chance against the French. The charge developed that Britain had shamefully neglected Commonwealth trade for many years. It should now be boosted by all manner of devices. Viscount Hinchingbrooke proposed a Commonwealth Payments Union and a Commonwealth Bank, to help finance British exports. All Britain needed, belatedly, was a positive policy for Commonwealth trade rather than for European trade. 'We shall have tremendous opportunities if Britain will really get down to it,' Turton vigorously enthused. The debates of 1961 and 1962 contained much wild thrashing about in search of economic nostrums, to avert the unthinkable political outcome.

The trading arguments, however, were not very convincing. They defied patterns that were already visible. For example, Commonwealth exports to Western Europe were already rising, while those to Britain were declining. The share Europe took of British exports was rising, admittedly from a low base, while that of exports to the Commonwealth was falling. This was from a high base (40 per cent), but the pace and quality of expansion in the advanced industrial societies across the Channel far exceeded what was likely to be available across the oceans, in countries that were in any case interested in diversifying their trade away from Mother Britain. There could never be a customs union with

Canada or Australia, Ghana or Malaya, for the simple reason that none of these places would have an interest in doing British exports a special favour against their own developing industries.

Besides, the Commonwealth was already showing its hand. Some members, like Canada, looked to the United States, some, like India and Ghana, to the Soviet Union. Others would soon be looking to the Common Market, with or without Britain, because of the quantity and quality of what it offered. The contempt of one Conservative MP, Peter Smithers, for the prevalent economic illusions was as withering as that of Walker-Smith, from the other side, for the political. How could a nation of 50 million provide the finance and know-how for a Commonwealth of 600 million? he asked. 'If we value the Commonwealth, can we really hope to hold it together all by our little selves? ... My belief is that the antithesis put before the House and the country of a choice between Europe and the Commonwealth – ayes to the right, noes to the left – is entirely false.' On the contrary, Smithers insisted, if we fail in Europe, the Commonwealth itself would probably have no future.

Thus even the pro-Europe faction was careful to protect the Commonwealth. An open federalist such as Jo Grimond, the Liberal leader, felt compelled to say that the Commonwealth has 'a great future', to which Britain must contribute. Roy Jenkins conceded that the Commonwealth was 'greatly valuable', before insisting that it couldn't be a substitute for Europe. Nobody could afford to say, because few allowed themselves to understand, that the Commonwealth was destined for the margins of world economic power, and therefore of the British economic interest, before another decade passed.

Hugh Gaitskell himself was in this pickle, but was reluctant to face it. Though he was born of Commonwealth stock, and was to conclude by appealing to its meaning with all the force at his command, in between he sang an uncertain song. He said different things about the Commonwealth at different times, just as he said many different things about Europe. As a leader, though he went out in a gale of rhetoric, he was more the weathervane than the wind of change. He was true, in short, to the British tradition of not being certain what to think.

He always maintained, like everyone else, that the historic links had to be sustained. Meeting the needs of the Commonwealth members must be a basic test, he said, of the conditions Macmillan was able to obtain. But he wasn't always intoxicated by the possibilities. 'Are you sure that in ten or twenty years' time the Commonwealth will be there?' he ruminated in front of a group of Commonwealth MPs, in July 1962.

The ties, he noted, were getting weaker anyway. India seemed to be drifting away, the African countries were drawing closer to each other, the old white countries might be looking more to the USA. Maybe Britain would soon become 'just a little island off Europe', he again speculated, which couldn't depend on the Commonwealth, since this wasn't a military alliance, nor a customs union, nor even 'entirely a community of democracies'. He openly feared Britain being 'excluded from a tough, strong European state', and he told the Commonwealth MPs not to traduce Macmillan for investigating the alternatives. 'It is not fair to denounce the Government as though [negotiation] was a plain act of treachery,' he said.

So Gaitskell was not an all-out nostalgia-merchant. His rational mind could make the Commonwealth sound like a bad bet. He understood its weaknesses. On the other hand, he allocated it a veto over Macmillan's negotiations, telling numerous Commonwealth leaders, as his position hardened, that if their summit, scheduled for September 1962, was not satisfied, 'then the Labour Party would come out in strong opposition to our entry'.[9] He almost goaded them to reject the deal. Commonwealth governments 'should know the power they have to influence British opinion ... is very great indeed', he said. He told the Australian Labour leader to 'regard it as your job to see that [Robert Menzies, the Prime Minister] does not sacrifice Australian interests'.

In reaching his final position, Gaitskell was naturally touched by his inner uncertainties, which were themselves influenced by the state of his party. In fact, he privately reflected on how well it would suit him if the agreement Macmillan was able to reach was so bad that the Commonwealth, the farmers and the Tory Party all vehemently rejected it. He did not *desire*, he said, to be obstructive, and he sometimes appeared not to be so. A party political broadcast he gave in May was judged to be a model of fairness, *The Times* remarking on 'his obvious devotion to truth and principle'. He was not, apparently, being oppositionist. The pro-Market forces in the Labour Party, a group of about fifty MPs for whom Roy Jenkins continued to be the most prominent spokesman, acclaimed his words as 'a great advance' – which reflected how they were more generally regarded, as a nuanced statement that came down, in spite of the recent, repellent meeting with Jean Monnet, in favour of British entry.

This ground which Gaitskell uncertainly occupied, however, was shifting beneath him. For few members of the Labour Party did Europe pose a clear issue of principle, and not all his colleagues on the right were reliably among them. The left, by now, were solidly opposed. But, when some of the key figures who had assisted him in his prior battles against the left, over nationalization and disarmament – Patrick Gordon Walker, Michael Stewart, Denis Healey, James Callaghan – began to move towards the anti camp, Gaitskell could not but take notice. Swinging erratically between his view of the Common Market, on some days, as a bore, on others as a test for Macmillan's negotiating skills, and on yet others as a matter of the highest principle, Gaitskell did not seem to have a secure anchorage. He could be mightily influenced by the last person who spoke to him. On a summer visit to Brussels, for example, he was destabilized when Paul-Henri Spaak made the unsurprising observation that the Community was destined to progress towards more political as well as economic unity. There was a terrible row. This continental line, which Gaitskell had heard many times before, now had a big effect on him. The man who had once called Europe a bore addressed the question with growing earnestness, but was also evincing more acrid scepticism.

This reached an interim climax when the Commonwealth prime ministers met together in early September, in London, where the Leader of the Opposition could be conveniently present in the corridors. Many had come with their own opposition leaders in tow, looking over their shoulders. Hostility abounded. For the terms negotiated thus far by no means satisfied all the Commonwealth demands. Though Foreign Office officials were able to paper over the disagreements, and achieve a public presentation of unity that later spin-doctors would have marvelled at, the white Commonwealth especially was seething, which provoked Gaitskell into mounting his highest horse of indignation. The personal bitterness between him and Macmillan reached a new pitch of venom. Referring to Australia, Gaitskell confided that the proposed terms were 'another example of Macmillan's smashing our relations with these people for personal political advantage'. Macmillan snarled in his diary: 'A very tense atmosphere everywhere. Gaitskell going about smiling . . . as if he had just kissed hands.'

The Labour Party conference now beckoned, and there was no doubt that Europe would be the vibrant issue. Gaitskell anticipated it with another broadcast, ripping into the emptiness of the promises Europe was prepared to make to New Zealand, Canada, India and the rest. He insisted he wasn't negative about Europe, but said the political case for entry derived largely from what the Commonwealth could bring to it. As a way of avoiding a choice, he searched for ways of yoking the two together. Bridge-building between First World and Third, between black, brown and white races, between the tight little crypto-federation of Western Europe and the world beyond the seas where the map was coloured red: these were now Gaitskell's criteria for blessing the enterprise. Although intelligible as an ideal, they were a distraction from the main question with which the country was confronted.

Gaitskell wanted to have it both ways, which is, arguably, what every leader seeks for his country. But, if that is the object, there has to be congruence in his approach to the competing interests. In particular, the short-term positioning required to satisfy one set of pressures has to avoid, as far as possible, foreclosing longer-term interests that point the other way. This rule the Labour leader now proceeded to ignore.

All along, as his private conversations show, he explained himself as a man who, at the right time and on the right terms, positively wanted Britain to go into the Common Market. He insisted that he was pro-Europe, pro-EEC, pro-British membership. He was aware that if he attacked Macmillan's terms too strongly he might be mistaken for someone who wanted to keep out altogether. There were plenty of people like that, and Gaitskell affected not to be one of them. He probably wasn't. 'The problem really has been how to maintain our position against going in on the present terms and yet reply effectively to the Government's obvious intention to take us in on any terms,' he told a correspondent later in October. To Alistair Hetherington, editor of the *Manchester Guardian*, whose diaries record more than a hundred private conversations with the Labour leader,[10] he claimed that Labour, on getting into power, would reopen negotiations with the Six immediately.

And yet, in defiance of all these cautions, outright opposition is what he finally produced, in language which nobody could mistake for a temporary, transitional, negotiating position. For that reason, Hugh Gaitskell deserves recognition as the first of the 'Euro-sceptics', in the rather special sense which that term gathered round itself. The label wasn't current in the early 1960s, and it later became a misnomer, because it conferred a spurious aura of detachment on a school of thought that was, in fact, passionately opposed, at any given time, to the project known as 'Europe'. The anti-Europeans of the Thatcher years were the first to lay claim to its undoubted seductiveness. But Gaitskell came before them, as the representative of a state of mind for which 'sceptical' was a misleading description. Just as William Cash purloined the epithet for a school of thought whose intellectual manners belied it, the scholarly Gaitskell chose to invest this same subject with a reviling, unsceptical passion that no one had ever heard from him before. It is probably fair to say that he was not, in the depth of his being, opposed root and branch to British Europeanism. He was by no means Europhobic. But it also has to be said that his political rhetoric in the autumn of 1962 conveyed entirely the opposite impression. It gave coherence to an attitude of out-and-out hostility.

For help in the preparation of his conference speech, he turned to one faction among his friends and not the other. The Jenkinsite segment of the right could already see what was coming. Peter Shore, the party's international secretary, a lifelong zealot in the anti-EEC cause, produced a draft party statement on Europe that Gaitskell forced him to revise. The leader thought it went too far. But it was Shore rather than George Brown, Gaitskell's deputy leader, who was privy to the process by which Gaitskell determined his final position. When Brown went to Gaitskell's room in the conference hotel the night before the speech, he was persistently refused sight of the text. Gaitskell kept it covered up on the table. Brown, who would have to wind up the debate, asked, 'You're not going to switch the line, are you?', and the leader embraced him, saying, 'You know me better than that. I'd never do a thing like that.' And that is doubtless what Gaitskell sincerely thought. It is certainly what Brown said about him later: that he did not really intend to do what he did. To the end, in short, he was determined to have it both ways: to blow Macmillan's project out of the water, while insisting that he was not in principle opposed to it.

The speech he delivered to a large audience at the Brighton ice rink on 3 October 1962 was, to some who heard it, the greatest he ever made. By modern standards it was of Gladstonian dimensions, lasting 105 minutes, and it began in a calm, evaluative tone of voice. The leader rejected some of the oldest shibboleths of his party: that entry into the EEC would be the end of socialist planning, or that the Community might somehow be wished out of existence by Britain's remaining outside. But this didn't last long. Although he continued to insist that his only objection was to the terms Macmillan would settle for, the entire message of the speech seemed to be that a version of triumphant British isolationism should stretch forward into the indefinite future.

For one thing, Gaitskell abandoned his earlier line, that the economic arguments were evenly balanced. Now he loaded them all one way, deriding the notion that Britain could expect any benefit from expanding her European markets while losing in Canada, Australia and the rest. He dismissed the view that a large domestic market of 250 million consumers offered an enticing prospect. 'Would we necessarily, inevitably, be economically stronger if we go in and weaker if we stay out?' he asked. 'My answer to this is . . . NO. Is it true to say that by going in we should become all that more prosperous . . .? Again my answer to that must be NO.' But economics was no longer what most interested this proudly rational man. What moved him was a series of arguments that could have been used at any time and in any circumstances, almost irrespective of the infamous 'terms', to exclude British membership indefinitely.

For membership, Gaitskell said, would change everything. Britain, he had discovered, would no longer be Britain. 'It does mean', he said, 'the end of Britain as an independent European state.' He would make no apology for repeating this, he said, his voice rising. 'It means the end of a thousand years of history.' For the EEC, he insisted, was all about European federation. 'How can one seriously suppose that if the mother country, the centre of the Commonwealth, is a province of Europe, which is what federation means, it could continue to exist as the mother country of a series of independent nations? It is sheer nonsense.'

Moreover, Europe itself harboured a series of menacing absurdities. These had now, apparently, become clear to him. Whereas the old dominions once stood beside Britain against continental enemies at Gallipoli and Vimy Ridge, he thought he had discovered in the Treaty of Rome evidence that the EEC itself, including the Germans and Italians and French, now had pretensions to becoming a military alliance. This was bad enough – but, in another field, there was much worse. The Common Agricultural Policy was 'one of the most devastating pieces of protectionism ever invented': so bad that mere negotiation away of its rougher edges could not meet the case.

All in all, Macmillan's project now merited the most strident language Gaitskell could produce. Europe's proposed treatment of the Commonwealth and the Government's assurances on that account were, he said, 'astonishing' and 'odious'. As for the assumption that only top people understood the issue, it seemed to imply that popular opinion should be excluded from the reckoning. Here was something no sentient politician could contemplate. It provoked Gaitskell to a peroration of purest demagoguery – 'what an odious piece of hypocritical, supercilious, arrogant rubbish is this!' – qualified only by a dying fall in favour of British entry. If the EEC would review this catalogue of its defects, maybe Britain could one day join.

'I still hope profoundly', this teetering Janus declared, 'that there may be such a change of heart in Europe as will make this possible.'

Before conference Gaitskell never had such a reception from the party as he had for this speech. Hardly anyone ever had. Throughout its length, 'nobody coughed or stirred', wrote the *Evening Standard*. For this one and only occasion, according to Peter Shore, Gaitskell 'won not only the minds but the hearts' of the conference. Backed by only half the right, the left, uniquely, supported him, which produced his wife Dora's famous *mot*: 'All the wrong people are cheering.' The leading dissident of the right, Douglas Jay, the only member of the Frognal Set who backed Gaitskell as strongly on Europe as they all did on Clause Four and nuclear disarmament, was still foaming with admiration two decades later. 'It was unique among all the political speeches I ever heard,' Jay wrote in his autobiography. 'It can only be described as an intellectual massacre.'[11]

Intellectual, however, is hardly the word to apply to Gaitskell's speech. It wasn't devoid of factual content, and it asked some hard questions about where the EEC thought it was going. Parts of it could be counted sincerely sceptical, especially about the meaning of union. 'Not all political unions are necessarily good in themselves,' he fairly noted. 'It all depends, does it not? ... It is not a matter of just any union, it is a matter of what are the effects of union. Is it an aggressive one? Is it damaging to others? ... Does it erect barriers as well as pull them down?' These were questions, he said, that had to be asked and answered, before deciding.

All the same, the speech wasn't intellectual so much as intensely, manipulatively emotional. For more than an hour, it plucked the mystic chords of memory. Gaitskell seemed so anxious to propitiate the past that he felt obliged to deny any real urgency about the future. He poured out all the most compelling reasons for Britain to believe that this was not a turning-point, nor the time to address the strategic question which underlay Macmillan's application to join the Common Market.

The speech was also, one must say, more than an instant success. One of Gaitskell's longer-term ambitions was clearly met, in that the party was commonly judged to be, for practical purposes, united. There was no great outcry against what he said, even though this offended an important group of Labour politicians: another way in which the Gaitskell period first exhibited trends that later made themselves felt consistently. Not only did this leader prove himself to be a sceptic in the vulgar as well as better sense, he also established that anti-Europe speeches usually got the loudest cheers and elicited the softest rebellions against them. This was to happen time and again, in Conservative as well as Labour epochs. There were salient exceptions, when anti-Europeanism had drastic effects on political leaders. Both the birth of a new party, the Social Democrats in 1981, and the deposing of an old leader, Margaret Thatcher in 1990, could be partly accounted acts of punishment against excessive displays of Euro-hostility. But a continuing thread of the pro-Europe cause has been its restraint in both victory and defeat. There are reasons for this, not the least of them being that this is the side that eventually won the argument, occupied power, saw its ascendancy take root, could therefore afford to be magnanimous: a complex, significant story. It remains a telling fact, however, that for most of this history it is the anti-Europe cause that has had the greatest resonance: made the most noise, named the most enemies, touched the most doubting nerves.

The post-Brighton politics of Labour saw the beginning of this pattern. Though many of Gaitskell's friends were disappointed, they were almost all forgiving. They did not stir up trouble, nor did they very vigorously fight back. Friendships did not collapse, and Gaitskell went out of his way to offer reassurance. 'He was still faithful to the old rule of the primacy of personal relations,' Roy Jenkins writes in his autobiography. Although there were meetings of hurt and puzzled pro-Europeans, who gathered to talk about ways of stemming the tide, the party was actually more united now than at any other time in the Gaitskell years, because the left, for the first and only time, were on his side. His enemies were his friends, and few of his friends became, even transiently, his enemies.

As an exercise in leadership, however, Gaitskell's European perform-ance does not stand up well to retrospective consideration. It was full of passionate doubt, but almost totally devoid of prophetic insight. It spoke with overwhelming eloquence for the importance of the past. The hard questions about the future it did not really address. It set a standard which others, over the years, were to follow, whereby the alternative to 'Europe' was never very coherently put together in the speeches of people who found this construct a hideous spectre which they couldn't accept.

At this stage in the argument, the economic picture was certainly confused. By far the most convincing doubt concerned the price of food. Entry into the Common Market, just as the Six were finalizing their Common Agricultural Policy, would mean a switch in the method for subsidizing farmers, and, after the elapse of a transitional period, the end of the system whereby Britain bought her food from wherever it was most cheaply available. By taxes and outright bans, the CAP would stop all that, and force British consumers to buy continental, often at higher prices than free trade would have allowed. There was no doubt about this, though the Government, naturally, slid over the detailed implications. Since 30 per cent of UK imports consisted of food, and the average family spent about 30 per cent of its income on food,[12] it was certain that such a change of regime would have important effects on British labour costs and on the balance of payments. This was an important downside to the project. For some protagonists, notably Douglas Jay, it remained the most reasoned reason for lifelong hostility to Britain belonging.[13] It also played a large part, as it had to, in the Treasury's unenthusiastic analyses, all the way from the 1950s to the 1970s, of the economic consequences for Britain of going into Europe.

There was, however, an upside to the project: or rather, a danger which loomed so large that, if she didn't enter the project, Britain would face disaster. She had to trade to live. The market of the future was growing next door, across the Channel, and the figures were already telling, there for all to see. In the old Commonwealth countries, let alone the new, imports had been moving slowly for years. They wanted to create their own industries, and were in any case inherently smaller scale than the US and Western Europe, to which world exports had more than doubled in the past few years. The trend was relentless, and the absolute figures, not just the rate of growth, were already showing it. In the first four months of 1962, as negotiations proceeded, 31.6 per cent of British exports went to the Commonwealth, 38.6 to Western Europe. This was before the full rigour of internal tariff-lowering had taken place in Europe. When the internal tariffs were gone, British exporters to Germany, France and the rest were certain to be badly hit in the market where, the evidence now incontrovertibly showed, expansion was going to be relentless.

That was the economic argument made by many MPs, in the two major Commons debates of 1961 and 1962. Gaitskell never frontally disposed of it, relying instead on plausible, but over-convenient, contentions out of the economist's locker: that Europe's expansion was not, in fact, due to the existence of the EEC as such, or that there could be no guarantee of Britain specially prospering under continental rules, or that regional blocs were a poor substitute, in the long run, for proper global trade bodies. The thread running through Gaitskell's economic agnosticism, as through the hostile doubts of others, was an exercise in self-persuasion. Probably the majority of British politicians at this time, whatever their long-term attitude to Europe, wanted to persuade themselves the economy was not in bad shape: the prospects were reasonable: industry was surviving, or better: and there was no overwhelming need, therefore, to plunge into the political pain – it always was a pain – of aligning our institutions with the EEC's, while spitting on the Commonwealth. That is what Gaitskell insisted. It seemed to be his way of avoiding what he called 'humiliation'.

It also pre-empted the pressure for a Great Alternative. If the problem wasn't terminal, why accept an argument that said: if not the EEC, what? So this, too, Gaitskell didn't speak of, though others did and produced a revealing glimpse of a debate.

To the extent that there was an economic problem, some argued, it should be met not by joining the EEC as a full member but by seeking mere 'association' with it. Some of the Tories were keen on that, and the Government's response wasn't always logical. When this dilute expedient was put to Macmillan – to become 'country members, so to speak', the club-man drawled – he said it had been considered but rejected, on the ground that it had no advantages. To become merely a free-trading associate, he said, would 'raise all the same problems for British agriculture and Commonwealth trade', without giving Britain a position of influence within the Community to address them.[14] In other words, all the duties without the say. Edward Heath put it rather differently. Britain seeking a free-trade relationship, he said, 'is one of the things that raises the deepest suspicions of everyone in Europe'. She had been trying to secure one, without success, ever since the Community got going. All that had happened was that in 1958 de Gaulle vetoed a British attempt to get a free-trade area for all of wider Europe, and Britain had to make do with a separate body, of the 'out' countries, called the European Free Trade Association, the weaker brethren, some of whom would now seek entry to the EEC on Britain's coat-tails. The problem, Heath implied, was the opposite of what Macmillan said: the belief, among EEC members, 'that we want all the advantages of the developments in Europe without undertaking any of the obligations of the other members of the Community'.[15]

Whichever was the real reason – and both men, as usual, said different things at different times – it is plain that the free-trade alternative did not enter the agenda, even of the main opponents of the

Macmillan deal. Gaitskell did not push it. He did not seem to believe, at this stage, that Britain's economic situation demanded any drastic rearrangement of external relationships.

It has to be remembered, of course, that he was operating in the hottest political environment. He was concerned as much with the next election, coming soon, as with strategic national judgement, so one can't take as conclusive the omissions in his public thinking. Perhaps it is fair to decide that his opinion was not yet ripe. Charitably, you might say he wasn't ready. In any case, speaking as a domestic politician, he had plenty to say about the mess the Tories were making of the economy. He just didn't seem to think the future of Britain was yet, necessarily, wrapped up with the future of Europe.

Charity, however, doesn't deal with all questions. Gaitskell's major premise was spectacularly wrong. He hung more of his argument on the Commonwealth than many in his party, but as a lynchpin of either the economic advance or the political influence of the off-shore island, the Commonwealth was unreal. Many people did see this, however decorously they chose to make it clear. There was nothing perverse or mysterious about their judgement. They were simply readier to apply a cool head to factual evidence, undistorted by wishes or nostalgia. They were right, and Gaitskell was found to have brought the Brighton conference to its feet on a series of emotional appeals which events did not take very long to falsify.

This must necessarily colour the assessment of what Gaitskell would have done later in the piece, when, perhaps, he had become Prime Minister. There developed a lively academic industry in Gaitskell studies, some of which was devoted to the question of what he really thought about the Common Market. He said more than once, in his meandering odyssey, that he was sure there would be another application if this one didn't come off. It was, he insisted, all down to the terms, and these, he sometimes speculated, would one day change, perhaps when de Gaulle was no longer the commanding presence on the scene. One of the more consistent themes Gaitskell voiced concerned Britain's vital role in diverting the EEC from the dire but, to many, plausible fate of what he thought might become an inward-looking, tight little regional federation. As late as 21 September, just days before he raised the roof in Brighton, he spent a party political broadcast ruminating about the desirability of a wider Europe, and saying what a force for good in the world it might be. He was not, in any crude or adamant sense, anti-European, and no trace of xenophobia disfigured him. On the contrary, the position he arrived at was driven by a concern for more global internationalism. The Commonwealth kept eating at him. He wanted 'a bridge between the Commonwealth and Europe', which could not be constructed 'if we destroy the Commonwealth by our entry'.

At the back of this was a claim he made with great emphasis to President Kennedy, that he did not object in principle to British entry. In December 1962, he wrote a long memorandum to his fellow progressive, explaining why he had taken the negative line he did. 'I myself and my leading colleagues', he said, 'all happened to believe and still believe that the arguments of principle were fairly evenly balanced for and against, and that the balance would be tipped in favour of entry only if our conditions were fulfilled.'

It is in the belying of that statement, however, that Gaitskell made his mark. Although he certainly believed it to be true – which means, in the major sense, that it *was* true – his political performance gave the opposite impression. Its impact was quite different. The small print and the qualifying clauses were effaced by the brute power of his categoric rejection. Far from being finely balanced, the argument from principle came from his mouth in an overwhelmingly one-sided way. Whatever he may have desired, he became a propagandist against the European project at home, as well as doing much to fortify the scepticism of anyone abroad who was already disposed to doubt whether Britain seriously wished to become a European country.

This stance had some important effects. It was a sort of bellwether for the future, marking the path for later leaders, setting a standard that others emulated. In two ways, in particular, we can see Hugh Gaitskell as the forerunner of many politicians who mistook the truth about what 'Europe' fundamentally required of Britain.

The first is elementary and, of the two, is much the more excusable. Europe was a divisive issue for Gaitskell the party leader, as it was to be for every Labour leader until Tony Blair. Party management heavily influenced his thinking. 'The terms' were for Gaitskell what they became for Harold Wilson: the pretext which allowed him to avoid taking a clear policy position that half his party might have opposed. 'If I had urged unconditional entry (thus going further than the Government),' he told Kennedy, 'there would have been bitter opposition from a minority which was basically hostile to our entry. If I had urged opposition whatever the terms, this would also have been bitterly opposed ... In either case, there would have been a major split in the party, which, following the great dispute on defence, would have been fatal to our prospects.'

The trouble was, though, that Gaitskell's chosen way of dealing with this did not present him as a man sitting on the fence. His decisive oration showed no positive sympathies whatever towards Europe. It was the pro- not the anti-Europeans he decided he could take for granted, a choice whose influence reached well beyond the Labour Party. It helped to spur anti-Europe feeling in the country. At the end of 1961, after the application, public opinion, while still heavily laden with 'don't knows', surged in support of the idea of joining Europe. Labour support increased along with that of loyalist Tories, and was at one stage said to encompass more than half of Labour voters.[16] As the Labour leadership became more sceptical, public support, though still far from negligible, somewhat waned. To the extent that Gaitskell wanted to keep open the European option, his impact on public opinion, with the extremity of his utterance, was poorly judged. He immediately became the chief rallying-point for Euro-scepticism.

And yet, in some ways, he did not intend to be so: and this is the second sense in which he was a trail-blazer for successors. There was a discrepancy between the outcome he desired and the method by which he chose to reach it. He wanted to keep the issue open, but played his part in helping to close it. Gaitskell's most obvious heir in this mode of politics probably never gave him a thought, but her identity proclaims itself. Gaitskell wanted, at some time, to see Britain join Europe, but he preached relentlessly against it. Likewise, Margaret Thatcher spent a decade taking Britain ever deeper into Europe, yet simultaneously did her best to rouse public opinion against everything that 'Europe' represented.[17]

Along with serial inconsistency, this discrepancy between deeds and words is the political style that infuses, time and again, the history of Britain-in-Europe. Fatally aberrant, often counter-productive, these are practices the political nation has regularly adopted as its only way of coping with the project that dominates its existence.

What Gaitskell 'really' thought became, by a fateful intertwining, an academic question. The veto, of course, swept aside any immediate interest in the ongoing reality of British entry. But, only four days afterwards, Gaitskell himself was dead. At the age of fifty-six, unfulfilled as a statesman of major rank, he died from a viral infection that got at his lungs and eventually his whole immune system.

An epitaph, however, had already, in a sense, been declared on his attitude to Europe, which, because of the timing of his death, became the position for which he was most sharply remembered. In early December 1962, not long after the Brighton conference, the former US Secretary of State, Dean Acheson, made a speech which contained a phrase that has never been forgotten. 'Great Britain', Acheson told the graduating class at the West Point military academy, 'has lost an empire and has not yet found a role.' It was a speech about larger strategic matters, but also went on to ridicule British pretences about 'a "commonwealth" which has no political structure, or unity, or strength'. The British self-image, whether as economic master of the sterling area or broker between Washington and Moscow, imagined, Acheson said, a role that 'is about played out'.[18]

The speech caused an amazing eruption of outrage in Britain. Everybody who was anybody had their say. Ambassadors on both sides of the Atlantic had to devote their full time, for some weeks, to smoothing out the trouble. Macmillan wrote an open letter to the people, rebuking Acheson for 'an error which [had] been made by quite a lot of people in the course of the last four hundred years, including Philip of Spain, Louis XIV, Napoleon, the Kaiser, and Hitler'.

There could be only one explanation for the depth of this outrage, namely that Acheson had touched a recognizable nerve. In a single pithy phrase, he summed up what the British, in their heart of hearts, knew to be the truth: the truth which Gaitskell's had been the most resonant voice to deny. I could find no evidence that the Brighton speech actually prompted Acheson to say what he said. But indisputably it was the most authoritative recitation of the fantasy which Acheson despaired of, and which Macmillan, to do him justice, was attempting to challenge and, as he hoped, extinguish from Britain's view of the world.

'You know, the Common Market breakdown was a bigger shock for us than you chaps realised,' R. A. Butler affably told the Labour politician Anthony Wedgwood Benn a month after the veto.[19] The misapprehension, however, was rooted in a reason that extended far beyond itself. Since Labour wanted the breakdown to occur, the party and its leaders took some time to address the scale of what it really meant.

6

JOHN ROBINSON

A Conspiracy of Like-Minded Men

A MONTH AFTER de Gaulle's destructive intervention, a memorandum arrived at the Foreign Office from the British delegation in Brussels. Entitled 'The Next Steps', it showed that some British officials could produce a more hard-headed response to the collapse of Macmillan's policy than by merely toying with elegiac quotations to season the speeches of their disappointed ministers. It was addressed to the head of the Office's European Economic Organizations Department, and reported on the post-veto mood of the Community with a sinewy sense of diplomatic purpose.

The despatch began by considering the Italians. The Italians, said the writer, were furious at what had happened. 'I am told that the Italians have said to the Dutch in Rome that their anger at de Gaulle's behaviour will last longer than the anger in Holland.' All except the Luxembourgers, he said, were disgusted with the French. They had wanted the negotiations to continue and, if possible, succeed.

On the other hand, London should be wary. Whitehall ought not to suppose that this sense of solidarity would last long. 'While there are many individuals (most Dutchmen ... the German Economics and Finance Ministries) who will not forget or forgive,' the memorandum advised, 'the anger at the French is bound to wear off.' Officials had their jobs to do, and would 'sooner or later want to fall back into the former rhythm'. Their anger, in any case, was not primarily sympathetic but self-pitying. It was 'based more on the damage done to Community co-operation ... than on the resulting exclusion of Britain from the Community'. Britain's exclusion, however regrettable, would soon be accepted as a fact. Therefore, the author suggested, the British should be aware of a certain urgency. Their objectives might not yet be finally decided, he noted, but whatever they were, 'it would be easier to realise them this month than next, and progressively more difficult as we advance into the spring and summer'.

There were other complications. The Five were by no means agreed among themselves. The Germans and the Belgians, though tempted by vengeance against the French, thought it impossible to hold up the work of the Community for long. Only the Dutch, the author judged, 'are seriously considering punitive action in this field'. While the Germans were interested in stopping the passage of any regulations that might create still more obstacles against Britain joining one day, they saw 'juridical difficulties' in an attempt by the Five to engage in subversive consultations. 'The French would, it must be assumed, not take part. In their absence it would be difficult for the Five to pretend to the French that they were not consulting us multilaterally. And there would be two substantial difficulties: first, Luxembourg would keep the French fully informed, and might be even more active on France's behalf; secondly, as time went on, it would only be realistic to suppose that one or other of the Five would have interests not altogether divorced from those of France, the united front of the Five and Britain would be broken, and our own position might be very difficult.'

Of one thing, however, the author was certain. The idea of mere 'association' with the Community, which had always been the ambition of Conservative politicians who wanted to have it both ways, was unacceptable. Many schemes to this end were already floating round Brussels, many ways of getting Britain at least half engaged in the European enterprise, with some of the benefits and fewer of the costs and much of the great advantage, as the Five saw it, of a British presence in counterpoise to the French. But those who favoured this 'do not seem to have thought out the practical difficulties in any detail'. 'I have firmly stated our objections to any form of Association,' the writer reported, 'especially the fact that it would not provide for "political" relations with the Community.'[1]

This was a grand announcement, especially coming from a relatively junior man on what remained of the UK delegation to the Brussels negotiations. The texture of the despatch – cold-eyed analysis, anonymous sourcing, conspiratorial realism – had a personal flavour. Its tone, confident, assertive and effortlessly Machiavellian, is to be found littered through the public records extending down many years of the British engagement with 'Europe'. Its author, in the British way with civil servants, was and is almost unknown outside the circle of government. Yet in Whitehall and Brussels his name acquired the aura of a legend, which is duly celebrated in the secret, official history of the negotiations that finally secured British entry into the Community in 1972.

'To get into the Community,' the Foreign Office's official historian wrote, 'this country had to follow an extremely strait and narrow path, maintaining the true objective, overcoming disappointments, above all resisting the temptations of plausible but inadequate alternatives. The man who did most for many years by rigorous argument and strong determination to hold us to this strait and narrow path is Mr John Robinson.'[2]

In 1963, John Robinson was thirty-eight, and in the middle of a Foreign Office career which had not by then taken on the aberrant aspects it later acquired. His formation was conventional: private education at Westminster School, followed by Oxford, where he read Greats at Christ Church – though a hint of perversity is supplied by the absence of either of these details from his entry in Who's Who. Between school and university, he did service in the Air Force, as a non-commissioned officer, just getting in on the war. In 1949, he sat the Foreign Office exam, and was one of eight applicants, out of 400, selected for entry: those were the days when the brightest and the best still saw public service as a career-option of unrivalled fascination. In his first six years, Robinson did a tour in Delhi, another in Helsinki, as well as time in the FO bureaucracy at home. It was an ordinary beginning.

In 1956, he was sent to Paris, to Gladwyn Jebb's embassy, and this was the beginning of something else. This something else, the unique attribute Robinson was allowed to acquire, was summarized by the official historian: 'For some fifteen years he has worked in Paris, Brussels and London, uninterruptedly on Community affairs, and has become an unrivalled authority upon them.' In a department famous for despatching Japanese linguists to Bogotá, and Arabists to Iceland lest they get too familiar with the natives of the Middle East, Robinson was allowed to become a real European expert.

When Edward Heath was assembling the team to do Macmillan's work, Robinson was, through previous experience in Paris, a natural candidate. When that work collapsed in ruins, furthermore, it was Robinson who stayed behind in Brussels for the next four years, reading the runes, working the chancelleries, laying the basis for what he could not help becoming: the keeper of the memory of every telling detail, and every significant character, in the lengthy saga that was played out between the preparation for Britain's first application in 1961 and the consummation of her last in 1972.

So this made Robinson rare enough. He was maintained in place, allowed to absorb a history, perforce became the continuity man during the lean years between the first and final acts. His performance at the climax drew an official verdict that verged on the ecstatic. 'In the negotiations, he knew everyone, understood everything, foresaw everything, did everything,' the history records. Yet even that, apparently, didn't quite say enough for Robinson, all things considered. The author wanted to be more precise. 'His most important service, I think, came in the years *between* the first and last negotiations.'

Robinson was not a conventional Foreign Office type. Though formed normally, he sometimes behaved abnormally. Urbanity, for example, was not his style. 'He was a wild man,' one ineradicably urbane contemporary told me. Another remembered that he did not always play by the diplomatic rules. There were better ways, he thought, to serve his country. When Heath was negotiating on Macmillan's behalf in 1962, Robinson's main task was to act as an intelligence agent in the rival camps. He moved behind enemy lines, gaining unrivalled knowledge of their intentions. 'At our meetings to work out the next week's negotiating problems,' a member of the team told me, 'Robinson would produce a complete dossier on the thinking of the French and the others. We thought he bugged their offices.'

'In brilliance, in knowledge of Europe, in his readiness to confront the grandest in the land, John was unique,' said Roy Denman, a Whitehall partner-in-belligerence.[3] But these very qualities made him, as it was said, 'difficult'. Robinson himself, when I met him in retirement in the mid-1990s, talked self-effacingly about the mundane life he had led in Whitehall, doing the job he had to do for 'my shop' – otherwise known as the Foreign Office. His conversation revealed little of the brilliance, still less of the burning commitment to European integration (this was the time of deep controversy over the Treaty of Maastricht, for which he did not seem to be an enthusiast), that his reputation led one to anticipate. But another of his contemporaries, David Hannay, himself no paragon of modesty, called Robinson 'unbelievably able'. 'He was a brilliant civil servant, he drafted beautifully, he was a superb, ruthless negotiator.'[4]

Yet what singles Robinson out for a place in both the history and the bureaucratic anthropology of these years is something else again. Not only is it unusual for a Foreign Office official to retain the same professional interest for more than a decade, it is rarer still for members of that department, especially junior ones, to become associated with –

indeed, to form the militant vanguard of – a distinctive policy position. The Foreign Office has been marked often enough by an attitude, a state of mind, an institutional bias that became in due course the object of wrath and castigation by those, whether contemporary politicians or retributive historians, who disagreed with it. But such intellectual phases have usually been driven from the top. The appeasement of pre-war Germany, the adulation of post-war America, the seductions of Arabism, the lure of power as against the case for an international morality: all are deformities plausibly laid at the door of the institution which has seen party politicians of every stripe take their transitory place under its grand imperial ceilings. And the collective orthodoxy of the Foreign Office throughout the 1950s was, of course, decisive in shaping, rather than challenging, the responses of politicians who, at bottom, wanted most of all to see their own anti-Europe prejudices reinforced.

In 1961, when Macmillan redefined Britain as a country whose interest lay in seeking to join the European Economic Community, the Office responded smartly enough. It did its duty without objection, for those who run it have always been realistic about the locus of power. It had begun, indeed, to do more than that. Among Whitehall departments, it showed the most enthusiasm for Macmillan's idea. It was beginning to share his anxiety about the condition of a Britain that was in danger of ostracism from the table of the great powers. Alongside the Treasury's pessimism about the economic case for British entry into the Common Market – otherwise put, the Treasury's blind optimism about the stand-alone potential of the British economy – sat the Foreign Office's burgeoning pessimism about the political consequences of Britain's exclusion from influence in Europe, something which the whole of British history had been devoted to retaining.

Even so, when the veto occurred, it could not be said that the Foreign Office was well prepared for the future to which Macmillan and the Government were committed. The European culture-graft had by no means fully taken. There were numerous officials, especially in the higher ranks, whose background left a stamp they found hard to obliterate, even in the rather rare cases when they tried. Trained in Anglo-Americanism, pickled in the heritage of Commonwealth, they were slow to remake themselves as Europeans. Many of the senior people never really did so. Throughout Whitehall, Europe was a generational, as well as an attitudinal, issue. Burke Trend, who was soon to be the Cabinet secretary, continued to show the hand he had exhibited as the author of the crucial pre-Messina exercise in Whitehall scepticism.[5] An inveterate

Commonwealth man, Trend once confided to a friend that his career would ideally have culminated not in the Cabinet Office but as high commissioner to Canada.

On the other hand, not only the Macmillan initiative but the passage of time left a significant residue of committed talent, of which John Robinson was but one element. The young men who had despaired of their superiors' hidebound disdain for the Schuman Plan and the Messina project were rising up the hierarchy. The emblematic figure of Michael Palliser, Spaak's son-in-law, having watched post-Suez politics from the Paris embassy, was made head of the Planning Staff in 1964, a plum position of influence. Donald Maitland, though still mainly an Arabist, was personally selected to be in charge of the vital task of press relations for the Heath delegation. Oliver Wright had moved into 10 Downing Street, as the foreign affairs private secretary.

And other contemporaries, later to play a significant part in the acting out of Britain's struggle to become – or avoid becoming – a European country, now begin to make their appearance. For the first time the name of Michael Butler, probing and enraging Gaullist circles from his position as first secretary in Paris, emerges in the PRO files, the beginning, as he rather grandly put it in a retirement memoir/polemic, of 'my long *servitudes et grandeurs européennes*'.[6] Butler, who rose through every important European policy job to become the UK ambassador to the Community during the sulphuric years of Prime Minister Thatcher, 1979–85, was, along with Palliser, the archetypal Foreign Office European, sharing with Robinson a trait that made both of them especially mistrusted in the rest of Whitehall. Neither was prepared to leave the accountancy side of the enterprise to the Treasury's exclusive judgement. Butler, like Robinson, could not be accused of being economically illiterate. Each man added this dimension to the otherwise threadbare credentials of most British diplomats to talk about the intricacies which are at the heart of all European negotiation. Whether calculating the odds on cereal deficiency payments or mastering the finer points of the hard écu, cocktail urbanity would never be enough.

Emerging here, in short, was a new, younger breed of Foreign Office orthodoxy, to replace the old scepticism. An elite regiment was taking shape. Europe wasn't yet the path of choice for every ambitious diplomat, but it promised to be much more interesting than the Commonwealth, and offered a prospect of influence greater than anything else available in a second-order power engaged with the global rigidities of the Cold War. By 1963, a corps of diplomats was present in and around the

Foreign Office who saw the future for both themselves and their country inside Europe. The interests of their country and their careers coincided. It was an appealing symbiosis. The fact that France had, for the moment, obstructed it was less a deterrent than a challenge to their ambition.

As a torch-bearer for this challenge, its most obdurate and devious exponent, nobody, as the historian implied, had a longer record than John Robinson. But one man, in the core years of the period, was more senior and therefore more important still than Robinson, and that man, as it happens, was the historian himself.

Sir Con O'Neill, the author of the secret history, was writing about the period when he was Robinson's immediate superior. O'Neill led the enterprise on which Robinson served, the final negotiations for entry, 1971–2. In the project of Europe, they were comrades: as exotic, by Foreign Office standards, as each other: a most potent combination of talents.

O'Neill's peculiarity lay not in his manner, which was diplomatic if somewhat professorial. Nor did he acquire enemies through an overbearing policy commitment that he was determined, by any devious means, to force past other Whitehall departments: the way Robinson is remembered. O'Neill, a man of great reclaim in Foreign Office mythology, was singular for twice quitting the department on matters of principle, or at least rebellion, beginning with a protest against the pre-war appeasement of Hitler. His role as official historian of his own work was the culmination of another sudden departure and return. Refused the ambassadorship to Bonn in the mid-1960s, he left the Office in a huff. But ministers summoned him back, having decided he was the indispensable figure to lead the official side of the negotiations. In that task, he regarded nobody as less dispensable than John Robinson, to whom he paid an extraordinary epitomizing tribute from one bureaucrat to another. 'I sought his advice many hundreds of times,' O'Neill the historian writes, 'and can scarcely remember an occasion when I failed to follow it.'

They became a professional pair, O'Neill the senior, Robinson his earth-scorching ally: Robinson the man of fire, O'Neill the restraining force. 'If Con hadn't been there,' said Michael Palliser, 'John might have wrecked everything by his single-minded determination to win, and not minding how he did it.'[7]

On the matter of Europe, O'Neill went back a long way: most distantly to his disgust for appeasement, but more recently to a misjudged response to the Schuman Plan. We have heard his name before.

After the war, employed as a leader-writer on *The Times*, he directed the paper's European policy with a sceptical bias against Churchill's grand effusions. 'A premature attempt by governments to force union on Europe, before it is wanted, can only make divisions deeper,' is a sample of his early post-war thinking about the earliest efforts that were being advanced, especially, by the Americans.[8] Back in the Foreign Office, he was posted to Germany in 1948, where he decided that the Schuman Plan could be ignored. 'I am ashamed to say that I did not realise its enormous importance,' he later told Michael Charlton.[9] The misjudgement, which was just about universally shared, did not damage his career. He served, with angular distinction, more an intellectual than a social man, in Peking and Helsinki, before returning to his prime focus of interest.

In 1963, O'Neill became head of the United Kingdom delegation to the European Communities (the plural signifying that there were still separate communities: for the Market, for Coal and Steel and for Euratom). Here he reacquainted himself with Robinson, whom he had previously met when they were both involved in the early phase of Macmillan's conversion, Robinson as an under-strapper, O'Neill in a more senior position. Robinson, in particular, was committed to this cause. His contemporary, Christopher Audland, remembers their time together, after Macmillan had begun to feel his way round the issue, sitting in the same Foreign Office room, sifting the replies from White-hall to the Prime Minister's questionnaire, shaping the responses in the right direction. They were not bloodless officials, but men who had decided what they thought and were now determined to help bring it about.

It is Audland's opinion that Robinson's contribution was the biggest of all, even though his rank was never high. 'He was the most influential official from 1961 to 1973,' he told me in 1994. 'He knew what he wanted. He was very clear strategically, but also tactically.' O'Neill, however, was the senior of the two, and therefore possibly the more important. Let us say that each, in his way, made a significant contribution to British history. In the middle years of the 1960s, followed by the early years of the 1970s, these two men had as much as anyone to do with keeping alive the conception that Britain belonged in the Common Market, and then bringing the embryonic idea to birth.

Something broader was also signified in their appointment to Brussels. It marked the establishing-in-place of the elite regiment. The Foreign Office was not yet run by Europeans, but the positions of influence on the Europe question were given to people who believed in its importance. They were a minority in the Office, but had majority control of the policy they cared about. The sceptics preferred to go, or were sent, elsewhere. Not that they were seen as sceptics. Such a term would imply the existence of an argument in which there had been winners and losers, an environment, such as developed in politics twenty years later, where sides had to be chosen and opinions were taken down in evidence. But in the early 1960s the new orthodoxy had not seized general hold. For many in the Office, and more in Whitehall as a whole, Europe was still a side-show. If anything, 'Europeans' were seen by their elders as a little off-centre: people who, because they happened to be captured by this unpromising cause which de Gaulle now appeared to have nullified, could be allowed to roam around their chosen playground.

The regiment, however, was disciplined. It knew where it wanted to get to, even though O'Neill and Palliser and Robinson and Butler were each men of different stamp, their intellects and emotions about Europe differently arranged. Whereas Palliser had a credal, not to mention family, affiliation, Robinson always claimed to be no more than a mechanic. He despised 'belief'. When I saw him thirty years later, he represented himself as a man who had merely done his best for 'my shop'. His allusions to his work, which were reluctantly given, emphasized its technical aspects: his reading of de Gaulle's intentions, his secret connections with the Dutch (always his best sources), the optimal ordering of papers to be circulated, or not, around Whitehall, the need to match the self-interested brutalities of the Quai d'Orsay. In the many interviews and conversations I had before writing this book, nobody's language was freer than Robinson's of the prophetic abstractions that so often accompany the European discourse. He was a practical man, from the beginning. 'I wrote a paper after the veto,' he said, 'pointing out how many telephones, how many refrigerators, how many washing-machines there were per 100,000 inhabitants of France. Things we'd been absolutely convinced we were superior in. But we were not superior. Nobody troubled to look them up, but I'd looked them up. My figures were accepted.'[10]

But not by everyone. At least, not by everyone immediately. For the elite regiment was taking shape before its generals, the politicians of the new Labour Government, had reached the same level of strategic certainty.

The story of the 1960s, after Macmillan and after Gaitskell, reveals a contrast of mentalities. On the one hand, officialdom, the diplomatic side of Whitehall, was beginning to nurture, at its policy-making core, a conviction that there was no alternative to British membership of the Common Market: a view accompanied by no less adamant professional vows that the French must be defeated in their refusal to permit this to come about. On the other hand, the politicians of the moment remained less sure. In politics, to begin with, nothing was changed by the veto. If anything, it stimulated a rebirth of the old hostility, and it certainly rekindled the old and chronic disagreements. Among the relevant politicians, with a handful of exceptions there was no matching clarity of purpose, no parallel willingness to shake off the incubus of past glories and future fantasies. De Gaulle's conduct, apart from rendering early entry impossible, had, for many politicians, only assisted in confirming their native dislike of Europe, and their suspicion of its schemes and stratagems.

This did not last very long. The influence of the committed soon began to bear down on the uncertain heads of those who would ideally have preferred not to be obliged to make a choice. The logic of the washing-machine was communicated from Robinson into the reluctant, but finally unresisting, mind of a new Prime Minister. Ultimately, the political class was cornered.

Two groups of public servants, who admittedly displayed different levels of angst, now made a serious effort to succumb to reality: the younger vanguard at the Foreign Office, and the inheritors, both young and old, of the mantle of British socialism. We are now entering the middle period of the saga of political ineptitude: of prolonged and agonized uncertainty, followed by the most grudging submission to trends that had been visible for a long time before.

*

LABOUR WON THE ELECTION, in October 1964, without any serious debate about Europe having taken place. The application for entry was Macmillan's last throw, and the veto was his last straw, as Rab Butler smirkingly indicated to Anthony Wedgwood Benn. So the issue was latent, a large failure added to the other disintegrations which his successor, Sir Alec Douglas-Home, was obliged, after thirteen years of Tory rule, to try and defend. But it was not made much of. The Labour manifesto clung to the old world, in which choices could be blurred. 'Though we shall seek to achieve closer links with our European

partners,' it said, 'the Labour Party is convinced that the first responsibility for a British Government is still the Commonwealth.' The party
stood by the five conditions it had defined as central in 1962: 'binding'
Commonwealth safeguards, freedom to pursue an independent foreign
policy, pledges kept to partners in EFTA (the residual second division of
non-EEC members), the right to plan the British economy, guarantees
for British agriculture.

Labour also had a new leader, with strongly anti-European credentials. Harold Wilson came from the left of the party, which had for many
years, after its early anti-American flirtations with European federalism,[11]
folded an anti-EEC position into its collection of socialist concerns.
Gaitskell, in declaring against the 1961 application, chose to betray his
friends before his country; for Wilson there was no such complication.
He had led the conference in rising to Gaitskell's glorious philippic. But,
to be elected leader, he did not need to state a position on European
integration: in the 1960s, as in the 1950s when Macmillan beat Butler
for the Tory leadership, the issue was low to the point of obscurity in
the assessment of the relevant electorate. More pleasing to the Labour
MPs of the day was Wilson's way with words, his brilliant capacity to
have it both ways, the scornful elegance he brought to bear on the
frailties of the other side. Although the veto, by keeping Britain out, had
saved her from the fate that Wilson as well as Gaitskell affected most to
fear, the new leader-presumptive did not hesitate to ridicule Macmillan's
failure. 'Naked in the conference room is one thing,' he told the
Commons on 31 January 1963. 'Naked and shivering in the cold outside,
while others decide our fate, is an intolerable humiliation.'

In the beginning, the new Government could believe its fate was in
no one's hands but its own. It, apparently, was the master now. That
was the state of mind in which it entered power. It seemed to recognize
that the Commonwealth, however keenly defended by Labour romantics,
did not close the argument about the British economy which, all Labour
spokesmen vowed, would be placed on the road to recovery only by the
application of socialist remedies. The economy, they knew, was what
mattered, and they did not doubt that the Tory record of low growth
and persistent balance of payments crises could be reversed. Shortly after
de Gaulle's veto, Richard Crossman, Wilson's leading propagandist, told
American readers that Britain's attempt to enter Europe had derived
from a pessimism spreading through Whitehall, industry and the City
which was 'completely foreign to the mood of the Labour Party'. 'Surely
it is a good thing', he added, 'that one of Britain's two great parties is

still passionately convinced that this country has a future – outside the Common Market.'[12]

This was what the party, with only a few exceptions, thought. Even the core of Labour pro-Marketeers grouped around Roy Jenkins, the *salon* of Gaitskell's *refusés*, found themselves for the moment put still further out of face by the General. Anthony Crosland, though not so committed a European as Jenkins, was a bellwether figure, the party's most celebrated ideologist. In the revised (1964) edition of his essential text, *The Future of Socialism*, there is no reference to the EEC.[13]

Other matters dominated the early months of the 1964 Government. A National Plan, designed to end the stop–go cycle that had been the curse of the post-war economy, was wheeled enthusiastically into place. Planning in one country was seen not only as the apotheosis of a modernized socialism but a repudiation of the European alternative: most of Wilson's main speech against the Macmillan application, delivered in the Commons in June 1962 when he was the shadow Foreign Secretary, had attacked the Treaty of Rome and the culture of its signatories on the specific ground that they were profoundly anti-socialist. 'The plain fact is that the whole conception of the Treaty of Rome is anti-planning, at any rate national planning,' Wilson then said. The only planning allowed in Europe was 'for the one purpose of enhancing free competition', he railed. To the enactment of this paean of belief in state economic planning the Wilson Cabinet turned most of its energies between 1964 and 1966. The European option was relegated to a negligible parenthesis.

This condition was replicated in Brussels, where the British option seemed equally void of relevance. One of Con O'Neill's jobs, as the new head of delegation, was to submit an annual report on the EEC's goings-on. At the end of 1964 he was obliged to record that British relations 'appeared to drift even further away from the foreground of Community thinking'. He added: 'The fact that our most positive contacts with the Community throughout 1964 concerned the subject of patents typifies the trivial level to which our working relations with the Community are now confined.' The Community itself, meanwhile, was developing fast. The rage against the French soon dissipated, and the regiment did not hesitate to warn its masters about what could be discerned. O'Neill quietly set down the ominous words. 'The inexorable process of adding little by little to the corpus of intra-Community decisions, doctrine and commitments has brought further divergence,' he noted.[14]

For a time, as it happened, this analysis was overtaken by events. In the middle of 1965, the Community experienced a heavy crisis that brought divergence within rather than without. The Treaty of Rome, one must always remember, was a beginning and not an end: since its signing, every year had been devoted to the practical evolution of its meaning in terms of real agreements, serious surrenders of national sovereignties, collective study and action on the common policies it envisaged. Through 1964, these had progressed so well – it was O'Neill's point – that the prospect arose of a full customs union, covering both agricultural and industrial products, being completed by mid-1967, more than two years ahead of the target date laid down in the Treaty. But in June 1965 there was another crisis of the French. The Council of Ministers failed to agree on arrangements for the future financing of the Common Agricultural Policy, the lynchpin of French design and interest. Not only did France, having failed to get her way, temporarily withdraw her ministers from meetings of the Council, bringing its policy-making to a halt, but General de Gaulle used the moment to launch a wide attack both on the powers of the Commission and on the very existence of majority voting in the Council, due, according to the Treaty, to start in 1966. Never an admirer of the Monnet–Schuman concept, the General came to power too late to stop it happening, but was regularly searching for ways to undermine its artefacts of supra-nationalism. An impasse developed. For the rest of 1965, nothing of substance occurred. For that period, the congruence between Britain's official lack of interest and the EEC's manifest inertia rendered O'Neill's gloom a little academic.

The inner momentum carrying the island towards the continent, however, had not entirely stopped. Although Wilson was comfortable with his anti-Europe railleries, and believed in his stand-alone National Plan, it is clear enough that he never repudiated Macmillan's ambition. Nor, at bottom, had Gaitskell done so. Gaitskell's summons to what sounded like a millennial battle for an independent Britain in fact concealed, as he disarmingly stated, the intention to resume the attempt to enter the EEC at some future date. Even in his ferocious defence of a thousand years of history, he kept open the door for a five-year change of mind. Deep down, and aware of the economic realities, he had to be ambivalent. Yet any ambivalence Gaitskell could muster was but a prelude to the efforts of Harold Wilson, a man whose entire political nature, what some might call his genius, was defined by his mastery of ambiguity.

Very soon, in the documents, the nuances are beginning to change. This starts, naturally, with the officials. Already in April 1965, Michael

Palliser, from the Foreign Office's Planning Department, gives an early glimmering of revisionism. Noting the abruptness with which some junior minister has recently invoked Labour's five restrictive conditions for contemplating accession to the Community, Palliser circulates an advisory rebuttal, cast in words of painful respect, suggesting that the reiteration of these conditions is no longer helpful. 'It is not for me to comment on the political importance within this country of laying emphasis on the five points,' Palliser disingenuously states. But the Government was now conducting 'a genuine reappraisal' of Britain's role in Europe, and 'any continuing insistence on the five conditions will seriously hamper HMG's efforts in this direction'. It would 'keep ... suspicion alive', and 'disturb our friends'.[15] Although it is true to say that, for much of 1965, the tone of the Foreign Office files reveals a state of extreme pessimism about Britain's prospects of *ever* getting into the Community, the regiment is plainly preparing to play a long game.

In the early days of 1966, it takes another stride forward. O'Neill, who has agreed to make a public speech in the Netherlands, submits the text of it for approval by the Office, with a mordant covering note that says, 'I think the general effect is fair and loyal enough to present British policy – or rather lack of policy.' He uses the opportunity to stress as much of the positive as he can, remarking how much attention the British were paying to the Common Market's French-inspired crisis, which 'proves how far my country has gone towards thinking of the fate and fortunes of the rest of Western Europe as inseparable from its own'. He has no doubt, this unelected officer says, that British public opinion is 'more and more coming to see our future as involving closer and closer connections with the rest of Western Europe'. He mentions the problem of sovereignty only, soothingly, to dismiss it: 'Experience in many fields has taught us that every international relationship affects our sovereignty and that exaggerated national independence is ineffective. ... The problem lies more in the practice than in the principles.' As for O'Neill's conclusion, which the Office does not restrain him from uttering, it is extravagantly prophetic. 'I venture to express the purely personal view', he told the Dutch, 'that, should we ever succeed in joining the Community, we may well be found to be the champions rather than the opponents of its "supra-national" aspects.'

To balance this enthusiasm, he counsels against excessive zeal, urging that the wish to join the Community was 'not the same thing as the wish to undergo conversion to a new religion'. Although some regarded the Treaty of Rome 'as Holy Writ, whose every comma breathes divine inspiration ... I hope the Community will not insist on baptism by total immersion'.[16] But O'Neill's underlying message, approved by London, speaks for a Britain whose eagerness is qualified only by stoic resignation to facts of life that are probably temporary.

And so it proves, at a higher level as well. Some time in January, the wheels begin to turn a little faster, not just among officials but among a secret group of ministers. On 26 January, a minute records the formation of a committee of top officials to recommence the work of examining the overall economic impact on Britain, especially of the Common Agricultural Policy. Chaired by Sir Eric Roll, a key member of the Macmillan negotiating team and now permanent secretary at the Department of Economic Affairs, it includes unusually senior people from the Treasury, Foreign Office, Board of Trade and so on, and will operate under special conditions. Its brief has been approved by Prime Minister Wilson and his Foreign Secretary, Michael Stewart, but no other minister is meant to know that the committee even exists. Collective responsibility will be delayed. The rubric is explicit. 'Officials would neither report to ministers that they were working on questions connected with our future relations with Europe, nor inform them how the work was progressing.' Only after the work was completed would the Prime Minister decide whether to inform his colleagues.[17]

Nothing of this tendency, so far, was public. At the March 1966 election, which he called to improve on Labour's modest 1964 majority, Wilson continues to present himself as a leader who holds the continentals in utmost suspicion. Scepticism is his tone, though he affects a grudgingly open mind. If the conditions are right, Britain will consider it, he says, parading himself as a hard-nosed negotiator. 'My own experience of negotiations goes back twenty years,' he told an election audience at Bristol. 'It started with the most difficult of the lot, the Russians.' His best-remembered line, reeking of John Bullish defiance, was a riposte to the recent welcome which his main opponent, Edward Heath, had given to the ending of the Common Market's crisis, and to new murmurings of fraternity from the French. 'One encouraging gesture from the French Government,' Wilson spat, 'and the Conservative leader rolls on his back like a spaniel ... Some of my best friends are spaniels, but I would not put them in charge of negotiations into the Common Market.'

Already, however, Wilson was setting course for an attempt at entry. Never did a cure-all economic nostrum have a shorter life than his National Plan. As the Roll committee started work, word was seeping out to supportive ministers like George Brown, the most senior and voluble pro-European in the Cabinet. It began even before the election. On 20 January, Brown goes to lunch with the newspaper tycoon, Cecil King, chairman of the *Daily Mirror*, who records in his diary Brown excitedly bringing the lunch forward a week 'to tell me that Wilson is deciding to enter the Common Market!'[18] The King diary, coming out of a newspaper that was close to Labour and strongly pro-Europe, tracks the private world of Wilson and Brown, the tycoon's regular lunch companions, through 1966. Wilson's own conversion seems to have been sealed much earlier than he let on. Less than three weeks after the election, on 19 April, after seeing Wilson for an hour, King recounts: 'About Europe, he said he thought we should be in in two or three years.'

It was not only the logic of the elite regiment that effected this change in the prevailing bias of the Government. Events themselves were exposing the thinness of the alternative analysis. Consider, for example, the Commonwealth. Wilson, like Gaitskell, was by temperament a Commonwealth man. Although the evidence of a long-term downward trend away from Commonwealth trade could not be refuted, this special British relationship with a multi-racial Third World was something with great appeal to the Labour soul, of which Wilson always considered himself the prime custodian. But the middle 1960s saw a rending of both the economic and political ties with the Commonwealth. In November 1965, Rhodesia declared for unilateral independence, which laid on Wilson's back the burden of trying to undo this intolerable exercise in white supremacy. The task preoccupied him, humiliatingly, for years, and he never succeeded. His failure, therefore, also provoked great bitterness against Britain from much of the rest of the Commonwealth, especially in Africa but also, before long, in white Canada and Australia. Sentiments of affection, which in 1964 were proposed as a central feature of Labour's world view and the viable basis for an alternative to Europe, began to vanish on both sides.

Simultaneously, the defence aspect of British globalism was being exposed as a costly charade. The country's role as a kind of deputy world policeman, alongside the US, could not be sustained. Here the soul of Labour had long been pressing the party's leaders to cut defence spending, but the leaders, for the first couple of years, resisted these emotional directives. In the case both of the currency and of the military, Wilson was bent on proving to the people and the world, and perhaps to himself, that Labour government was not to be associated with retrenching the symbols of national greatness. Such an ambition could not last long. Retreat from the world forced itself on the managers of the nation's finances, and in July 1967 the process culminated in a defence white paper announcing the end of Britain's presence East of Suez by the mid-1970s. The Commonwealth was shocked. The Australians were 'appalled and dismayed', the leader of Singapore, Lee Kuan Yew, was 'fighting mad' and threatened commercial revenge.[19] The American President, Lyndon Johnson, declared an epitaph, writing to Wilson of his disappointment 'upon learning this profoundly discouraging news . . . tantamount to British withdrawal from world affairs'.

But the consequence was, surely, obvious. With the political and the military engines of neo-imperialism all but turned off, a reassessment of Britain's role could produce only one conclusion. Whether or not she entered the Common Market, it was in her local region, grappling with her age-old neighbours, under the umbrella of Nato but also in some kind of new political and economic alignment, that her future was bound to lie.

The final awareness of this was borne in on Wilson only months after he had vowed never to be a spaniel. The Government experienced the first of several economic crises. In July 1966, a run on the pound was followed by a heavy deflationary package that put paid to the extravagant growth targets on which most of Labour's promises were based. The Crossman pronunciamento – 'this pessimistic conclusion . . . completely foreign to the Labour Party' – was shattered. As if to underline one inner meaning of this, in the Cabinet reshuffle that followed, George Brown became Foreign Secretary. To the enemies of 'Europe', this was a fatal signal. It could just as easily have happened that Brown should resign. At the time, he was making one of his frequent threats to do so. Had this been allowed to happen, reflected one of the enemies – deploying a level of hyperbole with which students of Britain's European argument would become more and more familiar – 'the application to join the Market would probably never have been made'.[20]

Crystallizing his plans, Wilson had to take account of these enemies. Not long ago, after all, he had belonged in their camp. But it is entirely improbable that Brown's presence, as a passionate European in charge of the department that would be responsible for implementing the policy, alone prompted the switch that they detested. Long after the event, anti-EEC politicians continued to ponder explanations for the volte-face that Wilson, their reliable friend, appeared to have performed. Douglas Jay,

President of the Board of Trade at the time, could barely credit it. Did not the political and economic case against entry remain exactly as it was when Wilson made his derisive election speech in Bristol? 'An intelligent man', wrote Jay, 'does not, on rational grounds, alter his entire view on a fundamental issue affecting the whole future of his country in six or seven months, when the facts have not changed.' Jay put the conversion, which he regarded as a kind of treason, down to Wilson's susceptibility to pressure, especially from the press, along with the arrival of George Brown to articulate it. The figure of Cecil King, 'a pro-Market extremist' and a friend and former employer of Brown, looms large in the Jay demonology. And, in the Wilson years, King was indeed a sinister presence who tainted them, not long after this, by seeking, until removed by fellow directors alarmed for his sanity, to deploy his newspapers in support of an anti-democratic coup against the elected Government and the installation of a ministry of unelected talents, including himself.

More reliable witnesses to the Wilson odyssey in this matter are to be found among colleagues who, while being almost as sceptical of Europe as was Jay, retained a certain dispassion in their observation of the leader's tactics. Both Richard Crossman and Barbara Castle, in their diaries for 1966, reveal mounting suspicion of what he was up to. Never did he openly explain what he intended. That was the Wilson way, surrounded as he was by Cabinet colleagues who split about evenly in their enthusiasms, with eight of them firmly against any new application for entry.[21] Although Wilson was going round among his non-political friends like King vowing to be 'one politician, and a Prime Minister at that, [who] is honest with the public', neither the public nor his colleagues were yet judged ready for the revelation. Mrs Castle, however, knew what he was doing, and summarizes a technique that describes his entire approach to managing power in the fractious Labour environment of those years. 'I remain convinced he is anxious to get in,' she wrote, 'and he has succeeded in guiding us into a discussion of the details, which is more effective than anything else in making principles look less important.'[22]

The regiment, meanwhile, was pushing Wilson forward. O'Neill, in particular, was active, after close consultation with Eric Roll. In August, he wrote a paper, 'How to get into the Common Market', in which his realistic analysis of French intentions concluded with a list of concessions Britain should make to gratify them.[23] He noted that the Ministry of Agriculture was against any softening of the terms, and the Treasury was increasingly alarmed by the short-term ('and not only short-term') disadvantages for the balance of payments. The economic advisers, O'Neill noticed, thought the economy would be unfit to enter the competitive world of a tariff-free Europe for another five years. But he himself saw the matter quite differently. He thought time was ever more of the essence. 'Though the consequences of early entry into the Community may seem economically bleak,' he wrote, 'the long-term economic consequences of continuing on our present relatively independent course look much bleaker; and as time passes, the difficulty and the price of entering the Community will both grow greater.'

O'Neill, in this crucial phase of Wilson's strategic evolution, had become an almost open proselyte. Wilson called an all-day Chequers meeting, on 22 October, at which the Cabinet, after being kept in the dark about Downing Street's machinations, would have its first full European discussion. The Prime Minister was about to spring upon them his own surprise. But among the mass of preparatory papers ministers received was a report from the head of the UK delegation in Brussels which opened with a lapidary statement designed to lift their minds to matters more elevated than mere accountancy: to a vision of high politics, in fact, of the kind that civil servants seldom feel it is their place to articulate.

'For the last 20 years,' O'Neill wrote, 'this country has been adrift. On the whole, it has been a period of decline in our international standing and power. This has helped to produce a national mood of frustration and uncertainty. We do not know where we are going and have begun to lose confidence in ourselves. Perhaps a point has now been reached when the acceptance of a new goal and a new commitment could give the country as a whole a focus around which to crystallise its hopes and energies. Entry into Europe might provide the stimulus and the target we require.'[24]

No politician could have said this in public, and few of the relevant ministers were prepared explicitly to contemplate it in private either. It was, after all, a painful condemnation of what their profession was supposed not to allow to happen. The idea that the country might not know where it was going, after two years of the blessings of Labour, was uncomfortable to contemplate – and some of the Chequers discussion, on the part of the less reverent participants, was devoted to demolishing the premise. Crossman's diary entry for 22 October reveals a strand of Cabinet opinion resisting the insinuation that lay behind the O'Neill note, its search for a new way of being Great Britain. The diarist spoke up for Little England. 'I regard Little England as the pre-condition for any successful socialist planning whether inside or outside the Common Market,' he stated. Along with this should go devaluation of the pound, which the Treasury said was the necessary concomitant of entry, but which Wilson would not hear of. When Crossman declared that 'they shouldn't go into Europe in order to remain great', some other ministers, he says, gave him 'a great deal of support'. Among them was a colleague who was in the middle of one of the many reversions and reconsiderations that have marked his own career. 'Tony Wedgwood Benn', Crossman writes, 'made an extremely good speech asking what was European about us and what was American and whether the Anglo-American relationship isn't worth a great deal more than entry into Europe.'

O'Neill's rendition, however, got close to epitomizing what was present, if only half articulated, in the mind of the Prime Minister. Wilson came to Chequers with a plan up his sleeve which he saw as the necessary prelude to another attempt at entry. He was meticulous, as always, in his dissembling. With a large minority of his friends dead against an application, he needed to couch his strategy as merely indicating a desire to probe the possibilities. But here and now, writes Douglas Jay, 'the fatal slide began'. 'There must be no leaks,' Wilson instructed. 'It would be fatal to have any suggestion which would commit us either for or against entry.'[25] But what he desired not to leak was a decision that had much significance as a gesture towards the truth of O'Neill's analysis. He and George Brown, he said, would embark on a tour of the EEC capitals to sound out the current state of opinion there.

The Probe, as it came to be officially called, was the beginning of a recognition on Wilson's part – never explicitly stated, but surely alive in his subconscious – that Britain did indeed need a new focus for 'its hopes and energies': that, what with Rhodesia and the economic crisis and the sense of drift that was everywhere a subject of media discussion, the Government itself would benefit from a revivalist project: that 'Europe', however regrettably, was becoming the only place to look.

The Wilson–Brown tour of Europe, from January to March 1967, was in many ways the acme of Wilsonian politics. It applied to Europe several of the defining traits of this remarkable leader. It put on show his fascination with tactics, his professional vanity, his impressionable mind, the grandeur of his self-confidence, his refusal to acknowledge the realities of international power. It was at times comical, at others almost calamitous. But, seen from this distance in history, it did, for all its travails and its ultimate nullity, deposit in the realm of inarguable fact the public commitment of a Labour Cabinet to British entry into the Common Market.

The tour, announced in the Commons on 10 November, began in Rome on 15 January. Already Wilson had enraged his Cabinet critics by stepping up the language of intent. 'We mean business,' he told the Commons and several other audiences – it became his pugnacious little catchphrase. The usage, according to Jay, 'went beyond the spirit of the ministers' agreement at Chequers'. Having Brown alongside, moreover, was no consolation to those who hoped this would indeed be no more than a probe. Wilson explained the two-man aspect of the act as being a matter of reassurance: he was the sceptic, Brown the zealot, and they would balance each other out.

Brown's presence, in fact, contributed more to the farcical than the substantive nature of what occurred. Although Wilson, in his own book,[26] records his colleague as giving capable and thorough accounts of the agricultural side of the problem in all six capitals, Brown, as a well-known European, was of small interest to the continental interrogators. His behaviour, in any case, was often an embarrassment. He was frequently drunk, as was his habit at home as well. As a man to work for, his aggression and unpredictability placed the heaviest strain on officials' respect for what they could see as the sound, intuitive, if not exactly Bevin-like, instincts of the unlettered working-class politician. 'When the buzzer went in the private office, one didn't know who would be sitting behind the desk,' Donald Maitland, who had a charitable recollection of working for Brown, told me. 'We were like subalterns leading troops over the top. Either the machine-gunner would open up, or he would be charming. He was completely volatile.' In Europe, he was given to a buccaneering familiarity with people whom, as a sound European, he always thought he could deal with. 'This little Brown,' de Gaulle allegedly once said. 'I rather like him – in spite of the fact that he calls me Charlie.'[27]

The man who mattered, plainly, was Wilson, whose intentions nobody in Europe could divine. And Wilson, from his earlier position of scepticism, now began to find the words that seemed to incorporate Europe into his grander political scheme. From being the enemy of planning, the EEC was now, apparently, the ally of another of his deeper-felt propositions: the need for Britain to become the molten creative centre of the 'white heat of the technological revolution', a phrase he had earlier used to distinguish his own modernizing, futuristic Labour Party from the anachronistic Tories. It now became his bond with

Europe. Much concerned with the danger of what he called the 'industrial helotry' of Europe vis-à-vis the USA, he presented Britain as
Europe's best agent of escape from this fate. What he wanted to see, he
said just after announcing the Probe, was 'a new technological community'. It was his way of persuading Labour that the European option
had a proper link with the party's modern credo. It was also a way of
amplifying one of France's well-known obsessions: of postulating, in
effect, a shared objective. *Le Défi américain* was not only the title of a
famous recent polemic[28] but a summarizing statement of French, and
especially Gaullist, alarm at the penetration of American industry and
technology into their country. Wilson waxed eloquent about the opportunity, together, to reverse the terms of trade.

At each stop, he returned to the technological community, which
had suddenly become, as he saw it, Britain's major selling-point. He
stuck to a hard line on the terms and conditions – the Commonwealth,
EFTA, agriculture, the sterling balances – but did his best to advance
positive messages in favour of a 'strong and independent European
computer industry' and much else on the cutting edge.

More striking than this, however, is the development of his public
discourse. Before the end of January, Wilson was giving the open
impression of a fully evolved European. 'We mean business' was left far
behind by a grand statement not only against industrial helotry but in
favour of the notion that the off-shore island was itself the creation
of the continent, its people indistinguishable from those with whom he,
as the British Prime Minister, was now conversing. Delivered in Strasbourg, the key speech summons up unmistakable echoes of another
speech delivered in the same place fifteen years before, with the same
gaseous promise of a Britain and a Europe that had much more in
common with each other than the actions of either speaker, in reality,
were ever prepared to underwrite.

Wilson's Strasbourg speech in 1963 resembled Churchill's in 1949.
Its appeal to history could not have been more different from those he
had previously uttered, in his guise as a worshipful defender of the
Commonwealth. Our kith and kin, previously the emotive bond with
Commonwealth interest, had, with brilliant facility, changed their location. Two thousand ago, Wilson said, the British people were already
created out of continental stock. And 2,000 years, the statistician typi-
cally noted, was only 'the last one-ten-thousandth' of the period for
which man was estimated to have been on earth, 'less than half a second
of man's hour of history'. A thousand years ago, he went on, the very

name 'England' reflected the origins of European invaders and settlers (presumably the Angles), and modern English law began with the super-imposition of Norman-French laws and forms. The nineteenth-century nation-state, Wilson also emphasized, had given way to concepts of unity and international co-operation. In short, Britain's very history, far from severing her from the continental vision, would apparently be betrayed were she to spurn this natural culmination, the logic of a perfect union.

Douglas Jay does not precisely record his reaction to this effusion, but it must have ignited his worst fears about a former friend for whom his memoirs, by this stage, can only summon up the words 'Wilson oracular, not to say incoherent'.[29]

The tour concluded. The French phase of it, which was obviously the most sensitive, was ruffled by nothing more disturbing than an outburst of boorishness by George Brown, directed at the wife of the British ambassador, Sir Patrick Reilly, whom he profanely chastised for the shortcomings of her staff.[30] But Wilson's approach to de Gaulle did not meet with universal admiration. Crispin Tickell, a coming member of the regiment, recalled being unimpressed by his presentation. Accompanying Wilson, he drew an embarrassed contrast between the Prime Minister's clutter of files and de Gaulle's capacity to hold in his memory everything he wanted to say. This was, Tickell thought, part of a wider pattern. 'I have noticed', he told me, 'that in Anglo-French dealings the French nearly always think their positions through more carefully than we do. We are quicker on our feet, because of ministers' training in the House of Commons. We are more inventive and creative. But in set-piece discussions we tend to be less well prepared, less directed.'[31]

Be that as it may, the encounter appeared to register some meeting of minds. Wilson, at any rate, thought so. When the General opined that he 'had the impression of an England which now really wished to moor itself alongside the continent and was prepared, in principle, to pledge itself to rules in the formulation of which it had played no part', Wilson replied that he felt this reference to 'mooring alongside' was 'important, even historic'.[32]

He soon persuaded the Cabinet that much had been achieved. His own momentum was now unstoppable. The colleagues were summoned, in mid-April, to be told there should be no delay in renewing the application for entry. He found them surprisingly compliant, 'a real turn-up for the book', he telegraphed to Brown, who was in Washington. The fence-sitters had moved over. Only Jay and Healey remained utterly opposed. Everyone else agreed 'we should "have a bash" and, if excluded, not whine but create a Dunkirk-type robust British dynamic'.[33] When, a few days later, Wilson presented a draft statement on the British application and requested unanimous Cabinet support, not one voice was heard to say no.

This now became a public fact – the announcement of the second try was made to the Commons on 2 May – and what is notable is how much had changed in public thinking about Europe during the six years since Macmillan first attempted to interest the British in a change of direction. Though the veto was a setback, it did not put an end to the European debate in Britain: rather, the opposite. After initial anger, the mood settled more closely into one of anxious alarm at what Britain might be missing. For example, Jim Callaghan, the Chancellor of the Exchequer, who was formerly hostile, announced his conversion in terms that probably spoke for many: 'My experience over the last two-and-a-half years has led me to the conclusion . . . that nations are not free at the moment to take their own decisions.' International factors, said Callaghan, had an effect 'which is much more than I had assumed when I took office . . . The argument about sovereignty is rapidly becoming outdated.' The arguments raged back and forth, but the weight of them, in the media and industry and the City and pretty well every interested forum outside politics itself, was leaning ever more consistently on the side of regarding British entry as a probable necessity – if not yet an inevitability.

A welcome sign of this was the increasing honesty of official statements, beginning with Wilson's announcement. In it, he did not pretend there were no uncomfortable aspects. Whereas Macmillan was terrified of specifying openly any of the inconvenient particulars, Wilson did not balk at the consequences of the EEC's now finalized agriculture policy which, he said frankly, would mean food prices rising by 10 to 14 per cent, and the cost of living by 2.5 to 3.5 per cent.[34] To this would be added negative effects on the balance of payments. These had always been the main fears of Jay and his allies, worked out in elaborate and scholarly papers which argued, in effect, that the food-price effect was so enormous, and its inflationary impact on wages so certain, that *nothing* could justify Britain contemplating membership of the Common Market. Wilson rebutted them with the contention, which became the core case for entry and membership for many years after, that, along with finding a place for Britain in the larger political world (a strong Europe, he said, would be able to exert more influence in world affairs 'than at any time in our generation'), membership would be worth all this economic pain because it would lead to a higher rate of industrial growth and an increase in exports.

With one of Wilson's audiences, this found overwhelming favour: the Commons approved the decision by 488 votes to 62. With another, its reception was sceptical to the point of insult: inside a week, de Gaulle, while noting 'with sympathy' Britain's apparent movement towards Europe, held a press conference in which he spoke of the danger of 'destructive upheavals' as a result of British entry into the Common Market, the 'complete overthrow of its equilibrium' that would result, the weakness of sterling and its unsustainable pretensions as a reserve currency.

Wilson was unperturbed by these mixed responses. It was time, instead, for his 'cheeky chappie' side, his stubborn defiance in adversity, not to mention his superior view of the forces of history, to take the field.

Although de Gaulle's verdict, while claiming not to be a veto, was as negative as any sentient observer could imagine, Britain's reaction, voiced by Wilson and not significantly disputed in the country, was to deny its meaning. The leader, committed to an exercise in national assertiveness, was insouciant. In June he visited the General for a tête-à-tête, to exercise what he regularly insisted was his professional gift for diplomacy. When Crossman urged that the Probe be conducted not by Wilson and Brown but by professional diplomats, Wilson had replied, 'I am a professional. I *am* professional, Dick.' 'Harold's illusions of grandeur in foreign policy scare me stiff,' the diarist recorded a little later.[35] The illusionist now assumed a patronizing attitude towards de Gaulle, telling him, as he reported to the Commons, 'why we do not intend to take no for an answer'. Privately, he informed George Brown of the impression he had gained in Paris: 'I found myself watching this lonely old man play an almost regal "mine host" at Trianon, slightly saddened by the obvious sense of failure and, to use his own word, impotence that I believe he now feels ... Against this background I feel paradoxically encouraged. He does not want us in and he will use all the delaying tactics he can ... but if we keep firmly beating at the door ... I am not sure that he any longer has the strength to keep us out.'[36]

Wilson actually told a French journalist that he believed de Gaulle would soon support British entry: a pathetic misreading, as Denis Healey, to do him justice, had always foreseen. He also stepped up his threats of the consequences that would follow any refusal by de Gaulle to acknowledge how seriously the British meant business. One of his junior, but personally intimate, ministers, Lord Chalfont, briefed journalists with a list of the retaliatory measures the Prime Minister was contemplating if the old man did not comply. They reeked of extravagant unreality: abandoning all Anglo-French projects, perhaps withdrawing the entire British Army of the Rhine, maybe refusing to renew the Nato Treaty. When journalists bridled at the improbability of this, the minister said he had come straight from Wilson and dared them not to print it. The little man had mounted his highest horse.[37]

But de Gaulle's impotence, far from inducing him to lower his resistance, soon led him to declare it absolute once again. Britain's own dire condition gave him the pretext, if he needed one. The words he spoke in May, casting doubt on the state of sterling, came ignominiously true in November, when Wilson and his Chancellor, Callaghan, having resisted devaluation for three years, had it forced upon them. From that, it was but a small step to another lecture from Paris, and on 27 November de Gaulle delivered it. It was the usual gnomic performance, critical of Britain's insistence on trying to enter, yet also sardonic in its account of her earlier refusals and delays. The Common Market, the General said, was incompatible with everything that mattered: Britain's relationship with the USA, the way she fed herself, the state of sterling, her enormous external debts. He was not without a certain condescending goodwill towards his wartime ally. He wished 'to see her one day make her choice and accomplish the enormous effort that would transform her'. But there was 'a vast and deep mutation to be effected'.

*

THE SECOND TRY assembled, for the first time, a critical mass of support among the political class for the proposition that Britain should become a European country. The Government was committed, the Opposition agreed, the moving powers in business were desperate, and the people did not dissent. Public opinion, though rattled by the ups and downs and still heavily laced with respondents who said they didn't know what to think, was broadly supportive. There was a national crisis in November 1967, but its cause was devaluation, the great Satan that Wilson had determined to repel which now had its debauching grip upon the currency. The Cabinet did not leave Nato, but it did lose the pound. If anything, Europe now seemed more urgently necessary as a way out of the British crisis. Far from inducing Dunkirkism, the

General's second veto intensified the island's desire to make common cause with the continent. Next day Wilson told the Commons he had no intention of withdrawing the British application. De Gaulle, he said, was in error on sixteen points of fact, which he then recited. 'The great debate will continue, not only in Britain but throughout Europe.'

There was, however, another reaction, which showed that the debate would not continue entirely on Wilson's terms. Coexisting with the anxious passion of the ruling establishment was an opposite sentiment. The conversion was not complete, and the anti-Market ministers by no means gave up. The leader's volte-face, had it produced a result, would have led, as he well knew, to a grand internal struggle: something he thought he could face with confidence but which others were delighted not to contemplate. Now, mercifully, the blurring did not have to continue. 'There was an overwhelming sigh of relief from a clear section of the Cabinet that de Gaulle had saved the Labour Party from having to go ahead with Europe,' one of its members recalled.[38]

This was not the feeling of the Foreign Office, where some new dispositions were being made. The best places were not yet all reserved for the regimental cadres, their allocation showing, rather, the purposeful eccentricity George Brown brought to his role as the maker of top appointments. An obsession with class drove even this passionate pro-European to assign Europe a lower place than some other matters. He promoted into the top job, as permanent under-secretary, Sir Denis Greenhill, not one of the obvious candidates, whose main credential in Brown's eyes was that he was the son of a railwayman. It didn't seem to matter than Greenhill was also soaked in Atlanticism and the Common-wealth, a man whose juices did not rise to Europe. More bizarre was the case of Con O'Neill, who should have been the obvious official ally of any Europeanist minister. O'Neill was due to move from Brussels and become ambassador in Bonn, a post he coveted; but Brown stopped it on the ground that, as an Old Etonian, O'Neill might be unappealing to the leader of the German Social Democrats, Willy Brandt. Annoyed at being passed over, O'Neill promptly resigned from the Office, for the second time.

But O'Neill was not finished, and his allies were moving ahead. The take-over of pro-Europeans in many of the nerve-centres of government was well under way. Michael Palliser, installed in 1966 as the Prime Minister's private secretary, felt he had to warn Wilson before taking the job that he was a passionate European and might therefore be a bad choice. 'We shan't have any problems over Europe,' Wilson assured him, and they never did.[39] Michael Butler, though no longer in line command, having left Paris in March 1965 for a senior post on the Joint Intelligence Committee, remained, as such, an influential watcher. Donald Maitland was Brown's private secretary. Crispin Tickell was head of Chancery in Paris. Increasing numbers of the Palliser generation, coming up behind Greenhill, were in position to fortify, shall we say, those ministers who wanted to pursue rather than challenge Harold Wilson's stated purposes.

Not to be excluded from their number was John Robinson. After four years diligently pursuing the British interest in Brussels, the hench-man and then, more formally, the deputy to O'Neill, he returned to London at the end of 1966. 'I expect you've had enough of the subject, after all these years,' noted a sympathetic young *naïf*, writing from headquarters to Robinson as he was about to leave Brussels.[40] But Robinson was only just beginning the core phase of his career on the European project.

His reporting from Brussels in the lean years was merely a prep-aration for his activities in Whitehall in the fat ones, lasting from the late 1960s through the early 1970s. He returned not to deal with Bolivia, but as a leading operator in the European Economic Organizations Depart-ment, a wanly neutral designation which he immediately set about lobbying to change. The names, he always thought, were revealing. 'It used to be called Mutual Aid, for God's sake,' he expostulated to me. 'That's the way it was looked at in the fifties, a sub-branch of economics which the Foreign Office could let the Treasury and the Board of Trade get on with.' In May 1968, Robinson became head of an office that soon declared itself with unvarnished candour to be the European Integration Department.

He took it over when integration was hardly topmost in the mind of many political leaders. This was an unpropitious time for governmental projects in either Europe or Britain. May was the month of *les événements* in Paris, the pivotal moment, in both time and place, of the social rebellion that marked the multiple liberations of the 1960s. At the height of the Vietnam War, recrudescent Marxism met the Age of Disrespect in an attempted undermining of the established order in many parts of the developed world, France and Britain prominently among them. In France, de Gaulle was struggling to control events inside his own country, let alone remake the shape of Europe. In Britain, devaluation, far from releasing the suppressed energies of the economy, had unleashed a wave of national self-mortification. 'I'm Backing Britain' was the cause to which people were being urged to attach themselves as a patriotic gesture, in lieu of any imperative market reason for doing so. A mood almost of apocalypse prevailed. It had been anticipated a few months earlier by Quintin Hogg MP, who told the Commons: 'Can anyone doubt ... that we are a people that has lost its way? Can anyone deny that the British people is in the act of destroying itself: and will surely do so if we go on as at present?'

Such was the atmosphere of moral decline, the distracting pessimism, with which those who favoured the integrationist project had to grapple. Yet, unpromising though it looked, the period had positive consequences. It turned out, indeed, to be pivotal in another way as well, the beginning of the end for Britain's most formidable antagonist. It set the scene for de Gaulle's final thrust against the British ambition to join the European Economic Community – and for the decisive victory the elite regiment of the Foreign Office finally gained against him.

The central player in this episode, which displayed the regimental influence with rare and brazen clarity, was not, in fact, one of them. This was more than an ironic detail. Brown's eye for unorthodox appointments produced some brilliant, as well as some absurd, results, and one of them was the decision to send as ambassador to Paris not a regular diplomat but a Conservative politician, Christopher Soames. It was one of many signs of the intention, felt by Wilson as strongly as Brown, somehow to 'get through' to de Gaulle, better to read his mind, to cosy up to France, to try and replace an arid defensiveness with intimations of something warmer.

On his frequent, lurching journeys to Paris, Brown found the embassy a terrible place. 'When I used to visit there,' he wrote, 'I seemed to arrive just as they were trying to get the dust-sheets off the furniture; sometimes they didn't even bother to do that.'[41] Soames could be relied on to change all that, being a gregarious man, large of both body and soul. But perhaps his best credential was that he was married to Winston Churchill's daughter Mary, a British connection that even de Gaulle would hesitate to patronize. He was a European of long, consistent stripe, with good French which he disguised in suitably Churchillian *gaucherie*, and an acquaintance with the continental political class that stretched back to the Hague assembly and the other post-war manifestations over which Churchill had presided.

Soames took up his job in Paris in September 1968 naturally intending an audience with de Gaulle to be one of his earliest priorities. The General did not readily make himself available, but on 4 February 1969, a Tuesday, he received the ambassador and his wife at lunch at the

Elysée Palace. For Soames it was a big moment, much manoeuvred for, long anticipated. For de Gaulle it was – who can be sure what it was? Nobody, in the incessant scrutinies that followed, was certain what the General had intended by the occasion: whether, indeed, he intended anything more to be heard than the vaporous ruminations of an autocrat at the lunch-table. Was this a calculated move in the highest of high politics? Or one of those conversations, of which high politicians are sometimes more victim than perpetrator, that acquire, by a series of accidents, a mythic importance far exceeding anything they intended?

At any rate, a conversation took place, the substance of which has resolved itself, over the years, into a residue that is not seriously disputed. It was more a monologue, in which the General described the kind of Europe he would like to see developing. This would be a very different 'Europe' from the EEC, a looser yet broader construct, with more members and wider tasks, yet liberated from some of the supra-national pretensions and invasions of national sovereignty that so offended Gaullist France. Such a Europe, de Gaulle speculated, would be led by the powers that possessed serious armies: France, Great Britain, West Germany and Italy. When Soames commented that the arrangement took little account of the existence of Nato, de Gaulle portrayed it as something necessary in anticipation of the day the Americans departed, and Europe had to look after itself. He did not, he said, conceive the idea as anti-American. But he did propose a radical alteration in the concept of what 'Europe' meant, and who should be allowed to constitute it. Ireland, Norway and Denmark would obviously belong, but most important was Britain, now offered not only membership of the group but a seminal role in discussions leading up to its possible formation. For what the General seemed to be proposing was a series of secret bilateral negotiations between Britain and France, to be followed, if they succeeded, by a British launch of the grand plan, which France would then be heard to endorse, and others invited to join.[42]

There are nuances in this scheme, if it was anything so definitive as to merit that word, which could still be disputable. Its substance was, at one level, not surprising, being of a piece with what the General was always known to believe. He had often hinted at his restlessness with the status quo. In January 1967, during the Probe, he dangled in front of Wilson mysterious talk about the need for 'something entirely new' in Europe, and he repeated the thought when administering his immediate near-veto in May. He never liked a Europe that did not look after its own defence, under the leadership, naturally, of France. And he was always irked by having come to power too late to abort the Treaty of Rome. More than many of his contemporaries, he was also gripped by the case for a Europe that was a player in the mighty hypotheses of the Cold War, a bulwark against the Soviet Union, a pillar of order in a possibly collapsing world. One British observer, close to Soames, read the initiative as a 'consequence of the events of May '68', and added that the occupation of Czechoslovakia by the Russians had also 'inclined him to open the doors of Europe to Britain'.[43]

Whatever his reasons, his proposition startled Soames, who rushed back to the embassy to begin to dissect its meaning, with the help of his diplomatic colleagues. This had to start with getting down on paper what the old man had actually said: not a simple task. Though Soames had many qualities fitting him for the ambassadorial role, retaining details of a conversation was not a skill that sat effortlessly alongside his expansive manners and somewhat unrefined intellect. 'He was a tremendous life-force, and he had a broad sweep of understanding of big problems,' said one of his admirers, David Hannay, the senior man on Soames's staff in his later incarnation as a Brussels commissioner. 'He could absorb masses of detail, though never in writing. It always had to be oral. He was one of the only grown-up men I've ever known whose lips moved when he was reading.'[44]

Even on the oral side, untrained as a professional diplomat, he had limitations. In the hearing of Crispin Tickell, who was among the embassy staff keenly waiting to hear what de Gaulle had said, Soames likened the process of recollection he now attempted to 'trying to tickle bits of garlic out from behind his teeth'.

The mouth and mind, however, were cleaned out to general satisfaction. So sensitive was the conversation that Soames sent a copy of his version of it to de Gaulle's office the next day, for verification. There were hazards in this procedure. The General, speaking as usual without notes, had made no record of his own, and his officials were uncertain exactly what had passed. But, three days after the lunch, word came back from the Quai d'Orsay that the Foreign Minister, Michel Debré, accepted, except for a few phrases, the Soames account.

In Paris, therefore, both the British and the French, while recognizing that something big may have been floated into the diplomatic air, conducted themselves with reasonably measured calm. Later, many of them had their say about what should have happened next. The British, however excited they felt, could have asked for further and better particulars: could have launched an orderly inquiry before giving a response: might then have insisted, if these inquiries got anywhere, that the Gaullist vision should be communicated to the Five, the EFTA countries, and in due course to the Americans, and altogether located in the regular channels that one might expect of an enterprise which, if it were to succeed, demanded fullest consultation with the many allies whose perspectives would be radically altered by it. Soames himself, reflecting later, thought as much. He told Cecil King in April, when the dust had faintly begun to settle on the most incandescent bilateral row between France and Britain since the war, that such a procedure, concerning an offer he personally took seriously, would have been proper. De Gaulle might not have agreed to it. But in that case the talks would not have started, and Britain, thought Soames, would have been 'out in the clear'.[45]

As it was, London's response was quite different. The Soames communiqué arrived in the Integration Department and caused immediate consternation. Here, in the spiritual home of the regiment, the enemy was seen to be striking at their central preoccupation. To John Robinson, as head of the department, and Patrick Hancock, his superintending under-secretary, it was perfectly obvious what de Gaulle had held out to Soames: the wreckage of 'Europe', and the discrediting of all Britain's ambitions to become part of it.

Hancock and Robinson immediately engaged the Foreign Secretary. George Brown, by this time, was no longer in office, his erratic emotions having driven him, finally, to resign. Instead, the Office was now run by the schoolmasterly, punctilious, sometimes rather moralistic Michael Stewart, an obliging pair of hands who had been drafted into the job once before, in 1965, when the chosen incumbent couldn't secure a parliamentary seat, and now returned after Brown had been caught drunk in charge of British diplomacy once too often. Stewart, though a faithful Wilsonian, was at this stage less interested than Brown in Europe. Vietnam and the Biafran secession from Nigeria were the questions that most engaged his capacity for passionate fluency in debate. But plainly the Soames–de Gaulle conversation was a matter of unavoidable priority.

The thesis constructed by Robinson, with Hancock alongside, was that de Gaulle's proposition constituted nothing but a devilish trap. Whichever way you looked at it, it presented Britain with ruinous options. What de Gaulle sought, Robinson insisted, was not to help Britain into Europe but to destroy her chances of ever building the alliances necessary to get there. She faced two possibilities, both of them congenial to de Gaulle's objective and destructive of her own. On the one hand, if Britain accepted the plan for secret talks to reshape and rescue Europe, she would be helping the General towards the kind of looser Europe he wanted and, in the process, would be revealed before the Five as conspiring against their project. To her friends she would be hardly better than a traitor. On the other hand, if Britain refused the bait, de Gaulle would increase his leverage with the Five. He would be able to say that he had offered Britain a role, had made the overture, but that the British weren't interested in talking.

Thus spoke the representatives of the regiment, and thus were they mostly heard. The conclusion that this was a Gaullist ploy, rather than the ruminations of an old man on the future of the world, was rapidly reached in official London, and subsequent events did not incline the main official participants to revise it. 'The analysis we made was right,' Palliser told me, years later. 'If we'd played it the General's way we might well have found ourselves being accused of breaking up the EEC, and if we didn't play it his way he would exploit that against us.' But, Palliser added, 'the handling of it was undoubtedly wrong'.[46]

The handling, however, had the effect the Palliser elite desired. It kept British loyalty to the EEC on track, in the eyes of people who would eventually matter more to Britain than de Gaulle did. But, before that could be established, time, chance and a show of remarkable Robinsonian ruthlessness had to work their way through the process.

The chance that intervened was a date, long scheduled in the diary, for Wilson to visit Bonn for a routine meeting with the West German Chancellor, Kurt Kiesinger. He was due in Germany even as the Soames telegram was being evaluated in London. Thus, de Gaulle's infinite cunning was now overlaid by a dilemma he could not have imagined being brought into play so soon. Should Wilson explain to Kiesinger anything of what had passed in Paris, thus risking the fury of the French at their secret overture being unilaterally disclosed? Or should he remain silent, play dumb about what de Gaulle seemed to be up to, and thus behave with unforgettable discourtesy to the power that was his strongest and most necessary ally in the quest for EEC membership?

Wilson's own first instinct was to say nothing. What de Gaulle had said privately could be explained away, if necessary, as simply repeating what he had said publicly about the need for 'something entirely new'. Britain owed no obligations to the Germans, at this stage. Palliser, his private secretary, was advising him otherwise, but, to Wilson, there seemed no great merit in '[presenting] ourselves as a rather priggish little Lord Fauntleroy who had resisted the General's anti-EEC blandishments'.

Britain should take her time, and if necessary get into further talks with him, an entirely proper thing to do as long as she kept the Five informed. So, at any rate, Wilson presents his attitude in the memoirs he wrote in 1971, after his Government fell.

The Foreign Office, however, determined on a different strategy. Robinson told me: 'It's the only occasion I can quote to you from my career where officials – I won't say dictated – but suggested policy, and it was accepted.' Michael Stewart took the line the officials pressed upon him. On the plane to Bonn, he advised Wilson to tell Kiesinger the gist of what had passed. There was a big argument among the politicians and the travelling diplomats about how this should be done. In discussions at the Bonn embassy late into the evening, Wilson writes, 'I continued to express my distaste for the proposal.' Robinson recalled him 'swirling the brandy and saying he was going to go to Paris to talk to de Gaulle and poke Kiesinger in the eye'. For Wilson, as Palliser told me, valued – 'over-valued' – his relations with the General. 'He was squirming at the suggestion of offending him.' However, goaded by telegrams from London, pressed by Robinson and others on the spot, he eventually agreed to mention 'in a few simple sentences', without lurid overtones, what de Gaulle had said.

When he did so, Kiesinger was at first baffled. Wilson put it as a casual thing: ambassador called in, the General suggests refashioning EEC, British a bit puzzled, and so on. Kiesinger thought the interpreter must have made a mistake, muddling up the EEC with the Organization for Economic Co-operation and Development, the successor body to the OEEC. Surely it was the OECD de Gaulle wanted reorganized, the Chancellor inquired. No, said Wilson, it was the EEC. Robinson remembered Kiesinger urgently sending an aide out of the room to call Paris and find out what was going on.

The fall-out from this relatively modest disclosure might have been containable. But something else, rather less defensible, had occurred. This was Robinson's finest, or alternatively his basest, hour. To prepare Wilson's mind for the Kiesinger meeting, and help ensure this went the way they wanted, the FO team wrote a memo. Wilson had asked that this be 'brief and anodyne', suitable to his modest purpose. When he got it next morning, he found it was 'the full works'. 'I made it clear that I was furious,' Wilson writes. He had to take trouble to avoid speaking directly from it.

His caution, however, was otiose. For the contents of the full works were already on the wire, despatched openly round all relevant British embassies, allegedly to keep them in the picture about developments of which, thus far, they were entirely ignorant. Both the contents of the Soames telegram, and the full conspiratorial take on it, were written up by Robinson's team, with effects that did not take long to materialize.

The French, whom Soames informed of the circulation, were soon enraged. Their first tactic, now they were forced into semi-public mode, was to challenge the version they had originally agreed, saying they particularly rejected the item that most offended the Five: the concept of a leadership group, a *directoire*, consisting of themselves, the Germans, the Italians and the British. Equally, they sniffed out what they said were deliberate British distortions, making the General's words sound more anti-American and anti-European than they were. The very act of requesting confirmation of the Soames version in the first place was now seen to have been a British trap. For, if the French said they had agreed the Soames version, that lent colour to the Wilson position. Yet by contesting it they put themselves under pressure to supply an alternative account, a demand that inevitably stuck in their throat.

There then began a battle of the leaks. Until the middle of February, two weeks after the Elysée lunch, all this was happening in secrecy. Nobody outside government knew that Soames had met the General. But inquiries were beginning to be made. Soon enough, a sketchy French version of the Soames Affair appeared in the Paris newspaper *Le Figaro*, which was the pretext for the Foreign Office's final act of vengeance, its conclusive gesture ensuring that de Gaulle's seductive manoeuvre was destroyed. Thus liberated from all normal protocols – 'We've got the bastards at last,' one FO man, who sounds very like Robinson, John Dickie quotes exulting – the Office's chief spokesman summoned selected correspondents, to 'correct' the French account. He read to them, verbatim and *en clair*, large chunks of Soames's original despatch, giving rise to an international furore that put paid to anything serious de Gaulle might have had in mind. 'De Gaulle's Secret Offer: Scrap Six', the headline read. Exposed to the public eye, it was an offer nobody could fail to refuse.

Was this a case of serious mishandling, as Palliser came to judge? Certainly it produced a great coolness between London and Paris. Soames was summoned and rebuked by the Quai d'Orsay for his Government's numerous malefactions. Diplomats, especially those committed to the enterprise in question, never like to fall out with such venomous feeling as temporarily engulfed the two capitals. As for de Gaulle, his biographer writes that 'it would have been quite impossible to describe the General's furious reaction', though he also asks: 'Could he expect the country of Pitt and Churchill to overlook the snubs of 1963 and 1967 and not resort to one of those acts of revenge that only very old families and very old diplomatic services are capable of exacting?'[47]

In Britain, those who certainly thought the episode an error were the group of ministers still committed against British entry. To them, the crack-up of the Community was a heaven-sent chance for Britain to do what they had always wanted: to have it both ways: not to be excluded from modest European enterprises, but not to be required to join anything so ambitious as the Treaty of Rome. They were aware that 'Europe' could do Britain damage if she did not belong, and were no longer entirely blind to the economic consequences of a common, becoming a single, market across the Channel. The de Gaulle proposition, for a Community that interested itself in foreign policy co-ordination but renounced its pooling of economic ambitions, left them with hyperbolic frustration at the ruin of what might have been.

Thus Crossman, the sceptic, delivered a punishing verdict on 'the infantilism of Harold and Michael Stewart, priggish children who showed moral disapproval of the de Gaulle overture'. Douglas Jay, the phobic, called this overture 'a new and wonderfully far-sighted offer to Britain, whose rejection by a muddled Government was as catastrophic a blunder as Chamberlain's rejection of Roosevelt's offer in 1938'. A group of Foreign Office officials, Jay went on, 'did an incalculable disservice to this country. Seen dispassionately in retrospect, the wrecking of this offer without even further discussion was a more calamitous error, because it may well prove irrevocable, than Munich or Suez.'[48]

Seen by those public officials, however, their tactics were in pursuit of a government policy that had now been extensively debated and, for the first time, agreed with all relevant majorities in the British body politic. Anything else was a side-show. The officials, seized of this policy, saw it as their job to protect ministers against being fatally distracted from it. That, at least, is the high-ground argument they can make. It was the special credit O'Neill gave Robinson, in his retrospective official history: the man deserved remembering above all for 'resisting the temptations of plausible but inadequate alternatives'.[49] By wrecking de Gaulle's destructive proposition, they were saving Harold Wilson from himself.

In the event, they were justified. The event was the passing of de Gaulle. Robinson thought he could see it coming. That is what he reckoned he was playing for. 'In February 1969, it seemed a possibility that de Gaulle would disappear,' he told me. 'It was worth keeping the rails open for that.' Had the General remained in place, the damage done by the Soames Affair would have lasted a long time. It is unlikely that he would have spoken to Soames again; Wilson himself would have had to go on his knees for an audience. As it was, the General remained in power for less than three more months, deposed by his own hand when he called a referendum on reform of the French constitution. Quixotically, he defined it as a vote of confidence in himself. When he lost, he resigned – and the regiment saw the vindication of its judgement.

*

LONDON DID NOT immediately respond to de Gaulle's retirement. There was no instant leaping into the arms of the Common Market. Gaullism remained in power in France, with the election of Georges Pompidou to succeed the General. Although Pompidou was a very different character, unencumbered by an historic obsession with Anglo-Saxons, and in principle more amenable to British entry, the brute fact of French interest remained. Indeed, it was in this period, not the earlier one, that a final obstacle was wheeled into place to impede the development of British enthusiasm for entry even though the basic decision, the great existential lunge of the political class, appeared to have been made. The French saw an opportunity to secure what de Gaulle had failed to get in 1965 and to use the eagerness of the Five for British entry as the lever. They insisted that the Six must conclude an agreement among themselves on the agricultural system and its financing, which was always by far the largest part of the Community budget. When this was hammered out in December 1969, it fixed in place a system that put the Community, rather than its nation-state members, in charge of its own resources, and allocated disproportionate quantities of these to the support of farmers, the most potent political lobby in France. This ensured that the food-price consequences of membership would become even more gloomily debated in Britain. It became a commonplace among both officials and ministers, watching in the wings from Whitehall, that the financial structure had been designed with the positive intention of raising the price of Britain's entry-ticket, without possibility of concession.

Wilson, however, did press on. He already had a minister for Europe, George Thomson, whose activities were beefed up before the end of the year. There were more tours of the capitals. 'There is no need to be obsessed by safeguards and the negative aspects of our application, though the Government has these fully in mind,' the Prime Minister minuted the Cabinet. 'There are plenty of positive points to put across about the opportunities that membership of the Community would offer for our influence abroad and economic well-being at home.'[50]

The Cabinet, of course, did not unanimously agree. And Wilson, getting ready for an election, took care not to cut off all escape-routes. The white paper he published in February 1970, on the cost of entering the Common Market, could not be accused of disguising unpalatable truths. The damage-assessment much increased the 1967 figures: food prices up by 18–26 per cent, the cost of living by 5 per cent, huge multiples to contemplate. The balance of payments burden could, the paper said, be anything between £100 million and £1,100 million. Although George Thomson told the Commons that this was about as useful as saying that a football game between his home-town teams might end 'somewhere between eight–nothing Dundee and three–nothing Dundee United', the propaganda effect was capable of being alarming. The Labour manifesto retained the old caution – for entry, provided the terms are acceptable – adding the defiant rider that 'if satisfactory terms cannot be secured . . . Britain will be able to stand on her own feet outside the Community'.

The large signals, however, pointed only one way. Speaking of the application, Stewart, the Foreign Secretary, told the Commons in February: 'It stands, we press it, we desire that negotiations should be opened, we are anxious that they should succeed.' If Labour won, Stewart was going to be replaced by Roy Jenkins. This had been agreed with Wilson: the placing at the Foreign Office of the man who, in the absence of George Brown, was the party's first European. The practical arrangements were all in place, moreover. Along with most of Britain, Wilson thought he would win the 11 June election, and he scheduled the renewal of his Euro-venture accordingly. The speech of application was drafted in the middle of the campaign, to be formally delivered in Luxembourg, by the newly mandated Foreign Secretary, on 30 June.[51] Everything was prepared for a seamless transition between one government and the next.

Except that the prophets were mistaken. Labour did not win the election, but lost it to a thirty-seat Conservative majority. And the seamlessness Wilson had prepared for turned out not to extend to the handover from one party to another, despite the fact that these parties fought the election on the same positive, if wary, platforms of support for entry. Having reached the brink of a commitment, and moved far enough to make Europe a seemingly common cause, Labour was about to prove that there was more life in the pattern of perpetual revisionism. Another story for another chapter.

Continuity, however, did not cease in the other part of government, John Robinson's shop. He remained in charge of Britain's European policy for another three years, stoking the fire, repelling all boarders from more sceptical departments, conducting himself as ruthlessly with Whitehall as he had always done against the French. Hardly anyone I came across in this inquiry wanted to qualify very much Con O'Neill's encomium for the man who 'knew everyone, understood everything, foresaw everything, did everything', though they usually remarked also on the enmities he created.

In the summer of 1993, I went to visit Robinson at home. It was more than a decade since his retirement from the Foreign Office, and he lived outside Cordes, at the heart of *la France profonde*, a choice of location that seemed to substantiate the label always put around his neck as a Euro-fanatic. In fact, he said, this was something of an accident. After Europe, his postings had been abroad, and he needed a house to retire to, in a country where he could take his dog without the expensive rigmarole of six months' quarantine. Plainly his tongue was in his cheek when he tried to persuade me of this. Actually his search had always been for a place in the sun, and his chief focus of study, before choosing Cordes, was the rainfall map. Neither his friends nor his colleagues ever doubted how strongly he was driven, well before Macmillan's decision, by the belief that Britain must get into the EEC. Married to a Swiss-French woman, with an Alpine plot to which he repaired every spring to plant his potatoes, he was a true continentalist, with a special under-standing, so one of his colleagues said, of the French administrative mind. But such are the defences a Whitehall official may need to erect, even in retirement, against the fatal charge that he was committed to a cause.

If Robinson had a single reason to live in France, I guessed, it was to escape the reach of an establishment to which he never belonged. He personified the FO line on Europe, but the institution was indeed 'my shop', and his approach to the work made him enemies along the way. Although he did much for Britain-in-Europe, Europe did little for him. This may have been more his own fault than anyone else's, but he takes his place in the line of public people whose careers have been blighted, sometimes ended, by the Europe question.

For one thing, it induced in him a conspiratorial attitude to life. Decades of trying to outwit the continentals, while suppressing the influence of other Whitehall departments, left their mark. Sitting in the sun in his garden, which he padded about in the guise of a gnarled French peasant – he was known locally as 'le fonctionnaire' – I got my first glimpse of it through the anxiety he expressed about the imminent availability of PRO files covering the Heath–Macmillan negotiations. He feared the exposure of his Dutch sources, possibly forgetting that he had seldom, if ever, committed their names to paper. Not surprisingly, he mentioned with some relish the fact that he had not long before destroyed all the files he kept on the Soames affair. I was further startled to be told, when he settled down to talk, that our interview could not be taped. It took half an hour to persuade him that, after my recording of many previous interviews in and out of Whitehall, such rule-book punctilio in the middle of the French countryside seemed a little excessive. Even then, there was much elaborate covering of the microphone at moments he still deemed sensitive thirty years on.

His former colleagues were not surprised to hear this. To them, he had never been able to shake the habit. 'Conspiracy was valuable when we were negotiating to get in,' said one. 'But, the day we joined, you couldn't afford to be conspiratorial any more. John couldn't adapt. You had to have open relationships with other ministries, and he wasn't prepared to do that. He intrigued, and kept secrets, and didn't tell people what he was up to. That might have worked in the French system, but it didn't work in the British.'

Nor did it work for Robinson's subsequent career, which he conducted with an unusual disrespect for the rules. After so many years engaged in the intriguing delights of multilateral diplomacy, the impositions of embassy life were as boring as they were bureaucratic. The Office finally inflicted its norm upon him, removing him from what he knew better than anyone, and Robinson did not react well.

His first post-Europe job was as ambassador to Algeria, selected presumably in recognition of his knowledge of the French. Although he survived his allotted three years, he didn't enjoy the work and didn't mind who knew it. Not long after getting there, he told friends in the Foreign and Commonwealth Office that he doubted the merit of maintaining a British embassy in Algiers at all. Certainly, he thought, two-thirds of its officials could be redeployed without any damage to its effectiveness. He was rare, possibly unique, in the annals of the foreign service as an ambassador who objected to an FCO inspectorate report because the staff cuts it recommended for his embassy were not deep enough. In assessing his host country he was no less rigorous. His valedictory despatch, circulated round the service, opened with a sentence that challenged the normal diplomatic niceties. 'Algeria is a country built on the organising principle of theft,' he mordantly wrote – a verdict which in the 1990s, when innocent Algerians were being murdered by the hundred, looked like an understatement.

His later appointments were no more satisfactory. Palliser, by now head of the diplomatic service, found Robinson a slot in Washington, as number two to Peter Jay, a prime minister's son-in-law, who was controversially sent there as ambassador in 1977. It was thought that the brilliant parvenu would be assisted, as well as quietly overseen, by the unorthodox veteran. Within an institutional framework, Jay thought, two intelligent men could work out any difficulties. But, again, the posting came to grief, Robinson's complaint being much the same as it had been in Algiers. There wasn't enough to do. He had been given a 'non-job', he told Palliser and Jay after a few months. He also brought his pro-Europe prejudices with him, which offended Jay, an instinctively anti-EEC man, like his father Douglas. By the end, the ambassador and his deputy were communicating only by letter, and Robinson, exiled to New York, would make business visits to Washington only after being assured that Jay was out of town.

The Office did not give up. A job fell vacant that at least involved serious work, the ambassadorship to Israel. Robinson went there in 1980, and before long was letting slip his opinion that the Israeli case against the Arabs was a weak one. Again, he didn't mind who knew what he thought, but this time the consequence was terminal. After a year, the ambassador was withdrawn, in the tacit knowledge that otherwise Israel would have demanded his expulsion. So he was obliged to retire, four years early, from the shop and office to which he had given exceptional service.

In recent Foreign Office legend, that is what Robinson is remembered for: the man who decided Algeria didn't matter, and exposed himself in Israel to the charge of being an Arabist of matchless indiscretion. When he died, in January 1998, a singularly crass obituary in *The Times* found little else to write about him, almost entirely neglecting the discreet but potent work at the centre of his career.

Having left the Office and disappeared to France, he returned deeper into the obscurity which he had always favoured when pursuing his métier as a European schemer. When I saw him, in his little rural fastness, he minimized what this European part had really been about. 'What was it based on?' he asked sardonically. 'Turning up at meetings and remembering what happened five years ago. Also knowing all the people, who hadn't changed on the other side. They always stayed put. At the Quai, it was the same old faces, again and again. I think there was a decision on our side to have at least one historical memory that went back over the months and years.'

Whatever the intention, the effect was something more: the creation of a single-issue diplomat, whose issue happened to set the path and dominate the argument of British politics and foreign policy for the next thirty years.

7

EDWARD HEATH

The Triumph of the Will

MANY FEATURES COMMON TO politics in every era and every dispensation are to be found in the history of Britain's reluctant binding to
Europe. There is vacillation and concealment. There is progress followed
by regress, and all the time an argument about the real meaning of each
of these forms of motion. There is, near the top of the list, the question
of national pride and what it means, allied to the question of the popular
will and how it can be handled: and there is the claim always to be
satisfying these potent values, while at the same time regularly redefining
them. Also present is genuine uncertainty. The leaders often did not
really know what would be the consequences of their action, or inaction.

Another thing that marks this history is the accident of timing,
especially as it touched the life of Charles de Gaulle. Had de Gaulle been
summoned to power a few months earlier than May 1958, it is possible
that the Treaty of Rome would have been unilaterally aborted, and the
Common Market as we know it never have come into being. A diverting
speculation. The other end of de Gaulle's political career produced a
more concrete fact – but again the consequences were fortuitous. A
conjunction occurred that produced results which would otherwise, in
all probability, not have happened in the same way, if at all. De Gaulle,
having put his position on the line and been defeated, was succeeded as
president by Georges Pompidou. A year later, Britain elected a new
government, led by Edward Heath.

These men were not almighty movers of events. Each was carried by
deep tides and other more fractured forces to the confluence they
reached. Impersonal pressures – economic demand, political push,
perceived strategic necessity – brought their two countries to a point
where Britain's desire to be admitted to the European Economic Community, and France's readiness to contemplate her reception positively,

were creating a coercive influence. Even without the men, the measure might have passed. Pompidou depended on anti-Gaullist allies and rivals, notably Valéry Giscard d'Estaing, who were more volubly pro-British than he was. He may not have been indispensable to the project. It is more debatable whether Harold Wilson, had he won the 1970 election, would have made the necessary connection with Pompidou, but the pressures might eventually have been strong enough to overcome even their mutually repellent personalities.

The chosen men, nevertheless, did matter greatly. In particular, Heath did. His presence rather than anybody else's at the helm of British policy from June 1970 until the moment of British entry, in January 1973, was singularly appropriate. He might not have been there. He could easily have lost the election, and before that he might well not have won the party leadership, in 1965. Had he failed to get that, the Tory leader and Prime Minister would have been Reginald Maudling, who was a sceptic about British entry and had been the enthusiastic point-man in Britain's doomed attempt to confine her part in the enterprise to a free trade area. As it was, Heath was chosen, without any special interest one way or the other in his European credentials, and thereby brought to the leadership, and then the job of Prime Minister, a collection of baggage which gave a clearer prominence to the European quest than any other Conservative politician at that time was prepared to offer.

Ted Heath, therefore, cannot help being the nodal figure in this story. The most qualified 'European' in Tory politics assumed the leadership of Britain at the time when the question of entry into Europe was ready for its final resolution. He was made a European, not least, by his formation, but he was made a European leader by his character. What he brought to the table, compared with every predecessor, was not merely a 'European' policy but exceptional single-mindedness in pursu- ing it. Not for Heath the anguish of Macmillan or the dissembling of Harold Wilson. For him the door to the future had been opened, to reveal a vision of blinding clarity, where every prospect led in one direction. That was how Heath thought of 'Europe'. Directing Britain towards it was a task he accomplished with an élan that put previous history to shame: a shame deriving not so much from the decisions as the indecision. Heath's performance in this matter was a text-book exercise in most of the arts of government, which produced a rare phenomenon, the complete attainment of a political objective.

So his place in the story is unchallengeable. He is, as he never let anyone forget, the father of European Britain, and for that is perceived worldwide as a statesman: the only post-war British Prime Minister in that category, distinguishable as such from Margaret Thatcher who, while more resonant and certainly more notorious than Heath, left no legacy that history will call, strictly, statesmanlike. Yet to say that of Heath is not to say everything. Such eminence brings with it responsibilities. The test he invites can't be satisfied merely by acknowledging that he took Britain into Europe, large task though that was.

At one level, he shaped an epoch. At another, his part was more enigmatic. What exactly Heath thought he was doing when he took Britain in is a different matter from the fact, the impressive fact, of doing it. What Britain-in-Europe was *for*, in his mind, is a question to which the answer is elusive. Closely related to it is the question of what the British people were told it was about and, still more puzzling, what this leader, having accomplished the brute fact of entry, did and didn't do to move the British towards starting to becoming truly European people. Heath brought an end to the unfortunate record of two decades. But he was by no means free of the foibles that rendered British policy, in some ways, as unsatisfactory after the event as before it.

*

HEATH'S CREDENTIALS began at the beginning. To be born, as he was, facing Europe, in Broadstairs, on the coast of Kent, within sight of the coast of France, is perhaps of no more than symbolic interest. One cannot pretend that the boy grew into a young man while staring with conscious forethought at his destiny. But at least Europe was not an alien place in his family. His mother, in service as a maid, had often travelled with her employers to the continent.[1] Although he came from humble stock, his father a carpenter, the family's cultural horizons were never confined to the English-speaking peoples.

As soon as he was old enough, the boy began crossing the Channel himself. When he was fourteen, he went to Paris on a school trip and fell immediately in love with the idea of travel. No particle of anxiety appears to have touched him as he wandered the streets of the foreign capital struggling with a foreign language. His memoir of the time recalls the 'heavenly anguish' of selecting which restaurant to enter, and the 'lucidity and clarity' of the French literature which, while he never became a very convincing exponent of spoken French, Heath always claimed to admire.[2] During summer vacations from university, he practically lived on the continent, especially in Germany, to which music drew him as much as politics. It was often forgotten, in later life, that Heath was an organ scholar at Oxford. He was steeped in European creativity, a condition that went well beyond the dilettante liking for a bit of Beethoven, which marked the cultural frontier of most English politicians.

These early excursions, however, had more to them than concert-halls and pavement cafés. When he got to Oxford in 1935, Heath soon involved himself in politics, through the Conservative Association, and displayed a seriousness about events on the continent that led to encounters which did decisively shape his European destiny. He had adventures that set him apart among Conservatives. In the summer of 1938, he went to Spain to see fascism in action, calling on the outposts of the anti-Franco government, being shot up and bombed as he travelled around the environs of Barcelona.[3] The young undergraduate spent days in intense political conversation with student-soldiers, assuring himself they were not primarily Marxists but genuine seekers after democratic freedom. He was not, however, lecturing them from the safe ground of British complacency. By his own account, he was obviously a serious fellow, drawn to the sea and soil of the Mediterranean, but engaged more by deep alarm at the tyrannies engulfing Europe.

Germany was where, in this formative time, he had the most astounding experiences. He became a wide-eyed tourist of the Third Reich. In Munich, in summer 1937, he made for the cellar where Hitler had first gathered the cronies who took him to power, and watched the changing of the guard at the Nazi memorial, 'steel-helmeted and goose-stepping with extraordinary precision', as he wrote. The German Embassy in London had given him an invitation to attend the Nuremberg rally. At the indoor conference preceding it, he witnessed Göring, Goebbels and Himmler at close quarters. As Hitler marched down the aisle, Heath was aware of him 'almost brushing my shoulder'. At the outdoor rally, he had a seat close to Hitler's box, and heard the leader's oration with traumatic horror. 'This man', he concluded, 'was obviously capable of carrying the German people with him into any folly, however mad.' Later, he went to a party where Himmler was the host – 'I remember him for his soft, wet, flabby handshake' – and Goebbels made himself known, 'his pinched face white and sweating – the personification of evil'.[4]

In the prelude to war, Heath had no doubt where he stood, against the appeasement policy of Prime Minister Neville Chamberlain. He took that side at Oxford, and helped fight a by-election in the cause. Even as war was on the verge of breaking out, he was to be found on another tour of future killing-fields, this time as far east as Warsaw. It was as if he could never satisfy his curiosity, just could not bear to keep away. It is an irony, therefore, that, when he volunteered for action, he should have spent most of the war years on the island, not the mainland. Only in the final year of combat did his unit move on from anti-aircraft duty, protecting Britain, into France and the Low Countries, participating, most memorably for him, in the liberation of Antwerp. The immediate aftermath, however, retained him on the continent, and deepened the meaning he took from what had happened. He went back to Nuremberg, this time for the war crimes trials, a spectator at the judgment on Göring, Hess, Ribbentrop and the rest, for their murderous depravities. 'As I left the court,' he later wrote, 'I knew that those evil things had been beaten back and their perpetrators brought to justice. But at what a cost. Europe had once more destroyed itself. This must never be allowed to happen again . . . Reconciliation and reconstruction must be our tasks.'

So this was a very European man. His collection of first-hand European experiences was as large and memorable as any young Englishman anywhere could boast of. Nobody from the traditional seed and shire of British Conservatism could get near it.

In his memoir, Heath claims to have had no foresight about what the war and its threat to European civilization would mean for his professional life. 'I did not realise that it would be my preoccupation for the next thirty years.'[5] But, indisputably, the experience entered into his blood and bone, as it did for those diplomats of his own generation, like Michael Palliser, whose lives were definitively shaped by the conflict they took part in. They were a particular kind of club, qualified in a different way from other kinds of public men. It probably mattered quite a lot to the direction of later events that in early September 1939, as Ted Heath was making it back to Britain from Poland by the skin of his teeth before war was declared, Harold Wilson was motoring to Dundee to deliver an academic paper on exports and the trade cycle, and that later, while Heath was training to run an anti-aircraft battery, Wilson became a potato controller at the Ministry of Food.[6]

Heath's opening bids in Parliament reflected this experience. Europe, especially Germany, was his prime, dominating interest. Germany bothered him, even as she absorbed him. In 1948, while wholly accepting Churchill's view that Germany must be readmitted into some version of 'Europe', he had no illusions about the Germans. He said his knowledge of their pre-war mentality led him to believe that many of them still looked back on the Hitler years with favour. They should be encouraged to recover, but not allowed to fight: an 'interestingly doubled-edged view', as his biographer notes.[7] By 1950, when he made his maiden speech, this clarified into a heartfelt certainty that the European project of the period, the Schuman Plan, should involve Britain as well as the continentals.

The maiden speech adds to the incremental symmetry which was to conclude with Prime Minister Heath leading Britain into the European Economic Community – the 'Monnet–Schuman system', as it continued to be regarded by *aficionados*. Characteristically, Heath was able to deliver the speech just after returning from a tour of Germany, on whose condition he reported to the Commons at first hand. Having talked to both Christian and Social Democrats, he said, he was convinced that they wanted reconciliation and that the Schuman Plan for a coal and steel community was the way to begin the task. The 'binding in' of Germany – the notion of a European Germany not a German Europe – was not a concept then explicitly articulated by anybody. It awaited another generation of German politicians to be put quite so candidly. But this was the thought that underlay Heath's speech, and the statement he made that Britain must be part of the enterprise. He scorned the Labour Government's argument that Schuman was a capitalist ramp. He feared the consequences for the British economy – 'a very great risk indeed' – of self-exclusion from a community that would galvanize our continental competitors. And he said this with quite searing conviction, which distinguished him from his leaders, Churchill and Anthony Eden. They, too, attacked the Government, but for crudely oppositionist reasons. They said we should be there, but they didn't mean it and didn't take their own chance to do something about it when they reached government next year. For Edward Heath, it was an article of faith: and it was rendered the more prominent in his credo, the more vital in his personal history, by the fact that it turned out to be not only his maiden speech but the one speech of any significance he made as a back-bencher in Parliament, before soon being hoisted into the Whips' office and thence, after nine years of managerial silence, to a front-bench position where he spoke from the despatch box.

It is appropriate that this speech should stand in such solitary isolation. It was a personal announcement, which rang down the decades, taking the position from which Heath never deviated, using arguments that swept aside what he would always regard as marginal irritations –

such matters as the effect of 'Europe' on national sovereignty, or the precise nature of the terms of entry. Coming from his heart as well as his head, it was the first piece of the political platform that launched him and his country, twenty years later, into the Common Market.

The second, of course, was that he had been there before. He had sat at the table, sweated through days and nights in the smoke-filled chamber, haggled with counterparts over pigmeat and cashew nuts and the sterling balances, watched his mind go numb absorbing the tenth new scheme for dealing with New Zealand butter. From his experience as Macmillan's negotiator, he was a master of the European scene, knew the shape of every committee-room and the frailties of the players in them, many of whom had not changed in the space of the decade.

Heath's sheer range of acquaintance was enormous, and on many of its members he had made the best possible impression. His opening statement at the 1961 negotiation revealed to them a more direct approach than Macmillan's. The application, he told them, was not tactical and wasn't based on narrow grounds. He swept aside the conceit, much cultivated by his party-fearing colleagues in the Cabinet, that this wasn't an application at all, but simply an inquiry to see if decent terms might be available. 'We recognize it as a great decision,' he had said on the first day, 'a turning-point in our history, and we take it in all seriousness.' It was what Macmillan meant, but not what he dared to say. This spirit Heath maintained until beyond the end. His speech after the veto culminated in a statement, partly penned in his own hand, which said that Britain would be back. The veto should not jeopardize European unity, he said. 'We are part of Europe by geography, tradition, history, culture and civilization. We shall continue to work with our friends in Europe for the true unity and strength of this continent.' It was one of very few occasions on which Ted Heath, earnest to a fault and one of the least inspiring speakers of modern times, brought tears to the eyes of some of those present to hear him.[8]

There has been argument about Heath's tactical appreciation of the dealing he was involved in. Did he drag out the negotiations too long? Miss a crucial opening in the summer of 1962, like some First World War general failing to anticipate a breakthrough in the Maginot Line? This is fertile ground for speculation in Euro-academia, whose output on the point approached industrial-scale with the opening of the relevant British files in the Public Record Office.[9] But the episode made no dent on Heath's reputation, supreme among all Conservative and most

Labour politicians of his era, as the man best equipped to take advantage of an opening across the Channel, should this appear.

Before it did, a third element of his relevant curriculum vitae began to disclose itself. He made himself into something of a Euro-intellectual, again an unfashionable development in a Tory politician. His conviction was clear from 1950, his experience established by 1963. Then, in 1967, he gave shape to his view of the future with a series of lectures at Harvard University.[10]

These caused little stir at the time. It was a period when the whole EEC project was becalmed. The world view Heath set forth, however, was strikingly Euro-centred, undeflected by Wilson's charge that his enthusiasm for Brussels and all its works could be likened to that of a submissive spaniel. It prepared the ground for a break not only with Macmillan's priorities – the Atlantic relationship, the Commonwealth – but with the ongoing sensitivities of the Conservative Party.

Heath summarized the state of things in Europe. Since the project was under the influence of French obstructionism, he said, British policy faced a paradox. 'On the one hand, if the Community gathers speed and begins once again to progress towards economic and political union, it will inevitably make fresh arrangements and develop fresh institutions to which Britain will then be asked to adhere without having had any say in their formation.' The once and future dilemma, what Russell Bretherton had noted a dozen years before: how to combine influence with exile. But now there was a new development. 'On the other hand,' Heath went on, 'a stagnant Community has proved increasingly unattractive to British opinion.'

To ward off such corrosive damage, he recommended a missionary approach. Public support would be recovered only if people knew what Europe was about. 'This can only be done by setting out the prospects honestly and showing that when we talk about the unity of Europe we mean not a vague concept, but the habit of working together to reach accepted goals.' Heath, in other words, was framing a political future for the Community, and the flesh he put on it was fattest in the realm of defence. He harked back to a European defence community, and in the process declared himself, by the standards of post-war convention, a less convinced Atlanticist than any other British leader. He talked up the sacrilegious idea of nuclear pooling between France and Britain, and openly canvassed for 'an eventual European defence system'.

This was the working out, in opposition, of new and distinct priorities which, while little noticed by the Conservative Party, became disturbing to the Americans. Heath was never anti-American, in the way the Labour left had spent a lifetime being. Yet here was the emergence of a philosophy, a harbinger of his years in power, which foretold a drastic change not only from Macmillan's intimacies with John F. Kennedy but from Wilson's cringing submission to Lyndon Johnson. In this, Heath was to remain consistent. Henry Kissinger, in his memoirs, recalled a Prime Minister who 'dealt with us with an unsentimentality totally at variance with the "special relationship"'. Unlike other European leaders, who 'strove to improve their relations with us . . . Heath went in the opposite direction'.[11] It was a conscious choice, based on the perception that the old concentric circles were no longer quite as equi-cyclical as they were when Churchill talked about them. Europe, in Heath's assessment, had to become the largest: a position that actually gave him much in common, paradoxically, with de Gaulle. From time to time, Heath made speeches that could be called Gaullist, talking about the need to 'redress the balance' against the dollar, and speaking with disapproval of 'an allegiance foreign to Europe'.[12] The Godkin Lectures at Harvard were where they took coherent shape.

Also while in opposition, he began to lose all patience with the third of these circles, the Commonwealth. It became as much of a curse for him as it was for Wilson, and he lacked any of the family background, the emotional bonding, that might have sustained the myth of kin against the glaring fact of irrelevance and even, on the matter of Rhodesia, enmity. From the moment Heath became Tory leader on 1965, white Rhodesia, declaring independence in the same year, gained virulent support from a faction in the Tory Party, which delighted to goad him. It would be wrong to call Heath a lifelong anti-Common-wealth man. During the 1962 negotiations, he worked hard to defend Commonwealth interests, and travelled across many red parts of the map to get agreement for the results. He was proud to say that, before the veto, 'these were worked out in great detail almost to the point of completion'.[13] But by 1970 such feeling as he had for the Common-wealth, black or white, had drained away.

It had become, along with almost everything else, a residual in the great equation he desired to make between Britain and Europe.

*

EVEN SO, Heath was cautious. While his personal commitment was deepening, so was the country's scepticism. The idea of Europe was seldom to be so popular as in the first flush of the early 1960s, when Macmillan's anxieties contrasted with the bright-eyed zeal that developed, especially in the business world, for an exciting idea which looked like the way of the future. The veto, followed by the EEC's inability to decide where it was going, topped off by Wilson's candour about the effect on food prices, took the shine off the vision. In April 1970, two months before the general election, a Gallup poll found only 19 per cent of voters favouring British entry, with more than half of them rejecting the idea of even getting into talks. Popular feeling for the whole idea was at rock bottom. Heath's manifesto was calibrated accordingly. Whereas in the first election which he fought as party leader, the 1966, the Tories promised to 'seize the first favourable opportunity of becoming a member of the Community', the pledge now was much more guarded. At the 1970 election, the Conservatives promised only to negotiate – 'no more, no less'.

The negotiating modalities, however, were already in place. Such was the seamlessness. Whoever won the election, the ground was prepared. All Heath had to do was pick up the briefs and files that had been in the making for three years. This bears a moment's contemplation, given what later happened in the Labour Party. The official historian records a depth of continuity that was greater than has often been understood. The Heath negotiation, he writes, was based 'in all essentials' on the statement made by George Brown on 4 July 1967, prior to Wilson's abortive venture. It wasn't a case merely of picking up the baton that de Gaulle's second veto had forced out of Britain's hand in November, but of being the beneficiary of unremitting work that had gone on ever since. Brown stated a position that never changed, and, right up to and through the election, the fine-tuning and detailed timetabling of a process scheduled to start on 30 June was going on. The historian lists the quantity of work that was by then out of the way: 'The decision to apply for membership; its endorsement by Parliament; the necessarily deliberate response by the Community, involving, among much else, an opinion by the Commission; the preparation of negotiating positions by the Community and by ourselves.' To Heath, he says, this was 'of enormous value'.[14]

Likewise, the team that would handle it was already in place. The biggest thing Heath wanted to do was done by people Labour had picked. The caravan was rolling, and by now it was full of believers. The Whitehall hesitations of a decade before had not entirely vanished, but the political commitment to succeed, through the men selected to do the work, was now pretty well absolute.

At their head was Con O'Neill, restored to the Foreign Office after his brief tiff with George Brown, and put back in place there thanks, in part, to the ministrations of John Robinson. Within days of de Gaulle's departure, the signal that serious business might begin, Robinson proposed O'Neill's return, and went round to his flat to make sure that, if drafted, he would serve.[15] Other members of the Euro-sodality were placed alongside. Robinson himself was the most prominent, O'Neill's trusted ally, the continuity man who knew where every French body was buried. Raymond Bell came from the Treasury, as he had in 1961. Freddy Kearns from the Ministry of Agriculture and Roy Denman from the Board of Trade were already steeped in Europe, through regularly negotiating with the Commission as part of their daily work. The members of the regiment and their allies were in place, before the election was held to decide which party they would be serving.

So was the structure within which they operated. It had been decided that the negotiation should be handled not, as last time, from the Foreign Office, an arrangement that tended to sharpen differences in Whitehall, but from the Cabinet Office, where it could be better subjected to central control. There needed to be smoother co-ordination, and a more reliable facility for riding over and dissolving the residual antagonism in Whitehall.

For antagonism there still was. Part of it was departmental: the bull-headed determination of the Ministry of Agriculture, for example, to defend the interest of British farmers against negotiating concessions. But the problem was more than sectional. While Whitehall officials were trained in nothing if not detection of the way the wind was blowing, active enthusiasm for the Common Market was still not universal.

One man who noted this was John Hunt, whom Heath appointed to run the Cabinet Office operation in the final stages of the negotiation. Not long after, Hunt was to become secretary of the Cabinet. To be aggressively keen on Europe at this time, Hunt thought, remained proof of slight eccentricity. With a pedigree by Treasury out of Commonwealth Relations, he had come to his own supportive opinions a little late, but, as Whitehall co-ordinator of the team, was struck by its members' maverick quality. 'Most were not naturally people who were going to go to the top of the mainstream civil service,' he later reflected. 'I think some of them had been shoved into this job because it was one that nobody else was keen to do, and they happened to believe in it.'[16]

This set them apart from their superiors. Burke Trend, the Cabinet secretary, as we have seen, was classically sceptic, vowing to defend Atlantic and Commonwealth links at all costs. 'He was profoundly against Europe,' Hunt told me. It led to much awkwardness with Heath, his direct master. But Trend wasn't alone. There was considerable twitching from the old order. When Wilson insisted on trying to negotiate, Denis Greenhill, Brown's appointee as head of the Foreign Office, came into Robinson's office, which overlooked Downing Street, and, staring across the road, declared with utmost gloom: 'I think it's a question of flogging a dead horse' – a statement of dissidence which Robinson found very shocking.

The Treasury, also, remained officially against British entry. That is to say, its judgement of the economic consequences was negative, and it submitted a paper to that effect. The permanent secretary, Sir Douglas Allen, was roused to unusually vigorous displays of disdain when the economic arguments for entry were set in front of him. Not for him the balanced agonizing of the 1950s. Now that the Common Agriculture Policy, with its massive disbursements for farmer-heavy countries like France, was set in place, the advantages, he thought, were far outweighed by the costs. Whatever the political gains, there would be losses both to the balance of payments and to the economy generally. The Treasury paper, however, was dismissed. When Heath came to publish a white paper, it simply buried the Treasury arguments. 'We were prepared to put the pros and cons,' Allen, by now Lord Croham, told me, 'but to argue that this would be beneficial to the economy, on the terms offered, was something we could not accept. Although the white paper said that, the official Treasury dissented.'[17]

By now, however, these views were a side-show. The momentum that had built up since 1967 overrode such fiddling particulars. On 30 June, a different minister showed up in Luxembourg: the Tory, Anthony Barber, rather than the Labour man who had supervised all this work, George Thomson. A different man again, Geoffrey Rippon, led the actual negotiations, owing to Barber's sudden elevation to the Treasury, on the untimely death of the ablest man in the Government, Iain Macleod. Rippon's presence probably made some difference. A more roguish and laid-back politician than Barber, though not a Heath familiar, he was a capable lawyer and a keen European, formerly chairman of the Tory delegation to the Council of Europe. He had a swift mind and a broad

brush, and an unlawyerly impatience with detail. Curious traits for a
negotiator, perhaps: but attractive to his official team, who were happy
to look after the mountains of small print while Geoffrey took care of
the big picture, along with the claret and cigars, marks of his personal
style, which delighted them almost as much as finding he was the first
man most of them had known who kept a telephone in his car.

The negotiations began without delay, and they were, despite all the
preparations, a process of extended complexity. They were sometimes
nasty, and occasionally brutish, and they were indisputably long, lasting
from July 1970 until January 1972. But they were also engulfed by a
paradox. On the one hand, they had to take place. There was no way
round the need to nail down every kind of transitional particular about
the way Britain – along with Denmark, Ireland and Norway, who were
also negotiating for entry, on the greater British coat-tails – would be
allowed to make her way into the burgeoning network of Community
governance. And yet there was a charade-like aura about them. In deep
reality, they were, according to a well-qualified participant, 'peripheral,
accidental and secondary'. For a large anterior fact dominated everything
that happened, namely the imperative that Britain should join the
continent. 'What mattered was to get into the Community, and thereby
restore our position at the centre of European affairs which, since 1958,
we had lost.'[18]

This lapidary opinion was no throwaway line. It didn't come from a
commentator, or a careless politician, or a *post facto* surveyor of events,
but from someone as close to the official British mind as it was possible
to be: someone, indeed, who arguably *was* the British mind: at any rate,
an interpreter of it second only to Edward Heath in his capacity to put
judgement into action.

The author was Con O'Neill himself, the chief official negotiator,
from whose work we have already heard in the last chapter. For nearly
thirty years, this secret text, the Foreign Office's own history of the
negotiation, more than 300 pages long, has lain in the vaults unread.
Quite early in my own inquiry, someone kindly slipped me a copy of
what is a *tour de force* of diplomatic writing, the ultimate insider's
account, which O'Neill completed, extraordinarily, within six months of
the negotiation ending. In its combination of narrative drive and
penetrating analysis, together with the unique authority of its standpoint,
there can be few state papers that surpass it. One cannot say it should
have been published earlier, for the enlightenment of the British people
about events that have bothered them ever since. It contains too many

candid indiscretions concerning the stance and character of Britain's interlocutors, particularly the French, many of them still alive. But as a source-book for the intricacies of the process – a case-study of how a certain kind of multilateral diplomacy is conducted between sophisticated operators in Europe – it is without rival.

It is, of course, only a British account. And it is vastly longer than a secondary author such as this one could accommodate. But I rely on it for the next few pages. Fragments seem worth exposing, for the light they cast on what happened in Brussels in the prelude to Heath's defining triumph. As to both tactics and method, they have a lot to say. As to the errors made, and the imperfections of the outcome, O'Neill is also not entirely silent: another reason, no doubt, for having withheld an eminently publishable tome from publication for as long as possible.

One gets from it, to begin with, a sense of the scale of what entry now meant, by comparison with 1961. There had been an immense accumulation of Community rules and precedents, even though half the decade had been spent, thanks to de Gaulle, in a condition of stasis. O'Neill puts with startling candour the fundamental fact that lay behind the negotiation, the existential reality about 'Europe'. 'None of its policies were essential to us,' he writes. 'Many of them were objectionable.' But they had to be accepted, for the larger purpose. They had grown up in our absence. If the British had been there, he says, 'we would never . . . have allowed a situation to develop which made it so difficult, for instance, to ensure fair arrangements for New Zealand dairy products or developing Commonwealth sugar, or to create a situation of equity in respect of our contribution to the Budget.'[19] These, along with fish, proved to be the most contested items in the deal. But, as a result of the British not being there from the start, the fresh enactments they had to address amounted to some 13,000 typewritten pages. By 1970, as a German official of the Commission wrote, 'an almost inconceivable flood of European law . . . had to be accepted by the candidates'.[20]

A great deal of this was absolutely non-negotiable. That stance was laid down from the beginning, and within three months the British accepted it. They started off by reserving the right both to try and change Community policy and to postpone some difficult matters for settlement until after membership had been agreed. 'By October 1970 we had shelved these possibilities,' O'Neill writes.[21] Even the countries most anxious for British entry, like Italy and the Netherlands, were determined to play a hard game. Their conversational flexibility proved to be 'little more than politeness and a desire to please'. The Community's principle, he adds, was 'swallow the lot', and, musing about why this should be – why they wouldn't accept 'some compromises, some fresh starts, some changes of existing rules' – he lights upon a truth that would apply throughout the Community's history, right down to the present day, with the close of the century in sight. It was an articulation of the famous saw, *Les absents ont toujours tort*, describing the predicament of every outsider trying to get in, not as a result of malice or political enmity but of simple inexorable fact. 'Almost every conceivable Community policy or rule or enactment', O'Neill concluded, 'is the resultant of a conflict of interests between members, and has embedded in it features representing a compromise between the interests.' Open it up, and the whole laborious compromise will fall apart. Make exceptions, just because the British argument is strong and the matter of no great importance, and you create a precedent. So the rule became: 'Swallow the lot, and swallow it now.'[22]

This, in turn, defined the limit of what negotiation could be about. It was, essentially, about mitigation not change, about transitional arrangements not the remaking of rules to fit a new situation. There were nuances to this. Actually, in the thickets of the argument about the access of Caribbean sugar producers to their traditional British market, or of New Zealand's butter to the country on which her economy substantially depended, the Community agreed to adjust its rules. But usually, only for a while: five years was the norm for the transition. Beyond that, there could seldom be any special privileges against free trading within the EEC, especially in agriculture, or against the imposition of tariffs on outsiders. For who were the beggars now, the *demandeurs*, in Euro-parlance? There had almost been a category-shift since 1961, when the British still felt strong enough, rightly or wrongly, to make their approach from a position of strength, inquiring if satisfactory terms might be available prior to them deciding, from their great height, whether to dignify Europe with their presence. Ten years later, it was a case of taking what they could get.

The physical arrangements for this work are not without interest. There were often more than a hundred people in the room, with delegations from each of the Six, as well as the Commission and the president pro tem of the Council – French for the first period, German for the second, Italian for the third – who was the only one allowed to talk for the Europeans. 'A series of short and stilted dialogues' ensued between the president and the British delegation. But this wasn't where the real business was done. Everything that mattered took place in the corridors, and the long interludes between quite short formal meetings. Even the all-night sessions were not as arduous as they have always been represented in European folklore, with British ministers tottering back to London after defending the national interest into the small hours. 'The general image was conveyed', O'Neill writes of his work in 1971-2, 'of the British Delegation locked for 15 or 20 hours at a stretch in debate with the Community Delegation, as statement or proposal, reply, rebuttal or rejoinder, compromise or counter-compromise were volleyed across the table. This was not the case.'

In fact O'Neill could not recall a single continuous session between European ministers and Geoffrey Rippon that lasted as long as an hour. By far the greater time was taken up – 'twenty or thirty times as much' – by the Community partners haggling with each other, rather than in meetings with the British. On the British side, many more weeks were spent in London, preparing for the next session and sorting out White-hall turf-wars, than in Brussels, though by the end of the piece more than 140 officials from seventeen departments had made the cross-Channel journey: testament to the immersion Europe already required of any applicant member, and a harbinger of what was to come – the infusion of European matters into the life of the bureaucracy more deeply than into any other class or category in the whole of British society.

Whitehall was the battlefield where John Robinson, in particular, came into his own. Guarding the negotiators' flank against enfilading fire from colleagues in the home civil service was his special task, carried out with the secrecy and conspiratorial dissembling of which he was the FO's acknowledged master. It was also Robinson who laid down a fundamental rule of British negotiating procedure. When there was a breakdown, he wrote, it would be crucial to pin the blame on the other side. In a formulation Machiavelli would have rated, he identified 'the all-important point that, if the Community cannot make joint proposals to us which lie within the range of what we would regard as reasonably negotiable, we want the Community to fail to agree on joint proposals to us. We want the crisis on each subject to be within the Six rather than between the Six and ourselves.' O'Neill thought so well of this strategy that he cites it specially in his history.[23]

From the start, the British had a date in mind. Their objective was to gain entry on 1 January 1973, which was what in fact occurred. Robinson drew up a critical path that proved to be extraordinarily prescient, marking down, two years ahead, often to within days of the event, what ought to happen when and where.[24]

Keeping the Community, and especially the French, to the wheel was therefore the first strategic priority, closely followed by a decision to bid low rather than high when putting forward proposals. Not too low, but, more important, not too high, on account of the publicity. For this was a negotiation, as everyone understood, conducted in public – which had its virtues and its vices. A merit of the Community, O'Neill drily notes, 'is that they find it almost impossible to maintain any security for their transactions'.[25] As a result, the British usually saw the texts of what the other side were going to say before they said it. The state of prior knowledge was 'virtually complete'. On the other hand, such habitual transparency in the Community culture carried penalties. A proposal pitched too high could have calamitous effects, for it had to be assumed that in Brussels there were no secrets. To fail to secure a British demand, even in those days of relatively calm journalism, was to court political disaster. 'Nothing', says O'Neill, 'could have created a more damaging impression, in the press and in Parliament, than for us to have demanded a particular solution, and then be seen to be beaten back . . . into having to accept something much more modest.'[26]

There were exceptions to this tactic. On the biggest imponderables – sugar, dairy products and the contribution to the budget – Rippon and O'Neill put forward 'maximum demands', in order to keep the producer lobbies in the Caribbean and New Zealand happy, and to establish a rigorous base-line for what they knew would be the hardest deal of all, over finance. Here, O'Neill records, both press and Parliament were obliging, and understood very well that the bids were certain not to succeed. On other matters, the team saw low bidding as a form of toughness. It was their own way of playing hard ball. From the armoury of recognized negotiating tactics, such an approach contrasted with the more usual continental flamboyance. 'We stuck to it as long as we could,' O'Neill writes, 'and refused to become engaged in a descending order of compromise.'[27]

The O'Neill history gives lengthy and meticulous accounts of the handling of each subject on the table. The chapters often run to dozens of absorbing pages, capable, even thirty years later, of arousing the interest, perhaps the outrage, of the industries that were made or broken in the process. We learn that while the Foreign Office received most letters on the question of sugar – Tate & Lyle, and the sugar industry generally, having a long record of successful pressure on Tory govern-ments – New Zealand butter and cheese was the likeliest deal-breaker, being the subject on which the parliamentary muscle of British kith and kin was most easily mobilized. If Britain, dealing on their behalf, accepted a settlement which the New Zealanders rejected, Parliament's approval could not be relied on. 'We were in a dilemma,' says O'Neill. 'The New Zealanders had us over a political barrel. They did indeed, to some extent, hold a veto over our entry into the Community.' The New Zealand Prime Minister, the historian judged, 'went on asking for more until, in almost every respect, he got it.' He was 'more successful in the negotiations than anyone else'.[28]

The most unexpected problem was the fate of the sterling balances, debts held in London, mostly to Commonwealth countries which had traditionally kept large quantities of their reserves there. 'No subject . . . was more elusive and mysterious,' O'Neill writes. 'In no case was it harder to grasp clearly and firmly what were the issues at stake and what we would be asked by the Community to do.' The French were the ones who most cared, linking the question to the weakness of the British economy, a consideration that remained, for them, one which they took very seriously. But the British couldn't get to the bottom of French concern. 'It was never quite clear whether the reserve role of sterling was more objectionable to the French as something which gave us an unusual privilege and advantage, or as something which would represent an unacceptable liability and risk.'[29]

The French, indeed, were permanently captious. Though others occasionally raised their own special difficulties, the negotiation was essentially with the French, on whose style O'Neill had every reason, by the end, to regard himself as a world authority. As one professional to another, he wasn't entirely unimpressed by the French. It was they, he complained, who for months kept all parties in 'unnecessary and agonising suspense'. But he admitted that in one way this paid off. By stonewalling, he concedes, France kept control of the sequence of events. This resulted in a linkage being made – an entirely adventitious nego-tiator's linkage – between a successful deal on New Zealand's dairy products and a settlement on the Community budget. This worked out much to Britain's disadvantage. To keep New Zealand happy, the British were forced to worsen their budget terms.

This was by way of being a secular French triumph. On the other hand, O'Neill decided, they often seemed to be playing games. 'The French take an unusual satisfaction in the conduct of negotiations for its own sake,' he writes. 'They like the tensions it can engender, and the careful orchestration of innumerable themes. For the French, negotiation is an art form, or even a sport.' At the end of one all-night session, he was greeted by his French counterpart who said: 'Congratulations! *Vous avez très bien négocié.*' 'It was as though we had just finished a particularly exciting, hard-fought and enjoyable game of tennis,' the author comments.[30]

As to who had won this game, O'Neill acknowledged only one British disaster. His history concludes with two chapters of evaluation. One of them asks: Did We Make Mistakes? The other: Did We Get a Good Bargain? For the most part, he answers no and yes, respectively – but with a single large exception.

On New Zealand, he thought, the Antipodeans got more than they deserved. Political pressure probably required it, but the price was too high. 'I still feel it is something of a blemish on the outcome that we ourselves had to pay so much on New Zealand's behalf.' New Zealand herself would have settled for less, had the British ignored the cunning threats of her Prime Minister. Getting what she got, because it involved concessions on the British budgetary contribution, cost the British Exchequer, O'Neill reckoned, £100 million in 1972 money over five years (or £750 million in 1998 terms).[31]

On the financial deal itself, there is also a modicum of self-criticism. Having started with an absurd demand, that Britain should pay only 3 per cent of the EEC budget in the first year, 1973, O'Neill and his negotiators had to settle for 8.64 per cent, rising to 18.92 per cent in 1977. Bidding too toughly here had a bad effect. The minuscule opening shot produced, says O'Neill, 'an exceedingly hostile reaction from virtually all quarters of the Community'. 'A better atmosphere might have led to a better settlement.'[32] On the other hand, he decides that, ultimately, the final deal could not have been very different from what in fact was achieved.

On fish, however, he enters only a modest defence. This is the great exception. It was a complex, disastrous story. The Community concluded its own Common Fisheries Policy within hours of the enlargement process commencing, which looked like an amazing piece of chicanery. Having hung fire for years, the issue of access to coastal waters was resolved between the Six to the extreme disadvantage of the four candidate members, who would bring to the Community far longer coast-lines and double the fish-catch. Of all the matters on the agenda, fish was therefore the least prepared by the British. Since it was also the one question on which the Labour Party wasn't hopelessly compromised by its own activities in government from 1967 to 1970, Harold Wilson and his colleagues leaped with special relish to attack the Government, driving home the scandalous nature of the deprivation facing in-shore

British fishermen at the hands of predatory Frenchmen who, at one stage, seemed likely to be able to fish 'right up to the beach'.

There were, and are, inherent conflicts of interest in the seas of Europe which were always certain to cause trouble. They could never have been resolved to everyone's satisfaction. But here, at least, O'Neill does admit to error. He and his team, he says, wholly miscalculated the support which the plight of plucky trawler-men could engender, vastly disproportionate to their numbers or their economic importance. The CFP opened the way for foreigners to enter what had always been regarded as British waters, and O'Neill could understand the consequences without finding a way of dealing with them. Sea fisheries, he noted, were the only significant economic activity of developed countries that are a form not of harvesting or processing but of hunting. So he diagnosed the feelings they arouse to be both deep and ancient. 'As a fisherman myself,' he wrote, 'I understand these feelings. If I ever find someone else engaged in fishing a pool which by law, convention or comity I have a better right to be fishing at that moment than he, I experience feelings of sheer rage.'[33] The thirty pages he devotes to the fish issue are the most brilliant in his history, recounting the apparent modesty of the issue at the beginning and the life-and-death struggle it became by the end. But they tell a sorry story.

O'Neill asks himself, in conclusion, whether, taking one thing with another and considering them all in the balance, Britain got terms that were 'reasonable, advantageous and not too onerous'. And he has no doubt about it. He answers with an 'unhesitating affirmative'.[34] Yet he does not claim all, or even the essence, of the credit. As he noted from the outset, his own negotiations were, for all their length, peripheral and secondary. What mattered was the politics, and the over arching agreement secured between two politicians.

We return to the role of Prime Minister Heath, and his fellow protagonist in the quest for a solidarity between national interests, Georges Pompidou. If these terms were satisfactory, it was because the leaders desired the negotiation to succeed. And, in particular, Pompidou desired it, as he showed by engineering – or allowing to be engineered, it matters little – a summit meeting between himself and Heath which was decisive in securing British entry. It is rare to be able to say as much about any moment of diplomacy. Usually, every moment belongs to a skein of events made up of complex interconnections, all or perhaps none of which seem to be absolutely crucial. But, in the British negotiation with Europe, one truth which nobody contests is that the

Pompidou–Heath summit on 19–20 May 1971 was the moment that decided everything.

Pompidou, though he had been de Gaulle's Prime Minister, was not in fact a Gaullist *croyant et pratiquant*. He was not another Couve. When I talked to M. Couve de Murville in Paris in 1994, he told me dismissively that Pompidou's interest in getting Britain into the Common Market was a matter of domestic politics. 'He wanted to show he wasn't like de Gaulle,' said Couve.[35] A banker and a countryman, proud of his peasant origins, Pompidou, it is true, had never been very interested in foreign affairs. Insofar as he had an interest, he was more inclined to be anti-German than anti-British, and lacked most of the Gaullist rage against the imagined conspiracies of Anglo-Saxons. As President he soon made foreign policy his private domain. Not least of his reasons for this was a determination to contest the dominance of the unreconstructed Gaullists, the heirs and allies of Couve, at the Quai d'Orsay.

The reasons why he favoured British entry, if he could secure conditions that continued to favour France, were the usual mixture of the political and the personal. It is ever thus: but here, perhaps, the personal, involving Heath, were indispensable.

In terms of politics, Pompidou thought, the time had probably come. His closest aide in 1970, Jean-René Bernard, told me in 1994: 'It was the right moment for a real choice. There were no special reasons to refuse, if the negotiation was good. If we refused, we would have had a severe crisis inside the Common Market. And we would have been on very bad terms with the British for fifty years.'[36]

There was a tide in the affairs of continent and archipelago, carrying them together. A Dutchman, Emile van Lennep, secretary-general of the OECD, saw a lot of Pompidou at the time. The French understood, he thought, that the Common Market would become weak and undirected if it did not grow. They didn't like it, because it would reduce their control, but they had to accept it. 'I found out very early that there was not to be another veto,' van Lennep recalled. 'Britain would succeed. Not because Britain had changed, but because the application couldn't be resisted any more. British membership became a political necessity not just for the British but for the others as well.'[37]

All the same, a question remained: who would do the deed? At the time these thoughts were percolating through the Elysée, the British Prime Minister, his application on the table, was Harold Wilson. Had Wilson won the 1970 election, the ineluctable forces of history might have had to bide their time. Roy Denman, one of the negotiators, says in his book (published in 1996) that, if Wilson had turned up in Paris for a summit meeting, he 'would have been shown the door and Britain to this day would have remained outside the Community'.[38] Michael Palliser, Wilson's private secretary at the time, recalled his own modified pessimism. 'I'm absolutely convinced he wouldn't have been able to persuade the French to let us in,' Palliser told me. Much is also made, in Foreign Office lore, of an unforgettable blunder the Prime Minister made in 1967, when he arrived very late for a dinner at the French ambassador's London residence. Pompidou, visiting as Prime Minister, was supposed to be his host. Not only was he unimpressed by Wilson's excuse, that he had had to attend a Commons debate on Vietnam, but the French saw a certain symbolism in Wilson's dishevelled appearance. 'You could almost feel the self-satisfaction when we met them next day,' Palliser remembered. 'They looked at this Government which had just had to devalue, which was in an economic mess, and there they were with the strong franc. It was a real reversal of roles, after years of us looking down on them.'[39]

More seriously, Wilson failed to pass the old Gaullist test, which still applied even though de Gaulle had gone. Did Britain really mean it? Was she prepared to make an unconditional commitment to Europe as it was? The French were not convinced in 1970 that Wilson could be relied on not to think first about the Atlantic and the Commonwealth.

Heath, on the other hand, was seen quite differently. He came with credentials, vouched for from within the vast freemasonry of his acquaintance. He told me about it himself. It all began on a beach in Spain, in 1960, where he had gone to diet. Whiling away the time, he noticed a Frenchman, sitting two tables away with his American wife and their son. One day, the Frenchman came over to him and said: 'If you don't eat any more, you'll never be able to deal with de Gaulle.' Thereafter, the two men lay on the beach for many mornings, drinking sherry and eating prawns. It was the beginning of quite a momentous friendship.[40]

It is typical of Heath's guardedness, as a source for almost any information about his life, that having told me this story he declined to tell me the name of his friend. Until he wrote his own memoirs, he was extraordinarily coy: possessive of anything to do with Europe, in particular: the jealous guardian, it seemed to me, not only of a certain point of view but of sacred details of the story that everyone else showed a bottomless capacity, whether malign or otherwise, to get wrong.

It wasn't hard to complete the picture, however, since coyness had failed to conceal the name from several of Heath's colleagues who got their memoirs in first. The man on the beach was Michel Jobert, who happened later to become Pompidou's private secretary. They kept in touch. Naturally, Heath sent his Harvard lectures to Jobert, who translated them for Pompidou, who pronounced himself delighted with their message, especially Heath's idea for Anglo-French nuclear sharing. 'This shows that Heath is European,' Pompidou told Jobert. 'Pompidou knows you are serious,' Jobert told Heath. 'That contributed very largely to the result,' Heath told me in 1994.

Although this sounds like an exaggeration, its truthful aspect should not be underestimated. It was important to Pompidou, if he was to change the French position, to be certain he was dealing with someone whose attitudes and commitment he could trust. Around the axis of the Heath–Pompidou relationship, the negotiations for British entry rotated towards a successful conclusion.

The climax came in Paris, in the middle of May 1971. Industrious though O'Neill and his interlocutors had been, progress until that point had been sticky. There was known to be a political will, in London and, at least in the person of the President, in Paris. Yet the negotiators lacked the power to make, on either side, the concessions to express it. Pompidou and Heath settled all that, in twelve hours of deeply private talks, with interpreters only, of which we know more about the essence than we do about the detail.

There had been a big build-up, the usual elusive feints and weaves, neither lot of diplomats wanting to be the first to propose the summit lest this show some sign of weakness. The French officials, indeed, who were Gaullist to a man, did not want to propose it at all. The divisions between the President and the Quai persisted, to such an extent that Pompidou stipulated to London, when the idea was in the air, that the French Foreign Minister, by now Maurice Schumann, should be told nothing about it. Con O'Neill's history describes the lengths to which the British were compelled (by Jobert, acting for Pompidou) to go to ensure that the Quai d'Orsay was 'completely excluded', and the French ambassador in London, Baron Geoffroy de Courcel – 'aloof, frigid and critical', says O'Neill – kept wholly in the dark.[41]

In some ways, however, Heath's role vis-à-vis his own officials was not dissimilar. The Foreign Office, as the history showed, had as deep a suspicion of the French as the Quai did of any breach with Gaullist orthodoxy. Preparing for the summit, Heath was on guard against the diplomats. 'PM cross with FO for, he thinks, anti-French mutterings,' Douglas Hurd, his political secretary, wrote in his diary.[42] He also

applied his own caustic interrogation of the Treasury's sceptical submissions. For several days, a length of time appropriate to the magnitude
of the moment, Heath sat on the Downing Street lawn, wading through
departmental briefs, challenging officials on the sterling balances, New
Zealand butter, Caribbean sugar and the rest. Even though there was a
shared intention that nobody should be a loser, he was getting ready for
man-to-man combat.

In the event, it was not a hard contest. An army of advisers journeyed
to Paris. 'The knights in full cry, especially on sterling,' Hurd noted, of
Britain's mandarin negotiators, after the first day. But their role was
mainly confined to gossiping in the corridors, as 'the great men strolled
and talked, and talked and strolled again', watched only at a distance by
auxiliaries who became increasingly puzzled as to what was going on.
Even when it was over, there was some uncertainty. 'We ran into an
unusual and potentially awkward situation,' O'Neill writes. The precise
nature of agreement on the main issues 'was not made known'.[43]

Such are the perils of staffless diplomacy. That the meeting was a
success, however, was eventually not in doubt. The two men, both highly
proficient at engaging with the detail, devoted many more of their hours
to the big picture. They disposed of the sterling problem – 'a totally
unexpected settlement', O'Neill recorded – in short order. Their aides
worried about the delays, but the principals were in fact progressing
towards the definitive deal. There were great meals, as there have been
from beginning to end of this history. Ambassador Soames gave a grand
lunch to which the President, unusually, came: a real tribute, in Heath's
opinion. Then Pompidou laid on his own splendiferous banquet. Such
was the paucity of outcome thus far, however, that Hurd, fretting, began
to think it was all going wrong. After the first day, he writes, 'we were
dismayed to find how little had been decided'. Heath, as he remembered
it, took mischievous pleasure in failing to reassure his political secretary
and the rest of his staff about what was happening. 'All the press thought
the thing was a flop and we were covering it up,' Heath told me,
smirking at the recollection, even twenty years later.[44]

The press conference to announce that it was far from a flop took
place at 9 p.m. on the second evening. With style and courage, Pompidou
arranged for it to take place in the Salon des Fêtes at the Elysée Palace,
the room where de Gaulle had announced the veto in 1963.

The negotiations, of course, were not over. There remained seven
months of detailed work ahead, before they were completely finished.
But the President gave the signal. 'It would be unreasonable now to

believe that an agreement is not possible,' he said. 'The spirit of our talks over the past few days enables me to think that the negotiations will be successful.' As for Britain and France, recent history could be regarded as undone. The ghost of de Gaulle was, apparently, laid to rest.

'There were many people', Pompidou told the press, 'who believed that Great Britain was not European and did not wish to become European, and that Britain wanted to enter the Community only to destroy it. Many people also thought France was prepared to use all kinds of means and pretexts to propose a new veto to the entry of Great Britain into the Community. Well, ladies and gentlemen, you see tonight before you two men who are convinced to the contrary.'

So: the political class had at last succeeded. The men of topmost power were finally of one mind. There is a guileless excitement about Heath's first literary effort to say what it meant to him. 'It was one of the greatest moments of my life,' he simply said.[45] Though there was more to do, he had done what mattered: come out, by his lights, triumphant, from what O'Neill calls 'by far the most significant meeting that took place in the whole course of the negotiations'.[46]

It was, however, only the beginning of his struggle: a point he never entirely got the measure of. After the captains and the kings, there was another constituency to take account of.

*

THE DEAL DONE in Paris, and eventually ratified in Brussels, was a big deal. But it was not about the biggest matters. It didn't address any of the great issues – future policies of the Community, its relations with the rest of the world, the reform of its institutions and how they should work. Nor did it have anything to say about the larger future of Britain. The deep, existential *meaning*, for Britain, of getting into 'Europe' was not considered. The way Britain would have to change had no place in the work of the technocrats. The future of the nation-state wasn't on the agenda. If the (unindexed) O'Neill history gives any attention to the question of sovereignty, I overlooked it.

At one level, this was to be expected. It wasn't the negotiators' business to open up these profounder matters. The great issue was taken as read: Britain was ready to make the national adjustments involved, as long as the technical terms were right. Indeed, there was a school of thought in London so passionate for entry that it thought the debate should be terminated there and then. A Tory MP, Sir Anthony Meyer, told the Commons in January 1971: 'Frankly, I do not think it depends on the terms at all. I believe it would be in the interests of this country to join the EEC whatever the terms.'[47] In the Lords, six months later, Lord Crowther said: 'You do not haggle over the subscription when you are invited to climb aboard a lifeboat. You scramble aboard while there is still a seat for you.'[48]

Heath, however, knew better. He had done for some time. Before the election, he coined a phrase that never died – one of the few he ever contrived – which was to become a text much pored over, twisted and turned, in the coming years. Speaking of the proposed enlargement of the Community by four more countries, he offered the opinion that this would not be appropriate 'except with the full-hearted consent of the parliaments and peoples of the new member countries'.[49]

This speech was actually meant to be a warning to the Six. It was saying: Don't press us too hard, we have to get this thing past our own democratic tests. It was a negotiator's speech, delivered when he didn't know whether he or Wilson would be sitting at the table. But it became a rod periodically lying heavy on Prime Minister Heath's back. Hurd wrote that it 'fell victim to Wilson's talent for distortion', in the sense that Wilson found it convenient to construe its meaning as the promise of a referendum – whereas neither leader, in those distant early 1970s, made any such commitment. The idea of a referendum was briefly discussed by Heath's team, only to be rejected as unBritish. Wilson, in office, thought the same. In the language of that time, it was apparent that what Heath meant by consent was the consent of Parliament, as filtered through a perhaps more than usually thorough awareness of public opinion.

The phrase, nonetheless, set a benchmark. It became, for ever afterwards, the test which the Heath Government, and its successors, could be said at convenient moments to have passed only by fraud. Full-hearted consent? When did the British people ever agree to be ruled by the bungling tyrants of Brussels? And so on.

But there is a subtler gloss to be made. It tells us something about the state of the argument at the time. In saying what it was that people had to consent to, Heath was very specific: it was the nature of the settlement. This, he said, must not be 'unequal and unfair', and the test that counted was 'primarily the effect upon the standard of living of the individual citizen'. He made little mention of those spacious questions about the future of Britain as an independent country. Although that was the question on which the people were later said not to have given their opinion, full-hearted or otherwise, it wasn't the question Heath meant. Heath was talking cost of living, not cost of nationhood.

Nor, to be clear, did that differ from the state of the national discussion as hitherto conducted. Returning with his deal, Heath faced a brand of scepticism that had changed little since the first negotiation. Compared with the furies emerging in the 1990s, the critics of EEC entry in his own party then remained severe but gentlemanly, and not very numerous. They were mostly concerned with the old issues, like the damage that would be done to the Commonwealth. Some contested the economic case, but none of them desired to bring down the Government. Although now, as before, some voices took the sovereignty point, they did not, with one exception, seize the public mind. Sovereignty wasn't what the main discussion was about in the Labour Party either: or at any rate, if it was, it was indirect, the old complaint that membership of the EEC was the kiss of death for the future of socialism in an independent country. Of the rich grammar of sovereignty, and the seductive investigations it prompted into the meaning of nation, little was heard in the early 1970s.

The exception, however, mattered. He was a bit of a prophet: not a successful prophet, because he roundly lost his cause, but a foreteller of the concerns that were eventually, much later, to grip the British psyche. He was the one thing that did register a change. Through him, for the first time, a demon began to stir that had not been fully wakened before, except briefly by Hugh Gaitskell. The pitch he made shifted the argument from fuddy-duddy concerns about the redness of the map to anxieties closer to home. Instead of worrying about other people's countries, the British were invited, by a harsh, haranguing, driven voice, to think about their own.

Enoch Powell, bringing overt and eloquent nationalism into the European argument, had the beginnings of a visceral effect. Along with the rod of 'full-hearted consent', Powell was a cross Ted Heath had to bear. He is worth a little inspection, for he was in many ways the godfather of the successor tribe, to whom nation was not merely something but everything. He had historic relevance in another way as well, as a perfect example of the oracular disfigurement that marks generations of British politicians talking and thinking about Europe: the louder the voice, the surer the chance that it is contradicting itself.

Mr Powell, former classics professor, compelling orator, One Nation Tory, MP for Wolverhampton South-West since 1950, was, it is true, always a kind of English nationalist. He could utter, without flinching, endless romantic paeans to those 'who felt no country but this to be their own'.[50] But, when Europe first came to the forefront of British politics, Powell evidently saw no contradiction between preserving such essential nationhood and entry into the Common Market. In fact, he had a special connection with the project. By an enjoyable irony, the one year Powell ever spent in anybody's Cabinet, as Macmillan's Minister of Health, happened to be the year, 1962–3, when entering Europe was the Cabinet's all-devouring purpose, something to which he raised no objection.

When the party was driven from power, and Heath became its leader, Powell's enthusiasm for Europe did not diminish. The One Nation group of MPs published a pamphlet, *One Europe*, that was little short of a federalist tract. Powell was not the only future sceptic to be associated with it. It was edited by his friend, Nicholas Ridley, then a passionate supporter of British membership of a united Europe and a federalist[51] who was later, when a minister under Margaret Thatcher, to be another exponent of the Principle of Voluble Contradiction. Powell, it was reported[52] and never denied, wrote 25 per cent of *One Europe*, a paper that advocated 'the full economic, military and political union of Europe'. Addressing the problem of sovereignty, the paper noted that already, through Nato, the IMF, the GATT and other international affiliations, 'we have lost much sovereignty', and that each move towards European unification 'requires that extra political step'.[53] Rather few British politicians have been associated with anything so extremely federalist as this effusion. In keeping with it, after the 1966 election, when his election address supported British membership, Powell, as shadow spokesman on Defence, objected to a Labour plan for withdrawing some troops from Germany on the very grounds that it would imperil the larger objective. 'All our professions of anxiety to enter the Common Market would be discounted,' he said. As late as April 1967 he attended a conference at Cambridge University, where he hob-nobbed with the likes of George Ball, Kennedy's hyper-keen European at the State Department, and Pierre Uri, a draftsman of the Treaty of Rome. The idea of the conference was specifically to promote European unification, and Powell was an uncritical participant.[54]

Not long after this, however, he underwent a conversion experience. As often happened on the right – it was especially noticeable among the intimate minions of Margaret Thatcher – this took radical form. From apparently supporting political union, Powell moved in four years to the opposite extremity. Instead of acknowledging political union, he utterly rejected it. It was the very essence, he said, of the horror of the EEC. As the leading voice of English nationalism, he became Heath's most implacable opponent. The people, he told the 1971 party conference, would not tolerate British 'sovereignty being abolished or transformed'. Fusing a rhetoric of anti-black immigration with a bitter discourse against all things 'European', he took the independence of old England, which he might reluctantly extend to 'Britain', further out than any politician since Oswald Mosley.

For Powell, in effect, wanted no alliances of any kind. He was an anti-imperialist from way back, and a scornful critic of the Commonwealth. Equally, he built a long record as a critic of the Atlantic alliance, ridiculing America's global pretensions and overtly hostile to her management of the Cold War. The distancing from Europe was therefore added to a portfolio of isolationism, which left the Soviet Union as the only international entity for which Powell offered his occasional support. 'We do not need to be tied up with anybody,' he said in 1969, when making his formal break with the earlier pro-Europe position. 'We earn what we earn by our work and our brains ... We are not a drowning man clutching at a rope and screaming for someone to throw him a lifebelt.' Britain Alone seemed to be the Powellite message from the moment Heath began.

This genius of international statesmanship nonetheless had his followers, indeed his worshippers. They were not upset by his lurching transformations. Nor did they explore with much rigour the way he justified them.

His talk-out was, for a man of fastidious intellect, confusing. The confusion might even be said to shade into a kind of unconscious dishonesty, if such is possible to credit to so self-regarding a mind. What Powell said, when interviewed on the question in 1994, was that in the 1960s he never really understood what the EEC was all about. He claimed to have judged the matter of the 1961 application entirely in economic terms. 'I said to myself,' he recalled, ' "That's going for free trade. I'm in favour of free trade." '[55] This was an odd statement, given that the EEC was not about free trade but precisely about a customs union that protected trade against the outside world. But it was even odder, given the plain recognition in *One Europe* that some kind of political unification was the inescapable meaning of a signature to the Treaty of Rome. Indeed, it is quite incredible to imagine Powell, a particular student of constitutional matters throughout his political career, being unaware that the entire nature of the EEC – visible in all its founding documents, spelled out in the countless speeches of its founders, recognized in numerous Whitehall studies prepared before, during and after the Messina conversations fifteen years earlier – tended towards the ever closer union of political Europe.

By saying that he had thought it was all about economics, however, Powell proved himself a kind of intellectual leader. He was an apologist for amnesia, a condition in which he had a host of successor-disciples. A similar case was made by many latter-day Euro-sceptics reluctant to recall their earlier Euro-enthusiasm, including some whose customary attention to detail rendered it especially hard to believe their pleas of surprise at the turn events had taken. What Enoch Powell said about the Treaty of Rome, Margaret Thatcher closely mirrored when she came to defend, in her new guise as a ferocious anti-European, her signature on the Single European Act in 1986. Nobody, she said, had told her what it really meant.[56]

Since these explanations are hard to credit, one must search for other clues. I suspect they are intrinsic to the psychological, as much as the political, aspects of the 'Europe' question in recent British history. In the Thatcher case rather more than the Powell, the record suggests a leader in an advanced stage of denial. The past, in some sense, simply did not occur. So engulfing is their present rage at what is happening that these people simply can't accept they were ever in a different condition, other than as a result of gross deception. Aware of their apparent inconsistency, they writhe in a serpentine struggle to deny the possibility that this same, sentient, political person could have taken one position – often acting under many heads to advance it – only to adopt another that implies they were once profoundly wrong.

Powell was the path-finder for this tendency. And in 1971, when Heath had to get the product of his negotiation through Parliament, he was the siren voice that summoned forty Conservative MPs to oppose what the Government was doing. This much affected, though it did not determine, the course of events.

At this stage, we may deal briskly with what happened in Parliament. Plainly, the governing party would be split, and its majority of thirty was not sufficient to accommodate the dissenters without help from some-where else. Since the Labour Party was also split, everything rested on the Government business managers selecting the most judicious tactic to maximize the chance that Labour pro-Europeans would endorse the historic moment that now appeared. They were highly motivated, but they needed the proper encouragement. They did not, of course, include

the leadership. In a collective renunciation, of near-Powellite proportions, Wilson and the majority of his colleagues made plain soon after
the election that the process they had begun could no longer rely on
their support. Later, they found, as they were bound to do, that the
terms secured by O'Neill and Heath were bad enough to justify the party
doing everything it could to ensure that entry did not happen. But
there were powerful resisters of this instruction – Roy Jenkins, Shirley
Williams, Harold Lever, others – who were to mark the history deeply.

Heath's contribution to securing their votes was, at first, astonish-
ingly unhelpful. Although he had been Chief Whip for many years, and
party management was supposed to be his forte, he persisted in the
stubborn pretences of party discipline until the eleventh hour, before
conceding to his Chief Whip, Francis Pym, that a free vote on the Tory
side was the surest way of liberating the principled rebels on the other
side. On 28 October 1971, this duly occurred, with sixty-nine Labour
MPs, led by Roy Jenkins, the deputy leader, walking through the
Government lobby, and helping to provide Heath with a majority of 112
in favour of the principle of entry on the terms he had secured.

Not everything was such plain sailing. During the passage of the
European Communities Bill, most of the Labour rebels did not feel able
to oblige. There were some narrow scrapes, though on every occasion
enough backstairs intelligence was collected by Labour pro-Europeans to
ensure that the Bill stayed on course. The Government majorities fell to
single figures several times. But there were 104 votes, and not one of
them was lost. The Bill passed unamended into law. And, on 1 January
1973, Britain entered the Common Market.

What, however, did people think they were doing when this happened? What did Heath think? How much was known, or unknown, or
perhaps concealed from view?

In making the great leap, how conscious were the British, either at
the top or among the masses, of precisely what it meant? These
questions, in retrospect, have acquired more than academic importance.
They will continue to reverberate through the story. They have become,
for some people, the essence of the matter. And since these people have
been among those most potently driving the debate – the apparently
unresolved struggle inside the national mind – a quarter-century later,
the aspersions they cast deserve to be studied: are, indeed, a central part
of the biography of Edward Heath.

For Heath, two epiphanies marked the triumph of his life. First, there was the conclusion of his meeting with Pompidou, the great moment, as he later wrote, that he could never forget. Second came the night when he got his majority of 112, which he celebrated, while everyone else was going to parties, by returning to Downing Street, sitting quietly at the clavichord he had installed in his flat and playing the first of J. S. Bach's forty-eight preludes and fugues. An awkward, remote, emotionally secluded leader experienced a cathartic victory. But what, in truth, was it all about?

At one level, not only was the purpose clear but it received the fullest possible attention from the organs of British democracy. Entering the European Community, the purpose of three successive governments since 1961, plainly and substantially changed the nation's direction, and everybody in the country was made aware of it. How could its meaning be missed, after a decade of vexed probing, several hundred hours of debate in both Houses of Parliament, a public discussion that surged, with only occasional ebbings, through the media, and an inexorably growing awareness that this was the question, for better or for worse, that preceded all others bearing on the future of Britain?

Nor did these deliberations suffer from a want of official guidance on the facts. From 1967, dossiers and statements poured off the government presses, explaining how both Labour and Conservative Cabinets regarded the available evidence on the gamut of economic and political consequences that would flow from the success of their policy. Especially substantial was Heath's own white paper, published in July 1971, which gave a long account of what had been negotiated. It was not a piece of special pleading. Heath admitted, for example, that food prices would certainly rise, though by rather less than Wilson had put forward eighteen months earlier. He conceded, at least by implication, that the British share of the EEC budget might become a serious burden unless – a likely story! – the Common Agriculture Policy was drastically reformed. Somewhere or other, it is possible to locate official texts and formulations covering every aspect of what Britain was about to do.

On the other hand, there were ways and ways of presenting them to the public, and the most open way was not always selected. That was especially true of the deepest, most inchoate question: what membership of 'Europe' truly meant for national sovereignty. This was the issue which, if it proved to have been falsely handled, lay in wait to invalidate at its innermost core the nation's 'full-hearted consent'. And, long afterwards, this became the argument. When Euro-scepticism secured its tightest grip on the throat of government, in the later years of John Major, the sense moved powerfully through the Conservative Party that British entry was originally approved on false, even fraudulent, pretences.

The Heath white paper, whatever its other merits, handled this matter with some opaqueness. Phrases were dreamed up that could mean all things to all men and women. 'There is no question of any erosion of essential national sovereignty,' the paper said. 'What is proposed is a sharing and an enlargement of individual national sovereignties in the general interest.'[57]

This was open, as intended, to many constructions. It conceded that entry into Europe would certainly do something to the popular concept of an independent nation. The curtailment of such separateness, and its replacement by selective immersions in a larger pool of multi-national power, presided over by a supra-national body, was the essence of the European idea. But by inserting 'essential' into the account of what would not be lost, the authors left it open to readers to make their own assessment of what aspects of sovereignty were included. Was the supremacy of European law a breach of 'essential' sovereignty? What about the special power of the Commission, as the sole permitted initiator of European policy? Where, on this scale, did one place the advent of majority voting, on issues which might thereby pass out of British control?

So 'essential' glided into the vocabulary of reassurance. It offered the Government deniability. For who could ever say the promise had been broken? The accompanying phrase – 'a sharing and an enlargement' – was even more impenetrable. How individual national sovereignty could be shared, while at the same time being enlarged, without compromising its individuality, was a question to baffle any casuist.

It was not entirely indefensible, if you assumed, as Heath did, that sovereignty wasn't a theoretical concept but a many-headed instrument – sometimes solitary, sometimes pooled, exercised separately or together according to the needs of the moment – to be judged by its pragmatic usefulness. Heath developed many metaphors to try and get this point across, including, in later life, the image of the miser. 'Sovereignty isn't something you put down in the cellar in your gold reserve, and go down with a candle once a week to see if it is still there,' was one I heard him proffer to a meeting in 1994.[58] The problem was, however, that the white paper phrases, however explicable, and even defensible, were a hostage to anyone who later desired to mount a case for saying there had been a crucial element of dissimulation in what the world was told.

If nothing else, they lowered the guard of a nation supposedly on watch for any fundamental change that entry into Europe was about to impose upon it.

This tendency continued in the House of Commons debates of 1971–2. Ministers did not lie, but they avoided telling the full truth. They refrained from stating categorically that the law of the European Community would have supremacy over British law. This was a conscious, much deliberated choice. The Bill did not contain, as it might have done, a clause stating in terms the general rule that Community law was to be supreme. There were, it could be argued (and was, especially by Geoffrey Howe), technical justifications for this. It could be defended as an economy of drafting, leaving it open to the courts, in due course, to make the necessary assertion that such supremacy was a fact.[59] But the more potent reason for leaving this inexplicit in 1972 was political. Spelled out in a clause that had to be openly debated and passed, Community supremacy would have had explosive possibilities. The Government lawyers knew perfectly well what the legal consequences were. 'Does he think we were all complete idiots?' one of them riposted, when a professor suggested many years later that the degree of subordination of British law to European law had come as a surprise.[60] Of course they knew. But the draftsmen had been instructed to tread carefully, knowing, in this man's recollection, that full and open admission of what was being done to parliamentary sovereignty would be 'so astounding' as to put the whole Bill in danger.

Nor did ministers state that the European Communities Act would be, in practice, irrevocable. They preferred to repeat the correct but essentially academic formula that what Parliament had passed it could always repeal. Somehow their capacity for dramatic excitement eluded them when it came to giving due emphasis to the startling proposition that Parliament was surrendering some of its independence to the clauses and powers of a written constitution, namely the Treaty of Rome.

They put it, in short, more gently, quietly, obscurely. Heath himself seldom talked about sovereignty being surrendered. He was not prepared to concede, in cold fact, that although there might be a gain in power there would be a loss of independence. Winding up the historic debate in October 1971, the word he chose was as soporific as could be: 'In joining we are making a commitment which *involves* our sovereignty, but we are also gaining an opportunity.' Geoffrey Rippon, his lieutenant, occasionally had more accurate formulations dragged out of him, but Heath himself declined to yield an inch of ground, even to those who thought the very point of the Common Market was to reduce national independence, and thereby enlarge the collective power of Germany, France, Britain and whoever else belonged.

This disguising was part of an intensely political process. Only by sweetening the truth about national sovereignty, apparently, could popular support be kept in line. There was another confusion as well, perhaps less calculated but also having its place in an intellectual contest that has never really ended. To what extent could the whole venture be called 'political' in its very nature? This too was much muddied, much obscured.

At the time, the vanguard of the Government's case was invariably economic, and the arguments gaining most purchase on the public mind concerned the impact of entry on jobs, on prices, on industry, on the likely fate of a once-great economic entity now seen to be lagging behind the continent. Whenever 'the political' was mentioned, it tended to be projected forward into a vague and indecipherable future.

Sir Alec Douglas-Home, the Foreign Secretary, was always reassuring. There would be no 'political' aspect of the Community without Britain's agreement, he insisted. All development would depend upon consensus. 'Decisions on the political evolution of the Community', he said in the October 1971 debate, 'are not for now, even for tomorrow, but for the future. Any decision made on political advance must have the unanimous support of all the members of the partnership.' Whether Europe would develop any kind of political identity was also addressed by Prime Minister Heath. In the same debate, he presented the issue as a blank sheet of paper. 'What we shall have', he ventured, 'is an opportunity, which we do not possess and will not possess unless we join, of working out schemes for the future of the major part of Europe.'

As stated, this was true enough. But, as an answer to the preoccupations that later came to obsess people, it did not meet the point. It contained its own form of deception. In later years, the intrinsic nature of the European project was always referred to as political – which, indeed, was the truth. Historians and participants alike agreed that, *au fond*, politics was what the Community was about and politics was what British entry was about. Heath himself, in elder-statesman mode, invariably used the most emphatic language to drive from the field the numerous antagonists who pretended not to have known that. 'From the first, the Community was political,' he stated in the first Franco-British lecture, in 1992. 'It is still political. It will always be political.'[61] His derision for those who imagined otherwise could not have been more eloquently conveyed.

At the time, however, Heath did not put things so clearly. To have done so might have frightened the horses. In any case, this wasn't what most bothered people who talked about the political ramifications of entry. What they meant wasn't the future aspiration of a political Europe, so much as the likely emasculation of a politically independent Britain. Both, eventually, mattered. But in the early 1970s, it was the latter rather than the former that was capable of being addressed with more certain clarity than Heath was ever willing to supply.

This charge of near-duplicity, when levelled during the ferocious Sceptic Years, drew a response of equal indignation. Heath himself, when I interviewed him in 1995, put it down to the ignorance of a new generation. They were simply unaware of history, and did not know how much he had said at the time about the political nature of the enterprise, and how much, in any case, the sovereignty of nations was already diluted by such bodies at Nato. Pressed to show that the people had been fully informed, he referred me to the phrase in the Treaty aspiring to 'an ever-closer union among the peoples of Europe'. 'That embraces everything,' Heath said, with conclusive satisfaction,[62] before embarking on a little lecture designed to show that, because Britain had been responsible for creating federal states in Canada and Australia, there was something contradictory about the British fear of a federal United States of Europe.

That isn't the only defence, or the best one. A better effort can be made by Geoffrey Howe, the chief political draftsman of the European Communities Bill, and a man with his own claim to a central role in the history. As a lawyer, Howe is and was a punctilious respecter of words, and has a large repertoire of evidence that the legal issue, in particular, was well addressed in 1972, as it had been ten years earlier, often by himself. And this is true enough. Legal supremacy, which was the prime *casus belli* of Conservative Euro-sceptics in the middle 1990s, became a settled question many years before Britain joined the Community. As early as 1963, the European Court of Justice pronounced that the Treaty of Rome had, among other things, created a new legal order in international law 'for whose benefit the States have limited their sovereign rights'.[63] Subsequent cases had clarified the point that Community law applied by direct effect in each member state. The Court, along with the Commission, the Council of Ministers and even the European

Parliament, possessed superior powers that were identified as long ago as 1962, by Macmillan's Lord Chancellor Lord Dilhorne, who laid them on the line. 'These organs', he said, 'have in the spheres in which they operate ... certain supra-national powers which override those of the national constitutional bodies, and which are also incapable of challenge in the national courts of the member States.'[64] No more limpid statement of lost independence is to be found from beginning to end of this history.

Howe himself, to clinch the proof he needed that everything was open and above board, gave a lecture in October 1972 which spelled out, as he would say, the circumstances in which United Kingdom laws would be rendered invalid by Community law. It was a long, detailed, pretty scrupulous performance. In later years, he would often point to it. It did contain words that could be said, in a roundabout way, to acknowledge the subordination of UK laws. And because the subject clearly bothered him, he kept returning to it with further academic lectures designed to prove that sovereignty had been dealt with properly and/or that it was not a problem.[65]

But it was also Howe's opinion, in retrospect, that he could have been clearer. In the Commons, his words read like calculated waffling. Where there was a conflict, he said in 1972, the courts would just have to do their best to reconcile the 'inescapable and enduring sovereignty of Parliament' with the need to give effect to Treaty obligations. They would somehow interpret statute accordingly, and if there was a problem, he concluded limply, 'that would be a matter for consideration by the Government and Parliament of the day'.[66] Nobody challenged him to fill the lacunae this formula obviously left. But surveying his performance twenty-five years later, Howe wrote to an old colleague: 'I ... remain at least plausibly exposed to the charge that less of [our] thinking than was appropriate was explicitly exposed to the House of Commons at the time the Bill was being passed.'[67]

Whatever was said, in any case, was directed to an academic audience, and not designed for the enlightenment of the mass electorate. The political emphasis was not on what would change but almost entirely on what would not change. Nobody talked about the new legal ascendancy in the way Lord Denning later did. The Treaty, he said in a famous case in 1974, was 'like an incoming tide. It flows into the estuaries and up the rivers. It cannot be held back.'[68] Instead, political leaders placed their heaviest emphasis on the inviolate continuity of the common law and the unfettered independence of English courts and judges.

In short: examining the record, scanning those hours of democratic argument, one cannot but be struck by the thinness of their attention to what became the preoccupations of the 1990s. Anyone outraged by what 'Europe' seemed to have become could easily find themselves scandalized by the absence of official statements saying that this is what would happen. From there, it is not too large a stride to the construing of a conspiracy of silence.

The case, however, is not conclusive. It neglects the historical context. For the 1970s were not the 1990s. In two respects, the violence with which Heath was later attacked depends on seriously aberrant hindsight.

First, the sovereignty question was much less on people's minds in the 1970s than twenty years later. This is not an accidental, still less a manipulated, fact, but one that says something about the condition of the country. Sovereignty did, of course, have its day in the court of Parliament. It was the devouring obsession of Enoch Powell. Another eloquent prophet of the end of British independence was Anthony Wedgwood Benn, as he was still known.[69] A scattering of MPs took up the point. It throbbed through the visceral concerns of dissenters on the Tory side. But it was not dominant. Questions of economics seemed to be far more important: would the Common Market *really* be good for British industry, could our manufacturers compete against the Germans, what about the balance of payments, and so on? Even the future of the Commonwealth, in 1972, attracted more parliamentary anxiety than the future independence of Parliament. The price of food was of more concern than the coming irrelevance of debate.

Why was this? One must recall another part of the context. Hovering around the Common Market debate in those formative days was the wider question of international security. The Cold War was at its height, and Britain still thought of herself as a major player in its evolution. Macmillan had sought British entry into Europe as a way of staking a position from which she could continue to matter globally, as he showed in numerous gloomy prognostics about the fate that might grip a small country caught in the sights of the Russian bear. Prime Minister Heath's speeches were less copiously internationalist in the same sense, but his Foreign Secretary, Douglas-Home, often showed that Macmillanism was not dead. A pamphlet Home wrote in July 1971 was introduced as one that 'raises the level of the debate from groceries to survival'. Pressing the case for entry, Home said it would be 'a step of the utmost political significance', by which he meant that it would be a way of shoring up Britain's security interests in a more collective Europe.[70]

Alongside the micro-economic questions, therefore, it was the pro-spective realignment of Britain internationally that moved the debate, more than her reduction domestically: the shifting of a nation that retained a certain political self-confidence, rather than its fearful sub-mission to the tyrannies of Brussels, and all the other impositions which, in the dialectic of the 1990s, allegedly reduced a once great nation to a satrap of scheming continentals.

In a word, the Britain of 1972 was not a nation dominated by fear. She did not doubt her future as a country that mattered. She was in economic trouble, but this had not yet drained her of self-belief. In particular, 'Europe' still seemed less like the threat it became, in some people's eyes, in the 1990s than the zone of promise it had been in 1960.

This is explicable by the second factor called to the defence of Heath. His critics tended to imagine he always had secret plans to achieve in and with Europe an integrated, or 'federalist', future which the people, had they been told about it, would never have supported. Again, the truth is messier. On the one hand, there was no such worked-out scheme. On the other, insofar as political leaders had thought about the future, they had done so very publicly.

In the early 1970s, the shape of the European Economic Community was in many respects uncertain. For a start, it was still known by that name, the *economic* community, designating economics as its prime sphere of action. Its political character was quite immature. The Euro-pean Parliament was still described, in the official English version, as a mere Assembly, and was not developing into anything much more than a talk-shop. The Luxembourg Compromise operated. This had been introduced in 1966 to surmount the impasse de Gaulle inflicted on the Community by refusing to accept majority voting. The Compromise conferred an informal right of veto by any member state that considered a 'very important' national interest was being imperilled: an important reassurance to the anxious British.

Such a level of uncertainty fortified several of the more thoughtful contributors to the Commons debates, including former or even present sceptics who decided there was no grievous threat to independent British nationhood. Sir Harry Legge-Bourke, for example, said he had originally been against the European venture. In 1951 he thought the Schuman Plan amounted to supra-national government, but now he thought differently. 'The more one studies the way in which Europe is working out,' he said in October 1971, 'the less likely it is that there will be close-knit federation.' He saw the 'old, traditional differences' between the nations alive and well, and did not believe that the final shape of Europe was anywhere near ready for definition.[71] Angus Maude, another Conservative MP, refused to support Heath, but based his case entirely on economic grounds. He thought the political argument of little importance. 'There is no political unity in the Six,' he said, 'and the likelihood is that there will not be any for a generation.' Nor did he believe 'that there is any serious risk of a major or total loss of sovereignty'.[72]

This perception, often deployed by Heath's defenders, has its problems. It does not sit comfortably with the parallel assertion they have made to squash all subsequent objectors: namely, that such people have no right to speak, since it was clear from the start what the country was signing up for. The Treaty of Rome says everything: the British signed it: end of story. So went the triumphalist case. The contempt inherent in it has been the greatest flaw in the prosecution of the pro-Europe cause in British politics for twenty years.

Nonetheless, the practice of reading into the era of the early 1970s the assumptions of the middle 1990s produced a false indictment. Heath's own speeches reflected uncertainty more than a grand, fixed plan. He was inviting the nation to engage with forces of history that had yet to show what they could do. 'Working out schemes for the future of the major part of Europe' was an activity he sincerely looked forward to, in the national interest. Presenting his case to Parliament, he enthused at the prospect of a summit meeting that had been called by France and Germany for some time in 1972, which he foresaw as some kind of Congress of Vienna, settling monetary and trading matters, and 'future political development'. When this summit came about, in October 1972, Britain, though not yet formally a member of the EEC, was present, and contributed to an outcome Heath never forgot. The communiqué that resulted from it, half of it written personally by President Pompidou, was, he stated on numerous occasions for years afterwards, 'the finest international communiqué ever written'.[73]

An element of this communiqué, moreover, challenges the other part of the charge-sheet: that the plan for the Community was secret. Far from it. Even before Heath became Prime Minister, Europe had pledged itself to something called economic and monetary union. At a meeting in The Hague in 1972, promoted by Pompidou and supported by the West German Chancellor, Willy Brandt, the Six pledged themselves to achieve EMU by 1980.

Although EMU didn't happen, its presence on the agenda makes another point. It was there, believed in by some, doubted by others, but arousing terminal hostility hardly anywhere. It may not have seemed real; and, very soon, turbulence in the exchange markets, together with the quadrupling of the price of oil, put paid to it for the duration. The 'snake', an arrangement by which European currencies – including sterling – locked into narrow bands of fluctuation against each other, was torn apart. But before that, as a concept, EMU aroused little outrage on constitutional grounds. At this first mooting, its role in history is surely to be the proof not of a secret federalism at large among the makers of Europe but of the indifference with which such possibilities were once regarded.

The critique to be made of Heath is real, but it is different from the one which is usually mobilized. As the nearest thing to Britain's father of Europe, he had significant shortcomings.

Though possessed of a great idea, he was congenitally unable to convey its resonance to the nation he wanted to believe it. Whether you liked it or not, his idea was the most discrete and particular Big Idea that any British leader had seized on since the war. Yet he could never make it sing. As already noted, he was an entirely uninspiring orator. For a people as reluctantly European as the British, this was an unfortunate conjunction. It meant that, in this formative period, when there was much cynicism to be lifted from the nation's soul, the voice at the top had the levitation of a lead balloon.

This wasn't merely a matter of rhetorical technique. In retrospect, what Heath seems to have lacked, rather surprisingly, was a coherent vision of what Europe, and British membership of Europe, ought actually to mean. If the message did not get across as it deserved to, perhaps this was because the content, as much as the form, was deficient.

Getting into Europe was plainly a Heath objective to which he applied every ounce of energy and resource. Nobody could fault his commitment. But there were officials who saw this as a purpose without a clear enough objective. Was getting in for its own sake, to Heath, enough? Michael Butler was a key panjandrum of the Europeanized Whitehall machine, who spent six years as Britain's permanent representative to the Communities. In Heath's time, Butler was head of the European Integration Department at the Foreign Office. As such, he talked to the Prime Minister often, and found him, he once told me, 'extraordinarily Gaullist'. That is to say, Heath saw the EEC not so much as a community of theoretical equals, rather as a theatre for his own domination. There were decisions in the early 1970s, for example about the location of an embryonic central bank, which Heath approached from the start with a veto mentality, Butler told me. Even though everyone else had agreed the bank should be in Luxembourg, Heath simply thought his own preference, which happened to be for Brussels, was the only solution. Though he was exultant at being at Europe's top table, Heath's temperament, wasn't really, in the concessive sense, properly *communautaire* at all. 'I always wonder to what extent Ted really understood what it was all about,' Butler said in 1993.

So did someone closer to him, Robert Armstrong, his private secretary, fellow music-lover and a zealous European. Armstrong saw Heath's Europeanism as rooted in the war. He shared with the continentals, thought Armstrong, the overriding belief that war must not happen again, and that the EEC was the way to avoid it. Britain should belong as part of this anti-war alliance, and also to subject her own industries to a reviving jolt from European competition. But Heath's larger purpose Armstrong found a little mystifying. He told me: 'It always seemed to me that, for him, getting in was an end in itself. I did not have the impression that he had at that time a coherent vision about what to do with it when we were in, how it would evolve and therefore how we would try and make it develop.'[74]

It was of much historic importance, all the same, that Heath remained in office for merely a single year after British membership began, in January 1973. It was probably a great misfortune. If Butler and Armstrong are right, one can't be sure how much Britain would have added any momentum towards a coherent, active 'Europe', had the Conservatives won the election in February 1974. The middle 1970s were a time of stasis in Europe, for reasons that transcended any one country's power to overcome them. But history would certainly have been different, if Heath had won: as different, perhaps, as if Wilson had won in 1970. There can be no doubt that Heath, the most committed European to lead the country between 1945 and 1997, would have tried to impose a personal stamp of Euro-enthusiasm. As it was, his year in office as an EEC head of government was not just pathetically brief, but was overwhelmed by domestic crises to which he was obliged, unavailingly, to give his entire attention.

Thereafter, he did not remain silent. And there was a long thereafter. In it, bitterness and rectitude vied to be the controlling presence in his output. In 1996, reviewing a new book, called *A History of Modern Europe*, he was not impressed. 'The sole reference to me describes me as "a yachtsman",' he complained.[75] An obtuse verdict, he felt, and sadly misinformed. But nautical metaphors are nonetheless in order. For the quarter-century after he was deposed from power, he wandered the world like some Flying Dutchman, destined never to disembark into the haven of a 'European' Britain which he should have been instrumental in creating. Alternatively, he was the Old Man of the Sea, symbol of a burden nobody else succeeded in discharging.

He remained, however, vigorous. He carried Europe with him wherever he went, castigating the fainthearts at home and abroad. I witnessed him at the age of eighty-one, in a seminar in Munich, rise from semi-slumber at the dinner table to deliver a word-perfect diatribe against doubts that had just been expressed by the Prime Minister of Bavaria about the wisdom of starting the European single currency in 1999. In his own mind, he was a major historical figure, justified in requesting, as he did, that the several parties his friends organized for his eightieth birthday in 1996 should be sure to include on the guest-list both the Queen Mother and the Prince of Wales, as well as every famous conductor old enough to be his contemporary. His contribution to Britain's destiny, he plainly felt, deserved nothing less.

And he was, in his way, not mistaken. Whatever shortcomings there were in his approach to the great adventure, he was the man who saw it through. He finally carried Britain over the threshold that the islanders for so long did not want to cross.

8

ROY JENKINS

The Fissile Effect

THE EUROPE QUESTION, ever since it presented itself, has been shot through with beguiling paradoxes for the British political system. It is not like other issues. For thirty years, it has not obeyed the rules.

It has, for example, ranged majorities against minorities, with aberrant consequences. Ever since Britain entered the Common Market, there has been a large parliamentary majority in favour of the enterprise – yet, throughout the period, this majority has at times had difficulty expressing itself. Dissenting minorities, for different reasons in different seasons, have had potent influence. There was a natural majority – 112 Heath got – for entering, in 1971, and a natural majority for remaining, throughout the years of Margaret Thatcher and John Major. But you might never believe it, looking at the history, whether in 1974, when Labour returned to power, or 1994, when the Conservative Party showed signs of incipient break-up after ratifying the Treaty of Maastricht. Europe tore politics apart, while enjoying steady majority support. The system, as organized, couldn't handle the issue in a way that reflected the majority consensus of the politicians the people sent to Westminster to represent them.

There are different ways of looking at this. It could be an example of politics at its most refreshing: men and women of conscience, liberating themselves from party disciplines, voting with their brains, holding out against the mighty power of government machines: a cross-party alliance of righteous free-thinkers, using all available procedures to impede the onward march of conventional, erroneous wisdom.

Alternatively, it could be something else: political failure on a heroic scale, the frustration of national purpose by unrepresentative ultras, a history of self-indulgent escaping from reality, through which the majority was regularly held hostage in the name of anti-Europe attitudes that were seldom formulated into a coherent alternative policy.

Whichever of these views has most appeal, one truth is incontestable. The closer Britain moved towards entry, the more ineluctably 'Europe' became a question that split the Labour and Conservative parties. Entry was meant to settle Britain's national destiny, but in politics it settled nothing. It was immediately an agent of fracture, not of healing, a propensity it has never shaken off.

The first victim was the father himself, Edward Heath. Losing office in February 1974, Heath could not blame the result on his Europe policy. It had nothing to do with the hideous mess he had made of a counter-inflation strategy that culminated with a battle against the coal-miners, in which the electorate failed to support him. But there was an overhang of Europe, in the insidious persona of Enoch Powell. Powell, who in 1968 had been sacked from the shadow Cabinet for a speech that fomented racial hatreds, had many complaints against Heath. 'One cannot but entertain fears for the mental and emotional stability of a head of government to whom such language can appear rational,' was his comment on one of Heath's defences of a statutory incomes policy.[1] But Europe did most to fire this devouring contempt. By 1974, Heath's 'surrender' of the sovereign powers of the Westminster Parliament had determined Powell to come out in support of the Labour Party which, so Harold Wilson said, opposed it. By force of oratory, as well as his mesmerizing disregard for party, Powell came close to dominating the last days of the campaign, and had some effect on the outcome.[2] Arguably, he swung enough seats, in a very close battle, to render Heath incapable of forming the new government. But whether he did or not, his conduct was a signal. It showed that, for some people, the Europe question transcended every other. Powell in 1974 was the harbinger of a faction for whom he remained an immortal hero in 1994. He was proof that Europe could divide a party and its leadership: the loudest voice to date in a long line of Conservative politicians – some before him, many after – whose careers Europe dominated and whose ambitions it, effectively, ended.

So the Tories were the first to be affected in government by the responsiveness of this great question to minority opinion. But Labour, in its turn, was also shattered. In the end, Labour was formally broken, along a line whose deepest cut was made by the Europe issue. The minority here had the opposite purpose from the Powellites. It enlisted itself, across party, in service of the broad majority which narrow party disciplines usually had the effect of frustrating. It had a determining effect on the 1971 vote, and on other occasions later. But it, too, was a symptom of the breakdown of a system. A system that was supposed to clarify political choices, through the deep, long rooting in of class- and interest-based parties, produced an outcome that was thoroughly confusing for the voters. The competing zealotries had almost nothing to do with divisions between the left and right which they were used to and could understand. For any voter who cared about Europe one way or the other, party was no longer a concept to be relied on.

Another paradox, therefore, shimmers to the surface. The people needed guidance, but they couldn't get it from the usual agencies. The parties wanted popular support, and the issue demanded the full-hearted consent Heath spoke of. But the average voter, deprived of clear party lines, was spectator to what seemed an increasingly private conflict, in which politicians showed many unsettling traits.

There was the divide within parties, the quartering rather than halving of the familiar political landscape between the two main protagonists. There was also the divide within politicians themselves: the near-impossibility of finding senior leaders who now thought the same as they thought ten, five or even two years before or who, if they did, hadn't reversed themselves, in some cases more than once, in the intervening period.

This was bound to be bewildering, especially at such a time. For it occurred in a context when the public was supposed to matter especially. Popular assent was required – yet the 'Europe' issue was already showing one of the traits it never shook off, an ambiguous relationship with public opinion. On the one hand, the combatants always claimed to be speaking for the public, often a public whose 'real' attitude was supposedly antagonistic to the whole European enterprise. On the other hand, the behaviour of politicians became increasingly like that of members of a private club. For twenty years their antagonisms, and the sacrifices some of them were prepared to make for their position, seemed like those of people detached from the wider world, engaged in a struggle to the death, over ideas that engaged the great mass of ordinary people with far less ferocity.

Never was such turbulence more in evidence than in the two years after Heath. They were the hinge moment, when anything might have happened. Entry was effected, but its permanence wasn't guaranteed. In the sceptic English dog, there was another bark yet. In fact there would be many, over the years. The people most responsible for silencing this, the first and decisive one, were, as they had to be, Labour politicians.

A Conservative leader took Britain in. But hardly less impact all round was made by the Labour politician who insisted that Britain must remain: the guarantor of Heath's majority, and architect, as it turned out, of Labour's crack-up.

*

WHEN HEATH LOST, and Labour took over the country, it also took over its own past. It could not avoid an encounter with the history for which it was responsible. In the recent phase, this had a distinct and ominous shape. When in opposition, up to and including 1963, Labour had opposed British entry. When in government, 1967–70, it had favoured and rather desperately sought British entry. When it was back in opposition, 1970–4, oppositionism asserted itself once again. Opposition, in short, gave control to the instincts of the party, government gave it to the perceived necessities of the country, and between these positions there was an absence of much grey area. The two attitudes were black and white. Moving from one to the other, in the early spring of 1974, barely a year after British membership had become an objectively existing fact, Harold Wilson faced a transition that would challenge even his famous mastery of manoeuvre.

Over all this period, one man mirrored and enhanced the dilemma through his own emphatic whiteness, or perhaps blackness. More than anyone, Roy Jenkins ensured that greyness, ultimately, was not an option. In government, he was Wilson's prop, little though he was welcomed as such: he stood for the position that Prime Minister Wilson found it inescapable to advance. Once George Brown disappeared into drunken oblivion, he was the leader of the Labour Europeans. But in opposition Jenkins was Wilson's curse, making it impossible for the leader to glide painlessly back into the arms of the sceptic party. With a group of allies, he stood inflexibly against the party line, an abomination for which he was not being readily excused even twenty years later. Interviewed in 1995, Barbara Castle, his Cabinet colleague of the period, asserted that she could still never forgive Jenkinsites for their 'party treachery' in 'putting Europe first', and recalled with relish how she had 'described the pro-Market fanatics as sanctimonious, middle-class hypocrites, and I meant it'.[3]

Jenkins always was a 'European'. Admittedly, he did not join Heath in supporting the Schuman Plan. For a young Labour MP to have jousted with Foreign Secretary Bevin would have been *lèse-majesté* demanding more confidence than Jenkins had at the age of thirty. He says that he 'meekly' accepted the party line.[4] But a few years later he went as a Labour delegate to the intermittent meetings of the Council of Europe in Strasbourg, a posting whose term was deliberately limited by the party to avoid its tenants going native. On Jenkins this precaution did not have the intended effect. In a total of seven weeks, spread over the two years, exposure to continental politics and politicians, he writes, 'sowed the seeds of my subsequently persistent conviction'.

By 1961, he was a fully fledged and active proponent of British entry. He had opposed EFTA, the second-division periphery Macmillan tried to organize into a rival grouping, and, when the time came, got himself made deputy chairman of the Common Market Campaign, already a cross-party affair, and then became chairman of the Labour Committee for Europe. From this period onwards, his commitment was steady, 'and at most times dominant in my life'. 'By the standards of the pioneers,' he adds a little sheepishly, 'I was a latter-day convert, although one well before the bulk of, say, the Foreign Office, City or Conservative Party opinion. When eventually enlightened I remained so, and with some fervour.'

He was not alone. Actually, the Labour Committee for Europe, as well as coming to the aid of a Conservative initiative, was in these early days cross-factional within the party. A number of MPs on the left continued to carry the banner of a united Europe once borne aloft by the likes of Michael Foot and Richard Crossman.[5] Names such as Eric Heffer, Sid Bidwell, Stan Newens and Marcus Lipton are to be found on the Europeanist roster. But the core of the cohort came from the liberal internationalist tradition more numerously represented on the right. William Rodgers made his maiden speech as a Labour MP in June 1962, supporting the Macmillan Government's policy for entry. Roy Hattersley was another, unbreakably consistent since 1958. Tam Dalyell, Douglas Houghton, Joel Barnett and a few others with a long parliamentary life ahead of them resisted their friend Hugh Gaitskell's determination to see the imminence of entry as the betrayal of a thousand years of history. Not all the right were with Jenkins. As well as Douglas Jay, Gaitskell's particular ally and intimate, some surprising younger men were still also hesitating. David Marquand, one of the most creative and influential thinkers behind social democratic revisionism in the 1980s, recorded his attitude to the Common Market as 'very sceptical, indeed hostile' when it first appeared as a British issue for decision.[6] But Europeanism was already a cult in the Labour Party, and Jenkins something like its high priest.

There was another aspect that helped give him that suitably awesome status. Although born modestly in Wales, he was a social as well as a political internationalist. He travelled much, conversed and wrote easily on a global stage, gathered a wide acquaintance, especially European and North American. He was as much at home in Tuscany, possibly more so, as in his constituency of Stechford in the bleak West Midlands. It would never have occurred to him, as it did to Douglas Jay, to carry a supply of British cornflakes on journeys he was required to make across the Channel. By 1970, he had had frequent personal dealings with just about every continental politician of note. Jean Monnet, Willy Brandt, Valéry Giscard d'Estaing, Helmut Schmidt, not to mention Kennedys, Achesons, Rockefellers, Bundys and a hundred others from points west and east of the British Isles, are grist to his memoirs, as they have been to his life.

This cosmopolitan figure was rooted in different terrain from other chieftains of his party, Wilson not least. The continent made Wilson uneasy. Europeans, 'especially from France and southern Europe', according to one of his close advisers, were to him alien. He disliked their food, 'genuinely preferring meat and two veg with HP sauce', and went on holiday to the Scilly Isles, 'which enabled him to go overseas and yet remain in Britain'.[7] Wilson was a miserly, north-country non-conformist, who delighted, as Jenkins never did, in keeping every particle of his background on display. James Callaghan, while perhaps a little more internationalist by instinct, also came from the part of the Labour Party that was, socially if not politically, cabined and confined. Jenkins, in this company, was a faintly exotic beast, which did little for his fraternal popularity. Among the baggage that went with it was a different relationship with 'party'. This shouldn't be exaggerated. He understood well enough that his party base was the source of all political power, and paid close attention to Stechford's requirements. But part of his 'European' stigma, among those who regarded it as such, lay in the distancing from traditional good old Labourism which it apparently signalled. There were faint traces, in the Jenkins of 1970–4, of the superior disenchantment – Barbara Castle's 'treachery' – that was to be exhibited, also somewhat de haut en bas, by Tony Blair after 1994. The link, as we shall see, was one of which Blair became extremely conscious.[8]

When Labour went into opposition in 1970, it did two things simultaneously. Its MPs elected Jenkins as Wilson's deputy leader. And the party as a whole, not discouraged by most of its leadership, moved into its familiar opposition mode of rejecting British entry into Europe as Heath was promoting it. This contradiction helped stave off the moment when opposition became absolute. But it exposed the split mind that eventually produced a split party.

Labour, under Wilson's guidance, eased rather than hurtled into rejectionism. Awareness percolated through even its extremer fringes that the U-turn should not be too abrupt. The party conference, which in 1967 voted by 2:1 to support entry, in autumn 1970 rejected, albeit narrowly, an 'anti' resolution. For the next three years, in fact, Wilson successfully prevented the conference from passing any motion of wholesale opposition in principle to membership. The old leftist opponents, supplemented after the election, especially by leading trade unionists, were held at bay.

The spirit, however, was with them. It called forth a countervailing force, which had the deputy leader at its head and was now free to exhibit a full emotional commitment. As prelude to its own scheme formally to oppose Heath's deal, the party's National Executive Committee summoned a special conference in July 1971, where feelings would be ventilated but no vote taken. On this occasion, the party's divisions became absolutely apparent, and, for the first time, the pro-Marketeers proved themselves the ultras in the argument. That was the flip side of the pattern, as between government and opposition. When Labour was in power, nosing towards entry, the leading antis had to keep their mouths shut. When Labour was out of power, preparing to reverse its position, no such restraint afflicted the other side.

Jenkins himself, being deputy leader, was not allowed to speak at the 1971 event. But his supporters reached full flood. John Mackintosh, MP for East Lothian, delivered a coruscating attack on the fainthearts who feared for national sovereignty and worried about economic growth. This speech was remembered in the annals for ever after. Re-read, it sharpens a large truth about the history: that, of all those who contributed to it, none has been more eloquent, more completely and defiantly committed to Britain's European destiny than the Labour pro-Europeans of the Heath period. They put Heath's own faltering locutions in the shade. Unencumbered by the need to negotiate, or to box the compass of a party navigating through fierce contrarian storms, they took the fullest responsible advantage of their lack of responsibility.

It was inevitable, when the question was put, that they would answer it in complete awareness of what they were doing. Europe needed them, Britain needed them, and they lived down to Mrs Castle's derisive expectation that they were the kind of people who would put these considerations before the overriding need, on the widest grounds of socialist politics and economics, to get the Heath Government out. On 28 October 1971, sixty-nine members of the parliamentary Labour Party voted with the Government to pave the way in principle for entry, and twenty others abstained from opposing it.

Without this support, the motion would have fallen. Almost certainly, Heath's effort would have been unsustainable in the British Parliament, and Britain would not have entered – then or, possibly, ever. The terrifying evidence of national decline might have impelled some future government to make yet another approach to Europe, but no one can have much idea what would have become of it. Jenkins and his people were thus determinant at one defining moment – and this wasn't the last.

By the protocols of parliamentary behaviour, their vote was a heinous crime. Once again, Barbara Castle can be our witness. 'I used to respect you a great deal, but I will never do so again as long as I live,' she hissed at Jenkins in the Commons members' dining-room, in the middle of the party imbroglio when he was making his intentions clear.[9] He didn't have the nerve to carry on in the same vein. When, after the paving motion was won by 112, the Bill itself came for passage, the rising, responsible men in the Jenkins group avoided voting with the Government. The majorities, clause by clause, came tumbling down, and were often crucially dependent on the saving interventions of a handful of Labour people – Tam Dalyell, Austen Albu, Michael Barnes, Freda Corbet – too old or unambitious to be intimidated, to keep the Bill intact. When Harold Lever, dutifully obeying Wilson, voted against the second reading of the Bill, he retired to the gentlemen's lavatory to be physically sick. Others, such as Bill Rodgers, felt demoralized, having voted tamely for the party after riding the high of their October principles. Jenkins, looking back, was penitent. He and his friends had been 'cowering behind the shields of these men older or younger than us who were braver'.[10] When he was challenged to run again for deputy leader, his ambition to keep the job made him blur his voting intentions as the Bill was in transit, and, even though this was enough to keep him in the post, he bitterly regretted it. 'It was weak and equivocating . . . a major tactical error,' he judged later.[11]

Nonetheless, the Bill went through, and Jenkins was the key accessory before, if not during, the fact. The October vote was a watershed moment. It established the presence of a hard-core Europeanism in the Labour Party, which others would ignore at their peril. It singled out a section of the party that was not prepared to be seduced by the ambiguity of others, separating them by style as much as content. In their way, these people were being unpolitical, if party and politics are to be treated as coterminous notions. They thereby ranged themselves against three types of ambiguity, the three threads of behaviour that evinced a quite different way of handling the 'Europe' question – even, one might say, a quite different political psychology.

The first was best personified by Anthony Wedgwood Benn, whose conduct about this time coincided with the prophetic elision of his name to fit the proletarianism which was to be Labour's signature theme in the coming years. At some moment, precisely unspecified, he had become Tony Benn. He had also become an anti-European.

Tracing Benn's personal European odyssey ought to be a relatively simple task, since his diaries constitute one of the most extended tours of a leading politician's mind ever made available.[12] The task is complicated not by lack of candour on the diarist's part, so much as by the mercurial approach, the ever imminent sense of messianic revelation, he brought to this subject in common with most others. His history plots a course from suspicion, through flirtation, into consummation, followed shortly by passionate rejection.

Benn was against the Macmillan application, proclaiming that he knew it would fail. And quite soon he was expressing admiration for the agent of its failure, General de Gaulle. 'I am really a Gaullist,' he says on 20 July 1964, 'and in favour of positive neutralism.' Gaullism litters his diary talk at this time, driven on by the dilemma he faced concerning the Americans. As a junior minister, Postmaster-General, in Wilson's first Government, Benn retained a leftist's deep dislike of America's military intentions, musing on 14 January 1965: 'The choice lies between Britain as an island and a US protectorate, or Britain as a full member of the Six, followed by a wider European federation. I was always against the Common Market but the reality of our isolation is being borne in on me all the time. This country is so decrepit and hidebound that only activities in the wider sphere can help us to escape from the myths that surround our politics.' Later that year, he solves the problem by offering covert support to colleagues working against British membership and in favour of 'an *all*-European group which I wholly support and have done for many years'.

Before the 1966 general election, he was still an anti, voting vainly against the manifesto phrase 'Britain should be ready to enter Europe'. But he was seducible. Later that year, seeing the way the wind appeared to be blowing, he prepared to yield before it. 'I came to the conclusion that Britain would be in the Common Market by 1970,' he writes with some prescience, after the October Cabinet meeting that approved the Wilson–Brown Probe. When the time came to decide, he spoke up clearly in Cabinet. 'I said we had to cut Queen Victoria's umbilical cord,' he reports on 30 April 1967. This 'created a favourable impression with the pro-Europeans, who thought me anti-European'. A week later, speaking as the Minister for Technology, he uttered a strong appeal for technological co-operation in Europe. This, he said, 'requires an integrated commercial market'. Bilateral dealings might have some value, 'with professors crossing the Channel both ways to read learned papers to each other'. But they would never be enough. 'If that is all we can achieve in Europe, then we shall be condemned . . . as a continent to the status of industrial helotry with all that that means in terms of world influence. And history may well say that we deserve it.'[13]

Benn thereby observed the pattern. In government, he favoured Labour's positive intention. In October 1971, equally, he conformed to type. What he once called the 'managerial phase' of his politics ended with the loss of power in 1970, and was succeeded by an ever leftward progression which included ever stronger anathemas against the Common Market. These began with a becoming linguistic modesty. 'I make no apology, in the course of having thought about this issue, for having changed the emphasis of my view at different stages,' he said in the great 1971 debate. Since the world was changing fast, what virtue was there in an unbending consistency? Besides, he confessed, he had had his doubts, even when supporting the application in 1967. It was, I suppose, his plea for recognition as a man who had never wholly changed his mind. But it hardly conceals the fact that Benn's reversion to his original hostility described a perfect parabola of contradiction.

This was one kind of ambiguity. It didn't guarantee Benn a wholly adoring reception back into the arms of those whose drive towards the last ditch never deviated: Barbara Castle, Michael Foot, Peter Shore, several others on the left; Fred Peart and a few others on the right. But together they composed one version of how Labourism, socialism, nationalism, internationalism, call it what you will, should answer the Europe question.

What united this school was the belief, above all, that Europe mattered deeply. That much they shared with Jenkins. The two sides reached opposite conclusions, but neither doubted that the issue touched the soul of the party and the future of the country. The contrast between them was in their attitude to it. The contrast between Jenkins and a second type of ambiguity was more subtle, and possibly more startling – certainly harder to comprehend – not least because it separated him from some of his natural political allies.

Denis Healey had a longer history in the matter than any of his colleagues. He was the international secretary of the Labour Party from November 1945 until he became an MP in 1952. For a young man who had seen war at first hand, this was an extraordinary time to occupy such a post: extraordinary, in particular, for the range of connection it gave him in European politics. Here he was, close to the heart of affairs, in the only socialist party then running a government in Europe, whose place as the dominant power there was taken for granted. Not only was Healey the intimate servant of Foreign Secretary Bevin, he fraternized incessantly with European socialist leaders. His catalogue of memories goes on and on. He was in at the beginning of the re-formation of the German Social Democrats. Ancient and modern socialists, from Norway and Belgium and France and Austria, received him gratefully in the post-war years. He knew the Italians, and in 1949 took a personal hand in selecting a suitable socialist leader for the Greeks. Further afield, he became best friends with Teddy Kollek, later Mayor of Jerusalem, close friends with Jayaprakash Narayan, and received Roy Welensky, the leader of the Rhodesian Labour Party.[14] He was, it can be seen, an impeccably international man. And so he remained. A feature of the superb autobiographies which both Healey and Jenkins composed in retirement is the reminder they provide of what expansive horizons some British politicians' lives encompassed in the first three post-war decades, something nowhere to be found in the 1990s, the first seven years of which were spent under the leadership of a Prime Minister who, before he became Foreign Secretary, had never visited the United States.

It follows from this history that Healey had a long engagement specifically with the question of European union. He was much involved in securing European socialist support for the Marshall Plan. In 1948, he wrote a pamphlet, *Feet on the Ground*, arguing against any idea of European federation, then much in vogue. Federation, he insisted, worked only in empty continents, like America or Australia. If European federation were imposed on countries that had separate national existence, it 'would require forcible sanctions against secession', for which 'the prolonged and bloody American Civil War is not an encouraging precedent'. He was and is a believer in the divisive relevance of the 'olive line', north and south of which, he contends, Europeans have different attitudes to authority, corruption and work.[15] The Mediterranean might be a good place to enjoy the food and pictures, but the littoral people were unreliable. However, Healey is at least willing to apologize for one thing he wrote in 1948, that Europe should concentrate on producing 'cheap cheeses for mass consumption instead of luxury cheeses like camembert and gorgonzola'. 'I still blush to remember,' he writes.

His anti-federalist position, reflecting that of most of the Cabinet he served, moved on to a higher plane. In 1950, he drafted another pamphlet, *European Unity*, which appeared under the party imprint at the very moment when the Schuman Plan was sprung on Bevin, and contradicted the emollient tone of the Government white paper. In retrospect, Healey was enough of a realist to regret the adamancy of Labour's hostility to Schuman, and more particularly the Conservative exercise in boat-missing at Messina. 'It was a terrible error,' he told me in 1995.[16] All the same, he was closely involved with Gaitskell's evolution into an anti-European who could not contemplate the end of a thousand years of history. He had reached the same conclusion.

He maintained this position in government, when he was Secretary of State for Defence, 1964–70. But here the shadings and complications begin. On the one hand, in this role, Healey negotiated the definitive post-war realignment of the British posture towards the world, by organizing and pushing for military withdrawal from East of Suez. He applied his powerful mind and rounded international expertise to the necessary task of locating Britain's mission within range of her economic capability – which is to say, broadly speaking, within Europe, the field of Nato. On the other hand, he continued simultaneously to oppose British entry into the Community, or at least any effort to secure such entry in the 1960s.

Healey was one of the last hold-outs against Wilson's 1967 venture, which was an object of his most hectoring scorn in Cabinet on the ground, he grandly stated, that de Gaulle would never take it seriously. When, in 1971, Labour swung into opposition to Heath, he therefore found it easier than almost anyone to argue with great brutality against the terms Heath got. He led for Labour at the beginning of the great debate, and took apart the speculative economic promises on which Heath's case was based. He didn't believe the growth forecasts, twisted the British budgetary contribution into its most dismal magnitude, and defined the project as being all about teaching the unions a lesson in a competitive jungle of Euro-capitalism that no decent Labour politician could stomach.[17]

This was preceded by his own version of the vacillation that has afflicted the majority of politicians in this story. For Healey, too, had his little flutter. In May of that year, he became one of the bigger catches of the Jenkinsites, as they rounded up signatories for an advertisement announcing support for what Heath was doing. This appeared days before Heath's climactic meeting with Pompidou, as if to emphasize the breadth of serious national backing the Prime Minister had, and Healey allowed himself to join a company of 100 Labour MPs to say so. He followed this up with other gestures, speaking for Europe in the shadow Cabinet and, on 26 May, publishing an article in the *Daily Mirror* under the headline 'Why I Changed My Mind'. It seemed to be the defiant assertion that a reasonable man could ultimately be persuaded of the whereabouts of the light. A reckless conclusion. At first it looked sound enough. 'I've changed my mind too,' he wrote. 'I know it's unfashionable. Some of my friends say it is politically inconvenient too. But the world has changed a lot in the last nine years and so has the Common Market ... failure in Brussels will be a great chance lost for everyone concerned.' But he was soon disclaiming responsibility for the headline, and pointing to the sceptic tone between the lines. 'If our economy is strong when we go in we should reap a splendid harvest,' he had written. But also: 'If it is weak, the shock could be fatal.' Having changed his mind within a month, he changed it back again within another. 'By July Healey was stridently back into the other camp,' Jenkins notes.[18]

The distinctive feature of Healey's position as against Jenkins's, however, was something different. The two men had been rivals, while also in a sense political brothers, ever since their years at Balliol College, Oxford. At that time, admittedly, Healey was a communist while Jenkins was already a social democrat, but their rise in parallel through the Labour Party was that of two immensely able progressive politicians, the cream of their generation. It was perhaps inevitable that they should have watched each other closely, and diverged in matters of style if not, in all seriousness, of content. Jenkins, though more distant from the soul of the Labour Party, was much the abler cultivator of party support, the more attentive to the arrangement of its factions at any given time. Healey, ostensibly the more emphatic in his opinions and certainly the more aggressive in conveying them to lesser mortals, was also more inclined to judge, flaunting his intellectual scepticism, that no issue was worth defining as a matter of incontrovertible principle.

So it was with Europe. Professional indifference became Healey's way of dealing with the passions that raged around him left and right. He thought Europe and the zealotries it induced were a distraction from what he regarded as the 'real issues'. He was joined in this posture by a man of similar intellect, but whose bias shaded in the opposite direction, Anthony Crosland. Crosland, a better friend of Jenkins and basically a supporter of British entry, also opined with some disdain that the Jenkinsites were making far too much of it. It wasn't one of the major questions of domestic politics, he thought.

This was the line that he and Healey persisted in through all the arguments in the Labour Party for the decade following the 1967 application. In one way, it may have had the merit of reflecting the attitude of the British people. It spoke for their agnosticism, trying to find a way of fending off the wild obsessions over Europe which have been an enduring difference between the political class and the voters who put them where they are. Is that enough, however, to justify the persistent refusal of senior politicians to give a lead to people who, unlike them, are not paid to have opinions, and who expect to be instructed on complicated matters?

Healey, evidently, thought so. When I interviewed him in 1995, as feelings over the Treaty of Maastricht swirled even more violently round the British political system than they had over the Treaty of Rome, he remained unapologetic. I accosted him with his shiftiness in the face of a hard decision, yes or no, on the idea of British entry, on which the people themselves, not long after, were required to give their own verdict. Were they not entitled to the clear opinion of one of the cleverest men in British politics? Healey replied with the consummate pride of the distanced intellectual, an approach almost as far removed from Jenkinsism as it would be possible to invent, short of outright Bennery: 'I made it clear that people should use their brains, as I was using mine, and take a final decision in the light of the situation as it developed.'[19]

So here were two strands of Labourism in the early 1970s. One, which finished by merging with the do-or-die opponents, reached that position having previously assisted the leadership's strategy for taking Britain in. The other, though opposed to the leadership plan, was even more opposed to those who most fiercely pushed it, and defined the issue as one not worth the attention focused on it. This was uncertain ground on which a leader might hope to base a firm stand of his own. In any case, such firmness wasn't Harold Wilson's natural mode of leadership even on simple questions. Inevitably, a third type of ambiguity assembled itself. It could have only one objective: to make sure these elusive strands continued to belong, alongside the uncompromising veins of Jenkinsism and Castlery, in the body of a single party.

More than anyone, Wilson bore the brunt of Labour's change of persona between government and opposition. One might say that he was himself, cynically, the essence of the shift, and did not try to resist it. After all, hardly anyone doubts that if Wilson had won the 1970 election he would at some stage have resumed his effort to get in. But that won't suffice as a verdict on his conduct when Heath took Europe back to the top of the agenda. Ambiguity was forced upon the Leader of the Opposition. Perhaps it even became more like duplicity. This can be called, nonetheless, one of Wilson's finer hours, in which he did for the Labour Party what at the time was his prime duty – to hold it mostly together.

It couldn't be done on Jenkins's terms. No amount of aggressive leadership would have altered the fact that, with the party out of power, a commitment to back Heath would have split the shadow Cabinet and been resisted by the party conference. But Jenkins's desired result, all the same, could be secured. That was what Wilson wanted. The one thing with which his conduct is consistent is a desire throughout that no organ of the party should commit itself to taking Britain out. Deep down, Wilson was, however reluctantly, a Marketeer. He never said as much. He may well have thought that he could get better terms than Heath: indeed, that if Heath fell he could immediately take over the negotiations and emerge triumphant. But he always stopped short of getting into bed with Barbara Castle.

Besides, he had another problem. The Europe issue did not stand alone, divorced from everything else that was happening in the party. The Labour Party of that time, from the mid-1960s to the mid-1970s, that is the entire Wilson period, was suffused by a permanent state of disloyalty at the top. It wasn't that overt plotting against Wilson went on all the time. There were whole years when his position was secure. It was just that faction and the rivalry between factions were a kind of given of Labour society. Manoeuvring around, if not against, the person of the leader was a condition of existence in the Cabinet, a necessary consequence of its division into left and right, a faculty without which any

Labour politician of consequence could hardly be taken seriously. Regular contestation between these groups was positively expected, was allowed for in all Wilson's decisions about who held what job, and was met on a daily, indeed hourly, basis by his own pre-emptive manoeuvres.

This wasn't, in other words, a government of straight and simple men. Europe, like everything else, played its part in larger battles, among them the question of the leadership. Throughout, Jenkins's ambition was the prime feeder of Wilson's paranoid anxieties. Jenkins, moreover, made little secret of it. His autobiography is honest about his desire to lead the party, and how his conduct fitted at any given moment into this life-plan. Actually, by that account, he had given up some of his hope a little earlier. His real chance, he felt, had been in the summer of 1968, when Wilson was presiding over a fractured government and deeply unpopular both inside and outside it. Looking back, Jenkins saw, after that moment, 'a career punctuated by increasingly wide misses of the premiership'.[20] When the Europe question exploded three years later, he might already have been out of the hunt. But that wasn't the way it seemed at the time to Wilson's friends – or his enemies. For some of these, 'Europe' was the instrument through which the treacherous little man might be disposed of. If they could trap him into supporting 'Europe', thereby sacrificing his traditional power-base on the left, the right thought they would have him by the vitals. Bill Rodgers is recorded as saying at the time: 'If Wilson loses his support on the left, he won't have any at all. And we'll cut his bloody throat.'[21]

So 'Europe' was not an academic argument between members of a respectful fraternity. Behind the issue was an ever present sub-text. Wilson was no keener to lose his head than to let the Jenkins ultras split the party.

The evolution of his tactics has been chronicled by several hands. In February 1971, he still thought trouble might be staved off. Jenkins went to warn him privately that, if the Government struck a deal with the Community, he and his faction would be determined to support it. The only way to minimize the coming upheaval, Jenkins suggested, was to have a free vote. But Wilson at that stage was saying he could do better. 'I am more optimistic than that,' he told Jenkins. 'I hope that we may be able to get the party officially to vote in favour.' The free vote would be a last, worst resort.

The year, however, saw a steady decline from this high expectancy. On 26 April, Wilson began to show tentatively anti-European colours, making a speech that canvassed the appalling possibility of an invasion

Hugh Gaitskell,
Labour Party
Conference, 1962:
cry God for England
and a thousand
years of history.

Douglas Jay,
President of the
Board of Trade, 1964:
never go abroad
without the
cornflakes.

A
RESEMBLANCE
OF
MANDARINS

John Robinson,
Euro-man 1961–73,
the keeper of the
memory.

Sir Roger Makins, the sceptic,
1947–52.

Sir Gladwyn Jebb, the sceptic convert,
1954–60.

Sir Con O'Neill, the fixer and historian,
1963–68, 1969–72.

Sir Michael Palliser, leader of
the regiment, 1966–82.

Sir Michael Butler, the numerate
persuader, 1972–85.

Sir John Kerr, the deal-broker,
1987–.

Labour changes course: Harold Wilson, prime minister, and George Brown, with Michael Palliser, private secretary, lurking between, Paris, 1967.

Dumbfounded by de Gaulle: Wilson and Chancellor Kurt Kiesinger, Bonn, February 1969.

The ambassador and the president: where the Soames Affair began.

Edward Heath,
prime minister
1970–74: there
is no alternative.

Heath and President
Georges Pompidou:
entente cordiale,
at last.

Two faces of 1972.
Enoch Powell (above):
ferocious sceptic.
Sir Geoffrey Howe:
cryptic zealot.

Into the continental embrace, 1972: prime minister Heath signs the
Treaty of Rome, flanked by Geoffrey Rippon, chief negotiator (right), Sir Alec
Douglas-Home, foreign secretary (left) and (far left) the documentation
of 'Europe' thus far.

of 'Italian black-leg labour' if Britain went in. It was the beginning of a precautionary populism, in which mood he was soon spurred to further lengths by the intervention of a man he feared more intensely, though perhaps less consistently, than Roy Jenkins: the former Chancellor and ever lurking shark, James Callaghan. In May, Callaghan delivered a burst of anti-Europeanism that would have sat comfortably in the mouth of a Tory Euro-sceptic of the 1990s. France's approach to the EEC, he said, would mean 'a complete rupture of our identity'. We were about to exchange our old friends in the Commonwealth and the United States for 'an aroma of continental claustrophobia'. Callaghan was especially concerned about the future of the English language. 'The language of Chaucer, Shakespeare and Milton' – late arrivals, one imagines, over Callaghan's known cultural horizon – was, he chided, threatened by the French demand for linguistic hegemony in the EEC. If French was to be the dominant language of the Community, then he had something to tell the Froggies in a demotic they might understand: 'Non, merci beaucoup.'[22]

For the rest of 1971 and through 1972, Callaghan vocally opposed British entry, and Wilson began to travel the same road. Callaghan invented a formula that Wilson seized on, to cover the charge of inconsistency with earlier policy: that entry was unacceptable on the terms Heath had negotiated. At the end of June 1971, Callaghan was telling Jack Jones, leader of the Transport Workers Union, that they should unite round three supreme objectives: to beat Heath, keep the party united and 'stop us going into the Common Market'.[23] At the special conference in July, Wilson, who had allied with Jenkins to resist its being called, made a speech of such negativity as to cast him finally and definitively, in the current terms of the argument, as anti-European. 'It was like watching someone being sold down the river into slavery, drifting away, depressed and unprotesting,' Jenkins said.[24]

Wilson's real depression at the time, however, had another source. Though few people believed he was really as hostile to entry as he felt it prudent to indicate in his conference speech, this did not secure him remission from the harsh verdict of the pro-Europeans. Quite the opposite. They felt he should be more honest. On 9 June, he had allowed Jenkins to give him a little lecture about straightness. While conceding that the leader had a hard problem to deal with, the deputy told him, insufferably: 'What is most damaging to your reputation and position in the country is that you are believed, perhaps wrongly, to be devious, tricky, opportunistic.' By sticking to the Europe position he had taken in government, said Jenkins, Wilson would not only do some good to the cause and the country but might make people see him as a man of principle.[25] Not only that – here came the twist of the knife – but he would be rewarded by a guarantee that the Jenkinsites would not endeavour to replace him, with or without the intriguing Callaghan.

The leader, writes Jenkins, received all this 'with perfect good temper'. Such tolerance seems all the more heroic, since the homily was delivered in response to Wilson's complaint about his difficulties, toying with an agonizing choice, which he compared self-pityingly with the simplicities confronting a man like Jenkins whose choice was already made. Later, he put the point more graphically. Exasperated by his posturing colleagues, he told them one day: 'I've been wading in shit for three months to allow others to indulge their conscience.'[26] When Jenkins, shortly after the July conference, delivered a scintillating pro-Market philippic to the parliamentary party, Wilson was beside himself, ranting to Tony Benn, a visitor to his home in Lord North Street: 'I may just give up the Party leadership, they can stuff it as far as I am concerned.'[27] 'He was full of boasts,' writes Benn, 'but underneath was desperately insecure and unhappy.' He was beginning once again to see Jenkins's people as an anti-party fifth-column, just like the Gaitskellites in an earlier phase, gathering in private rooms and flats to plot against him. 'A party within a party is not less so because it meets outside the House in more agreeable surroundings,' he told the parliamentary Labour Party, with vintage sarcasm, the very night he was telling Benn he might quit.

Come October, of course, he was still there. He always was, until a moment, years later, when he stunned the world by resigning with clear blue skies apparently all round him. Now, squeezed between right and left, Europe and anti-Europe, he told the world that what he wanted was a united party, a phrase which at this particular moment meant that the pro-Europeans should not be penalized. It was apparent, as Jenkins had warned, that significant numbers would refuse to be dragooned into opposing the vote-in-principle for entry, and the leader felt obliged to make the best of it. In exchange for the freedom to do that, they would sacrifice their freedom to support the passage of the Bill, and Harold Lever would take his conscience to the lavatory. Wilson, for his part, would sustain the line that all he objected to were the terms, the infamous and terrible terms by which Heath had failed to secure a decent deal in the cause of a great leap forward which the Labour Party continued to imply that it did not, in principle, oppose.

There was, however, one more condition, another shard in the mosaic of Wilsonian ambiguity. He found an additional way to confuse the matter, in order to simplify his life. It had first emerged some time earlier, out of the teeming mind of Tony Benn. In his new raiment as man of the people, Benn had proposed that Europe was so large a question that it should be put to a referendum: not a wholly new idea, but one which he laid on the table at the perfect moment. What the party could not agree, let the people settle! It was an irresistible lure to a leader pressed by short-term considerations of party unity.

At first, Wilson opposed the referendum. 'I understand you are suggesting a plebiscite on the Common Market,' he said acidly to Benn on 5 November 1970. 'You can't do that.' When Benn put it to the party's National Executive around that time, he couldn't find a seconder. But he persisted, writing a long letter to the electors of Bristol, the seat of his constituency, presumptuously challenging a more famous message delivered to the same electors, in which Edmund Burke, on becoming the MP for that parish in 1774, laid out the doctrine of representative government: 'Your representative owes you, not his industry only, but his judgement; and he betrays you, instead of serving you, if he sacrifices it to your opinion.'[28] 'If people are not to participate in this decision, no one will ever take participation seriously again,' Benn riposted. A less romantic voice, impressed by the needs of party rather than the voguish concept of participation, was that of Callaghan. He was among the earliest to dabble with the referendum, calling it 'a rubber life-raft into which the whole party may one day have to climb'.

The whole party, however, declined to do so. Although Wilson changed his mind under pressure from the left, Jenkins and his friends saw the referendum as the beginning of the end. It became, for them, a *casus belli* requiring an extreme response.

Though achieving a measure of unity in the short term, its ultimate role was the opposite. In the end, it marked a stage on the road to a great sundering.

Wilson never liked it. In deflecting Benn, he only repeated what he had said when asked the question during the election. All three party leaders had rejected a referendum, none more vehemently than the Prime Minister. 'The answer to that is No,' he said. 'I have given my answer many times ... I shall not change my attitude on that.'[29] Nor did he want to do so. A referendum, while superficially attractive in certain circumstances, has the large disadvantage, to a party leader, of surrendering control. Only a more threatening source of such prospective impotence could induce him to revise his opinion.

The process of emasculation now unfolded. Adamantly negative in November 1970, Wilson, under slow torture, was obliged to switch sides in March 1972. The regular 1971 party conference, in October, came close to deciding against entry in principle. Those were still the days when massive union bloc votes, wielded by grotesquely power-proud barons, affected to determine party policy, and only the jousting of the Transport baron, Jack Jones, against the Engineering baron, Hugh Scanlon, ensured that the line was held. By another typical perversity, the conference at that point rejected the seductive middle option, a referendum, by a larger margin. But this wasn't the end of the matter. As the European Communities Bill began passage through Parliament, the Heath Government was in trouble on many other fronts. To the Labour Party, Europe or no, it presented an irresistible target. Any issue on which it could be defeated roused the blood of every Labour politician not prepared to regard entry into the Common Market as a sacred purpose. The referendum became such an issue.

Its transforming into party policy was engineered by its latter-day inventor, Tony Benn, a master not only of rhetoric but of manoeuvre. On 15 March, the shadow Cabinet, despite the rage for unhorsing the Government, had considered and rejected support for a referendum that would have thoroughly embarrassed Heath. On 22 March, Benn got a gently lisping little motion carried by the National Executive asking the shadow Cabinet if it would be good enough to look at the referendum again. This was passed 13–11, with Wilson, Callaghan and Jenkins absent. A Tory back-bench amendment to the Bill, promoted by Enoch Powell among others, was due to test Commons opinion very shortly. So, a week after the NEC, the shadow Cabinet did what it was asked and, this time, reversed itself, voting 8–6 to support Powell's parliamentary ploy.

The ploy, as it happens, got nowhere. When it came to a vote, there were enough Labour abstentions to kill the amendment. Inside the party, however, this proved to be a truly historic moment: a second occasion when Jenkins was determinant. He, Lever, George Thomson and others lower down regarded the referendum not merely as defective in itself and a betrayal of parliamentary democracy, but, perhaps more important, as a device designed, should they support it, to nullify what they had achieved by voting against the party line and sending the Bill exultantly on its way the previous October. To them, it was as much a matter of what would happen to their faction as what would happen to their cause. Watching Wilson's switch, particularly his willingness to call the second shadow Cabinet meeting, Jenkins concluded that 'he must have fixed upon a strategy of forcing us into submission or resignation'.[30]

If so, the strategy succeeded. Not long after the shadow Cabinet vote, Jenkins resigned as deputy leader, taking Lever and Thomson with him. Alongside and below, the advice to him split on lines that are of interest. They began partly to foretell the shape of future allegiance. Roy Hattersley, though a totally committed European, was emphatically against resignation. David Owen, then a Labour European of similar stamp, advised against but, says Jenkins, supported it 'almost enthusiastically' when it happened. Bill Rodgers, while not wanting to put the pressure on, was thoroughly pleased. Lever, back from playing the tables at Deauville, said simply, 'Thank God.'

What Wilson said was nothing much. He made a token attempt to change his deputy's mind, but was otherwise calmly acquiescent, especially when Jenkins assured him that he would not be making a challenge for the leadership, at least in the coming autumn.

The Jenkinsites, after all, were isolated. Even as they gained approval in the press, they soon became unpopular in the party. Most of the younger ones opted not to leave their front-bench jobs, and Wilson, fortified by the referendum commitment, was able to see off what he regarded as the threat that mattered most, the left's demand for exit. 'Harold said that to be committed to come out would be impossible for him, and that he would have to resign,' Benn's diary records on 3 May 1972. An exit resolution loomed at the party conference. In fact, it was defeated, by the narrowest margin – 2,958,000 so-called votes in favour, 3,076,000 against – and Wilson, on the basis of a colourful promise of what could be gained by root-and-branch renegotiation, achieved the impression of unity which was, to him, what counted most.

Looking back, many have criticized Wilson's handling of events. Bill Rodgers once went so far as to say of the October 1971 vote: 'He could have held the party together by voting for entry.' So widespread was moral repugnance against Wilson's deviation, Rodgers thought, that the damage it did was far worse than any split provoked by the opposite course. Many more than sixty-nine MPs, he judged, would have voted for Europe if the leader had led them in that direction.[31] On the same retrospective occasion, Jenkins himself reflected that a lot of trouble might have been avoided if Wilson had chosen to act, in a sense, even more ambiguously than he did: keeping the temperature down, not imposing the whip, allowing free rein to party disagreements, not taking a black-and-white position himself.

Outright support, the Rodgers line, was, I think, impossible. The presence of anti-Europeanism, both numerically and emotionally, was dominant in the Labour Party of this period. It was supplemented by the usual ferocious anti-Tory feeling that justified, for many Labour politicians, adversarial combat on any and every issue. Overt backing for Heath's initiative would not have been tolerated.

On the other hand, only an illusionist could seriously suppose that the opposite approach would produce a settled unification. A time of functional tranquillity might now eventuate; but it was the calm before the crack-up.

*

WHEN WILSON walked into Downing Street in early March 1974, for his second tour as Prime Minister, Britain had been a member of the European Economic Community for fourteen months. It would have been easy for an outside observer, especially a European, to conclude that she did not intend to stay there much longer. The early gestures of the ministers that mattered seemed to signal hostility, verging on contempt.

Jenkins did not matter. Though at one point slated to return to the Treasury, he was obliged to settle for a more remote reprise, at the Home Office, which he had last run in 1967. Here he was parked well away from Europe, which was placed, instead, in the beady care of Callaghan, the new Foreign Secretary. The Labour election manifesto had pledged the party to a 'fundamental re-negotiation of the terms of entry', a promise decked out with some spacious presumptions. The manifesto said, for example, that pending a successful renegotiation Britain would feel free to ignore Community rules which didn't suit her. There was more of this kind of posing arrogance. Callaghan set about engaging in the Euro-world with a notable brutality of purpose.

Ambassadors were summoned to London for induction into the new coolness. Having spent a year trying to demonstrate that Britain was now keen on 'Europe', they were told to reverse course. 'I want you to understand that all this European enthusiasm is not what we're in business for,' the Foreign Secretary instructed one of them. 'I need to know whether you can do the job.'[32] Michael Butler, under-secretary in charge of the European Community, who prepared the Foreign Office briefing papers in response to the manifesto pledge, was called to a man-to-man meeting. Callaghan thanked him for the papers, but added an admonition. 'They tell me you really care about Europe. Is that right?' he asked the official. Butler, though worried about hanging on to his job, nevertheless said yes, that was so, he did care a lot about Europe. 'Very well,' the Foreign Secretary replied. 'But just remember. I really care about the Labour Party.'[33]

He carried his offensiveness abroad. Visiting Brussels for the first time, he wasted no charm on François-Xavier Ortoli, the president of the European Commission. 'He was extremely rude, and treated Ortoli like a second-rate official,' said a witness. The negative effect of the aggressive formal statement he made to a meeting of the Council was mitigated only by a sudden distraction: the death of President Pompidou was announced in the middle of it. But in his hostility Callaghan spoke for a new regime infused by suspicion of Brussels and most of its works. Other visiting ministers varied in their handling of the problem. Though Peter Shore, the Trade Secretary, was the most fundamental of critics of British membership, he behaved, from officials' point of view, impeccably. Tony Benn, the Energy Secretary, intrigued more deviously against Community initiatives. He was now an out-and-out enemy of Brussels, declining to conform to pattern. Reappearance in government made no difference to Mr Benn. 'I felt as if I was going as a slave to Rome,' he wrote on 18 June. 'My visit confirmed in a practical way all my suspicions that this would be the decapitation of British democracy without any countervailing advantage, and the British people, quite rightly, wouldn't accept it. There is no real benefit for Britain.'

In the topmost reach of government, however, the old normality prevailed. Staying in was Wilson's objective, through dense veils of hostile obfuscation. While Callaghan seldom relented in his aggression, even allowing it to be put about that, like it or not, a British exit might be inevitable, that doesn't seem to have been his end-game, and it certainly wasn't Wilson's. Renegotiation, a term that promised everything but might mean rather little in the end, was to be the salve for Labour's gaping wounds.

It could not begin in earnest until there had been another election. In March, Wilson was a minority Prime Minister unable to put forward proposals that the Community would have to take seriously. Every week, the talk was not of governing but of the next election, to acquire a proper majority. When the election happened, in October, the majority it produced was only three, enough to rule if not enough to dominate, and the inescapable basis on which anti-Marketeers could increase their influence over the renegotiation process.

Interestingly, they had not been able to insist on a categoric commit-ment to a referendum. In October, as in February, the pledge the party made was only to 'consult the people through the ballot box' after new terms had been negotiated. Even now, Wilson and his friends recognized the importance of the Europe faction enough to use these ambiguous words, as Jenkins writes, 'rather than to flaunt the red cloth of "the referendum" in my face'.[34] But this was indeed no more than face-saving. A referendum, rather than yet another general election, was clearly the instrument of choice. The balance of forces favoured the anti-Market side. They were, after all, in a majority in the conference and related organs. They had a strong grip on the Cabinet and the parliamen-tary party. They stood for an attitude, an emotion, a defiant rejection of the capitalist imperatives that the Market then seemed to embody, which Wilson had done little to argue down.

He did, however, hold the initiative, and something that could be called a renegotiation began. It was not without substantive potential. Certain matters had been postponed by Heath, most obviously the size of the British budget contribution. After so short a period of member-ship, the presence of serious financial inequity, sufficient to trigger the correcting mechanism the Heath deal contemplated but did not define, was hard to establish. But its likely occurrence was widely agreed. Brussels's own forecasts showed that the inequity – Britain contributing more than she would get, and more than her national income indicated as her due – would get worse in future years. Likewise, the Common Agricultural Policy, the source of most of this imbalance, was penalizing New Zealand, for which Wilson had a special soft spot, and the Caribbean. All the old issues, in other words, were deemed fit for grievance-mongering by the British. And all were in some manner at least addressed in the process which the British obliged the continentals, saddened but resigned, to reopen.

It was an extended process. Wilson briefed himself diligently on each of the seventeen aspects of the Heath deal Labour said were unacceptable. Over the winter of 1974–5, Callaghan flew to and from Brussels incessantly. The existing apparatus of Cabinet committees was fortified by another two, one for Euro-strategy, one for tactics. Regional policy, industrial policy, energy policy, overseas aid policy, the policy for Value Added Tax: these were just the beginning of the struggle. The entire structure of O'Neill's negotiation, if the static generated by ministers was to be believed, was up for detailed discussion. At the heart of it was the money, a matter on which Wilson regarded it as important to be able to show he had got something back.

Three aspects of the renegotiation, however, are more telling in retrospect than the barren matter of the sums. The sums, in fact, added up to very little. Despite the length of the process, which reached its climax at a summit in Dublin, Britain gained nothing that could be counted. The German Finance Ministry dreamed up a new formula for calculating a British rebate, to apply once Britain's gross national product per head was lower than 85 per cent of the Community average. In the event, it was valueless. According to Michael Butler, the British official closest to the renegotiation and one of the few Foreign Office men who does not look back on it with scoffing cynicism, it 'never produced any financial results'.[35] Since it was the only item in the list that was strictly quantifiable, rather than susceptible to linguistic blurring, this could have been damaging to Wilson's strategy. But its emptiness became apparent only after the moment of political crisis had passed.

And politics was the issue. This is the first aspect worthy of attention. 'It soon became clear to me', said Michael Palliser, at that time the ambassador in Brussels and a key player in the renegotiation diplomacy, 'that the whole object of the exercise was to keep Britain in, and get something that could be presented to the British as politically adequate.'[36] What was actually obtained mattered much less than the impression that, whatever it was, it was quite enough. This was part of the reason for the elaborate, long-drawn-out nature of the dealing.

Quite early in the piece, Wilson was daring to let it be known that he wanted a success, and that when the ensuing referendum took place he would be in a position to support a Yes campaign. For Jenkins especially, this was an important moment. It signalled that Wilson had, in effect, changed sides. Instead of sucking up to the left with anti-Market nuances, he was putting himself in a position where he had to make common cause with the Jenkins faction, little though he cared for them. 'By December I was not in serious doubt that Wilson would recommend a "yes" vote and that Callaghan as Foreign Secretary would do the same,' Jenkins writes. 'I did not therefore feel that there was any need for me to contemplate a second resignation.'[37] Subsequently, Wilson had so hard a time from the left – 'He was almost beside himself . . . The venom poured out of him,' wrote Barbara Castle, after an especially heated confrontation with his old allies[38] – that he once again waved around resignation threats. The renegotiation, thin though its eventual outcome was, in effect obliged him to come out for the first time as an open pro-European.

The second piece of hindsight to which this gives rise concerns the forbearance of the Europeans. Never was their desire for British participation so sharply manifested as during the elaborate dance that Wilson now conducted with his party, a period of uncertainty which occupied another fifteen months after the mere fourteen that Britain had so far belonged.

Wilson's peer-group of European leaders put up, first of all, with his theatrically extreme demands, some of which appeared to be challenging the very clauses of the Treaty of Rome. They went along with the implication that British membership thus far had somehow lacked political legitimacy. They put themselves to much trouble, going through the motions of meeting and deliberating and haggling, with a view to producing what might be represented as a fresh basis of British membership. With some boldness, they even brought their own skills to bear on the British political process direct, through the intervention of the new German Chancellor, Wilson's fellow leftist, Helmut Schmidt.

When Schmidt became Chancellor, in place of Willy Brandt, he was commonly construed to be an Atlanticist rather than a European. This was how Callaghan saw himself, and the false dichotomy, so popular in British politics, was planted on the Germans as though they were as much in thrall to it. Callaghan looked forward to dealing with an American German. But Schmidt, while certainly a friend of Nato, was not a critic of European integration. More than that, he was willing to argue for Europe in the temple of British anti-Europeanism, the Labour Party conference. In November 1974, he came to the platform at Central Hall, Westminster to speak, in effect, in Wilson's cause, and brought the rapt assembly of sceptics to their feet. I was present myself, as a journalist. It was hard to know which to admire most, his command of irony in a second language, or the way he elevated the Europe discourse to a level which the British were so seldom capable of addressing: its geo-political, even its moral, dimension as a force for good in a dangerous world.

Schmidt's presence that weekend was key in another way too. It encouraged Wilson to align his public mind with his private intention. There was a session between the two of them at Chequers, at which the German promised his British counterpart enough help with the renegotiation to satisfy Wilson that it would succeed. In return for German backing, he induced the Prime Minister to prepare to come out into the open, and to visit Paris to inform the new French President, Valéry Giscard d'Estaing, as well that he was about to do so.

Interviewed twenty years later, Schmidt took a sardonic view of this whole encounter. The renegotiation, he said, was face-saving, a cosmetic operation for the British Government. 'If, from British hindsight, it worked as a cosmetic operation, then the rest of the members were successful,' he reflected drily.[39] But at the time, his presence looked entirely different. It had a galvanizing effect. One official who was present at the Chequers session regarded it, indeed, as the final conversion of Harold Wilson to a course of conduct that concluded by keeping Britain in the Community.

'After Schmidt had gone,' the official told me, 'Wilson retired to his room. He spent about three hours there. He made one telephone call, to Jim Callaghan. By the time he came out, he knew exactly what he wanted to do and where he wanted to go. He clearly understood that if he tried to pull us out of the Community, he would split his party and Roy would take out however many people. He would get the Cabinet to agree to have a referendum, to agree that it was government policy to stay in, but that Benn and Shore and Castle would be free, exceptionally, to argue that we should come out. I think he had thought all that out as a tactical operation when Schmidt left. After that, it was just a question of making sure it happened.'

'I don't think it was a matter of principle for Wilson,' added the official, a man who saw many British ministers at close quarters throughout his life. 'But I thought his performance was staggering.'

He now had to carry it into the Cabinet room. With the renegotiation formally concluded in March, he needed to count the heads before the inevitable division, which he was prepared to legitimize for this one occasion, became public. It took two days, and the spilling of a great deal of acrimony. Presenting himself as an open-minded doubter to the end, Wilson, like Callaghan, spoke for a positive recommendation only on the second day. His attitude, in fact, remained Healeyesque. 'The decision is a purely marginal one,' he told Barbara Castle a little later. 'I have always said so. I have never been a fanatic for Europe. I believe the judgement is a finely balanced one.'[40] But there came a point, and it was now, when he could not avoid staking himself to a position that did not admit of such convenient cerebration. You were either for it or against it, and as Prime Minister, having promoted the entire process that culminated with this choice, you would find it harder than most to pretend that there was somewhere in between.

Some of the Cabinet were enraged. The diarists, especially Barbara Castle, excel themselves in their depiction of Wilson's alternation between fury and self-pity, as his dream of a well-mannered disagreement – 'a dignified parting of the ways', Ben Pimlott writes[41] – gave way to violent exchanges of abuse. Driven into alliance with his scheming rival, Jenkins, he boiled over with indignation at Jenkins's growing contacts with pro-European Tories getting ready for a Yes campaign in the referendum. 'Most unusually for him, Wilson was out to make himself unpleasant,' Jenkins writes.[42] To his oldest friends he seemed to be self-flagellating, as he contemplated the break with them. 'Harold was talking of resigning or of calling the whole thing off,' Michael Foot recalled. 'He kept saying the humiliation was so awful, the attacks of the press were so awful . . . He was in a state of emotional fury about it.'[43]

Such was the condition of the Prime Minister, as he edged the apparatus of politics in the direction he knew it had to go. His near-derangement, which was not construed by anyone as a tactical invention, did not, however, divert the course of events. The Cabinet majority of 16–7 for a positive recommendation of the new terms included five members previously on the other side, who were now won over by a combination of wheedling and enforcement, mainly by Callaghan.[44] Without them, the vote would have been 12–11 against staying in the EEC. For all his inner, and sometimes outer, turbulence, Wilson managed to guide the machine of government against the opinions of all his closest political friends, not to mention most of his personal coterie of advisers who were committed anti-Marketeers.

He also did so against the bulk of opinion throughout the Labour Party. However open Wilson is to the charge of slipperiness, and of complete, studied, sedulous failure to lead popular opinion in the direction he presumably wanted it to go, his managerial talents – deployed, it would seem, only semi-consciously, with him half-resisting himself all the time – produced an extraordinary reversal of political normality. When the Cabinet decision was put to Parliament, it received a large majority, entirely thanks to the Tories. But, of Labour MPs, 145 were against, only 137 in favour, with 33 abstentions. Counting all ministers, fewer than half voted for the Government line. Later in April, at a special party conference, there was a massive majority, 3.7 million to 1.98 million, for coming out of the Common Market altogether. Wilson had to remind them that coming out was not yet the issue: this was what the referendum of the people, not the party, would decide.

All the same, true to the position he had taken throughout this latest phase, Wilson made a speech that nowhere contained a statement saying he was personally in favour of staying in Europe. Already, thus, he was hedging against a No verdict. One may look with awe on his tactics in the Cabinet, but there is surely a limit. Even while he was judging an issue so important that it had to be sent to the people, he was reducing to the minimum his own responsibility, guarding against the worst, omitting to rise with even a single enthusiastic phrase to the occasion.

But there is something else worth noting about this phase of Wilsonry, which has particular piquancy in the 1990s. It is the third large insight to be legitimately enriched by hindsight.

As early as April 1974, scarcely a month into power, and still baring his teeth at anyone who looked like a pro-European, Callaghan was already beginning to learn something about the EEC that he liked the sound of. There began to emerge a collective opinion that the Community should find ways of taking a more active interest in foreign policy: what was known, in the language, as political co-operation. This was not entirely what he had looked for. As a noted Atlanticist, he watched with some distress the fiasco of the so-called 'Year of Europe' which his friend, Henry Kissinger, the US Secretary of State, had invented as a way of diminishing transatlantic rivalries. The resignation of President Nixon, running from impeachment, was one of several events that compromised the Year of Europe. But it did become apparent to Callaghan, pushed by the Foreign Office, that some kind of consultative approach to foreign policy by the Nine – Nine, instead of Six, was now the number, Denmark, Ireland and Britain, but not Norway, having seen their applications through – might be a way of increasing Britain's weight in the world.[45]

At the time, this awareness played its part in Callaghan's adjustment – conversion would be far too strong – from an adversarial to a mildly co-operative role in the renegotiation. Seen from afar, its casual treatment in 1975 recalls the lack of neuralgic sensitivity which then attached to anything that resembled political collaboration. Such ideas were then part of an ongoing, exploratory dialogue, towards a possible end which nobody could clearly foresee but which nobody fundamentally opposed. It is one example of how the context has changed, but also a cautionary item to insert into the 1990s argument about the alleged deceptions being perpetrated twenty years before. The observable historic fact is that, while political collaboration – a version of political unity – was in the air, it wasn't concealed. Rather, it was almost completely ignored in the debates that went on about the future of the nation.

There is parallel evidence of this in the still more neuralgic field of the currency. Economic and monetary union, EMU, was, as we have seen, on the Community agenda at the time Heath signed the Treaty. Serious leaders of serious governments made a commitment to introduce it in 1980. When Wilson displaced Heath, this objective was still nominally in place, though the oil shock meant that most bets were off. Nevertheless, it appeared on the agenda of a summit Wilson attended in Paris in December 1974, and he signed up to the declaration which said that, on EMU, the will of heads of government 'has not weakened, and that their objective has not changed'. 'The time has come', it went on, 'for the Nine to agree as soon as possible on an overall concept of European Union.'

Wilson, it is true, signed this in a spirit of confident agnosticism. He thought it wouldn't happen for some time. Other governments, he told the Commons, now had a different attitude towards 'the practicability of achieving EMU by 1980'.[46] He said the objective had been 'tacitly abandoned'. And plainly he did not want it. In their grapplings with him, the anti-Europe keepers of the diaries show him caustically promising that EMU is out of the window.

But fury at the prospect, all the same, was muted, by comparison with what came later. It didn't touch the British at that time on a spot where Europe really hurt. Although that can be attributed to its remoteness from reality, it dilutes the case of the conspiracy-theorists, whose retrospective vision depends so heavily on the notion that Europe was, all the time, cooking up plans that neither they nor their leaders knew anything about.

Few people, in truth, knew exactly where they were going. And now it was time for the British people as a whole to make what they could of the prospect.

*

IN THIS GREAT ARGUMENT, the people had thus far been only occasional contributors. Their voice had not been heard. Or perhaps they didn't have a voice. This was as real a possibility. The people hadn't spoken, in part, because they hadn't been asked. But also they didn't always have much to say. Now they were invited to take part in a referendum which, though termed merely consultative, would be decisive. It was the first national referendum in the history of the United

Kingdom: an alien deviation from the trusted path of party and parliamentary government.

'The people' were always hitherto a tool in the debate, their feelings handled warily by pro-Europeans, deciphered with confident presumption by the other side. But, insofar as they had been able to give a political opinion, this was inevitably buried in the mix of a hundred issues that were at stake in parliamentary elections. Their real responses, when put to it, were a bit of a mystery. Nobody had reason to be certain *what* they felt about this single question.

From public opinion polls, which were taken regularly from the late 1950s when Europe first became an issue, it was possible to deduce three characteristics of the public attitude to Britain's entry and membership. It was changeable, ignorant and half-hearted.

At the beginning, it tended to be favourable by a wide margin.[47] A Gallup poll in March 1959 showed that those in favour of opening negotiations to join outnumbered the antis by four to one, an order of magnitude that broadly held good until the beginning of the Macmillan event. This was a period of some excitement at the prospect of what beckoned, though there were palpable class differences: Europe has always been an idea more favoured by middle-class voters than the rest. Between June 1961, when Macmillan was preparing to decide, and January 1963, when de Gaulle administered his veto, there were fluctuations. Possibly the most significant figures, thrown up at different times in 1962 by Gallup and National Opinion Polls (NOP), were those showing the 'don't knows' as quite often larger than either the pros or the antis.

After the veto, it didn't take long for a majority to say it wanted negotiations to resume: 46 per cent against 25 per cent, according to Gallup in June 1963. The later 1960s, however, were not a good time for the European idea in Britain. In fact, an enduring shift began in the year Wilson decided to make his first overture, 1967. Disapproval of the initiative stood at 26 per cent in February, 41 per cent in May (when Wilson announced it), 45 per cent in November when the General said no again. Ignorance and indifference were still conspicuously prevailing conditions, measuring well above 20 per cent at all times. Of one feature there could be no doubt throughout the period: the high proportion of the people who found themselves unable to share the fascination of the politicians with this subject.

Not surprisingly, therefore, Europe never achieved then, and hardly

ever has done since, what opinion pollsters call salience. It did not stand
out, among the range of matters that troubled the typical British mind.
It was seldom a preoccupation, by comparison with prices and jobs and
schools and health and the other quotidian realities. The popularity of
the Community has had its ups and downs, and has never been so high
as it was in the late 1950s when Britain did not belong. But even at the
depths of its unpopularity it did not really set the electorate's pulses
racing. There were always things that mattered more. In October 1974,
only 10 per cent of voters logged it as an important question. Through
the 1980s, this was consistently down to low single figures: between 1986
and 1988, the monthly average was 2 per cent.[48]

Now, however, the voters were obliged to take it seriously, because
they were being asked to vote. The question could not be avoided. 'Do
you think that the United Kingdom should stay in the European
Community (The Common Market)?' And at the moment the question
was put, they were readier to give the answer the Government wanted
than they had been for a long time. For all the shenanigans in the
Cabinet, the coolness of the national leadership and the limited popularity of all things European, as the inevitability of the campaign came
finally into view the polls showed Yes votes outnumbering No votes by
two to one, a lead they never lost.

The referendum was happening, it should be remembered, at a time
of considerable national anxiety. In thirty years, the atmosphere had
completely changed. When Ernest Bevin and Clement Attlee decided to
have nothing to do with the Schuman Plan, they did so as leaders of a
country still deeply conscious that it had won the war, and still imbued
with a grim self-confidence to match: still blind, also, to the comparative
industrial weakness that loomed not far down the track. 'Europe'
remained a speculative venture, all right for other countries, quite
unlikely to come to anything, and, in any case, a project that could never
dent the immortal verities that sustained the independent British state.
Had there been a referendum in 1951, asking whether Britain should
enter the Coal and Steel Community, it would have produced an
overwhelming majority in favour of roast beef and Old England, along
with the near-universal opinion that our Spitfire pilots surely had not
died in vain.

In 1975, it was all quite different. The national psyche had been
battered by many intervening events, not least those of recent memory.
For one thing, the country saw itself as being in desperate economic
straits. Crises of several kinds seemed capable of destabilizing it, begin-

ning with the aftermath of the event that had pushed Heath out in the first place. In the winter of 1974, the British underwent the economic damage and national trauma of a three-day week brought about by a dispute between the Government and the miners. Alongside this disruption was a world oil crisis, further weakening people's expectations of normality. This was a time of great churning, even a certain panic. Inflation had lately reached 25 per cent, and Britain was simultaneously experiencing widespread, sustained unemployment for the first time since the 1930s. So unpredictable were world events that responsible pundits and politicians began to fear for a shortage of raw materials and basic foodstuffs: a phenomenon, incidentally, which neatly finessed any argument there might be about the cost of the Common Agricultural Policy. In this context, the Common Market had become a reassuring fixed point in the status quo. The people looked ready to be persuaded that anything which put jobs at risk, and might add yet another element to the turbulence, was an adventure not worth undertaking. Christopher Soames, by now the senior British Commissioner in Brussels, was widely quoted as saying: 'This is no time for Britain to be considering leaving a Christmas club, let alone the Common Market.'

Nor was it just a matter of the economy. Political developments also hung like an albatross round the national mind. There was the horror of Irish terrorism on the British mainland: the bombings now reached out of Belfast and Derry to London, Guildford, Birmingham. In Scotland and Wales, votes for national independence peaked in the October election, another disturbance. Scottish nationalism, which took 30 per cent of the vote, was to become a familiar feature on the British scene over the next decades, but at this time the English had difficulty putting it into perspective. They thought it could be the beginning of a break-up, against which, ironically, Europe might provide some kind of unchanging bastion. These things played their part in the formation of a consensus, in the middle of 1975, which was always going to be hard to persuade to take a plunge into what amounted to the unknown. Already, perhaps oddly, Europe was normality. *Quieta non movere*, let sleeping dogs lie, an axiom of British political management ever since Robert Walpole, was likely to work to the advantage, in such a climate, of the most revolutionary change in constitutional status visited on the country since that venerable eighteenth-century leader first introduced the title of prime minister into the English language.

The consensus, certainly, was wide and strong. Roy Jenkins, fittingly, was placed at its head. As a senior minister, he carried the authority of the state. As an enthusiast for Europe, he divested Wilson of responsibility for a cause the leader did not himself care for. The arrangement was, relatively, congenial to all parties.

It was also supported by most organized segments of British society. Business, of course, was universally in favour of a Yes vote. A survey of company chairmen, carried out by the Confederation of British Industry, showed no fewer than 415, out of 419, saying that Britain should stay in the Community. Donations poured into BIE, Britain In Europe, the umbrella group set up to conduct the Yes campaign. The press was equally united. Though some newspapers opposed the holding of a referendum, and all treated the conduct of it as more or less of a bore, none campaigned for a No vote. The *Daily Express*, once the last bastion of Empire loyalism and, in 1962, a dedicated enemy of what Macmillan was trying to do, had by now come round to the view that there was no alternative to the Common Market. There was no lack of coverage of the No campaign,[49] but nor was there ever a sense that this was an argument that evenly split the leaders of opinion in any sphere. Even in church, it was impossible to get away from the uplifting case for Britain's place in Europe. Every Anglican bishop supported it, prayers were said in half the Anglican churches, any lingering whiff of Europe as a project designed for the furtherance of rule by the Vatican was thereby helpfully dispelled.

What happened was that all the acceptable faces of British public life lined up on one side. While Jenkins led the cross-party campaign, Heath was just as active and Jo Grimond, the leader of the Liberals, had equal standing. Whitehall set up its own task forces and liaison committees with the unfamiliar role of supporting one side in a quasi-electoral argument. The old begetter of the deal, Con O'Neill, was recruited as the chief administrator of BIE, though he found the chaos of electioneering, the sheer disorder of politics as against diplomacy, hard to handle, and he was quietly sidelined. A fraternity of the middle-minded carried all before it, towards the continent many of them knew rather well. The historian E. P. Thompson thought of them as people who defined 'white bourgeois nationalism as "internationalism"', and he satirized their cultural habits. 'The Eurostomach', he wrote, 'is the logical extension of the existing eating habits of Oxford and north London. Particular arrangements convenient to West European capitalism blur into a haze of remembered vacations, beaches, bougainvillaea, business jaunts and vintage wines.'[50]

The No campaign, by contrast, enlisted a different breed. What

united them wasn't just their attitude but their effect: their oddity, by
and large, their position outside the mainstream of governing politics,
their resistance to the edicts of centrism in both its behavioural and
intellectual mode. Enoch Powell, Tony Benn, even Peter Shore, certainly
Dr Ian Paisley, the leader of the Ulster Democratic Unionists: these were
not smooth, concessive or readily pleasing politicians. They were edgy,
passionate, admirable for their very refusal to conform: not qualities
often rewarded by the mass of a cautious and conservative nation. A
Harris poll taken at the beginning of the campaign tested public
reactions, on a personal level, to twenty-two leading political figures who
were involved in it. Each of the fourteen pro-Market names drew a
positive reaction. Six of the eight antis scored negative, Powell and Benn,
their most important voices, among the most extremely. Paisley, the
worst, racked up 62 per cent who did not like him.[51]

They were supported by groups and hangers-on who were usually
still more outlandish. The National Front made its presence felt at too
many meetings. Missing from the mix was any ballast from an institution
the public could respect and understand, such as a political party. For
although the Labour Party in conference had voted to pull out of
Europe, and the majority of its MPs agreed, it was forbidden to have any
presence in the No campaign. Wilson and the leadership insisted on
silence from the party, obliging the licensed dissenters to make no official
connection with it.

There were attempts, by both sides, to submit a conclusive economic
case. For economics was what the campaign ranged most consistently
around, and in particular the question of prices. Prices were the key: that
was felt by Robert Worcester, the head of MORI, pollster for the Yes
campaign.[52] He found that for 58 per cent of people the cost of living
was the prime concern, and for 37 per cent food prices specifically.
Unemployment, by comparison, worried only 15 per cent. Yet although
these were the prime subjects of debate, and had the attraction of
apparently being quantifiable, they existed, in the end, more in the realm
of fear and speculation than in that of hard evidence. The No campaign,
for the most part, said that prices would rise, and that the iniquitous
CAP would be a blight on the British housewife. Probably the height of
its effectiveness was reached with a scare story launched by Tony Benn,
to the effect that 500,000 jobs had already been lost to Europe. This
contradiction of the assurances that Heath had given three years earlier
secured a lot of publicity. For its part, the Yes campaign could do little
more than go on making the same point. It found a hundred different

ways of saying, though none of proving, that the general economic prosperity eventuating from Britain's deepening membership of the EEC was a prospect it would be insane to give up.

In the late 1990s, however, the interest of the 1975 referendum campaign lies in something different. What was really said about the issue that came to matter most? In what state of mind, as regards the future of the British nation, did the people make their choice? Were there things they did not know, whose absence from the debate somehow invalidated the verdict? Was there, in particular, a conspiracy of conceal-ment about what Europe meant for national sovereignty?

As Euro-scepticism reached a crescendo, driven with special vituper-ation by politicians who had been part of the Yes campaign twenty years before, these questions acquired new potency.[53] The answers are more complex than they were sometimes made to seem.

The sovereignty issue was raised with passion and prominence by the anti-Marketeers. This camp divided into two: those like Barbara Castle and Douglas Jay, whose main concern was food prices, unemploy-ment and related economic matters: and those like Enoch Powell and Tony Benn, who, while also plunging into the economics, preached great warnings about the end of Parliament and the abolition of Britain's independence. The official No campaign's propaganda document ran through the fundamental dangers. The Common Market, it said, 'sets out by stages to merge Britain with France, Germany and Italy and other countries into a single nation ... As the system tightens – and it will – our right, by our votes, to change policies and laws in Britain will steadily dwindle. ... Those who want Britain in the Common Market are defeatists; they see no independent future for our country.' This was distributed at government expense to every household in the country.

Along with it went verbal paeans to the greatness of the nation that was and is. 'What the advocates of membership are saying, insistently and insidiously,' Peter Shore declaimed as the campaign was ending, 'is that we are finished as a country; that the long and famous story of the British nation and people has ended; that we are now so weak and powerless that we must accept terms and conditions, penalties and limitations, almost as though we had suffered defeat in war.' This was the kind of line heard much from Michael Foot as well. 'The British parliamentary system has been made farcical and unworkable by the superimposition of the EEC apparatus,' Foot said. 'It is as if we had set fire to the place as Hitler did with the Reichstag.' On the whole, it was the more floridly effective parliamentarians who voiced the most eloquent concern for the shell that Parliament, they said, was about to become. But they were often not very specific. There certainly were losses of specific bits of sovereignty – legal supremacy especially – involved in membership of the Community. But these critics, by and large, preferred the grand sweep of their own unhorizoned rhetoric, prophesying the end of life as we know it: a tactic that may not have assisted in diminishing their faintly crackpot aura.

The Yes campaign dealt with the matter differently. I traced no major document or speech that said in plain terms that national sovereignty would be lost, still less one that categorically promoted the European Community for its single most striking characteristic: that it was an institution positively designed to curb the full independence of the nation-state. Seldom, if ever, did the leading speakers address specifically the implications of the European Court of Justice. There was plainly much wariness about exactly how much to say, and in what context. The official Yes campaign document described the legal question, for example, as follows (italics in the original): '*English Common Law is not affected.* For a few commercial and industrial purposes there is need for Community Law. But our criminal law, trial by jury, presumption of innocence remain unaltered. So do our civil rights. Scotland, after 250 years of much closer union with England, still keeps its own legal system.'

While not untrue, this could be said somewhat to understate the matter. It certainly conformed, as did the entire Yes campaign, to the old familiar rule, the golden thread of deceptive reassurance that runs through the history of Britain's relationship with the European Union up to the present day: our entry was essential, our membership is vital, our assistance in the consolidation is imperative – but nothing you really care about will change.

On the other hand, it cannot be contended that the Yes campaign was silent on sovereignty. The words are there, the allusions are made. They just sought to change the way people thought about the concept. 'So much of the argument about sovereignty is a false one,' the document said. Sovereignty wasn't a 'dry legal theory', but had to be tested in the wider context of British interest in the world. 'The best way is to work with our friends and neighbours,' it said. If Britain now said No, 'the Community would go on taking decisions which affect us vitally – but we should have no say in them. *We would be clinging to the shadow of British sovereignty while its substance flies out of the window.*' The Community, it went on, recognized that every nation was different.

There was a balance to be struck between national and communal desires. '*All decisions of any importance must be agreed by every member.*'

While again it can be said that all these statements are defensible, they begged some questions. What did *any importance* mean, in the last one? The Treaty of Rome provided for majority voting, for example about agriculture. The agreement of every member wasn't always necessary. That was part of the point about the Community, but one the Yes campaign did not dare address. It did not deal, in all its subtle intricacy, with the straitening of the sovereign nation, or the climate of collaboration that would begin to produce majorities which it became impossible or imprudent to resist. The pro-Europeans did not try to foretell, in other words, the extent to which *political* union would begin, as a matter of political reality, to emerge. Their statement did say in terms, disposing of another 1990s canard, that while some people 'want us to be half-linked to Europe, as part of a free trade area', this wasn't possible because 'the European Community doesn't want it'. But the extent to which the project was political at all became masked: another well-chewed bone of contention with 1990s sceptics, who blame Messrs Heath, Jenkins and the rest for having failed here, above all, to tell the truth.

To this charge, Heath and Jenkins have their answer. They sometimes sound incredulous. When I interviewed Jenkins in 1995, he said the campaign had been almost all about politics. 'We're accused of having presented the case as just a useful trading arrangement and not facing up to the broader political issues,' he said. This was the reverse of the truth. He remembered a celebratory dinner, after the referendum, at which he and Heath had sat on a sofa together and shared experiences on this very point. 'We both agreed', he told me, 'that we had had some great meetings, very well attended, two thousand, three thousand people. In all of them, it was when one talked about the political issues that one got those moments when there is a sort of silence, a positive silence that meant one was gripping the attention of the audience.'[54]

Heath himself remembered the same kind of thing. When, in early 1997, he was goaded into contesting the claim that he had always disguised the political implications of going into Europe, he replied by producing chapter and verse from long-forgotten statements. Had he not said, to *The Times* on 7 April 1975, 'Britain – as a member of the Community – now belongs to the greatest political grouping in the world'? And what about this from the *Guardian* a month later: 'For the first time in their history, the ancient nation-states of Europe are coming together to learn the lessons of history and to avoid a repetition of its mistakes ... We have a unique and crucial role to play in building a Europe others have only dreamed of: free from tyranny and bloodshed, living in peace and prosperity, and meeting its responsibilities in the wider world'? To anyone who said he had not talked about the politics, he simply said, as he once said to me: 'They're just ignorant.'

This is not quite good enough, however. The arguments about Europe, like many political disputes, often come face to face, only to pass each other at the moment when they should lock horns. While it is true that membership was always a political act, and also true that it was discussed as Heath, Jenkins and many others remember it – as the avoidance of war, the closer union of friendly peoples, and so on – those weren't the hard issues. They were about Europe as a political entity, but not about Britain as a country constitutionally altered. They were politics in one sense, but not the other. As to that other sense of politics, the combatants today are apt to fall back on the suggestion that everyone knew that national sovereignty couldn't last anyway. Pressed on the suggestion that he had evaded the issue in 1975, Jenkins said: 'I don't think one ever dodged it. But certainly I would never have pretended – because I always believed it was absolute nonsense to say that you will preserve every bit of your sovereignty.'[55]

So the pro-Europeans' defence, in retrospect, is not satisfactory. Its frailties, however, are to a substantial extent made good by two aspects of the 1970s often lost on the fevered minds of the 1990s.

The first, already touched on, is the genuine and almost universal uncertainty about where the Community was going. The British referendum took place at a time, after the oil shock, when Europe was inert. Nothing much was happening. Jacques Delors, the next urgent driver towards more integration, was almost a decade away from taking the presidency of the Commission. For a minister to say, as many did, that nothing big could be decided without Britain's agreement was no more than the truth at the time: and, since nothing big of any kind was on the horizon, it was not a statement that immediately aroused speculative curiosity. The enemies of the project did their best to chill the people's blood, but their scenarios were drawn from their version of the literal meaning of the Treaty – its meanings and possibilities, on which they turned out to be quite largely correct – not from actual future programmes that anyone knew were in the works. Even EMU, though affirmed as an objective, was, as Wilson spotted, no longer very real.

The second point is still more telling: a natural trap for modern sceptics to fall into, but a trap all the same. The truth, incredible though it may seem twenty years later, is that the public were not interested. The potential loss of sovereignty did not bother them. Not all the rhetorical feats of Bennery could make them take it seriously. If the voters said Yes to Europe, it was because they did not care about the arguments pressed hardest on them to make them say No.

This is not merely a deduction. It can be measured. In the MORI opinion poll already cited, which showed 58 per cent of people concerned about the cost of living, the number registering alarm about sovereignty or national independence was no more than 9 per cent. Nor was this an aberration. Polling by NOP, which asked the same question at regular intervals between June 1961 and July 1971, found that, in a list of the aspects of Europe which people most disapproved of, having 'no say in our own affairs' scored remarkably consistently: at 3 per cent rising to 4 per cent.[56] If not enough was said by the Yes campaign about these matters which later became so sensitive, it may partly be because the campaigners knew that prices rather than independence, money rather than nation, was where the voters needed reassurance.

There was a congruity between these points. The absence of a future integration plan and the absence of public concern about integration no doubt reinforced each other. That doesn't mean 'Europe' did not develop, as sceptics were to claim, in ways unimagined by the voters of 1975. But it does raise a question about the percipience of those, especially the professional politicians, who claim to have been comprehensively hoodwinked when the Community, with Britain a compliant and fully voting member throughout, developed in the way it did. Misjudgement, maybe: conspiracy, surely not.

At any rate, the vote was won. The margin stayed the same, 2:1, as the polls had said it was in mid-March, though further polling implied that the campaign had not been entirely wasted, since perhaps 14 per cent of people changed their mind one way or the other. What settled it, by common agreement, was fear rather than exultation: the fear of the unknown, as represented by a world outside Europe which the No campaigners were unable convincingly to describe: not, alas, the enthusiasm of the British people for dealing in their newly discovered destiny. Just as there was a great contrast with the atmosphere that made membership of 'Europe' unthinkable in 1951, so there was another with the mood prevailing in 1961–3, when the EEC debate revolved round such confident questions as whether Britain would 'realise her full potential' in the EEC or as leader of a multi-racial Commonwealth. Now sullen apprehension was more the ticket. Survival, rather than potential, was what dominated the national mind. One woman's story spoke for many. The day after the referendum, a Cabinet minister told a civil servant outside the Cabinet room: 'I went to my constituency and an old lady said to me, "I don't like this Community, but I voted to stay in for my grandchildren." '[57]

What, however, did the outcome mean? It was supposed to be conclusive. The people had spoken. Robert Armstrong, later to be Cabinet secretary, said in my presence a few days later that, as a strong European, he was delighted to think that the issue had finally been put to bed. He spoke for the entire establishment of the political class and their auxiliaries, who had first opposed the referendum but then, after winning it, thought it would exorcize doubt at every level, from the Euro-stomach to the European peace.

It wasn't merely the winners who took this view. Tony Benn himself was man enough to embrace the outcome of the enterprise he had got under way. The populist did not unsay what the people said. 'I have just been in receipt of a very big message from the British people,' he came to his doorstep to declare on the morning after. 'I read it loud and clear. By an overwhelming majority the British people have voted to stay in and I'm sure everybody would want to accept that. That had been the principle of all of us who advocated the referendum.'[58] It sounded as though the participants might now go back to their party benches, and normal hostilities resume.

For careful observers, though, there were more interesting signals to consider, which raised some doubt about that. The meaning of party, and its connection with the Europe enterprise, might perhaps have been fatally compromised.

For one thing, it was obvious who had been most exhilarated by the campaign. 'It is a perverse but indisputable fact', writes Roy Jenkins in his memoirs, 'that the event I most enjoyed during 1974–6, my second and last period in a British government, was the one which I had striven most officiously, even to the point of a resignation which may have cost me the prime ministership, to prevent taking place.'[59] At the head of a cross-party organization, a truly national leader for the first time, Jenkins had made a temporary escape from the body that both succoured and, increasingly, alienated him, the Labour Party. It was the beginning of what might become a habit. Europe had supplied the excuse for this separation. It could yet become the pretext, the inescapable reason, for something more enduring.

The real leaders of the Labour Party, meanwhile, had conducted themselves with an equal and opposite lack of interest. While Jenkins was rising above party to preach Europe, Wilson and Callaghan rose above Europe to maintain, as they saw it, party. Their lack of zeal in the campaign was singular to behold. They refused to be seen under the cross-party umbrella, and did not speak at BIE occasions, for which stance Callaghan offered a significant rationale. There were, he said, three sides to the argument – the pro-Marketeers, the anti-Marketeers and 'the truth', which he represented. The BIE, though campaigning for the outcome the two men were banking on, was stained by prejudice, and therefore beyond the pale. They appeared occasionally under the banner of the Trade Union Alliance, but never under that of the Labour Campaign, a sub-group within BIE. Wilson made eight speeches, often at ill-arranged meetings, and Callaghan five: far fewer than they would do in an election campaign. Wilson's most memorable line used a cricket metaphor, uncomfortably mixed with sailing, to express the wholly defensive nature of the case he was presenting. Britain could not maintain world influence, he said, 'by taking our bat home and sinking into an off-shore mentality'. All in all, both men took care to remain eloquently distanced from the action.

Wilson carried his coolness even to the moment of victory. On the steps of 10 Downing Street, he gave a prepared speech which noted the size of the majority – bigger than any government ever got at a general election – and said it mapped the way forward to 'join wholeheartedly' with the rest of Europe in working together. The result, he added, meant that fourteen years of argument were over. But he refused to say he personally welcomed the result. Advised to do so by Bernard Donoughue, the only pro-Europe man in his entourage, he pointedly declined.[60]

And somebody else was absent from the popular consultation, Wilson's opposite number in the Conservative Party, Margaret Thatcher, who had been elected leader in Heath's place a few months before. She made her excuses, and let others carry the torch. She counselled a Yes vote, but said she thought Heath should take the thunder. Like Wilson, she had nothing to do with Britain In Europe.

Both main party leaders, therefore, were disclaiming some portion of responsibility for the watershed. They chose not to be fully engaged. It was a telling sign. The parties, through these leaders, distanced themselves from Europe in a way they would never contemplate over any other issue. It was as if, great though it was, they did not see it as a party question. They shrank from it personally, but they also recoiled from the political implications of an issue which party could not accommodate. It was unavoidably fissiparous – and the agent who might prise apart the fault-line was still at large.

*

THE REFERENDUM did not determine much. It settled the argument in British politics for a while. Not for some time was there any more talk, even from the serious anti-Europeans, about getting out of the Community. The decisive vote seemed to be the end of that debate. At the same time, it was the start of almost nothing. It failed to ignite a new collective effort in the chambers of government to take positive advantage of the Europe connection. In terms of British policy, as opposed to Labour politics, it was almost as if the referendum had never happened.

In less than a year, Wilson resigned the premiership, Callaghan replaced him, and Jenkins signified his intention to depart from British politics, accepting a four-year term as president of the European Commission.

Callaghan was not the man, any more than Wilson, to see in his post-referendum situation an historic opportunity. Presented with this result, this apparent settlement of a dispute that had rendered full-hearted membership, *croyant et pratiquant*, of the Community impossible, he allowed little of his natural scepticism to be reconsidered. The voice of the people had no effect upon him, perhaps because he didn't believe that, even with such a clear discrepancy between one side and the other, it was in any meaningful sense 'pro-European'. He construed the voice as identical with his own: cautious, suspicious, defensive and – most complacent of Callaghanesque postures – famously pragmatic. As a factual description, this was probably correct. What it left out of account was how a political leader, if he had any ambition to change the world, might steer Britain into making sense of what had now been definitively confirmed as the main part of her political destiny.

Callaghan's attitude, however, was congruent with his weak political position. By the time he became Prime Minister, his party had lost its majority and the anti-Europeans in his cabinet and party had not surrendered their opinions. Although the exit option had gone, the line of least collaboration remained stubbornly attractive. Any more positive engagement with the Community, besides offending many of the antis, would have been a distraction from other problems that were crowding in. In the autumn of 1976, after all, the economy appeared to be in such parlous imbalance that the Government became a supplicant at the court of the International Monetary Fund, whose officers temporarily seized control. Neither the leader nor his circumstance were conducive to truly constructive reconciliation between the island and the mainland.

For Jenkins, the prospect was very different. He may have been finally frustrated in his desire to be Prime Minister: he secured only 56 votes out of 314 in the contest to fill the Wilson vacancy. But he was, at last, a European leader. Taking up the presidency in January 1977, he made his break with British and Labour Party politics, to which, interestingly, he had already indicated to Callaghan he would probably not return. This wasn't made public at the time. But he told Callaghan that he 'did not want a future in British politics in their existing shape'. He could only envisage returning to 'a reshuffled pack', in which Labour's anti-European prejudices had somehow been finessed. 'Callaghan', Jenkins writes, 'looked surprised and pensive rather than hostile.'[61]

In his new task, he was at first frustrated. Impasse and lack of optimism still prevailed, the continuing fall-out from the oil-based recession. But eventually he became the prime instigator of the modern Community's most far-reaching project to date, a forerunner, in its way, of the system that was to come to full flower in the 1990s, leading, indeed, to many of the developments which ensured that 'Europe' would remain for the duration a festering source of division in British politics. In effect, Jenkins invented the European Monetary System, within which was sited the Exchange Rate Mechanism, out of which was begat the economic and monetary union that became scheduled to start for real on 1 January 1999. The dream so sanguinely defined by Pompidou and his colleagues in October 1972, having sunk almost into oblivion under the weight of quadrupled oil prices, now acquired definition once again.

Jenkins did not, of course, bring the EMS about. Though still in once sense a political leader – the first in his post, incidentally, to be admitted as an equal partner to world summit meetings of the Group of Seven – he was now formally an official. He could propose but not dispose. He did propose an outline for the EMS, dreamed up, as he records, on a picnic outing to the Forêt de Soignes – shades of Jean Monnet, devising the shape of the Coal and Steel Community as he strode across Alpine fields.[62] The case for a new currency regime, it seemed to him, was overwhelmingly made by a comparison between the 1960s and 1970s. In the 1960s, with fixed exchange rates, European economies had done well, at least keeping pace with America and Japan. In the middle 1970s, with rates unpegged and oscillating sometimes wildly, the performance had been dismal. For a few fleeting weeks, Britain had belonged to what was called the currency snake, the 1972 agreement allowing Community currencies only narrow fluctuations against the dollar, and so against each other. By 1976, it had been abandoned under the pressure of events, by all members except Germany and the Benelux countries. Now a 'zone of monetary stability', possibly leading to full monetary union, became Jenkins's crusade, as much, it would seem from his own account of it, because it might be a device to relaunch the flagging European idea as for its substantive virtues.

After breaking it to the world in a speech at Florence, he did much private politicking to enlist the support of the political leaders who mattered, Helmut Schmidt and Giscard d'Estaing. Though both were wary, and both otherwise preoccupied, it appealed to some of their pre-existing instincts. Giscard had to be ready to face down Gaullist resistance in his own coalition. Schmidt was initially reluctant, but then suddenly changed his mind, an occasion on which Jenkins lavishes a self-conscious cliché. Schmidt's enthusiastic account of the benefits of an EMS was the turning-point. 'I shall never forget how my heart leaped during that exposition,' the stylist apologetically writes.[63] The usage is a measure of his commitment to the project – which did not, however, find much favour with Callaghan.

It was, first of all, sprung on Callaghan unawares, at a summit in Copenhagen in March 1978. Although Callaghan had in fact heard Schmidt expounding a version of it before, he had not been listening, because he was simultaneously trying to get Schmidt to listen to his own initiative for closer links with the dollar. On that occasion, Jenkins writes, they 'had passed like two friendly ships in the night, close but not seeing or at least not listening to each other'.[64] But, in any case, Callaghan was by no means a solitary British sceptic. He was advised by the senior Treasury official on hand at Copenhagen, Kenneth Couzens, to reject it: and though he did not do this *tout court*, showing Jenkins an unaccustomed measure of polite interest, there was never much doubt that the Cabinet would find reasons to resist any active British involvement.

In fact, the Prime Minister himself seems to have become, if anything, a little more interested in the EMS than his Cabinet colleagues. 'World statesmen', wrote Edmund Dell, a Cabinet sceptic, later, 'have often proclaimed the benefits of stability in currency markets': they were attracted by 'an excuse to interfere' in the erratic and irrational perform-ance of the markets, where the recent era of floating rates had a poor record.[65] When the Government produced a green paper, designed as a basis for rejecting the Jenkins–Schmidt–Giscard initiative, the Prime Minister insisted that it at least contain a commitment to the *principle* of stable exchange rates. Indeed, Callaghan's flirtation with the idea grew stronger in his memory as time passed. He apparently regretted accepting what was in 1978 the conventional Treasury and Whitehall, as well as political, advice. Some years later, when Giscard came to deliver the annual Ditchley Lecture, at Ditchley Park outside Oxford, he alluded to Britain's failure to join the operative element of the EMS, the Exchange Rate Mechanism. The meeting was chaired by Sir John Hunt, the former Cabinet secretary, by now Lord Hunt of Tanworth, who thanked the former French President for his brilliant presentation, remarking, on the side, that he himself had always believed Britain should have joined in the first place. Lord Callaghan was sitting in the front row, and said in a voice that echoed round the room: 'Pity you didn't say so at the time.'[66]

The European Monetary System came into operation in March 1979. In May, Britain elected a new government, which did not immediately manifest any greater desire than its predecessor to plunge whole-heartedly into the European enterprise. And even as it was in the throes of being elected, Jenkins was given what turned out to be his opportunity to make good what he had Delphically foreshadowed to Callaghan before he went to Brussels: that when he returned, he would be reluctant to re-enter the tribalism of British party politics as then arranged. The fissile effect of the European experience was about to reach its explosive moment.

It would be a simplistic error to say that the founding of the Social Democratic Party was due wholly, or even mainly, to the disagreement about how Britain's European relationship should essentially be con-ducted. It answered a more pervasive call, in and out of the Labour Party, for a new grouping on the centre-left. It sprang from histories, arguments and rivalries going back a long way, reaching deep into the very fundaments of Labourism and socialism, Marxism and Methodism, all the competing strands that had brought the party to a pitch where they had ceased, in practical effect, to coexist together as a governing force. Europe was only one of the questions at stake. There was nationalization, there was defence, there was the constitution of the party, there was so-called elitism versus so-called populism, there was a host of dissatisfactions that drove a collection of professional politicians, supported by many unprofessional but active citizens, to depart an old allegiance and fashion a new one. However, Europe was, of all these questions, perhaps the most specific catalyst.

It played this role in several ways. First, there was Jenkins himself. The prophetic send-off, which Callaghan could scarcely believe, was amplified during his time in Brussels, where he became both fully European and ever less fully a British politician of the kind his life thus far had shaped him into. At the end, the EMS mattered far more to him that what the Labour Party thought about the EMS. Though he was incessantly busy, ranging round the continent and maintaining dialogue with every European figure that mattered,[67] he attained a distance from the British scene that gave him the opportunity to deepen his perception that it was in serious trouble.

He put this into words in late 1979, when the absent statesman was given an hour's free time to address the nation on BBC television. Jenkins's Dimbleby Lecture, as it was called, became a text marked down as an early pointer towards political reform, in which he proposed to play a major part. It was a philippic against excessive partisanship, a diatribe against the sterile party system, a paean for the virtues of coalition government. It sought to map out a new political creed, towards which such coalitionism might lead the country: less penal taxation but better public services, more respect for market forces but less unregulated worship of them, more state benignity but less state omnipotence, objectives, he called them, which 'could be assisted by a strengthening of the radical centre'.

The lecture rose above Europe, barely mentioned it. But it came out of Europe, and affirmed respect for modes of politics, such as coalitions, that were and are European. This was before the Labour Party lurched towards the extremity favoured by Tony Benn, but Jenkins spoke in the full knowledge that Europe would be a war zone for the now unconstrained Opposition. His own history, culminating in his departure from the deputy leadership, had singled Europe out as the issue above all others that moved his wing of the party to do unusual things. Though most of them felt as strongly about nuclear disarmament, this wasn't something they'd had to fight for so hard, since here the Wilson leadership felt the same. By many devices – calculated resignation, organized defiance of the whips, even the building of something close to a party within a party – Labour pro-Europeans had shown for many years the special potency of the attitude Jenkins stood for.

This points to the second European stream in the confluence of the SDP. It was a matter of organization as much as ideology. The referendum campaign blurred the Labour divisions but laid bare the way they might later be pursued. Many significant people acquired the habit of structured disagreement, discovering the pleasures, not to mention the culminating triumph, of working outside normal party lines. The list of pro-Europe activists in 1975 can helpfully be read alongside the roster of founding members of the SDP. William Rodgers and Shirley Williams were high in the councils, and other names leap off the page. Among Labour MPs later to go over were George Thomson, Dickson Mabon, Tom Bradley, David Marquand, Ian Wrigglesworth, John Roper, all of whom were heavily engaged as Jenkins lieutenants. Dick Taverne, who had gone so far as to resign his seat at Lincoln to fight a mid-term by-election in March 1973, to make his point against Labour's anti-Europe position, was another prominent cross-over.

There were exceptions. Roy Hattersley, a prime and undeviating Labour Europeanist, was also a categoric and unflinching Labour loyalist. He never contemplated surrendering either Europe or Labour, and by the middle 1990s, while mutating into a Grand Old Man of Labour orthodoxy in face of the New Labour model of Tony Blair, was happy to declare himself a European federalist.

David Owen was another case again. Like Hattersley, he spoke and voted for Europe in October 1971, having been a combative pro-Europe MP from the moment he got into the House in 1966. 'My political career has been dominated by the question of British membership of the European Community,' he starkly wrote in his autobiography.[68] He resigned from a junior post, with Jenkins, in 1972, and then again in 1980, from the shadow Cabinet, when Michael Foot became leader of the party. Though rather slower than Rodgers or Shirley Williams to welcome Jenkins's path-defining Dimbleby Lecture, he signed up with the two of them to make the Gang of Three that was preparing to leave the Labour Party, and then the Four that made the SDP.

But for Owen, it seems, Europe never had quite the prominence, as a mould-breaking issue, that it did for Jenkins. He was by this time more concerned with the defence question, and the attempted reconstituting of Labour Party power away from its MPs to the unions and the rank and file. In 1977, Callaghan had made him Foreign Secretary at the age of thirty-seven. He thus spent two years dealing with Jenkins, in a sense, as his political superior: the youthful politician surpassing the now unelected bureaucrat. During this time, moreover, the politician had acquired a certain dyspepsia with Europe, priding himself on the difficulties he was able to cause the Brussels bureaucrats, and rooting out the 'federalists' he thought were dominating the upper reaches of his department.[69] These people, he said, were the 'biggest source of friction' he had to contend with. When he had left office, he once marked the card, for my benefit, of an entire generation of Foreign Office grandees, divining several of the top men as lacking prime loyalty to the British nation. 'I have never been at any stage a federalist,' he writes, preferring to guard more jealously the independent muscularity – 'the sinews of nationhood' – that also might be said to describe, exactly but fatally, his own political style.

For Jenkins, however, Europe was the source of his ultimate liberation. It drew him out of one party into another: and with him much, in the end, of the tradition he stood for. This awaited reabsorption, more than a decade later, into something also exalting itself, in terms, as the radical centre: the old party becoming New.

9

MARGARET THATCHER

Deutschland Über Alles

FOR THE FIRST SIX YEARS of British membership of the European Community, Britain was led by men who were otherwise engaged. Ted Heath, preoccupied with domestic survival, did not begin to make an impression. Harold Wilson and Jim Callaghan, though compelled to give the matter some attention, were always trying to fend it off. Their successor was the first in the line to see Europe as a subject not for apologetic reticence but for triumphal prominence. For eleven of the first seventeen years, the tone was set and the policy made by someone who, at important moments, gave Europe the loudest place on her agenda.

This had a transforming effect. As the inheritor of unfinished business, Margaret Thatcher was well cast to conclude the deal neither Heath nor Wilson could close. But the loudness eventually brought with it confusion and calamity. As British steward of the Europe connection for twice as long as anyone before or since, she imposed on it a contradiction that had an influence no other leader came near to matching.

This was the Thatcher hallmark. In her time she took Britain further into Europe than anyone except Heath. Institutions and markets and laws became far more deeply imbued with the Europe effect. In one shining case, with the British leader's creative and voluble support, the project underwent a step-change from unanimous to majority rule. This was big, adventurous stuff, in a period of rich expansion for the Community idea. Mrs Thatcher, at every stage, was part of it. Yet simultaneously all her political energy was directed against what she herself was doing. Even as she took Britain further in, she stoked the fire of those who opposed this every step of the way.

One way of describing her performance was put to me by Robert Armstrong, now Lord Armstrong of Ilminster, her Cabinet secretary for much of this time. As a pro-European, Armstrong was impressed. 'She was more skilful than anyone I've ever met', he said, 'in combining rhetoric which was faithful to her principles with policies that were totally pragmatic.'[1] But another reading also has to be considered: that the rhetoric so far drowned out the pragmatism as fatally to complicate the most elementary task of the politician – securing popular support for the policies her Government is actually pursuing. As time went on, she allowed her very personal obsessions to confuse, even corrupt, her role as a national leader.

Seldom in the recent record of democracy, and never in this story of Britain-in-Europe, has a lengthy course of events been attributable so particularly to a single character. For all her eleven years, Prime Minister Thatcher was in disagreement, on Europe, with most of her significant ministers. In this central phase of Britain's accommodation to the reality it had finally chosen, the country had a leader who was more potent than any since the war, but was formed by influences which could have been selected, unless she overcame them, to bring her into collision with the European idea.

To begin with, she was Britain's first post-war Prime Minister. That is to say, she did not know the war at first hand, whether as a potato controller or a soldier. Born in 1925, she was still at school when it began and at Oxford when it ended. She could not, like the Macmillans and Heaths and, for that matter, Pallisers, call to mind images of a continent reduced to rubble, which left such men with the inextinguishable belief that European nations must devote their future lives to ever closer union. The echoing afterlife of remembered battle was not available. So she did not participate in the experience that defined the convictions and fired the practice of the main contemporaries who gathered with her, decades later, round the table at the European summit.

Her war, instead, was spent in the small middle-England town of Grantham, thinking about the Germans. Her father, Alfred Roberts, the shaper of her mind and life, was intensely suspicious of foreigners. Whereas the Heath family's gaze drew on experience across the Channel, the Roberts family were navel-watchers, supremely proud of Englishness. 'I would sooner be a bootblack in England', Alfred told the Grantham Rotary Club, of which he was president, in 1937, 'than a leading citizen in a good many of the other leading countries of the world today.' He seems to have detested, in particular, France, which he called 'corrupt from top to bottom'.

It was Germany, inevitably, that dominated table-talk in the Roberts household. 'I knew just what I thought of Hitler,' Margaret Thatcher recalls in her autobiography.[2] It is hard to decipher, as one reads this work, how much of it is a genuine recollection of the time, and how much the pasted-on hindsight of a retired politician. Whether, for example, the thirteen-year-old girl was as conscious as she states of the iniquity of Hitler's invasion of Sudetenland is difficult to judge: as is the representation of herself as someone who always knew that the pacifism in Britain in the 1930s was not exclusively, as she insists, a disease of the right. However, her retrospective conclusion about the Germans is eloquent. That even 'a cultured, developed, Christian country like Germany had fallen under Hitler's sway' showed that civilization, in the hands of weak people, could never be taken for granted. As the bombers droned over Grantham, the nature of the enemy, and the contrast they made with the British, impressed itself on a youthful mind. 'I have to admit', she writes forty years later, 'that I had the patriotic conviction that, given great leadership of the sort I heard from Winston Churchill in the radio broadcasts to which we listened, there was almost nothing that the British people could not do.'[3]

Europe, as this child's mind reached adulthood, acquired no prominent, still less a visionary, place in its hierarchy of interests. There is no record of what she thought of the Schuman Plan. By the time of the Macmillan application, she has reached Parliament, and is, as a dutiful Conservative MP, in favour of it. Indeed, she remembers thinking, after the event, that we had missed the boat at Messina: 'There was a general sense, which I shared, that in the past we had underrated the potential advantage to Britain of access to the Common Market.'[4] All the alternatives, she also thought, were inadequate: neither EFTA nor the Commonwealth nor the USA could meet Britain's trading needs.

With hindsight, however, she is a wistful Gaullist. It is the earliest of many regrets, misjudgements, errors and reversals that litter the Thatcher career on this subject. Writing in 1995, she confesses she did not know at the time what the Treaty of Rome was all about. She was in favour, she says, of a common market, 'and neither shared nor took very seriously the idealistic rhetoric with which "Europe" was already being dressed in some quarters'. Again in retrospect, she looks on de Gaulle's veto as an opportunity that should, in ways she does not describe, have been somehow seized. He had said, in his veto statement, that the breakdown of negotiations need not prevent 'an accord of association designed to safeguard exchanges', or 'close relations between England

and France'. This, the elder stateswoman reflects, would have been better than British membership on the terms eventually negotiated. She concludes: 'We may have missed the best European bus that ever came along.'[5]

Such a perception had not been borne in on her by 1971. When Heath made his second try, she was a Cabinet minister and 'wholeheartedly in favour of British entry'.

De Gaulle's departure had 'transformed the prospects'. Though a mere onlooker at the detailed negotiations, she had the opportunity to contemplate the meaning of Community membership for the grand principles of sovereignty, both national and parliamentary. Enoch Powell and others, after all, brought them to everyone's attention and Powell was one of her heroes. But she looked on his arguments as 'theoretical points used as rhetorical devices'. She did not, at that time, dispute what Geoffrey Howe, piloting the European Communities Bill through the Commons, said about the potential conflict of laws, namely that in any dispute 'the courts would . . . try to interpret statute in accordance with our international obligations'. For it could not be disputed. Only much later did she come to regard the white paper's talk about there being no loss of 'essential' national sovereignty as 'an extraordinary example of artful confusion to conceal fundamental issues'. In 1971, it evidently made perfect sense.[6]

By 1975, the year of the referendum and of her ascent to the leadership, it still made sense. She wasn't, at that stage, too keen on the referendum device, and made her maiden speech as party leader attacking it. Again we find a belated confession of error. At the time, she argued that a referendum, whose implications for parliamentary sovereignty would always be 'profound', was conceivable only 'in cases of constitutional change'. The Europe connection, in 1975, evidently did not measure up to this requirement. Twenty years on, now positioned somewhere between the sceptic and the phobic concerning British membership of the European Union, Baroness Thatcher found herself to have been mistaken in supposing that the Treaty of Rome did not entail a constitutional change. It was 'at least part of the way' towards a written constitution, she now considered.[7] By this time, the middle 1990s, a referendum on the next development, a single currency, had become, in her raucous opinion, essential.

As party leader, she had from the beginning a world view shaped much more by the Cold War than by the European Idea, and it was in this respect that she was able to muster most enthusiasm for the meaning of the Nine. 'I did genuinely believe that it would be foolish to leave the Community,' she writes. But she always saw the bond between West European countries as a strengthening of freedom against the menace of the Soviet bloc, and from time to time urged them, while not diminishing from Nato, to strengthen their attitude to collective security. Speaking in Brussels in 1978, she said: 'Who is there in the EEC deliberations to speak up for defence? I feel no assurance that all these connected matters are being looked at together.' In December of that year, it should also be noted, she was even derisive of the Callaghan Government's refusal to get involved in the foundation of the Exchange Rate Mechanism (ERM) of the European Monetary System. 'This is a sad day for Europe,' she said in the Commons, under a Labour government 'content to have Britain openly classified among the poorest and least influential members' of the Community. She seemed to want in. But the defence dimension concerned her most. For all the economic collectivism of Brussels, which became a source of maximum suspicion, strategic collectivity was an attitude to be encouraged.

Member though Britain was, however, the Community, even before she had to grapple with it, represented much that Mrs Thatcher did not like. She may have brushed aside as meaningless its absurd aspirations, but there was no getting away from its history and composition. For someone as instinctively suspicious of Roman Catholicism, for example, the spectre of *Europe Vatican*, once to be found among the nightmares of socialists like Ernest Bevin and Denis Healey, was not entirely absent. Catholic social teaching, if not the threat of papal conspiracy, was a menace to the project of a leader bent on liberal market economics. Worse than that was the very style of politics that Europe lived by. It had been exalted by Heath, frantically trying to pull election victory out of the fire in October 1974, when he suddenly proposed a so-called Government of National Unity, a non-party administration of all the talents, to tackle the British crisis. Mrs Thatcher silently seethed against the very idea. That was one reason why she took little part in the referendum: the Yes campaign was a plain affront to the supremacy of party, and the war between parties, which was the only political style she understood. Europe, in its larger way, constituted a lifelong exercise in the haggling and dealing, the compromise and consensus, that the lady most despised.

To the objective problems Europe presented to any Prime Minister, therefore, was added, in Mrs Thatcher's case, a more personal challenge. Christopher Soames, whom she put in her first Cabinet, had a good phrase for her, and the truth of it endured at least through her office-holding, Europe-engaging life. 'She is an agnostic who continues to go to church,' he once told me. 'She won't become an atheist, but on the other hand she certainly won't become a true believer.' Europe contended with most of her natural instincts, none of which she desired to overcome. Thatcher *contra Europam* was the stance that she adopted. Although it produced some significant positive results, her long tenure was more notable for its encapsulation of the vices, the English diseases, to be found at one time or another throughout this history.

Somewhere, they can all be seen in the Thatcher years. There is straightforward inconstancy: once routinely favouring Europe, she became its passionate enemy. There is more than a touch of dissimulation: though apparently the upholder of the sovereign nation, she acted to increase the collective powers of the Community. There is the preaching of illusion: as Prime Minister she fully understood the interlocking of Britain with Europe, but when she left she flirted with the dream of Britain Alone. There is contradiction: leading Britain further in, she tried to talk Britain further out. And there is incompetence: she lost four senior ministers to the Europe question, a record of instability that culminated in her own eviction.

One does not need to be a critic of the Thatcher approach to pick out the shape of this saga. The country she took over was in a poor way. What Sir Henry Tizard had said all those years ago – 'We are not a Great Power, and never will be again. We are a great nation, but if we continue to behave like a Great Power we shall soon cease to be a great nation' – received, at the very moment of her arrival in power, an eerie modern gloss from the British ambassador in Paris. Sir Nicholas Henderson, whose confidential valedictory despatch in June 1979 contrived to be published in full, offered a less elegant, but no less telling, update. 'Our decline in relation to our European partners', Henderson wrote, 'has been so marked that today we are not only no longer a world power, but we are not in the first rank even as a European one.'[8]

The three parts of Mrs Thatcher's response to this condition were phases first of triumph, then of confusion, and finally of collapse.

*

NOT ALL THE EUROPEAN business she inherited was unfinished. The thing had not been a total failure for Britain. Since the moment of entry, there had already been some gratifying successes. Food prices were one example. Predicted, even by Heath, to rise by 16 per cent, in the first two years they actually fell – by just over 1 per cent.[9] Britain paid that much less inside the Nine than she would have done outside, because world food prices happened to rise above the level at which they had been fixed in the Community. In some later years of the 1970s, Britain did have to pay more. But here was a case that showed how little was predictable in the finances of the Common Market.

More viscerally pleasing was what had happened to the status of the English language. This was a triumph to satisfy even the most sceptical Thatcherite. In the Heath negotiations, language had been a problem. Con O'Neill even offered the opinion that France's fears for the primacy of French 'had lain for years behind earlier French determination to exclude us from the Community . . . It was seldom referred to in public; but it loomed and swelled in the background.'[10]

Heath, to placate Pompidou, had said that the old linguistic ascendancy would be sustained, and he instructed British officials, when they arrived in Brussels, to continue the practice under which all negotiation was conducted in French. It was a moral obligation he felt it incumbent on him to fulfil. The Danes and the Irish, however, had given no such undertaking, and made clear from the start that they wanted to speak English. Even though the Dane in question spoke excellent French, he was under instruction from Copenhagen to use his even better English. Once that happened, the Englishman, Michael Palliser, decided it was a practical impossibility for him not to do likewise. At that point, however, other national representatives were under their own instructions to take defensive action against both English and French. An elaborate minuet began in the Committee of Permanent Representatives, or Coreper, in which the Italian, another good French speaker, started speaking Italian, and the Dutchman Dutch. Michael Palliser, the Englishman in question, recalled: 'We had the effect, more through the Danes and the Irish, of turning the committee into a Tower of Babel.'[11] But the consequence was to erode the supremacy of French. Texts in other languages slid quietly into Euro-practice. By the time Mrs Thatcher came to power, French was no longer the exclusive first-draft usage. English was on the way to a place of equality, even, in practice, superiority.

Money, however, remained an unresolved problem. The Heath arrangement had left open the possibility that, if an 'unacceptable situation' arose concerning the British contribution to the Community budget, something would be done. That was what the Wilson renegotiation had mainly been about; but it had produced no more money. The formula depended on many elements, the net effect of which was to disadvantage a member state which (a) collected more tariffs and levies on goods imported from outside the EEC, and (b) had an efficient agriculture sector, with much lower manpower costs than other members, and was therefore rewarded with much lower subsidies from Brussels. This was a description of Britain. Labour had got the formula adjusted, to give more weight to national wealth: gross national product per head. By 1970, after all, Britain was already less rich, in those terms, than France, Denmark or the Netherlands. However, with North Sea oil on stream by the later 1970s, the Wilson formula produced nothing. Some richer countries continued to be net beneficiaries, while the new Thatcher Government was looking at a net contribution in 1980 of £1,000 million, rising fast.

The very calculation of this figure was, in its way, a heresy. Community idealism had always frowned on the concept of a fair national return, the infamous *juste retour*. This was not supposed to be the way true Europeans thought about their joint endeavour, an elevated view which did not, however, exclude certain more familiar considerations. The net beneficiaries didn't want the net balances even to be published. 'The Danes, in particular,' writes Michael Butler, one of the Foreign Office's champion number-crunchers at the time, 'were passionate in their opposition, lest giving publicity to their net gains lead to their erosion.'[12] So great was the commitment to the pooling of resources, after their collection according to the neutral formula laid down, that some continentals had serious difficulty understanding why the British had a problem. Butler and David Hancock, the Treasury man in charge, were reduced to drawing elementary graphics in order to explain how British taxpayers' money was being routed into the pockets of German farmers. 'There was a real intellectual problem,' Hancock told me. 'Some of them couldn't see what the fuss was about.'[13]

The new Prime Minister, immediately briefed, had no such difficulty. The sensibility of 'Europe' was soon swept aside, and the *juste retour* enshrined in the demotic: 'our money', sometimes corrupted into 'my money', became the watchword, and the demand for its return the focal point of all Mrs Thatcher's early forays into European diplomacy. It was, for her, an almost perfect issue. The problem suited her angular mind and her instinct for aggression. It was very black-and-white. The outcome, instead of being lost in swathes of Euro-babble, would be starkly measurable. There would be a winner and a loser, and only the winner would have justice on her side.

The battle over the budget contribution, however, set the scene for contests which lasted much longer, against two categories of enemy that became a demonic presence in Mrs Thatcher's world throughout her decade in power.

In the first category were the other European leaders. She met them early, and did not like what she found. Her first foreign visitor to Downing Street was Helmut Schmidt, the German Chancellor, with whom, in one way, she got on quite well. Though Schmidt, as leader of the Social Democrats, was theoretically a socialist, she sometimes joked with him that, being seriously interested in market economics, he was well to the right of half her Cabinet. Their relationship testified to her ability to rise above, or perhaps descend below, mere ideology to make instantaneous judgements about whether X or Y was someone with whom, almost chemically, she could do business. I even found the same myself: despite producing a good deal of critical journalism, I was somehow never banished to the darkness, and was even credited as a person with 'convictions'. So it was, at a much superior level, with politicians. Just as there were progressives she could tolerate, there were conservatives she disliked, and high in this category was Schmidt's European partner, Valéry Giscard d'Estaing, the French President, whom the British leader thought cold and patronizing. 'Olympian, but not patrician', she acutely called him.

Over the budget question, they were both her enemies. When the matter came for what was supposed to be settlement, at a summit in Dublin six months after she got in, she inaugurated the new, Thatcher, era of European diplomacy. It was to be characterized, on her part, by hideously plain speaking, and a triumphant lack of sensitivity to other people's problems.

The Europeans behaved badly at Dublin. In response to her unsubtle demands for a fair deal, they were rude and derisive, and determined not to meet her anywhere near halfway. Roy Jenkins, a witness, writes that Schmidt feigned sleep during one of her harangues. At another point, Giscard had his motorcade drawn up at the door, engines revving, to signal that he would delay no longer. 'I will not allow such a contemptible spectacle to occur again,' he said as he departed. On the other hand, the lady's own performance had broken all the rules. She marked out the last ditch she would defend with total intransigence for as long as it took. The smootheries of conventional diplomacy, the spirit of give-and-take on which the whole European edifice depended, were plainly values she could never be relied on to observe.

No deal was done at Dublin, and, as the argument rumbled on, the other object of Mrs Thatcher's undying suspicion began to emerge clearly into view: the Foreign Office, and – a rather larger compass – all who stood in unquestioning emulation of the Foreign Office attitude to international life.

Quite a lot had happened to the Foreign Office since the days of Roger Makins and Gladwyn Jebb, and even since those when John Robinson was holding the European fort. Europeanism, non-existent in the 1950s, remained an eccentric allegiance as late as the middle 1960s. Since Britain was still outside, Community affairs hadn't yet become the obvious career-path of choice for all young diplomats in search of stimulus and influence. Older men had to see their careers out, and older men were Commonwealth or American men, not, by and large, Europeanistas. Equally, however, the middle generation was moving towards the higher reaches, and this group was different, being constituted by many of the people who had once despaired of the Euro-scepticism above them.

In the topmost place, when she got in, Mrs Thatcher found ensconced none other than Michael Palliser. Palliser, a two-time veteran of the Paris embassy, hand-holder to both Wilson and George Brown during their European ventures, first UK mission chief to the European Communities after the joining, continued to regard the closer union of Europe as the core British interest the Foreign Office should be defend-ing. He had lived and breathed it throughout his professional life, and was now at the head of the institution that could do most to advance it.

He was not alone. The Office Mrs Thatcher inherited was, according to David Owen, who bequeathed it, a hotbed of Euro-federalism. In his memoirs, Owen writes about this aspect of his time as Foreign Secretary with some venom. A number of officials, he says, 'had become zealots for the European Community and all its works'. Instead of behaving like diplomats, they had taken up 'a campaigning role'. Too many were reluctant to do anything that would put them at loggerheads with the rest of the Community, still less to 'spill a little blood on the diplomatic carpets of Europe', which was Owen's own ambition from time to time. Nor did they easily submit to political control. Owen notes scornfully that the politicians they mainly associated with – Heath, Jenkins, Gri-mond – 'were federalists, and when I joined the Foreign Office they too easily assumed ... that I would be too'.[14]

With uncharacteristic tact, Owen withholds the names of the officials he has in mind. And he probably exaggerates the semi-conspiratorial influence he attributes to them. There were certainly diplomats who didn't accord with his description. But it is not hard to know the people he was talking about. One of them, I easily surmise, is Palliser, a man Owen says he 'liked and respected', but whom he then compares, under the thinnest disguise, with the patriotic high-flyers of the Quai d'Orsay who 'talk European and think France', who 'fight at every level for France', unlike the British, who mostly lacked the tenacity to do likewise. Another name surely marked by Owen's federalist stigma is that of Michael Butler, a cunning, thick-skinned negotiator, whose passion for 'Europe' nonetheless implies a view of the British interest that would be uncongenial to a nationalist politician, whether one at heart a European, like David Owen, or an anti-European, like Margaret Thatcher. Other figures who could easily have attracted Owen's suspicion were John Fretwell, later ambassador in Paris, Michael Jenkins, a Europeanist many times over, who finished his career as ambassador to the Netherlands, and Christopher Mallaby, soon to go to Bonn.

It is not a crime to be a federalist, and, besides, the term has a variety of meanings. Few of these distinguished public servants would accept the label without careful qualification. The two I asked, Palliser and Butler, denied the charge as made, each producing a set of definitional nuances that rendered it meaningless. Nevertheless, officials are not elected politicians, and are wont to have less sensitivity than ministers to problems of popular consent. Their institutional bias is to get things done, to wrap up the business, to achieve consensus between the high negotiating parties without excessive regard for the possibly cussed reaction of the mob: indeed, perhaps seeing their public duty as being to help their minister forget such considerations, which might otherwise divert him from the national interest. Making 'Europe' work, which inevitably meant reducing to their lowest the imperatives of narrow nationalism, was the institutional bias of the Foreign Office when it came under Mrs Thatcher's command.

She had some difficulty commanding it. When, a little later, she found an ambassador in Paris by the name of Reg Hibbert, who urged her to keep up the heat on the French in some negotiation, she was amazed, and inquired how he had ever been appointed.[15] In fact Hibbert, a noted contrarian, whose previous ambassadorship was in Outer Mongolia, was put there by Owen. For the rest, she found people who far from satisfied her requirement that they be One of Us. 'I think she tended to feel that the Foreign Office was so committed that it wasn't on our side at all,' Lord Hunt of Tanworth said.[16] Along with its ministers, it was horrified by what had happened in Dublin, and these ministers, Lord Carrington and Sir Ian Gilmour, wet Europeanists both, were left the task of picking up the pieces.

Another lesson in diplo-Thatcherism had to be taught them first, however. The Dublin offer was for a refund of no more than £350 million, one-third of the British deficit: quite unacceptable. The Thatcher demand was for 'broad balance' in the sums, which, interpreted literally, would have required the whole imbalance to be wiped out. The Foreign Office set its sights on two-thirds, and, through a series of complex formulae and adjustments batted to and fro with Schmidt's and Giscard's people, got close to a net figure which was near that. But it offered no permanent promises for the future. The discrepancies produced by the system would remain as irritants every time the budget came up. It took another FO negotiation, using FO methods, which included a modest amount of stick as well as carrot, to reach the two-thirds reduction for two years, with the promise, in certain circumstances, of a third.

What was seen as a triumph by Carrington and Gilmour was regarded differently elsewhere. This was the lesson. No negotiation could be permitted smoothly to succeed if it was conducted by a minister other than the Prime Minister. Farcical and phoney scenes had to be gone through before a deal was recognized as done. The ministers, arriving at Chequers uncertain what to expect from the compromise they had agreed over the midnight oil in Brussels, were met by the leader's almost uncontrollable wrath. As she appeared at the door, Gilmour recalled, she was 'like a firework whose fuse had already been lit; we could almost hear the sizzling'.[17] She accused them of giving in, and settling for a worse deal than she had already rejected. Officials were summoned to settle the point one way or the other. The Treasury official, Rachel Lomax, then a relatively junior economist who happened to be on duty when the telephone rang, briefed herself in the car to Chequers, and proved, perhaps woman to woman, to be the only person capable of persuading the Prime Minister, calmly but insistently, that the figures added up to Britain's advantage. 'It was beautifully done,' writes Gilmour. 'What a pity, I thought, that Mrs Lomax is not in charge of the economy.'

After many hours of rancid discussion, followed by a full Cabinet meeting, the new arrangement was accepted, though in the leader's case still through gritted teeth. As an early indicator of the Europe problem and the Thatcher way of meeting it, the episode had aspects which are of some enduring interest.

At this stage, for example, the issue remains one of cost, not sovereignty. The lady's ferocity is addressed to the unfairness of the balance-sheet, not the existence of the enterprise. Though exulting in her freedom to break the diplomatic rules and cause maximum annoyance, she is playing the Community game, albeit with a ruthlessness hitherto visible only behind the better manners of the French.

Moreover, she was addressing a real, undeniable problem. The budget imbalance was the product of a financial scheme quite deliberately set in place, under French direction, before the Heath negotiation began, to ensure that within the existing *acquis*, the European patrimony, another item was stacked against the British. It wasn't the first time such a ploy had been worked. Both the Common Agricultural Policy and, even more particularly, the Common Fisheries Policy, were concluded under pressure of the applications for membership from a country, Britain, that stood to be disadvantaged by them. The loophole in the budget rules – the allowance for a possibly 'unacceptable situation' that needed to be changed – was one of which the British were absolutely entitled to take advantage, if they could negotiate an outcome. The seven-year transitional phase Heath and Pompidou originally negotiated was, in any case, coming to an end as Mrs Thatcher took over.

But, in the negotiating task, normal manners had got nowhere. Though both Roy Jenkins and Ian Gilmour claim in their memoirs that the Thatcher style gained nothing extra, several officials I interviewed – Palliser, Butler, Hancock, David Hannay, most of the suspect *galère* – more or less disagreed. Some with reluctance, others like Hannay with bullish enthusiasm, thought her method, which was not always their method, had paid off. The budget question had to be settled, and her abrasion contributed to what amounted to a three-year deal. The spectacle of Helmut Schmidt kicking the furniture and unleashing a volley of German oaths after Mrs Thatcher had left the room, during an intervening summit in Luxembourg, was one that Michael Butler appears to have found thoroughly amusing.[18]

The story, moreover, had a satisfactory outcome. We leap forward four years from the Chequers fiasco: past the Falklands War, past the 1983 election landslide, into the middle Thatcher years when she was operating in all her amplitude. In that time, the 1980 formula had produced mixed results, again contingent on the impossibility of predicting EEC budgetary flows, which were themselves mainly influenced by the vagaries of agricultural production. For example, in 1981, amazingly, the British contribution netted out at merely *2 per cent* of the 1980 forecast.[19] In 1982, by contrast, the agreed deal was higher than predicted. But, in any case, these year-by-year haggles could not last. Though there had been the three-year comfort period, it guaranteed nothing for the future. The potential for continuing inequity, with Britain the substantial loser, remained. Any Prime Minister, whatever their position on the spectrum, would have been obliged to fight hard against it.

The 1984 contest ranged Mrs Thatcher against a new cast of main characters, who were to have more influence than their predecessors on her life. By now she was plainly at least an equal, rather than the tyro needing to go to extreme lengths to establish her position against Schmidt and Giscard. This was the mature Thatcher, who was dealing, however, with two new men who, in different ways, personified the Europe that disturbed and finally unhinged her.

Schmidt was succeeded in 1982 by Helmut Kohl who, as a Christian Democrat, nominally a conservative, might have been expected to be more like a kindred spirit to the British leader. But the law of perverse outcomes, an ordinance frequently at work in the radiations of the Thatcher personality, continued to operate. Kohl, a pawky Rhinelander, was a very German politician. He was not by instinct or formation an internationalist, like Schmidt. Nor was he, as a Christian Democrat, fully versed in the liberal economics now raging through the decimated heartlands of industrial Britain. Schmidt made no secret of his disagreements with Mrs Thatcher, and his near-contempt for her view of the EEC as an arena where the only thing that mattered was to be seen as 'winning': in conversation with me in 1985, he likened her, in this respect, to Harold Wilson.[20] But Schmidt she could understand, whereas Kohl she spent eight years regarding as a pain: verbose and difficult, and, more to the point, a leader whose views of the European project conferred on it steadily larger grandeur, even as hers were moving in the opposite direction towards, if possible, the complete unfettering of the nation-states.

They could not, for a start, speak the same language, a misfortune that partly lay behind her nickname for him: the gasbag. Often though they met, they never seemed to get any closer. For this she was most to blame, according to one of her devoted admirers, Charles Powell, her foreign affairs private secretary for six years. Powell, whose own Euro-scepticism marched in line with hers, described to me how courteous Kohl invariably was, bringing her little gifts he had personally chosen, escorting her round his home town, trying to convince her that he was

'not German but European', as he once confided to the private secretary.
'I think Chancellor Kohl deserves great credit for working very hard on
the relationship,' Powell said. 'To be honest, he worked harder at it than
she did.'[21] But he did not succeed. Mrs Thatcher was both careless and
atavistically alarmed. Once, visiting the Rhineland-Palatinate in Kohl's
company, she responded to the welcoming ceremony by saying how
much pleasure it gave her to be in France.[22] Throughout, as Powell
reflected elsewhere, she was in thrall to childhood memories. 'For a small
girl growing up in Grantham,' he said, 'the Germans were about as evil
as anything you could think of.'[23] This opinion, though displaced by the
rise of Soviet communism, was never entirely abandoned.

As regards Britain's budget problem in 1984, however, Kohl was not
the prime object of Mrs Thatcher's attention. The moment of decision
coincided with France's term as president of the Council, which elevated
to critical prominence the other new butt of the Thatcherite approach to
Europe, François Mitterrand.

Giscard's successor as French president, a socialist, was, in historic
terms, hardly new at all. He was elected president, after many years'
trying, in 1981. Like Kohl, he came out of the deep past, formed and
tempered by the defining event that had been the origin of this 'Europe'
in which all leaders were now engaged. More passionately than Schmidt
and Giscard, Kohl and Mitterrand articulated an emotional commitment
to the European idea fashioned in the experience of war, which Kohl
(born 1930) had spent as a young spectator in the killing fields along
the Rhine, and Mitterrand (born 1916) as a shadowy operator in the
Resistance who still managed to keep his connections with the Vichy
Government.

These men were almost different species from Margaret Thatcher.
But the German and the Frenchman had swapped places in her esteem.
She admired Mitterrand almost as much as she disliked Kohl. Despite
being a socialist, Mitterrand had intellectual quality. 'He is a philosopher,
which she would like to be but isn't,' Powell once told me. Beside an
extraordinary political career, in which he was the left's presidential
candidate against de Gaulle as long ago as 1965, and then against Giscard
in 1974, ran a capacity for grandiose reflection which, oddly, Mrs
Thatcher did not always resist. A scornful enemy of Euro-guff – the
sweeping visions and journeys-without-maps which were alien to British
temperaments far beyond her own – she nevertheless appreciated a class
intellect when she saw one. Mitterrand's broad literary culture – he

could recite from memory the last lines of 'Ulysses', for example[24] – was something she could admire without ever approaching it herself.

Mitterrand, for his part, was fascinated by the lady, at least at the beginning. She was not without charm, and he not without a susceptibility to it. He once famously advised his Minister for Europe, Roland Dumas, to be aware of her dangerous qualities. 'Cette femme Thatcher!' he reputedly said. 'Elle a les yeux de Caligule, mais elle a la bouche de Marilyn Monroe.' Claude Cheysson, the Foreign Minister, observed the two together often. 'I've always been amazed by their mutual fascination,' he said. 'Each looked at the other, wondering how someone so strange could exist, trying to grasp who he or she was.'[25]

In 1984, they had each reached an important moment. For its first few years, the Mitterrand Government all but ignored Europe. The French Socialist Party was pursuing socialist economic policies that put it at odds with Germany. By March 1983, with the leftist faction in command, there had been two devaluations of the franc inside the European Monetary System, from which France was threatened with exclusion if she attempted a third. Only at this moment did Mitterrand change course, reinstating a more conventional economic policy and, at the same time, determining to get much more involved in the evolution of Europe. Indeed, he intended 'relaunching' Europe, along with himself. A senior French diplomat observed sardonically: 'Monsieur Mitterrand's term as president of the European Council has become his road to Damascus.'[26]

His involvement in this presidency was arguably greater than that of any national leader occupying the same six-month position in the history of the EEC. He began by touring all the capitals of the Nine, while Foreign Minister Dumas engaged in regular shuttle diplomacy between Paris, Bonn and London. Just as Pompidou's 1971 démarche over British entry had to be kept secret from the officials of the Quai d'Orsay, these efforts by Mitterrand were conducted against the opposition of the Quai and also his own left wing. Nonetheless, in this short period he met six times each with Kohl and Thatcher for bilateral talks. 'Europe', he had warned at the start of his term, 'is beginning to look like an abandoned building site.'[27] He was entirely committed to resuming construction, the principle edifices being agricultural reform, the accession of Spain and Portugal, the liberalization of the internal market and an increase in Community funds. Looming as an obstruction to all this dynamism, though, was the net British contribution to the budget.

This had already gone through many phases. The 1980 formula did not preclude an annual haggle over its particulars. Now, however, there appeared a possible parting of the ways. For, although Mitterrand wanted the question settled, he wasn't prepared to make all the concessions. It was in 1984 that talk of a Europe of two speeds – the ins and the outs, the core and the periphery, other incessantly deconstructed metaphors of what he now called *la géométrie variable* – began seriously to be heard, though it had been canvassed a decade earlier, in the Tindemans Report, as a way round the impediments placed by a previous British (Labour) government. With a summit due in June, at Fontainebleau, both Kohl and Mitterrand made clear their determination to move forward on a unity agenda, towards the completion of the internal market and more majority voting. Kohl said that the 'decisive conditions had been created'. Dumas, on Mitterrand's behalf, said that, if a budget agreement was not reached, France would call a meeting without the British to discuss political reform.

Thus, a repeat beckoned, on a smaller scale, of 1955, with another display of self-excluding British stubbornness which could never be relied on to impress the continentals. This has been the pattern of the relationship for half a century, hardly less visible in the 1990s than at moments in every other decade. The tactic of leaving an 'empty chair', and obstructing all Community business by refusing to attend, may have been exclusively a French device. But the British deployed an opposite and equal effect. They alone were able to exasperate other members almost enough to have an empty chair forced upon them.

On her way to Fontainebleau, Mrs Thatcher told the British officials travelling with her that she thought the meeting was doomed. Just before, she had let it be known how unimpressed she was by the threat of a two-speed Europe, and what it really meant. 'Let me tell you what I mean,' she told a newspaper, with characteristic subtlety. 'Those who pay most are the top group and those who pay less are not.'[28] In the car, she said: 'We're never going to settle this thing.' Her belief was that Mitterrand would refuse to move, even though it had been Kohl who got in the way of a previous near-deal in March. After all, any concession to the British, however justified in equity and logic, would be paid for by larger contributions from the others, which meant, in major effect, Germany.

By the time they reached Fontainebleau, the matter was down to a single issue. The structure of the arithmetic on which the British abatement should be calculated – the VAT factor, the tariffs and levies factor, the scalings down and leverings up, the link with an increase in the Community's total resources, and all the other haggled computations that are the stuff of Euro-negotiators' lives while remaining for ever outside the comprehension of every normal European citizen – was just about agreed. What it came down to was a percentage figure and a time-span. What per cent of the contribution that Britain was due to make under the regular rules would be deducted on account of Britain's special position? And would this last indefinitely?

Mrs Thatcher was determined to get 66 per cent, worth around £1,000 million of public spending: the cost, say, of the entire family doctor service in Britain. The occasion was laid on with a grandeur that fitted the spacious ambitions Mitterrand had set himself, but it got off to a start of precisely the unbusinesslike kind the lady most detested. First the French, aided by the European Commission, sought to set a time-limit on any deal, and to hustle it through in two hours before dinner. Then the President spent much of the meal briefing the col-leagues about his recent visit to Moscow, which was followed by Kohl's interminable account of a journey to Hungary he had recently returned from. These were pitiful distractions from serious business. The British briefed scornfully against the Germans. Mrs Thatcher, retreating to confer with her officials, fumed against the general lack of gratitude. 'How on earth can Britain be treated in this way?' Robin Renwick remembered her saying. 'After all, we saved all their skins in the war.'[29]

When they got down to business next day, it was after all-night negotiations between officials. But the business, at European Council summits, is unusually dependent on the performance of the principals. Officials are seldom admitted to the room. Prime Minister and Foreign Secretary have to do the work themselves, and quite often the Prime Minister is alone with the peer-group. This was an aspect of the task at which Mrs Thatcher was uncommonly good. Not only was she briefed in great detail, a British style growing out of Question Time in Parlia-ment, and also out of the British cultural obsession with the precise rather than the aspirational aspects of negotiation. She could take and remember the briefing to formidable effect, and was always armed with little lists, known to the officials who supplied them either as 'stiletto points' or, alternatively, 'handbag points', with which she would prick or batter her adversaries.

When the end-game started, most of the others, according to Michael Butler, who was in the thick of it, were talking a maximum of 55 per cent, while the leader's instruction to the British was to talk about

70.[30] 'It was quite *impossible* to go below that,' one of them was told, 'there could be no whisper of a thought of it *in any circumstances whatever.*' Many hours intervened. Talking along these lines continued. The Germans, 'a rugger scrum . . . round the massive figure of Chancellor Kohl', writes Butler, eventually said that 60 per cent was their limit, while Mitterrand, desiring to be the orchestrator of a settlement, said he might be pushed to 65.

Gathering her officials together, Mrs Thatcher found them of one mind. These were not, it should be noted, a collective from yester-year, the old gang, as she had perceived it, of typical Foreign Office gentlemen always prone to regard the other side as having a decent, or even the better, case. Butler and Renwick were hard-headed, highly combative men, aggressive and devious to a fault. Together with David Williamson, an old Community hand whom Butler describes as a born negotiator, they reached the conclusion, as did Geoffrey Howe, the Foreign Secretary, that they had got everything they could. And she agreed. 'It's time to settle,' she immediately said – but with one more shot to call, a percentage point which, if gained, would be worth at least £150 million to Britain over the next ten years. Approaching Mitterrand once more, she duly got it. It would be very helpful, she said, if she could hit the two-thirds mark, 66 not 65 per cent, to last for as long as the Community's take from VAT collected was pegged at the new ceiling of 1.4 per cent. The EC's desperate need for this new ceiling, up from 1 per cent, to pay its escalating farm subsidies, gave the British their negotiating leverage. And the Council, led by the President, surrendered, as the price for moving on to other things – such minor matters as the liberalization of the internal market, the abolition of customs controls, the radical reform of the institutions.

Mrs Thatcher, in her hour of victory, appeared to go along with these signs of the relaunch Mitterrand had set himself to getting started. She talked quite happily in terms of forward momentum. Reporting back to Parliament, she said: 'The way is now clear for the completion of the Common Market in goods and services.' Speaking to the Franco-British Council, she sounded almost ecstatic about the possibilities for collaboration across the board, listing as European objectives 'greater unity of the Community market, greater unity of Community actions in world affairs, greater unity of purpose and action in tackling unemployment and the other problems of our time'.[31] What a litany! No line was drawn, or so it seemed, beyond which 'Europe' might not have a beneficent role. Language which no Conservative politician, even of a pro-Europe persuasion, would comfortably be using in a decade's time now cascaded from the Thatcher lips. The deepest-dyed symbols of an entente were, at this stage, capable of being congenial to her. Visiting Paris in November 1984, for example, she took the first diplomatic steps towards Anglo-French agreement to build a tunnel under the Channel.

Such was the personal effect of a famous victory. She had been very effective, laying waste all critics of her confrontational methods. Emile Noël, the legendary French civil servant who was secretary-general of the Commission from the EEC's inception until 1987, told me that she 'obtained much more than was reasonable', an achievement for which the British taxpayer ought to be grateful.[32] 'The British got more than they really needed – in the opinion of a poor official!' The cost to the other members, Noël thought, had been outrageously high.

But, from now on, things got more complicated.

*

THE THATCHER TECHNIQUE was brilliantly successful in a certain task. It got the money back. She could measure the victory, and gloat over the consequences. But it had its costs, and these weren't a matter of mere caprice or jealousy on the other side. The confrontational method, even when deployed only once, cashed in a lot of chips, in a game where every player has only a limited number and can't acquire more by simply shouting.

Winning on the budget, especially in the way she chose, which was probably the only way she knew how, meant *inevitably* paying a price in other spheres. Her bad manners were certain to worsen the manners of everyone else she would need to help her at some other time. They raised the temperature and burned in the memory. They were the weapons of a leader who took a narrow view of her objective, forgetting that every other leader round the table was as much or little a sovereign leader as she was, with pride to salvage and voters to please, and just as deeply held a view of how Europe should develop. This was, after all, meant to be a team, an alliance, a jousting but ultimately fraternal partnership. For a body created to prevent war, battle was exquisitely inappropriate as the driving metaphor one of its members brought to the table. The Community way, which grew out of the coalition politics every continental politician absorbed at kindergarten, involved give-and-take, log-rolling, back-scratching, all rooted in a concept of 'victory' that couldn't be defined by anything as simple as the short-term interest of one country.

The mismatch between the Thatcher mind and the European mind took time to reach a climax. She went on thinking she could fashion Europe to her advantage, and in some measure she did. But in the second phase, the transitional sequence, there began to emerge the unsettling sense that she didn't know what she was doing.

As she told Parliament after Fontainebleau, the way was now open for great developments. The period of stasis, though she never used such a regretful expression, could be ended, with the Common Market being stripped of its protectionism and made truly common or, better put, free. She now had a project for Europe, the single market, to which, banishing most traces of scepticism, she was able to apply her talent for messianic zeal. It was the high point of her vision – the only time, indeed, when such a word could be aptly applied to her continental attitudes – yet within it can be seen the start of her undoing.

The single market was not a Thatcher idea, but a collective aspiration. As everybody knew, it made no sense, in a so-called Common Market, to have succeeded in lowering customs barriers but to leave in place many other blockages to open business dealings. So-called 'non-tariff' barriers, brought on especially by the 1970s recession, were ranged throughout the system: all the panoply of different national standards on safety, health, the environment: of half-closed frontiers across which labour and capital and services could not freely move: of discrimination against foreign products or tendering for public procurement: all the fences and ditches and slopes and biases that precluded the creation of that distinctively 1990s cliché, the level playing-field. The market could not be free or single until these had been removed. The Commission had long desired to do this, and the lists of what needed to be done had languished in its drawers for years. But now a critical mass assembled for action. To Mitterrand's desire for a relaunch, and Mrs Thatcher's perception of a single market beckoning, was added a third element, the arrival in the Commission presidency of a politician who wished to make something significant out of it, Jacques Delors.

Delors, at this stage, was a man the British much admired. There were, as ever, complications about the succession to his crucial post, which in theory was meant to go to a German. It was the Germans' turn. But they had recently done rather well in the international market for big jobs, and, in any case, also said they did not have a suitable candidate for the new vacancy. They ceded their place to France. Britain much preferred Delors to the Frenchman who was first put up, the Foreign Minister Claude Cheysson. Cheysson was regarded as uninterested in liberalizing the market, and besides, according to Robin Renwick, he had been 'absolutely hopeless' during the budget negotiations.[33] Delors, by contrast, was the Finance Minister who master-minded Mitterrand's reversion from socialism. He was a financial disciplinarian. 'He began imposing our policies,' Howe noted with admiration, 'a finance minister after our own hearts.'[34] Though talking left, he acted right. On Europe, however, he was an unknown quantity, as Howe, speaking ten years later, rather plaintively remembered: 'One never knows, you see, when people arrive in that job.'

It did not take Delors long to hit on his own project for the relaunch of Europe, though he came to it from an unThatcherite position. He favoured the single market because it made political sense: it was congruent with the right-wing ascendancies then to be found in many of the member countries. It also made economic sense, with a period of strong growth – always the condition in which the Community thrived – on the horizon.[35] But, for Delors, it had little to do with any deregulatory passion shared with the British. He was a tough, *dirigiste* French socialist, out of the Catholic social tradition. He was also an acquiescent, though not recklessly proactive, federalist. He became, in the European context, the enemy Mrs Thatcher often seemed to need for the successful prosecution of the politics of battle. The names of many defeated enemies were gouged on her tally-stick: Galtieri of Argentina, Scargill of the miners, Heath of Old Conservatism. Here was a European candidate who might soon be fit to join them.

This wasn't the tenor, however, of the first phase of Delors. There were difficulties, of a personal kind that Mrs Thatcher, as many rivals found, had an uncontrollable instinct to inflame. She was very patroniz-ing, as if the president were no more than a bureaucratic flunky. At one early press conference which they were supposed to be conducting jointly, she left no space for him to speak, and, as her long harangues drew to a close, addressed him thus: 'Would you very kindly confirm that what I said was absolutely strictly accurate and that you are looking forward to this, and rising to the challenge it represents, and that you will hope to solve it during your coming two years of presidency of the Commission?' To Delors' monosyllabic grunt, she responded: 'I had no idea you were such a strong silent man.'[36] It was a snubbing Delors did not forget.

But in the beginning they shared an objective. And to advance it they brought in a man they both admired, though not at the same time. The Delors Commission, which started work in January 1985, produced a general post among commissioners and, most spectacularly, the rise to prominence of one of the odder protagonists in this story, a man named Arthur Cockfield.

Cockfield was an operator in the interstices between business and government, of long pedigree but almost zero visibility. Qualified as a barrister, he had joined the Inland Revenue as a tax inspector as long ago as 1938, rising high in that organization before starting a new career at the head of Boots Pure Drug Co., which he ran for much of the 1960s. He had his first public job under the Heath Government, as head of the Price Commission, a nerve-centre of the corporatism of the day. But hardly had Mrs Thatcher, the anti-corporatist, supplanted Heath as Tory leader than Cockfield was handed a peerage and a seat beside her as a kind of ideas-man, an apolitical wheeze-merchant, her loyal, unambitious, creative antidote to the scheming, soft-headed paternalists she was obliged to keep in the Cabinet. In 1982, Cockfield reached the Cabinet himself, as Secretary of State for Trade, a post in which his eccentricity proved as notable as his business sense. Reluctant to travel without his wife, but having a wife who resisted travelling anywhere by air, he once conducted a trade negotiation with Nigeria standing offshore, like an antique son of Empire, aboard an ocean liner.

To liberalize Europe's internal market, both Delors and Mrs Thatcher regarded Cockfield as the best-qualified agent. He set about the task with a purposefulness that soon proved more pleasing to the former than the latter, effecting as swift a transfer from the Thatcher project to the Delors as he had from the Heath to the Thatcher. Cockfield was that sort of man, anchored in the internal logic of whatever task he had been set, rather than riding the captious tides of what a real politician might call political reality. The technician became, in his way, an ideologue. What Howe, in his memoirs, called Cockfield's 'tenacious commitment' grew, as Mrs Thatcher saw it, into something more menacing. He seemed to move from deregulating the market, an authentic Thatcher goal, to reregulating it in the Delorsian name of harmonization. So zealous was he to strike down every barrier, even to the point of harmonizing national tax systems, that he became, she writes, 'the prisoner as well as the master of his subject'. 'Unfortunately,' she goes on, 'he tended to disregard the larger questions of politics – constitu-

tional sovereignty, national sentiment and the promptings of liberty . . .
It was not too long before my old friend and I were at odds.'[37]

It was a Frenchman who paid Cockfield the ultimate compliment,
by comparing him with Delors. Delors, he said, was the more intuitive
and flexible. But 'Cockfield is a cool Cartesian, whose logic is so deadly
that he can push systematically to extremes. You need that kind of mind
to work through the consequences of abolishing frontiers.'[38] Such a
laudatory epitaph from Paris was a kind of death-warrant in London.

Cockfield produced a white paper identifying 297 imperfections in
the single European market, with timetabled proposals for eliminating
them by 1992. At this stage, when they were still mere proposals, they
accorded with what Mrs Thatcher thought she wanted. She was still, by
her lights, in a 'European' phase – which is jolting to look back on from
the phobic years of her retirement. In the middle of 1985, she put
together and circulated a paper she calls 'ostentatiously *communautaire*',
which indeed it was. Not only did it talk about completing the internal
market, with decision-making changes to match, but it made the case
for a stronger European foreign policy, under the rubric of political co-
operation. The Falklands War, in which not every EC member had come
up to scratch, was still for her a living memory, and she thought 'how
valuable it would be if all Community members were prepared to
commit themselves to supporting a single member in difficulties'.[39]
'Europe: The Future', the document in question, might even be described
as a tentative approach towards that entirely unBritish concept, a phrase
never uttered by a British statesman in half a century, 'The Construction
of Europe'. Mrs Thatcher didn't go that far. But there was a whiff of
collaborative promise. This was a period in which the French newspaper
Le Matin could write of 'the spectacular evolution of the British position
. . . which will confuse those critics normally sceptical about Britain's
European enthusiasm'.[40]

There was, however, a limit. Britishness necessarily intervened, only
to be balked. How was the Cockfield–Delors programme actually to be
imposed? Mrs Thatcher and her Foreign Secretary favoured the informal
approach.

Plainly there would be no end to protection, no effective creation of
singleness, if any one country was able to block something it didn't like.
There would have to be, as all concerned seem to have recognized from
the start, an extension of qualified majority voting: a mechanism which
allocated voting weight to each country roughly according to its size,

and permitted a majority of such weighted votes to secure a decision binding on all members. It was known as QMV: one of the alphabetic short-hands which, along with ERM and IGC, came to occupy a special place of neuralgic infamy in Britain's later consideration of what 'Europe' meant, or might mean. But the method by which QMV would be installed, across a far wider range of Community business than it had ever touched before, was a question.

The Thatcher–Howe proposal was for a kind of constitutional convention – 'a concept more familiar to Anglo-Saxon than to continental minds', Howe concedes.[41] There would be a gentlemen's agreement, written but without legal force, to treat all the single-market agenda as though the unanimity rule had been set aside. For the British, accustomed to such half-worlds, this would be quite enough for QMV, and would have the merit of forestalling the need for an IGC, or intergovernmental conference, whose legalistic outcomes would in turn be capable of invoking the activity of another suspect abbreviation, the ECJ, or European Court of Justice. An IGC was the normal, indeed the only, way of securing amendments to the Treaty of Rome. The trick would be to pretend that QMV did not require such amendments. Above all, Britain wanted to avoid an IGC, which ministers felt might open the way for uncontrollable constitutional ventures, themselves likely to be federalistic, certain to be legalistic and, all in all, guaranteed to operate against the British interest. Even Howe, the European, felt this, though the Baroness, in her memoirs, charges him with giving in about it.

They were both, however, defeated. It was the first serious calamity of the Thatcher era, a pay-back, some said, for her discomfiting budget triumph. The Thatcher rule of negotiating conduct said that 'compromise' was an unmentionable word. This was formally laid down by No. 10, a curse on all normal diplomatic behaviour. In their briefs to the Prime Minister, throughout her time, officials were never allowed to use the term, commonplace though it was: they had to invent all kinds of circumlocution, if they were to do their job of giving tactical guidance on upcoming meetings. But in Milan, in June 1985, the tables were turned. No-compromise became the weapon of the other side. The European Council, the summit of leaders, did something it had never done before, taking a vote, which required only a simple majority, over the British leader's writhing, fuming body, to call an IGC.

The British went to Milan seriously believing this could not happen. They thought they had fixed enough support for their idea of a gentlemen's agreement. But meanwhile, there had been other developments propelling things in a different direction: the formal, dramatic, declaratory, treaty-bound direction most members usually preferred. At the very same time the budget deal was done at Fontainebleau, a committee was set up to investigate ways of making another leap forward in Europeanism. Chaired by an Irish politician, James Dooge, it was told to suggest improvements in European co-operation: which, by the time the caravan moved on to Milan, it had duly done.

Some of the Dooge proposals were congenial to the European Thatcher. They met her two largest demands: for a smoother internal market and closer political co-operation. But they were also, as she could see even then, ominous. They were an expression of momentum, of process, of the endless quest for ever closer intimacy under the Brussels umbrella. They talked about the 'achievement of a European social area', about 'institutional reform' and about the promotion of 'common cultural values': menacing portents of a new and pervasive unity, to be topped off by the rebranding of the Community as the 'European Union'. When the captains and the kings arrived in Milan, this was waiting on the table for their approval and, more particularly, for the summoning of an IGC which would certainly be the only way to enact its ambitious propositions.

At the beginning, it looked as though this might be avoided. Under the hand of Bettino Craxi, the Italian Prime Minister, the Thatcher approach seemed to gain ground. Craxi was 'sweetly reasonable' when the two of them talked, luring the lady into a state of security. 'I came away thinking how easy it had been to get my points across,' she writes.[42] Besides, she had taken trouble to get the Germans on side, entertaining Kohl for an entire, painful Saturday at Chequers. The first stage of Milan saw unanimous approval both for Cockfield's white paper and for the British proposal on informal improvements to decision-making.

But that didn't settle the matter. Both the Italians and the Germans turned out to be treacherous jades. The British idea wasn't seen as an alternative, but as a prelude to the real game. Discussion grew more rancorous, as Mrs Thatcher struggled to resist formal Treaty changes and the erosion of the Luxembourg Compromise – the Gaullist device of twenty years before, that had protected the veto rights of individual states. 'Margaret,' writes Howe, 'with more excuse for tetchiness than usual, contrived to get us emotionally aligned with [the Greek Prime Minister] Papandreou at his worst.'[43]

Then Craxi sprang his little trick. Without warning, he pressed for a vote on whether to hold an IGC, and easily secured his simple majority, a success Howe explains as 'a reaction above all to the sharp tone of British leadership'.

A decade later, Michael Butler, one of the posse of hard-faced Foreign Office men by Mrs Thatcher's side, was still ashamed of his lack of foresight. 'I was horrified at my own failure to see that this was what they would do to us if we went on being intransigent,' he told me in 1993. The British became nothing more than spectators at the Italians' 'enormous satisfaction' when they pulled off their coup.[44] For her part, the leader was furious at being bulldozed by a chairman she regarded as disgracefully partisan.

Her anger, however, did not yet drive her to folly. There now unfolded an example of something that became a Thatcher pattern through many of her European, and not only European, ventures. 'I saw it happen a thousand times,' said Butler, 'her reason overcoming her prejudices.' Instead of roaring out to denounce Craxi to the press, she listened almost immediately – it only took the lunch-break – to officials who pointed out the folly of declaring that she would have nothing to do with the IGC, which was her first instinct. The same prudence attended her report back to Parliament. Neither in hot blood nor in cold did she make anything so unwise as a pledge to reject any Treaty change. On the contrary, she sent her officials off to negotiate the kind of changes that would expedite internal-market decisions.

By this means Mrs Thatcher, instead of being the chief obstacle to further European union, became one of its chief architects. The Single European Act, which six months later became the concrete product of the Milan summit, was a fusion between the visions of Margaret Thatcher and Jacques Delors for the future of Europe. But for Thatcherites, and for the whole British argument against Europe, it has been alternatively a problem and an embarrassment ever since. So it merits some careful attention.

As the IGC proceeded, a sprawling agenda was laid before it, just as Mrs Thatcher feared. It was due to end in Luxembourg six months on, a tight schedule which assisted in limiting the scope and doing so quite largely in accordance with British desires. The British were the minimalists, and, since any changes needed unanimous support, the minimalists were strongly placed. They weren't alone. Other members, sometimes less voluble in their rhetoric, were as cautious in their surrenders of power, for example, to the European Assembly, now about to be called, at last, a Parliament. Small accretions were allowed to this body. Equally, the strengthening of co-operation on foreign policy was easily agreed.

There was more trouble over EMU, the dreaded economic and monetary union first cited as an aspiration in 1972 and never expunged from the gospel. Most continentals wanted to upgrade it to a Treaty objective, but the British would rather it weren't mentioned at all. They thought the Monetary System was progressing well enough on an informal basis. Here they lost a point. The Single European Act contains the first formal Treaty reference to EMU, albeit in a cautious mode that was to have much significance later. Any evolution of the Monetary System was listed as requiring unanimous approval: a condition which came controversially into its own, further down the line, in the Treaty of Maastricht 1992. The taxation ideas, apotheosis of Cockfield's harmonizing lunacy, as it was seen, were also kicked into the long grass with a heavy British boot.

These were satisfactory curtailments of what the Euro-visionaries, the Delors Commission among them, had hoped for. But the Single Act needed its positive side as well. This was the whole point of a strategy, the imperative British strategy, to liberalize the internal market in all the ways the British thought, for practical as well as ideological reasons, they could profit from. The new Treaty, if Treaty it had to be, needed to provide a thoroughgoing extension of majority rule for the immense range of decisions that touched on market matters. This was, in British parlance, a 'federal' proposition. It consciously diminished the power of nations, in these specific but large areas, to frustrate the collective will. Yet this did not debar it, in the slightest, from the approval of the British. Indeed, such a way of imposing a genuinely free market was allocated its own, faintly triumphalist, campaigning slogan: 'Thatcherism on a European scale'.

The British demanded, and got, one big exception to the regime of unimpeded movement. The island nation wanted to keep its right to control immigration. But, for the rest, the British placed their country not merely in compliance with, but rather in the vanguard of, the most practical advance towards the abolition of national frontiers and national powers that the Community had undertaken in the whole period of British membership. It had another wrinkle to it, moreover. There was a change in the power under which individual countries could secure exemptions. Under the Luxembourg Compromise, a nation could simply demand and exercise this power. After the Single European Act, a nation that needed an exemption from single-market rules by reason of *exigences importantes*, as they called them, put itself in the hands of the European Court if any other nation launched a challenge. The Court, along with the Commission – these supra-political embodiments of 'Europe' – were handed the power to determine what the Single Act, in hard cases, meant.

The Single Act was, in part, a triumph for Delors and Cockfield, though it didn't satisfy the president, who expressed himself dolefully about how little had been achieved. Most of Cockfield's 300 items had been put forward before by the Commission, but had always been rejected by the nation-states. The skill and drive of the two Commissioners now saw the Act past innumerable pitfalls. But it was also a triumph for Mrs Thatcher, in that, by common consent, the final agreement on most substantive issues satisfied the British more than anyone else.[45]

It certainly satisfied Mrs Thatcher. When she got back home, she called the result 'clear and decisive'. This reflected the general atmosphere in the Conservative Party at the time. Hardly anyone criticized the Act as a piece of crypto-federalism which wasn't all that crypto. The Prime Minister's enthusiastic report to Parliament was accepted in similar spirit.

Passage of the necessary measure was just as untroubled. When the European Communities (Amendment) Bill came to the Commons in April 1986, six days were required to see it through all its stages. After a mere three sessions in committee, a guillotine motion to cut off debate was proposed by the Government, through the mouth of the leader of the House, John Biffen. Biffen, who had been a Powellite on the subject of Europe many years before the term Euro-sceptic was invented, spoke to the motion with wry but determined awareness of what was now required, and it was carried by 270 votes to 153.

In the light of what happened later, the debate on the Bill deserves passing scrutiny. The Single Act, after all, was a major constitutional measure. Just as remarkable as the size of the majority for the guillotine was the indifference attending the matter in the minds of many MPs. On that occasion, with the Labour Party still supposedly in anti-European mode, there were 200 absentees from the vote. When it came to the third reading, the final moment of passage, there was an even more paltry tally of 149 supporters to 43 opponents. During the debates themselves there were contributions which, at the end of the 1990s, seem a little startling. Some of the usual suspects with whose names a later generation became all too familiar – Teddy Taylor, Tony Marlow, Nicholas Budgen – are to be found dominating the brief discussions that did take place, grinding on for some hours about the powers of the

European Court of Justice, and attacking, with Enoch Powell, the change of nomenclature by which the Assembly was to become a full-blown Parliament. But none of them joined their grand old hero in voting against the guillotine. Riotous rebellions on the Government back-benches, such as accompanied endorsement of the Treaty of Maastricht seven years later, were nowhere to be seen.

A fair number of latter-day sceptics supported the argument made with most notable passion by one George Gardiner, the MP for Reigate and a devoted Thatcher disciple, who in 1997 was so disgusted with the remnants of official Conservative Party enthusiasm for Europe that he fought the election in the interest of the Referendum Party instead. A decade earlier, Gardiner is to be found uttering a paean of desire for the 'economies of scale' of a united Europe to take on the Americans in high-tech industries, and making the case for qualified majority voting as the only way to defeat national protectionism.[46]

As we shall see, Gardiner was not alone in his painful lurching from one passion to another.[47] After a few years, many Conservatives were singing a different song about the Single Act. They came to regard it, not as a lynchpin of the liberalized market, but as an instrument through which the ever closer union of Europe made its way forward. They saw it, increasingly, as a moment of serious defeat, possibly of treachery against the nation: a treachery, even, for which they themselves might be somewhat responsible, and might therefore have a duty to make condign repentance by reneging on their own handiwork – however embarrassing such a manoeuvre is for any politician. Among these apostates was Baroness Thatcher herself. The architect of the Act became seriously disillusioned by its operation.

This raises quite a list of questions for the by-standing, voting citizen, who has no choice in high politics but to leave such important matters to the leaders of the day. What is he or she, who played no part in either the writing or the passing, to make of it? Was there some element of betrayal here, and if so, who betrayed whom? Did the continentals circumvent the revised Treaty of Rome, to accomplish more than they ever let on at the time? Or was it more a case of the British leader first misunderstanding what she was doing, and then, along with her allies in the party, searching for scapegoats to cover up what was either a change of perception or a change of heart?

There is no disputing that the Single Act worked both better and worse than its different founders intended. Delors and Thatcher saw it in different ways, and got different things from it. The more obvious parts of this outcome are the worst, the places where rather little happened, which Mrs Thatcher, presumably, should have had most cause to regret. For long after 1992, there continued to be many imperfections in the freedom of internal trade and movement. Some state-owned airlines, Air France conspicuous among them, were still being grotesquely over-compensated for their commercial failures, and the free markets in such sensitive services as banking and insurance were opened with agonizing reluctance. The cultural differences between the free-trading tradition, mostly but not entirely represented by Britain, and a continent with a long history of both social protection and privileged state enterprise, could not be wiped out by a single measure. The Act was the beginning not the end of a negotiation that would never cease.

This was one part the British didn't like. Nor were they invariably impressed by the ways in which the famous singleness – the harmoniza-tion, the union – did come about. They were soon confronted by the habit of the entire Euro-apparatus, mainly the Commission and the Court, of construing in a spirit of integration, when in doubt, the words with which the Act presented them. Incorporated in it, for example, was an article designed to achieve common standards of health and safety at work, a measure included in those that were manoeuvrable, like other level-playing-field items, by QMV. But what was 'health and safety', and where did you draw the line between it and general social policy, which required unanimous agreement? When attempts were made to broaden the definition, the British rightly felt cheated.

On the other hand, are we seriously to suppose that Mrs Thatcher had not examined the words she put her name to? This was the implication of the charge, familiar in the pathology of Euro-scepticism, that 'Europe' had somehow pulled a fast one. But, as to the words, there is copious evidence that she was aware, as her fascination with texts of all kinds would lead anyone to expect, of everything. I pressed a number of her officials about this. David Williamson, who at the time was her senior Europe adviser, said: 'I was present in 10 Downing Street on one occasion when Mrs Thatcher came down the stairs and said to me, "I have read every word of the Single European Act." '[48] For Michael Butler, any other behaviour would have been an offence against nature. 'I never remember an occasion in the six years when I worked for her', he told me, 'when she negotiated something without knowing what she was talking about.'[49] Geoffrey Howe says in his memoirs that she sat with the other leaders 'for no less than twenty-seven hours in two working days' talking through the draft of the Act, which was in any case quite largely a British text.[50]

So the notion that the Act, which she hailed as a triumph in December 1985, got past her on the basis of some kind of fraud will not do. But that doesn't mean she fully understood it. There is no necessary contradiction between British Tories, led by her ever more vocally in her retirement, saying that the Act did more than they intended, and this having come about, more than anything, through the peculiar combination of their innocence and hubris. Perhaps Mrs Thatcher wanted the Act to mean what she said it meant, and was simply not prepared to recognize that it might mean something else as well.

What it said in Article 1, for example, was: 'The European Communities and European Political Co-operation shall have as their objective to contribute together to making concrete progress towards European unity.' This came after a preamble that talked about furthering 'the European idea', protecting Europe's 'common interests', and 'investing this union with the necessary means of action'. Such federalist verbiage Mrs Thatcher, while signing up to it, was inclined to dismiss as claptrap that could safely be ignored. Asked about it in the Commons, she both chided and exonerated her continental counterparts: 'I am constantly saying that I wish that they would talk less about European and political union. The terms are not understood in this country. In so far as they are understood over there, they mean a good deal less than some people over here think they mean.'

But they didn't. They expressed an aspiration which it suited Mrs Thatcher, like almost all British politicians, to ignore by pretending it didn't really exist. This was a practised condition. In 1983, the British leader put her signature to the Stuttgart Declaration, which spelled out a pledge, supported by twenty pages of detail, to the cause of much more European union. It was the first big statement, promising institutional reforms of an intensely unifying kind in every field, that modern 'Europe' had ever attempted. The British, while signing, despised it. Looking back, Geoffrey Howe says the attention they had given it was 'less than we should have done'.[51] The Thatcher memoir says: 'The document had no legal force. So I went along with it.'[52] But the truth is they preferred not to address the language of their partners with the seriousness it deserved.

They thought of it as Euro-guff, or Euro-twaddle, a bizarre, cultish worshipping at the altar of Jean Monnet, which would mercifully never get anywhere near full transsubstantiation into the body of revealed and meaningful law. There had been similar words in the texts from the beginning. The Treaty of Rome, for example, placed high among its purposes 'to lay the foundation of an ever closer union among the peoples of Europe'. But few of the British, even among the political leadership, properly absorbed this. They never really penetrated the words, and, if they did happen to be vouchsafed a moment of enlightenment, it was to see them as a challenge, rather than a credo that had much to do with the island race. From that long history of recoiling from what Europe meant, the pretence followed almost naturally that the aspirations of the Single Act could best be treated in the same way.

Alongside this misperception was a mismatch in the British attitude to negotiation. In Europe, negotiation never ends. Membership is a process not an event, Howe once said. There is a sense in which nothing is ever finally settled. An agreement favourable to one country is merely the beginning of the next deal, and often vulnerable to being reopened under a different heading. Little is quite cut and dried, and, since cut-and-dried-ness was the part of her style in which Mrs Thatcher took most pride, there were always likely to be incandescent difficulties between her and the people she resolutely declined to see as partners.

Nevertheless, the Single Act was a fact. It surrendered sovereignty, accelerated momentum. That, at the time, was what the British leader thought she wanted, and urged the people to applaud. Though it wasn't what Jacques Delors envisaged, it seemed to signal Britain's open-eyed engagement with the dominant culture of the Community. Everyone in the Thatcher Cabinet backed it, and so did almost everyone in the Thatcher Party – storing up trouble for the day when it became an inconvenient memory.

For their eyes weren't open, and they couldn't really face the consequences of what they had done.

*

ONE OF THE MOST compelling, if unsung, visionaries of 'Europe' was Emile Noël, the first, and until 1987 only, secretary-general of the European Commission. For forty-five years Noël devoted himself to the cause, thirty of them as the wily, dedicated, self-effacing but all-knowing official at the heart of the Community's central machine.

Noël was, of course, a Frenchman. No other breed would have been considered for the top job in a bureaucracy fashioned on French lines to serve French purposes. But he rose far above nationality to become the complete European, wise in the objects of the enterprise, steeped in its history, dedicated to its oneness, observant of the foibles of the many political leaders who came and went. A measure of his importance, and the affection in which he was held by true Euro-cultists, was an all-day meeting held in London after he died in August 1996, to hear tributes from all manner of former Commissioners, ambassadors, directors-general and the like. Here he was placed, to general acclaim, in a bracket with Monnet, Schuman, Adenauer and Spaak as one of the great Europeans.

When I met Noël in 1993, he was in his retirement job, running the European University Institute in Florence. A small, quiet, unimposing figure, he still exuded the tireless absorption of the bureaucrat in the project on which he had spent his life. He loved talking about Europe, to whose history he brought a formidable memory, capable of instant recall of the proceedings of every summit he had ever attended. But this vast accumulation, together with the length of time, rivalling the monarch's, which he had in one job, supplied him, as well, with a conspectus of the ages.

Emile Noël watched the Thatcher phenomenon in Europe with interest and some admiration. He thought she got too much money at Fontainebleau, but saw this was to her credit. 'She was a real states-woman, very efficient, very clear, knowing every significant point,' he judged. 'I cannot agree with the content of her position, but she was a very effective Prime Minister for a certain length of time.'[53]

Exactly when this time ended, Noël thought, was a matter for debate. He argued with himself as between 1984 and 1988. After the budget deal was done, he said, 'the Thatcher method became less and less efficient, year after year'. But the Single Act was a sort of victory. And in 1988, the battering-ram technique produced a refinement of the budget deal, locking the British rebate into a wider reform of agricultural spending. At that same meeting, on the other hand, occurred a more dismal Thatcherite watershed, showing how far she was from controlling the agenda any longer. Britain wasn't satisfied with the agriculture reform and threatened to veto it, a gesture that provoked a decisive move by the other eleven members. Noël said: 'This was the first time they were prepared, and even preferred, to go ahead without the British if the decision was opposed. It was the first time it was so clear.'

Whatever moment one might try to select as definitive, a trend established itself in the middle 1980s with which Mrs Thatcher could not easily cope. Settling the British budget problem was a doubled-edged event. It brought her back 'my money', but opened the way for new developments. Victory was the necessary prelude to something more unpleasant. Until it happened, the continental integrators were in balk. That is why Mitterrand needed to make concessions at Fontainebleau. After it happened, a sequence of events was liberated, all of them discomfiting because all spoke for the kind of momentum the British leader would prefer to think did not exist. At each colloquium of the leaders, in what became a decade of Community dynamism to follow the decade of stasis, something new was always edging forward. The agenda was always multiple, overlapping, relentlessly evolving. Just as the Single Act grew out of the budget deal, something more ominous began to take shape even as the Single Act was being finalized. The allusions to economic and monetary union, murmured during the build-up to the Act, turned out no longer to be mere aspiration but to describe the next great project.

From 1985, in fact, money began to be the core issue. If there was to be a single market, why then should there not be single money as well? This, to Margaret Thatcher's obvious bafflement, was something several of her peer-group, the leaders of Europe, apparently believed in, at least as a long-term goal. From now until the end of her prime ministership, aspects of the single currency – its preliminaries, its legitimacy, the prior binding of national exchange rates, the settlement of this goal as the new holy grail of 'Europe' – dominated an expanding acreage of the politics and economics of what used to be known, in distant halcyon days, as the Common Market. The prospect drew out the Thatcher scepticism, followed shortly by the Thatcher aggression. It came to dominate her political life, seizing her mind, devouring the unity of her Cabinet, to the point of being her nemesis.

For in parallel with this new momentum came another development. She began to show both an intensity and exclusivity of commitment on the Europe question that had hitherto been kept at bay. Early disagreements with Foreign Office ministers about how to handle the budget row had been superseded, on the whole, by a unified determination. She won the argument among her ministers, the prelude to winning the battle in Europe. Geoffrey Howe, Foreign Secretary from 1983, stood shoulder to shoulder, tolerant of her disdain, a solid ally in struggle. But for the colleagues, as for the Europeans, the new phase marked a change of atmosphere. There began to be a new argument, and new dissent. The politics of the personal began ever more insistently to intrude upon the politics of the nation. How currencies were managed, and how the Europe relationship was factored into them, were questions that called forth remarkable events in the annals of a prime minister and her government.

One strand concerned the currency itself. The European Monetary System (EMS) encompassed an exchange rate mechanism (ERM) locking the member currencies within bands of stability from which they could not, without agreement, shift. While embracing the innocuous aspects of the EMS – the 'zone of monetary stability' it proclaimed, and the European Curency Unit (écu) it controlled – Britain had kept out of the ERM ever since the Callaghan Government, saying only that sterling would join 'when the time was right', or alternatively 'ripe'.

So the ERM, in 1985, wasn't a new venture, wasn't part of some grand new European initiative. For Britain to join it, on the other hand, would be a European signal, as well as a decision to base economic, and especially anti-inflationary, strategy on the exchange rate, rather than on monetary indicators (M3, M0) whose chronic unreliability were at last depriving them of their mystic power over the minds of all true Thatcherites. In 1985, the leading minds in this category, Geoffrey Howe and Nigel Lawson, who was Chancellor of the Exchequer, made a big push to get into the ERM. Their reasons were economic, not European. But they didn't allow the European dimension to compromise their economic judgement. 'Europe' had not reached neuralgic status in the Tory Party, and besides, Howe, if not Lawson, was a lifelong devotee of all things continental.

The argument, at the economic level, had gone on for some time. Lawson was flirting with it as early as 1981, as a junior minister. Running the Treasury since 1983, he had grown more enamoured of the case, until it became for him the driving strategic objective. He was convinced that linking sterling to the Deutschmark, which was in effect what ERM membership meant, was the route to economic stability. It would protect business from exchange-rate gyrations and foster an anti-inflation climate. But he was unable to instil this opinion into those immediately around him. For most of two years, the senior Treasury officials and the top people at the Bank of England were, according to Howe, respectively 'sceptical' and 'cautious'.[54] The leader herself was still more heavily barricaded against conversion. Even after Lawson had managed to swing the Treasury and Bank, by early 1985, she still resisted. She didn't like the entrapment of fixed rates, the loss of political discretion and economic freedom. And she had an adviser off-stage, Alan Walters, who opposed ERM membership, in Lawson's phrase, as 'the work of the devil'. Walters, an aggressive professor of free-market persuasion and an intellectual base more American than European, was a Thatcher guru, an early presence in Downing Street fending off the wetter Cabinet ministers, who continued to exert much personal influence on his patron even after leaving London.

Lawson, however, did not surrender. As 1985 wore on, the lady herself seemed to be teetering. Howe records a moment when he caught her 'speaking of "when" not "if" we joined the Mechanism'. Joining was now almost conventional wisdom among mainstream Tory opinion. A meeting to fix it was set for 13 November.

This meeting wasn't strictly a "European' moment. The clash of mind-sets still related more to economic than to political ideas: to the currently inner meaning of economic Thatcherism, not yet the existential crisis about the future of an independent Britain. It was, nevertheless, significant in the evolution of Mrs Thatcher into a leader whom Europe would eventually undo. It marked the most strident moment yet recorded of her assuming a personal command that swept aside collective opinion, not by argument but by crude personal assertion, in a field adjacent to the Europe question.

Lawson presented the case he had long prepared the ground for, having circulated all present with reams of papers and tables laying out the economic advantages ERM members were gaining over Britain, and exposing the much lowered risks, in present circumstances, of deciding to belong. His listeners made an interesting collection. The Treasury and the Bank, both represented by their chiefs, were now solidly behind him. So were Howe, Deputy Prime Minister William Whitelaw, the Trade Secretary, Leon Brittan, and the party chairman Norman Tebbit, a man who later kept his elderly name alive by becoming a rabid Euro-sceptic. The chief whip, John Wakeham, offered the clear opinion that entry would induce no important back-bench rebellion. Only John Biffen, the sceptic from way back, opposed what Lawson wanted to do. Insofar as the collective was being consulted, it voted overwhelmingly to support the Chancellor.

But this was beginning not to be, in the old sense, a collective government. Having heard the opinions of her colleagues, the leader said sharply that she disagreed. Over her shoulder, it was apparent to Lawson, loomed the absent figure of Walters, and on her desk, plain for all to see, was a Walters communication. He had lately written an academic treatise denouncing the ERM root and branch.[55] Having delivered a crisp philippic against the entire idea of the European Monetary System, Mrs Thatcher responded to those who continued to make their pitch by saying: 'If you join the EMS, you will have to do so without me.'[56] In other words, the principle of time's ultimate ripeness was overturned. Government policy, which had hitherto accepted that one day Britain would join the ERM, was reversed by fiat of a Prime Minister who regarded her word alone as sufficient to kill it, apparently, for ever.

For Howe, it was all very bewildering. 'This was the first time that any of us had contemplated her exercising a veto of this kind,' he snuffles in his memoirs. Getting such high-handedness reversed, he muses, might require him and his friends 'to go almost off the constitutional map'.[57] A mysteriously menacing phrase. What could it mean? Impeachment? Or perhaps a rare, Howe-like mumble of total disagreement? Lawson felt much more explicitly outraged. It was 'the saddest event of my time as Chancellor', he writes, 'and the greatest missed opportunity'. He felt particularly vexed that it came about under the influence of a man, Walters, who had no place to speak at all, and he railed at the spectacle of the leader reversing Government policy without ever formally renouncing it: a recipe for confusion – but one, as we can now see more clearly, that was to become increasingly characteristic of Mrs Thatcher's dealings with the European Community.

The episode gave rise, in any case, to another bizarrerie. The passions let loose in this territory were beginning to produce many irregularities for constitutionalists to ponder. A Prime Minister personally reversing a policy was not an act without precedent, though this would normally – in the case of Harold Wilson, say, or Ted Heath – imply the presence of an unspoken Cabinet majority on the same side. By contrast, a Chancellor pursuing an exchange rate policy so secret that it is never disclosed to the Prime Minister, and a Prime Minister apparently so blind that she doesn't see what is happening until she reads about it in the newspapers, pushes forward the frontiers of the para-normal. Yet this is what began to happen little more than a year after Lawson was spurned in his desire to enter the ERM. Almost as a private frolic of his own, he began to have sterling shadow the Deutschmark, aiming to keep its value down to DM3.00. Selling sterling, the Bank doubled its foreign currency reserves within a year. Whether this really was secret from the Prime Minister, or something from which she preferred to avert her gaze, is a question to which the definitive answer is lost in the haze of muteness that sometimes surrounds actual financial operations. Eddie George, deputy governor of the Bank, later said: 'At no point did Nigel Lawson tell us there was to be a policy of shadowing the Deutschmark.' On the other hand there plainly was a shadowing, described by one Treasury official to Philip Stephens thus: 'It was exclusively a Lawson operation . . . [But] you will not find any papers in the Treasury setting out the policy of shadowing the Deutschmark.'[58]

These utterances from an arcane world are not satisfactorily clarified in the memoirs of any of the principals. What was indisputable, and required no great crystallizing, was the argument that underlay the matter. Argument, in fact, is too decorous a word. The contest of wills about exchange rate fixing, conducted with increasing rancour between the Prime Minister and her Chancellor, was a harbinger of what Europe at large, beyond the currency question, could do to the personal relations – the very solidarity – of her Government. The Prime Minister was ceasing to be all-powerful, even though in March 1988 she abruptly forced Lawson to end his intervention against the pound. Senior ministers, who had grown up as her protégés, were ceasing to respect her exclusive wisdom on matters either economic or European. A fissure was opening up, under the influence of acrid personal politics, and of developments in Europe itself which now became the dominating pre-occupation of Mrs Thatcher's life.

This was the second strand of what it is hardly too much to call her slow disintegration. There were tides she could not control, and it became a matter for mounting rage that this should be so. Such was the nature of 'Europe', once that elusive entity was experiencing economic growth, and a certain political confidence, and was under the hand of a man who knew where he wanted to take it.

For the middle 1980s were also the palmiest days of Jacques Delors. Whereas for Mrs Thatcher the Single Act was, desirably, the apogee of Europe's trajectory, for the Commission president it was but a way-station on the path to a still more integrated future. Behind this vision, Delors gathered the great majority of continental leaders, including all the biggest ones. In 1988, it exposed itself, in ways that the British leader could neither endorse nor obliterate.

Delors was nominated, first of all, as master of the future of economic and monetary union, EMU. This followed his reappointment, *nem. con.*, to another term in the presidency. 'We were saddled with M. Delors,' the Baroness writes, and in the end she even seconded his name, finding to her annoyance that her favoured horse, the Dutch Prime Minister, Ruud Lubbers, refused to run.[59] A note of defeat is beginning to infuse her estimation of events. As foreshadowed in the Single Act – its stated 'objective of progressive realization of economic and monetary union' – progress was simultaneously set in train towards EMU. A committee was required and Delors was put in charge of it. 'I was having to recognize that the chance of stopping the committee being set up at all was ebbing away,' is the doleful Thatcher memory.

She secured some crumbs of comfort. The slant of the Delors committee was directed away from a possible European central bank: 'I restated my unbending hostility.' She even renewed an argument she had proffered earlier, that the terminology of the Single Act, buried in its ambiguous entrails, contemplated only economic and monetary 'co-operation' rather than union. The membership of the committee itself she also believed she had influenced to her advantage. It was to be composed of central bankers rather than officials: reliably flinty realists and sceptics, as she thought, about anything so delicate as tampering with currencies. The head of the Bundesbank, Karl-Otto Pöhl, almost resigned over the presence of Delors as the chairman, deeming him not to be a qualified 'expert'.[60] The governor of the Bank of England, Robin Leigh-Pemberton, was the British member, to whom, along with Pöhl, the Prime Minister looked 'to put a spoke in the wheel of this particular vehicle of European integration'.

Delors' agenda, however, was much wider. Elated by his nomination for a second term, he immediately repaired to Strasbourg, the home of the European Parliament, to set out an overview of where the Community might be going. There could hardly have been a more frontal challenge to the British leader's opinion, not merely of Europe but of the liberal *Zeitgeist* she was bent on infusing into the new age. Matching Delors' belief in a Single Act was his determination that Europe should be something more than a paradise for unchained capitalism. He believed in a 'social' dimension: took it, indeed, as a good socialist, to be a cardinal priority for his presidency. Addressing the parliamentarians, he sketched out the implications of both a social and 'political' Europe. Law-making, he said, was bound in some part to shift from the nations to the federalistic centre. 'In ten years,' he specified, '80 per cent of the laws affecting the economy and social policy would be passed at a European and not a national level.' He went on: 'We are not going to manage to take all the decisions needed between now and 1995 unless we see the beginnings of a European government.'[61]

Delors, a subtle as well as strategic man, saw this speech as a warning. It was not a mission statement so much as a provocation to national parliaments, inviting them to consider the political realities likely to flow from the momentum unleashed by the Single Act.

That wasn't how Mrs Thatcher read it. To her it seems to have come as a straightforward power-grab by a megalomaniac. She went on the radio to denounce Delors, saying that he had gone 'over the top'. He was frightening people with his visions. 'He would never say such extreme things to me,' she said. They were entirely 'airy-fairy'.[62] And they soon became even more intolerable. On 7 September, the French imperial socialist – no longer the man Howe once approved as 'after our own hearts' – was received with acclamation in a south coast resort by the British Trades Union Congress. Addressing the brothers and sisters, he assured them that the single market would have a social dimension and protect workers' rights. In return, they serenaded him with a rendition of 'Frère Jacques'. He shed an uninvented tear. The occasion marked an important moment in the conversion of the British left to 'Europe', not yet for its internationalist, still less its federalist, potential, but as the only available hammer that might dislodge Margaret Thatcher from her unsettling ascendancy.

By this summer, however, Mrs Thatcher, in a larger way, had had enough. Everywhere she looked, it seems, she saw developments that proved 'Europe' was getting out of hand. It was the final dawning of a light she had hitherto been finding many ways to resist: the light that gleamed from the formal pledge, written thirty years before, to an ever closer union, the illumination which showed there were many significant people who meant this seriously.

She writes about it in her memoirs with the fury of one belatedly discovering a truth that had been withheld. The European Commission, she found out, was being very active. It wasn't like the British civil service, the tool of elected ministers: hadn't, indeed, been set up like that in the first place. One of the uniquenesses of the Community from the start was the exclusive power it gave the Commission, the supra-national *apparat*, to initiate proposals, ideas, advances. These had to be approved by ministers before they could become part of Community law or practice. But the Commission never was as self-effacing as Whitehall, and was now, according to the raging adversary of Delors, excelling itself.

Assembling a charge-sheet, her officials listed what it was doing in 1988. She was appalled. It was 'pushing forward its "competence" into new areas', she writes.[63] These included culture, education, health, social security. 'It used a whole range of techniques.' It set up advisory committees 'whose membership was neither appointed by, nor answerable to, member states and which tended therefore to reach *communautaire* decisions'. 'It carefully built up a library of declaratory language, largely drawn from the sort of vacuous nonsense which found its way into Council conclusions, in order to justify subsequent proposals.' 'It used a special budgetary procedure, known as *"actions ponctuelles"*, which enabled it to finance new projects without a legal base for doing so.'

Most seriously of all, she goes on, 'it consistently misemployed treaty articles requiring only a qualified majority to issue directives which it could not pass under articles which required unanimity'. These were part of a tendency so pervasive and pernicious that it entirely overshadowed the merits of particular cases. The Baroness chronicles her difficulty in arguing against populist environmental and health regulations, for example, that came under this heading. Cunning Commissioners kept 'presenting themselves as the true friends of the British worker, pensioner and environmentalist'. And if ever they were challenged in court, the ECJ lined up with the Commission, 'twisting the words and intentions of the Council', always favouring 'dynamic and expansive' interpretations of the Treaty over restrictive ones.

Such was the catalogue of disgust. The more she considered it, 'the greater my frustration and the deeper my anger became ... I had by now heard about as much of the European "ideal" as I could take.'[64]

She therefore decided to say so, in whatever undiplomatic words she could get away with. A speaking engagement was already scheduled for early September in Bruges, at the College of Europe, a good platform from which to deliver the new vision of what Europe should be about.

The lecture she prepared was a clear break with the implicit consensus for which every British leader, herself included, had spoken since 1973.

It partly depicted Europe as a threat to what she had done for Britain. 'We have not successfully rolled back the frontiers of the state in Britain only to see them reimposed at a European level, with a European super-state exercising a new dominance from Brussels': this became the Bruges speech's single most famous line. But its deeper message was that Europe itself must redirect its priorities in the world. What mattered in Europe was not the Community, but the wider Europe to the east. 'We shall always look on Warsaw, Prague and Budapest as great European cities,' she said. In their enmity with the Soviet Union, these were the places where the lamp of decentralized liberalism really shone. As prisoners of Moscow, they valued nation-statehood more highly than the

West, where too many Community members wanted to move in the opposite direction. 'Willing and active co-operation between independent sovereign states' was the way to build a successful European Community, a 'family of nations' the image insistently preferable to anything that smacked of a single endeavour.

There was more in this vein. It was a long, vibrant, intentionally challenging speech, with a peroration that exalted above all else the Atlantic community – 'our noblest inheritance and our greatest strength'. By the time she wrote her memoirs, the author had enhanced the range of her European vision to stretch from the Urals to what she rather fancifully termed 'the New Europe across the Atlantic'.[65] Anything to lower the presumption of what was now no longer even the European *Economic* Community, but, menacingly, the European Community *tout court!* But just as interesting as the content of Bruges were its preliminaries and its aftermath. They throw light on her two *bêtes noires* respectively.

Before the speech, there were fierce exchanges between the Foreign Office and Downing Street. I have glimpsed some of the secret official papers, and they expose not only the mutual contempt now existing between the two power-centres, but also something of the tactics inside the Foreign Office as the mandarins considered how to deflect the lady. From scanning them, one learns quite a lot about the state of things in the mature years of her prime ministership.

The draft was prepared in Downing Street, by Charles Powell, her closest official. He sent it across to the FCO asking for comments and suggestions, and noting that 'it has been seen by the Prime Minister, who is quite attracted to it'. The draft was undeniably strident. Powell included, among other choice readings of his mistress's voice, a passage that talked about Britain alone having saved Europe from being united 'under Prussian domination', and some triumphalist paragraphs on the success of the British Empire by comparison with the imperial failures of France, Spain, Portugal and Holland. Similar tactlessness abounded, along with some threatening allusions to the growth of qualified majority voting and the intolerable loss of national independence.

This had a pained reception across the road. Foreign Secretary Howe was appalled. His private secretary, Stephen Wall (who ten years later was head of the UK delegation to the European Union), minuted the head of the European Department, John Kerr (who ten years later was permanent under-secretary, the top official in the Foreign Office), listing a series of *bêtises*. There were 'some plain and fundamental errors in the draft', Wall began. It also tended 'to view the world as though we had not adhered to any of the [European] treaties'.

The Foreign Secretary, he went on, 'does not like the suggestion that we were more successful colonialists than other European countries. Is it not anyway a fact that we lost our North American colonies before Spain lost her South American colonies?'

Nor was Powell's appropriation of freedom as an exclusively British concern acceptable. It 'implies that we alone fought against tyranny and for freedom, which is presumably what the French revolutionaries thought they were doing'. As for the proposition, declared by Powell–Thatcher, that we should 'forget a United States of Europe – it will not come', this elicited another tart history lesson. 'The Secretary of State agrees that a stronger Europe does not mean the creation of a new European super-state, but it does, has and will require the sacrifice of political independence and the rights of national parliaments. That is inherent in the treaties.'

After receiving and absorbing this minute, Kerr set about rewriting the draft. Circulating it to colleagues, he said that Powell's original 'seemed off-beam' and in some parts 'needlessly provocative'. He was also struck by an omission. In all the fervour of the lecture, it seemed to him 'eccentric to pass over in complete silence one of the principal themes of the UK's EC policy in recent years' – the need for evolutionary change in the Community. He therefore included a new passage on that, and sent the whole to other Euro-concerned departments – Treasury, Department of Trade and Industry, Ministry of Agriculture – though with a pre-emptive ban on letting Downing Street know who had seen it. 'I think it would be good tactics *not* to reveal this to No. 10 at this stage,' Kerr instructed. Let these departments make known their approval of the FCO version – but it will be best if 'such advice appears *sua sponte*'.

In his covering note to Powell, by contrast, Kerr was all emollience. The authors of *Yes Minister* couldn't have made it up. It was too beautifully tendentious even for them. 'The Foreign Secretary believes that the scope and structure of your draft are generally well judged,' the under-secretary purred. But to avoid 'rejoinders or rebuttals', it might be prudent to consider some reformulations such as are herein proposed.

A week later, Powell sent back another draft, 'substantially rewritten', which Kerr regarded, so he circulated colleagues, as 'buying 80 per cent of the suggestions sent out by the FCO'. In a further redraft, he tried bidding for another 10 per cent, saying that 'the remaining 10 per cent don't really matter (and concern areas where No. 10 are probably incorrigible)'. All in all, he could reflect on a Whitehall job well done. 'It looks as if our damage-limitation exercise is heading for success.' The Bruges speech might not take any tricks in Europe, but it would cause no trouble. Howe, by now travelling in Africa, didn't need to be disturbed.

As to the battle of the drafts, this was only partly correct. After the final exchange, some of the sentences got souped up again before delivery. But, as a prophecy, Kerr's conclusion was more seriously in error. There had been some pre-emptive damage-limitation, both by the softening that remained and by warning Brussels of what was coming – thus enabling Delors, for example, to cancel his plan to attend. But the speech, of course, made its mark with the enemies in Europe, and thus fulfilled the Prime Minister's intentions rather than the Foreign Office's. In her chapter on this passage of her premiership, subtly entitled 'The Babel Express', she can hardly contain her delight at the anger she had caused. 'Not even I would have predicted the furore the Bruges speech unleashed,' she writes. The reaction was one of 'stunned outrage'.[66]

Writing privately to a British official in Brussels, Powell defended the speech as a warning. This is also recorded in the secret file just cited. Perhaps Mrs Thatcher was trading warning for warning with Delors. The speech was directed against future losses of national sovereignty occurring 'by stealth rather than by design', Powell explained to William Nichol, who had a senior post at the Council secretariat. The outcry, he added, had come from 'those who did not like the implications of their small steps being exposed to public scrutiny'. In any case, the speech had been an exceptional political triumph. It attracted, he noted, 'more support and favourable comment than any since the Prime Minister has been in Downing Street'.

Recounting his own memory of the Bruges speech, parts of which he calls 'sheer fantasy', Howe sees it as the moment when his leader finally ceased to allow her head to rule her heart. Her rhetoric, certainly her private posturing, had often smelt like this, but her policies had invariably been pragmatic, not least under the helpful hand of her Foreign Secretary. '*No. No. Yes.*' described the usual parabola of the Thatcher mind in addressing European suggestions, according to a later Foreign Secretary, Douglas Hurd. Now, it seems, she had moved beyond reason. 'She began readopting arguments which she and I had had no difficulty in rebutting in debates over the Single European Act only a couple of years before,' Howe writes.[67] The rupture between them was, he seems to have found, traumatic. 'It was, I imagined, a little like being married to a clergyman who had suddenly proclaimed his disbelief in God.'

Europe, however, moved on. So, for a time, did the power and influence of Howe and Lawson. This was the other oddity of the later Thatcher epoch. Though the Bruges speech set out a new agenda, and achieved maximum effect in the public arenas of politics, it stopped nothing happening. Nor did it have an instructive impact on any of her senior ministers other than to stiffen their resolve to defeat the philosophy it proclaimed. Apparently the height of presidentialism, it exercised little authority and attracted no respect among the colleagues who were, presumably, supposed to make it work.

There were, admittedly, differences between the two lieutenants. Howe was much the more 'European' in the old sense. He believed in the sweep of history, with himself somewhere near the centre, that must carry Britain, willy-nilly, closer to Europe; and he had no difficulty, in this context, imagining the congruences required by economic and monetary union. They did not frighten or repel him. Lawson, by contrast, more of an economic intellectual, was fiercely and publicly opposed to a single currency. He distinguished between the ERM and EMU, declining, unlike most of those who backed the ERM, to regard the one as mere prelude to the other. The ERM he saw as 'an agreement between independent sovereign states . . . economic and monetary union, by contrast, is incompatible with independent sovereign states'.[68] For Lawson, 'Europe' could never be a cause strong enough to override his mistrust of a continental central bank and – Churchillian dream, or nightmare – a United States of Europe.

For the moment, however, the ERM was the issue: the diabolical invention that Mrs Thatcher had thus far successfully warded away from Britain, but the item on the European agenda that no single leader was able to snuff out. On this point, Howe and Lawson were together, indifferent to the ordinance of Bruges, and willing, as it turned out, to face down the leader whose declaration in September 1988 was supposed to shock Britain, as well as Europe, into a new way of thinking.

The momentum was continuing, inexorably. Lurking in the wings, unstoppable, was Delors' committee on EMU itself. The central bankers were working away, and the British representative, Robin Leigh-Pemberton, kept the ministers informed. At this stage they were anxiously agreed that Delors, while certain to propose a general signing up to ERM, should be restrained from plotting a definitive path to EMU;

and the governor, a Thatcher appointee, agreed on tactics to achieve this. But others, unfortunately, did not. The head of the Bundesbank, Karl-Otto Pöhl, having first resisted the very presence of Delors anywhere near the sacred ground of currency-management, edged feebly – 'a broken reed', writes Lawson – towards acquiescing in an EMU scheme. When the committee arrived at a three-stage programme for monetary union, Leigh-Pemberton, too, signed up, protesting to Lawson that he did not want to be in a minority of one. That was not a posture likely to recommend itself to the Prime Minister. After writing to her to explain himself, he never received a reply. I was told that, after the Delors Report was published, she refused ever again to talk to Leigh-Pemberton, crucial though his position was, about anything to do with Europe.

Thus far, Lawson, though favouring the ERM, was with her. But this couldn't last. These matters were not the stuff of a debating society. While EMU might unite the colleagues, EMU itself, here and now, was only peripherally the issue. The question posed by the Delors committee, which came for final settlement at a summit in Madrid at the end of June 1989, was whether or not Britain, though well understood to be more minimalist in her vision than other members, would sign the pledge – Stage One, as it was called – to enter the ERM. The way things had evolved, in this new Europe which had discovered a certain dynamism, meant that a negative answer to the question would imply a negative approach, in effect, to Britain's continuing presence as a big player in the entire 'Europe' project. Through the Thatcher eyes this might be seen as perverse, absurd, enraging. But it was a fact, of somewhat epic proportion. And it gave rise to events, where politics and personality entwine around each other, of similarly awesome moment.

Howe and Lawson were quite determined that the answer at Madrid should be yes, and went to considerable lengths to break down the lady's opposite opinion. At Howe's suggestion, the Dutch Prime Minister, Ruud Lubbers, one of the few Europeans she approved of, was invited to Chequers for a day's discussion. Though he was a potential ally in resisting Delors' proposal that Stage One should *inevitably* lead to Stage Three, the full EMU, the British leader destroyed her opportunity by lecturing Lubbers both on EMU and on his alleged feebleness over the modernization of Nato. When the Dutch Finance Minister suggested that her opposition to EMU would be much more influential if it came from within the ERM, she rounded on him with fury. The whole occasion, Lawson writes, was 'ghastly and embarrassing'.[69]

As their own preparation for Madrid, the two then composed a memorandum, with the aid of Treasury and Foreign Office officials who were now, it seemed, behind them to a man. It was a seductive memorandum, cleverly contrived, beginning with the strategic suggestion that the British priority, which was to derail EMU, would indeed be better achieved by first joining the ERM, or at least stating the firm intention to do so. To that extent, it played winningly to its audience of one. But it went on to say other things that were less ingratiating. The Howe influence was visible in his usual mantra about the risks of isolation in Europe, and both ministers, after much consideration, raised the ante further by proposing not merely a declaration for the ERM in principle but a deadline by which entry would be accomplished: at first shot, within a year, but then, in a spirit of pragmatism, the end of 1992.

The argument was a mirror-image of what had often come before, and what, indeed, would also continue to come afterwards. It was the case – the incessant, unexhausted, unembarrassed case – for the merits of being inside a European venture, helping it to happen: ranged against the case for being outside, watching it succeed or fail, and half hoping, let's face it, for the latter outcome. The Delors Report, the ministers said, was going to be accepted, whatever the British said. It was certain to have some kind of life and future. An attempted veto would not stop anything happening: would, indeed, make the project more likely to advance, and the emergence of a two-tier Europe more likely to occur.

This was a foretaste of a future argument – to name one moment out of many – to be held in 1997, when EMU had become a near-reality. Much the same parade of agonized sophistries, as between inning and outing, would unfold in the early months of the Blair Government. Then, at least, there was a difference of methodology. For one thing, the Howe–Lawson memorandum's curtain line was not yet applicable after six months of Mr Blair. 'Could we discuss this with you?' the Chancellor and the Foreign Secretary plaintively requested. Such was the state of the Thatcher collective.

Their hesitancy proved to be well judged. To begin with, the answer seemed to be no. Instead of meeting her senior ministers to get ready for Madrid, Mrs Thatcher assembled her senior Downing Street staff, who now included, as a returned adviser in full fig, the same Alan Walters who had set her against the ERM in 1985, as well as a chief policy man of similar kidney, Brian Griffiths. Powell, the Foreign Office sheep long since attired in Thatcherite clothing, was also there, along with her influential press secretary, Bernard Ingham. But the leader was the only elected politician. This was the kitchen cabinet which had now replaced the formal Cabinet as the forum of influence, and together it agreed that the Howe–Lawson memorandum was unacceptable. The ministers were altogether too soft. The conditions they wanted to propose to Europe – the universal end of exchange controls, fully free movement of capital – were insufficient. The prior requirements must now reach into realms that some might call unreal, including the complete deregulation of all national banking systems. There should be no acceptance in principle of the ERM, but instead the Europeans would be told at Madrid that the only worthwhile priority was another push to complete a long list of single market measures which had been either evaded or forgotten.[70]

Howe and Lawson could not stand for that. Rare though it was for two ministers, alone, to engage in what amounted to bilateral warfare with the Prime Minister, they now raised their firepower, insisting that she should meet them together, and not, as she would have preferred, singly. According to Lawson, it was 'the only instance in eight years as Cabinet colleagues when we combined to promote a particular course of action'. At a meeting on 20 June, she heard them out, and even promised to 'reflect further' on what they said. When, following a riposte from Downing Street, they sent a second joint minute and requested a second meeting, she tried to fend them off with separate telephone calls. But this underestimated their purpose. They were determined to push her to the limit. On the very eve of the Madrid summit, she felt she had no alternative but to receive them in Downing Street, where she heard, apparently to her astonishment, a solemn declaration from Howe, followed in like manner by Lawson, that if she remained totally unwilling to move forward on the ERM neither of them would feel able to remain members of the Government.

This was a new nadir for the Thatcher engagement with 'Europe'. In her book, it was an 'ambush' mounted by a 'cabal', a strange way to depict the posture of her two most important colleagues but not unjustifiable. This was what she had driven them to, by trying to gather to herself the exclusive, transcendent control of a national policy which she had reduced to a personal obsession. In the televised version of her book, when she gave her account of 'this nasty little meeting', the memory of it contorted her visage, even four years after the event, into one of loathing. The recollection of failure, as well as enmity, was etched on her mouth and in her eyes.[71]

For failure is what it was. Next day, she and Howe flew to Madrid.

They were on the same plane but did not speak. Howe's memoirs conjure up a state of things so bad that communications between them were passed back and forth, in written notes, through separately curtained enclosures on the aircraft. That evening, the Thatcher party, which included Powell and Ingham, declined to attend the British ambassador's dinner-party, leaving Howe and his entourage feeling 'strangely relaxed' at the table.

When the summit began, it was to hear, very soon, a speech from the Prime Minister whose content, Howe said, had not been vouchsafed to him. He had no idea what she would say. But, when she spoke, he was agreeably surprised, as much by the content as by the manner. She was 'calm, quiet and measured',[72] he writes. And she made the necessary, if unexpected, statement: 'I can reaffirm today the United Kingdom's intention to join the ERM.' It was as if there had been no other possibility. She stipulated some conditions, and declined to specify a date. She also reminded those present to remember that adoption of the single currency, EMU itself, would not be acceptable to the House of Commons. But the essential concession was made. Finance ministers could now get ahead with the preparation of a full ERM, and Britain would take her place within the process.

There were other developments. A proposed social charter, another Delors initiative, reached the table, only to be flicked at least halfway off it by the British. All in all, Madrid was seen to be a British victory: within that, moreover, a victory which both sides in the British argument could live with. Howe and Lawson had got just about what they thought they needed, and Mrs Thatcher, making much of the conditions she had imposed and the continuing imprecision of timing, had not lost face. She really could persuade herself it was her victory, over none more saliently than the enemy cabal within.

Once again, as with the Single Act, the House of Commons and the media greeted with unsullied acclaim the return of a Prime Minister who had authorized an advance in 'Europe'. They somehow persuaded themselves it was another victory for the nation over the tribe of Jacques Delors. The leader herself, in her own memoirs, has grown a little less self-deceived on this point. 'Only someone with a peculiarly naïve view of the world', she writes, could have expected the Madrid conditions for the ERM to modify the pace towards its happening – though that is rather what she was trumpeting at the time. In another respect, however, her recollection of triumph is undimmed. It is the triumph over Howe and Lawson. At the first Cabinet meeting, she gloatingly remembers, she did not, as was her habit, sit at the table while the members trooped in. 'This time . . . I stood in the doorway – waiting.' She was eager to watch the expressions, see as early as possible what anyone might be planning to do, after her great success. 'But there were no resignations.' The nasty little meeting a week earlier had been, to her satisfaction, turned against the men whose conspiracy produced it.

It wasn't long, moreover, before this was driven home. In the cool of the following month, the leader did not behave like someone whose victory reinforced her position, so much as one with the memory of insult, and the fear of its repetition, ringing through her mind. Quite suddenly, the Cabinet was reshuffled, and Geoffrey Howe, the great, grey, slowly flowing, never ceasing artery of Thatcherite, and for that matter Heathite and Macmillanite, Conservatism, was choked off from the heart of power. He was compelled to leave the Foreign Office, and offered, after a fair amount of jockeying and confusion, a job that didn't matter much, as Leader of the House of Commons.

'Something had happened to Geoffrey,' Mrs Thatcher darkly writes, implying perhaps that he had gone slightly off his trolley. In fact, it was simpler than that. He had ceased to be ready to agree with her, come what may, about 'Europe'. She also thought he was enjoying himself too much, jetting about the world at government expense with dubious regard to the national interest, and enjoying the grace-and-favour official residences where he could entertain her enemies. 'I was determined to move him aside for a younger man,' she explains, with parodic unawareness of the resonance of the dissembling cliché.

She would have reason to regret this ruthless sentiment. In due time, Howe made her pay for it with condign severity, and in retrospect she expresses some doubt about whether she did the right thing. But only because of the misfortune that was heaped upon it soon after. Nothing to do with what happened a year later. Unlike Howe's departure, Nigel Lawson's was not precipitated by her. Often though they had argued, and furtively though he had operated, she evidently did not want him to go. But Lawson went, a few months later, exasperated beyond endurance by the undermining interventions of her special adviser, Alan Walters. 'Perhaps if I had known that Nigel was about to resign I would have kept Geoffrey at the Foreign Office for at least a little longer,' the Baroness writes.

By October, both were gone, and she was left, as she thought, with more malleable successors, readier to pursue her vision of 'Europe'. This, however, was now menaced from a different quarter – by another tendency which the Iron Lady could not control.

*

IN THE COMPLEX of prejudices, whether rational or, just as often, visceral, that Mrs Thatcher brought to 'Europe', none was more potent than her attitude to Germany. Both positive and negative surges of sentiment concerning the European Community were warmly affected by it.

On the positive side, Germany was close to the heart of the matter. As we have seen, European security interested her more than economic integration. Well before she became Prime Minister, she earned the Iron sobriquet by declaring her non-negotiable hostility to the Soviet Union, and her determination to see that Britain made stronger contributions to the defence of freedom in Central Europe. Germany, the divided epicentre of this region, couldn't avoid being the focus of her interest. In 1978, she made a speech, entitled 'Principles of Foreign Policy', that spoke of the need to advance democracy throughout the world so as to reduce the risk of war. In this sense, she powerfully desired the Community to assume a political role. 'I did not regard the EEC as merely an economic entity,' she writes. 'It had a wider strategic purpose.'[73] The Community, because it bordered on the communist world, was the showcase and the magnet that might draw people away from communism.

To that extent favouring, if anything, a stronger political presence for the Community, Margaret Thatcher upheld the idea of 'Europe'. Indeed, she took it further than most of her contemporaries. She thought the EC should be the defender of freedom, alongside Nato but also in some sense additional to it, a view not shared by many continental leaders, who were wary of such a dimension. These doubters included German leaders themselves, of all parties – Kohl every bit as much as Helmut Schmidt, or Schmidt's predecessor, the architect of *Ostpolitik*, which the Iron Lady much disapproved of, Willy Brandt. It was, in a sense, a tribute to her fearlessness in face of what conventional opinion might term a contradiction that she was prepared to be, in one sense, a stronger integrationist, but, in another, the opposite.

The defence of German freedom, as part of Europe's freedom, was therefore a high purpose that excited Mrs Thatcher's interest in 'Europe'. Her doubts about the Germans, on the other hand, spoke differently.

What Hitler's war fired in an adolescent breast in Grantham did not disappear. The images fixed by Hitlerism extended into a picture of Germany as an expansionary power, out to dominate by peaceful means the Europe it had almost destroyed by war. Whoever was leader of Germany at any given moment, these feelings were seldom far away. Laced into them were threads of envy at the speed and depth of Germany's post-war recovery, which she thought was somehow unfair. That was the opinion of Charles Powell, who once instructed Helmut Kohl's closest adviser, Horst Teltschik, in the significance of his boss's 'wellspring of instinctive anti-Germanism'.[74]

For a full decade after 1979, the instinct ebbed and flowed with variable importance. No German was exempt from its consequences. Kohl, with whom she cohabited, as it were, for eight years, was never graced with forgiveness for his nationality. He it was who bore the brunt of an opinion she summarizes with remarkable candour in her memoirs. Dismissing those who think the German problem 'too delicate for well-brought-up politicians to discuss', she offers an emphatic view of her own. 'I do not believe in collective guilt,' she says. 'But I do believe in national character.' Since the unification of Germany under Bismarck, she opines, 'Germany has veered unpredictably between aggression and self-doubt.' 'The true origin of German *angst*', she rather more mysteriously writes, 'is the agony of self-knowledge.'[75]

Though these were awkwardly deforming opinions for one close ally to hold about another, they had no catastrophic consequences until 1989. In that year, however, the fall of the Berlin Wall and collapse of the Soviet Union put both the positive and negative segments of the broader Thatcherite view of Europe under grave strain. The positive side began to lose its rationale, while the negative side threatened to billow to bursting-point. With the end of the Cold War, what, any longer, could be relied on as the security argument for a more cohesive European Union? And with the death of communism, what, any longer, could keep the separate sectors of Germany, the Federal Republic and the Democratic Republic, apart – their only acceptable condition, in the eyes of anyone who was alarmed by what they saw as Germany's grandiose ambitions?

For Mrs Thatcher, this was a terribly destabilizing conjuncture. Nothing could have left her more conflicted. The Iron Lady rejoiced to see Moscow ruined, but was appalled to imagine Berlin reborn as the home of a new Reich. Not that many people expected this to happen. Weeks before the fall of the Wall, with Mikhail Gorbachev dismantling

Soviet tyranny, a *Financial Times* columnist was thought very daring when he wrote: 'The future period during which German unity could be regarded as feasible has suddenly shrunk from a matter of decades to perhaps only 10 or 15 years.'[76] The prophecy of Professor D. Cameron Watt, a celebrated international scholar at the London School of Economics, seemed nearer the mark: 'There will still be two Germanys 50 years from now.'[77] This was certainly what Mrs Thatcher wanted, as she did not hesitate to inform Kohl, Gorbachev, the American President George Bush and – the only Westerner who agreed with her – François Mitterrand.

Attempting to stop German reunification was one of the more bizarre initiatives in the Thatcher foreign policy record. But that is what she did. It took less than a month for her to fail, with Chancellor Kohl having the nerve to set out his own ten-point plan for a German future which included the goal of federation between the two Germanys, to be followed by 'the reattainment of German state unity'. Germany was deciding her own future, with the support, incidentally, of British voters, whom opinion polls in October 1989 registered as 70 per cent in favour. This did not console their leader. In the first half of 1990, she exposed her doubts to all who would listen, telling the House of Commons, the Polish Prime Minister and the Board of Deputies of British Jews, among others, that boundary changes in Central Europe were governed by the Helsinki Final Act and should not be attempted without 'massive consultation'. Her attitude towards the old enemy was more intransigent, and ruinously outspoken. In July, at the fortieth-anniversary celebration of the Konigswinter Conference, the Anglo-German get-together that had done much to improve relations between the two national establishments, she told a former German ambassador it would be 'at least another forty years before the British could trust the Germans again'.[78]

So this was a settled opinion. And it had recently received intellectual endorsement of a kind which, in her opinion, clinched the point. Earlier in the year, she had registered the special place of Germany in her concerns by organizing, extraordinarily, a day-long conference at Chequers. What other nation ever got such treatment? None. Not even the Soviet Union – with whose leader, Gorbachev, she was in any case now rather more cosily in sympathy than she was with Kohl. The Chequers seminar on Germany became part of Thatcherite Britain's downward slide, away from European fraternity, into the grip of the leader's private world.

It assembled half a dozen academics, American and British, to speak to an agenda prepared by Charles Powell.[79] The agenda set out the persistent Thatcher concerns. 'What does history tell us about the character and behaviour of the German-speaking people of Europe? Are there enduring national characteristics? Have the Germans changed in the last 40 years (or 80 or 150 years)? Is it better psychologically to "stand up to Germany"? Or to pursue a friendly approach?'[80] Scores of similar questions, homing in on the German national character and what could best be done about it, were listed for the academics to think about.

During their day's discussion, they did not wholly satisfy Mrs Thatcher's requirements. Though they were a mixed bunch, among whom were three of her known political supporters, the more she talked, the more anxious they seem to have been to disabuse her of some of her assumptions. One of them, George Urban, later set down his own account of what happened. Urban has the historians unanimously challenging some of the Granthamite generalizations the leader found it hard to let go of. To the suggestion, for example, that the German people had not changed, Urban himself, along with the two other sympathizers, Hugh Trevor-Roper and Norman Stone, responded by saying that Germany herself had changed a great deal. Germany had remade liberal democracy, reinforced her institutions, shown every sign of being a constructive and pacific European power. Likewise – another Thatcher *idée fixe* – German minorities scattered round Eastern and Central Europe would not, these scholars thought, become a fifth-column working to destabilize the continent. All in all, they declined to subscribe to the nightmares summoned up by Mrs Thatcher and her faithful scribe, Powell. Before arriving, they had not known who else would be present and had not got together, yet, according to Urban, several of them remarked, as they departed, on the similarity of their assessments.[81]

What happened next, however, was indicative of the lady's intellectual methods, as well as her incorrigible attitudes. Powell's fidelity as a scribe proved more closely pinned to prior prejudice than to the truth. His minute of the meeting became famous, because it was leaked some months later to a newspaper. According to this account, the seminar had reached conclusions which gratifyingly confirmed most of what the leader suspected. It had picked out the essence of the German national character: 'angst, aggressiveness, assertiveness, bullying, egotism, inferiority complex, sentimentality', according to Powell. It had found reason to fear for the future in the Germans' 'capacity for excess, to overdo things, to kick over the traces ... to over-estimate their own strengths and weaknesses'. It had agreed there were still questions to be asked about 'how a cultured and cultivated nation had allowed itself to be brain-washed into barbarism', and whether 'the way in which the Germans currently used their elbows and threw their weight about in the European Community suggested that a lot had still not changed'.[82]

Such was the collective wisdom it pleased Mrs Thatcher to come away with. It is interesting that in her memoirs she makes no attempt to soften the verdict, or correct the impression the public – and the Germans – got of the Chequers seminar. Could the Germans be *trusted*? That was the question, according to Urban, to which she kept returning, while reciting many reasons to give a negative answer. Although the participants were quite prepared to consider that there was a complex of issues that might be summarized as 'the German question', they did not go along with the simplistic version from which the Prime Minister could not be shifted. Another of those present, Timothy Garton Ash, told me Powell's account was 'extremely tendentious'. No one has contended otherwise, save Powell himself, who responded with a combination of bullying and vanity that aptly reflected the tenor of the times in Downing Street as the Thatcher era drew to a close. 'I've been taking minutes for a long time but nobody has yet accused me of fabrication or inaccuracy,' he bellowed to the participants who challenged what they read.[83]

The fact is that angst was more prevalent among the British leadership than the German. They worried about the Germans more than the Germans worried about themselves, fiercely conscious though Kohl was of the need to placate European anxieties over the message of history. He himself did worry. That was the reason for his large, undeviating commitment to the unity of Europe, and the axiom he had placed at the base of his political life: Thomas Mann's famous affirmation – 'not a German Europe but a European Germany'. But his worries did not exceed those of Mrs Thatcher and her friends, who thought nothing of saying and believing about Germany things which, if a German had ventured similar generalities about the British, would have precipitated a nervous breakdown in the tabloid press.

Even Mrs Thatcher was obliged to recognize some constraints of political decency. When Nicholas Ridley, the Trade and Industry Secretary, attacked Germans in an open interview, she accepted his resignation. In the summer of 1990, it seemed some manner of taboo still operated. By stating to a magazine editor that European integration was 'a German racket designed to take over the whole of Europe', Ridley somehow put himself beyond the pale. German behaviour, said the minister, was 'absolutely intolerable', and Kohl would 'soon be trying to take over everything'. The Germans were a menace 'because of their habits'. Six columns of this stuff provided sufficient circumstantial static, the editor thought, to justify him running a cartoon depicting the Chancellor as the reincarnation of Adolf Hitler: which in turn affronted public opinion so much that Ridley had to be asked to leave the Government.[84]

But Mrs Thatcher was sorry to lose him. Not only did he know about the Germans, he understood the frailties of the ERM. On this point, he was 'almost my only ally in the Cabinet', she writes.[85] There is an eloquent beauty about this combination of truths and accidents. They are a kind of epitaph anticipating the lady's fall. A minister who agreed with her, on both the questions that now most gripped her mind, was obliged to depart. She could not save him. He joined the line of ministers, all likewise once her close allies, who, one way or another, had also left because of the Europe question: a question that by now was raised to a new pitch of explosive sensitivity by her handling of it: a question which she thrust to the forefront of British politics, even as her treatment of it ensured no other colleague who mattered agreed with what she wanted to do. Could there be a more ominous foretelling of Armageddon?

New ministers, meanwhile, were in place. But they did not prove more malleable than Howe and Lawson. One of them, Douglas Hurd, could never have been expected to. As Foreign Secretary he had entered the place for which his life hitherto was preparing him, which meant, by definition, that he was unlikely to agree with his leader about the Germans. Over Europe, he was not a federalist. In fact, as the 1990s proceeded and the issues became yet more divisive, Hurd was to show himself less steeped than Geoffrey Howe in the juices of European integration. But he was a Foreign Office man to his roots: trained there as an embryonic mandarin, embraced there as Heath's private secretary when the 1971 negotiation took place, already with form as a junior minister there in the Thatcher years, altogether an entirely unsuitable appointment for a Prime Minister whose stance towards the place was studiously adversarial. It is a commentary on the condition of the Government that Hurd selected himself. By late 1989, no other candidate for the post was remotely as credible.

Alongside Hurd, from the same date, was a new Chancellor of the Exchequer who, on the face of things, might have been more persuadable to the Thatcher viewpoint in his particular field of operations, the ERM.

John Major was, to all appearances, a Thatcherite, personally nurtured by the leader through a career that saw him rise from his first junior ministerial post into the Cabinet in less than four years. Major had no form, one way or the other. He seemed a willing follower of the orthodoxy of the leader, without diversionary ideas of his own. It was the only position for an ambitious young Tory, without previous convictions, to adopt. That, along with a general industrious competence, was the way he had got on. Compared with Lawson's formidable, aggressive intellect, Major's was untutored and, on matters of economic theory, apparently timid.

The Thatcher orthodoxy on the ERM, however, was contested. And Howe, bearer of the old wisdom, remained, unlike Lawson, in the Government. Even from a backwater as Leader of the House, he could still make speeches, and he lost little time in emphasizing in public, for example, how imperative it was that Britain 'stuck in good faith' to the ERM terms agreed at Madrid. This wounded the leader. She later called it an act of 'calculated malice'. But the fact was that orthodoxies could not necessarily be shifted by a reshuffle. Inside the Treasury which Major took over, the ERM lobby was fully formed. His officials were by now entirely in favour of entry as the route to a more solid basis for the war against inflation. Though Mrs Thatcher exerted episodic influence from No. 10, thereby inflicting some confusion in the early days of Major, he soon became a Chancellor with an agenda that decisively preferred the economic orthodoxy of the Treasury to the political imperatives of Downing Street. With Hurd as his reliable ally – they met regularly together for breakfasts that appeared on nobody's public schedule – he soon began to reinforce rather than challenge the Madrid commitment. In this period, Hurd, when asked privately about daily speculation then occurring on ERM matters, was quite happy to reply that his young colleague Mr Major, far junior to himself on the time-line of Tory hierarchy, was the most powerful man in the Government: even, he would mischievously imply, more powerful than the Prime Minister herself.

For both Hurd and Major knew they were in a strong position. Having already lost both a Chancellor and a Foreign Secretary, even a leader as well accustomed as Mrs Thatcher to riding out storms of her own creation could hardly afford to lose another from either post. The two of them began a process of persuasion, and ultimately enforcement, which casts a strange light on her eternal reputation for getting her own way. By the time she reaches this part of her memoirs, faced with the forces ranged against her, she is almost bleating with self-pity, as well as implied self-exoneration. 'There are limits', she writes, 'to the ability of even the most determined democratic leader to stand out against what the Cabinet, the parliamentary party, the industrial lobby and the press demand.' Wrong though she thought it was, this majority, alas, might finally be capable of imposing itself upon her. With only Ridley for an ally, she goes on, she was not strong enough 'to state that on grounds of principle we would not have sterling enter the ERM now or in the future'.[86]

It took time for Major and Hurd to get there. There were a number of intervening moments.[87] Apart from the objective need for technical preparations, and a reasonable alignment of economies, the argument itself continued. The leader did not end her struggle, and her colleagues were not so adamantly convinced of their rightness as to fight her in open court. Major, for example, was happy to engage in the distracting quest for an alternative to the goal of EMU, a search that had been legitimized at Madrid. An old Lawson idea for 'competing currencies', whereby all twelve national denominations would be legal tender in every EC state, was explored, as was a complex scheme promoted by Major himself for a so-called 'hard' écu – the European Currency Unit, the basket of national currencies in which much Community business was done. This was conceived as a possible but highly contingent route towards full EMU, more experimental and less frightening than the big bang the Delors committee proposed. Major espoused it strongly, as an appealing way to persuade the leader towards an ERM that would not, if the écu scheme triumphed, necessarily be the prelude to full EMU. It involved him in many hours of linguistic negotiation, to ensure the right nuances of conditionality. The 'would–could–should' problem became famous in the conversations of the higher Treasury at the time. 'The écu would be more widely used,' Major said when he announced the plan in June. 'It *would* become a common currency for Europe. In the very long term, if peoples and governments so choose, it *could* develop into a single currency. But that is a decision we *should not* take now, for we cannot yet foresee what the size and circumstances of the new Europe will be.'

These ideas, however, received little support in Europe. 'Competing currencies' was simply dropped, and the main value of the hard écu was political: the luring of Mrs Thatcher, along with Ridley while he still mattered, towards the moment when entry into the ERM, as long as it could be portrayed as much less than an automatic staging-post to EMU, was deemed to be inevitable. Even as such, the hard écu did not attract unanimous agreement. The game kept being given away by other players. The Prime Minister might say, as she did, to the Commons: 'Those who wish to use the écu in place of their own national currency may. I do not believe we shall.' But the governor of the Bank could not help but describe the hard écu as a step on the way to full monetary union. Nor could the entire Thatcher philosophy of Europe avoid being seen as a minority position, standing against an attitude for which the new Foreign Secretary spoke as firmly as the old – his counsel against Britain being 'prickly, defensive or negative', his fear lest 'we isolate ourselves by shutting ourselves off, raising the drawbridge of argument, acting as if we were a beleaguered island'.[88]

When the fateful moment of entry arrived, on 5 October 1990, the circumstances were related intimately to the past, the present and the future of the island's relations with the mainland, and the Conservative Government's custodianship thereof.

It happened then because it had not happened before. The force of events, almost unanimously supported by the political class of all persuasions at the time, drove sterling in. Yet entry took place when the relevant exchange rate index stood at DM2.95 to the pound, a rate that was already higher than it need have been and, within two years, was to prove unsustainable. In the matter of timing, the decision was calamitous. It thus takes its place in a category that has become familiar in this history: of climactic moments long postponed, then urgently desired, then achieved at a conjunction of time and place producing less, sometimes much less, advantage than might have been previously attainable. The sequence began in the 1950s, and would be equally visible in the later 1990s. It was now operative at the start of the decade. Once again, what appeared to be the logic of the present cast heavy doubt upon the judgement of the past.

In the case of entry into the ERM, indeed, this absence of an earlier decision perhaps had an especially corrosive effect. It contributed to the building of a conventional wisdom that turned out to be as potent as it was unfortunate. Though seemingly a success for the European wing of the Cabinet, it eventually helped to strengthen anti-Europe feeling, especially in the Tory Party. Although Thatcherite opposition to the ERM rested as much on an ideology of floating exchange rates as on hostility to 'Europe', the counter-attack, welling up in most corners of business and the press, and much of the parliamentary party, was in part born of resistance to the entire direction of the leader's European policy.

Out of her excessive hostility grew the misdirected zeal of the other side, which allowed itself to be deceived into ignoring the downside of entry into the ERM at the chosen moment: a moment that came about not through any perfect economic logic, but more because it happened to be the moment when the leader's resistance at last collapsed.

In the longer term, this had a still weightier effect, redoubling the scale of the defeat that awaited those who thought that, by entry, they had won. The mistimed entry, when followed two years later by humiliating exit, discredited the very concept of a fixed exchange rate in the period when EMU, from being a speculative dream, had become an imminent reality. When a serious British debate about EMU should have begun, it was impeded not least by sick memories of the ERM experience. For years after October 1990, all British politicians found it hard to speak of the ERM without being drowned in hoots of derision. In Conservative circles, the infamous alphabetic sequence was literally unmentionable. In the Blair Government, it was considered so explosive that the then Chancellor of the Exchequer, while announcing that Britain would enter EMU if and when the time was ripe, felt obliged to deny that he had any intention of joining the ERM beforehand, as the prevailing Treaty stipulated.[89]

The ERM, in short, became the Great Satan. It was placed beyond the edge of rational discussion. Such was the consequence of the October climax in 1990, for which the supporters of 'Europe', it can be seen in retrospect, were as much to blame as the enemies. Indeed, since it was only later that a good many of these supporters became enemies, perhaps one should say that the 1990 friends of the ERM were almost entirely to blame for the disastrous connotations which thereafter hung around it.

Politically there was a more immediate result. Joining the ERM was the penultimate episode in the self-destruction of Margaret Thatcher. Never before had she been driven to an action she was so reluctant to endorse. Even the 1985 Anglo-Irish Agreement, which she signed with gritted pen, had, by comparison, its merits. After the ERM moment, it was very soon apparent that she could not forgive herself. Her response was in keeping with the general tendency to over-compensate for defeat, which was by now infecting all sides of the 'Europe' argument in Britain. This mighty Prime Minister, once the lord of so much she surveyed, had lost the decision. But she was determined not to let the consequences slip away from her. The decision must in some way be countermanded. She therefore set out to make clear what this baleful defeat for her did not mean.

It was the beginning of the end. And the scene of its unfolding opened, fittingly, in Rome, home of the originating Treaty that was responsible for luring the island towards this benighted continent in the first place. At a summit called there by the Italians, EMU was eased relentlessly on to the agenda. There emerged a plan to fix a date by which the second stage of the Delors committee's proposal should be set in place. Thus, a mere three weeks after Britain dragged herself into the ERM – Stage One – the continentals were already plotting something else: a rather vague, but nonetheless insistent, pushing forward.

In fact the summit turned out less threatening than it might have been. It agreed to delay the Stage Two deadline by a year, from January 1993 to 1994. The communiqué made no explicit commitment to a single currency in the future. But the Thatcher boiling-point was lower than before. The very looseness of the communiqué, shaped in part to suit the lady, attracted her scorn for its 'grand and vague words'. She made a vigorous assault on 'non-urgent and distant things' that were far from 'the nitty-gritty of negotiation'. 'People who get on a train like that deserve to be taken for a ride,' she said at a press conference when the summit closed. The vehicle was on its way to 'cloud-cuckoo land'. When M. Delors predicted that a single currency would be created before 2000, she retorted that the British Parliament would never agree to it, and would stop it in its tracks. 'We shall block things which are not in British interests, of course we shall,' she promised, goaded onwards by the reckless aggression of much of the tabloid press. It was to this moment that the *Sun* pinned the famous ranting headline – 'UP YOURS DELORS'.

Returning home, she had not cooled off. True, as quite often happened in the Thatcher decade, the relevant Whitehall officials effected a certain hosing down. In her report to the Commons, Mrs Thatcher read out a text that gave off a different level of heat. By comparison with Rome, she sounded almost emollient, even alluding with approval to Major's hard-écu plan and acknowledging the possibility – the remote and undesirable but nonetheless real possibility – of it eliding into a single currency if the people and governments chose that route. But this was merely the text. When she came to the questions that followed it, and there was no text to hold her down, the politics of the intensely personal resumed their sway.

The European Commission, she said, was trying to 'extinguish democracy'. She would never stand by while a federal Europe was created 'by the back door'. This is what a single currency would amount to. Having suggested earlier that the écu could develop into a single currency, she now insisted that it would not, in the real world, be widely used. Therefore it could not develop. Therefore, by implication, there could never be a single currency.

As for M. Delors, he had many federalizing schemes. For all of these she had a simple answer. It became, in its monosyllabic brutality, the rubric of one of her most famous parliamentary moments, leaping with rage, ringing round the chamber, startling even those who in eleven years had much experience of the Thatcher vocabulary on Europe. 'No ... no ... no,' she bawled, her eye seemingly directed to the fields and seas, the hills and the landing-grounds, where the island people would never surrender.[90]

*

LOOKING BACK FROM 1998, one finds it hard to credit the circumstances of Margaret Thatcher's undoing.

Here was a Prime Minister who had won three general elections, and still bestrode politics. The people had elected her, kept on electing her, and her party in the country continued to greet the super-star wherever she went. She was not a fading force, nor had she suffered the kind of parliamentary defeats that begin to unpick the position of a leader in place for more than a decade, as she had been. All these were points of astonishment when her assassination occurred, but the aspect of it that grew most arresting as time passed was different. In 1998, it was utterly jarring to recall that the prime cause – at least the indispensable pretext – of Mrs Thatcher's removal was that Conservative Members of Parliament were unable any longer to trust her hostile conduct of British relations with Europe.

There were other influences. She seemed to some of them to be losing her touch in a more general way. The most worrying proof of it was her inability to draw the deadly electoral sting of the new local property impost, the so-called poll tax, which she had been determined to put in place. This tax roused even the stoical British to riot in the streets, an event whose rarity made it very potent. The poll tax also hit Tory MPs where it hurt them, often being a gauge, measurable between one locality and another, of their prospects of holding on to their seats at the next election. Anxiety about survival, their Government's and their own, was the *sine qua non* of the uprising in the parliamentary party that drove Mrs Thatcher from office.

Europe, however, fired anxiety to its decisive pitch. It was her performance at and after Rome that determined the manoeuvres of the decisive players against her. It supplied them with the material for attack, and enriched the atmosphere of alarm into which they deployed it. The leader was suspected, even by some of her supporters, of becoming wayward, excessively emotional, often, in the bar-room demotic of the Commons, a little crazy. One Cabinet minister told me around this time that she was 'absolutely barking' – which, coming from an opponent of ultra-Thatcherism, was discountable, but, because it reflected what was being loosely put about by a wider range of politicians and editors, suggested her position might be crumbling. Even though her climactic roar in the Commons, the triple negative, was answered with deep-throated pulsations of approval behind her, the Tory Party in the autumn of 1990 was inwardly conflicted. It still warmed to the defiant chauvinism that was her standard mode of speech. But it could also respond to the inducements of those most worried by the stance which she was, incorrigibly, taking.

The pro-Europe segment of Conservatism secured the strongest purchase on these contradictory feelings. Mrs Thatcher was challenged by people whose sharpest identity was 'European'. She was voted out of office by a party which, at this time, came to be repelled by the extremity of her anti-Europeanism. Written in 1998, that is a statement it is hard to come to grips with. By 1998, there was almost no limit to the Euro-scepticism that would find favour in the Tory Party. But in 1990 it was Mrs Thatcher's almost demented fervour over Europe that convinced enough Tory MPs of her wider ineligibility to be the leader who could guarantee them a fourth election victory.

The first signal came a year before. After Lawson and Howe left the great offices, turbulence in the party did not abate. The Tories hadn't recovered from their last electoral disaster, the European elections in summer 1989, when the leader's ferocity was given full expression in party propaganda – to unimpressive effect. The campaign was conducted on the basis that Europe was the enemy, and its Parliament a near-absurdity. This did not strike a chord with the British people. Urged to be fearful of 'a Diet of Brussels' and suchlike puerilities, less than 28 per cent of those who turned out voted Conservative, the lowest share of the vote ever recorded by the party in a nationwide election.

The leader, therefore, was challenged in December 1989. The challenge did not succeed. But the man who made it, an otherwise obscure baronet, Sir Anthony Meyer MP, was best known for his European dimension. Though generally unsympathetic to all that Thatcherism stood for, he responded to a specific stimulus. 'I made no secret of the fact that it was her manifest distaste for everything that emanates from Europe that finally decided me to launch my challenge,' Meyer writes in his own memoir.[91] He persuaded sixty MPs not to vote for the lady. It was a harbinger. Although she paid little attention, it rendered thinkable what had previously been viewed with incredulity.

The same definition, the European, applied with much greater sharpness to the man more seriously lurking in the Conservative politics of the later 1980s, the politician who, shortly after the débâcle in Rome, was obliged to conclude that his time had come.

Michael Heseltine stood for nothing if he did not stand for Europe. The continental connection infused, with Heath-like intensity, every part of the politics that interested him. There were differences with Heath. For Heseltine, the drive had less to do with worshipping alongside the post-war cult of Jean Monnet than with a view of economics, especially the economics of size, and the over arching necessity of Britain submerging herself in the only entity that would give her a chance of survival in global competition – except that survival was not a concept Heseltine ever discussed. His obsession was with 'winning'. The pitch he always made for Britain-in-Europe was that this was the only road to 'victory', the mythic objective beloved of many politicians: an expression which comes from the same root as the Thatcher concept of 'battle'. Heseltine, who wrote a substantial book on the subject, called it *The Challenge of Europe: can Britain win?* – a question to which there was a positive answer, but only on one condition.

In 1990, Heseltine had been absent from governing politics for nearly five years. He had walked out of the Cabinet in 1986, ostensibly on a Europe question – the obscure but fiery matter of whether Britain should build military helicopters under licence from American or European suppliers. Surrounded by static of the most explosive kind, emanating from the Thatcher personality and the Thatcher style of governing and Heseltine's lordly impatience with his inability to get his way, that was the core issue in what became known as the Westland affair. Every week and every month thereafter, Heseltine devoted himself to avenging not just the personal defeat he had suffered – always the most powerful impulse, demanding the ultimate retribution – but also the political misjudgement he thought this defeat entailed. He was passionately committed on Europe. He wrote his book, which was a serious, thorough, constructive compilation, and a polemic in favour of closer integration.[92] He also spread the word. I saw him a number of times during his wilderness years, and never failed to receive a lecture about the leader's European follies: how she had got the Germans hopelessly wrong, had put a succession of anti-Europeans in charge of Britain's trading policy, did not know or care about the needs of British business. 'Germany and France will go ahead with some sort of monetary union,' he told me in March 1990, 'and Britain will simply slide slowly out of the picture, mainly owing to one woman's prejudice.' He was appalled to think there was nothing more to it than that.

But Heseltine had to be careful. Though it was common knowledge that he thirsted to depose the woman, prudence said he should never indicate, by a half-sentence of public disloyalty, that this was the case. The quantity of his menace depended on the quality of his silence. Maintaining his air of mystery, Heseltine loomed ever larger as the raw lineaments of Mrs Thatcher were finally demystified. It required the intervention of another force, creating another climacteric of the European argument, to bring him into the open.

The most avid listener to the triple negative had been a minister who was supposed, under collective responsibility, to endorse it. Geoffrey Howe was still a member of the Cabinet. But after hearing it, and reflecting on the excitement it induced on the benches behind, he decided he had had enough. A relationship which, he mordantly calculated, had stretched through at least 700 meetings of Cabinets and shadow Cabinets, was brought summarily to an end by his resignation. Or rather, its positive aspect was concluded. Their twenty-year professional connection had one more element to disclose, a final disgorging of emotion laid out for the witness of the world.

They exchanged letters of departure with mutual incomprehension. He wrote: 'We must be at the centre of the European partnership, playing the sort of leading and constructive role which commands respect.... I now find myself unable to share your view of the right approach to this question.' She wrote: 'Your letter refers to differences between us on Europe. I do not believe that these are nearly as great as you suggest.' They were ships passing in the day, never mind the night. She also wrote, material for greater retrospective puzzlement, 'We want Britain ... to be part of the further political, economic and monetary development of the European Community.'

But these were merely the formalities. There remained the opportunity for speech, and Howe determined to make the most of his: the resignation speech, customarily heard in silence by the Commons, in which he would explain himself with the most devastating effect he could summon from a rhetorical style never previously noted for its power. It is another measure of the 'Europe' question, its capacity to grip the hearts as well as the heads of many different kinds of British politician, that, at this terminal occasion, it propelled Geoffrey Howe to heights of oratory more disdainful and more lethal than he had ever reached before.

It was the occasion, as much as the words, that mattered. The words were damaging enough. They spoke of Europe and they spoke of style, intimating that Cabinet government, over Europe, had all but come to an end. They described as 'futile' the task of 'trying to stretch the meaning of words beyond what was credible and trying to pretend that there was a common policy'. They offered self-laceration, from a man who had 'wrestled for perhaps too long' with his conflict of loyalties. But what made the moment decisive was its timing. Enough MPs knew, in their inward minds, that Howe was not speaking out of pique so much as desperation. They recognized, even if silently, the picture that he drew. They looked to their own seats and their own future if that picture was permitted to prevail. And they were aware of both the man and the moment that might supply an immediate opportunity for relief. If the annual leadership election, provided for in party rules though never activated before 1989, had not beckoned, nothing might have happened. As it was, after Howe spoke, the calendar set the tumbrils rolling.

For Heseltine, it was now or never. Howe's speech drew him from cover. The urge for a contest reached even those who never wanted Heseltine to win it. They could not deny the divisive nature of Mrs Thatcher, in substance as well as style. One of her most obsequious flatterers, Paul Johnson, was driven to write in the *Daily Mail* of 'the real weakness of Mrs Thatcher's leadership – her inability to unite the party over Europe, or even to convince it that she is doing her best to keep it together'. And so enough of the party thought, proving the truth of the perception by splitting almost down the middle when it came to the vote. There were 152 votes for Heseltine, 204 for Mrs Thatcher – a majority four short of what the arcane rules required for a first-round victory. The lady was now for burning.

There was something dramatically satisfying about these final days. The locations were somehow appropriate. After spitting on the Treaty in Rome, the leader was on her way to Versailles when she first heard that she was to be consigned to the guillotine. She did not immediately offer her head. Having heard, while in Paris for a European meeting, that the vote had left her short, she fulfilled her Versailles engagement with aplomb. Her old adversaries were considerate. François Mitterrand, the host, delayed proceedings for an hour until she arrived. Helmut Kohl, she records in her memoirs, came straight to the point, advising her not to bottle up her feelings. She had plenty to say against Kohl but at least, she writes, he was 'never devious'. 'He had been determined to devote this evening to me as a way of demonstrating his complete support.'[93]

Kohl, however, did not have a vote. And it must be doubted whether, if he had had one, he would have cast it in favour of survival. As it was, the leader did not survive, falling by her own hand two days later, when she was persuaded by a stream of colleagues that a second round of voting would not supply the victory, or at any rate the mandate, she needed to carry on.

So passed the longest-lived leader of Britain's European connection. Though Heseltine plunged the dagger, after Howe had drawn the first blood, he did not succeed. He could spark the party into a negative act, but not a positive one on his own behalf. Instead of him, it elected as replacement the most obscure of the candidates, with the most opaque record on all matters, Europe among them.

As to what this meant, hindsight is again a good and faithful servant. Only at a distance is it possible to reckon out the truth, and get a measure of the ambiguity in the Conservative Party at that time.

Ostensibly, the deposing of Margaret Thatcher was the conclusive triumph of Tory Europeanism. Here was the largest Conservative, now ranging the party openly against the objectives of the Treaty of Rome – 'an ever closer union among the peoples of Europe'. She might cavil at that description, saying that a union of peoples should be distinguished from – would be violated by – a union of governments or states. No matter: addressing Europe's evolution as attained by 1990, she was anti-'European'. And she lost. She terminally antagonized two major figures, both of them paradigm 'Europeans', who routed her from the field. What Helmut Schmidt called her defining characteristic, her love of war, was not enough to win the last battle. This was decided not just by Heseltine and Howe but by the party at large, in Parliament and, to sufficient extent, outside as well. When she left, the nation and much of the party exhaled a long sigh of relief. They were relieved at the new possibilities: of collective decision-making, of reasoned discussion, of government that started from the belief that Europeans were not enemies but colleagues with whom business could be done. The first continental act performed by the new man, John Major, was a declaration that he wanted Britain to be 'at the very heart of Europe'.[94] It seemed to settle the tenor of a more stable time.

Such was the apparent truth. But it was wholly deceiving. Actually, these events were the prelude to something like the opposite. After a brief period of tranquillity, the expulsion of Mrs Thatcher led to more turbulence than ever before. It settled nothing. 'Europe' was the pretext for the great defenestration, but settling the Europe question was not what the party was in any state to do. By her departure, Mrs Thatcher gave way to the 'Europeans' – yet also exposed how little they had prepared the ground for their own victory.

A question was answered: for how long could the country stand a leader whose Europe policy, founded on aggression, became totally divisive? But another question was asked: how could the party that first took Britain into Europe still be vulnerable to the prejudices which the bloody victors thought they had expelled?

10

WILLIAM CASH

Europe Made Me

EURO-SCEPTICISM, though it did not enter the language until the 1980s, penetrated the bloodstream of the Conservative Party in the early 1950s. From the moment 'Europe' began to be invented, there were Conservatives who thought Britain should have nothing to do with it. There were Labour people too. The names have changed, the numbers surged and fell, but the institutions have always harboured this strain of feeling. It is a persistent, rooted thing, which some Tories and some progressives alike cannot regard as inconsistent with their party allegiance, even when party leaderships have been long committed to Europe. Indeed, especially on the Tory side, they see their tenacity as a noble duty, for which they will one day be rewarded by seeing their party redirected towards the course of national righteousness.

This phenomenon is not in the least surprising. What is at stake has always been fundamental. It hasn't always been presented that way. Enthusiasts for entry, as we have seen in the cases of Edward Heath and Geoffrey Howe, felt it prudent to mask the radical nature of the transaction they were proposing. But 'Europe' involved an organic shift in the nature of the nation-state. This hit some people in their guts. They could never get over it. It broke with a history they revered, notably the Commonwealth connection. It seemed to imply a threat to the heart and soul of Britishness. For some politicians, driven by a sense of existential crisis, opposing it became the central purpose of their life.

Some of the early opponents of entry proved to be less driven. Peter Walker, later a Cabinet minister under both Heath and Mrs Thatcher, is an example. As a youthful tyro, Walker acquired notoriety for tramping round the Commonwealth to oppose the Common Market. Getting into Parliament in 1961, he immediately set about attacking the Macmillan negotiations then in train. His reasons were mainly to do with a judgement about trade, laced with his preference for the multi-racialism of the Commonwealth. He came at Europe from the left of the party. 'It was proposing external tariffs against the rest of the world,' he later wrote. 'And it was totally white, while I believed that Asia and Africa were the emergent powers.'[1] Walker seriously believed that Commonwealth trade could build the future of British prosperity. But not for long. By the end of the 1960s, with Heath on the brink of office, Walker had seen the error of his ways. 'I became more and more convinced of the wisdom of my conversion,' he writes, 'when I became a minister, attended EEC Councils of Ministers and began to see the value of co-ordinated European action.'

This element of self-interested rationality – the lack, in the end, of gut feeling – helps account for Walker's rare status as a committed sceptic who then enthusiastically went over to the other side. There were more startling versions. In June 1971, Nicholas Winterton secured the Tory nomination for the Macclesfield by-election as an anti-Marketeer, and won it in September as a pro-Marketeer.[2] The conversion experience litters this story, but mostly, as time goes on, the other way. Economics was never enough to breed undying hostility. For that, it was necessary for the viscera to be fully engaged.

In history, the core of scepticism has been about the visceral question. In the 1972 debates, the few incorrigible Tories who opposed Heath were moved by thoughts of nation more than economics. Their parliamentary resistance was mannerly, tenacious and almost entirely uninfluential. Insofar as they mattered, it was to achieve the ironic effect of pushing alarmed ministers to dissemble about what they were doing. They had no effect on the decision. But they kept the flag flying, and a sceptic core intact, and some of them still mattered a quarter-century later.

John Biffen, for example, was proud to have voted more often against the European Communities Act 1972 than any other Tory. He even beat his hero, Enoch Powell, on the count. In the style of that era, he maintained a stance of perfect parliamentary civility, which carried on through a career that crested as a member of the Thatcher Cabinet. Biffen's lightness of touch, combined with the remarkable bipartisan regard in which he was always held, made him a kind of licensed sceptic even when belonging to a government which officially embraced the European project. But on this subject, he was granite. He believed in nation as the only entity capable of commanding popular authority. For many years he carried in his wallet a dog-eared sheet on which he had inscribed a quotation to remind him where he stood. It came from de Gaulle's memoirs. 'Now what are the realities of Europe?' the General asked. 'What are the pillars on which it can be built? The truth is that those pillars are the states of Europe ... states each of which, indeed, has its own genius, history and language, its own sorrows, glories and ambitions; but states that are the only entities with the right to give orders and the powers to be obeyed.'[3]

Biffen didn't make many speeches on the subject. Compared with later sceptics, he was as short on didactic ranting as he was on bile. He thought enlargement might be the answer, but underestimated the capacity of the Community to absorb new nations without sacrificing its momentum towards integration. In 1977, he wrote that the accession of Greece, Portugal and Spain, then being discussed, would make the Common Agricultural Policy a dead letter, and monetary union 'well nigh impossible'. He added: 'I am certain the Treaty [of Rome] cannot prescribe the political forms to govern a Europe of Twelve.'[4] None of this having come to pass fifteen years later, the arguments continued and Biffen was part of them. The Twelve had become Fifteen and Brussels was not broken. But it might be. A new generation of Tory MPs arrived in the Commons, equipped with Biffen's firm purpose and their own brand of streetwise ferocity. In 1992, as a back-bench elder statesman, Biffen rejoiced to see himself as teacher and strategist, the old brain behind the young. He once told me that he was now the Fagin of Euro-scepticism.

This school had other ancients who went back to the beginning. One of them was a Scotsman, Teddy Taylor, also present at the creation which he adamantly opposed. Unlike Biffen, Taylor bore all the signs of becoming a single-issue politician, as well as an unlucky one. Having fought the Heath application, he was installed in the Thatcher shadow Cabinet but then lost his seat at the 1979 election. Re-elected, for a seat in the south of England, he was never invited on to the front bench again, largely because he was an anti-European. This stance he took with unshakeable earnestness, though again, like Biffen, he was short on acrimony and capable of self-mockery. 'You see I am terribly obsessed about the European Community,' he told an interviewer, looking back on his life, in 1996. 'This is probably a problem. I am the biggest Euro-bore there ever was.'[5] Though he participated keenly in every anti-European rebellion of the 1990s, unlike most of his friends he didn't need the sting of betrayal to get him going. He knew in 1972 what Europe meant for national independence. He thought entry would be a disaster, and left the Government on account of it. But Heath, he said, also knew what it meant and did not conceal it. Unlike all the modern ultras, Taylor never pleaded deception by the former leader as the reason for an uprising. 'He didn't hide the consequences,' Taylor reflected. 'The tragedy is that few listened.'[6]

So here were two exemplars of a steady trend. There always were Tory politicians who detested British membership of the European Community from start to finish, top to bottom. They were part of the scenery, to whom nobody objected because fundamentally they didn't matter. They were admitted, sustained, even promoted, in polite society. But for many years they also seemed irrelevant, a fringe group of tolerated cranks. What they stood for had, after all, been defeated. Minorities deserved to have their voice, but this one was faced by some inconvenient developments.

The first was the 1975 referendum, in which all the Tory sceptics of the time naturally played a part. The result of the referendum appeared to close the gut argument. Belatedly, the anti-EEC position had been displayed and tested before the people, of whom two-thirds turned out not to be impressed. There remained plenty of negotiating to be done, to defend the British position, but the fundamentalist line was finished: a reading emphatically reinforced by the second development, the election of Margaret Thatcher. Everything about Mrs Thatcher's prime ministership seemed to render the sceptic cause, politically, void of rebel fire. On the one hand, she absorbed it into her own strategies towards Europe, especially over the budget. On the other, by taking Britain into more intimate congress with the Community, she seemed to be confessing that there was no longer any future in root-and-branch hostility. As proof of this, nothing could have been more eloquent than Biffen's own piloting of the Single European Act through a guillotined House of Commons.

When the lady herself was overthrown, this reading seemed to be confirmed. It was surely implausible to suppose that the forces of reason, of power, of acquiescence, of establishment conformity – everything that 'Europe' conventionally represented – could now be displaced. If that were to happen, it would argue for the presence in the Tory soul of a force quite different from the ineffectual fragment of gentlemanly politicians who disclosed themselves twenty years before. This force, if it existed, would have to be outside the realm of the hitherto known: a voracious beast not yet sighted: a spirit still capable of being moved uncontrollably by the visceral impulses most people thought had been put to sleep.

*

WILLIAM CASH was not present in 1972. But he was there in 1990, and still there in 1998. As the personification of the Tory Euro-sceptic spirit in this new, unfettered guise, he became the single most notorious operator, at a time when these people finally came to matter. In his person he does as much as anyone to show how and why, after Mrs Thatcher was deposed, the beast that had failed to defend her was let loose, avenging the years of impotence, on what was now supposed to be a European country.

Cash was born in May 1940 – on the day, as it happens, that Churchill became Prime Minister – child of a father killed in Normandy four years later. Whether this was already a defining moment is hard to say. It cannot have given the Germans a high place in the youthful Cash's hierarchy of esteem: and Germany bulked large in the nightmare visions he later had of Europe. Another feature worth pondering is his Catholicism. Educated by the Jesuits, at Stonyhurst, he might, simplistically, have been expected to gravitate towards the pro-Europe camp. After all, wasn't the Community a Catholic conspiracy, orchestrated from the Vatican, mistrusted on that account by Ernest Bevin and Denis Healey, not to mention, in fragmentary moments, Margaret Thatcher, a notorious incomprehender of Catholicism? It is a feature of modern scepticism, however, that the religious stereotype has been copiously reversed. Maybe this attests to the dwindling power of the Vatican, maybe to the fact that other spectres came to dominate the fear-filled minds of those who dislike everything epitomized by 'Brussels'. Among the more tireless critics of British policy, and even membership, in the 1990s were well-known Roman Catholics such as the editor of the *Daily Telegraph*, Charles Moore, the former editor of *The Times*, William Rees-Mogg, the incontinent columnist Paul Johnson. The Catholic fraternity included converts, both to their new Church and/or to a view of Europe opposite to the one they had held before: suggestive indicator, perhaps, of a cast of mind that entertains flexibility of doctrine, while needing it to coexist with blazing doctrinal certainty at any given moment.

Cash was a Catholic from the start, but not an anti-European. As it happens, I knew him in our youth, when we played cricket together on the fields round Sheffield. He remained a fanatic for the English game, captaining parliamentary teams into later middle age. But more formative was his induction into English history, which he read at Oxford. The appurtenances of history began close to home, with his descent, as he seldom missed an opportunity to recall, from John Bright, the Victorian social reformer. When totally immersed in the anti-Europe cause, he sometimes raised his eyes from the latest statutory excrescence to remind one that he was not, like most of his factional colleagues, a right-winger. In his early days, he was saluted by Shelter, the housing charity, and also recognized as a campaigner for the relief of Third World debt. But the defence of the nation, as a nation, became his cause, and revelling in its history was his pastime. His country home in Staffordshire, he was proud to think, once belonged to the British ambassador to Hanover in the late 1690s.

Cash started professional life as a lawyer: useful avocation for what was to come. Installed first in a family firm of solicitors, he took up the recondite work of a parliamentary agent, assisting businesses and local authorities with the promotion of private bills. At a young age he was a legal adviser to the Confederation of British Industry. Later he got deeply involved with large-scale measures such as paving the way for submarine pipelines and repatriating the Canadian constitution. It was activity that kept him in the purlieus of Westminster, and made him familiar with statutory exegesis: a talent which, in later years, his contemporaries, obliged to watch him deploy his indefatigable capacity for deconstructing European legislation, had as much reason to regret as to admire.

It took Cash some time to reach the heart of Westminster. As a young man, he worked away at the party grass-roots, spent holidays helping older MPs keep their seats. His power-base, if it could be called such, was the Primrose League, an antediluvian Tory sub-group, originally the magnet for the party's recruitment of women, which, according to one reliable history, had 'passed its peak in most areas by 1906'.[7] At least fourteen parliamentary seats declined to make Cash their Tory nominee, before he closed in on Stafford and won a by-election in 1984. He was no worse a candidate for politics than a hundred other Tories. He was pleasant, serious and committed to the public good, if prone to deeper-delving obsessions than his contemporaries. But he came with neither the connections nor the charisma for stardom. Arriving in the House, he seemed destined for an ordinary career of public service that would never make him famous.

Almost immediately, however, he plunged into the Europe question.

Somebody recognized the textual appetites of the budding legislator, and put him on the Select Committee on European Legislation, which has the task of trying to scrutinize the outpourings from Brussels. The job put Cash's Europeanism on the line.

For he regarded himself as a European; and he certainly wasn't a cradle sceptic of Biffenish mien. In the 1975 referendum, he voted Yes, and was then involved in founding something called the Westminster-for-Europe Group. More than that, he prided himself on his Euro-awareness from a legal point of view. Long before Britain signed the Treaty of Rome, he urged his law partners to remember that this would be a superior law, when it came into force. The European Court of Justice would hand down superior judgments. He thought the partners should know this, and prepare for it. Always a fearless letter-writer to the powers-that-be, the young Cash widened the audience for his message. 'I wrote to the President of the Law Society and the Prime Minister to get people to realize that they had to have course studies for the solicitors' exams in European law as an absolute fundamental,' he told me.[8]

While anxious to open other people's eyes, however, it turned out that he had not fully opened his own. Neither the statutory nor the political momentum towards integration, which the Treaty expressed, had apparently crossed his consciousness. He did not believe in momentum, nor in the desire of some Europeans to achieve it. His arrival on the select committee seems, for all his vaunted attention to the subject, to have produced a terrible awakening. 'It was then that I realised what was really going on,' he writes. 'The European Community was in danger of rapidly becoming a political federation.'[9] A visit to Brussels with the committee exposed the fuller dimensions of the nightmare. 'I was disturbed by the number of officials I met from the European Commission whose federalism was beyond doubt.'

Shattering though it was, this *aperçu* did not at first divert Cash from supporting the Government's own Europeanism. No sooner did he arrive in Parliament than the Single European Act reached the agenda for debate and decision. At this stage in the evolution of the 'Europe' question, he played a role that confirmed the innocence of his legal understanding, while simultaneously enraging those with a longer sceptic pedigree than he had. It was where, however, he first established a reputation, the *sine qua non* of 1990s Euro-scepticism, for interminable fascination with the small print behind which one should always assume the likely presence of ministerial subterfuge. He was making his mark as a Euro-bore, even as he rebuked others for mistrusting the Single European Act more than he did.

On second reading, he warmly supported the Act. Though he thought the Community's 'mechanisms' needed careful watching, and cautioned that 'we must be sure we know what we are doing', he pointed to the global competitiveness the single market would bring, and added a reassurance: 'We tend to exaggerate the dangers of majority voting.'[10] On the committee stage, which was dominated by the sceptics, he again affirmed the obvious truth, that majority voting could work to Britain's advantage. He twitted Enoch Powell with the reminder that, in 1972, the sage had prefaced his attacks on British entry with the words: 'I come to speak to you as a European, among Europeans.' Not having been present himself in 1972, Cash felt free to patronize those who had missed the point about what the Treaty of Rome really meant. They had been 'a little disingenuous ... and did not consider the treaty in its full context ... They should not be so surprised to find that these things are happening now,' he solemnly chided.[11] Given his own seeming lacunae of understanding, his listeners could have been excused if they regarded this as faintly insufferable. Whereas Teddy Taylor, Enoch Powell and others voted steadily against the Bill, Cash reliably supported it, even speaking in favour of the guillotine, albeit on condition that time be allowed for some substantive speeches by all those, himself included, who hadn't been allowed to say enough.

On third reading, he did open up some anxieties. The generalized alarm about the looming, spreading, all-consuming monster of Brussels was beginning to express itself. Familiar buzz-words vaporized across the sky. 'It is essential', he said, 'to maintain the democracy of this House and its sovereignty and to ensure that we do know that the legislation done in our name is known to have been done on behalf of the people of this country.'[12] Indeed, he had tabled an amendment asserting, with the kind of grandeur that teeters between the definitive and the meaningless, that 'nothing in this Act shall derogate from the sovereignty of the United Kingdom Parliament'.

But the amendment was ignored, and Cash's vote was unaffected. Essentially, he was a Thatcherite. What Mrs Thatcher believed, he believed as well: that the preambles and codicils about closer union did not mean what they said, and that Britain, in any case, could, under the lady's vigilant leadership, prevent further outrages occurring.

He had, however, now been ineradicably infected with the pleasures and the pains of notoriety as an anti-Brussels, if not wholly anti-Europe, politician. The pleasures, on the whole, were ascendant. The by-line of William Cash began to appear with some regularity, especially in *The Times*. These pieces, in turn, would be alluded to as reinforcements of his speeches in the Commons. He began to travel the continent in search of kindred spirits, journeys from which he would return with extensive lists of names to be dropped and many hours of intimate discussion attested to. A German banker here, a French Gaullist there, seminars in Madrid, weekend conferences in Schloss this or that, all were fluid matter for Bill's torrential, single-issue conversation, the proof that he was not alone in the scepticism he felt about the European project.

An obscure, even mildly comical, politician was on the way to becoming an international celebrity, whose voice counted for something in a government to which he would never belong.

*

THOUGH MRS THATCHER WENT, Cash did not. Nor did any of the others who thought like he did. In the leadership contest, they were defeated by the forces of reason, of fear, of, among other things, 'Europe': the defenestration was opposed by every sentient Euro-sceptic. But then they colluded in the nomination of her successor. John Major, the chosen leader, was supposedly their man. He could not have been elected without them. They had a veto on the alternative possibilities. While the lady's departure seemed to signal the triumph of the Europeans, less remarked was that Major's installation was contingent on the anti-Europeans. This was a party already in subterranean conflict with itself, even as it rallied round a new, more collegiate, more consensual leader. The mainstream establishment had won. But the potential of Euro-scepticism, lurking just below the skin of the staid and stolid centre of the party, was greater than anyone understood in November 1990.

It came in several clusters, which had different roots.

The old guard was still represented. Many veterans of 1972 were dead or departed, and Biffen's impersonation of Fagin awaited the 1992 election, when the new young boys would come aboard. But there remained the hardest of hard-liners, including Teddy Taylor, and a farmer named Richard Body who had pushed the cause for twenty years. Body's opposition embraced any forensic attitude that lay to hand, not excluding a paranoia that qualified him, from way back, to keep company with the younger Euro-phobes. It was Body who in 1975 first sought an audience for the claim that the CIA station chief in London was the hidden hand behind the Yes campaign in the referendum.[13]

A second group, almost as strongly pedigreed, came to full flower during the Thatcher years. Nicholas Budgen, Powell's successor in Wolverhampton from 1974, was a thinking, practising sceptic who joined Taylor and Co. opposing the Single European Act. So did names of past and future obscurity such as Ivan Lawrence and Bill Walker. Edward du Cann, former party chairman and never much of a supporter of what Heath did in the beginning, was of the company.

But the case of the Single Act presented problems which foreshadowed divisions in scepticism that continued, in various forms, to dog it as a source of belief and unified allegiance. Down the years it attracted free traders, on the one hand, protectionists on the other: currency fixers as well as currency floaters: the right and, occasionally, the left: Little Englanders, yet alongside them globalists who regarded Europe as too small a span to work with. On the Single Act itself, an exemplary figure is that of George Gardiner MP. This was a politician so loyal to Mrs Thatcher that he spent the years from 1990 to 1997 conspiring against her successor, and so full of loathing for European union that he finally bolted the party. But in 1986 he was more emphatic than Bill Cash about the need to pass the Act, making, as we have seen, a speech in praise of the economies of scale as the only way by which Europe could challenge America's technological supremacy. Gardiner's attack on national protectionism, and his defence of majority voting to make the market function better, could not have been improved on by Ted Heath himself.[14]

This highlights a third strand of the sceptic phenomenon: numerically, and politically, the most arresting. Bill Cash and George Gardiner were not the only converts. This was a church full to overflowing with apostates of one kind or another, and it was the brutal eviction of Margaret Thatcher that tended to persuade many of them to clarify their new position. Many who had served in her Government, but were not inclined to break with her even after they had left it, came forward with an anti-Europeanism freshly minted. Her departure removed their heroine, in some cases their very reason for supporting Conservatism. Exposing anti-Europe feelings at least as strong as hers was one way of securing revenge for what the other side had done. Not all the scepticism that soon began to swirl round her successor can be attributed to such personal sourness. But what is indisputable is that the parting of Mrs

Thatcher from her job accelerated the parting of many politicians from their support for the official party line on Europe.

The conversions came in many times and shapes. There is a variety of motive and explanation, of fame and obscurity, to be sampled.

The sceptics of the 1990s included some exceptional enthusiasts of the 1970s. An example was John Wilkinson. As Conservative MP for Ruislip Northwood, he joined every group, however disloyal, that strove to make life insupportable for the Major Government on Europe: the most obdurate Old Etonian to be found on that side of the argument. Yet who is this, during the pathfinding debate of October 1971, leaping from his place to harry and hector anyone who dared challenge Heath's great scheme? The same Mr Wilkinson, then MP for Bradford West.

In 1965, a Labour MP named Woodrow Wyatt wrote to *The Times* announcing himself as a European more *pur et dur* than the grand master, Heath himself. This was during the wilderness phase, after the failure of the Macmillan negotiation and before Harold Wilson had begun to think about taking up the cause. Wyatt pleaded for a gesture that would cut through the agonizing, saying: 'We should make the historic and brave decision to sign the Treaty of Rome as it stands.'[15] He held to the pro-Europe line through and beyond the referendum. But, having shifted parties, in conformity with a powerful adoration of Mrs Thatcher, he also reversed his attitude. His experience resembled that of Cash. The enterprise turned out to be not as he imagined. What he had once regarded as 'unattainable pious hopes' now offended him by their apparent substance. The European Court of Justice, a basic lynchpin of the Community idea, now had no acceptable place. 'The court,' Wyatt wrote, 'steeped in continental law, expresses its judgements in terms frequently offensive to our understanding of law.' 'We are as alien to the major players on the mainland as they are to us,' he went on.[16] By the end of 1996, Wyatt was advocating Britain's immediate exit from the European Union.

A similar odyssey was traversed by another convert peer, the historian and scholar Max Beloff. In 1969, Beloff published a book on British foreign policy arguing that Britain's destiny was to assume the leadership of Europe 'which she rejected almost a quarter-century ago'. The logic of the argument that the European nation-state is 'for many purposes obsolescent' was, he wrote, 'unanswerable'. It followed that Britain should 'come out as an advocate of a European federal system'.[17] Yet in 1994 he was telling the Lords that Britain was 'becoming simply a unit in a federal system', and on that account might justifiably be expelled from the Commonwealth of independent nations. It was Gaitskell's old point. Why should the other countries, Beloff argued, 'be prepared to regard as an equal a country which has no more constitutional status than that of, let us say, an American state or a Canadian province?'[18] In 1996, another Beloff book directly contradicted the thesis of thirty years before, contending that the basic differences of outlook between island and mainland, combined with the deception by which successive statesmen had sought to bury them, cast fundamental doubt on the future of the European Union.[19]

There were more vulgar and spectacular shifts. In 1975, Alistair McAlpine, wealthy scion of a construction business, served as an active treasurer of the European League for Economic Co-operation (ELEC), the all-party body that fathered the Yes campaign. By 1997, after several years as chief fund-raiser for Mrs Thatcher's election campaigns, he had moved to the Referendum Party, founded by Sir James Goldsmith as the chief gathering-place for anti-Europeans. For McAlpine, who scorned Major more loftily *de haut en bas* than his own formation, either social or educational, in any way justified, was the extreme case of a convert fired by Thatcherite revenge. He simply adored the lady. Goldsmith himself, though, also did service in 1975, chairing the food sub-committee of the Yes campaign – where, according to one admiring colleague, he was 'extremely creative in finding arguments to justify the CAP'[20] – before turning into the most florid, profligate opponent of 'Europe' in the history of Britain's membership.

Some of the Euro-patterning was, by contrast, subtle. Jonathan Aitken is a case in point. Great-nephew of old Lord Beaverbrook who spoke for Empire in the 1950s and 1960s, Aitken voted Yes in the referendum, but No, as an MP, to the Single Act. The Single Act, he thought, was the beginning of the end for Parliament, where he and Teddy Taylor had spent many a fruitless night dividing the House against Brussels directives that would otherwise have gone through on the nod. On the Treaty of Maastricht, by contrast, he was heterodox in his scepticism. As we shall see, the Treaty became fount and focus of the most violent hostility to Europe that ever managed to assert itself. But to Aitken it was acceptable. By then he was a minister, but told me that, had he been a back-bencher, he would still have supported Maastricht, on the ground that it gave Britain all necessary protections.

So Conservative Euro-scepticism, beginning to erupt even as it saw its heroine depart, had rich and various origins. It was a confederacy of zealots and lurchers, with the latter amply outnumbering, and often outreaching, the former. One might venture some conclusions from their history. Some were moved by disappointment born of failed ambition. They resented their exclusion from office sufficiently to allow an embryonic scepticism, hitherto suppressed, to prepare them for full rebellion. Others were pushed, by personal loyalty to Mrs Thatcher, over an edge they had already spent some time looking across. They hadn't all cast an anti-Europe vote, insofar as one was available, in the leadership election. Biffen, for instance, voted for Douglas Hurd, and Richard Shepherd, whose position sprang from an almost Cromwellian romance with the historic sovereignty of Parliament, supported Heseltine. But, for them both, Euro-scepticism served what they had long known. Others again, Cash-like, thought they now knew what they didn't know before.

Considered as a group, they were cantankerous, mostly humourless, and acquired a single-mindedness sufficient to elude, in a way the British system cannot readily tolerate, party discipline. The lurchers, however late, became zealots.

The two categories shared in common one overriding consideration. They were determined, above all else, not to let themselves or the country be deceived. Deception, they felt, was close to the heart of the story so far. The old believers were never misled. That was the source of their particular pride. They had always known what Europe meant and, knowing it, rejected it. The converts, by contrast, had something to answer for. All these protestations, whether by William Cash or Woodrow Wyatt or Max Beloff or, supremely, Margaret Thatcher, that they never really knew what Europe stood for, cast doubt on their political judgement, and secretly they knew it. They needed to make up for it. An element of the post-Thatcher zealotry, among Thatcherites including the lady herself, was a kind of guilt at the errors of the past: at their complicity in the momentum towards European integration which they imagined was not really happening. For more than a decade, after all, Mrs Thatcher had been running the country while the incremental growth of European common rules and action – community, in another word – was developing under her very eyes, and sometimes under her active hand. For a visceral anti-European, this was a shameful record to have to contemplate.

All conversion events have their ambiguity. There is a gain, for those who experience it, in terms of truth. Here and now, the converts, as they imagined, could at last see Europe plain. This was offset, however, by a certain weakening of credibility. Were such erratic insights really to be trusted? No matter. If the occasion arose again when the European juggernaut could be stopped, it would be met by a resistance that poured repentance for all those errors of the past into one mighty last stand.

*

ALTHOUGH THESE PEOPLE counted for little in November 1990, from April 1992 they counted for everything.

John Major won the general election, but with a majority of only twenty-one. The result consigned him into the hands of politicians who, though they had mostly chosen him to be their leader, spent the next five years tearing his leadership to pieces. The beast was let loose. And an occasion appeared that brought into the open the pent-up rage which the years of surrender to Europe now, in feral eyes, required.

There was nothing sudden or unexpected about this moment. It arose, as ever with Europe, out of the continuities. The Delors committee on economic and monetary union had reported. Mrs Thatcher had uttered her shrieking triple negative against it. But the momentum to implement it, and much else besides, had not been impeded. An inter-governmental conference, necessary to change the Treaty of Rome, was scheduled. It would take, inevitably, a large stride towards a greater Europe, unless it was stopped. And it could not be stopped. Convened for its decisive session in December 1991, in a Dutch town which until then had impinged on the mind of hardly anyone in Europe, the IGC produced the Treaty of Maastricht: a name to live in infamy in the annals of British Euro-scepticism.

The Maastricht Treaty was a watershed. It was, formally, a Treaty on European Union. 'The Union' became an entity in international law, and those who lived within its borders became 'citizens of the Union'. The British, already optional possessors of burgundy-coloured, malleable Euro-passports, replacing the straight-backed navy blue of home, would now be holders of European citizenship whether they liked it or not. Words like the 'coherence', 'solidarity' and 'borders' of 'the territory of the Union' were enshrined in treaty language. The word 'Economic' was dropped from the old designation, European Economic Community: a deeply sinister development. And that was only the beginning. In institutional terms, the Treaty had much to offer, much to threaten. It increased the power of the European Parliament, installing it as a co-decision-maker, in some circumstances, with the Council of Ministers. It extended the reach of a common social policy. It struck out in the direction of 'the eventual framing of a common defence policy'. It provided for more collaboration on foreign policy, and proposed 'a single institutional framework' within which matters of justice and home affairs would also, in due course, be encouraged to fall. Most specifically, it provided for the creation of a European central bank, the non-accountable, non-democratic power-centre that would invigilate 'the irreversible character of the Community's movement to the third stage of Economic and Monetary Union'.

From some of these particulars, Britain secured exemption.[21] She removed herself from the protocol redefining the social chapter that appeared in the Treaty of Rome. She asserted, and it was agreed, that, unlike every other member state except Denmark, she would not automatically take her currency into the monetary union once economic conditions made it eligible for membership. These were serious exemptions, tenaciously negotiated. But they did not prevent the Treaty, if ratified, from existing. They did not alter the character of the Treaty of Maastricht as it was regarded by its architects, particularly President Delors and Chancellor Kohl.

'In Maastricht,' said Helmut Kohl, 'we laid the foundation-stone for the completion of the European Union. The European Union Treaty introduces a new and decisive stage in the process of European union which within a few years will lead to the creation of what the founding fathers of modern Europe dreamed of after the last war: the United States of Europe.'[22]

For British sceptics, that was exactly the problem. Kohl put in a verbal nutshell what they knew 'Europe' now to mean. For some, Maastricht was the confirmation of what they reckoned they had always known but been unable to instil into the convictions of the brethren. For others, it was the final eye-opener. It put indisputable words round the proposition they had hitherto found ways of obscuring: that the Single Act was indeed but a step along the path to something greater. Kohl and the sceptics, in effect, had a meeting of minds. They agreed about the object, while utterly disagreeing about its desirability. Together they left John Major and the Government floundering somewhere in between. The Kohl analysis, endorsed with horror by more British politicians than had ever shown their faces before, gave rise to the climactic battle of the Thatcher–Major era: the bitterest struggle, indeed, of the entire period of British membership of the Community.

Maastricht provoked, first of all, a flowering of the sceptic intellect.

There was a great outpouring of books and tracts. William Cash, now consumed by his life's work, was first into the lists. Characteristically, he got in there ahead of time, with his dense volume *Against a Federal Europe*, which appeared while Maastricht was still in negotiation.

The book revealed the fruits of many journeys to and from the continent, into and beyond the minds of a great variety of Europeans. It was anxious to establish that the author wasn't anti-Europe, only anti-'Europe'. No xenophobe he. And this wasn't a false claim. Nobody who disliked foreigners could have spent as many hours as Cash parading through the ante-chambers of European chancelleries, offering their occupants the burden of his limitless knowledge. On the other hand, Germany kept recurring as an object of suspicion. The more journeys Cash made, the more confident his generalizations became. 'The problem of German national identity has been intractable,' he wrote, 'largely because there is simply no credible political model in German history for the Germans to follow.' 'For long Germany had a political inferiority complex,' he further ventured. 'Germany's failure to achieve political greatness further encourages the view that she has a great future before her,' he cunningly opined. 'As Nietzsche wrote', 'as Fichte addressed the German Nation', as Adenauer implied, as Genscher hinted: the texts came thick and fast, all tending to suggest that Germany was an arrogant menace to the peace, epitomized in the observation that 'her previous bids for power have been made in the name of "Europe."'[23]

Engulfed within the German menace was, in Cash's confident belief, the coming end of British sovereignty. The draft texts of what became Maastricht were already available, and foretold the ascendancy of central banks, the sacrifice of national autonomy to common policies of numerous kinds. This gave rise to ominous reflections. 'One of the most baffling phenomena in the debate about Europe is that Britain seems to be the only country worried about national sovereignty,' the author wrote. He demystified the matter by asserting that no other country was sufficiently interested in parliamentary democracy.

But above all what Cash saw – what nobody, actually, could deny – was the irrevocability of the scheme that was on the verge of enactment. Once created, the new currency was intended to be for ever. The structure supporting it would become a permanent government. There was to be no opening for exit or, quite possibly, refinement. Moreover, the existence of British opt-outs from the social chapter and the single currency would be of modest consequence. They would not stop the Treaty happening. And the Treaty, once written into law, would affect every European Union member, whether or not they signed up to every piece of it. It would be the new norm, the base-line, the objectively existing fact against which every country would be obliged to measure its real independence. What was signed in 1991, and ratified in 1992, would become one more item in the integration of Europe, another stage on this long and stealthy journey, obliging Britain to travel on – or risk exclusion from the engine of the train she had joined twenty years before.

The fact that Maastricht would be irreversible was an electric prod. It finally galvanized British Euro-scepticism to assemble the accoutrements – ferocity, stubbornness, venom, suicidal will – appropriate to a last stand. For Maastricht needed the support of every member state. Britain, along with the others, had power of veto. And if the leadership wouldn't use this veto, which Major hadn't, perhaps Parliament could be made to use it instead, by rejecting the necessary legislation and thereby bringing the entire Community venture to a juddering halt.

Investigations into doubt therefore ranged much wider round the Conservative Party. This was the period of maximum growth, in an output where scepticism elided readily into phobia. By the time the Maastricht Treaty came to dominate politics, no fewer than twenty-seven separate organizations existed in Britain with the sole purpose of contesting this or that aspect of European unification.[24] In the wake of the Treaty, pamphlets flooded from the presses attributing its acceptance by the Government variously to national self-hatred, castles of lies, the road to serfdom or a hundred different varieties of incomprehension as to the consequences of economic and monetary union.

Conservative MPs, not usually counted among the book-writing classes, followed Cash into the literary field, driven by the common perception that what was now at stake was the survival of Britain. In *A Treaty Too Far*, Michael Spicer expressed the bewilderment of a European who had perhaps misled himself.[25] Like many Tories, Spicer's main interest was in free trade. His book rehearsed the patchy history of the implementation of the Single Act, and while he refrained from the callow criticism that the Act had produced far too many Brussels directives – how otherwise could the market be made free and fair than by imposing Europe-wide regulations? – he found that Britain was the only member state genuinely acting out its belief in free markets. The case for 'working from within' was, for Spicer, finished. The evidence proved that Britain's influence was feeble. She was constantly being outflanked by the scheming continentals.

The thinking, though often phobic, didn't always reek of phobia. Phobia is a sort of madness. Like Spicer, a good many adherents to the sceptic cause were now developing a reasoned critique. The Commons debates, over the period, had at times the air of an extended seminar in the higher constitutionalism. Fertilizing the guilt about the past was a scholarly demand for exactness about the future.

'The most extraordinary thing about the United Kingdom is that traditionally expenditure and taxation were decided by the House of Commons,' said Sir Trevor Skeet. 'In future these matters will not be decided here for many of them may be transferred to Europe.' 'Are we prepared to put our signature to a treaty which will erode the power and influence of Members of this House to such an extent that they are incapable of delivering the natural and legitimate aspirations of their constituents?' asked Christopher Gill. 'What have we joined? We have joined a centralized unitary state, and at some stage we shall have to ask the people, "Do you want to go this way, or do you not?"' said Sir Teddy Taylor. James Cran said: 'I am concerned only about the kind of Europe that we will have. I wish to see an evolutionary Europe. Institutions are much better if they are allowed to develop slowly. I take exception to the fact that the people who are deciding matters at inter-governmental conferences want to force the issue of unification far faster than I would wish.' On 20 May 1992, when the Maastricht Bill came for its second reading, these words were as quizzical as they were emphatic. Scepticism seemed a well-merited designation. From the real meaning of subsidiarity to the presumed logic of a common foreign policy, the aspirations of the Treaty were subjected to worried scrutiny.

It was not, however, an academic exercise. It might have been that. In fact, almost everyone expected it would be. These solemn utterances, after all, came a very few weeks after the Government had won its fourth election victory. Governments at that time in the cycle usually get their way. And, at the beginning, Major did get his way. The second reading of the great measure, the European Communities (Amendment) Bill, was won by 336 votes to 92, with Labour officially abstaining and only twenty-two Tories declaring themselves incorrigible sceptics by voting against. That was on 21 May. The next stage, committee, was scheduled for 4 June. The Government planned to whip Maastricht through with all deliberate speed, on the tide of victory, leaving an autumn uncluttered for other legislation. The collective beast of scepticism, sublimely convinced though it was of its own rectitude, did not believe it could roar its destructive way through the whipped acquiescence of conventional political lore and practice.

But then something happened that opened the cage. Ironically, a European country paved the way for attack by Britain's anti-Europeans. On 2 June, even as the Whips were finalizing their plans for disciplined passage, a referendum in Denmark produced a negative result. By 50.7 to 49.3 per cent of the vote, the Danish people refused to endorse the Treaty. If Denmark said No, then the Treaty would become a nullity everywhere else as well. Short of by-passing Denmark – in effect, expelling the Danes from the EC – there was no way the architects of Maastricht could hope to get their creation into place. It was a moment to test the entire apparatus of the Euro-debate, not least in Britain, where the argument was much more sulphuric than anywhere else. The moment revealed the rather different temper of the Cabinet from that of its die-hard opponents in the ranks.

The Government temporized. It promised statements, immediately choosing not to drive home its election victory and carry on regardless but, rather, to fall into the arms of the Euro-sceptics and see what they would accept. The House, ministers conceded, needed to be told what the Danish vote meant. The committee stage should be postponed, pending clarification.

The sceptics, on the other hand, were jubilant. They saw their moment. There is nothing like the possibility of victory to shift dithering souls from one camp to another. The twenty-two dissenters of 21 May grew to sixty-nine, who signed a motion against Maastricht on 3 June. They immediately diagnosed a gap wide open for the total renegotiation of the Treaty, a 'fresh start with the future development of the EEC'. They were tremendously excited. Having shown them a chink of hesitation, Major, with his small majority, was about to surrender himself into their hands. 'It seems irrefutable', said Kenneth Baker, 'that last week tore a gaping hole in the Maastricht Treaty . . . The Danes have given us an opportunity to think again about the next step forward.' Baker, as Home Secretary, had belonged to the Cabinet that negotiated and approved Maastricht. During the election, he was particularly robust in its defence. But Baker had now lost his job. Not for the first time, this experience of loss helped ease the machinery of a flexible mind. The conversions were coming as if by mass baptism. The parliamentary veto now beckoned, Major having so signally failed to do his duty and force the whole of Europe to march in step with the island race.

I had several conversations with Bill Cash around this time. He was a man the Government now took quite seriously. Douglas Hurd, emollient diplomat, had tried to buy him off with a job. These blandishments seemed to produce in him equal amounts of pleasure and contempt. In 1991 there was apparently a parliamentary private secretaryship on offer, which might be traded up in due course for a minister of stateship. But Bill would have none of it. He was also asked by Hurd to contribute draft material to the 1992 manifesto, another gesture that suggested his European opinions were beginning to get a grip, which was far more important to him than office. As the Maastricht negotiation was coming to a head, he seems to have had ready access to the top people. 'I saw John Major the day before he went to Maastricht,' Cash told me. 'He asked to see me. I said, "You must use the veto and you must stop what effectively would be a German Europe, because I think that's the direction in which all this is going." '26 Having neglected to take this advice, Major had to face the full weight of the sceptics' punishment. There is a sense in which they were now controlling, if not quite running, the Government. Certainly it was true that Major could hardly make a move, at home or abroad, without first considering the response it would receive from the likes of William Cash.

The parliamentary history of the European Communities (Amendment) Bill, once its timing had succumbed to the vagaries of the Danish voter, was a drama containing some elements unprecedented in this century. Having put off the committee stage until the autumn, the Government gave scepticism free rein to establish itself at the centre of political debate. At last it moved in from cranks' corner, becoming the main dynamic element to which all other forces had to adjust. It was boosted by a cognate government disaster, the forced removal of sterling from the European Exchange Rate Mechanism in the middle of September.27 No Euro-sceptic could have written a more perfect script to legitimize the contention that 'Europe' was bad for Britain, and the entire project of currency alignment a malign federalist fantasy. The righteousness of scepticism discovered no more potent image than that of the Chancellor of the Exchequer, Norman Lamont, scuttling white-faced from the pavement outside the Treasury after announcing, on 16 September 1992, that British membership of the ERM was over. It set the stage for a process which, while it ended in the passage of the Bill, destroyed the fabled unity of the Conservative Party, perhaps for decades.

The Bill was driven through every imaginable legislative contortion. Each vote had the capability of being lost. The business managers kept being forced to buy off trouble with the promise of future votes, or underpin the critical moments of passage by threatening votes of confidence. They began with a so-called 'paving' debate, promised after the Danish fiasco, which itself was nearly lost. It was carried by 319–313 only after the Prime Minister had been obliged to assure the sceptics – curious testimony to the sovereignty of the British Parliament – that completion of the Bill's passage would be delayed until after the Danes had held a second referendum. So the dance went on. Tactical manoeuvres by the Labour Party ensured, as they often had in history, that the natural Commons majority for Europe which, now thanks to Labour, still existed, might not necessarily express itself. At the last throw, in July 1993, weeks after the formal stages of passage were complete, on another special vote that the Government had been obliged to concede in order to worm out of a byzantine trap set six months earlier, they were actually defeated. At this high moment, twenty-two Conservatives voted for destruction, only to be overturned by a confidence motion the following day.[28]

This performance, lasting from June 1992 until July 1993, provided many field days for Euro-sceptic ultras. Cash was prominent among them. The period was, in a sense, his apotheosis. It was not quite true, as he told me later, that he 'organized the whole thing'. There were several contenders for the title. Factions on the right are no less vulnerable than factions on the left to the old political truism that the more passionately an ideology is preached, the more vicious are the jealousies, and sometimes the disagreements, between those who preach it. The Euro-sceps and the Euro-phobes who flourished under the Major Government had their sub-sections. Cash's relentlessness, and the fame that clung to the tall ungainly figure in the stridently chalk-striped suit, did not enjoy universal approval even among his allies in the division lobbies: perhaps, on occasion, especially among them. Nonetheless, it is a fact that he personally crafted 240 amendments to the three-clause Bill, and that he was proud to have voted forty-seven times, more than any other MP, against the Government when three-line whips were in place. He was the most frequent as well as the most creative exploiter of the parliamentary facilities to hammer home, regardless of what anybody thought, the Tory opposition to the newest, most menacing artefact of European union.

As such, he was part of something wider as well. He belonged within a segment, almost a movement, that was changing the terms on which Tory politics were done. In the political generation that was growing up behind him, Europe was producing a new breed of politician, harsher and more disrespectful than any Tories that had gone before. This is what Europe, among other things, did. Ambitious young MPs would tread modestly during their first few months in the Commons. Cash had done that himself. And nobody could accuse him, in these middle years, of modesty over Europe. But, just as Cash was rougher than Biffen, there were younger men a lot rougher than Cash. Within weeks of arriving in the House, they were strutting about as the saviours of party and country from the European menace.

Running into a group of them in the autumn of 1992, I was given a dose of their aggression. In ascending order of passion, they were against the ERM, against Maastricht and against the party leader. Their deconstruction of the texts produced cries of mirthful triumph, as they discovered yet another sub-clause proving the Treaty's menace to sovereignty, or its irrelevance to Europe, or – a favourite insight – the inherent likelihood of it leading to a new European war. But their real passion was for deconstructing John Major. Six months after he had won them their seats, they wanted him out. The longer the Maastricht crisis could be made to last, they felt, the more satisfactorily it would eat away his authority. Though admitting they would have voted for him had they been MPs in 1990, they now thought him a traitor to the right, who had acquired a European conviction in outrageous defiance of those who put him where he was. They were the first significant cohort of Thatcher's children, as they called themselves, to get into Parliament. There had been a time-lag before this happened, producing a Thatcherized party only after the heroine had gone. But these people had won their rightist spurs at university. They were 'combat-trained', as one of them, Alan Duncan MP, coolly put it to me. They could bide their time before they really took over the party, meanwhile marking the cards of Major's successors with ideological severity. They wanted Major to fail, not least over Europe. And they thought he would.

In the days when Biffen, and then Cash, entered the Commons, such treacherous conversation would have been unthinkable. Issuing from the mouths of tyro parliamentarians, it would have crossed all frontiers of political propriety. But it would also have seemed, in the watches of the night, seriously deluded: a speculation outside the realms of political reality. In the old days, party leaders were far beyond the reach of such underlings. It wouldn't have occurred to a single member of the intake of 1970 or 1979 that they were in a position to conspire against Mr Heath or Mrs Thatcher.

The combination of Europe and John Major, plainly, was different. The potency of the one and the weakness of the other changed the rules of political conduct.

*

THE TREATY OF MAASTRICHT was, however, ratified. There were no backsliders. All twelve member states of the European Union pushed it through. Denmark was smuggled back on board, after securing still wider exemptions than Britain and running a second referendum that produced a majority of 56.8 per cent. France, where a referendum was very nearly lost in 1992, resumed her customary role at the heart of European activities. Germany, perversely, was the last to ratify, after Maastricht had been taken to the Constitutional Court. Britain's final act of passage, in July 1993, was eased by the politics of personal survival. Neither William Cash nor anyone else, save a single abstaining eccentric, was prepared to withhold support from a confidence motion. They were, after all, professional politicians. Their own frailty stared them in the face. No Conservative, whatever his state of combat-readiness, wanted to fight a general election which the party was certain to lose by a landslide. So the governing establishment won. It is a moment to survey the wreckage.

By 1994, Euro-scepticism was a, perhaps the, factor the Conservative leadership had to reckon with. It had become a term of art, as well as a famous force. This was a period, also, when its different designations began to matter: just as there were factions within the faith, there were labels registering different levels of refinement. 'Scepticism', an attractive state of mind implying a quest for objective truth, scarcely seemed to do justice to some of the raging furies that sheltered behind the name. To some observers, therefore, 'phobia', with its staring-eyed connotations, now became a truer designation for certain members of the camp. So the sceps became the phobes, at any rate among Euro-philes who wanted to make a propaganda point. But the philes, in turn, resented such labelling on their own account: philia could sound even more dangerous than phobia. A contest thus established itself for ownership of the most sententious vacuity: 'Euro-realism'. We are the Euro-realists now, every faction claimed. As a convenience, and a courtesy they hardly deserve, I will continue to refer to Cash and his rivals as Euro-sceptics.

By now they had a considerable grip on the parliamentary party.

Around the Major Government's mid-term, some academic research investigated the attitudes behind this.[29] These were pretty extreme. No fewer than 56 per cent of Tory MPs wanted an Act of Parliament passed which would 'establish explicitly the ultimate supremacy of Parliament over EU legislation'. Behind such an apparently righteous clarification lay a radical idea. It meant, quite simply, tearing up the Treaty of Rome. But how many of the respondents understood this, even as elected legislators, may be doubted. Some of the other answers were contradictory, revealing an alarming incomprehension about the most basic elements of Community life. For example, 55 per cent of these MPs thought the European Court of Justice 'a threat to liberty in Britain', but 67 per cent said they wanted the ECJ to have greater powers – to enforce the single market, which already represented much of its active jurisdiction. This seemed very muddled thinking. But there was no mistaking the sway of the sceptics. The sense of the majority was clear enough. They wanted to turn back the tide of integration, with a reduction in qualified majority voting and an attack on the powers of the European Commission. In the ideal world of the average Tory MP, both the Commission and the European Parliament would be put back in boxes that could never be opened except with the approval of national legislatures.

There was no let-up, either, in parliamentary activity. Maastricht's passage merely fuelled the sceptics' capacity for outrage. Buried in the Treaty was a pledge, agreed to by Britain, to increase the annual contribution of member states to the EU budget. This had to get through Parliament as a separate matter. By the time it came up, by-election defeats had whittled the Tory majority down to fourteen, so Major moved once again to make the matter one of confidence – a vote no Tory MP could dodge with impunity. Eight MPs, however, dodged it. Their own opinion that the vote, as framed by the Government, was a constitutional outrage met the response that their abstentions were a disciplinary disgrace for which the only appropriate punishment was withdrawal of the whip. Joined by one other, the 'Whipless Nine' were born: including Taylor and Budgen and Gill and Shepherd and Wilkinson and Body, of the names already mentioned: supplemented by politicians who strained to breaking-point the decorous intellectualism implied in the bearing of a sceptic. Teresa Gorman, MP for Billericay, and Tony Marlow, MP for Northampton North, brought to the Europe argument the complacent, guttural boorishness of the authentic British nationalist. Marlow, indeed, was regarded by some party managers as possessing attitudes so far to the right on these matters that he did not properly belong in the Conservative Party.

Bill Cash refrained from joining this company. He thought Community finance was the wrong issue on which to break with the party, he told me. But not far distant from this stance were the ever present strands of personal rivalry. Politics may usually be thought of as a trade conducted by means of collective action, as party solidarity, but in the taxonomy of Euro-scepticism there were almost as many categories as there were Tory politicians espousing that general allegiance: each of them with a slightly different history, his own studious analysis, a mildly divergent set of obsessions, a discrete tactical appreciation, a more or less grandiose vision of his own contribution. Cash, in a sense, was just such a solitary. He did his own thing, to which he brought the necessary degree of passionate certainty, together with enviable indifference to the effect he sometimes had on others. But he remained within the encampment, to play his part in the irresistible growth of Euro-scepticism that was making its inexorable way, as Biffen once put it, 'like weeds through concrete'.[30]

What, however, was this designed to achieve? What world did it stand for? What was the mind-set that drove it forward?

The sceptic mind, belying its label, was prone to anxieties that were the opposite of cool. Paranoid fear became one part of its stock-in-trade. An image Cash seized on, and often toyed with, was one that Geoffrey Howe had once used when explaining how sovereignty should be seen as fragmented rather than solid. Consider a bundle of sticks, said Howe. That, he recalled, was how he once heard a Cambridge professor talking about the freehold ownership of property: something which could be likened to the possession of a bundle of sticks, each of them deployable as a different form of ownership – lease, partnership, licence and so on. So it was with sovereignty. Like property rights, 'sovereignty may be seen as divisible, and exploitable, in the interests of the nation whose sovereignty it is, and in a thousand different ways and circumstances'.[31]

This might be thought a somewhat recondite metaphor, not best calculated to clear the mind of the ordinary citizen puzzling over political abstractions. It struck Cash as tremendously significant. 'It is difficult not to notice', he wrote, 'that the "bundle of sticks' is reminiscent of the Roman *fasces*, the bundle of rods with a protruding axe-head, carried before Roman consuls as a sign of the state authority of Rome, and adopted by Mussolini as a symbol of the movement he led to power in 1922, whence the word "fascist." '[32]

Cash stops short of calling the EU and its supporters fascists, though clearly the parallel with the *fasces* made a big impression on him. He came back to it – 'sticks wrapped in a silken cord' – when I interviewed him in 1998. To him, the unaccountable authoritarianism of Brussels and all who support it is, at the least, fascistic. The fear of fascism also overhangs the sceptic vision of what could most easily go wrong in Europe if there is any more integration: a disorder not so much of Brussels as within nation-states that can no longer express their independence, especially over economic policy. 'I think we're heading for the possibility of a new fascism on the back of unemployment,' Cash said. This is a more respectable fear than the spectre of European Commissioners parading with their *fasces*. But the word became easily thrown around, tossed lightly into the demagogic pot, sometimes by voices, such as that of the plutocratic James Goldsmith, which themselves seemed to have a closer affinity with fascist tendencies than any Cockfield or Jenkins or Delors.

Reaching further into the murky depths, the Conservative historian Andrew Roberts published a futuristic novel, *The Aachen Memorandum*, built round the heroes of a body called the English Resistance Movement.[33] Their sacred task is to resist the new Nazi Reich which the European Union has re-created. This totalitarian monster features German functionaries embarking on the extinction of old English virtues. They assassinate Baroness Thatcher, punish women who shave their armpits, rename Waterloo Station after Maastricht, force letter-writers to use the postcode. The Movement takes vengeance against them, retrieving the Union Jack from the ignominy depicted on the cover of the book, where it is shown being burned away to reveal yellow stars – ambiguously Jewish or European – beneath. This version of patriotism locates Europe with communism, Jewish finance and black immigration as the enemy of the British, more particularly the English, people.

Roberts's idiom was satire, but his meaning was plain. As an extreme English reactionary, he certainly wasn't satirizing himself. He was exalting the past, over which no shade broods more lushly than the hero of this school of Englishness, Enoch Powell. 'Backward travels our gaze,' Powell once epically intoned, 'and there at last we find them, or seem to find them, in many a village church, beneath the tall tracery of a perpendicular east window and the coffered ceiling of the chantry chapel. From brass and stone, from line and effigy, their eyes look out at us, and we gaze into them, as if we would win some answer from their inscrutable silence. "Tell us what it is that binds us together; show us the clue that leads us through a thousand years; whisper to us the secret of this charmed life of England, that we in our time may know how to hold it fast." [34]

A blunter version of this romantic quest came readily to the minds of a certain class of Tory politician. The Roberts satire was not a joke. During the 1980s Europe induced a more fully developed paranoia concerning the future of the British essence than it had done thirty years before, sometimes coming out *en clair* and directed at the dark forces that now ensured the supremacy of European thinking in the secret cabals of the power elite. Alan Clark, then Minister for Trade, on encountering a Foreign Office official who seeks to enlighten him on some aspect of European Community policy towards Chile ('All crap about Human Rights'), notes in his diary: 'This man is exactly the kind of mole who is working away, eighteen hours a day, to extinguish the British national identity.' [35]

So the supposed defence of Englishness was one impulse of political Euro-scepticism. However honestly the fears were felt about the homogenization of a nation under rule from a distant capital, they did not produce a debate that was either generous or enlightened. Vicious language and poisonous thought abounded in the Tory Party. 'It is a party where one Conservative hostile to the European Community can accuse another in favour of it of being "a Pétainist" adapting himself to the new European order, as one such person did to me only two nights ago,' Lord Thomas of Swynnerton reported to the House of Lords. 'This mood derives not from national pride or even a memory of past greatness but from a new mood of provincial nationalism which is extremely destructive.' [36]

Woven into this feeling – those viscera talking again – was the pain of an inner intellectual conflict. Should sceptics want 'Europe' to work or not? In particular, was the legal order, which the Treaty of Rome created, something that should impose itself on the constantly wayward continentals, who were always wanting to blur its effect, for example, on the enforcement of the single market? Or must it at all costs be stopped from imposing itself on the sovereignty of the British Parliament – even, in the more extreme version, the supremacy of the British courts? It couldn't do both things, couldn't bring French protectionism into line without extending its reach into the regulation of the British fishing industry. British sceptics forced themselves into painful contortions to have it both ways.

Plainly there had to be a European Court of Justice. Its role was fundamental to the functioning of the Community from the start. It also had to apply its jurisdiction equally between the members. That was the whole point of the enterprise. This did not impede the onset of ever more insistent appeals for British exceptionalism. Aware that the ECJ could not be abolished, some sceptics began to work up arguments for special opt-outs. One of them introduced a Bill, for example, 'to provide by Order in Council for the disapplication within the United Kingdom of judgments, rules and doctrines propounded by the European Court'.[37] Introducing it, Iain Duncan Smith sought to undermine the strictly legal basis of the ECJ. It was, he said, 'a political court'. It had 'huge licence to make legislation that national governments must obey.' Parliament, therefore, must reclaim its sovereignty, review the judgements 'and, where necessary, seek to change them politically'. It must, in other words, amend the British Act of 1972, from which all this had sprung.

The measure got nowhere. But it was a *cri de coeur* against what have unquestionably been the integrationist tendencies of the Court. The ECJ paid attention to the preambles and codicils, as well as the formal texts, of the treaties. It developed into a constitutional court, gradually establishing, as one scholar put it, 'an overarching legal order which is greater than the continuing consensus which originally created it'.[38] The effect has been 'the creation of a European federal legal system to which the legal orders of the member states of the Community are subordinated'. Although implicit in the Union enterprise, and discernible as happening many years before Britain became a member, this can rightly be called a political evolution. It discomfited and enraged a growing segment of the Tory Party, including members of the Government. The Home Secretary of the period, Michael Howard, while part of an administration that often invoked ECJ jurisdiction, became spokesman for radical proposals to escape what the British didn't like about it. 'Some countries', Howard said in 1996, 'may wish to withdraw from elements of the treaties.' 'This may indeed mean', he went on, 'that some states would be able to repatriate powers which are currently exercised in Brussels.'[39] Repatriation, a vogue word for the old Tory right when Enoch Powell was inflaming the populace with his responses to immigration, was reborn as their magic solution to the problem of a court they couldn't escape but had come to detest.

The apostate Lord Beloff put it more graphically. Laws made in Brussels and adjudicated by the ECJ were 'a challenge to Britain's sense of identity'. Most of the British, he went on, 'have an idea, however vague, of the benefits they derive from the common law and of its superiority to continental codes'. The continentals were natural law-breakers, 'prepared to vote for anything at Brussels in the confident knowledge that they will only enforce what suits them'.[40] So spoke the Oxford scholar, striking a chord that rang sweetly, though without avail, through the noisy forums where sceptics assured each other of the terrible fate that had befallen Britain.

Their inner conflict went further. United by the infamies of Brussels, they were still a mass of disagreements within and between themselves. Majority voting posed such a quandary. A Euro-sceptic who wanted to minimize the role of Brussels on the matter of funds for the Common Agricultural Policy could only favour any system that reduced the power of small countries to block reform. Extension of the dreaded QMV could, in some fields, enhance the power of large member states like their own. But, as a totem looming over national sovereignty, it had to be regarded, at some higher level of principle, as a menace. In short, the Euro-scepticism of a fully paid-up EU member could not readily accommodate the contradiction such a stance entailed. For a people that was inside the Union, the quest for solutions, to satisfy the ever more passionate anxieties of a class of politician that could not abide what was happening, was destined to be frustrating.

At the peak of these frustrations was the climactic problem. What could the sceptic mind offer as an alternative to British membership of the European Union? This intellectual instrument, a mélange of logic and rage, became well practised in arguing the case against the EU. William Cash had his own litany, much recited. The EU was bureaucratic and centralized. It would not take seriously the Maastricht promise of more 'subsidiarity' – power to the members. It was moving outside political control. It wasn't doing enough to make the single market real. It was spreading its tentacles, largely through the Court, into areas it should never touch. It had ambitions, sometimes open, sometimes secret, for wholesale political union. It was the heart of an emerging super-state. It was run by majority rule, which might leave Britain on the thin end of an argument. Even where unanimity was required, the EU had its own momentum. It couldn't be stopped without a massive, perhaps destructive, effort. All these features rendered it an unlovely, sometimes highly dangerous, menace to the British way of life and government. Above all, perhaps, it was not British. As the years passed, a critique developed which asserted that the differences between island and mainland were written into history: were unalterable: were, sadly, part of the ineluctable order of things. There is, wrote Michael Spicer, 'a fundamental difference in the philosophy which lies behind the British constitution and those of her continental partners'.[41] The one, he added, wasn't necessarily 'better' than the other. Just different, as it always had been – something everybody ought to have realized long ago.

So what should be the response to this? One approach, the Government's, was to develop the concept of 'variable geometry': different members moving at different speeds, with different opt-outs and the like. The images acquired their own surrounding theology. Variable geometry, implying some kind of structural measurement, did not stand up to rigorous examination. 'Multi-speed', on the other hand, got close to implying a multi-divisional Europe, which was obviously dangerous ground. Nor did 'concentric circles' do the trick for everyone.

The harder sceptic was not in favour of any of this. Cash was especially emphatic in his denunciations. 'A two-tier or two-speed Europe *is a most unattractive idea* [italics in the original],' he wrote in the manifesto advice Hurd asked him to prepare for 1992. 'We would be marginalised, lose authority and involvement, and would not catch up.' The concentric circles were even worse, implying France and Germany at the centre, and Britain on the fringe, of an organization to which she would nevertheless have to subordinate large swathes of her legal independence. 'This is a lego-political power-play,' Cash obscurely sniffed.[42] He was especially horrified by a suggestion that once came out of Helmut Kohl's office, proposing 'observer status' for any member state unwilling to join a full United States of Europe.[43] This smacked of relegation, perhaps along with the Baltic states and other fringe supplicants, into some kind of 'Association of European States'. Cash smelt a federalist rat of peculiar pungency. 'How *communautaire* is it for Britain to face the threat of being forced out if she does not comply unquestioningly with proposals to which we have never agreed?' he asked.

So Cash, at this stage, seemed to favour staying in the EU at its very centre. The proper solution would have been to veto Maastricht outright, making it impossible for the EU to proceed as the majority of its members wished. But short of that, it seems, the Cash position saw variable geometry as a trick. Yet this surely contradicted another strand of sceptic thinking: the proposition that Britain should renegotiate her terms of membership. In the 1990s, the idea of a merely trading partnership began to acquire friends in the Tory Party. It seemed the perfect way to secure the economic benefits of EU membership without making the political sacrifices, as Tories saw them, presently required. Michael Spicer was representative of this opinion. He had ambitions to see the whole EU revert to 'an association of freely trading and co-operating independent states', but, failing that, he thought Britain should go it alone. Those European countries outside the EU, he believed, had done better economically than EU members. Mimicking their position had no dangers, he thought. Trade would continue as before, since this would be in the EU's interest. The 'fresh start' a lot of Tories signed up for saw 'a place for Britain in a loose European commonwealth'. She would have her own currency and her own market liberalism, thereby rejecting, among other things, 'the specious fear of isolation'.[44]

Seductive though this sounded, it took incomplete account of the evidence. True enough, Sweden, Finland and Austria, outside the Community in 1990, had a higher per-capita income than either Germany or Britain. Each, however, was seeking to get in, and later did so. Rich though they were, they judged exclusion from the EU, despite the burdens of membership, to be imprudent for their countries. This seemed to turn part of Spicer's case against him. He did not explain, moreover, how the sweetheart deal he envisaged for Britain – all the benefits, none of the burdens – would be consummated with a Union that might not look kindly on a partner who lived by different rules of market conduct, and was seeking to retreat from full membership precisely in order to secure advantage on the notorious unlevelled playing-field.

Among honest sceptics, in short, there was a lot of thrashing about. They knew there was a problem. They didn't hesitate to join the more phobic elements by seizing every opportunity to intensify anti-Europe feeling. Without a blush they could expostulate against Beethoven's 'Ode to Joy', chosen as the theme tune for Euro 96. How could German music be allowed to infiltrate the European Football Championship England was hosting? They couldn't modify feelings that were intestinal in origin. In fact, these became steadily more powerful. Yet the logic of the alternative caused them problems every time they confronted it – mainly because of their reluctance to embrace the true logic of their guts, if not always their minds, which was for Britain to leave the European Union.

It took some time for such a dramatic option, full exit, to begin to emerge, even as a rhetorical possibility. Even the less rarefied sceptics were aware it might not be popular. Quite apart from their own intellectual problem, there was the political question, which exposed another of their awkward contradictions. Much of their case rested on the contention that the EU was deeply unpopular: that the people were being led by a smooth, deceiving political class: that another referendum on Europe would turn the tables. Yet they also weren't sure enough of that to make an open case for a new arrangement which faced the people with the awesome possibility of actually disengaging from 'Europe'.

The first time this happened, it caused a bigger row in the Euro-sceptic camp than in the world outside. The first serious politician to try it on was Norman Lamont, the former Chancellor of the Exchequer, a prime negotiator of the Maastricht Treaty, on whom, however, the experience seems to have left an indelible loathing of the Union. It was the Cash and Thatcher case all over again: the self-hatred, among other things, of the politician who had once voted for 'Europe' but now had his eyes opened. At Maastricht, Lamont suddenly discovered what he was dealing with. He had been a minister for twelve years, many of them spent negotiating in European councils, but evidently hadn't understood what was really going on. 'For the first time in my life,' he told me, 'I really came face to face with people who in private would say to me "There will be a United States of Europe and I want to see it."'[45]

Lamont began to ventilate the case for exit at the Conservative Party conference in 1994. 'I do not suggest that Britain should today unilaterally withdraw from Europe,' he said. 'But the issue may well return to the agenda.'[46] Britain was 'on a collision course' with her partners. She was frustrating their plans, and they were understandably annoyed. She couldn't simply veto new political developments. Far preferable would be to negotiate 'outer tier community membership . . . which involved only the free trade parts of the Treaty of Rome'. This wouldn't be a 'two-speed Europe'. It would simply recognize that Europe was moving in 'two completely different directions'.

This was a somewhat fumbling approach to exit. It still pretended to have things both ways, wanting all the trade benefits and none of the political consequences. But it opened up the real argument. It began to face anyone prepared to listen both with the extremity of one Conservative opinion and with the adjustment that serious scepticism, applied to the real world of running Britain, would involve.

*

It did not, however, please William Cash. Only part of this displeasure arose from the challenge Lamont's thesis presented to the notion, espoused by Cash and many others, that to favour two speeds, outer circles and all that stuff was to cave in to the Eurocracy. Lamont's 'exit' headlines irritated not Cash the thinker but Cash the impresario. His school of scepticism had taken a new turn, and recruited a tigerish force with the capacity to propel the cause far beyond the picayune world of Parliament. In Parliament, after all, it had failed. Maastricht was law. A national movement was now required, and Cash, with some important assistance, placed himself at the head of it.

The same day Lamont made his speech, a new body, named the European Foundation, held a rally in a Bournemouth hotel, where the room was packed with the sweating bodies of Conservative Party activists in town for the conference. It wasn't the first such meeting, but it was the most exultant, and it introduced fully frontal into the political arena the most imposing grotesque to enter the modern Euro-debate, Sir James Goldsmith. Cash, the Foundation's founder and only chairman, led up to the Bournemouth stage Jimmy Goldsmith, its biggest patron, a man of gigantic wealth who had the quixotic idea of using some of it to promote the anti-EU cause in Britain.

Goldsmith was, in a special sense, a European, having a mother who was French and a life-style that bridged the Channel as well as the Atlantic. A formidable private accumulator, he had hankerings to be a public man somewhere in the regions of politics. In the 1970s, he tried to force his way in by starting a glossy British news magazine, which failed. From time to time, he would be heard from on trade matters, where he had become an articulate protectionist, railing against the damage done by global corporations, not dissimilar from his own, to the life of Third World countries in particular. Then, earlier in 1994, he entered politics proper, by founding, with others, a political movement in France that went by the name of L'Autre Europe. Europe, he thought, was, while protectionist within its borders, another iniquitous agent of the evils of globalization. It was also bureaucratic, and distant from democracy: the creation and feeding-ground of what he called, in conversations I had with him, 'the political caste . . . the elite that begins to think it owns what it runs, which can be a nation-state or a local community, the Mafia or Europe'.[47] This was the breed that Goldsmith most detested, and from which he saw his own entry into politics as offering some kind of rescue.

It will be seen immediately that he was far from the model of a Conservative Euro-sceptic. Apart from his grand manner and bottomless pocket, his ideas about trade were anathema to most Tories. But this they put on one side. Under the banner of his new party, Goldsmith got elected as a French Member of the European Parliament in summer 1994, prepared to take his scorn for the entire EU project to Strasbourg

– though in the event, as was true of many MEPs elected on party lists in France and elsewhere, his attendance in the Parliament was seldom recorded. In his other home, England, he set about creating a movement which, under guise of neutrally pressing for a referendum on British membership, mobilized phobo-sceptic opinion wherever it came from.

Another way Goldsmith was different was that, in his way, he was an intellectual. Having made his pile, he went into retreat to improve his mind, journeying privately round the globe to conduct ground-level investigation of the case for protection. He published books – *The Trap, The Response* – that spelled out with statistical support the dire state of the world resulting from the mismanagement of everything from education to nuclear power.[48] The books reached far beyond the question of Europe. But their alignment was sensitive to the author's different European constituencies.

The French edition of the first, *Le Piège*, argued for a strong Europe, which could 'protect its economy against America and Japan as well as developing countries'. Brussels, said Jimmy (he was James only in Britain), must have 'central powers' to control diplomacy and defence, the latter 'consisting of exclusively European forces'. How this sat with his general loathing for 'Brussels' was never fully explained. He even argued, in the French version, for a European central bank, to prevent 'competitive devaluations'. But none of these prescriptions appeared in *The Trap*. There he called the European Parliament 'either a waste of time or downright destructive', words that don't appear in the French text.[49] To the French he was as pro-Europe as, to the British, he was anti, offering the indignant excuse, when pressed about these apparent contradictions, that they were differences brought about by 'the evolution of my ideas' (*Le Piège* appeared in Paris a year before, in 1993) or mistranslation. To the innocent observer, it may have seemed only that he had taken to characteristic extremes a trait of the profession he most despised. He had become, with tycoonish contempt for subtlety, a politician.

It was as a politician that he agreed to meet me. He said he was used to complicated contracts, but had seen nothing like the Maastricht Treaty. 'I've spent three years studying the Treaty and the protocols, the way it works, how the institutions work,' he told me. 'I've done practically nothing else. Twelve hours a day.'[50]

By this time, rivalling Cash as the world's greatest living expert on Maastricht, he had moved on from the European Foundation to full-blown campaigning activity as leader of his own party, the Referendum

Party, which was getting ready to run a candidate in every seat in the 1997 election. The only exceptions would be places where the sitting MPs, through conviction or terror, were persuaded to come out for a referendum on their own account. Otherwise, £20 million of the Goldsmith fortune would be available for the great assault, the best-breeched single-issue campaign in the history of British democracy. 'I've had tens upon tens of Tory MPs coming here to plead with me not to run against them,' the grinning autocrat told me in his Belgravia drawing-room. There had been some attempt to negotiate at a higher level as well, with Prime Minister Major engaging in more than one conversation, in which the vague promise of a referendum was dangled in front of Goldsmith in the hope that he might withdraw.[51] This showed as much naïvety about his pliability as about his calculated interest in what he might actually achieve. He assured me that even if he secured only a single vote, his own, the Party would have been worthwhile. 'I do what I must do,' he said. To an important extent, the whole campaign was a self-indulgent ego-trip, not susceptible to conventional inducements from the governing class.

'I vomit on the Government,' Goldsmith said to me more than once, sitting in his private booth in Wilton's Restaurant, readying himself for action. Such was the unsettling force under whose generous sway quite a number of Tory Euro-sceptics, in both the Commons and the Lords, were happy to place themselves in the post-Maastricht period.

But, all in all, Goldsmith was an embarrassment rather than a credit to the cause. For one thing, his £20 million got it nowhere. When the election took place, the Referendum Party, fighting nearly 550 seats, got an average of 3.1 per cent of the vote. This was better than any minor party had ever done before; it was also consistently better – as it should have been – than the other anti-Europe entity, the shoestring UK Independence Party. Goldsmith had some influence. Arguably his mere presence deepened the split in the Tory Party, by increasing the number of Tory candidates who felt obliged to trumpet their sceptic tendencies as a way of trying to see him off. But the number of seats his party's presence swung was minuscule, if indeed they existed at all. The most learned scrutiny concluded, after poring over a complicated matrix of hypotheses, that there might have been four Tory seats lost because of the Referendum Party's intervention, offset by three that were probably held for the same reason. 'Insofar as the objective of Sir James Goldsmith's campaign was to inflict losses on the Conservatives,' the scholars write, 'it must largely be deemed to have been a failure.'[52]

More problematic still was what he left behind for the politicians, not least William Cash. When Goldsmith got his party going in 1996, as a rival to the Conservatives, the Foundation had hurriedly to regroup. Cash, about to fight the election in the Tory interest, couldn't go on getting money from a political opponent. He was always coy about how much Goldsmith gave, and more emphatically reticent about the donor who stepped in briskly to replace him: Baroness Thatcher. 'Who is the lunatic who advises her on these things?' asked one back-bench Tory, faced with his former leader funding an operation diametrically opposed to the official party line.[53] She was certainly warm to Bill.

He continued, inexhaustibly, to perform, unimpressed by the status of his opponents. Germany still bulked large in his forebodings. When Chancellor Kohl dared to suggest that Europe, without a political union of the EU, might slide into war, Cash and a colleague composed an entire pamphlet in rebuttal.[54] 'We have no desire to return to the nation-state of old,' Kohl said. 'It cannot solve the great problems of the twenty-first century. Nationalism has brought great suffering to our continent.'[55] Cash, echoing a lot of sceptics, rejected this inconvenient recollection of why the European Community had been started in the first place. He could see why Kohl was bothered. 'Germany has in the past found it difficult to reconcile nation-statehood and democracy,' he sneered. But for other countries, like Britain, it was different. She had no problem with democracy, nor the slightest need to fear a war – unless it came about through the forced unification of Europe under German domination.

Nor was Cash's zeal diminished when his faction had lost their power over government. The old language continued, even though delivered into the political void represented by the benches opposite: the massed ranks of Labour politicians with a majority of 179, who could afford to relocate him where he began – as a bit of a joke. This didn't deter him in the slightest. By now he could call on some of the appurtenances of a budding elder statesman in the cause, remarking to the tyros that he was in his fourteenth consecutive year as a member of the Select Committee on European Legislation, of which commodity, he warned them, there was 'masses in the pipeline' that would be 'a fraud . . . on the people of this country'. When the next post-Maastricht event, the Treaty of Amsterdam, was debated in December 1997, his fulminations were divided between 'the ideology of the European Coal and Steel Community, which stinks', and all the measures on which the new Government was embarked, which 'are inviting the chaos, the disorder and the implosion of the European Community'.[56]

This was an article of faith. Having failed to stop the momentum of the Union, sceptics were resigned to sitting back and waiting for the end. They had made the most of their period of potency, avenging the past, including, in many cases, their own past. But it hadn't been enough. Faced by a new government which aspired without ambiguity to be pro-European, they got most of their kicks by looking back: towards the ministers whose own weakness had made them, for five years, strong – and whose influence they wanted finally to extirpate from the modern Conservative Party.

11

JOHN MAJOR

At the Heart of Darkness

IT IS THE FATE of modern British governments, however sceptic they are in theory, to be in practice 'European'. The facts of life are European. Europe shapes the everyday reality with which all public people have to grapple. What Lord Denning said of law – 'the Treaty is like an incoming tide. It flows into the estuaries and up the rivers. It cannot be held back' – could be said as graphically of governance. The existence of the European Union is a condition infusing the bloodstream of every British official and politician. But it reaches deepest into the life of ministers especially. Where others protest and complain, ministers act. Others lament, but ministers carry on. They are not only the governing class of Britain, they belong to the governing class of Europe: knowing each other, haggling together, cutting deals, a kind of masonic fraternity, assisting daily in the onward passage of a project they regard, however much they may sometimes dislike it, as a given. No member of the Union can operate in its own national interest without a leader who understands the meaning of this axiom.

One person who understood it, for most of her time, was Margaret Thatcher. She fought the Union, but lived under it and did much to advance its integration. When the Conservative Party came to choose her successor, it never occurred to anyone to seek a leader who rejected it. No such candidate existed. In fact, there was barely an MP – certainly not Bill Cash – who subscribed to any other idea than continuing acceptance of this norm of British life. We are all Europeans now, they could still credibly declare in 1990.

There was a range of options when the choice arose, within which, admittedly, the European credential of the available leaders was an element to be considered. Two of the candidates were prominently European. Douglas Hurd had worked with Ted Heath, and was tarred as a Foreign Office alumnus from the beginning of his career. He was thus assumed to be, among other things, a Europe man, which, by and large, he was – though he usually spoke with a more guarded sense of distance than, for example, Geoffrey Howe. Michael Heseltine was more fiercely of the faith, having written a book-length panegyric to Britain's coming 'victory' on the continent, and having placed the issue in the vanguard of his argument against Mrs Thatcher. If the party had chosen either of them, it would have announced that it was opting with enthusiasm for Europe simply by the fact of rejecting the third candidate, who seemed perfectly to exemplify what it thought it needed: nothing more nor less than constructive agnosticism. Both parts of that label mattered equally. There had to be a lack of zeal, which was a matter of character. But there should also be an intention to build rather than destroy, which was a matter of politics.

John Major was made leader for other reasons than his ideas about Europe, but his general political character, which is what got him the job, imparted itself to that question as well as all others. Where Mrs Thatcher was strident, he was emollient. Where she burned with conviction, he could see all sides of the argument. Where she tore the party apart, he was elected to keep it together. Where she became the enemy of 'Europe', he pronounced himself its friend, and was chosen for the very reason that, by style as much as content, he would enable hostilities to cease. Though approved by the allies of the departed leader, he was picked as someone who would not give full voice to their prejudices.

He was, in other words, a simple party man. He actually liked the Conservative Party. Long before he became its leader, it was by far the most important influence in his life. Keeping it one and whole was to be the defining task of his leadership. When he had retired from the front line, after Cash and his friends had brought this task close to the most ruinous failure, Major said to me, musing socially, by way of explanation of all he had done: 'I love my party. That was the point. She never loved the party. That was the difference.'[1]

Major's origins supplied no formative twist to his ideas about Europe. He neither fought the Germans, nor heard the Luftwaffe overhead, nor lived with the oppressive knowledge that his father had been killed in action. In his roots, there was nothing to indicate that he could aspire to be a public man, let alone dream of the heroic course his life might take.

He was born in 1943, in a forgettable patch of suburbia on the southern edge of London. For many years the only exoticism in his life was supplied by his father, a circus artiste, later the owner-operator of a business manufacturing garden gnomes. The family was chronically short of money, and its youngest child short of sufficient ambition to keep him at school past the age of sixteen. In adolescent years, therefore, he was constructing no intellectual hinterland, historical or otherwise. When his contemporaries were preparing to go to Oxford or, as mostly happened for his generation of Conservatives, Cambridge, he was looking for clerical work, or helping his father and brother with the gnomes. Ambitious young Tory swells of the period began to strike attitudes round the Macmillan application and the de Gaulle veto. For someone coming of age in the early 1960s, it was the issue of the moment, which might mark the definitive end of a politics still trapped in the penumbra of the Second World War. University Conservatism billowed with earnest argument about the Common Market, and its superiority, for a modern-minded person, over the Commonwealth. On the streets of Brixton, where the young Major lived, such matters were barely heard of.

The boy did, however, discover politics. After school, his further education was supplied by the Young Conservatives. With their help, he ceased to be a rather lonely social reject. His frontiers stretched out from Brixton to the alluring seaside resorts where the Conservative Party held its annual conference. The party, he later said, brought him alive. Quite soon, he became a political junkie, hooked on street politics, tramping the far corners of the local borough in search of a seat on the council, advancing a career that reached an interim apotheosis as chairman of the Lambeth housing committee. It was the prelude to fulfilling the ambition he formed quite early in his startling shift from drop-out to mainline politician: to enter the House of Commons.

This was an intensely local beginning. Major reached Parliament, in May 1979, without having been obliged to express, possibly even to hold, an opinion on any international question. He was apparently present as a Yes voter in the 1975 referendum on Europe, but at the time of the debates on entry, in 1972, he wasn't heard from. His tireless official biographer could find nobody with a recollection of him having taken a position.[2] Whereas for many future Conservative politicians, the Heath event, the successful entry, was a defining moment, which shaped their very commitment to modern Conservatism, the future leader was not engaged.

He may even have been something of a closet sceptic. While persistent deviation from the party line would have been out of character, he did give one indication of less than reverential loyalty to the European

Idea. Six months after getting into Parliament, he signed a letter to *The Times* which addressed itself to the Community budget negotiations Mrs Thatcher was then furiously embarked on. This called for fundamental reform of the Common Agricultural Policy, as the necessary basis for 'new and permanent financial arrangements'. Such thoughts were commonplace; all Tories agreed that we should get 'our money' back. But the letter concluded on a note of sulphuric menace that was not often heard at the time. 'Unless we can jointly work out the radical changes needed and put them speedily into effect,' it said, 'the case for Britain staying inside [the EEC] becomes increasingly difficult to sustain.'[3] Appearing in November 1979, this was a lonely sentiment to be heard from anyone outside the ultra-phobic bunker. Since one of Major's cosignatories was Tony Marlow MP, a lifelong and unregenerate anti-European, it is fair to assume that the climactic recommendation was seriously intended.

For Major, however, it represented only a brief squirt of rebellion against conventional wisdom. He had put his name to something no other ambitious mainstream Tory would have dreamed of uttering. But then he disappeared into the silence of junior office, first as a whip and then in the necessarily parochial enclave of social security administration. These were the days of the final European budget negotiation – the 'new and permanent arrangement' – and then of the Single Act, neither of which required a junior member of the Government to take any other position than the acquiescence that was now, on all subjects, Major's natural demeanour. He was making his reputation as an efficient minister and amenable Thatcherite, on whose relatively inexperienced head the lady's eyes were coming to be trained with serious admiration. She was ever watchful for allies who might become protégés, younger politicians to earn admission to the rank of One of Us. Many, after early promotion, failed to satisfy her expectations. A Cabinet in which the most senior posts continued to be held by men she successfully made into her enemies was in need of loyalist replenishment, and Major fitted the description. He duly received preferment, on an unusually fast track from the back-benches. As Chief Secretary to the Treasury, which he became in 1987, he conducted himself with punctilio and charm, winning more friends than enemies among the spending ministers whose ambitions it was his job to curb. When larger posts fell vacant, owing to the furies let loose around the work of, first, Geoffrey Howe, and then Nigel Lawson, the same capable, deferential replacement was standing quietly by, eager to accept the extravagant patronage of his leader.

The first of these promotions took him wholly by surprise, and required him, among other things, to make his first serious excursion into the 'Europe' question. Until then, he had still managed to remain outside it, even as a Cabinet minister. The Thatcher–Howe and Thatcher–Lawson imbroglios largely passed him by, though he was in Lawson's ministry. Faction, at that point, had not established itself as the organizing mechanism of the Conservative debate on Europe. But, suddenly, Major became Foreign Secretary, a task for which his background in no way prepared him. He was the minister for Europe, without a record of experience to draw on even from ministerial visits to the plethora of European Councils, since his particular jobs had seldom required them.

He was an *ingénu* and he knew it. When he got the news, he told Douglas Hurd how impossible he thought the job would be. 'He was rocked right back on his heels,' Hurd told me. 'He was very unhappy.' Elsewhere Hurd has recorded the reason for this. Major had said to him: 'There's a world full of 150 countries, always exploding into bits and pieces, there are boxes full of stuff about places I have never heard of. And I am expected to take decisions about that!'[4] It is true enough that, in the later twentieth century, it is no longer the ambition or aptitude of every rising Tory to follow in the footsteps of Curzon, redrawing the map of the world. But, even in his own time and place, the Foreign Secretary Mrs Thatcher chose to appoint in July 1989 was uniquely under-qualified for the work.

As it happened, Europe was not the place that felt the consequences of this disability. Major occupied the post for barely ninety days, July to October, for part of which the continent was on holiday. Other matters – Cambodia, Hong Kong, a Commonwealth conference – pressed unavoidably in. It was also as Foreign Secretary that Major made the first trip of his life to the United States. The global rather than the regional was what arrived on his desk in this short span.

He was not, however, silent on the Europe question. And since the politics of the matter had been given a new dimension by Mrs Thatcher's speech at Bruges in September 1988, it was beginning to become impossible for any ministerial utterance to be taken at face value. In this period of endless textual deconstruction, the Bruges speech set a benchmark, with its assault on the socialism emanating from Brussels and its aggressive defence of the nation-state. The nightmare of the super-state, in particular, was born. Any speech that failed to amplify it was capable of being seen as subversive.

Yet the Bruges philosophy was not one with which the new Foreign Secretary was instinctively imbued. Though expressed by the Prime Minister, it remained more a defiant challenge than an agreed definition. Least of all was it well regarded in the department which this unformed man, this unlettered internationalist, had been put in charge of. If there was a teacher and a student in their bureaucratic relationship, the leader and the led, departmental orthodoxy inevitably began by having the upper hand. Naturally, therefore, what Major said about Europe reflected the wisdom Mrs Thatcher had not yet succeeded in rendering unconventional. Delivering the annual British *tour d'horizon* at the UN General Assembly, a year after Bruges, he spoke of the need for a 'stronger, more united Western Europe', and asserted that 'our active membership of the Community is a fixed point in our future'. In normal times, these would have been trite banalities. In 1989, they were seen by the Thatcher circle as signs of the new man's susceptibility to the Foreign Office, an impression not diminished when they were repeated in the Foreign Secretary's speech that year to the Conservative Party conference.[5]

Yet to have said anything else would have been, for the ministerial Major, an offence against his nature. Even at this early stage in his prominence, he behaved like a man whose task was not to amplify the more abrasive messages of his leader, but the reverse. He wasn't an anti-Thatcherite. Though Mrs Thatcher was his patron, and the definer of his core ideas about economic policy, he wasn't burdened with her extreme convictions, and positively disapproved of the disunity these brought with them. Over Europe, he was already seeking to dissolve differences and heal wounds.

Such was to be his mission as leader too: a period that could later be regarded as a six-year exercise, painfully unsuccessful, in trying to persuade the Conservative Party there was a middle way between the anti-Europe passions of its most vocal minority of politicians and the pro-Europe necessities that came with the task of government.

Undefiled by awkward prejudices of his own, Major naturally clothed himself in the orthodoxy that was the pragmatic wisdom of the moment. As Foreign Secretary, this led him to the extraordinary insight that British membership of the Community had its merits. In his next post, however, it required something a little more daring: a posture and a choice, in fact, that turned out to touch his life for many years ahead.

It was at the Treasury, not the Foreign Office, that the 'Europe' question drove into the heart of Major's political life. Once again, he arrived at a new department in the wake of the personal turbulence which Mrs Thatcher made inseparable from her governing style. Nigel Lawson had resigned, and not the least of his grounds for doing so was the persistent intervention in his work of Alan Walters, the leader's personal economic trainer, who was particularly exercised over the matter of the European Exchange Rate Mechanism (ERM). Walters assisted Mrs Thatcher in preventing Lawson from doing what he wanted. The ERM, as we have seen, was then the fiercest *casus belli* in the Thatcher Government.[6] While it largely passed Major by when he was at the Foreign Office, at the Treasury it became the issue that defined him as what he was: an absorber of establishment wisdom, and a tenacious functionary in the task of seeing it to enactment.

He first addressed it as a sceptic: or rather, a more suitable designation for Major, as a man without opinions. 'I am an agnostic,' he told a Foreign Office official.[7] In his early days at the Treasury, he remained in the same condition, but was surrounded by some objectively existing facts he was never likely to resist. The Government was already committed in principle to entry to the ERM, when the time was ripe. That was the consequence of the blood spilled at the summit in Madrid in June: the victory over the leader that had cost Howe his job as Foreign Secretary. More than that, by autumn the entire senior collective at the Treasury were of the opinion that the time had come to convert the commitment into fact.

Seldom, indeed, in the entire history of Britain's membership of the European Community has there been such unanimity, concerning the next integrationist development, as that to be found in the debates about entry to the ERM in 1989 and 1990. This did not, it is true, indicate a sudden upsurge of Euro-idealism. The proximate cause was the decline in the value of the currency throughout 1989: the pound, worth DM3.28 at the beginning, dropped to DM2.72 by the end, a fall of 17 per cent. This gravely damaged the prospects of a fall in the inflation rate, and became a self-accelerating vortex that threatened to consume defenders of the exchange rate, chief among them the new Chancellor of the Exchequer. The need for a reliable counterweight, an anchor, became apparent.

All the same, it is remarkable that the ERM, which existed as a studied preliminary to a European single currency, was almost universally seen as the right way to construct the anchor. Officials, politicians and other observers had been through a variety of intellectual odysseys before reaching this position. Lawson himself, for example, while an unwavering believer in the ERM and fixed rates, was powerfully opposed, in all circumstances, to entry into a single currency. At the Bank of England, Eddie George, the future governor, was less sure about the ERM than Robin Leigh-Pemberton, the present governor, whose signature on the Delors committee's recommendation of a critical path leading to EMU had infuriated Mrs Thatcher.[8] But, as the currency slid and inflation rose, the Chancellor soon decided that the ERM offered him his best hope, and he had almost everyone who mattered on his side, from the Treasury to the Bank to the Foreign Office, from the old guard like Howe and Lawson to his new, most intimate colleague, Foreign Secretary Hurd, from the CBI to the Labour Party, from the *Financial Times* to the *Guardian, The Times* and the *Daily Telegraph.*

His conversion was due to economics, but not entirely devoid of a sense about European politics. As befitted a politician who was nothing if not sensitive to the locus of power, he knew that entry into the ERM club would also align Britain more favourably in discussions about the future of Europe. Such discussions – how relentless was the European dynamo! – were already scheduled. The leaders had agreed in December 1989 to call an inter-governmental conference – the Maastricht of two years ahead – to agree the changes to the Treaty of Rome that were necessary for a single currency. Major didn't need to be Howe-like in his Euro-philia to want to influence this, if necessary by joining the ERM. It was the normal instinct of any minister not barricaded behind an over-mastering scepticism about the European project – which meant almost all ministers except the leader herself, who was, even at this late stage, wholeheartedly supported only by one Cabinet minister on the verge of departure, Nicholas Ridley, and another too junior to matter, Michael Howard.

However, once Major was himself persuaded of the case, she had to be carried to the point of decision. It was not a simple task. He did not, to begin with, show his hand. After all, for a new, young Chancellor to presume to push the Prime Minister off the course she still preferred was a large ambition, even though Hurd was his ally. Hurd and Major met frequently for breakfast, picking a way forward, in the knowledge of realities that favoured their ambition. The first of these was that any reneging on the Madrid commitment would have a disastrous effect on the Government's credibility in the City, the second that they were both uncommonly secure in their positions. Neither, in effect, could be sacked. They were therefore well placed to impose upon Mrs Thatcher, a point she appears to have taken with some bitterness. As her discussions with Major proceeded in the spring of 1990, she could see where he was headed. 'I was extremely disturbed to find that the Chancellor had swallowed so quickly the slogans of the European lobby,' she writes in her memoirs. 'It was already clear that he was thinking in terms of compromises which would not be acceptable to me, and that intellectually he was drifting with the tide.'[9]

He dabbled with alternatives to the culminating concept of full economic and monetary union. These had been half formulated in Lawson's time: the notion, for example, of 'competing currencies', whereby the market rather than a European central bank would determine how far sterling was replaced in daily transactions by the Deutschmark and the franc. The contribution of Major himself was to encourage development of another idea, partly fathered by the old Eurocrat Michael Butler, for a 'hard écu': a possible stepping-stone to a single currency, but not inevitably destined to produce one. Each of these schemes, besides any virtue it had in itself, was designed to render more palatable to the leader the case for entry into the ERM. Each, however, was without significant support elsewhere in Europe. They were of little more than academic interest: steps along the way, down a path Mrs Thatcher would eventually find it impossible to impede.

When she conceded, on 13 June, it was to Major personally. 'I had too few allies to resist and win the day,' she laments. By that time, even her personal staff, from which Walters had retired, were pushing in the same direction. The logic and the pressure, orchestrated by the Chancellor, set Britain on the threshold, after a decade's resistance, of absorption into the European monetary project. His instincts, moreover, were already pointing him beyond that. He was at least toying with the politics of EMU itself. He saw the possibility, as he minuted the Prime Minister in April, of a 'two-tier Europe', from which Britain would be excluded if she did not take EMU seriously. He plainly thought this would be very bad news. The leader's recollection of his message is witheringly scornful. Major, she thought, had 'a tendency to be defeated by platitudes', and should not have cared about the two tiers 'if the other tier is going in the wrong direction'.[10] But, on the immediate question, she had had to bow to him. All that remained, as regards the ERM, was to settle the date of entry, which was finally agreed between them to be 8 October – as long as it was accompanied, at her insistence, by a 1 per cent cut in interest rate.

For anyone watching Major's evolution as a European, this saga offers a number of illuminating lessons, the first of which concerns his susceptibility to the fashion of the moment. There was nothing wicked about this preference, nothing that was even aberrant: after the ERM decision was debated in the Commons, only eleven Conservative MPs, led by John Biffen, refused to support it. When the overwhelming weight of expert opinion, both political and economic, lies on one side of an urgent argument, the stubbornness required to resist it can derive only from the kind of systemic prejudice that had no part in Major's make-up. Even that cussed quality, as Mrs Thatcher herself proved, was not enough. The fact remains, however, that the decision came to be almost as widely criticized after the event as it was supported before. Not *quite* so widely. In the controversies that rattled round the Tory Party's European debate for years ahead, there were always defenders of the therapy which ERM disciplines had worked on the economy. But it did become commonly agreed that the pound, which after falling so far in 1989 appreciated steadily in 1990, was put into the mechanism at a rate, DM2.95, which was higher than could be sustained, even within a 6 per cent band of flexibility either way, and much higher than any figure reflecting the real competitive relationship between the German and British economies.

Major knew most of this at the time. 'It was the only occasion I ever witnessed him having a fundamental row with Margaret Thatcher,' one of his closest political friends told me. He had wanted a lower rate, she an even higher one. Later, Major himself, in my hearing, specifically denied the existence of such a disagreement. But the final figure was certainly a compromise, which also had to reflect, of course, what the existing members of the ERM would accept.

Whatever the array of forces on this point, the material consequence was a lowering cloud over Major's career. What he had joined together as Chancellor, he was obliged to put asunder as Prime Minister two years later. His conduct generated a feeling, moreover, that he was a politician for whom conviction tended to follow action, rather than vice versa. Not many people thought, looking back, that he had ever really believed in the ERM from a position of principle. He took it up as an anti-inflationary weapon, but, for him, it did not fit into the kind of grand European scheme of thinking which persuaded some of his contemporaries, who had had a different education, of the need always to take one side in the great European debate – for fear of being stigmatized as a member of the unwashed and unenlightened. It was as a trimmer, not an ideologue, that Major led the making of a decision that became the first item in the charge-sheet his former friends eventually raised against him.

But, secondly, another signal was there for those who wanted to see it. Major was not a visceral anti-European. He had, at this stage, no particle of the faith that might persuade him to worship at the same altar as William Cash. His form, on the subject of Europe, was shallower than that of Hurd and Heseltine, and much less rooted in the past, but it was also fresher. It had been proved, as it were, in battle. He had shown that his gut feelings didn't carry him into the same blazing empyrean, afire with anti-continentalism, where Margaret Thatcher defiantly took up residence in her final months.

He was therefore never really qualified for the task which his supporters, retrospectively, reviled him for failing to fulfil. Hurd, his friend and rival, always knew this. Major never was a rightist, in this or, for the most part, any other matter. He slipped into the mainstream of the moment, always moderately rather than with Thatcher-like zeal. 'We used to have lunch occasionally, when I was Home Secretary and he was Chief Secretary,' Hurd said some years later. 'He talked perfectly clearly about his views. I've never understood (a) why she thought he was a protégé, or (b) why the right wing in 1990 thought "Here's our guy."'[11] They all just wanted to believe it, Hurd thought.

Major, moreover, was happy to allow them. Also dating from his time as Chief Secretary, a journalist recalled an evening at a party conference when he had 'bumped into one of the most pro-European Tory MPs' and later 'had a drink with a fiercely Euro-sceptic right-winger'. Both had been impressed by the little-known Mr Major. 'Why? Because he had given both of them the impression that he agreed 100 per cent with their views.'[12]

Such was the figure in whose hands was now placed the task of sustaining party and government into another election, while pursuing the work that was axiomatic to Britain's place in the world: the recovery of some influence in Europe.

*

As Prime Minister, Major wanted, above all, to restore normality. The period of one-woman rule, an unsuccessful experiment in quasi-presidential government, should come to an end. Not least was this so over the question that had brought the lady down. The very night of his election as leader, he kept a date in the inconvenient town of Altrincham to make a party speech, in which he said, among other things, that he thought Britain should stop shouting from the terraces and start playing on the field of Europe.

This was a mood he was fully permitted to engender: the change of leader was, for a time, cathartic. It would not be long before the historical rhythm which the great Arnold Toynbee divined in his survey of the ages, whereby every action is eventually followed by a hostile counter-action growing out of it, would reassert itself, to memorable effect, in the annals of the Conservative Party. The underlings at Major's back would soon make sure of that. More than 130 Tory back-benchers had joined what they defiantly named the Bruges Group, to keep faith with the famous text. But they had also chosen Major, and they wanted him to succeed. For a while, therefore, the governors governed. Their perspective, rather than that of their tormentors, was reaffirmed. Events could be seen from their point of view, rather than that of a rank and file that was not yet driving events. The sides coalesced, to resemble a fully functioning political party.

There came a time when this would not be easy to remember – but it did happen, in Major's first few months.

He started with the advantage of not being repelled by foreigners. He was intensely English, and, in his somewhat self-conscious attempts to fill out an otherwise vacant personality, Englishness was pushed to the fore. One of his few extra-mural passions was cricket, and the author he most regularly said he read was Anthony Trollope. When I saw him, later in his time, in his flat in Downing Street, he proudly displayed his cricketing memorabilia; and the collected works of Trollope, he said, lay alongside *Sense and Sensibility*, which he was re-reading, by his bed. One of the lines that clung to him was pilfered from George Orwell, to convey an image of Englishness he exalted, reaching back from the 1990s, as he recited it in a speech, to another England of 'long shadows on county grounds, warm beer, invincible green suburbs, dog-lovers, and old maids bicycling to Holy Communion through the mist'. This reeked of nostalgia. Warm beer came to seem a refreshment that was especially congruent with the Major personality. But he was not the kind of Tory who needed to define his love of one country by the ferocity of his dislike for others.

In particular, he had no hang-up about the Germans. He knew they were the key to a more diplomatically constructive future for Britain in Europe, and was critical of his predecessor for her neglect of this. He once gave me a learned little lecture on exactly why her attitude –

reflecting, it must be said, what successive British leaders had done ever since the war – contrived to perpetuate Britain's most unfortunate missed opportunity.[13] It had been, he said, 'an historic error of very great proportions'.

His opening gesture as Prime Minister was to set about correcting the error, by seeking the special friendship of Chancellor Helmut Kohl. Kohl was by now in his prime as a statesman: after German reunification, indisputably the dominant European figure. From the beginning, the two men warmed to each other in gratitude: the one for his release from the didactic tyrannies of Mrs Thatcher, the other for the sympathetic understanding he received from the more experienced politician.

It was natural that Major should choose Bonn as the place where he would make his first speech as Prime Minister outside Britain, and almost as predictable that it would aim to establish a tone that was different from what had gone before. This much it did. But it also became something of a *cause célèbre* in Major's evolution, and as such repays a little study.

His main purpose was indeed to change the climate. After lauding what the Conservative Party and Kohl's Christian Democrats shared between them – 'the great Conservative values: stability, opportunity, community, identity' – he talked about his vision of a free-market Europe, and an enlarged Europe open to the new democracies in the East. He made clear that, so far as monetary union was concerned, 'we think it best to reserve judgement . . . we cannot accept its imposition', and he offered a finely inconclusive assessment of the proper place of nation, in the scheme of things, as against Community. 'Europe', he said, 'is made up of nation-states: their vitality and diversity are sources of strength. The important thing is to strike the right balance between closer co-operation and a proper respect for national institutions and traditions.'

But the most remembered passage was the one that really did appear to foretell a change of aspiration: 'My aims for Britain in the Community can be simply stated. I want us to be where we belong. At the very heart of Europe. Working with our partners in building the future.'[14] So important were these words to Major that some of them appeared on the draft in his own hand: 'At the *very* heart,' he wrote.[15]

It is in the aftermath, as much as the fact, of this speech that its interest lies. It sounded like a manifesto for at least the long-term purpose of shifting Britain closer to the centre of the Community: not towards agreeing a federalist agenda, but surely breaking with the insistent separatism that had hitherto spoken from most of the sub-texts. Yet it turned out that this was not quite meant to be so. While, at the time it was given, the speech caused rather little turbulence, and passed the test of substantive, if not tonal, consistency with what had gone before – the *Daily Mail* rejoiced to conclude that 'the carping has stopped' – this verdict eventually changed. When the Euro-sceptic atmosphere reheated in the Tory Party, the speech became subject to revisionist assessment.

A minor sign of this is to be found in the flexible verdict of Charles Powell, Mrs Thatcher's influential, and brazenly loyal, foreign affairs adviser, who stayed on with Major for his first few months. At the time of the Bonn speech, Powell pronounced it satisfactorily Thatcherite. There was nothing in it, he said, that could not have been said by his former mistress.[16] Later, Powell had a different recollection. He told Major's biographer that he had said the speech 'went much too far in the Europhile direction of Heath'.[17]

Such, apparently, was the suppleness of judgement exacted by the changing circumstances in which it had to be delivered. But Major himself also came to rewrite his purposes. He had never intended, he later insisted, to say what his words apparently said. What he meant was not that Britain should be at the heart of Europe, but at the heart only of the European debate. 'I emphatically did not mean ever Britain slavishly following on at the behest of whatever the fashionable European majority opinion of the day happened to be,' he said in 1995. 'What I meant is that we should engage in the argument . . . and argue the British case from the heart of Europe.'[18]

This was a retrospective apologia. One thing that certainly did not happen under Major was the location of Britain at the heart of Europe, and some explanation was now required for those who had briefly been led to expect otherwise. But the regime did change in other ways.

One of them was via the ascendancy allowed to Hurd, and with it the rehabilitation of Jacques Delors, the Commission president, as a man with whom it was not only necessary but valuable to do business. Hurd was a serious admirer of Delors, a case of one quality mandarin recognizing another of the breed. Although Hurd spent his entire time as Foreign Secretary insisting he wasn't a federalist, and cautioning against the centralist tendencies of Brussels, he always saw Delors as an ally, rather than the demonic enemy of Thatcherite imaginings. We need Delors 'to keep us straight', he said to me on one occasion. He regarded the Commission as mostly a guardian of practicality, and Delors himself, in particular, as someone who understood the need to decentralize: a proponent of 'subsidiarity', the ugly abstraction that entered the vocabulary of Euro-speak in the 1990s. Delors had often told him he wished some of the other Commissioners – for example, an Italian transport Commissioner trying to lay down the law about British roads – 'would not be so silly'.

Hurd himself pushed in this direction, urging Brussels to keep out of 'the nooks and crannies' of national life. But his main contribution was as a tutor in foreign affairs whom Major was happy to learn from: a key influence, therefore, on the calmer, more moderate, more bureaucratic context in which, the leader hoped, 'Europe' affairs would once again be conducted.

For he couldn't escape the heat indefinitely. The Maastricht summit beckoned. There was no getting away from it. Some kind of deal had to be arranged that would satisfy both Major and the party: satisfy Major *because* it satisfied the party. The relationship was symbiotic. The party chose Major, and wanted him to succeed – but on its terms. Major accepted the brief, and wanted to deliver – but on terms which he, as a national leader, could pragmatically live with. Running up to Maastricht, which was fixed immutably for early December 1991, the Prime Minister began to show the tortuous subtlety for which, devoid of any excessive zeal, he was to become well known.

There are other ways of describing that faculty. The time came when it would have to be called weakness, or empty deviousness, or bare-faced contradiction. But, before and during Maastricht, Major was subtle, prescient and pretty effective. The regime outfaced its opponents, abroad and at home.

The opponents abroad wanted Maastricht to be something big. After the Single Act, it would be only the second substantial revision of the Treaty of Rome since the great document was written in 1957. Not one but two inter-governmental conferences, one on economic and monetary union, the other on closer political union, were labouring towards conclusions. For federalists, therefore, it was a moment of opportunity and truth, and they did not want to waste it.

At their head, it turned out, was the Dutch Government, who would be in the chair at Maastricht. The Dutch weren't always enemies of the British view of 'Europe', but in their present configuration they were, in British terms, 'federalist', and first used their presidency to favour proposals massively enhancing the power of Brussels. The political union IGC was all about this argument, and especially the extent to which foreign and security policy could and should be drawn under the Community umbrella. The Gulf War was only just over when the argument got going, and the terrible bloodshed in Bosnia continued throughout, a rebuke to the inability of 'Europe' to act together on its eastern doorstep. The Dutch, ditching more cautious proposals that were on the table, produced a draft treaty that put both foreign policy and interior-ministry affairs under the hand of the Commission and the Court of Justice. This was federalism writ heavy. Besides risking confusion about the role of Nato, and the Americans, in the future defence of Europe, it would constitute a serious step towards political union, if not, yet, exactly a European government. To explain and justify it, its defenders offered the image of the Community as a tree, springing from deep roots into well-spread branches which grew, however, from a single trunk.

Not only Britain but France rejected this. A creative Frenchman propounded the rival model of Europe as a Greek temple, whose façade consisted of three pillars. Although these all propped up the Council of Ministers – the national government leaders – only one consisted of powers that were truly integrated: the existing Community, based on the Treaty of Rome, and covering mainly matters of markets and trade. The other two would consist of foreign-and-security policy, and justice/home affairs/immigration and so on. These, while expressing a European dimension, would admit of less intervention by the Commission, the Parliament, the Court, the artefacts of 'Europe'.

Naturally, this model appealed much more to the British, and they appropriated it as their own. In the intensive discussions that revolved around the shape of future political union, moreover, they played a more constructive role than had been true in the recent past.[19]

The British, of course, never wanted a treaty at all: that was still their fundamental position. As a journalist, I was reminded of this, at moments when the Maastricht process was striking them as especially arduous, by just about every minister involved. The Treaty was the tool, they thought, of politicians who took seriously that very unBritish term 'the construction of Europe', and was therefore, at some level, deeply undesirable. To that extent, a certain seamless continuity prevailed from Thatcher to Major, indeed from Major, interrupted only by Heath, all the way back to Ernest Bevin and Winston Churchill.

But Major and his people played a decent hand. This required a great deal of diplomatic energy, coupled with a modicum of reassembled goodwill, which would not have been available under the previous dispensation. For there were plenty of other points of contest, notably about the role of the European Parliament, which the Germans especially, as their price for economic union, wanted to see enhanced in a matching upgrade for political union. Delors himself, though an integrationist on foreign policy – and a constant lamenter of the weakness of the political side of Maastricht – joined with the British in resisting the extension of Commission 'competences' into such fields as energy, tourism and disaster relief. In all these preliminaries, the Major style did roughly what seemed to be required by the people who had been so horrified by Mrs Thatcher's declarations of war. It got to grips with the reality of continental negotiation. There was a lot of fine-tuned preparation, for an agreement to which the British, for once, were as committed as the Europeans – as long as they secured some important positions.

For the Thatcherites had not gone away. They were the opponents at home, who had equally to be propitiated by the party manager. He did the work with aplomb, and a certain amount of political courage.

The Cabinet was kept involved with a thoroughness to which few of its members were accustomed. It contained, as we shall see, its quota of naturally severe Euro-sceptics, who were biding their time. But the leader comfortably boxed them in. It was a member of this group who exulted to me about how attentive Major was being in keeping them informed. 'There has never been a European summit on which so many ministers were able to have their say,' this man said. Parliament was given the opportunity to speak as well, before Maastricht began. Major, rather riskily, laid his position on the line. He would accept no taint of federalism in the Treaty, he said. He would insist on his 'pillars', would reject any compulsion, such as the other countries were contemplating, to join up to economic and monetary union.

The temperature was beginning to rise. Led by Mrs Thatcher, some sceptics could already see the Maastricht trap, as a now-or-never last chance to exercise a British veto over integration which would, if it was enacted, be irreversible. Opt-outs and special British exceptions were in the air, but they wouldn't stop the caravan moving forward. At the head of her friends, Mrs Thatcher demanded at least the gesture of a promise to hold a referendum on EMU, should Britain ever decide to join, and called Major arrogant when he refused either to rule out for ever British membership of the single currency or to promise a national consultation if the time came.

An issue thus was born, Yes or No to a referendum, which was to invade Tory politics for the duration, the litmus-test of his honour, his nationalism, his respect for party – his whatever – that Major kept facing for the next five years. This, also, was when William Cash came to thump the table.

But only six Tory MPs, including Biffen and excluding Cash, voted against the pre-Maastricht declaration of support. Sent on his way with a parliamentary majority of 101, Major arrived at the place, whose unheard-of name would one day be engraved dolefully on his heart, with his Cabinet and his party behind him, and with skills that had now been honed in the European arena for a year. He might not be a visionary, but the little lessons in dealing with people, acquired in Lambeth street politics, developed in the corridors of the Commons, enhanced at the Treasury, were what he thought would see him through.

He was, indeed, a student of people, the lowest and the highest. It was his special trick. Douglas Hurd noted it as one of Major's early consolations when he was plunged into foreign affairs. 'He is a collector of people,' Hurd told me, after retiring from the Foreign Office. 'In a way, going into foreign affairs was like enlarging his collection.' At the negotiating table, watchfulness, along with an intense application to detail, was his principal weapon. 'He's a student of body language,' Hurd went on. 'He watches, more carefully than anyone I've ever known, how people conduct themselves when they're with him. He used to say to me, because I was often with him at diplomatic discussions, "But you didn't watch what his hands were doing. You didn't see what he was doing with his hair at that point." Which I hadn't.'[20]

When I once put this to Major, he cringed, but did not deny it. His own body visibly stiffened. Plainly I had stumbled on the protective device of an outsider from way back. 'Yes,' he said, his cover blown. 'I look at the body language at least as much as I listen to the words. I have always done it, as far back as I can ever remember.'[21]

At Maastricht, these were necessary, though not sufficient, skills. Since national leaders are decisive figures at European summits, often negotiating only with a foreign minister beside them, their personal faculties matter keenly. But Major's tenacity was as important as his sensitivity. When it came down to the wire, there were two issues that mattered more than any others to the British.

One was EMU, not a new problem. It had been obvious for more than a year that EMU would be at the heart of Maastricht, its central purpose. It had been equally obvious that Britain, for one, would be unwilling to collude as a signed-up member in a scheme that required the solemn disclaimer of monetary sovereignty for an indefinite, perhaps permanent, period ahead. If the Maastricht version of EMU contained such a sense of both the automatic and the perpetual, and if it was to be accomplished within the legal order of the Community rather than as a separate enterprise outside the Treaty of Rome, Britain, and perhaps others, would have to retain the option not to belong.

How was this to be arranged? The months before Maastricht were occupied with numerous arguments about the shape of EMU, the role and status of a new European central bank, the number of currencies necessary to make a viable quorum, the relationship between coercion, veto and arbitrary exclusion as these might affect different countries. Of particular controversy was whether Britain should be treated uniquely. Britain didn't want to be. Norman Lamont, the Chancellor, at the last meeting of finance ministers before Maastricht itself, argued for a generalized opt-out, on which any country could draw, something that might conceivably prove attractive to the Germans, always the most delicately poised, as regards EMU, of the continental powers. But Lamont did not gain his point. Only Denmark, in any case, was as interested as Britain in retaining freedom of monetary manoeuvre. The Lamont proposition was defeated 11–1.

In Maastricht, the final EMU opt-out was secured only with difficulty. The precise text of the protocol, giving Britain her special privilege, had to be agreed, and the others insisted on going through it. This was the day Lamont later said that his eyes were opened to the hideous federalist impulses of his fellow finance ministers. It was also a moment concerning which some ugly little retrospective squabbles broke out, prompted by the now Euro-phobic former Chancellor, as to who precisely deserved the credit for the British opt-out. There had been stories of dramatic walks-outs from Maastricht committees, and the Chancellor banging vainly on the door of a room where Major and the Dutch leader, Ruud Lubbers, stitched up the final deal. 'I just produced a piece of paper at the last meeting deleting everything and saying it didn't apply to Britain,' Lamont later claimed. And of the opt-out: 'I did that.' At which Major said he was 'very surprised . . . [and] so will everyone else be who was actually there at the Maastricht negotiations'.[22]

The second British point was less well prepared for. Bruges 88 lived in the collective Tory memory, and its statement of revulsion against the reappearance of socialism via the ordinances of Brussels was shared throughout the Major Government. Since Maastricht was destined to include an expression of the 'social dimension' of Europe, this had to be eluded as firmly as EMU. It brought back some of the arguments from the very origins of 'Europe', which the Labour Party had first opposed, among other reasons, as a capitalist plot. In a certain context, 'Europe' was an exercise in free-market protectionism: in another, it could be seen as a form of Christian socialism. It all depended where you looked from. In fact the British, taken as a whole, were never consistent about where to place the EEC on this left–right spectrum. The critics in either party could always find convenient reasons to put it at the opposite end from their own. But in 1991, without doubt, Maastricht's prospective social chapter seemed wholly ominous to the reigning British orthodoxy.

It was not, however, easy to dispose of. And the way this happened, while successful in the outcome, was a harbinger of the Tory struggle which, in due course, insinuated its way up from the back-benches into the Cabinet itself.

The issue was not the fact but the content of a social chapter, and on this the continentals at first seemed ready to negotiate. Some of the partners – French, Italian, Belgian – saw it as a text that should seriously enhance the rights of workers to be consulted about decisions in the enterprises where they worked. Major's position was that this would impose huge costs on industry, and sacrifice jobs. But since there had been no agreement in principle before Maastricht, one way or the other, a poker-game ensued. As things stood, Britain could wreck the Treaty by rejecting the chapter, and for most of the two-day summit the Europeans judged that Major wouldn't dare to carry his resistance that far. They thought he must be bluffing.

But Major had some uncompromising forces at his back, whom he seemed almost to beg to apply their pressure. The Employment Secretary, Michael Howard, had stated his own unyielding hostility to any version of social chapterism. Although he wasn't at Maastricht, Major instructed that he be kept informed and given, in effect, a veto on what might be proposed. So Howard, when asked by telephone, seized his chance, threatening that he might resign if Britain signed up.[23]

This early version of a regular Major tactic – 'the more you pressure me, the more readily I will agree with you' – had the desired effect. When Lubbers, who as the summit chairman needed to save the Treaty, sought to seduce him with a much watered-down social chapter, Major said no as clearly as he knew how: words to the effect, according to his biographer, of 'It's no good asking me. I can't do it. And I won't do it.' For the last six hours of Maastricht, in fact, Major sat solemnly, almost pleasurably, declining to accept the logic of being one against eleven, sticking to his solitary negative on several issues, periodically reminding his colleagues that it was they, not he, who wanted the Treaty anyway. Finally impressed that the British meant what they had been saying, Lubbers produced his own alternative – a social chapter that was technically outside the Treaty, which meant that Britain's dissent, her formal refusal to sign up, could be permitted without jeopardizing everything else.

And so a Treaty of Maastricht was agreed. The process had a number of aspects, some of which are so startling that they deserve a special place in any reflection on Britain's relations with this mysterious collection of countries and cultures across the Channel.

The least surprising concerned Major himself. He conducted a canny, patient negotiation. He wasn't the main architect of Maastricht, a title which undoubtedly belongs to Ruud Lubbers, Dutch grand-master of the politics and game-playing required to keep a complex coalition of political interests moving forward. The only mistake Lubbers made, he told me afterwards, was in not appreciating the adamancy of Major's position on the social chapter. As the author of the chapter, he thought he had contrived the proper degree of unoppressive subsidiarity within it, sufficient for Britain to sign up. As he reflected on what had gone wrong, Lubbers took an almost academic interest in his own chairmanly performance. 'If I had known that John Major needed in all circumstances an opt-out, I would have played it differently,' he said.[24]

But he admired Major's trajectory as a negotiator. 'There are two models of negotiation,' the scholarly deal-maker explained. 'The model of using arguments, trying to convince people, doing that in a good sequence, with good timing. And then you have the other model, negotiating emotionally. However strange this may sound, most political leaders do it emotionally. Margaret Thatcher. Helmut Kohl. Also Mitterrand, a bit less. They shout at you that such-and-such is absolute nonsense. But John Major never. A gentleman, well briefed, rational, well informed.'

It was not surprising, either, that Major should make the most of what had been achieved. His spokesman went too far in saying that the result amounted to 'Game, set and match' to the British. Even had this been true, it was a foolish piece of triumphalism that was pinned, owing to the anonymity behind which British official spokesmen then sheltered, to the Prime Minister. Even though he didn't say it himself, he offended both Lubbers and François Mitterrand. 'Mitterrand was very irritated,' Lubbers told me. 'It was as if he said to Mitterrand, "I managed

A united vision: Harold Wilson goes European, with Helmut Schmidt, the German Chancellor, Labour Party conference, 1974.

All about the price of bread: Barbara Castle (left), shopping for a No in the referendum, June 1975.

Margaret Thatcher and friends: the Dublin summit of the European
Council, 1979.

The President and his patrimony: Jacques Delors, European
Commission, 1985–95.

Margaret Thatcher: disdaining Europe and, with Helmut Kohl (below, right), failing to understand the Germans.

The phobic faces of the 1990s: Sir James Goldsmith (above),
and William Cash.

John Major, prime minister, 1990–97: my hesitation is final.

Bastards and others: John Redwood (to the right of the blazer), and his campaign team for the challenge to Major, June 1995.

Roy Jenkins: from Wilson to Blair, and goad to god-father.

The militant tendency: Conservatives for Europe, Kenneth Clarke (above) and Michael Heseltine.

Tony Blair, Paris, March 1998: *Je suis un homme d'Europe.*

Maastricht, not you, or Kohl, or anyone else."' It also incurred Lubbers's disapproval for its crassness as a piece of domestic political management. 'After all, he was apparently saying that all the elements of Maastricht where I *don't* have an opt-out are excellent! Because I managed it! If you're going to say that, you should at least go hell-for-leather for parliamentary approval, instead of leaving time for a controversy to start.'

That, as we have seen, is not what happened. However, given that there had to be a treaty, this one was as good as Britain could have expected. Besides, there was an excuse for Government exuberance in the ecstatic reception the conquering hero received on his return from the Netherlands.

Given the odium subsequently heaped on Maastricht, and its luminous place in the catalogue of infamy that became the bible of Conservative Euro-scepticism, it is worth recalling what these people were saying at the time. This is another testament to the waywardness of judgement that has been characteristic of many a sceptic mind: its capacity for sharp reversals of opinion not only about the matter of principle, but about the correct interpretation of matters of fact: its sheer want of scepticism, in the proper sense, at moments of excitement.

For the anti-Brussels camp also, like Major himself, thought he had had a triumph. 'He went. He stood firm. And he prevailed,' said the *Daily Mail*. 'When the test came, Mr Major was ready for it. The moment found the man of consensual instinct with more than a touch of steel.'[25] Paul Johnson wrote: 'John Major's Houdini-like escape from the toils of the Eurocrats at Maastricht is a personal victory which may well go into folklore.'[26] 'In almost every sense, it was a copybook triumph for Mr Major, the stuff of Foreign Office dreams,' reported the *Daily Telegraph*'s man in Brussels, Boris Johnson.[27] The *Telegraph* itself editorialized as follows: 'Mr Major deserves the heartfelt gratitude of his party for averting a disaster which might have made election victory unattainable.'[28] *The Times* leader described the whole event as an 'emphatic success'.[29]

What unifies these voices most remarkably is not that they approved of Maastricht and Major in 1991, but that each one of them, in less than a year, came to write about Major in the most scathing terms, and cite the Treaty of Maastricht as the main evidence against him. A variety of explanations might be ventured. Since all supported the Conservatives, and an election was coming, they were doubtless eager to fortify the leader of their party at what might otherwise have been the wrong sort

of turning-point. In addition, the very fact of doing down the continentals, by securing the opt-outs while remaining somewhere near the centre
of European activities, could only be a source of pleasure to papers and
writers much concerned about the future of British national sovereignty.
Once again, we seemed to be having it, rather comfortably, both ways.
In any case, the level of these people's expectations for Britain in Europe
was different from what it became. For one thing, they still wanted
Britain to be in there, making the most of the EU and pushing the
British interest. The *Daily Mail* verdict, for example, was predicated on
the need for what it called an effective defence 'of our country's interests
in shaping an ever closer European union'. The paper speculated
optimistically on a new currency that would one day 'be worth having'.
A few years later, no reader of the *Mail* would believe it could ever have
taken such positions.

Nothing, however, had changed about Maastricht in the intervening
time. The Treaty was the Treaty was the Treaty, for better or for worse.
Only later, it seemed, did these unsceptical sceptics fully understand
what it was about: or at any rate decide to bewilder people with second
thoughts which they seldom, if ever, acknowledged as such.

Another thing that happened, though, was that Major became
committed to the Treaty. He saw himself as its maker. From the British
point of view, he owned it. Seeing it ratified was, for him, a matter of
honour as much as politics. However loud the roars and devious the
manoeuvres of the Cashites, there could never be a question of withdrawing the European Communities (Amendment) Bill from the
parliamentary process. He would use every disciplinary device, and all
his political capital as leader, to prevent Britain being responsible, by her
non-ratification, for the failure of Maastricht to become a fully functioning treaty of the Union.

This was the high point of Major the European, the governing man,
declining to be fettered by the party politicians around him. But it
marked the last real ascendancy of the senior colleagues – a dwindling
collection, as it turned out – who backed him in his earnest desire,
ineptly expressed, to be at the heart of Europe.

*

On 9 April, Major did what he had been chosen to do, in the general
election which almost nobody expected him to win. To common
amazement, he acted out the scenario that was only a wishful dream for

most Conservative MPs. There were a good many reasons for this, which had less to do with him or his party than with the Labour Party and its leader. But the election took place in the shadow of Maastricht. The campaign unfolded, therefore, within the outer edge of the phase when the Treaty was still being written about as an unqualified triumph, burnishing Major's name as a man of competence. To that extent, Europe played its role in helping him to win the 1992 election.

If anybody saw this at the time, however, it was only for an instant. No election, won by a clear majority, has been followed by a sharper reversal of the mandate which it might normally be thought to have created. Never in modern British democracy was so much confidence, given by so many people, so swiftly removed from the Cabinet on whom it was conferred. If Major's version of Europe helped him win, it was also responsible for withdrawing the palm at record speed.

For the disagreements in the party had not been resolved, merely forgotten as a pre-electoral act of convenience. They were, in fact, incapable of resolution. They related to a question, the very nature of an independent Britain, which was, in the eyes of quite a number of Tory politicians, uncompromisable. These ultras did not exist merely at the lower levels, where Cash sported and Teddy Taylor played. They had their representatives all the way up the Government, reaching into the Cabinet itself. Such sceptics had been silent until now. Sometimes, as with Michael Howard and the social chapter, the leader was careful to humour them. Their presence at all levels constrained his negotiating stance – though in directions with which he himself was, for the most part, content. At no stage could Major have been called a thunderous Euro-phile. But now he was about to discover a different order of disagreement among high colleagues, a new brand of hostility to himself within the privy group, which he was driven to match at similar levels of revulsion. Such, within a few months, was the dire influence of 'Europe' on the Conservatives' fourth, apparently triumphant, term of office, now about to be destabilized by men whom the Prime Minister defined in a word seldom heard as an officially listed category of colleague: 'the bastards'.

Events, rather than people, started this descent. There was the Danish referendum on Maastricht in June 1992. What the British voters gave – newly mandated tranquillity – the Danes were allowed to take away. This transformed the realm of the possible, galvanizing anti-Maastricht feeling, reopening the Tory divide that had been more or less disguised since the removal of Mrs Thatcher. It soon exposed the fact that this was not a strong government, but a brittle one, with pieces flaking away as readily as in the Thatcher years. But there was a difference with the Thatcher experience. Whereas, under her, dissidence over Europe produced six sackings or resignations from the Cabinet, under Major the dissidents, in every case except one, remained inside, free to argue and corrode, challenge and dissent, from within the portals of power. A style first welcomed as the soul of consultative collegiality, after years of Thatcherish autocracy, became a vehicle for entrenching treachery on the one hand and weakness on the other. It was the defining element in the decline and fall of John Major's Government.

This first surfaced, appropriately, in the person of a Major ally. Norman Lamont had been, after Mrs Thatcher, his most important friend. In some respects, he was all that Major wasn't. After schooling at Loretto, a famous private establishment in Scotland, he moved on to Cambridge. In 1964, the year Lamont, as president of the Cambridge Union, was reaching the pinnacle of a conventional political apprenticeship, Major was a clerk in a dead-end job at the London Electricity Board. What they shared from that period on, however, was a dedication to Conservative politics, and an inexhaustible desire to succeed. The crooked path of political ambition had carried them, by 1990, to a point where one, Lamont, was subordinate to the other in their Treasury posts, and became, by inevitable and self-interested osmosis, his closest ally in the contest to get the top job. Lamont managed Major's campaign, and Major rewarded him with the chancellorship. Thus were they bound together in what became a crisis far exceeding the Danish referendum in potency as the unraveller of the mandate.

For Lamont was by now presiding, *ex officio*, over Britain's membership of the European Exchange Rate Mechanism, the ERM. This was Major's baby, his claim, in a sense, to be a man of power: certainly the policy initiative that had carried him through the fire against Mrs Thatcher, in defence of which he had emerged triumphant on the other side. But, Chancellor Lamont was now in charge, the man who had to worry every day about the exchange rate and the interest rate that supported it.

By the summer of 1992, it was clear that the story of the ERM was not an entirely happy one. Sterling's membership had served one purpose, as a suppresser of inflation, pretty well. But as the second year of the experience progressed, the economy was caught in a familiar, alarming bind. A startling aspect of the election victory was that it had been achieved against a background of rising unemployment and economic recession. With house prices falling and business bankruptcies almost as rampant as they had been in the early Thatcher years, however, restiveness on the Conservative back-benches wasn't stifled by the recentness of MPs' return to Westminster. It was infiltrated by their other discontents, mainly Europe and the imprisonment which Europe, via the ERM, was enforcing on what they liked to think of as the sovereign domestic economy.

Along with the fresh-discovered, supra-national evils of Maastricht, in other words, came a more ominous count against the continental enterprise. For the ERM required sterling to be held within fixed bands against the Deutschmark, and during 1992 this was proving difficult to achieve. The markets' faith in the maintenance of the rate, given the parlous state of the economy, was beginning to drain away, demanding, if the Government were truly serious, a rise in interest rates. Yet such a rise was exactly what the depressed national economy did not require. The viciousness of the circle could hardly be more apparent, and nor could the vulnerability of the British situation to external developments, such as a rise in Germany's own interest rates for Germany's own domestic reasons.

Much of the summer was spent in semi-public arguments about how this dangerous impasse might be addressed. There was a case for raising interest rates. There was a case for 'realigning' sterling in the ERM, a euphemism for devaluing. There was even a case for leaving the ERM altogether. There were reckless shouts from some Tories in favour of lowering interest rates, and to hell with the ERM. And over all these arguments hung an air of impending crisis, which the Government chose to resolve by a statement of adamant support for the currency as it was, inside the ERM, within the present bands. Lamont made the statement.[30] It was a ringing defence of the principle of fixed exchange rates, and a challenge to anybody who dared to say that Britain's present economic difficulties had anything to do with ERM membership. Floating or devaluing, said the Chancellor, would lead not to lower interest rates but, in all probability, higher, because of the influence exerted, in or out of the ERM, by interest rates in Europe.

The political significance of this speech, in the evolving pathology of Euro-scepticism, became apparent only later. For Lamont subsequently laid claim to being a deep sceptic at heart, so his utterance, which I witnessed him giving with severe and unchallengeable assertiveness, becomes one more display-piece in the well-stocked museum of inconstancy on the subject of Europe. At the time, however, it stated an official policy which no minister seems to have contested.[31]

It was also the prelude to disaster. Having pledged themselves to the ERM and the rates it required, Major and Lamont were driven to tactics and performances they would later have preferred to forget. The management of Britain's exit from the mechanism – the sundering of what Chancellor Major had joined together – was one of the most embarrassing, as well as politically calamitous, episodes in the post-war history of British economic policy, a period not short of contenders for the title. Major always defended entry, seeing it, he once told me, as a lynchpin in the assault on inflation which he regarded as his central political task, and whose success he was incorrigibly proud of. 'Between 1990 and 1996 we moved from an inflation-prone country to a disinflationary country,' he said. 'I am happy to let history make a judgement about whether the short-term pain was right for the long-term gain.' But on the coming-out, he thought, history could already speak. 'It was a disaster, a political disaster. There is no doubt about that. It was an embarrassment for the United Kingdom.'[32]

Such clinical blitheness did not prevail when events were unfolding. They featured, mainly, the blundering of Lamont, a man of whom it was often rumoured that he would no longer have been Chancellor at all, but for the surprising defeat of an abler politician, Chris Patten, in his seat at Bath. In the event, this was perhaps a mercy for Patten. From the moment the Cabinet decided to remain in the ERM, mere ministers lost control to the overwhelming power of the financial markets. On 26 August, Lamont stood on the Treasury steps to announce that 'we will do whatever is necessary' to maintain sterling's parity. The world was to have 'no scintilla of doubt' about this. On 4 September, he travelled to Bath for a meeting of EC finance ministers which he was chairing. Dismal scenes ensued, in which the Chancellor took it on himself to lecture the Bundesbank on the need to cut interest rates, and advanced an extensive critique, to anyone who would listen, of German policies. He seemed to be following, punily, in the Thatcher line, emulating her performance in Dublin in 1979 which almost caused Helmut Schmidt to walk out. Now Lamont performed a little foot-stamping of his own that had the same effect on Helmut Schlesinger, the chief German central banker. It was 'the most ill-tempered meeting I had ever attended', another banker recalled to Philip Stephens. The opening, that might have existed, for a negotiated realignment of sterling's value was lost in the rage that Lamont, on Britain's behalf, felt at the suggestion of the pound being treated in the same way as the peseta and the lira.

Major, too, was firm. Maintaining the pound's value had become for him, as for many of his predecessors, a totem. Their wretched history in this matter did not caution him. Rather, the reverse. 'All my adult life,' he told Scottish industrialists on 10 September, 'I have seen British governments driven off their virtuous pursuit of low inflation by market problems or political pressures. I was under no illusions when I took sterling into the ERM. I said at the time that membership was no soft option. The soft option, the devaluer's option, the inflationary option, would be a betrayal of our future.' He recalled the Harold Wilson devaluation in 1967, doubtless imagining there was no possibility of his being forced down the same track. He spoke with contempt of those who would, as Keynes said, 'debauch the currency'.

The speculators were active, however, against currencies both in and out of the ERM. Early on 16 September, the game was almost up. The pound continued to slide, and, to begin with, the Major–Lamont response was to raise interest rates from 10 to 12 per cent. When this had no market impact, they announced another rise, to 15 per cent, for next day, in a last, near-hysterical punt to defend their sterling policy. They got all the leading Cabinet ministers lined up in support of this, 'to put their hands in the blood', as Kenneth Clarke described it. These ministers had not been directly included in policy-making up to this point, and not made aware, at the time when it was still relevant, of the options that might have been available. But the more emphatic pro-Europeans – Clarke, Hurd and Heseltine – were especially implicated, and especially willing to test the 'European' option to the limit, though more than $10 billion had already been spent by the Bank, to no effective purpose other than the enrichment of speculators.

This could not last. As night fell, Lamont made another appearance outside the Treasury, to announce that his economic strategy had been destroyed. 'Massive speculative flows', he said, were continuing to disrupt the exchange markets. So the judgement now had to be reversed. The 15 per cent interest rate already announced would be revoked, and sterling's membership of the ERM would be suspended. Most of the words in his July speech, he might have added, had now to be eaten.

Though the overt events of this disaster were bad enough, it had other layers and reverberations which, had they been known at the time, would have heightened the sense of a government out of control of events: something governments are never meant to be. Some of these

were merely comical, if revealing. The absence of command reached into
the most elementary areas. It happened, for example, that Downing
Street was under repair at the time, and Major was occupying emergency
quarters in Admiralty House, where, though this was 1992, there was no
proper telephone switchboard and no direct line to market information.
The high command of British economic management, including the
governor of the Bank and the First Lord of the Treasury, were huddling
over a crisis they were unable to measure from moment to moment.
Even a radio could not be found when it was wanted.

More enduring was the memory of some of the ministers who were
kept out of the information loop for more purposeful reasons. Although
Douglas Hurd was Foreign Secretary, and therefore running a Europe
policy of which the ERM was a central element, he recalled later how
shocking these events had been. The day was immediately known as
Black Wednesday, a correct label for what was a national humiliation,
though one which was in due course reversed – White Wednesday – as
a political statement by anti-'Europe' elements wishing to emphasize the
therapy of liberation from the ERM. Hurd thought he should have
known about the possibility of Black Wednesday some weeks before it
happened. So did Kenneth Clarke, the Home Secretary, who discovered
most of what he knew about Lamont's Treasury operations from reading
the newspapers. He told a group of journalists some years later: 'I
reflected on that day that I'd never been in a government that didn't
have an economic policy. I waited with interest to see what it would be
by the end of the day.'[33] None of this was a happy augury for the four
years in which Britain was liable still to be governed by the Major
Administration.

But the most testing impact of these days and weeks was felt,
naturally, by Major himself. To him, the outcome was a failure he took
very personally. It bothered him deeply. There is good evidence that he
considered, on a day-to-day basis, the case for his resigning. Hurd was
one person who listened to him agonizing. 'Quite clearly, he and the
Government would have to start again from the bottom up,' Hurd
recalled. 'He was not sure he was the right person to do that.'[34] Major's
official biographer has amplified this account, reporting that on 23
September the Prime Minister got as far as drafting, in his own hand,
the script of a resignation statement he would broadcast to the nation,
prior to making way, as he hoped, for his preferred successor, Clarke.
He showed the text of this to one of his private secretaries, Stephen
Wall, who refused to contemplate the possibility. 'Wall and Major talked

for two hours,' writes Anthony Seldon. 'Major subsequently regarded this conversation as crucial to his decision to carry on.'[35] According to Hurd, he was still thinking about quitting a fortnight after Black Wednesday.

London wasn't short of people who thought he should do so. It was from this period that can be dated the unprecedented accumulation of enemies gathering round Major's person. There had been nothing like it since the depths of Harold Wilson's unpopularity – and Wilson, reviled though he often was, lived in a time when a minimum of good manners still applied to the media's performance. It wasn't permissible, nor even contemplated, even in Wilson's worst days, for a newspaper to imply that he was mentally deranged. Nor did editors vilify him to his face. Throughout the Thatcher decade, indeed, they had lost the habit of sceptical detachment of any kind, when addressing the leader. For Major, after the ERM débâcle, different rules applied. And it was apparent that Europe, including some sharp revisionism concerning the Europe of Maastricht, was the driest tinder on the fire.

A heavy rumour circulated that, at some point on 16 September, Major was so completely laid low by the destruction of his policy, and the colossal outflow of reserves, that he had some kind of nervous breakdown. So great was the pressure on him that a brief retreat from reality might have been understandable, though also, of course, discreditable. I made intermittent efforts over the years to get the episode confirmed, but the quality of the denials was impressive: enough, at any rate, to render any perpetuation of the rumours thoroughly dishonest.

But this did not deter all newspapers closer to the moment. *The Times* published a lengthy examination of the Prime Minister's mental health, by two reporters whose lack of medical qualifications, let alone their distance from the scene, did not deter them from asking whether Major 'can take the strain' and concluding that quite possibly he could not. They adduced a variety of gossipy circumstantial evidence, from 'dramatic weight loss' to the fact that he 'has given up alcohol' and was 'having his hair tinted at Trumpers'. He was 'lonely', 'unhappy', and might well be suffering from conditions that are triggered by extreme stress, of which 'heart disease and mental ill health are possibilities'.[36] On this miserable basis, it wasn't hard to construct the picture of a disintegrating Prime Minister.

While not all papers were so extravagant in their speculations, many began to cause Major problems. They drove a reasonably balanced man into a species of neuroticism. There is no sight quite so characteristic as that of the British press hammering a man when he is down, a practice that gains in venom when the same organs have been largely responsible for raising him up in the first place. So it was with Major, who heard multiple voices around this time telling him he should quit, and became an obsessive accumulator of resentments concerning material he couldn't stop himself reading. A kind of fusion was beginning to appear between strands of polemical opinion that were to remain ever present in the future demeanour of most of the Tory press: a ferocious line in Euro-scepticism, bound together with a deepening contempt for the unleaderlike leader who was failing to show the same exuberance for the cause as they did.

Major didn't often call up newspaper editors on the telephone. But over the ERM he later admitted to doing so. To small effect. Self-serving though it is, the account given by the *Sun* editor, Kelvin MacKenzie, of one such conversation is worth putting down. When the Prime Minister called, shortly after the débâcle, MacKenzie alleges he said to him: 'I've got a large bucket of shit on my desk, and tomorrow morning I'm going to pour it all over your head.'[37]

But another fusion materialized, forming a critical mass with potentially still greater explosive qualities. There were people in the Government whose visceral feelings about Europe resembled those of the editors: had probably existed, indeed, for rather longer. A consequence of the ERM humiliation was the reassembling of these feelings by ministers who had tended to suppress them, but who saw September 1992 as a watershed that ought to carry the Conservative Party back towards its latter-day preference for floating currencies, as well as a proper hostility for further European integration. What united most of these men was their intense, sometimes tearful, loyalty to Margaret Thatcher in the hour of her deposing: an emotion so spacious that it could entirely overlook, when the ERM exit occurred, that it had been Mrs Thatcher who authorized entry in the first place. Attitudes to the ERM became the touchstone of a neo-Thatcherite revival, crystallizing the presence of enemies within as well as behind and below the Government. These enemies were a mixture, as ever, of erratic converts, their ambitions thwarted, and discreet zealots, with ambition awaiting satisfaction.

In the former category, Norman Lamont was the leading member. He struggled on as Chancellor for eight months after the cataclysm, his life increasingly marked by a lack of either public or personal discipline. The man who, in July, said ERM membership was the irreplaceable centrepiece of his economic strategy reported, in September, that he had been 'singing in the bath' when exit was accomplished. Explaining himself afterwards, Lamont always said he had been agnostic-to-sceptical about the ERM in the first place, but, having inherited the policy when Major gave him the Treasury, had gone along with it uncomplaining. A pliant politician had blown with the wind.

It took the loss of office to sharpen Lamont's decision as to where his agnosticism ended. Before this trauma, he gave little hint of the depth his Euro-phobia would soon reach. What he said was certainly not enough to spare him the merciless hounding of the Tory press which, on that point, might have been willing to protect him had they known what he really thought. When Major sacked him, in May 1993 – the only political enemy to suffer that fate in six years – Lamont trampled derisively on the leader's grave, delivering the effective curtain line that his Government gave 'the impression of being in office but not in power'.[38]

Having left government, it must be said, Lamont became one of the more serious scrutineers of the EU. He developed a critique acknowledging, as we have seen, the need to consider the truth that momentum could draw Britain in one of two directions: towards greater federalism or, alternatively, towards a looser relationship that amounted to a form of exit.[39] But he entered a category already created by another departed minister, Kenneth Baker, a Home Secretary who did not survive past the 1992 election, and then discovered, having been a key supportive figure in the Maastricht negotiation, that he was a Euro-sceptic after all. There was something tainted about these reconsiderations. The attraction that might be claimed for an open mind was nullified by the sense that loss of office, rather than any irresistible novelty of evidence, had something to do with stimulating the conversion.

The same charge could not be made against the sceptics who remained in high office, and were, if anything, cosseted and promoted by the Prime Minister. Their self-defined though usually unadmitted mission, at the heart of government, was to achieve an ever greater distance from the heart of Europe. They weren't in the topmost jobs, but they were both a threat and, as Major saw it, an indispensable necessity to the leader. That was the context in which he gave them their famous name, while talking on an inadvertently open microphone to a television reporter in July 1993. Beset by the fiery divisions attending the final parliamentary vote on Maastricht, Major bemoaned the size of his majority and the incipient split that he was striving to prevent. People, he noted, were always telling him to do 'all these clever, decisive things', to reassert his control on the Europe question among others. But the party was still 'harking back to a golden age that never was'. In this fantasy-land, he speculated, 'You have three right-wing members of the Cabinet who actually resign.' But what happens then? They simply join the ranks of the dispossessed, causing all sorts of trouble. 'We don't want another three more of the bastards out there,' he concluded.[40]

He could as easily have said four not three, though he apparently thought of Michael Howard, whom he had made Home Secretary, as excluded from the coven. Howard, along with the two of them then present – Peter Lilley, the Social Security Secretary, and Michael Portillo, Chief Secretary to the Treasury – had pressed for Maastricht to be abandoned after the Danish referendum: the voices of Cashism above the salt. They had pressed the case further, after the ERM fiasco, when it looked likely that a referendum in France might kill the Treaty anyway: a prospect which Major himself, Lamont told me, saw as an escape-route from his troubles. According to Lamont, Major hoped the Danes would vote Yes but then the French No: which, if true, is a neat measure of his passing disillusionment. When the French failed to oblige, and Maastricht became a commitment the Cabinet could not avoid, the bastards were the ones expressing an inability to see why the British should exert so much effort to rescue a Treaty they had never wanted in the first place.

Lilley was the senior among them, who had been in the Cabinet the longest. Born in 1943, he was a right-wing economist of quite serious pedigree, an investment adviser before getting into politics, who wanted not just to halt but to reverse the process of European integration. In private, he advanced the concept of a 'nuclear Switzerland' as a model the British should aim for, believing it to be wholly absurd to suppose that a country with 56 million people couldn't survive as an independent economy making trade agreements with its neighbours. Lilley was quite an absolutist. For instance, the political nature of the European Court of Justice, in his view, didn't even need to be debated. It existed as an ominous, repellent fact. He was also an optimist, believing with some certainty that 'Europe' would wither away, once the old men, Kohl and Mitterrand, had faded from the scene, and the rest of Europe came to see that genuine reform, of such matters as agricultural and regional policies, would be achieved only at the expense of national interest – and would therefore never be attempted. This prospect, with its potential for the long-term destruction of the EU project, Lilley found agreeably exciting.

He was a studious figure, notably lacking in charisma. In polls that were taken to find out which ministers were best recognized by the public, there were years when Peter Lilley barely troubled the scorers, though he had been minister for a decade. His one occasion of prominence, when he paraded a different personality, was the party conference. Here the shy, high-voiced nonentity tried hard, not without success, to sound like a ranting demagogue, with a strident line of invective against the continentals, in their guise, for example, as welfare scroungers. At the 1993 conference, Lilley seemed to revel in his new bastard ranking, treating the faithful to a speech of xenophobic ridicule which also, in its sub-text, tweaked the Prime Minister's nose.

A rather different place in the *salon des salauds* was occupied by Michael Portillo, who began the Major period as Chief Secretary and finished it as Secretary for Defence. Portillo, potentially a larger politician than Lilley, was driven by opinions that extended beyond law and economics. What bothered him was the future of Britain and Britishness in their grandest meaning.

How much this was due to Portillo being the son of a Spanish immigrant was a question to evoke any amount of amateur psychology in reply. Whatever the reason, this was a very *British* right-winger who, in conversations I had with him over a three-year period, often lamented the absence of more national pride in his countrymen. He seemed to regard British irony, including self-irony, as a disease not an attribute, comparing it unfavourably with the Germans and, especially, the French, who expressed old-fashioned attitudes to the superior merits of their own goods and services.

He wasn't always a sceptic on the Europe question, however. It didn't present itself to him as an issue until late in the 1980s. He had voted for the Single European Act, he once told me, without any reservation. He simply didn't know anything about its deeper meaning, he confessed. But then came Maastricht and the single currency, to which, while keeping silent in public, he was fiercely opposed. He admired the meticulous way Major had handled the politics of Maastricht, culminating with its appearance as a manifesto commitment. But by 1994 he had reached the conclusion that it had become impossible to keep the Tory Party together while keeping the EU together, in its present shape, at the same time. Besides believing that the single currency simply would not work, unless it was supported by an equivalent political structure, he adopted a hard attitude towards the need, at all costs, to preserve national power unfettered. It was the veto, not the size of Britain's weighted vote in Community councils, that concerned him. The British interest, he thought, almost never lay in getting things done, almost always in stopping things we didn't like. There had never been an occasion, he contended, when Britain had been frustrated in her objectives by other countries mobilizing a majority vote against her. He was utterly convinced that only the veto, the undying symbol of a negative attitude to Europe, could defend the British way of life.

The strength of his opinions about this led Portillo to circulate the news of where he stood, but without ever being disloyal. He was not the most deft performer on the tightrope, though he knew that the sentiments of the back-benches were collecting themselves into a reliable safety-net for anyone of his persuasion. He, too, couldn't resist the lure of the party conference, raising the roof, as Defence Secretary in 1995, with some spectacularly tawdry jibes at the inferiority, even the cowardice, of the European partners. These followed a reckless charge that many European students were 'cheats' who got their degrees by paying for them. On each occasion he had to withdraw or rephrase what he had said. But his mistakes, he seemed to think, were merely tactical. On the substance he was moved by juices for which he would never apologize. For another conceit was that he held his convictions about Europe more strongly than anyone on the other side held theirs: and this, in his belief, guaranteed that in the fullness of time there could be only one outcome to the story which had begun with the historic error made twenty years before, when Britain misled herself into believing that 'Europe' was her inevitable destiny.

Here, therefore, were two alien presences alongside Major, not yet formidable for their political weight, but known to hold opinions about the Europe policy that echoed those of the volubly sceptic cave on the benches behind. Despite their obvious hostility, Major chose to do nothing about them. Indeed, in May 1993, he added to their number, bringing into the Cabinet John Redwood, who was made Secretary for Wales.

As a candidate for bastardy, Redwood was in some ways the most eligible of the three. Certainly in the eyes of Major's friends, he became the most ridiculed and reviled. Again with a pedigree in the City, he was also a former Fellow of All Souls, the Oxford college distinguished as a scholarly enclave but seldom as a supplier of durable performers in the practical world of high politics. Redwood was a Thatcherite by specific definition, having headed the policy unit at 10 Downing St in the middle 1980s. He climbed, as an elected politician, under his patron's welcoming eye. When she was removed, he was among the most despondent of her followers but, because he was cleverer than many high Euro-sceptics, he became accepted as one of their necessary representatives in government in the post-Thatcher world.

But Redwood was a disturbing figure, a kind of *idiot savant* as some saw him. He was obviously very bright but, equally obviously, rather unreliable. There was something other-worldly about him, a quality that might be attributed to his academic origins but was supplemented by an appearance which the press could not resist turning into a joke, depicting him as a Vulcan from outer space. Redwood knew he had this effect on people, and trained himself in attempts at populism: for example, while Welsh Secretary, modifying his reputation as a rigorous Thatcherite enemy of public spending by mobilizing a campaign in defence of local cottage hospitals. But on 'Europe', he was the most ultra of ultras, a powerful disbeliever in integration, and an expert casuist in defence of the common sceptic proposition that being against the European Union was the only way, in truth, to show that you were a real European.

Major did not like these people. As dissenters from the Maastricht process through the first half of 1993, they remained within the bounds of formal propriety while being, in their hearts and deeper stratagems, unreliable colleagues, as he indicated by his private crudity about them. By the end of Maastricht's passage, he was utterly exasperated. Yet this was an emotion he did not feel able to take much further than a muttered aside to an accidental television microphone. The bastards, allied with the friends of William Cash, had another effect as well. By the autumn of 1993, Major was beginning to understand how he might need to make common cause with them. This was the moment when that famous capacity to convince each faction in the argument that he was really on their side can be seen slipping one way rather than the other.

From now on, Major's survival instincts started the process of converting him from a genuine sceptic – quizzical, calculating, negotiating – into something more like what 'sceptic' had become as a term of art, which is to say an enemy of 'Europe' and a disbeliever in its driving purposes. How much this was due to canniness under pressure, and how much to what passed for his genuine convictions, became a subject of some controversy. He was indignant that anyone should suppose he ever acted out of anything but his real beliefs. The fact is, however, that he now made his first utterance to rank with the Thatcher speech in Bruges. He declared for a kind of British scepticism that puzzled and dismayed the continentals as severely as that famous eruption had in 1988. After a five-year interval, the world was put on notice that British Conservatism, in this as in most other respects, had not actually changed.

Significantly, Major chose not to place this statement in the Euro-phobic press, or to make a speech before a select audience, but to write a piece in a magazine, the *Economist*, with an international audience.

He sounded extraordinarily hostile to what 'Europe' was now doing, and positively jubilant at Britain's reluctance to go along with it. 'We take some convincing on any proposal from Brussels,' he proudly wrote. 'We counted the financial cost of our membership. Others counted their financial gain. We subjected each proposal to the scrutiny of Parliament. They relaxed in the sure knowledge that their public opinion uncritically endorsed the European idea. Hang the detail. Never mind the concession of power to Brussels.'

The future, he said, recapitulating the Bruges address, must be built around the nation-state. Insofar as the vision of Monnet and other founders had proposed a weakening of nation, the time for any more of that was over. 'The new mood in Europe demands a new approach ... It is for the nations to build Europe, not for Europe to attempt to supersede nations.' As for the main project now on the table, EMU, this would, in Major's opinion, simply not happen. 'I hope my fellow heads of government', he wrote, 'will resist the temptation to recite the mantra of full economic and monetary union as if nothing had changed. If they do recite it, it will have all the quaintness of a rain dance and about the same potency.'[41]

As a piece of prophecy, this joined quite a long line of British misjudgements. But, as a piece of politics, it showed that Major the man of government had decided, once Maastricht was safely written into law, to allow himself to be gradually superseded by a character with ambitions that turned out to be more futile: Major, the man of party, susceptible to the most insistent voices that could be heard at any given time.

*

HE WAS NOT a failure, as a European governing politician. He entered the freemasonry with aplomb. Ruud Lubbers and Helmut Kohl were not the only leaders to notice and relish the change of style he brought, after the wholesale depredations of Mrs Thatcher. He could carry on, as a regional diplomat, even when under the most extreme pressure as a domestic leader.

The hideous débâcle of the ERM, for example, occurred in the half-year when Britain took the presidency of the European Council, and Major was therefore chairing all meetings among the leaders. He continued to do this punctiliously, and to some effect. A summit held in Birmingham shortly after the ERM exit was very testing. He had called it, partly to make up for such destabilizing events as that one. The Danish and French referendums also seemed to call for some reaffirmation of the Euro-order, an acknowledgement of discontents. Major hoped Birmingham would see an increase in subsidiarity, handing powers down to the national level, and a reduction in the reach of the Commission. Jacques Delors wasn't pleased, and Anglo-German relations were still suffering from what the British regarded as the Bundesbank's betrayal of Kohl's apparent promises to help keep the pound in the ERM.

But the regular summit at the end of the presidency, held in Edinburgh in December 1992, was regarded as a little masterpiece of Major-ry. He was the consummate chairman, of an unusually heavy agenda. There was the Danish position to be agreed: how many more opt-outs could Denmark be permitted as the price for getting a second referendum launched and carried? This was essential if Maastricht could survive. There was the perennially delicate issue of the Community budget, over which Major used the chair to secure a lower increase than many other members, especially the small ones, hoped for. Enlargement, subsidiarity, changes to the European Parliament: all these required the preparation, the mastery of detail and the nerveless elbow-gripping of the quiet fixer Major liked to see himself as being. Now, too, his study of body-language was attaining senior-wrangler excellence. His swotting up of European history evidently enabled him to make some uproarious little jokes featuring the medieval St Hubert of Maastricht in the punch-line.[42] Now he had made it quite apparent that he was determined to see Britain ratify rather than destroy Maastricht, despite his difficult parliamentary situation, pretty well everyone in the masonry was his friend and admirer once again.

In particular there was Kohl, his original friend, who held for him and his entourage a special fascination. Kohl was terribly helpful at Edinburgh, taking instruction from Major on the quiddities of the British parliamentary system as the reason why, contrary to the demands of Delors and others, Britain could not guarantee to pass Maastricht by a given date. Later, Kohl, an exacting judge of the mastery he thought all leaders needed to show over their parties, was to become very scornful of the British leader. There was a severe withdrawal of affection. But in 1992 the reappearing spectre of Margaret Thatcher, now situated in the eccentric but unavoidable legislative assembly called the House of Lords, united them in watchful understanding. The Majorites could never think of Kohl without a certain toffish mirth, especially at his physical presence, eloquent even before it began to move. They relished the memory of him in Major's Edinburgh hotel suite, almost crushing the low-slung furniture, 'this great bull on a little velvet chair', slapping down any colleague who dared raise an objection, the antithesis of any posture Major could hope to bring to his own situation. British condescension for the foreigner could extend even into the most pro-European circles of government. 'I would guess there must be about 20 stones' worth of Jerry there,' a jocularity perhaps permissible in private conversation, was a phrase committed shamelessly to print by none other than the minister for Europe at the time, Tristan Garel-Jones.[43]

Garel-Jones was an under-strapper, but men like him, the pro-Europe figures, were essential to the Major prime ministership. They were the counterpoise to the sceptics, the other force the leader had to reckon with: the ones who, in their way, he necessarily relied on, and whose line, as a governing man, he supported while never wanting to be so clear about this as to rouse the fury of the other side. That, essentially, was the story of John Major's term of office for the last three years: holding a balance in which, as part of the task, he deemed it critical never to disclose for certain where he finally stood, or what might be regarded as his bottom line: a task rendered manageable, however, by the palpable fact that he didn't really know what these positions were himself. He was prepared to settle for almost anything, as long as it satisfied the cardinal necessity of sustaining, in formal terms, the unsundered union – though not, of course, the unity – of the Conservative Party.

To finesse their difficulty, the men of government came up with a verbal formula, of which Douglas Hurd seems to have been the main author. He developed the conceit that Europe was 'moving our way'. Those who called on him heard these words often. So did the Cabinet. They were a way of arguing that, if you took the long view, the problem between, say, Portillo and a pro-Europe man like Michael Heseltine might be said not really to exist. For Britain's objectives were coming about anyway. 'The climate is changing,' Hurd told me on several occasions between 1992 and 1996. The Commission, repeatedly, was said to have got the message about subsidiarity. So had Delors and Mitterrand personally. There was now a new stream of higher wisdom percolating through the Community from its source-bed in London. Ideas that had once been regarded as 'heresies, eccentricities of British thought' were now beginning to prevail, a development that made it 'not sensible to back off into noisy and destructive isolation'.[44]

Major himself also believed this. He was convinced the Germans would soon be as keen decentralizers as the British, spurred on by the demands of the *Länder* for their regional rights to be recognized against Brussels' impositions. France, he thought, was moving in the same direction. More than once, I saw him gleaming with certainty that the priorities of the big three EU countries would conspire in favour of the British view, on this subject at least, and that future enlargement would bring about the wholesale review of EU spending he always wanted.

Nor was this posture always nervous and defensive. Though Major cultivated a Hamlet-like demeanour in the matter, Heseltine continued capable of bursting on the scene with the dismissive fierceness of a Falstaff. Preparations for the 1994 European elections began in an atmosphere of anxiety, reflecting the divisions in the party and the tormented dithering of its leader. Ministers came and went, suggesting to the manifesto committee the compromises they thought essential in any form of words the party wrote. When Heseltine's day arrived, he made a statement of unmitigated Europeanism, explaining to the assembled functionaries that the present climate of scepticism was nonsensical, and that he personally would play no part in the election campaign unless the party line returned to the heart of Europe. He challenged them to account for their feeble-minded collapse into the arms of the anti-Europeans. Hurd, who was chairing the committee, thanked him for his robust statement, but the bald declaration left everyone stunned. The intervention was barely comprehensible. 'It was so utterly unfamiliar to hear anything like this from a minister,' one witness told me next day. And the party, incidentally, fell some way short of the eruptor's demand, when the time came.

Hurd and Heseltine were large figures. Though Major had defeated them in the leadership contest, they were, in a sense, larger than he was. He won not because he had the most friends but because he had the fewest enemies: on account not of his forensic brilliance but of his emollient competence. Hurd and Heseltine, Foreign Secretary and President of the Board of Trade, stood for something, not only as leftist

Conservatives but as politicians whose experience in government gave them considerable standing outside. They personified the governing world, the politico-business establishment, the whole inheritance of which Europe was deeply a part. Together with Kenneth Clarke, they formed the bastion that protected Major against the sceptics' onslaught, while also preventing him from sliding, as he sometimes seemed about to, wholly into the sceptic embrace. They were his haven of escape from the bastards, without ever becoming, however, a force strong enough to erase the strong neo-Thatcherite colouring that Major soon felt obliged to give his Europe policy.

As Chancellor from May 1993, succeeding Lamont, Clarke was in as prominent a position as his colleagues. He was a robust, often aggressive character, more than a match for the sceptic snipers behind him, meeting fire with fire and eschewing the sibilant formulations of some other Europeanists. Heseltine, for example, usually took the line that public rows should be avoided. However emphatic he was in private, he declined to retaliate against the steady stream of anti-Europe speeches – coded from the front bench, ever more scathing from the rear – on the ground, as he would say, that 'I won't stir it up unless I'm forced to.' Clarke was temperamentally less willing to leave the field to the enemy. As the Major years wore on, he became defiantly assertive in his positioning, so much so that by the end of them he had been promoted to the top demonic rank in the sceptic calendar.

For the notion of Europe 'going our way' was constantly under challenge. These governing figures of high Tory politics could never rely on events to bear them out. Eminent though they were, they had to live with both the neuralgia of the party and the capacity of the leader, in his tortuous uncertainty, to make a difficult situation worse.

One episode put all these features on display with an especially lurid clarity. For Major it was his worst crisis since the ERM exit, and for Hurd 'the worst episode', he said, in nearly six years as Major's Foreign Secretary.[45] For the governing class, its outcome put them closer than ever to being overpowered by the bastard rabble beneath.

Its origins lay in a Europe policy that Britain not only supported but had promoted: enlargement from a Union of twelve members to one of sixteen, with the addition, if their people agreed, of Austria, Finland, Norway and Sweden (though the people of Norway, once again, voted No). Enlargement, for any member state that rejected the integrationist model of the existing EU, was a natural objective, but it had inevitable consequences for the balance of power. In particular, for the zones of

EU action that were subject to qualified majority voting (QMV), additional members would raise a question about the size of the majority needed to act, and of the numbers needed to qualify it. Under rules that had existed for quite a time, votes were weighted according to each country's size, and twenty-three such votes were enough to create a 'blocking minority' – the collective veto, which Michael Portillo was not alone in believing to be the vital fall-back weapon in defence of the British national interest. If the EU was enlarged, should twenty-three votes still be sufficient to block? If so, a smaller proportion of the whole would be able to frustrate the wishes of the majority. Twenty-three votes could already be assembled merely by two large countries and one small one, but, under enlargement, small countries could get together to defeat what all the larger powers, notably France, Germany and Britain, might want. Plainly this was a serious issue, which would require fundamental attention, as to the size–vote ratio as well as the scale of the blocking minority, when enlargement actually occurred. But meanwhile, without changing the votes-per-country to reflect population size more accurately, the majority of members wanted to raise the twenty-three to twenty-seven – well short of the figure that would have accurately reflected the change in numbers that was about to happen, but still a dilution of existing veto power.

At that modest level, the change did not need to present itself as a massive question. It might have been treated as almost technical in nature. To the bulk of people outside the political class, and a good many within it, it was, if not unintelligible, extremely obscure. Before it attained incandescence, quiet compromise, pending more permanent arrangements, might have been available. Differently handled, the bulk of sceptic Tory MPs would, in the judgement of several of them after the event, have settled for twenty-seven, this being so much smaller than it might have been. But here Major's famous talents as a manager completely deserted him. For most of March 1994, he became the author of a political exercise that ended in near-disaster, especially for himself.

Hurd could see what was coming, but Major declined to go along with him. Isolated in the foreign ministers' council, Britain nonetheless decided to appeal to the grandstand of domestic public opinion by declaring that this was a great test of national sovereignty. She would settle for twenty-three or nothing, even if this meant her being solely responsible for delaying the next stage of enlargement, on which Major had hitherto played a constructive role, encouraging the momentum for entry in the applicant states, especially during his presidency. 'We aren't going to do what the Labour Party do, which is to say "yes" to everything that comes out of Europe without any critical examination,' he shouted to the Commons. 'We will not be moved by phoney threats to delay enlargement.' The Labour leader, John Smith, who challenged him, was dubbed, in the relentless, faintly whingeing locutions of sub-cockney, known as 'Estuary English', that Major retained, 'Monsieur Oui, the poodle of Brussels'.[46] In its invocation of the dog, this recalled Harold Wilson on Ted Heath: in its deployment of a bit of French, the sarcastic knowingness of Jim Callaghan playing to the gallery before the 1975 referendum: a wretched, but telling, ancestry.

The Cabinet, offered the opportunity to tie Hurd's hands when he went into the negotiation, duly did so. With two exceptions, all the voices favoured sticking at twenty-three. Neither of the contrary opinions, it should be noted, came from Heseltine or Clarke: a measure of how fast the issue became one of national pride, and how sensitive even these pro-Europeans were to the desirability of being seen on the pro-British side of the argument, in the event of the leader's position becoming untenable.[47] For the vultures were circling. Major's future was the stuff of daily speculation. The post-ERM frailty reappeared, and with it the sense that he very likely could not last. Discussion was openly taking place as to why Heseltine, having recovered from a recent small heart attack, could now be considered to have overtaken Clarke as the party's likely favourite.

When the foreign ministers met, at Ioannina, Hurd had a very hard time. The absolutist position was untenable, and he had been left a small amount of leeway, something about 'preserving the substance' of the existing position. This he proceeded to exploit, with help from the Germans, who in effect supplanted the Greeks as the deal-makers, and from his friend Jacques Delors. Only by keeping the French out of the room at a critical moment was he able to construct a communiqué which had a chance of satisfying his colleagues without imperilling the next stage of enlargement. Even by Europe's standards, the compromise was convoluted, stating that if the potential blocking minority mustered between twenty-three and twenty-six votes, then, though that didn't meet the agreed figure of twenty-seven, the relevant Council would do 'all in its power', within a 'reasonable time', to reach a consensual solution. The deal had stretched everyone's diplomatic powers, and risked enraging those who were excluded from the final fix. 'I could never do this again,' Hurd mordantly reflected to me soon after returning.

His reception, however, was far from grateful. The Ioannina compromise made Major very nervous. In the political arena, it would be seen only as a climb-down, however much sense it made as an act of government: the more sense, indeed, given the real world of actual European decision-making, where these computations of voting power would hardly ever come into play. This was a supremely totemic controversy. Symbol, power, ambition, politics: all mattered more than the substance of the issue. Such was the state to which Britain's 'Europe' problem had once again degenerated.

The Cabinet sceptics, naturally, opposed Ioannina. Howard made the main statement of dissatisfaction, which the other side found 'long and able', Hurd told me. Portillo, Lilley and Redwood chimed in. Clarke, however, did not. Having spoken before for twenty-three, he was prepared to settle for Hurd's 23–26 deal. His governing persona reasserted itself. Not only Hurd but Major needed to be guarded against the fury of a party that now seemed gripped more widely than ever by the sense that its leader, irrespective of the line he took, was forfeiting its confidence. Quite a number of middle-of-the-road MPs were unable to understand how he had ever got into the Ioannina crisis in the first place, and others were more brutal. Tony Marlow had been his collaborator on the occasion of Major's first known Europe intervention, writing a letter to the papers favouring possible exit from the EEC. To him, Major must have been a particularly sad disappointment. Now Marlow stood up and told him to depart, with a directness no backbencher had summoned up since Anthony Fell said the same thing on the same issue to Harold Macmillan – 'make way for somebody else who can provide the party and the country with direction and leadership'.[48]

I saw Major to interview him around this time. He much resented the common belief that he was being pushed around by forces he couldn't control. Too many people, he thought, were in the grip of a fallacy. 'The fallacy', he said, 'is that I am wholly reactive, and only concerned with one side of my party or the other. It might perhaps occur to people that I feel pretty strongly myself about what is the right thing to do . . . I happen to be doing what I believe to be right.'[49]

In his own eyes, his role was still more creditable than that, both abroad and at home. His calculations about Europe, he said, had to take into account the line-up on the other side, especially the fact that the other powers all had natural friends – 'an entailment of allies', as he rather curiously put it. 'Partly because we are an island, partly because of history, we don't have an entailment.' The skills he brought to this national condition, he thought, were just as valuable on the domestic front. Indeed, they were probably irreplaceable. Gazing round the empty Cabinet table at which we were sitting, the embattled Prime Minister checked off the ghosts in the chairs, enumerating the reasons why each of them, were they to take his place, would split the party. 'If there hadn't been a consolidator sitting in this chair since 1990,' he said, 'I think it would all have broken up.'

The process of consolidation, nevertheless, tended now to move all in one direction. What might be called Major's genuine feelings did play some part in this. He had begun thoroughly to dislike what he called the continental way of doing things: the refusal to be precise, the preference for grand generalities, the slack briefing, the reluctance to conduct a meeting in the cut-and-dried way the British favoured. But more, surely, had to do with a political predicament in which he knew where his most potent enemies were to be found.

His speeches and stances became more desperately appealing to them. One strand tried to reassure them, and perhaps himself, of the unreality of their nightmares, especially about the single currency. 'My scepticism is about the economic impact of it,' he told a German magazine in April. 'You would need proper convergence of the econ-omies across Europe. They would all need to be operating at the same sort of efficiency. I know of no one who believes that is remotely likely. It is simply not going to happen.'[50]

During the European election campaign, which culminated in June, he delighted Euro-sceptics by putting fresh words to his vision of Europe. We should now see the Union, he said, as 'multi-track, multi-speed, multi-layered'.[51] This was a new British formula, first alluded to by Hurd, to permit the continentals to make swifter progress towards integration, while ensuring Britain's legitimized separateness. But the speech did not appear to have been well worked out. A few months later, close to the anniversary of his groundbreaking effusion in the *Economist*, Major contradicted himself. 'I see real danger', he said at Leiden in Holland, 'in talk of a hard core, inner and outer circles, a two-tier Europe. I recoil from ideas of a Union in which some would be more equal than others.' This was puzzling in the detail: having favoured a multi-speed Europe in May, how could anyone but a hair-splitting casuist recoil from a two-speed version in September? But there was no mistaking the consistency of tone. Major was now speaking for nation more than Community. 'The Maastricht Treaty strained the limits of acceptability to Europe's electors,' he said. 'Europe's peoples in general retain their favour and confidence in the nation-state. I believe that the nation-state will remain the basic political unit for Europe.'[52]

These declarations of independence were not confined to the verbal. The 1994 John Major was happy to cast a solitary vote against the agreed successor to Delors as president of the Commission, Jean-Luc Dehaene, the Belgian Prime Minister, who had been approved by every other member. Reasons were invented for stigmatizing him as a federalist, a designation that could just as easily be applied to the fall-back candidate who eventually got unanimous support, the Luxembourger Jacques Santer. This was pettiness by Britain – but pettiness with a domestic purpose: the invention of a defect, said to apply uniquely to the porky Belgian, for no better reason than the pleasure of being able to demonstrate, to a press and a party thirsting for continental blood, that nothing could cut more sharply than a bit of British steel.

*

THIS WAS NOT ENOUGH, however, to staunch the flow of bile around and out of the Tory Party. To accomplish that, the leader judged he owed them, in the last analysis, the opportunity to dispose of him.

Major was, by comparison with other prime ministers, a quite frequent contemplator of resignation. It hardly needs to be said that he had a lot of iron in his make-up, the material without which he could never have made his unassisted journey from Brixton to Downing Street. But there was also a certain self-effacement, a looming excess of modesty: a vulnerability, therefore, to depression when things were going badly, and a capacity at least to wonder whether, in all circumstances, he continued to be the right man for the job. There is no record of any such apprehensions having crossed the mind of Edward Heath or Jim Callaghan, though Wilson planned his exit, for reasons of exhaustion as much as anything, more than a year ahead. When Mrs Thatcher talked about quitting, which she did quite frequently, it was, on all occasions save one, a threat designed to pull people into line behind some policy they seemed in danger of not supporting.[53] She threatened, as it were, from strength. Major thought about it from weakness, at different moments of the Maastricht ratification process, and then, folded into that, when he had to get out of the ERM.

In June 1995, however, he produced a different effect. Surrounded by enemies, he exercised his right to surprise, by jauntily walking on to the Downing Street lawn and announcing that he had resigned as leader of the Conservative Party. There would now have to be a leadership election, in which he would stand as a candidate. Under party rules, every autumn brought the possibility of such an election, and every autumn since 1992 there had been discussion of some enemy or other making use of this opening to challenge him. By the summer of 1995, two years from the end of the present Parliament, and with three years of accumulated fire banked up against the leader, the talk of an autumn challenge was more unquenchable than ever. The Government was being chronically destabilized. So Major threw down the gauntlet to his party. 'It is time to put up or shut up,' he said.

This was a challenge, essentially, to the Euro-sceptics. Although he had been appeasing them with almost every gesture he could find, the appetites of the people who thought like William Cash and Michael Portillo were, as is usually the case with the appeased, insatiable. To their ideological hostility was added the dismay of a wide variety of Tory politicians who, if the opinion polls were indicative of any durable truth, faced the imminent end of their careers. For the first time in many of their lives, the Labour Party was a credible alternative government, now twenty-five points ahead.

Thus challenged, the sceptics duly rose. Lamont, skulking, was the first bet to lead them. But Lamont was not the most undamaged of goods. Redwood also lurked, unable to decide. Portillo hovered, waiting to see what Redwood might do, and thinking he might come into the contest if the first round was inconclusive. Portillo, by this stage, was extraordinarily alienated. The pervasive European issue of the moment was the prospect of another inter-governmental conference, the follow-up to Maastricht, which would take the EU into further realms of integration, with more QMV, more streamlined institutions, perhaps a more powerful Strasbourg Parliament. On this, Portillo favoured the most radical of British nationalist strategies. Complete rejectionism – the antithesis of the way Major and Hurd did business – was the right line both for Britain and for the electoral prospects of the Tory Party. The straddling of the sides should end. Portillo was even prepared to talk, in my hearing, about the desirability of a formal splitting of the party.

But Redwood it was who ran, and scepticism paraded in full regalia behind him. At his first appearance, the nine MPs from whom the whip had been withdrawn were his prominent henchmen: a bad start. His alternative programme proved more eccentric than substantial, though it promised a clear and absolute No to Britain joining the single currency. The sceptic press came out in force. 'Redwood vs. Deadwood' is what the *Sun* called the contest. Elsewhere, it was Major's lack of leaderly qualities, his shortage of officer-class command, as much as his want of Euro-phobia, that gathered the voices against him. But, to him, the presentation of himself as a man who could appeal to the sceptics as much as anyone else was a crucial objective. When Clarke, for example, emerged with typical brutishness to say that an ultra right-winger like Redwood could not win an election for the Conservative Party 'in a thousand years', Major's people were horrified.[54] They feared this might make their man sound insufficiently right-wing. And when Hurd let it be known that he would resign as Foreign Secretary immediately the election was over, the word went out that his replacement might well be a sceptic.

With the help of these signals, and the slightness of the opposing candidate, the parliamentary party was persuaded to reinstate the leader. More than a third of them didn't vote for him: he won by 218 to 89 votes, with twenty abstentions. Immediately announced as a decisive victory, it did become, as far as Major's ongoing position was concerned, conclusive. But, as regards the issue, the result was no more than cosmetic. It settled, after a fashion, nothing. For the pro-Europe people, Major was, of course, the only option – though there were some, possibly even some who secretly went as far as casting a tactical vote for Redwood, who thought Heseltine, coming in after a non-result, might be their saviour. But the anti-EU faction simply resumed the struggle for Major's mind, and the enforcement upon it of their visceral prejudices.

The degeneration of the Conservative Government, therefore, entered its terminal phase. A ruse designed to solidify it actually produced no change in its condition. And this happened at a time when the great question continued to obtrude, quite unrelentingly, on the consciousness of politics.

On the one hand, EMU beckoned – with decisions required, of both an economic and political character, by 1997. Choosing between 'never' and 'some time, maybe' was not the most uplifting of arguments to be having, but it was around that bleak axis that the entire end-game of the Major period would now revolve. At the same time, the IGC, equally undeflectable, had to reach its conclusions either shortly before or shortly after the British general election. What Europeans saw, as they made their own preparations for another group of epic developments, was a government in London that was not so much indecisive as, quite probably, incapable of taking a decision. It was no longer a question of seeing which side the British would come down on, but of addressing the palpable, if rather pathetic, reality that their internal condition debarred their leader from being taken seriously, whatever he said.

Government did go on. The seat at the table continued to be occupied. Hurd duly departed, to be replaced by Malcolm Rifkind, the Defence Secretary, whose past performance did not appear to qualify him as the promised sceptic. If Rifkind had a definable origin, it was on the left of the party, as a supporter, for example, of Scottish devolution, and a rising minister who was not entirely trusted by Mrs Thatcher. Amid a cluster of vaguely centrist positions was thought to go a more Hurdish than Portilloite attitude to Europe. That perhaps was the case. In my own first conversation with him, however, soon after he became Foreign Secretary, he greeted these suggestions cautiously. When I noted that he was a pro-European, he instantly denied that he had ever been a strong one 'if by that you mean someone who wanted more integration'. He challenged me, with a gleam of triumph, to find a single press release throughout his career that might indicate otherwise – although I knew that in a previous role, as Minister of State in the Foreign Office, and the British representative on the Dooge committee in 1985,[55] he had had to be restrained by none other than Geoffrey Howe, then his boss, against being too European. Rifkind hoped to show he had never changed his mind, but he seemed like a piece of fluff blown on the sceptic wind now breezing irresistibly through the party.

Nothing could happen without reference to this torrid zephyr. It generated, simultaneously, the oxygen on which most of the Tory Party existed, its life-support system, yet also the poison that seeped through it, corrupting all coherence.

Adventitiously, too, scepticism was given another twist, and Major an uncontrollable blow, by a threat to the nation's health that had nothing directly to do with either Europe or political leadership, but soon carried both issues to a yet deeper nadir of aggravation. In March 1996, the Government was forced to disclose that a cattle disease, BSE, might be linked with brain disease in humans, a new strain of Creutzfeldt-Jacob, or CJD. Though BSE had been present in the nation's beef herd for some years – a consequence, it was often argued, of the deregulatory, anti-inspection prejudices of high Thatcherism – the human link had not been authoritatively made. Now a Government scientific committee said it might exist, and ministers felt they had no choice but publicly to endorse the finding.[56]

The statement produced an immediate national panic but, almost as importantly, a series of repercussive degradations – if that were possible

– in relations with the European partners. For Britain exported beef and its products to Europe, and the European Union, as the controlling agency of both trade and public health rules, imposed an immediate British beef ban not only in Europe but worldwide. Farming was put on the rack. A great British industry, which was a traditional bulwark of the Conservative Party, found itself a prisoner of Brussels.

Evaluating the Major years after they were over, some Downing Street insiders called the BSE crisis the most difficult single issue of the premiership.[57] Heseltine told a group of journalists at the time that it was 'the worst political problem I have ever had to confront': a large statement for one whose ministerial career went back twenty-five years. The successor Government, after an early trawl through its Whitehall inheritance, said the BSE problem, which was still quite unresolved, constituted much the most chaotic mess it had to deal with.

For Major himself, however, it was the intermingling with Europe that caused him most grief. Part of this was his own, rather typical, British fault. A decision had been taken, when the CJD link was first adumbrated, not to advise, still less consult, the European Commission beforehand. Justified on the grounds of preserving secrecy, this showed some contempt for the body which, after all, would have decisive influence on the regulatory consequences, and represented millions of European nationals whose health was potentially under threat from British negligence. It was a studied choice, contributing to a long-drawn-out absence of mutual co-operation, which in turn did much to transmute the scepticism of many of the island Tory politicians into downright phobia for the continent and all who made decisions there.

The crisis swiftly escalated. At its first emanation, a summit in Turin to launch the plenary stage of the post-Maastricht IGC, the Europeans were actually quite helpful, promising Major financial help for the destruction of older cattle on a vast scale. But he took an abrasive line, attacking the beef ban as an exercise in 'collective hysteria', and already preparing the ground for what became the most surreal, yet strangely persistent, feature of the British position: that 'Europe', rather than Britain, was responsible for the BSE catastrophe. As the ban continued, Britain got ready to retaliate. A number of options were prepared, including a counter-ban against European meat products and, more dramatically, the leaving of an empty chair at all EU discussions. This, the de Gaulle tactic of the mid-1960s, could not have had the same paralysing effect as it did then. The only victim would have been Britain,

unable to exercise her veto. A substitute ploy was therefore invented: to
obstruct all decision-making that required unanimity. After the veterin-
ary committee in Brussels had persisted in its dissatisfaction with
Britain's safety measures, Major rose to his full parliamentary height to
announce a policy of 'non-cooperation' with Europe,[58] as a result of
which British ministers succeeded in blocking as many as seventy
measures, including several, for example against EU fraud, which they
themselves had been promoting. With very little to show for this, after a
month's obstruction, serious thought was given in London to refusing to
attend the next EU summit, in Florence, at the end of June.

The overall effect of the grand gesture of non-cooperation was
merely to increase the number and deepen the resonance of the Prime
Minister's critics, wherever they were. It was the worst breakdown since
Britain joined the Community in 1973. For the Europeans, it marked
the beginning of the end of their respect for him. Though the bastard
faction in the Cabinet, led by Howard, were pressing for the empty
chair, Major did, of course, go to Florence. He thought he could get
some kind of beef deal, which, in the event, he did. The ban would begin
to be lifted, in line with a cattle-slaughter programme that EU vets
would invigilate and approve: a conjunction, as it turned out, which
took a very long time to come about. But the damage done to the British
leader's relations with his continental peer-group was considerable, going
on terminal. Before Florence, the Commission president Jacques Santer
spoke of an imminent 'moment of truth' for Britain, a menacing phrase
which nonetheless reflected the genuine opinions of most of the member
states. They could not but see Major, occupying what they ridiculed as
the 'half-empty chair', as increasingly petulant, and obviously not in
control.

Pressing on him more strongly, however, were the people who
supposedly belonged to the same political enterprise as he did at home.
Stamping his foot in rage at what he regarded as the unscientific
politicking of the continentals was an attitude which, far from gladdening
the Tory Party, only rendered its divisions more combustible. The beef
row somehow excited the famous viscera to more turbulent agitation
than ever. Was this because the substance at issue was the Roast Beef of
Old England, the complete culinary symbol of British eating? Major
himself, hinting as much to a Spanish audience, called beef 'part of the
psyche of our nation', to be reckoned alongside forests for the Germans.[59]
Might poisoned lamb, or contaminated chicken, have touched a less
sensitive national nerve? Or was the problem that this aggressive interfer-

ence from Brussels, even on a matter requiring urgent attention, exposed to apparent ridicule Major's much pleaded case for subsidiarity, and Douglas Hurd's insistence that things were 'moving our way'? Whatever the reason, BSE unleashed the media dogs, barking at Major with renewed ferocity. Around this time, one measured comment, not untypical of the general tone, said that here was 'a weak man trying to look strong', who presided from his half-empty chair over 'a half-dead Government'.[60] Having excited the mob by going to war, Major had inflamed it yet further by retreating into peace and calling this, emptily, a victory.

Sceptic appetites had been whetted by an earlier gesture, concerning the matter that vibrated with still more potency than BSE. For the manoeuvrings over the single currency never ceased. Though Major was an open sceptic on this matter, he never wanted to declare against EMU in perpetuity. The governing man in him regarded that as hopelessly imprudent, though the political man kept inventing formulae to put off the evil day when he might have to confront the other side of the party, whether at Cash's level or Portillo's, with the choice.

This political man had thought of a device that might assist him towards a haven of tranquillity, where the forces around him temporarily ceased to battle. For a year or two, he was toying with the case for promising a referendum. This, he privately suggested, could be pledged to happen before any decision was taken to put sterling in the single currency. It became the touchstone of most Euro-sceptic politics from now on. Anyone opposed to a referendum announced himself, by implication, as an anti-populist and probably an anti-democrat. So said the body of Euro-sceptics. They were goaded by the overbearing Jimmy Goldsmith, who made an all-embracing Europe referendum the core purpose of his new party. But they worked out to their own satisfaction that, in a referendum on EMU *tout court*, they couldn't fail to win the argument to which many of them had devoted the prime of their political lives.

The referendum, therefore, became the question, as the factions in the party looked fit finally to split apart. But the referendum did not enjoy universal approval, even among Euro-sceptics. Portillo opposed it on democratic grounds: also, perhaps, because he could see more clearly than some of his colleagues that it was a duplicitous expedient which, if it endorsed the wrong decision, would close the argument, and pre-empt parliamentary sovereignty, for the indefinite future. The more important opponent, however, was Kenneth Clarke. He it was, as Chancellor and man of unshiftable conviction, whom Major knew he had to carry in all these matters.

But Clarke was manoeuvrable, if not directly carriable. The referendum argument rumbled through the Cabinet before and after the BSE bombshell burst; its outcome became part of beef's collateral damage. It appeared, in late winter, that some sign of official sympathy for a referendum would be the most promising way to sweeten the atmosphere in the party that was now boiling with hatreds. One day in the Commons, Major duly dropped the hint. There would be study of the subject, he said. That was as good as saying that there would be a referendum pledge very soon. Clarke was not amused. He detested the way he had been bounced, and so did Heseltine.

Heseltine was to murmur, some time later, that the Tories' commitment to a referendum on EMU was one of the great disasters of the final months. Once made, it would extract, he thought, a matching commitment from Labour – which it duly did. And, once that happened, any government's EMU options would sharply close – which they did. To both Heseltine and Clarke, placing the single currency in hock to the popular will would immensely complicate the task of remaining anywhere near the centre of Europe. Nonetheless, the commitment was made, in a protocol stating with rare public formality that if a newly elected Conservative government were to contemplate entry into EMU, it would hold a referendum first. This was issued not from the Government but, eloquently, from Conservative Central Office. There was no signature, but those silently taking the pledge were Major, Clarke and Heseltine, with the sceptics alongside, and Rifkind piping up for the usual pretence that this was all part of an ordered continuity. 'The Government made quite clear some considerable time ago,' he said at a press conference, 'that we are not going to rule out the possibility of joining a single currency in the next Parliament.'[61]

From the anti-sceptic point of view, there was only one merit to this document. Its promise was restricted to the life of a single parliament, and was solemnly, if privately, sworn to be the last concession Major intended to make to the Cabinet's bastard strain. There would be no further yielding, Clarke was given to understand, on the policy that the Government would 'wait and see' if sterling should one day belong to the single currency. The famous bottom line – or was it the infamous line in the sand? – was now definitively drawn. O fond illusion!

The pressure for another pledge did not let up. The real goal of Euro-scepticism, about which the Tory press, quite unimpressed by the referendum decision, kept hammering on, was to secure sworn testimony from Major that he would not enter EMU. Between the referendum pledge and the election campaign, exactly one year passed. There was no week when this question failed to intrude upon the life, and dominate the manoeuvres, of the grimly tormented figure in 10 Downing Street.

In the middle of this period, I had a conversation with him, in which the subject of Europe could never be far away.[62] He presented himself as a man of competing convictions, yet also one who denied the need to make certain kinds of choice. He seemed puzzled by what confronted him.

Like all post-war prime ministers before him, he rejected any suggestion that 'Europe' represented some kind of an alternative to the Atlantic relationship. America's defence role in Nato was central to European security, and 'we are the second nation of Nato'. In his experience, there had never been a serious difference between Britain and the Americans on the big issues, a fact which pointed the way towards one of Britain's most necessary interests. 'Every time the Europeans have tried to do something without the Americans on defence,' he said, 'they have made a bog of it.' All this suggested to him that the British problem could never be resolved by making a strategic choice, loaded one way rather than the other. 'Unlike any other European nation, we are genuinely split as to where our interests lie,' he said. The country, he thought, was 'pretty evenly split' about which way to go. 'So I ask myself,' he said, 'why do we have to choose one or the other? Why should we make an artificial choice when our interests are almost equally divided between two great blocs – the Americas and Europe? My answer is that we would be mad to make such a choice.'

It followed that we would be equally mad to contemplate leaving the European Union, as some sceptics were now implying. 'It is nonsense, copper-plated nonsense,' he said, 'that we would leave the European Union and form some Atlantic alliance.'

At the same time, however, the Europeans were 'going too far, too fast'. They were moving in the wrong direction. They should be thinking about enlarging to the east, letting in the poor countries like Poland and Hungary, rather than deepening relations among the rich Western nations. 'I profoundly believe that is the wrong choice after a century, for half of which these countries have been to all intents and purpose enslaved.' It was all very well for Helmut Kohl, who also wanted enlargement, to be pushing for more integration. He had the luxury of being in charge, 'driving the motor'. Equally, Major could see why Spain and Portugal wanted a strong European Union: 'not all that many years ago, they were run by men in epaulets and dark glasses'. But for Britain, he said, it was otherwise. 'It is a different prospect for a nation traditionally used to doing things in its own way, suddenly finding that it may not be able to do so.'

In particular, he added, the single currency would make for a situation that was very different. It would remove power and responsibility from elected politicians. 'I wouldn't like to be the Chancellor of the Exchequer', the Prime Minister mused, 'who went to the despatch box and said: "Well, I no longer have any control over interest rates. I am sorry they've gone up by three per cent but it's nothing to do with me, Guv!"'

What seemed most to frustrate him about the present situation was his own confusing locus, blown about between the people of Britain and the European ruling class. The people, on the one hand, he regarded as not being fundamentally chauvinistic. 'They are not anti-European at all,' he said. What bothered them, he thought, was that 'we often seem powerless to prevent things happening'. On the other hand, it was the perception of public opinion, and its effect on him as leader, that weakened the message he was constantly trying to get across to the Europeans. The press, falsely representing the people, was responsible for this. He was unable (as he did not say) to discover a way of asserting his command over the deluge of polemic and propaganda it evacuated over him. The 'nature of the debate here' was unhelpful: that was the way he put it. 'The problem I face in Europe', he concluded forlornly, 'is that the Europeans are never certain whether the position I take is because I believe it or is a reflection of political necessity.'

Whichever of these two influences was the greater, one more, fateful stride had to be attempted, into the arms of the anti-Europeans. Though the referendum pledge was supposed to be the last such move, Major was uncomfortable with the vague, procrastinating, palpably evasive, intentionally contorted words he was being required to say about the single currency. Much of the last part of 1996 was spent, on the one side, trying to make sense of them, and on the other trying to take them apart. It was another period of textual deconstruction, sufficiently reductivist and passionate to recall the medieval school-men. Every word spoken on the subject of 'Europe' by Major, by Clarke, by Rifkind, by a club of bastards that was growing in number, was scrutinized for its inner meaning with respect to possible shifts on the single currency, probable rejection elsewhere in the party, and proof that the leader either was, or was not, about to convert fully to scepticism, perhaps either before or after sacking his Chancellor of the Exchequer. The quotation about a notional Chancellor, cited two paragraphs above, which appeared in a piece of mine published in February 1997, was just one example of an utterance seized on by the media, held up to the light and rotated through all planes of inspection, before being pronounced incontrovertible proof that Major had changed his mind again.

It seemed he half had. Certainly he imposed one more sceptic concession on Clarke, who regarded it as impossible to resist, on account of the proximity of the election. Again, looking back, one can hardly see in this the cause for civil war. What the Cabinet agreed was that it should now be said the single currency was 'very unlikely' to start, as intended, in January 1999. Further, 'if it did proceed with unreliable convergence [of the economies of member states] we would not of course be part of it'.[63] This was a neat way of avoiding the sceptics' stipulated demand, that the Tories should fight the election pledged against entering EMU in the first wave of currencies to join it. By postulating delay, the Cabinet could be said to neutralize the question. But this wasn't the way the adjustment was interpreted – or intended to be. It was a sop to the Euro-sceps, falling short of sufficient provocation to Clarke to resign.

This was the posture in which the election was fought – or rather, in which the leader tried to fight it. 'Wait-and-see with extreme scepticism' might be a way of encapsulating it. But the message, already baffling enough to voters less schooled in medievalism than Conservative politicians, was overlaid by the more strident complication that more than half the party's candidates rejected it. As Major, with the support of some of his Cabinet, stuck doggedly to his final final position, many Tory election addresses were being crafted with words of total commitment against a single currency in any circumstances. Financed by a phobic businessman named Paul Sykes, and under the gun from Jimmy Goldsmith, a great cohort of would-be Members of Parliament sought to arrive there on the basis of a position that swept aside the agonized syntax – his last attempt to present himself as all things to all Tories – of the party leader.

For the man whose chief credential, when he became party leader, was supposed to be his mastery of the arts of political management, ironic is hardly the word to describe his fate. Over the seven years, the Conservative Party, under his decent and well-meaning hand, had all but disintegrated. And it duly lost the election, in which the Labour Party secured a majority unimaginable by any post-war government, ending 179 seats ahead of all its rivals put together.

What was the role in this cataclysm of 'Europe'? Directly, a rather small one. The Tories could not make it a great question, since that would only draw attention to the party's divisions, a condition which voters, waking from slumber to pay their quinquennial attention to the political scene, are known particularly to dislike. Apart from one rather passionate statement, in which he pleaded – pleading was by now the only mode he knew – for his party not to 'bind my hands', Major didn't talk about Europe much. Labour, for its part, took up a circumspect position, desiring above all to give no hostages to sceptic fortune. So the most divisive issue in British politics was not presented in full vigour to the electorate, at this classically healing moment in the democratic calendar.

On the other hand, Europe was proxy and proof for other things, to do with leadership style and party credibility, with competence and with plausible purpose. On all those counts, it did more than any other issue to wreck the Tory Government and obliterate any possibility of it being re-elected. And the outcome of Major's handling of it summoned up some troubling ghosts.

He was the sixth Conservative Prime Minister since Churchill to have grappled with the Europe question. In a way, he was discernibly of the lineage. In his particular time and place, fifty years on, he represented in his person some of the same hesitations and anxieties that had afflicted all his predecessors save one. In Churchill's case, the divided national psyche was barely visible, beneath the imperial certainties and the grand continent-building for which he spoke. But the separateness of the island and the unthinkability of it itself being part of the continental project were a part of almost all Tory instincts. Under Eden, who disdained to go to Messina, this continued, only marginally abated. Under Macmillan, followed by the afterthought of Douglas-Home, the balance changed but the divide remained. In their hearts, very many Conservatives were only half ready for the enterprise which de Gaulle saved them from having to choose. They backed Macmillan's attempt to edge Britain towards a different kind of future, but few hoisted into their minds a true understanding of what it would mean. They thought they could probably go on having it all ways, without the need to make a new statement of dependency, still less allegiance, as the founding fact of existence in the European Community.

Heath, of course, was the aberrant case. He was unreserved in his belief, if not wholly clear or candid in his vision. Had Heathite Conservatism survived more than a year after entry, winning rather than losing elections, no one can know how different Britain's European settlement would have been, or whether the Euro-scepticism that destroyed Major would have had half the purchase it subsequently gained on the Tory Party. But Heath lost, and his cause, while rooting itself in the practical business of British life, captured the minds and hearts of Conservatives only imperfectly. A decade of Mrs Thatcher, exciting the Tory divide even as she conducted policies that were supposed to carry the nation, gave Major a legacy whose true nature was unresolved. It matched, all too aptly some would say, his own uncertainties. If the Conservative Party in 1990 needed the firm stamp of a European, ready to embrace the destiny towards which Britain had limped for fifty years, Major was certainly not the man to deliver it.

In some ways, even, the past spoke more loudly through him than the future. Churchill, after all, had at least welcomed every sign of European unification. He was the benign, and not inactive, spectator at a process he regarded as essential. Integration, at that early moment, was something even the Labour Government could acquiesce in.

By Major's time, the prevailing attitude was different. His true forebear, perhaps, was Eden. By Eden's time, while the agreement to European unity was still extant, the belief that it would work was fraying. When the next stage of it, the Common Market, was being conceived, the main British attitude was that it didn't stand a chance. R. A. Butler spoke, consummately *de haut en bas*, about the comical 'archaeological excavations' going on at Messina. This was the beginning of a line of analysis, often repeated, which consisted of the British persuading themselves that the Europeans were engaged on an impossible endeavour. Apart from producing a series of false prophecies, this did not make for fraternal warmth. It wasn't seen as the thinking of a friend. In international affairs, predictions of failure do their bit to ensure their own fulfilment.

The last days of Major eerily replayed them. First, he decided it was time to tell the European Union to rethink its place in the world. Rifkind, the Foreign Secretary, was sent on a tour of the capitals to explain to a succession of political and business elites that they were leading Europe in the wrong direction. The Union should become less integrated, more of a partnership of nations. Rifkind began his tour, calculating on special resonance, in Zurich, where Churchill had launched his own vision of a United States of Europe in 1946. Did he imagine he could lay claim to the smallest scintilla of Churchill's authority, or the tiniest fragment of his audience, for the view Britain was now, in her wisdom, prepared to vouchsafe to her continental neighbours? His lectures continued, round half a dozen capitals, chipping away at EU institutions, warning against 'jumping blindly' towards more integration, pressing the virtues of British parliamentary democracy.

Coming from a strong government, credibly committed to the European enterprise, this might have been a little hard to take. A German foreign minister, touring Britain with a series of Euro-philiac lectures, was a spectacle as hard to imagine the Germans proposing as the British permitting. But the Rifkind exercise was launched by a government no European had listened to for a long time, which was on the verge of collapse, and whose every word on Europe, as they saw it, was dictated not by a serious judgement about how the Union might develop but by sceptic stranglers with their hands round the party's neck. Rifkind's final journey was one of the most humiliating, as well as ridiculous, acts of British foreign policy in the fifty years of which he was so proud to speak.

It wasn't the only echo of the past, however. Still more damaging was a replication of the prophecy made with such confidence in 1955 that the Common Market wouldn't come to birth. Nor, Major and his Government were almost certain, would the current project of economic and monetary union. In 1993, someone had produced for Major the uncharacteristically vivid phrase he was proud of, in which he said that EMU had 'the quaintness of a rain-dance, and about the same potency'. This was still the analysis, which lay, among other things, behind the pre-election compromise, making the wish father to the thought that EMU would not happen at the appointed moment in January 1999. Even Clarke and Heseltine thought that much. Major and most of the others thought more. They believed, both before the election and for some time after it, that EMU was essentially nonsense. Even the Europeans, when they stared it in the face, would surely see this, and retreat before political and economic realities so fraught with danger.

So saying, the British made themselves pretty much detested, certainly ignored, by the leaders whom Major had once imagined he would join at the heart of Europe. These leaders had pursued difficult policies, sometimes strongly against the pattern of their nations' economic history, in the belief that they could make EMU happen. They were now about to do so. What could be said for Major was that, in his error, he himself had exhibited a certain historical consistency. Most of his predecessors would have recognized his problem – though vacillation, the chronic disease, took none of them as close as him to the heart of darkness.

12

TONY BLAIR

Leading from the Edge

JOHN MAJOR was removed from office in the twenty-fifth year of
Britain's membership of what was now the European Union. The
anniversary, when it finally arrived on 1 January 1998, went unre-
marked. There were no newspaper supplements, no television retrospec-
tives. In a media world that feeds avidly on the convenient predictability
of such moments, the silence was remarkable. But it was also eloquent.
It spoke for the dismal state of relations Major left behind. By far the
greater portion of the belonging had been spent under the hand of
ministries, culminating in Major's, that never – not too strong a word
– found a single thing to exalt about membership of 'Europe'. Destiny
had dragged Britain there, but the British discourse seldom moved
beyond the narrow modes of complaint, lecture and demand. Sympathetic recognition of the quarter-century would therefore have been,
as a mirror of history, somewhat unreal. Celebration was out of the
question.

Whether this would have been any different if another group had
been in power for all or some of the time is, of course, an academic
matter. For nearly twenty years, Conservative politicians and politics
shaped the relationship alone. But the speculation isn't worthless, and
the most likely conclusion to be drawn from it is salutary. Although the
Tories were in power, they weren't opposed, for much of the time, by a
coherently organized party able to see Europe more clearly than they
did. They were at the head, one might say, of an entire political system,
the very structure of British politics in the 1980s, which allotted the
'Europe' question an auxiliary, and almost always negative, place. The
Liberal Party had long been a minority voice for closer union with
Europe, but it was almost never heard. The Liberals' small importance
only emphasized the extreme apprehension, sharpened by erratic

aggression, with which both the big battalions habitually treated the subject.

The Labour Party's history in the matter promised terribly little. Go back to the last time they were in the frame of government. It was the culmination of extensive deviousness. Harold Wilson, as shown above,[1] played a critical role in keeping Britain in Europe, by organizing the 1975 referendum. The Labour leadership was then, to that extent, European. But this was after a series of shifts that spoke for a collective scepticism, a riven and unresolved party mind, which would have been hard for any party leader, even from the seat of government, to fashion into the kind of positive Europeanism that Margaret Thatcher, despite the many integrationist steps she took, spent a decade teaching the people to vilify. Wilson and his successor, James Callaghan, let's not forget, opposed the Heath Government's negotiated entry, having spent the three previous years themselves seeking to take Britain in. And they played the smallest part they could in the referendum campaign.

It can be said that these leaders were prudently hedging their bets. On their own account, they would probably contend that my version of what happened gives too little weight to Wilson's problems of party management at all stages. Maybe so. Like John Major, Wilson was prepared to abandon any consistency, let alone vision, as regards Europe for the sake of keeping his party in what could be construed as one piece: and this purpose, though ultimately unsuccessful, wasn't indefensible. But in the case of the last Labour leaders in government, before the two-decade ice age of powerlessness, it also expressed their personal ambivalence. Neither Wilson nor Callaghan were, in any but the most reluctant and instrumental sense, 'Europeans'. They did nothing whatever to teach the party or the country to embrace the continental connection. It is hard to imagine how their immediate successors, if miraculously given the opportunity, would have produced a very different atmospheric context from the one Mrs Thatcher set about creating on her first encounter with European leaders, and never ceased to poison thereafter.

On the other hand, something did happen to the Labour Party in this time, which might not have happened if it had been in government. Under the curse of what seemed to be the interminable status of opposition, it evolved. This occurred not because it saw the light but because it tired of the darkness, the experience by which most political change is propelled. Labour didn't suddenly become seized of the higher Euro-wisdom, perhaps after re-reading the sacred texts of Jean Monnet or Roy Jenkins. No great access of supra-national idealism could be detected, percolating round the corridors and smoke-filled rooms of Blackpool and Brighton, as the party struggled through its annual conferences during the barren years. What happened was a reaction to the much larger political reality that dominated its existence: the hegemonic rule of Mrs Thatcher. Challenge and response, action and reaction: eventually, the classic pattern began to surface through the tundra.

Largely, though not entirely, because Mrs Thatcher was anti-Europe, Labour became pro-Europe. Because Thatcherism dominated the power-structure of Britain, socialism, as it was still called, sought and found another outlet. Over time, strands in the progressive left that had parted fused together once again. Europe, which had contributed mightily to their division, became a kind of therapy, even, in some ways, a unifying balm.

The middle 1990s were the first occasion, in all this history of British membership, when Europe not only brought parties together, but, in due course, ceased to be a destructive agent at the heart of government.

*

AFTER 1979 and the Thatcher victory, Labour reverted with great speed to the anti-Europe stance that had been its instinct to adopt at almost all times when the party wasn't burdened with office. Even in government, it had never been the party of Europe. Ernest Bevin, under Attlee, was the Foreign Secretary who sanguinely watched the Schuman Plan pass him by: the first leader of the left who rejected 'Europe': the man who stood at the earliest gateway and was certain Britain's future lay in turning her back on it. In opposition, as we have seen, Labour's heart persisted in this prejudice for the next twenty-five years. Now in opposition again, the party reassumed the line, almost as if it had had nothing to do with the unfortunate accident that put a Labour government in charge of Britain-in-Europe for five of the country's first six years of the relationship.

Labour had already shown something of its hand. At the last conference before the 1979 election, party instructed government in an impossibilist agenda, supporting a resolution which asserted a series of unilateral priorities. Britain, the conference said, should pass a law enacting Westminster's power to override any EEC regulation: should abolish the CAP, insist on the right of nation-states 'to pursue their own economic, industrial and regional policies', and reject any increase in the powers of the European Parliament (then still a mere Assembly). This, let's say again, was the party still in charge of national policy, still the Government. For the bulk of the party, plainly, the 1975 referendum meant little. It was only natural therefore that, when office was removed, it should make the next leap, after demanding impossible reforms from within, to the straightforward position that Britain should leave the Common Market. A motion to that effect was duly passed in October 1980, exchanging the scorned religion of Europe for something more pantheistic. The next Labour Government, it said, should 'disengage Britain from the EEC institutions and in place of our EEC membership work for peaceful and equitable relations between Britain and all nations in Europe and the rest of the world'.

This was carried by 5 million to 2 million, a result greeted with exultation by Tony Benn, the one-time pro-Europe man and inventor of the referendum whose result, at the time, he had humbly accepted. 'That is sensational, a fantastic victory,' he wrote in his diary on the day of the 1980 vote.[2]

Anti-Europeanism hadn't always been the position of the Labour left. It was the left's flirtation with European federalism, back in the post-war period, that particularly enraged Ernest Bevin. The left, at that time, saw nascent 'Europe' as the desirable counterpoise to the American super-power, an attitude Bevin abominated. But time, naturally, changed everything, and long before 1980 the 'Europe' question divided the Labour Party on left–right lines which placed the left, almost entirely, on the anti-Europe side. In the afterburn of the 1979 defeat, Europe became part of the radical leftist catalogue that captured the party: a reversion somehow rendered more satisfying by the fact that one of those old federalists, Michael Foot, who had long ago forgotten he ever embraced such heresy, was elected to be the Labour leader.

In parallel with this, as we have already seen, was a compatible development. Roy Jenkins, having left London to become president of the European Commission, gave every indication that he would make good his private vow at that time never to return to the Labour Party. Six months after the 1979 election, he delivered the Dimbleby Lecture, canvassing a new, coalitionist party of the centre. Not long after that, when he began to attract allies to this cause, they came from among people moved first and foremost by the anti-Europe stance that Labour was already taking.

The fissile effect of Europe on the Labour Party was thus matched by its coagulant influence on everyone, high and low, involved in the

construction of something else. It wouldn't be true to say Europe was
the biggest single motivating element in the formation of the Social
Democratic Party, the SDP, under Jenkins's leadership. Nuclear defence,
and the Bennite onslaughts in the name of party democracy, were still
more jarring pretexts for some of those involved. But Europe was first in
time. The most authoritative history of the SDP records the moment.
After the first Labour *démarche* to unpick the primacy of the referendum
verdict, Shirley Williams met David Owen and William Rodgers in her
flat. The date was 6 June 1980. They were all, in different degrees, strong
Europeans, as well as former ministers, high in the Labour hierarchy.
They agreed to issue their first joint statement of dissent from a party
position, and agreed it must focus on Europe, though on condition that
this 'would be only the first thing they did together'.[3]

Europe, therefore, had become a defining reason for some senior
people to leave the Labour Party. By the same token, it was by now an
issue on which the party insisted that an unyieldingly negative position
should be adhered to by all who stood in the Labour name. The
departure of the SDP MPs cut the ground from under the already
waning support for Europe. There were a few resilient members of the
right and centre, whose personal record on Europe would have made
any surrender of their position laughable even by the relaxed standards
of consistency on this issue that British politics has long observed. But
only they could afford to make clear their dissent from the line Foot
keenly favoured, and with which he led his party to the most spectacular
electoral defeat in its post-war history. For the most part, there was at
least token solidarity for a simple repudiation. 'British withdrawal from
the Community is the right policy for Britain,' said Labour's 1983
election manifesto. This would be 'completed well within the lifetime of
the Parliament'. In one easy swoop, a Repeal Bill would abolish the
present powers of the Community in Britain, and then repeal the 1972
Act once negotiations on withdrawal were complete.[4]

What role this startling commitment played in the near-terminal
withdrawal of the British people's support from Labour at this election
cannot be precisely assessed. In a document that was described by one
of its more sardonic dissenters as 'the longest suicide note in history',
degrees of culpability as between the promise of unilateral nuclear
disarmament, the pledge to renationalize swathes of industry and the
commitment to get out of the EEC are hard to distinguish. Suffice to say
that, on Europe, the opinion polls at the end of the campaign were
putting the Tories 23 per cent ahead, one of their largest measured

advantages on a policy issue.[5] When Foot was ushered off the scene, soon after the electoral disaster, his Europe policy was one of the first that began to disappear after him.

One of its apparently more ardent supporters became the promoter of, once again, a Labour reversal of position. But on this occasion it was a reversal in favour of a more positive line, conducted, not grudgingly under the pressure of being in government, but with all deliberate urgency, after the party had finished an election with 188 seats fewer than the Tories and come close to being relegated to third place in the popular vote by an alliance of the Liberals and the SDP.

Neil Kinnock, a man of the left, had always been, in conventional terms, an anti-European. His attitude was gathered almost blindly into the familiar leftist cluster. But when Kinnock became party leader in the autumn of 1983 he soon understood that a shift was compellingly desirable – if for no better reason than that elections for the European Parliament were due in June 1984, and supplied an early focus for the revisionism that the recent catastrophe indicated was necessary across the board. But there was more to it than that, Kinnock subsequently indicated. He represented himself as never having been an anti-European in the manner of late-period Tony Benn. Changing the line on this subject, one of his associates confirmed, was nothing like so difficult for him as the personal renunciations of conscience involved in abandoning unilateral nuclear disarmament or supporting the sale of council houses, two requirements of political realism he accepted through gritted teeth. He was already, he himself once told me, dissatisfied with the straight pledge to get out of the Common Market: and he also wished, as he looked back on it, that when he began to change the party line he had done so more emphatically. As it was, he indicated at the start of his leadership only a conditional resumption of a hypothetically pro-Europe position. The EEC had to prove itself 'a source of tangible value to the British people', he wrote. 'We could only realistically accept enduring membership if, at the very least, we suffer no significant material loss or disadvantage.'[6]

This was a cautious advance, conducted against the grain of a still highly militant left. Kinnock wrote those words while a miners' strike, which he felt obliged against his better judgement to support, was testing the very life of the Thatcher Government. He had to be careful with this other inflammatory issue. But, in any case, the new stance conformed to the barren realities of all but a small fragment of British Europeanism. It was defiantly minimalist: pragmatic, rather than in any way visionary. It posed the test of economic advantage, which was the way most Labour people ever since Wilson preferred to look at the matter. Insofar as it touched on more philosophical issues, Kinnock's statement represented Europe as a concept to be considered within the approved canons of nationalism, rather than by acknowledging any positive virtue in sinking some of Britain's economic identity into a larger whole: again, a familiar stance for all British party leaders, with the partial exception of Heath.

The change was, however, significant. And it became decisive. It was cabined and qualified by all manner of oppositionism, and by a persistent reluctance to admit that Labour was now a European party. In 1986, the party opposed the Single European Act, putting up one of its most stalwart pro-Europeans, George Robertson MP, to say that this measure was 'wholly irrelevant', and 'a diversion from the real task before us'.[7] Under Kinnock's successor, the better-credentialled European John Smith, Labour's incessant parliamentary manoeuvres, against a government without a majority, almost succeeded in destroying the Treaty of Maastricht. The tradition of putting party before issue, and victory before anything discernible as a principle, was carried over seamlessly from the Wilson era. But the course was set for a different sort of Labour approach to Europe. The recognition was established that, without this, the party might find it much harder to exploit the growing frailties of the Thatcher, and then the Major, Government.

For the first time, one is beginning to see, Europe became, in the late 1980s, an arena whose role in British politics was changing. While it continued to tear successive Cabinets apart, there appeared the novel prospect that, to other politicians, it might offer some advantage. Perhaps, they dimly saw, there was actual political gain to be made by adopting a stance that was positive rather than negative.

Labour lost the 1987 election, even though it abandoned its Year Zero extremism on Europe and several other matters. But Kinnock was becoming a European politician, at least in Europe. He was an assiduous attender at meetings of continental socialist parties, and became friends with leaders such as Willy Brandt, in Germany, Michel Rocard, in France, and the Italian nemesis of Mrs Thatcher, Bettino Craxi. In 1985, he was invited to Spain by the Prime Minister, Felipe González, to speak in the local referendum campaign to authorize accession to Nato.[8] These were socialists with actual experience of real power, the proof that progressive politics need not consign its leaders into the oblivion which Thatcherism had thus far dealt to the British Labour Party.

The European Community, moreover, was itself an embodiment of that kind of politics. What post-war Labour saw, not incorrectly, as a threat to the freedom of the great British nation-state to organize its coal and steel industries under public ownership had become, by the lights of the Thatcherite world, a repository of socialism. 'We have not success-fully rolled back the frontiers of the state in Britain', the lady said at Bruges, 'only to see them reimposed at a European level.' As well as marking the moment of her new belligerence, this signified the very reason why, in the same month of September 1988, the British Trades Union Congress received the president of the European Commission, Jacques Delors, as if he were a prophet. Delors, whom the brothers serenaded as Frère Jacques, to the tune of the only French song most of them knew, came from Brussels to explain that there was another world, beyond either the free market or the command economy, which 'Europe' existed to promote. His words became a mantra, his very presence a beacon, for the beleaguered rabble that the island's Labour movement, after a third election defeat, was in danger of becoming.

This was, once again, more a facing of reality than a deep conversion experience. Europe, for Kinnock's evolving Labour Party, did not repre-sent a dream of union but the Utopia where power might lie. The debates which began to revolve around it in the party concentrated, as usual, more on the economic than the political dimensions. Could the Community become a power-house of economic growth, or were the anti-inflationary biases of the Bundesbank a threat to British industry? The discussion that ensued had a rationality, notwithstanding the strength of the sceptic left, that barely allowed itself to be touched by the primeval demons simultaneously at large among Conservatives. National sovereignty was an issue that no longer stirred the left. Kinnock himself, after all, was Welsh. John Smith, his successor, was Scottish. Many of their strongest lieutenants were also Celts. Such politicians, coming from a tradition steeped in forced submission to the English, were always less likely to be disturbed in their viscera by the occasional importunities of what might be decided in Brussels.

A collection of influences was therefore developing that now united rather than divided all the important forces opposed to the Conservative hegemony. This wasn't enough to save them from yet another election defeat, in 1992. But both the old party, Labour, and the new party, known as Liberal Democrats and still significantly peopled by those who had left the old in acrimony, now made common cause on the principle of the Europe connection.

There were still hold-outs on the further left. Tony Benn continued to preach, a voice of undiminished eloquence: in support of a case, however, of much diminished political strength among his fellow leftists. Benn's allies were on the Government benches. He spoke with enthusiasm of young William Cash, though he would never join Cash on a platform, and wrote with horror of his nationalist opinions.[9] Among the centre left, hardened by its decades of impotence, a moderate degree of Europeanism now seemed the touchstone not only of distinctiveness from the other side, but of Labour's fitness, at last, to be taken seriously by the people.

*

IN THIS EVOLUTION, some Labour politicians played a more heroic role than others. The old found it considerably easier than the young. Only the most ancient allegiance to 'Europe' was enough to fortify resistance to the party line in the early 1980s. Indeed, it was only through having lived and fought the struggles of the 1960s and 1970s, or so it seemed, that a Labour politician of the Year Zero period was capable of attaching any real importance to the continental question, as something he or she needed to think about. I have been unable to trace any Labour MPs, making their first entry into Parliament in 1983, who proclaimed themselves opposed to the party's pledge on immediate exit from the Community.

Certainly, the aspirant Member for Sedgefield, in the county of Durham, didn't. And the absence of such a statement from Tony Blair's first successful personal manifesto is indicative of a number of truths.

One is that Europe, at this stage, had entirely lost its inspirational place in social democratic, or indeed any other, British politics. Seen from 1983, the idealism that once swirled round this issue, the oxygen that pumped the very heart of Roy Jenkins, John Mackintosh and their friends in the Wilson era, was untransmutable into a contemporary force. It did not reach the youthful progressive mind. This was partly because the Community, now that Britain belonged, had become a banal, merely functional extension of the business of governing, and as such incapable of inspiring anyone. But it also reflected the decade since entry, in which Europe was downplayed by Wilson and Callaghan, prior to resuming its place as nothing more than a commodity in the marketplace of Labour faction: an issue whose main sensitivity for an ambitious politician, therefore, was that it should not be seen to damage him.

Europe, in other words, was something on which hardly any sensible young Labour person would dare to challenge the orthodoxy. It simply wasn't big enough, as a question on which to break with the party so early in a political life. It wasn't even a subject where one tended to have terribly prominent opinions either way, certainly not in a favourable direction.

This illuminates something else behind the Blair abstention from dissent, which is immediately worth noting given what happened later. In that era it was possible, often essential, to sublimate personal conviction, on almost any subject, to the quest for preferment in the party. The true state of a tyro Labour mind was very often impossible to discern. Opinions didn't seem to be the point, as the prudent tyro was the first to see. Routine promises of fealty were the way to get ahead: which, in Blair's case, at least placed him, on Europe, as securely in the line of his ancestors as John Major was in his. He was true to the past in one definitive respect. Like every other Labour leader before him, when Blair assumed the succession in July 1994 he had to account for the fact that he had apparently changed his mind on Europe.

Whether this really was a change raises quite profound questions about the nature of conviction. Certainly Blair *said* he was against British membership of the Community. But at that time virtually any opinion a Labour person had could be regarded as an opinion of convenience. Blair's real opinions in 1985 were often as obscure as, ten years later, they were clear. Dissimulation and agnosticism were among the intellectual diseases from which he began to release the party when he became leader. But in his personal case, on the 'Europe' question, the cure was quite a long time coming.

Born in 1953, Blair matured when the Second World War was a distant memory. The formative events of 'Europe' had made no impact on him. He was two when Messina happened, ten when de Gaulle said no, fifteen when Wilson tried again, twenty when Britain got in. Besides, he was not, in the conventional sense of most progressive youth, political. The son of a barrister who was also a law lecturer, he imbibed such politics as he did from, as it were, the wrong side of the fence: Leo Blair was chairman of the Durham Conservative Association. Subsequently, Tony Blair would recollect that it was the disabling stroke his father suffered at the age of forty that started him, the son, on the road to politics. He rather consciously took over some part of his father's frustrated ambition for a public life, albeit with a different party base. Occurring when he was only ten, the illness and its consequences for the family also seem to have supplied the first stirrings of ideas such as service, and community, and fairness, and the need to do something about them.[10] However, Blair did not become a university politico. Going up to Oxford in 1972, he might have become involved in all manner of political causes. His years there coincided with the degeneration of the Heath Government under the weight of some massive industrial struggles, and the return to power of a Labour leadership roiled in much disputation. For any young man drawn to politics, there was a great deal to argue about. But Blair appears not to have been interested, finding the greater part of his moral development, and his concern about public questions, in the religious rather than the political sphere.

One of his earliest recorded political acts, as it happens, was European. He voted Yes in the referendum in 1975, the year he also joined the Labour Party. This didn't signify a crusading interest in Europe, which could hardly, in any case, have been a sufficient reason at that time to persuade any person, young or old, to sign up with the party. It was simply a natural marriage of positions for any burgeoning progressive who did not side with the hard left. It was a normality Blair observed, without making any fuss about it or needing to strike any kind of posture, but it can surely be said to have defined him as by instinct a pro-Europe man: a regular, unzealous absorber of Europe into the routine attitudes of someone who was now beginning to think he might like to be a politician.

By the time this became a possibility for him, however, the definition of what was routine had changed. His first intervention in national politics was as Labour's candidate at a by-election in the Tory stronghold of Beaconsfield, in May 1982. With Michael Foot at the helm, the official party line already proposed exit from the EEC, and the youthful candidate did not openly dissent. According to his biographer, indeed, he 'made Europe one of his main themes'.[11] He wasn't quite categoric in his adoption of the exact party position, which stated, in *Labour's Programme 1982*: 'We do not believe a further attempt to change the nature of the Community would be worthwhile. . . . Britain must therefore withdraw.' Blair voiced a faintly less extreme position, with a timid parenthesis in a letter to the local paper, which supported 'the Labour Party's present leadership' on all important matters, including, he wrote, 'withdrawal from the EEC (certainly unless the most fundamental changes are effected)'.[12] He was anxious, he also made clear, not to be labelled 'a Benn-backer'; but he took up something close to the Benn position. His way of putting this was interesting. He said he had come to these positions, which included nuclear unilateralism, 'as a Labour Party man, not as a "Bennite" or any other "ite" '. It was the same, evidently, with Europe. 'Come out if we must, but not as an article of socialist faith,' was how he described it to the *Guardian*.[13] And all his specific observations were critical. 'Above all, the EEC takes away Britain's freedom to follow the economic policies we need,' his official election leaflet said.

How much he agreed with all this is a moot, and perhaps an academic, point. When he became more prominent, it was normal to assert without qualification that he never had done.[14] But in the general election a year later, when he fought the safe seat of Sedgefield, was he also, therefore, expressing false sentiments? His election address said: 'We'll negotiate withdrawal from the EEC, which has drained our natural resources and destroyed jobs.' These words subsequently gave him trouble with the Tories, who used them to undermine his image as a sincere and, above all, consistent party leader. A talk-out has been constructed, to the effect that they were written in a hurry, after he got the Sedgefield nomination very late, and that they merely summarized party policy: what his leaflet called 'Labour's Sensible Answers'. His 'Personal Message', on the other side of the leaflet, contained no mention of Europe – evidence, so it is contended, that he didn't really mean it.[15]

All that this demonstrates, perhaps, is the problem of conviction, in that era of Labour politics. There is not much reason to doubt that, in his heart, Blair had little problem with British membership of the EEC – but had still less problem with adapting his public words to get into Parliament, and thus position himself to help rescue the party from the attitudes that were making it unelectable. When Tories attacked his seeming shift, they were misunderstanding the nature of the Labour debate on Europe – as if to say that every piece of positioning on the matter was like their own, drawn from the bone and soul and gut. Very few of Blair's generation in the Labour Party felt anything like that about Europe, or any other issue save the need to get rid of the Tories and install the progressive left in government.

It has to be said, nonetheless, that these sinuous duplicities, however well intentioned, became, justifiably, an embarrassment. They were yet further examples of the confusion that has been the mode in which the British political class chose, times without number, to present its views on Europe to the people. In his early days, Blair treated Europe as a subject about which it was dangerous to tell the truth: risky, even, at his early stage of initiation into the class, to decide and stake out a position on what the truth really was. While plainly untouched by Cashite nationalism, he was reluctant in the beginning, whatever he actually believed, to address the fact that being pro-European might require a commitment to look Euro-scepticism square in the face and stare it down.

The youthful Blair was the exponent of a national habit with a long pedigree. Whether he could shake the habit was to become one way of defining the challenge Europe presented to his quality as a political leader.

In the contest that put him in that place, after John Smith died in May 1994, the 'Europe' question played no part. The Kinnock evolution was carried on by Smith and, apart from unregenerate Bennites, attitudes to the European Union had long since ceased to be a litmus test of whether a Labour politician was sufficiently red or blue. The years after Bruges, and then Maastricht, imparted to the Labour Party not only a warm acquiescence in what 'Europe' might do to revive social democratic politics, but a considerable satisfaction in their own beautifully moderated unity compared with the turmoil on the other side. They could sit quiet and smug, as the bloody oppositionism that reached into the Cabinet itself performed, more than adequately, the task of giving the Prime Minister a hard time. Not the least damage, indeed, that the state of the Tory Party did to the 'Europe' issue for most of the 1990s was to absolve the Labour Party from seriously engaging with it.

I had many conversations with Blair in the five years of the 1992 Parliament.[16] Whatever his judicious hesitations in the past, he was by now plainly a proper European. Once installed in the Commons, he had been totally supportive of the Kinnock–Smith shift, and now personified the sense in which every mainline Labour politician of his vintage could be presumed automatically to be, with greater or lesser zeal, pro-EU.

With him, this opinion was more than automatic. Quite regularly, he would describe himself as 'passionately' European, and he was never less than realistic about continental developments. As early as May 1993, barely six months after the ERM débâcle, he was expressing his disappointment that the entire press, which had pushed so hard for British membership, now directed the same unanimity in the opposite direction. He could already see that EMU and the single currency were likely to continue being pushed forward by most other EU members, and he meditated on the certainty that the case for some kind of British attachment to the ERM would be revived. What was most striking at this time, however, was the way he located the 'Europe' question within the wider Labour predicament: that, along with Kinnock's other shifts on the importance of markets or nuclear defence, the conversion on Europe had been a matter of expediency not conviction. The party was still addressing all these matters, Blair thought, as if nothing fundamentally needed to change. 'Conversion', as such, was almost being avoided: certainly relegated to a second-best option, pending the moment when the timeless Labour values and positions, in faintly new cosmetics, could be reaffirmed. That might be necessary for party management, he thought, but was quite insufficient as a way of making Labour credible in the wider world.

This attitude prefigured Blair's strategy when he became leader. From the moment he began his leadership campaign, up to and through the moment when he won the 1997 general election, he took it as axiomatic that Labour must change 'from within', and be seen to do so. This didn't touch on the party's Europe position anything like so sensitively as on many other questions: in the context of the time, the party was already seen, and saw itself, as 'European'. But it meant, for example, that Labour shouldn't fear to concede that there were occasions on which the British interest was served by adopting lines that ran with the grain of Europe rather than against.

This, when Blair began to put it into words as leader, had a startling effect on the climate. His position, he said, was that 'the drift towards isolation in Europe must stop and be replaced by a policy of constructive engagement'. He wasn't uncritical of the EU or the Commission, but he wanted to establish an atmosphere in which criticisms were not assumed to denote anti-Europeanism. Britain should be 'at the centre of Europe', 'should set about building the alliances within Europe that enable our influence to grow'. This, he thought, was about more than fulfilling our national interest. To hesitate before our European destiny, he rather more boldly said, was 'to deny our historical role in the world'. The role was to be 'a major global player', and would be forfeit unless we accepted Europe as our base.[17]

This was a measured beginning, a cautious introduction to what Blair called 'the patriotic case', in which he quoted Palmerston and Kissinger but neglected to name with approval a single continental politician, living or dead. It provoked, nonetheless, a sensation in the Conservative Party. In the course of his speech, Blair proposed that qualified majority voting, the dreaded QMV, might be extended to social, environmental, industrial and regional policy decisions taken in the EU Council. It was a modest suggestion, carefully and conditionally couched, but to many Tories it seemed like a staggering gaffe. The 'four vetoes' and the pathetic innocence with which Blair had 'thrown them away' became the mantra of many a Conservative seeking succour from the Government's own crises. I met a number of ministers around this time who were almost literally foaming with disbelief that the young man could have said such a thing, their reaction lurching between the jubilation of party politicians who were certain they had got him, and the dismay of national chauvinists who saw Britain on the brink of being sold down the river to Brussels.

But Blair made one or two other speeches reiterating the position, and trying to broaden the impression of a leader thinking in a quite different spirit from the reigning sceptic orthodoxy. Their defensiveness reflected the spirit of politics at the time. They were hot for European reform, especially of the institutions and the agriculture policy, and they stressed the need for popularizing what Europe might mean for people's everyday lives. 'If we do not now make persuasion the condition of moving forward,' he said in Bonn, 'then the initiative will pass to those hostile to the whole project of Europe.'[18] He wanted to make very clear, to the Europeans, that they could expect, if Labour won, something better than the impotent posturing of Major: while also making it clear enough to the British that the national birthright would be safe in his hands. He was convinced, he always told me, that the country wasn't anti-European in the Tory way, and that the task was carefully to convince it that it was losing out as a result of Major's imprisonment by his party.

Here was another aspect of Europe, for Blair the student of political authority. It was blinding evidence of the single thing he most despised about the other side, to which he was determined never to succumb – control of the leader by the party, rather than the party by the leader. The same perception drove him with equal rigour to minimize the opportunities for forces to arise that might be beyond the leader's power to resist.

His opposition leadership, therefore, was marked by tactical manoeuvres, not all of them very creditable. Under his predecessor, as already noted, Labour had risked wrecking the Maastricht Treaty for the sake of possibly bringing down the Major Government. The jockeying went on through Blair's three years. He used to be opposed, for example, to another Europe referendum. When the question arose over Maastricht, he rejected the idea emphatically, saying in 1992: 'The right place for the debate to take place is in Parliament, where people can express different views.' He also said, in 1993: 'Our mandate is derived from our ability as Members of Parliament to represent our constituents.'[19] But in 1994, in his very first joust at Prime Minister's Question Time, he chose to try and goad Major into pledging a referendum on further European integration, knowing it to be a live issue between him and Kenneth Clarke. Not long after that, he made a commitment on the point himself. In the event of 'a major and fundamental constitutional change', said the Leader of the Opposition, 'there is clearly a case for ensuring that the decision can be very clearly taken by the British people'.[20]

Referendum politics continued to dominate, as EMU became the most crucial question on the table. In my talks with him in the earlier 1990s, Blair never expressed any hostility to EMU, or the single currency, in principle. He explicitly said he favoured it, if it could be made to work. By mid-decade he was being more sceptical, in the proper sense. His anxiety always was a practical one: whether, as the undoubted route to greater stability and lower transaction costs and (probably) lower interest rates, it could be sustained within the vast economic discrepancies between the different regions of the EU. This greatly bothered him, and he gave voice to the sceptic sentiment often enough in private, it seemed, to awaken the mistaken excitement, once again, of the Tory Party. Themselves mired, throughout 1996, in Major's strife-torn hesitations about exactly what words, to strike what policy, the party should be using about EMU, some Tory managers became convinced Blair was about to commit Labour against entry in the life of the next Parliament – the very line they were pleading with Major to adopt.

I asked Blair at the time about this rumour, and he was bewildered. Such a position was never on the cards. On the other hand, after Major promised an EMU referendum, Labour promised the same thing a few months later. It feared any challenge to its populist credentials. The leader took a lot of trouble to explain that this was merely the logical consequence of the fact that EMU itself was now impossible for any country to decide on before May 1997, the last date for a British election. This meant there couldn't be a manifesto commitment on entry, which in turn meant that a later referendum was the only way to secure the people's consent. It might look like a surrender to the anti-Europeanism which the Tories had long cultivated in the country, but it wasn't.

'My strategy is *not*, underline three times, to run as a Euro-sceptic,' Blair told me. It was, instead, to wait and see, just like the Conservatives. Or rather, since each party had improved on that tepid usage, Labour's plan was to 'protect and advance' – a formula fresh from the same words factory as its resounding Tory competitor, 'prepare and decide', a phrase much trumpeted by the ever resonant Michael Heseltine. Labour would presumably *protect* the issue by the referendum promise, then in due course *advance* the argument for a Yes: which was perhaps less bleak than the insinuation from the other side, that Britain would *prepare* for a single currency other people were inventing, and then *decide* not to buy it.

This, then, was the basis on which Blair moved into the election campaign which nobody except he and Major thought he might conceivably lose. In it, Europe played a smaller role than many Tory managers wanted it to, and Blair was therefore not put to a question that might compel him, in his caution, to appear more sceptical than he felt. If Major had done what the managers urged, and forced Clarke to swallow an outright pledge against EMU entry in the coming Parliament, he would have hoped to throw down a gauntlet to his Labour rival – yet there was no reason to believe the rival would have picked it up. Watchful EMU-readiness, moderate Euro-enthusiasm, a worldly-wise absence of zeal on either side of the question: these were the vibrations Blair sought to convey, which he knew were quite enough to distinguish him from the Conservatives, and reassure the electorate that it would be safer with him than with them.

This was what he won with. And immediately he had won, the caution of it was swept up into the more spacious rhetoric growing out of the greatest British election victory of modern times. 'Europe', along with other matters, became infused, as an issue, with the self-confidence, the freshened certainties, even the didactic exuberance that naturally comes over a party which has had such an uplifting experience at the hands of democracy.

For the first time in all this history, Britain had a 'European' government with a long life ahead of it. If there were resisters in the governing party, they were irrelevant, all importance drained by the massive numbers of MPs who would do anything the leader asked of them. It is not too much to call this a revolutionary moment. It was – could be – the moment when passion dulled and struggle ceased: when vituperation and bullying and gut-driven piety and the sanctimony of exclusive patriotism, all the coinage of permanent threat which had been the currency of political trade in this matter almost since the beginning, finally lost their power of command. This was the opportunity the leader had made for himself. As a therapy for the nation, it would be disturbing, after so many years in a different psychological condition. How, one had to wonder, would he use it?

He had already foreseen the early days in power, and dwelt upon how they would be handled. The European calendar laid down a post-Maastricht summit, concluding another long-drawn-out inter-governmental conference, to be held at Amsterdam within weeks of the election. He had thought about how different he would make the British tone, how altered would be the atmosphere in the Commons, as compared with the triumphalist bull-pit favoured by both Mrs Thatcher and John Major, when he reported back from the summit. He would use the language of collaboration not confrontation. He would claim positive results not negative triumphs. It would be the signal that, as well as what happened to Britain, what happened in Europe would matter too: the theatre where Labour's victory was displayed could be, in a sense, all-encompassing.

And so it proved, after a fashion, to be. In Opposition, Blair put an old Euro-sceptic, Robin Cook, in charge of foreign affairs. Cook had campaigned for a No vote in the 1975 referendum. But the Cook who became Foreign Secretary had long since changed his own mind, and become a European: quizzical, practical, Scottish, but European. The Conservatives, who had built Amsterdam into an occasion when the very lifeblood of the British nation would be in danger of dripping from the table, sincerely believed that Blair would be incapable of preventing it. How could anyone lacking the matchless experience of their own, battle-hardened, superlatively successful Mr Major hope to take on the likes of Helmut Kohl? But this turned out to be a false apprehension. Extravagantly so. It was true that the European leaders welcomed their counter-parts from the new British Cabinet. The change of atmosphere was instant and, to them, stunning. Accustomed to British delegations that were not only hostile, but incapable of guaranteeing the passage of any agreements they did manage to complete, the continentals were now dealing with a country that aspired to make Europe work, and a leader, aided by a Foreign Secretary, whose skills as a bargainer immediately made themselves felt in the Treaty of Amsterdam. 'You can't imagine how wonderful it is to feel you are actually being listened to,' a British official, steeped in the pessimism of the Major years, told a journalist.[21]

But nobody could say that Amsterdam made large integrationist strides. It left institutional reform in abeyance, and only with difficulty managed to keep EMU on track. It was, in the end, a minimalist conference which witnessed, among other things, the ironic spectacle of the British prime minister seeking to extend majority voting which, in some of the most important cases, was resisted, for their own domestic political reasons, by the Germans. What emerged, in fact, was a possible confluence, further simplifying the British task, between the greater readiness of London to enlist for a positive European project and the status of that project in the minds of many Europeans. Maastricht, many thought, had already brought to an end the full Monnet vision of ever closer integration, concluding with a United States of Europe. The pillared structure, dividing up the areas that would remain with governments from those that were covered by the EU Commission, Court and Parliament, was, from the viewpoint of fully centralizing super-statists, an eyesore; and Amsterdam did little to improve the landscape.

Just as Blair, in other words, was taking the heat out of 'Europe' by the fact of his victory, Europe, with the fiery exception of EMU, looked as though it was cooling down to an atmosphere dominated by compromise, and endless, boring, relatively uninflammatory pragmatism. At Amsterdam, the British confirmed their border controls, backed more collaboration on crime control, did more than they ever had under the Tories to try and rescue the lost cause of the domestic fishing industry. It was unglamorous, mostly uncontentious, stuff. Within six weeks of the election, Europe was rendered into a part of quotidian banality.

Blair's area of contest, in fact, was different. But he did choose one. It was the sign that a big victory did bring with it a certain arrogance. Having won Britain as new Labour, he soon set about persuading Europe that new Labour's remedies were the route to salvation for social democrats everywhere. Within a month of gaining power, he had been to Noordwijk in the Netherlands and Malmö in Sweden, and delivered what amounted to lectures on the liberal economy and labour market flexibility, the notorious Anglo-Saxon economic model the continentals were supposed to learn from. In effect, he was asking them to abandon the social Europe of Jacques Delors, or at least minimize its place in the big picture. *Le grand tableau* was the catchphrase, virtuously self-conscious in its chosen language, with which Blair invariably reminded himself and his colleagues that the broad brush made the images that mattered. Always remember *le grand tableau*.

In Blair's Euro-version of the big picture, the man with the most enviable mandate in the Union began to redraw the ideological map which most of his peer-group had grown up with. Government's job, he said, was to enable people to make the most of themselves, 'in an

economy based on knowledge, skills and creativity'. 'This is the third
way,' he told the European Socialists Congress, 'not old left or new right,
[but] a new centre and centre-left agenda.' It was the route, among other
things to 'a people's Europe'.[22] If nothing else, Blair wasted no time in
conveying to his audience his mastery of the essential modern art of the
soundbite.

This kind of lecture might be said to have something of the Rifkinds
about it. It was, after all, telling the Europeans what to do – though it
refrained from explaining how to run 'Europe' as such, and did come
from the mouth of a new leader whose sympathies in that respect could
not be doubted. There was still the faint whiff of hubris. After Malmö,
the Dutch Foreign Minister, Hans van Mierlo, was heard to remark
sardonically that some things never changed – another British leader
telling the Europeans where they were going wrong.

All the same, as most continentals recognized, Britain had changed.
The leader *saw* himself as European, and didn't fear to say so. For one
thing, he felt quite at home in their countries, holidaying naturally in
Tuscany and speaking French with facility. When he delivered a speech
in French to the National Assembly in Paris, in March 1998, there was
wild excitement on both sides of the Channel: as much a tribute to the
stubborn mono-linguism of his predecessors as to his own rare brilliance.

His political relations with the French were not perfect. Lionel
Jospin, elected Prime Minister at just about the same time as Blair,
personified the socialism that had never died in France, and whose
success at the polls was a rude counter to the Blair thesis that the 'third
way' was the only way progressives could win. Jospin was also of a
slightly different era, not quite part of the 'young continent' Blair wanted
to position alongside the 'young Britain' which he had fashioned as the
defining, if somewhat vacuous, image of his time and place. Though not
as old as Helmut Kohl, whom the Blair people, come 1998, were
beginning to paint as yesterday's man, Jospin was an awkward ingredient
in the 'modernized' Europe for which the British leader seldom stopped
preaching. As a leader who prided himself on having no enemies, Blair
took time to find himself congenially alongside the French socialists.

In his European role, however, he enjoyed the blessing of old men.
He was a source of relief to Kohl, in whose presence I sat for some hours
in October 1997, listening to him expatiate not only on the future of
Europe but on the role it was now open for Britain to play there.[23] Blair,
one of the Chancellor's staff said, had told Kohl, when they met for their
first intimate talk, that he looked forward to 'a relationship of equals'.

But Kohl had forgiven such startling presumption. Britain now had a leader, he was pleased to say, who saw the point about Europe. With Mrs Thatcher, any dialogue on the point had been 'hopeless'. With Major, who at least understood the problem, it had been almost as bad, because he had put so many anti-Europe people in his Cabinet. With Blair, Kohl believed, there was a good chance of fulfilling the maxim to which he had always held, that Europe could ultimately succeed 'only if Britain joins in'.

Another old man could also feel a sense of vindication. Blair's arrival in Downing Street completed, in a sense, the odyssey Roy Jenkins had begun. The party Jenkins left had become the party he would not now have needed to leave. The 'Europe' question, on which he mainly left it, was being addressed with more effortless aplomb by Blair than by any Prime Minister of his lifetime. There was something singularly fitting in the fact that Jenkins was now permitted to become a man of influence once again, the private godfather, some called him, to a leader who had still been in short trousers when Jenkins first began trying to persuade Labour leaders – Gaitskell, then Wilson – to adopt the cause to which he gave the largest part of his political energy. Blair was Jenkins's natural heir. He seemed to be launching a decade in which Britain would move, for the first time, full-hearted into Europe.

Yet the past could not be shed quite as easily as that. It lingered heavy in the air. There was a limit to Blair's Europeanism. No longer fearful of the 'Europe' that compromised old definitions of the nation-state, Britain still hesitated to follow the continental agenda. The traditional posture – fifty years of history, in a sense – remained palpably present in the consciousness of politics, an emanation the new Prime Minister did not desire instantly to ignore. While in favour of 'Europe' in general, the Government was ambivalent concerning the project that most countries of the Union cared most about, economic and monetary union, EMU: the project, indeed, on which the very future of 'Europe' was now most heavily staked.

Tony Blair, as we have seen, never wholeheartedly believed in an EMU which included, from the start, the pound sterling. He placed himself in the classic line of those British politicians who, while not part of the Whitehall conspiracy to wreck Messina, were sceptical about the success of the weird integrationist scheme, and argued that we must wait and see if the Common Market worked, which it probably wouldn't. The same line of reasoning would apply to the single currency. The propaganda of the deed, after all, has always played the most persuasive role in Britain's eventual embrace of 'Europe'. In the autumn of 1997, when Blair made the British decision not to join the monetary union that was scheduled to start on 1 January 1999, he submitted to a tendency that was hallowed not only in the politics but, one might say, in the culture and psychology of his country.

The occasion was a moment of mismanagement as well as disagreement, frailties which showed that Europe could still be a neuralgic issue, even behind a Commons majority of 179. While Labour, through Blair's own voice, had long ago declared there to be 'no overriding constitutional barrier' to EMU,[24] the question of the promised referendum had not been settled. Where, exactly, should it be fitted into the critical path of the Government's progress towards a second term? In October 1997, the leader took the line of least resistance. The pledge which neither he nor Major was prepared to offer before the election, that they would exclude entry into EMU in the lifetime of the coming Parliament, was now, bizarrely, made good.

Much confusion attached to it. It became the most damaging item in the process – an incessant deformity in the Government's methods – by which ministerial spin-doctors, the new masseurs of information, sought ascendancy over each other on their masters' behalf. The chain of half-promises and quarter-denials through which the decision eked into the public realm supplied an early lesson in public disbelief for what any unelected Labour spokesman had to say. But on 27 October the Chancellor, Gordon Brown, told the Commons that more time was needed. Britain and Europe were at different stages in the economic cycle. Brown was known to be less sceptical than Blair about the workable merits of EMU as a technical construct, but he had not fought hard against the prevarication he was now announcing. As well as the convergence of economies, the better preparation of opinion was required. This was what the Government would now embark on, but the task could not hope to be completed, on either the economics or the politics, until another election had taken place.

Six months after the 1997 election, this was a bathetic apotheosis for Tony Blair, on the issue where he hoped to make a serious difference. As such, it was unfortunate, but revealing. Maybe it would, in the end, be a temporary position. But, for the moment, it showed him straddled between the intensity of pressures from the past and the extremity of his ambition for the future.

The past was not represented by members of the previous government, since they were now irrelevant. Nothing the Conservative Party had to say could make any impression on the public. But their scepticism still had its proxy messengers, which Blair took much more seriously. The loudest voices in the print media remained Euro-sceptic, and were virulently opposed to the single currency.

It was perhaps a reflection of Blair's belief in the transience of political power that he regarded these voices as a threat which even his luxuriant Commons majority could not be sure of repelling. And no anti-EMU voice was more influential, he thought, than the one which most of both old and new Labour united in abominating, that of the Australian-American tycoon, Rupert Murdoch, speaking through his four national newspapers and, less important, his monopoly satellite TV station. Blair gave inordinate attention to cultivating Murdoch before the election. Now, by sidelining EMU from immediate decision, he was pre-empting a Murdoch onslaught which, he feared, might undercut his prospects of a second term.

That wasn't the only reason for delay. There were genuine disjunctions between island and mainland economies, though it wasn't clear, if this was to be the test, when and what manner of convergence was to be expected. The media priority, however, was there. Blair took the view, he had often said, that once the economic argument was convincing, public opinion could be won in favour of EMU. But he was anxious, I think, about the process. He foresaw an all-or-nothing battle, which the referendum would constitute. Ranged against him would still be the product of two decades' worth of accumulated scapegoating of Brussels and all its works: the ferocity of printed xenophobia, which a reasoned case found hard to match: the baying voices of publicists and politicians ready to die in the last ditch, in defence of a Britain that was as sentimental as it was vestigial, but which nonetheless, if challenged at the wrong moment, might rise and smite its leader. He wanted to be certain he would win.

Until this test was faced, however, Blair's claims for his future European life were bound to be ambiguous. He stated his purpose. He wished to be a leader of Europe; and he had both the domestic base and the political charisma to make this a credible possibility. But hard on his self-exclusion from EMU came the involuntary, though entirely predictable, exclusion of Britain from the committee that would shape and run the single currency from the moment it became a near-reality. Blair and Brown mishandled that, provoking a further excitation of sceptic rage by insisting Britain should belong, even when every argument undermined the case, as the French Finance Minister said with notable relish, for the marriage-chamber to be occupied by anyone except the wedding party.

It was an irony, but not an empty one, that the first half-year after Blair pulled back from EMU was occupied by Britain's turn in the presidency of the European Union. The Prime Minister conducted this with much efficiency. The Foreign Office lived up to the reputation it had enjoyed since John Robinson's day, as the most professional, best-resourced diplomatic service in the Community. Much was quietly done, for example, towards the enlargement of the Union – though not as much, inevitably, as the trumpets had predicted. In the slow progress of Europe – now accelerating, now retarded, here sometimes gliding, there more often stumbling – Britain was now able to play a part no longer poisoned by sectarian aggravation.

But the climactic act Blair performed as President produced a moment of uncomfortable symbolism. He was an umpire not a player, on 3 May 1998, when eleven members of the Union took the field and pledged to complete their economic and monetary union. He chaired the meeting, but did not sign the pledge.

He left his country, for the moment, in limbo, back from darkness and willing to be saved, but not yet ready to name the day or the hour when the old world would end.

*

THE WAY IN WHICH the new world would ultimately develop was a matter of far-ranging doubt. The single currency, the euro, was about to be minted in the tabulations of bankers and accountants. In eleven countries there would soon no longer be national coins of the realm. But the future of the European Union – its shape and its numbers, its power and its relevance – were debated seriously. One could easily forget, in the often crude cacophony of the British argument, that the EU had genuine problems, about which responsible intellectuals could take sober, critical positions.

On the large scale, what was the EU any longer for? Born out of one war, it had prospered during another. The Monnet people conceived it, and secured the political argument for it, as a compact to prevent Germany and France from ever destroying the peace of Europe again. That was the provenance, and the point had now been made. One of the beauties of Six, then Nine, then Twelve, then Fifteen groups of national politicians spending their waking hours in wearisome dialogue with each other was that the experience left no possibility of war. Moreover, anachronism was surely redoubled by the ending of the Cold War and the redrawing of the internal continental frontiers. Neither hot nor cold war any longer made 'Europe', as hitherto understood, an axiomatic necessity. The deeper unification of what used to be Western Europe was arguably a project that took too little account of greater Europe: was perhaps, indeed, inimical to the countries struggling to rebuild their economies and democracies after the communist catastrophe. What did Brussels have to offer Warsaw and Budapest, let alone Latvia and Bulgaria?

Timothy Garton Ash was an intellectual whose credentials as a European were quite satisfactory: one of those, for example, who had been summoned to Chequers to instruct Mrs Thatcher in the iniquities of Germany and been dismayed to experience the depth of her anti-German sentiments.[25] But in 1998 Garton Ash was a sceptic about the need for, or wisdom of, the pursuit of unity. Post-war integration, he noted, was the product of external influences, first the Soviet Union and second the United States: Moscow driving Western Europe together for its security, Washington encouraging this process as a precondition of the Marshall Aid that rescued Europe's economies. Together with the cutting-off of Eastern Europe, these pressures created 'a historical constellation that was particularly favourable to a particular model of West European integration'. But the end of the Cold War had ended the need for it.[26] Now, it could be argued, the EU was a threat to the liberal order rather than a guarantee of this paradigm being broadened and deepened around the continent. If integration succeeded, Garton Ash seemed to say, it would be a threat to the greater Europe and possibly the world. If, more likely, it failed, the formidable achievements that were to the credit of those who had built the European Community could well be destroyed.

At a still loftier level, the Anglo-American scholar Tony Judt was pessimistic about the continuing value of any attempt at unity. 'I am enthusiastically European,' he wrote in early 1996. 'No one could seriously wish to return to the embattled, mutually antagonistic circle of suspicious and introverted nations that was the European continent in the quite recent past.' But, he went on to argue, 'A truly united Europe is sufficiently unlikely for it to be unwise and self-defeating to insist upon it. Unlike Jean Monnet, the founder of the European Community, I don't believe that it is prudent, or possible, to "exorcise history", at any rate beyond moderate limits.' Judt therefore urged the 'partial reinstatement . . . of nation-states', and contended that it might be 'the better part of wisdom' to stop promising the former communist states of Eastern Europe that they could expect to become members of a fully integrated continental system.[27]

The fumbling performance of the EU, in trying to construct a policy that inserted 'Europe' into the Yugoslav tragedy of the 1990s, fuelled the pessimism of this and other observers. It had shown, Judt wrote, 'the compulsion to avoid engagement, and the absence of any agreed strategic interest beyond maintaining the status quo'. 'The myth of "Europe"', he went on, 'has become little more than the politically correct way to paper over difficulties, as though the mere invocation of the promise of a united Europe could substitute for solving problems and crises in the present.' Events in the Balkans had shown that this Europe was 'fundamentally hollow, selfishly obsessed with fiscal rectitude and commercial advantage'.[28]

The possibly overreaching ambition of EMU wove itself into this thesis. Monetary union is a high-risk project, based on a very optimistic assessment of how the economies of eleven countries, and the politics of those economies, can be made to coexist and fructify. It imposes huge demands for economic reform on societies that are not necessarily prepared to abandon the social protections which more market-driven, liberalized economic rules will imperil. The usual flexibilities, whether of wages or jobs, that need to exist within a zone that has a single interest rate will take years to develop. The central controller of monetary policy will be not a group of elected politicians, but the European Central Bank, whose susceptibility to political influence is one of the most imponderable elements of the future 'Europe', but whose likely propensity to favour deflation is well attested and is, indeed, enshrined in its formal rubrics. Who will be to blame for rising unemployment? Garton Ash's answer exposes one of the many problems EMU will encounter. 'As elections approach, national politicians will find the temptation to "blame it on EMU" almost irresistible,' he writes. 'If responsible politicians resist the temptation, irresponsible ones will gain votes.'[29]

The case that has driven EMU has not been, essentially, economic. It is a political venture, as its critics have inexhaustibly pointed out. But the economic test is the one it has to begin by passing. Its prime – indispensable – justification will be if it produces more reliable economic growth, behind lower interest rates and the illumination of transparent prices. One of the extraordinary features of the euro, in anticipation, was the depth of the uncertainty, on every side of the argument, whether, and if so when, this decisive economic improvement would begin to happen. Similarly absent was any agreed prediction about the role of the euro vis-à-vis the US dollar. But, irrespective of the politics, the euro's creators were placing themselves behind a massive bet that the economic effects would be positive. And on top of that there certainly will be the politics: the asymmetry between regions, the contest between nations with different interests at any given time, the relationship between belongers and non-belongers, the impact of these great issues on the future of the EU as a sustainable, developing enterprise.

At more mundane levels, forty years on from the operative beginning of the Treaty of Rome, there were many problems too. Enriching the accountability of 'Europe' to the people was a task in which several generations of leaders in every member country had failed. The bureaucracy of Brussels, though numerically smaller than some individual Whitehall departments, continued to defeat the political intention that its power should be reduced – or at least was perceived as doing so. After Maastricht, there was meant to be more 'subsidiarity', used as a synonym for national decision-making. It was taking time to come about. Even Helmut Kohl, bestriding Europe as the prophet of closer integration, attacked Brussels as a place out of which came 'a lot of nonsense'. 'It is full of people who never face an election,' he said at the occasion described above. 'When you go on the hustings, you have to answer questions.' A question he was having to answer, in a country now ready to overcome its reluctance and endorse his case for abolishing the Deutschmark, was how 'Europe' could be said to belong to the people.

On behalf of the British debate, it could be said that these and other questions had at least been raised. The ferocity of the Conservative argument drove an intense public discussion of what 'Europe' meant, what it might or might not do to the British nation, what role Parliament could any longer play. The British parliamentary culture encouraged the adversarial approach, and when the Government was in daily danger of being defeated, maximum coverage in the press and on television was assured. This was true, as in no other country, from the beginning to the end of the Major years. Major's first EU summit as Prime Minister, in Rome in December 1990, was a big moment on the road to EMU, and the occasion for extensive debate on all British TV channels about what it meant. Its outcome got blanket treatment. By contrast, on the final night the main 8 p.m. television news in France had no report from Rome, though on the midnight bulletin the communiqué did scrape in as the tenth item.[30] For many years, the question of Europe held little importance for the domestic politics of the continental member states, a condition that had its merits but also carried its penalties. It showed that Europe had become an everyday reality of life, hardly worth reporting: a norm which all parties accepted. But it also deprived both people and politicians of the obligation to examine serious questions. Jacques Delors, the great high priest, was one of those who most deplored this. 'You have to keep the British in the EC for their democratic tradition if nothing else,' he once said. 'They have the best journalistic debate, the best parliamentary committees, the best quizzing of prime ministers after a summit.'[31]

Insofar as this was true, it came about not as an observance of text-book democracy but as a consequence of passion. Sheer intensity of feeling, boorish and blinkered though its exponents sometimes were, produced an air of combat that invigorated the democratic challenge to executive action which other countries dozily nodded through. Yet it is hard to take Euro-sceptic passion, after all these years of deploying everything it's got, as a persuasive matrix for the Blair Government's approach to the new world.

It remained, for one thing, incorrigibly petty, beneath its grand themes of national survival. Its antagonisms knew no limit. When Beethoven's 'Ode to Joy' was chosen as the theme tune for TV coverage of Euro 96, the soccer competition for the European Championship, Tory MPs attacked the BBC's suspect patriotism, the party chairman said fans would be upset because this was the EU anthem, and the Education Secretary, Gillian Shephard, called for a 'rousing' work by an English composer to be played instead.

British Euro-scepticism was seemingly unembarrassable. It formally complained about a children's TV programme because this 'contained positive statements about EU membership and nothing to indicate there were other viewpoints', a charge to which, in the climate of the times, the BBC director-general, John Birt, felt obliged to assent.[32] A hideous episode in serial paedophilia, occurring in Belgium, was seized on by the *Daily Mail* as something much more than a sex crime. How appropriate, wrote one of the paper's star performers, that the Belgian capital should also be the capital of the EU. Her tortured reasoning produced a linkage typical of the sceptic mind. Thanks to the paedophiles, she asserted, 'the Europhile fantasy that Belgium was a successful precursor of a European super-state, happily uniting all ethnic, religious, language and histori-cal divisions, now lies in tatters'. The Belgian political class, 'and by extension the EU political class', would now (somehow) realize that 'cosy deals, cosy corruptions which exclude the people can no longer be tolerated'.[33]

Not all anti-EU material reached such a depth of xenophobia, but the instinct often lurked. Fear and loathing, far beyond the realm of Bismarckian exegesis, was present in many of the attitudes to Germany. The Mafia-corruption of Italians, and animal torture by the Spanish, were national stereotypes regularly deployed as part of a mentality deeply preoccupied not just with the defence but with the inherent superiority of Britishness.

Britishness, however, is complicated. This was another problem with the Euro-sceptic synthesis. It proposed a rather simple narrative for our island story, as dubious in its descriptive accuracy as it was confused in analysing Britain's contemporary options. It depended on a claim to the purity of Anglo-Saxon lineage which the facts do not sustain. In this sense, Englishness, as an identity to be defended in the last ditch, was as unconvincing as Britishness. The English, like the British, were an ethnic mixture going back into the mists of time, wherein we find the Teutonic tribe of Saxons, and thus an early German connection. The inter-penetration between island and continent, beginning with the British monarchy, obscured exactly what specialness of national character was being threatened by the continental connection.

Besides, many points of reference that had uniquely defined the British were now in jeopardy, for reasons quite apart from the existence of the European Union. Linda Colley, in her book *Britons*, identified them. Protestantism, once the vital cement, no longer had much influ-ence on British culture. Recurrent wars with continental Europe, in which identity had been forged against the enemies without, were a thing of the past. The commercial supremacy of the eighteenth century, and the imperial hegemony of the nineteenth and twentieth, were gone. 'No more can Britons reassure themselves of their distinct and privileged identity,' writes Colley, 'by contrasting themselves with impoverished Europeans (real or imaginary), or by exercising authority over manifestly alien peoples. God has ceased to be British, and Providence no longer smiles.'[34]

This is not to say the British don't have different customs and manners from their closest European neighbours, the French. At every level, from politics and the structure of the state, to sport and culture and the arrangement of leisure and, indeed, the manifestations of chauvinism itself, these are distinctive countries. They each have traditions to protect, and national rules of conduct their people resolutely decline to modify. So does every other country in the EU. This very fact, however, throws doubt on some of the nightmares peddled by anti-EU propagandists in Britain. Six of these countries have been together in this Union for forty years. They have created a single market, subjected themselves to common laws, taken seats in a European Parliament, sunk some of their economic sovereignty in the institutions of Brussels. But who will say that any particle of the Frenchness of France has been sacrificed, or the Italianness of Italy, and so on? If such attenuations have occurred, they derive from the universal impact of American culture and commerce far more visibly than from the impositions of the Union.

Here, then, are two unpersuasive weaknesses in the spirit of anti-Europeanism at large in Britain. Its scepticism has a phobic edge, and its fear for the national identity is, on the available evidence, a hallucination.

It can be argued, however, that even these, though powerfully felt, are not the point. And they may not be. In some ways, Euro-sceptics, especially at the lower end of print journalism, make the worst of the case by constantly harping on about them. The serious case, surely, is not about the survival of cricket versus *boules*, or even about the relative propensity of French and British dock-workers to take direct action against the travelling public, but about national control over big decisions. The European Union renders collective a decision-making process, in some areas, that was once exclusively national: and sometimes without the protection of a veto.

But this is where the anti-EU case begins to wobble, attacking the status quo but unable to mark out a foothold on a different sort of future. Lack of realism has been its problem throughout the history, and this continues. At every stage, those of the British who did not want 'Europe' to develop have predicted it would not: and in every case, except over the European Defence Community in the mid-1950s, they were wrong. False prophecy about EMU, the total improbability of it actually happening, was uttered with mandarin certainty by a variety of Cabinet ministers, right up to 1 May 1997.

Similar unrealism affected the main thrust of the sceptic attack on the way the EU actually functions. The European Court of Justice was a frequent target. During the later Tory years, ministers developed a deep-felt line that the Court should be brought to book. The 'repatriation' of its powers became a familiar theme of the then Home Secretary, Michael Howard. The proposition was discussed as though this was a matter for Britain alone, omitting to address the elementary fact that any body like the European Community or Union needed some mechanism for resolving disputes, and the further fact that one of the main beneficiaries of this arrangement was Britain. Since, from the start, it was one of Britain's distinctive peculiarities to observe Community rules, and the practice of many other members to evade them, the ECJ was not obviously an institution that operated against the British interest. Yet sceptics were enraged by its integrationist tendencies, when interpreting the treaties. So they seemed to think nothing of unilaterally demanding its reform, and overlooking the need to persuade not merely some but all member states of what they had in mind.

A deeper speculative fantasy came to pervade them, as the years went by. This was the belief that the European Union somehow did not constitute 'Europe'. There was a decent impulse behind such a conceit. Some Euro-sceptics, unwilling to be cast as xenophobes, desired to parade their international, and especially their European, credentials. 'I have always been a supporter of moves to greater co-operation in Europe,' wrote William Cash.[35] He spoke for many, aware of the pitfalls of simple nationalism. Tuscan home-ownership and gastronomic tastes were proofs, so they said, of a veritable lack of insularity. More seriously, the collaboration of free nation-states was what they said they had always favoured. The post-Cold War world, as many added, created an opportunity to expand the true dimensions of the European House, which the existing definition circumscribed. At its worst, some said, the single currency could lead to disintegration, if not war. They, the true Europeans, were here to prevent that happening.

The possible narrowness of 'Europe' was a legitimate concern. But the notion that the EU did not constitute 'Europe' was wishful thinking. The Union existed, the product of several decades' history. This history could not be undone. It had created, for better or for worse, the main framework within which the great majority of European nations wished to pursue their own development. EMU itself, problematic though it was, was backed by an enormous collective political will to make it work. For all the EU's frailties, there were far more countries wishing to join it than depart. In fact, with the possible exception of Denmark, none even thought about quitting. For some reason, all were content with the prospect that their economic decision-making would now partly become collective, and confident enough to stake their future on what could be made, for the betterment of things, out of the extraordinary experiment set in train by the Treaty of Rome. The European Union was, quite simply, the largest fact objectively existing across the terrain of the continent and its archipelago.

The discomfort that this engendered was displayed in the Conservative Party's debate. It was a very awkward fact to have to confront. The discussion, both before and after the 1997 election, thrashed about, pitching between horror, as most Tories now felt it, at the prospect of further European integration, and inarticulate timidity, as their leaders showed, before the task of defining an escape-route from this fate.

There were attempts. William Waldegrave, for seven years a Cabinet minister, made an ambitious one. Though a pro-Europe man, Waldegrave always had a certain scrupulousness about what this meant. Long before, as Edward Heath's political secretary, he was so disgusted by the dissembling and evasion he saw in the Yes side's preparations for the referendum that he withdrew his services for the duration of the campaign. But he belonged to the party's European wing, and never qualified as a term-of-art sceptic. While in office, however, he was privately thinking about ways of escape from the continental clutch, and preparing to recognize, he once told me, that claims for British global influence might have to be abandoned. The need for this influence, paramount possession of an old imperial power, was the case most pro-EU politicians made. Only through Europe, they said, could Britain count or, in the Heseltine formulation, 'win'. Waldegrave decided that counting might not matter. He set supreme store by what he thought could still be called the sovereign independent nation – despite the network of international obligations and uncontrollable pressures that binds every modern country within it. His plan, published after he lost his parliamentary seat, was for 'a sort of European Canada'. This way, Britain, having left the EU, could remain prosperous, in the shadow of a more powerful state: free of central economic control, yet benefiting from the proximity of a vast market. 'No more sitting at the top table any more,' Waldegrave ventured. 'No more punching above our weight.' After a decade or two, he blithely admitted, 'we would have as little say over what happened in our end of the continent as do the Canadians in theirs: not *no* say, but not much say'.[36] But we would not be under Brussels's thumb.

This was a very unTory attitude, challenging the party's age-old assumption that Britain must, above all, count. As such, it was far too painful for many Tories to think about. It also overlooked the influence Brussels still would have. Continuing free trade with the EU required submission to EU rules, while surrendering influence over how those rules were made. Norway, the model more commonly put up for emulation, was the proof of it. Though Norway wasn't in the EU, it was subject to all the laws in the EC treaties, through membership of the European Economic Area, the basis for its trading relationship. The entire apparatus of EU rules on immigration, transport, manufacture and trade in goods and services applies in Norway. Norway's courts and companies live under law as interpreted by the European Court in Luxembourg. This is the precondition for Norway's trade with the EU, unmediated, however, by the presence of any Norwegian ministers at the political table.

Still, the Waldegrave version had the merit of intellectual honesty. It went further than some of the earlier logicians, like Norman Lamont, who favoured permanent exclusion from EMU, while being unwilling to describe what would happen next in respect of membership of the EU. Even the most serious and deep-dyed of Euro-sceptics quailed before this task. Michael Portillo, like Waldegrave and Lamont, was also out of the Commons, and therefore, it might be felt, free to explore what had previously been unthinkable. In April 1998, he gave a serious speech, dissecting the dangers of a common European foreign policy, and calling for some 'honesty' in Britain. Honesty, he thought, had been most conspicuously lacking. 'If we adopted an honest policy from now on,' the former minister said, 'we could hope markedly to improve the esteem in which our partners hold us, and so increase our influence.'[37]

We would, however, still be partners. Portillo did not propose a British exit. Yet he said that 'we in Britain have in mind a completely different destination from that cherished by our partners', and attacked the failure of successive politicians to make that clear. Our willingness to criticize, but then acquiesce in, Europe's project 'makes us look ridiculous ... robs us of influence,' he said. It was, further, 'a myth that we can influence the development of Europe by being an enthusiastic participant in its future development' – the scornful opinion Portillo had always had of the Major–Hurd belief in a Europe that was 'moving our way'. Britain needed the 'courage to move against the throng', and should not fear to instruct Europe in the overriding virtue of liberal markets and sovereign nation-states. But, even in Portillo's view, it seemed that Britain should still be there. Some might say he revealed a lack of personal courage, or perhaps an access of private realism, by not being ready categorically to say otherwise.

If official Conservatism represented one pole of the British argument, it stood in deep, but suggestive, confusion. Waldegrave and Portillo defined the long-term problem, but left it unresolved. At the same time, the party leader, William Hague, teetered between rejecting EMU for five years or for ten, concluding with the longer period. Those in the party who thought a certain fluid agnosticism would be more prudent were, for the moment, routed. But, silently, they mattered. A part of Hague's dilemma was that, hardened sceptic though he was, he was also ambitious, and knew somewhere in his head that the business wing of the party had to be retained: something unlikely to be made easier if the euro happened, and did not fail to work, and young Mr Hague were still found sitting on the shore beneath the white cliffs of Dover declining to learn the lesson King Canute had vainly tried to teach.

Pending the divulgence of this moment, most sceptics were limited to making prophecies of doom. They said that EMU would not work. They went through the motions of adding that they hoped they were wrong. For the failure of EMU would certainly be a catastrophe for every economy in Europe. But, as politicians, they had vested much in being right. Their intellectual position left room for no other outcome than the collapse of the project. They needed EMU to fail. 'Its end will come,' Lamont intoned. There was certain to be 'a massive political crisis'. 'The people will kill the euro,' said his last, lapidary piece of wisdom before the die was cast.[38]

The impression one had of Conservatism summed up the image of another King, famously cavorting on the same outcrop of land. Here, surely, was an existential condition more like that of Lear, railing against unalterable Fate: aware of the tragedy of history that had brought Britain, at the hands not least of many of the Conservatives' own leaders, to a destiny which their inheritors now regretted – but could find no way to change.

As a model for a new government, this was not encouraging. Though politicians like Portillo and Waldegrave asked serious questions, their responses conformed with those of the rest of the sceptic school, and added up to a counsel of despair. The world they defended seemed, in the end, to be nostalgic and narrow: assailed by demons, racked by existential confusion. They were incapable of absorbing the possibility that 'Europe', by immensely strengthening the post-war local economies, might have been the making not the breaking of the nation-state in the modern world.[39] They could see no future good, of that or any other kind, in 'Europe'. All in all, by 1998, many had lost the faculty of rational detachment. Their opinions were strongly felt, but incoherent: sincere, but baffled: certain, yet unsure: speaking from the gut, but incapable of satisfactory engagement with the neurons in the head.

Behind their inchoate power, also, was a challengeable piety. 'The people', who Lamont thought would kill the euro, had played an important part in the sceptic demonology for many years. Indeed, mistrust of what the people would stand for ran through the history of both sides. It explained Macmillan's hesitations, as well as Heath's reluctance to explain the drama of the revolution he was proposing. Claims about what the people wanted had been the cat's-paw of every politician, assuring some, alarming others. Yet British public opinion about Europe was always hard to gauge reliably. It did not take 'Europe' for granted, as opinion did among the people of the original Six. It varied from age to age. If it revealed a consistent pattern, however, it was this one: that the people tended to go wherever they were led by the political class.

As a new political class settled in for a long innings, a significant question bonded the future to the past. It was the question that Tony Blair, if he wanted to lead from anywhere more fruitful than the edge of Europe, needed to address more urgently than any other. What was the real relationship between the voters, the politicians and Europe, and how could this be intensified, for the first time in twenty-five years, as a force for positive rather than negative developments?

The truth about opinion on Britain's Europe connection was that it ranged between fickle and indifferent. For example, there wasn't a single month, between September 1974 and November 1991, when it had higher saliency – mattered more – than prices or law-and-order or education, in the public mind.[40] As the Conservative blood-letting over Maastricht began to dominate the news, this changed a bit, though even then most of the bread-and-butter issues bothered people more. In the week when the political class, in the shape of the Major Government, came closest to collapsing in the wake of a Maastricht-based confidence motion in the Commons, unemployment, the NHS, law-and-order and the state of the economy were regarded as more important than the European issue.[41]

Against this background of relative indifference, the British could not be listed among the most consistently pro-Europe people. When asked specific questions, they have reflected the vagaries of the time. The European Commission maintains a 'Eurobarometer' of public opinion, inquiring into issues of the moment, which is published twice a year. Among the questions regularly asked is: Do you think the European

Community is a Good Thing, a Bad Thing, or Neither? In 1973, the year of entry, 31 per cent of the British said it was a Good Thing; in 1975, referendum year, 50 per cent; in 1981, the depth of the Thatcher winter, 21 per cent; in 1989, the penultimate Thatcher year, 52 per cent; in 1991, Major's first year, 57 per cent; in 1997, his last, 36 per cent.[42] So the picture changes, between pretty wide extremes. There doesn't always seem much rhyme or reason about it.

The same lack of steadiness emerges in answer to the opposite question, though perhaps, in this case, with an explanation that shows a growing awareness of practicalities. Asked, after ten years of membership of the Community, if Britain should withdraw, 42 per cent of people said yes. When the same question was asked after twenty years, the percentage for exit was down to 17.[43] Some might say, given the unrelenting barrage of hostility to Europe which the dominant political class delivered in this time, that it is surprising to find any serious percentage of the British still expressing positive opinions. But in 1991, even the unenthusiastic *Daily Mail* gave prominence to a poll it had commissioned, which found that 43 per cent favoured joining 'a federal Europe', with only 31 per cent against.[44]

As EMU approached, the percentages in favour, already unimpressive in several European countries, weakened. In Britain, announced as a non-candidate for entry, 61 per cent said in April 1998 that they would vote No in a referendum.[45] But the question could be differently asked, and get a different kind of answer. A MORI poll for the European Movement found that 57 per cent believed EMU membership 'could offer advantages, but Britain should only join when the economic conditions are right'. Seven out of ten people were also found to agree that Britain 'should support closer co-operation between the countries of Europe'.[46] Another trend also diminished the succour which sceptics could take from these surveys. It appeared that the pro-integrationists were generally younger and better educated than the antis. A MORI poll in June 1996 showed that pro-Europe feeling was ahead by 35 per cent in social class AB, the upper-income professionals, and by 30 per cent among voters aged between eighteen and thirty-four.[47]

The only safe conclusion to draw from the history of these surveys was that opinion was not settled. The propaganda of the deed was working. When asked, irrespective of their preferences, what they *expected* to happen, most people registered their belief that the European Union would become more important in their lives. This, they thought, was an inevitability. But the propaganda of the word, to explain and justify it, had hardly started. The question remained enmeshed in the damaging perception that it wasn't primarily the business of the people anyway: that Europe was owned, as it always had been, by the political class.

Such, indeed, had been its history. Escaping from this history, and rectifying the disastrous record of this class in this arena, was the best summation of the task Tony Blair had to undertake if he was to begin making good his desire to be a leader in Europe.

The British political class. These are the people this book has been about. And it is true enough that Europe has been their preoccupation, far more than the people's. Out of this grows the common depiction of 'Europe' as a conspiracy against the people, the most potently felt of the righteous arguments made against everything that has happened. The case is falser than its makers contend – yet also truer than those who resist it have ever been prepared to recognize.

The Euro-sceptics, who make this case, themselves belong to the political elite. They are of the class they criticize, and as vulnerable as their opponents to the charge that they speak from and about a private world. To a significant extent, their concerns are about that world rather than the wider world. They hate 'Brussels' not only because they don't like the decisions that are made there, but because the place supersedes *their* place, which is Westminster. The more honest of the sceptics are prepared to admit this. Portillo once conceded as much to me. The prospect of losing power makes occupancy of political position so much less attractive. There is a way of locating this argument on the high ground: by talking about the loss of national and parliamentary sovereignty, and the damage this does democracy. But the low ground is more important than is often admitted: the place where MPs posture and speechify, where national ministers like to think they are making big decisions: the playground from which the decision to join the European Union removed some favourite toys.

That is one reason why the issue has become most loudly owned by the chattering classes – but not just by one faction among them. The elitist disease, spreading through the hot-house of Westminster, affects all sides. The sceptic chatterers fear, as much as anything, their own diminishment, in the grand political role they probably once imagined it would be their life to play.

As a case against 'Europe', this is badly flawed. Even granting that politicians are entitled to the sensation of power, one cannot say that 'Brussels' has uniquely prevented modern Members of Parliament from enjoying it. All national parliaments, like all national governments, now live under a range of inhibitions. The power of markets, like the influences of intermeshing alliances, have cut them down over a long period. No land is an island, least of all this particular scepter'd isle and blessed plot, which was always global in its range and now depends on the Europe connection to protect what remains of its worldwide reach. But the reduction of Westminster's power and glory belongs to a wider trend, which has not happened by accident. Decentralizing government is supposed to be the acme of modernity, agreed on all sides. While Conservatives didn't agree with the Labour hand-over of regional power to Scotland, they defend subsidiarity as a principle. Under the Blair Government, starting with Scotland, it is happening. 'Europe' is but one of the agents draining the decisive life out of Westminster. Theoretically, Westminster will still be sovereign over Scotland, and retains the power to revoke devolution. In practice, such sovereignty is a chimera. It will not be exercisable. Power has gone, as it has also gone to the European Union. So railing against Europe on that account makes a seductive, but hardly a sufficient, case.

What we have here is more like another illusion – passionately felt, but remote from the facts. Just as it is doubtful whether Euro-scepticism has any special connection with some embittered, unrepresented, forcibly silent majority, so it is misleading to portray the spokesmen for this cause as protecting Britain against an onslaught uniquely threatening to the British national character, or the British sovereign Parliament, or both. What these people more exactly represent is the sceptic elite's collective inability to tolerate the notion that the future of Britain now depends on securing the agreement of politicians who come from other countries.

The British failure to absorb this, however, isn't only, or even mainly, their fault. Another elite has been part of the performance. More clearly than the sceptics', its record measures the scale of the task Blair took on when he vowed to move his leadership from the edge to the centre of Europe.

One of the most instructive talks I had, while probing around this subject, was with the former Dutch Prime Minister Ruud Lubbers. He said something I never forgot. Here he was, a modern leader of one of the founding Six, which was a country usually to be found among the most keenly integrationist, renowned for its European instincts, living proof that the smaller countries feel little need to be defensive about their nationalism, and have electorates who don't give a second thought to membership of the European Union. Yet it was Lubbers's opinion that none of this was immutable. 'If I and others went on television for a few nights, to make a case against the integration of Europe,' he told me, 'I think the Dutch people could easily turn round.'[48]

One way to read that is as proof that 'Europe' is indeed an elitist project. In the beginning, like all original ideas in democratic politics, it certainly was. Lubbers was saying that this, in a way, continues. 'It is a very difficult idea,' he said. 'You have to keep nurturing it, supporting it.' In other words, it remains an experiment. What began as a structure to rule out war continued, he implied, to be vulnerable to the human propensity for conflict. Nationalism remained a force, perhaps the strongest force among people who were given any encouragement to express it. The duty of the elite was to exercise their skill and wisdom against this force, as well as creating the political context that under-pinned the huge benefits Europe stood to gain, in the global context, from economic integration. While the EU had popular support – was part of the unquestioned order of things – this was still always contingent on leadership. If the elite gave up, the experiment would fail.

That certainly describes a project which can be defined, or stigma-tized, as the work of the political class. Such were the people – Monnet, Schuman, Spaak, Beyen – who thought it up: and equally the people – Pompidou, Schmidt, Mitterrand, Delors, Kohl – who applied the further impulses that made it live. The European Community was a heroic endeavour, undertaken against great odds, which built a record of assisting peace and prosperity among European nations that has not been surpassed. The political elite of the continent, though open to criticism for many false steps that had to be corrected, created an entity that justified their claim to leadership.

The British pro-Europe elite has more to answer for. Leave aside its collective lateness to get the point. Forget the recurrent theme of individual hesitation and serial apostasy. Consider only the scale of what it did, beside the puny skills it brought to the task of proclaiming what this meant.

One signal weakness was misrepresentation. It was as if the makers did not dare to tell the truth. Though Edward Heath showed the tenacity to do what had to be done, he could not liberate himself from the nation-state mythology to which his country was in thrall. Beginning with him, the idea that one of the virtues of the EEC lay in its dilution of national sovereignty could seldom be openly described. During the 1975 referendum, Heath spoke, quite reasonably, not only of 'extending

Britain's influence in the world', but also of the 'controlling interest' which membership of the Community would confer on this one country.[49] A version of this triumphalist philosophy always remained in currency. While no British leader could seriously talk for much longer about 'control', the sense of 'winning' a constant series of zero-sum games against partners who were really opponents continued to be the narrative-line of the story governments told. I have found no trace of any Prime Minister, from Heath to Blair, returning from an EU summit to report that he had supported, or else opposed, a decision solely because such a course was best for the future of 'Europe'.

Starting from such an attitude, the political class failed to convey, perhaps even to experience, a sense of idealism about the project. It has been an ineffective missionary for the change it brought about in 1973. This was true almost from the start. David Watt, reporting on the referendum campaign, detected little positive enthusiasm on either side. He found both the pros and the antis were essentially negative, worrying about the price of food or the effect on jobs. 'Idealism of any kind does not enter into the equation,' Watt wrote, 'and there is neither zest nor vision in most of what is being said on platforms up and down the country.'[50] True in 1975, this became more apparent in the decades following, when the sceptical tone of successive prime ministers helped to dampen such ardour as existed among the lower ranks.

In place of zeal came its natural opposite, complacency. The most corrupted trait I kept encountering was the sense, so prevalent among the Euro-elite, that having won the decision, they had won the argument. Many exhibited the unmistakable opinion not only that the battle was over but that the other side, however loud it shouted, had simply lost and should now shut up. The noisier the contest became during the early 1990s, the heavier the silent gloating that accompanied it, from the class that knew it commanded every operational forum from the ante-chambers of Whitehall to the board-rooms of big business, from Brussels committee-rooms where a thousand lobbyists thronged, to the outposts of the Commission whence arrived the subsidies that were, for many people up and down the land, the way they got to know most about the European Union.

'Europe' was extraordinarily bad at preaching its message. So were the politicians, designated, *ex officio*, to be its intermediaries. They talked, for the most part, to each other. Dank seminars for the enlightenment of the converted took precedence over effective proselytizing of unbelievers. Out of the back-streets of Westminster, from the offices of the

European Commission or the European Movement, came messages that reflected chronic uncertainty about how to deal with the British condition. In sum they rendered the pro-Europe side as cultish a faction as the sceptics: a private group, with the establishment behind it, baffled into near-obscurity by the belligerence of those whose weapon of choice was the Union Jack. So deep-seated was the British tradition of aggression towards Brussels that it cowed into calculating reticence even those whose entire purpose was to advance the opposite case.

In this climate, there were some severe derelictions. Consider one of them. A consistent weakness of the EU, as perceived by sympathizers as well as sceptics in the British Parliament, was the inadequate scrutiny of its decisions by democratic assemblies. This became a constant complaint, and it was justified. Westminster, in keeping with its claims to be a superior parliament to any other in the Community, made more effort than many, but this was still inconsequential. Commons sub-committees toiled over Brussels directives, but had meagre success in persuading Parliament as a whole to take their reporting seriously and still less in influencing the words that became Community law. This was a democratic affront, yet nobody did much about it. Nobody dared suggest that, if Parliament meant what it said about dictatorship from Brussels, it might itself sit a few more weeks of the year to ensure that the ministers who act as legislators in the Council are properly accountable to it: an example, perhaps, to less developed assemblies. That would not have been convenient to the executive. It could have been proposed by serious pro-Europeans, or, for that matter, by the Thatcher camp. But in those years ministers of neither stripe felt moved to do this.

The losers from this negligence were the citizens of Britain and, dare one say it, Europe. The underinvigilated network of national bureaucracies, together with the Commission, continued on its way. But the political losers in Britain were the Euro-elite. For a quarter-century, they were prime accomplices in the failure of 'Europe' to infuse itself into the democratic culture, preferring that it should be retained in the executive zone of private deal-making and unaccountable, invisible decisions, for fear of being exposed to the incessant hostilities of the other side.

As a result, the practical benefits of the Europe connection were, for most of this period, minimized. There were many areas where these existed – but often in the teeth of British politicians' resistance rather than with their creative support. The huge inward investment by car and electronics industries into Britain in the 1980s was a direct result of the European Union. Britain became the main access point for Asian businesses into the continental market. But the explanation for this was a matter of discomfort to the governing party. At the 1996 Conservative Party conference, the Scottish Secretary, Michael Forsyth, and the Welsh Secretary, William Hague, each recited his magnificent record in steering investment into his territory. But in neither case could they acknowledge, by even a word, the indispensability of Europe to this performance. The Union, though central to the lives of these ministers, was literally unmentionable, except perhaps as an expletive.

The omission went wider. European oversight was heavily responsible, for example, for cleaner water and beaches, and other bits of environmental progress. Yet most British ministers built a record of resisting rather than advancing it. It took its place in the expletive-driven world that passed for the British European debate, where the language of antagonism singularly failed to elicit a matching vocabulary of support. Likewise, over a far longer period, human rights in Britain were fortified by the European Convention on Human Rights, administered by a court and commission in Strasbourg. The Convention was actually a British creation of the post-war years, long predating the Treaty of Rome. But by the end of the Conservative years the very fact that it occasionally produced judgments overturning British practice was swept up into the tide of ministerial hostility to all things European, which the other wing of the political elite made only feeble efforts to challenge.

This was Blair's inheritance, as the first British Prime Minister elected on a ticket that said he was entirely comfortable to be a European. The aura of Euro-scepticism was still palpable, especially in the press. The sense of Britain being, among other things, a European country was not yet coursing strongly through the land. In many influential minds, the belief that the European Union would, for the indefinite future, be grappling with enormous problems still half effaced the belief that Britain must be centrally involved in addressing them. Escapism, combined with vilification, continued to lure a segment of the political class, pulling some of the intellectual and journalistic class behind them.

Blair started from a quite different position. He could look forward with some confidence to a decade of power, in which these national attitudes might be fundamentally altered. It would be a many-faceted task, turning round the accumulations of fifty years which successive leaders had always shrunk from addressing squarely. But, in the likely process, two broad elements were perhaps discernible.

The first was the work of persuasion. A government united in a

sense of Euro-realism would set about demystifying – better, disinflam-
ing – the question. The discourse would become sober, rather than
perpetually contentious. In place of a government that rejoiced in the
failures of 'Europe', and returned from every summit defiantly proclaiming that it had again been defeated by the mad continental integrationists, a new leadership began telling the country something it was actually
better pleased to hear. In due course, one might expect some explicit
statements that the EU brought advantages to Britain which did not
deserve the neurotic suspicion the people had long been taught to apply
to everything coming out of Brussels. This shift was unlikely to encompass visionary paeans of adulation for the great European Ideal – but
then, those had stopped being heard, anywhere in Europe, years ago.
The Blair approach would need, first, to carry him past the EMU
referendum which it was plainly his intention to conduct, if possible,
before the notes ands coins of euro-land came into circulation on 1
January 2002. But, even before that, the teaching process was gradually
beginning. It was already plausible to believe that, deprived at last of a
government it thought it could overturn, the Euro-sceptic minority was
being set back.

Whether this would soon create a sense of European community in
Britain was another matter. Truly European consciousness is an elusive
faculty on the off-shore island, and dependent on a popular involvement
that certainly hasn't been available by means of politics, though travel
and culture and the general first-hand experience of non-political Europe
have surely changed the national outlook: changed it, perhaps, closer to
the attitude Ernest Bevin articulated, but did nothing to bring about,
when he claimed that the object of his foreign policy was a world in
which he could 'go down to Victoria Station here, take a ticket, and go
where the hell I like without anybody pulling me up with a passport'.[51]

That was in 1945. Closing on 2000, the millennial leader spoke at
least for a frontier-free mentality, if not the abolition of passports. He
brought an end to defiance, as the leitmotif of Britain's self-image. A
master of public rhetoric, especially on the electronic media, Tony Blair
was unlikely to miss his opportunity to reposition the national mind,
and thereby permit a more angst-free contribution by Britain to the
great questions concerning the future of Europe: the enlargement of the
Union, its economic management, its political institutions: all in all, the
diversity it was prepared to tolerate within its integration, without
speeding its own dissolution.

Secondly, however, there were facts. The European Union existed. It had survived for many decades. Its leaders were determined that this should continue. It would be the context, the given reality, round which their other problems would revolve. It would set the terms on which these problems would have to be addressed. There wasn't any other way, they thought, to protect and advance their nation-states. That, as it turned out, was the way for Britain too.

This was not a new truth. The history suggested strongly that no alternative had existed for fifty years. But there was now a Prime Minister who did not fight it, and, untroubled by the demons of the past, prepared to align the island with its natural hinterland beyond.

Notes

1. Winston Churchill: Rule Britannia

1 Michael Charlton, *The Price of Victory* (BBC Publications, 1983), 12.
2 William Beveridge, *Pillars of Society* (1943), cited in Kenneth O. Morgan, *The People's Peace: British History, 1945–1989* (Oxford University Press, 1990), 3.
3 Herbert Read, *The English Vision* (1933), cited in David Gervais, *Literary Englands* (Cambridge University Press, 1993), 134.
4 In *Return to Bestwood*, cited in Gervais, *op. cit.*, 99.
5 The phrase is stolen from Freeman Dyson, *Weapons and Hope* (Harper & Row, 1984), 129.
6 George Orwell, *Homage to Catalonia* (1938).
7 George Orwell, *The Lion and the Unicorn* (1941).
8 George Orwell, *The English People* (1944).
9 *Saturday Evening Post*, February 1930.
10 John Colville, *The Fringes of Power: Downing Street Diaries, 1939–1955* (Hodder & Stoughton, 1985), 13 December 1940.
11 'Morning Thoughts': Notes on post-war security by the Prime Minister, 1 February 1943, appears as Appendix V in Michael Howard, *Grand Strategy*, iv (London, 1972), 637–9.
12 BBC Home Service broadcast, 23 March 1943.
13 See W. F. Kimball (ed.), *Churchill and Roosevelt: the complete correspondence* (Princeton University Press, 1984), ii, 222.
14 *Saturday Evening Post*, February 1930.
15 *Federal Union News*, 23 December 1939, cited in John Pinder, 'British Federalists 1940–47: from movement to stasis', a paper given to a conference of historians, Brussels, May 1993.
16 Altiero Spinelli, *Come ho tentato di diventare saggio: Io, Ulisse* (Bologna, 1984), 308.
17 Martin Gilbert, *Never Despair* (Minerva, 1988), 267.
18 See below, pp. 224ff.
19 Interview, Lord Hailsham, 12 January 1993.
20 Harold Macmillan, *Tides of Fortune, 1945–1955* (Macmillan, 1969), 175.
21 *Ibid.*, 217.
22 CAB 129/1 CP (45) 112.

23 Margaret Gowing, *Independence and Deterrence: Britain and atomic energy, 1945–52*, vol. i (Macmillan, 1974), 230.
24 *The Times*, 25 May 1945.
25 James Morris, *Farewell to Trumpets* (Penguin, 1979), 473.
26 Eisenhower Library, Ann Whitman Files, State Department dinner 12 April 1954.

2. Ernest Bevin: Great Brit

1 Quoted by Roy Jenkins, *Nine Men of Power* (1974), 75.
2 *Ibid.*
3 C. R. Attlee, *Labour's Peace Aims* (Labour Party, 1939), 13.
4 29 November 1945, quoted in Alan Bullock, *Ernest Bevin, Foreign Secretary* (Heinemann, 1983), 198.
5 FO 800/493, 5 May 1947, cited in Bullock, *ibid.*, 396.
6 Frank Roberts, in Michael Charlton, *The Price of Victory* (BBC Publications, 1983), 48.
7 Bullock, *op. cit.*, 857.
8 Cited in Charlton, *op. cit.*, 54.
9 Anthony Sampson, *Anatomy of Britain* (Hodder & Stoughton, 1962), 311.
10 FO 371/40741.
11 Anthony Adamthwaite, 'Britain and the World, 1945–49: the view from the Foreign Office', *International Affairs* (Spring, 1985).
12 Roger Bullen and M. E. Pelly (eds), *Documents on British Policy Overseas*, series ii, vol. i: *The Schuman Plan, the Council of Europe and Western Europe Integration, 1950–1952* (HMSO, 1986), No. 102.
13 Cited in Adamthwaite, *op. cit.*
14 FO 371/66546.
15 House of Commons, *Hansard*, 5 May 1948.
16 Charlton, *op. cit.*, 55.
17 FO 371/62732.
18 Charlton, *op cit.*, 59.
19 *Ibid.*, 74.
20 *Ibid.*, 72–3.
21 *Ibid.*, 70.
22 *Ibid.*, 71.
23 Richard Mayne and John Pinder, *Federal Union: the pioneers. A history of federal union* (Macmillan, 1990).
24 Walter Lippgens and Wilfried Loth (eds), *Documents on the History of European Integration*, vol. iii: *The Struggle for European Union by Political Parties and Pressure Groups in Western European Countries, 1945–1950* (de Gruyter, 1988), 698.

25 House of Commons, *Hansard*, 13 November 1950.

26 Ben Pimlott, *Hugh Dalton* (Jonathan Cape, 1985), 568. The friend who reported it was Nicholas Davenport.

27 To Christopher Mayhew, his junior minister: Charlton, *op. cit.*, 77.

28 *Daily Telegraph*, 9 September 1949.

29 Cited in Anthony Nutting, *Europe Will Not Wait* (Hollis & Carter, 1960), 25.

30 The initial circumstances of the Schuman Plan are especially illuminated in 1950 PRO documents: CE 2141, 2219, 2328, 2330, 2339, CAB 130/60, GEN 322/3; CAB 134/293.

31 Kenneth Younger, Diary, 14 May 1950, cited in Peter Hennessy, *Never Again: Britain, 1945–1951* (Jonathan Cape, 1992), 400.

32 Interview, Georges Berthoin, 1 July 1994.

33 Conservative Party conference, October 1993.

34 Karl-Gunther von Hase, spokesman, German Foreign Office, 1958–61, quoted in Charlton, *op. cit.*, 209.

35 Lord Gladwyn, *The Memoirs of Lord Gladwyn* (Weidenfeld & Nicolson, 1972), 176.

36 Younger, *op. cit.*, 14 May 1950.

37 Quoted in Charlton, *op. cit.*, 121.

38 *Ibid.*, 95.

39 Dean Acheson, *Present at the Creation* (Hamish Hamilton, 1969), 385.

40 Dean Acheson, *Sketches from Life of Men I Have Known* (Hamish Hamilton, 1961), 44.

41 Interview, Douglas Allen (Lord Croham), 27 May 1993.

42 Interview, Roger Makins (Lord Sherfield), 6 May 1993.

43 For the later passages of decision-making on the Schuman Plan, see 1950 PRO documents: CE 2342, 2376, 2468, 2470, 2526, 2568, 2569, 2615, 2659, 2772, 2773, CAB 129/40, CAB 134/293, CAB 128/17.

44 Bernard Donoughue and G. W. Jones, *Herbert Morrison: portrait of a politician* (Weidenfeld & Nicholson, 1973), 981.

45 House of Commons, *Hansard*, 26 June 1950.

46 Most eloquently by Edmund Dell in *The Schuman Plan and the British Abdication of Leadership In Europe* (Clarendon Press, 1995), a masterly history of the episode.

47 House of Commons, *Hansard*, 27 June 1950.

3. RUSSELL BRETHERTON: THE SACRIFICIAL AGENT

1 Anthony Nutting in Michael Charlton, *The Price of Victory* (BBC Publications, 1983), 169.

2 Robert Carr in *ibid.*, 157.

3 According to Roger Makins in *ibid.*, 151.
4 For detailed survey of the Fyfe–Eden conflict, see H. J. Yasamee, *Anthony Eden and Europe, November 1951* (Foreigh Office Historical Branch, Occasional Paper, 1987).
5 Paul-Henri Spaak, *The Continuing Battle* (Weidenfeld & Nicolson, 1971), 227.
6 FO 371/116040.
7 For Foreign Office reactions to Messina, see PRO documents FO 371/116038–40.
8 FO 371/116038.
9 Charlton, *op. cit.*, 194.
10 T 230/394, 18 June 1955, cited in Simon Burgess and Geoffrey Edwards, 'The Six Plus One: British policy-making and the question of European integration, 1955', *International Affairs* (Summer, 1988).
11 Charlton, *op. cit.*, 190.
12 For Whitehall debates over British response to Messina, see 1955 PRO documents: CAB 134/1026, CAB 129/76, CAB 128/29, T 230/394, FO 371/116042.
13 FO 371/116042.
14 CAB 128/29, 30 June 1955.
15 Charlton, *op. cit.*, 169.
16 Interview, Sir Roy Denman, 1 February 1994.
17 Charlton, *op. cit.*, 178.
18 Robert Rothschild, head of Spaak's Cabinet, in *ibid.*, 180.
19 CAB 134/1044, 1955.
20 CAB 134/1026, 1955.
21 Charlton, *op. cit.*, 184.
22 For Whitehall analysis and tactics re the Spaak committee, see 1955 PRO files: CAB 134/1044, CAB 134/889, T 232/433, T 234/181, FO 371/116045–8, FO 371/116054–5.
23 Sir Roy Denman (interview, 1 February 1994) gave me this account, which he had heard from a member of the French delegation, J.-F. Deniau.
24 Charlton, *op. cit.*, 188.
25 T 234/181, 1955.
26 Late November exchanges in FO 371/116056.
27 Interview, Lord Armstrong of Ilminster, 3 December 1993.
28 Charlton, *op. cit.*, 194.
29 BT 11/5402, 1955.
30 *Ibid.*

4. HAROLD MACMILLAN: AGONIZING FOR BRITAIN

1 There was a second treaty, signed on the same day, which set up the European Atomic Energy Authority, known as Euratom.
2 Interview, Sir Donald Maitland, 4 February 1993.
3 Interview, Sir Michael Palliser, 4 July 1993.
4 Lord Gladwyn, *The Memoirs of Lord Gladwyn* (Weidenfeld & Nicholson, 1972), 2.
5 Cited by Alan S. Milward, *The European Rescue of the Nation State* (Routledge, 1992), 128. Several statistics in this passage come from Milward's ground-breaking work.
6 Peter Oppenheimer, in Robert Skidelsky and Vernon Bogdanor (eds), *The Age of Affluence* (Macmillan, 1970), 146.
7 Interview, Roger Makins (Lord Sherfield), 6 May 1993.
8 Interview, Douglas Allen (Lord Croham), 27 May 1993.
9 Interview, Sir Roy Denman, 1 February 1994.
10 CAB 134/889 (1955).
11 Interview, Emile Noël, 28 October 1993.
12 *Ibid.*
13 Miriam Camps, *Britain and the European Community, 1955–63* (Oxford University Press, 1964), 77.
14 FO 371/124421, cited, along with several other documents in this passage, in James Ellison, *Harold Macmillan's Fear of 'Little Europe'* (Leicester University Press, 1995).
15 Keith Kyle, *Suez* (Weidenfeld & Nicolson, 1992), 556.
16 *Ibid.*, 464–5.
17 Roger Bullen and M. E. Pelly (eds), *Documents on British Policy Overseas*, series ii, vol. i: *The Schuman Plan, the Council of Europe and Western European Integration, 1950–1952* (HMSO, 1986), Nos 406, 424, 437.
18 Alistair Horne, *Macmillan, vol. i: 1891–1956* (Macmillan, 1988), 351.
19 John Colville, *The Fringes of Power: Downing Street diaries, 1939–1955.* (Hodder & Stoughton, 1985), 30 May 1952.
20 Sir Nicholas Henderson, speaking on *The Last Europeans*, Channel Four TV, 26 November 1996.
21 Cited in Ellison, *op. cit.*
22 PREM 11/2133, 18 April 1957.
23 PREM 11/2133, 15 July 1957, Macmillan to Thorneycroft.
24 Charles de Gaulle, *Memoirs of Hope* (Weidenfeld & Nicholson, 1971), 188.
25 PREM 11/2679, meeting at Chequers, 29 November 1959, cited in Milward, *op. cit.*, 432.
26 FO 371/150282.

27 CAB 130/173, CAB 134/1820, 1955.

28 CAB 129/102, 1955.

29 Michael Charlton, *The Price of Victory* (BBC Publications, 1983), 258.

30 FO 371/150369, 1955.

31 PREM 11/3325, 1961.

32 According to Georges Berthoin, chief representative of the ECSC in London at the time. (Interview 1 July 1994).

33 Camps, *op. cit.*, ch. 10.

34 *Ibid.*, 371.

35 FO 371/171449.

36 John Newhouse, *De Gaulle and the Anglo-Saxons* (André Deutsch, 1970), 211. Newhouse's brilliant book offers a very full account of the Rambouillet meeting, which appears to derive from close inspection of the official minute taken by the British.

37 See Camps, *op. cit.*; Charlton, *op. cit.*; Richard Lamb, *The Macmillan Years, 1957–1963* (John Murray, 1995); Alistair Horne, *Macmillan, vol. ii: 1957–1986* (Macmillan, 1989); and, interstitially, every political memoir and history of the Macmillan period. See also Nora Beloff, *The General Says No* (Penguin, 1963); Robert J. Lieber, *British Politics and European Unity* (Berkeley, 1970); J. W. Young, *Britain and European Unity, 1945–1992* (Macmillan, 1993); George Wilkes (ed.), *Britain's Failure to Enter the European Community, 1961–63* (Frank Cass, 1997). A monograph I found useful here: N. Piers Ludlow, 'A Mismanaged Application: Britain and EEC membership 1961–63' (paper presented to the European Liaison Committee of Historians, March 1996).

38 Interview, Sir Edward Heath, 8 February 1994.

39 Several figures in this passage are taken from a useful study: David Dutton, 'Anticipating Maastricht: the Conservative Party and Britain's first application to join the European Community', *Contemporary Record* (Winter 1993).

40 Rt Hon. Harold Macmillan MP, *Britain, the Commonwealth and Europe* (Conservative Political Centre, September 1962).

41 *Ibid.*, 6–7.

42 Interview, Sir Michael Butler, 30 January 1993.

43 Sir Edward Heath, speaking on *The Last Europeans*, 26 November 1995.

44 Interview, Maurice Couve de Murville, 30 June 1994.

45 FO 800/889, 1963.

5. HUGH GAITSKELL: PROGRESSIVELY BACKWARDS

1 R. H. S. Crossman, 'British Labour Looks at Europe', *Foreign Affairs* (July 1963).

2 Philip Williams, *Hugh Gaitskell* (Jonathan Cape, 1979), 702–49 contains many of the quotations that follow in this passage.
3 Roy Jenkins, *A Life at the Centre* (Macmillan, 1991), 145; Douglas Jay, *Change and Fortune* (Hutchinson, 1980), 282.
4 House of Commons, *Hansard*, 2 August 1961.
5 FO 371/150369.
6 Dennis Thompson, *The Rome Treaty and the Law* (*Crossbow* supplement, July–September 1962).
7 House of Commons, *Hansard*, 3 August 1961.
8 House of Commons, *Hansard*, 6 June 1962: which, along with the August 1961 debate, is the source of all the quotations in this passage.
9 Letter to Arthur Calwell, Australian Labour leader, August 1962, cited in Williams, *op. cit.*, 721.
10 The most easily available source for these is Philip Williams's biography, *op. cit.*, which uses them copiously.
11 Jay, *op. cit.*, 286.
12 Central Statistical Office, *Annual Abstract of Statistics 1965*.
13 See, notably, Jay's contribution to Brian Brivati and Harriet Jones (eds), *From Reconstruction to Integration: Britain and Europe since 1945* (Leicester University Press, 1993).
14 Harold Macmillan, House of Commons, *Hansard*, 2 August 1961.
15 Edward Heath, House of Commons, *Hansard*, 3 August 1961.
16 Kenneth Younger, 'Public Opinion and Foreign Policy', *International Affairs* (January 1964).
17 See Chapter 9.
18 See Douglas Brinkley, *Dean Acheson: the Cold War Years, 1953–71* (Yale University Press, 1992), 176–82, for the text of Acheson's speech and a helpful discussion of it.
19 Tony Benn, *Out of the Wilderness: diaries 1963–67* (Hutchinson, 1987), 20 February 1963.

6. JOHN ROBINSON: A CONSPIRACY OF LIKE-MINDED MEN

1 FO 371/171420, 8 February 1963, Robinson to Keeble.
2 Sir Con O'Neill, 'Report on the Negotiations for Entry into the European Community, June 1970–July 1972' (Foreign Office, unpublished, 1972).
3 Interview, Sir Roy Denman, 1 February 1994.
4 Interview, Sir David Hannay, 26 August 1994.
5 See above, p. 91.
6 Sir Michael Butler, *Europe: more than a continent* (William Heinemann, 1986), 4.

7 Interview, Sir Michael Palliser, 7 May 1993.

8 Leader, *The Times*, 15 May 1947.

9 Michael Charlton, *The Price of Victory* (BBC Publications, 1983), 105.

10 Interview, John Robinson, 20 August 1993.

11 See above, p. 41.

12 R.H.S. Crossman, 'British Labour Looks at Europe', *Foreign Affairs* (April 1963).

13 Noticed by Donald Sassoon, *One Hundred Years of Socialism* (I. B. Tauris, 1996), 237.

14 FO 371/182299.

15 FO 371/182377.

16 FO 371/188327.

17 FO 371/188328.

18 Cecil King, *The Cecil King Diary, 1965–70* (Jonathan Cape, 1972), 20 January 1966.

19 Reported by George Thomson, the minister sent to convey the news. See Philip Ziegler, *Wilson: the authorised life* (Weidenfeld & Nicolson, 1993), 331.

20 Douglas Jay, *Change and Fortune* (Hutchinson, 1980), 363.

21 Jay identifies these accurately: Denis Healey, Fred Peart, Herbert Bowden, Dick Marsh, William Ross, Barbara Castle, Anthony Greenwood and himself, with Jim Callaghan and Richard Crossman 'wobbling'.

22 Cited in Ziegler, *op. cit.*, 334.

23 FO 371/188346.

24 FO 371/188347.

25 Richard Crossman, *The Diaries of a Cabinet Minister*, ed. Janet Morgan, vol. ii (Hamish Hamilton and Jonathan Cape, 1976), 22 October 1966.

26 Harold Wilson, *The Labour Government, 1964–70: a personal record* (Weidenfeld & Nicolson, 1971), 327–44.

27 Lord Jenkins of Hillhead, speaking on *The Last Europeans*, Channel Four TV, 26 November 1995.

28 Jean-Jacques Servan-Schreiber, *Le Défi américain* (Paris: Denoel, 1967).

29 Jay, *op. cit.*, 363.

30 Ben Pimlott, *Harold Wilson* (HarperCollins, 1992), 439.

31 Interview, Sir Crispin Tickell, 19 January 1993.

32 Wilson, *op. cit.*, 341.

33 Ziegler, *op. cit.*, 335.

34 Cited in Elizabeth Barker, *Britain in a Divided Europe, 1945–70* (Weidenfeld & Nicholson, 1971).

35 Crossman, *Diaries*, vol. ii, 21 April 1967.

36 Ziegler, *op. cit.*, 335.

37 This episode, on 26 October 1967, became known as the Chalfont Affair,

and is well described by John Dickie, *Inside the Foreign Office* (Chapmans, 1992), 171–5.

38 George Thomson, 'The Labour Committee for Europe: a witness seminar', *Contemporary Record* (Autumn 1993), 393.

39 Sir Michael Palliser, cited in Ziegler, *op. cit.*, 332.

40 FO 371/188348.

41 George Brown, *In My Way* (Victor Gollancz, 1971), 131.

42 Apart from interviews with officials cited in the text, the published sources relied on here for the content of what de Gaulle said to Soames are: Jean Lacouture, *De Gaulle: the ruler, 1945–1970* (Harvill, 1991), 475–7, Dickie, *op. cit.*, 166–71, Wilson, *op. cit.*, 610–12.

43 Bernard Ledwidge, *De Gaulle* (Weidenfeld & Nicholson, 1982), 392–7. Ledwidge was the minister in the Paris embassy at the time.

44 Interview, Sir David Hannay, 24 August 1994.

45 King, *op. cit.*, 21 April 1969.

46 Interview, Sir Michael Palliser, 7 May 1993.

47 Lacouture, *op. cit.*, 477.

48 Jay, *op. cit.*, 433.

49 See above, p. 175.

50 Ziegler, *op. cit.*, 337.

51 George Thomson, 'The Labour Committee for Europe', 394.

7. EDWARD HEATH: THE TRIUMPH OF THE WILL

1 John Campbell, *Edward Heath* (Jonathan Cape, 1993), 5.

2 Edward Heath, *Travels* (Sidgwick & Jackson, 1977), 10.

3 *Ibid.*, 40.

4 *Ibid.*, 31.

5 *Ibid.*, 115.

6 Ben Pimlott, *Harold Wilson* (HarperCollins, 1992), 69–70.

7 Campbell, *op. cit.*, 65.

8 According to Sir Michael Butler, who was in the room (interview, 30 January 1993).

9 Much of it helpfully summarized, as well as added to, in George Wilkes (ed.), *Britain's Failure to Enter the European Community, 1961–63* (Frank Cass, 1997). See especially ch. 12.

10 Edward Heath, *Old World, New Horizons*, Godkin Lectures, delivered in March 1967 (Oxford University Press, 1970).

11 Henry Kissinger, *Years of Upheaval* (Weidenfeld & Nicolson, 1982), 141.

12 See House of Commons, *Hansard*, 16 November 1966.

13 Heath, *Old World*, 30.

14 Sir Con O'Neill, 'Report on the Negotiations for Entry into the European

Community' June 1970–July 1972' (Foreign Office, unpublished, 1972), ch. 34, para. 9.

15 Interview, John Robinson, 20 August 1993.

16 Interview, Lord Hunt of Tanworth, 13 January 1993.

17 Interview, Lord Croham, 27 May 1993.

18 O'Neill, *op. cit.*, ch. 36, para. 1.

19 *Ibid.*

20 *Ibid.*, ch. 4, para. 11.

21 *Ibid.*, para. 8.

22 *Ibid.*, para. 16.

23 *Ibid.*, ch. 7, para. 16.

24 See *ibid.*, annex 1, section B.

25 *Ibid.*, ch. 6, para. 4.

26 *Ibid.*, ch. 7, para. 10.

27 *Ibid.*, para. 11.

28 *Ibid.*, ch. 15, paras 15, 22.

29 *Ibid.*, ch. 14, paras 1, 4.

30 *Ibid.*, ch. 32, para. 16.

31 *Ibid.*, ch. 35, para. 3.

32 *Ibid.*, para. 20.

33 *Ibid.*, ch. 25, para. 2. This and the next two chapters discuss the fisheries question.

34 *Ibid.*, ch. 36, para. 4.

35 Interview, Maurice Couve de Murville, 30 June 1994.

36 Interview, Jean-René Bernard, 1 July 1994.

37 Interview, Emile van Lennep, 18 June 1993.

38 Roy Denman, *Missed Chances* (Cassell, 1996), 232.

39 Interview, Sir Michael Palliser, 9 July 1993.

40 Interview, Sir Edward Heath, 21 May 1994.

41 O'Neill, *op. cit.*, ch. 33, para. 15; ch. 32, para. 5.

42 Douglas Hurd, *An End to Promises* (Collins, 1979), 62.

43 O'Neill, *op. cit.*, ch. 7, para. 19.

44 Interview, Sir Edward Heath, 21 May 1994.

45 Heath, *Travels*, 5.

46 O'Neill, *op. cit.*, ch. 33, para. 17.

47 House of Commons, *Hansard*, 20 January 1971.

48 House of Lords, *Hansard*, 27 July 1971.

49 Speech to the British Chamber of Commerce, Paris, 6 May 1970.

50 Cited by Robert Shepherd, *Enoch Powell* (Hutchinson, 1996), 248. Several of the quotations that follow were first collected in Shepherd's valuable book.

51 See Nicholas Ridley MP, *Towards a Federal Europe* (European Forum, 1969), published text of a speech delivered at a European federalist conference.

52 Andrew Roth, *Enoch Powell* (Macdonald, 1970), 372.

53 *One Europe* (One Nation Group, 1965).

54 G. R. Urban, letter, *Sunday Telegraph*, 29 December 1991.

55 Shepherd, *op. cit.*, 248. The interview was conducted for a Channel Four TV programme, *What Has Become of Us*, screened November–December 1994.

56 See Chapter 9.

57 *The United Kingdom and the European Communities* (HMSO, July 1971), Cmnd 4715.

58 European Movement meeting, London, 7 May 1994.

59 Which they duly did, though only with categoric finality in 1989, in *R* v. *Secretary of State for Transport, ex parte Factortame Ltd*, 1990 ECR 1–2433.

60 Private information.

61 Franco-British Lecture, delivered at the Foreign Office, 15 October 1992.

62 Sir Edward Heath, interview for *The Last Europeans*, Channel Four TV, July 1995.

63 Case 26/62, *Van Gend en Loos* v. *Nederlandse Tariefcommissie* (1963) ECR 1.

64 House of Lords, *Hansard*, 2 August 1962.

65 Notably: 'Sovereignty and Interdependence: Britain's place in the world', the London School of Economics Alumni Lecture, 8 June 1990, published in *International Affairs* (October, 1990); and 'Euro-Justice: Yes or No?', a paper delivered at the Bar Conference, London, 30 September 1995, published in *European Law Review* (June 1996).

66 House of Commons, *Hansard*, 13 June 1972.

67 Private information.

68 *Bulmer* v. *Bollinger* [1974] 3 Weekly Law Reports 202.

69 See, notably, House of Commons, *Hansard*, 27 October 1971.

70 Sir Alec Douglas-Home, *Our European Destiny* (Conservative Group for Europe, July 1971).

71 House of Commons, *Hansard*, 21 October 1971.

72 House of Commons, *Hansard*, 27 October 1971.

73 I heard him say this in the Franco-British Lecture, *op. cit.*, and modified versions of it on several other occasions.

74 Interview, Lord Armstrong of Ilminster, 2 December 1993.

75 *Sunday Times*, 7 July 1996.

8. Roy Jenkins: The Fissile Effect

1 *The Times*, 30 November 1973.

2 The measurable Powell effect is helpfully discussed in Robert Shepherd, *Enoch Powell* (Hutchinson, 1996), 448–51.

3 Barbara Castle, interview for *The Last Europeans*, Channel Four TV, July 1995.

4 Roy Jenkins, *A Life at the Centre* (Macmillan, 1991), 104. Other references

in these paragraphs to Jenkins's early positions are drawn from the same source.

5 See above, pp. 41–3.
6 House of Commons, *Hansard*, 27 October 1971.
7 Bernard Donoughue, 'Renegotiation of EEC Terms: a witness account', in Brian Brivati and Harriet Jones (eds), *From Reconstruction to Integration: Britain and Europe since 1945* (Leicester University Press, 1993), 204.
8 See Chapter 12.
9 Jenkins, *op. cit.*, 323
10 'The Labour Committee for Europe: a witness seminar', 12 June 1990, *Contemporary Record* (Autumn 1993), 409.
11 *Ibid.*, 416.
12 There are six volumes, covering the years 1940–90.
13 House of Commons, *Hansard*, 8 May 1967.
14 These and many more are itemized in Denis Healey, *The Time of my Life* (Michael Joseph, 1989), 70–96.
15 *Ibid.*, 116.
16 Denis Healey, interview for *The Last Europeans*, June 1995.
17 House of Commons, *Hansard*, 21 October 1971.
18 Jenkins, *op. cit.*, 318.
19 Denis Healey, interview for *The Last Europeans*, June 1995.
20 Jenkins, *op. cit.*, 260.
21 Ben Pimlott, *Harold Wilson* (HarperCollins, 1992), 583.
22 Speech, Southampton, 25 May 1971.
23 Kenneth O. Morgan, *Callaghan: a life* (Oxford University Press, 1997), 395.
24 Jenkins, *op. cit.*, 320.
25 *Ibid*, 319.
26 Healey, *op. cit.*, 360.
27 Tony Benn, *Office without Power: diaries, 1968–72* (Hutchinson, 1988), 20 July 1971.
28 Edmund Burke, *Speeches at his Arrival in Bristol*, 3 November 1774.
29 Quoted in David Butler and Uwe Kitzinger, *The 1975 Referendum* (Macmillan, 2nd edn, 1996), 11, on which I have drawn for some other details in this chapter.
30 Jenkins, *op. cit.*, 343.
31 'Labour Committee for Europe', *op. cit.*, 397.
32 Private information.
33 Sir Michael Butler, speaking on *The Last Europeans*, 3 December 1995.
34 Jenkins, *op. cit.*, 389.
35 Sir Michael Butler, *Europe: more than a continent* (William Heinemann, 1986), 93.

36 Interview, Sir Michael Palliser, 3 September 1993.

37 Jenkins, *op. cit.*, 399.

38 Barbara Castle, *The Castle Diaries* 1964–70 (Weidenfeld & Nicolson, 1984), 19 March 1975.

39 Helmut Schmidt, speaking on *The Last Europeans*, 3 December 1995.

40 Castle, *op. cit.*, 26 April 1975.

41 Pimlott, *Harold Wilson*, 656.

42 Jenkins, *op. cit.*, 405.

43 Pimlott, *Harold Wilson*, 657.

44 Bernard Donoughue, *op. cit.*, 200. Donoughue, a key Wilson aide at the time, names the five as Merlyn Rees, John Morris, Fred Peart, Reg Prentice and Lord Shepherd.

45 Butler and Kitzinger, *op. cit.*, 32.

46 *Hansard*, 18 April 1975.

47 See F. Teer and J. D. Spence, *Political Opinion Polls* (Hutchinson, 1973), 108–19, from which several of these figures are taken. Also Butler and Kitzinger, *op. cit.*

48 According to MORI's monthly polls.

49 See Butler and Kitzinger, *op. cit.*, 228, 240.

50 *Sunday Times*, 27 April 1975.

51 Butler and Kitzinger, *op. cit.*, 256.

52 'The 1975 British Referendum on Europe: a witness seminar', 5 June 1995, *Contemporary British History* (Autumn 1996), 98.

53 This phenomenon is discussed at greater length in Chapter 10.

54 Lord Jenkins of Hillhead, interview for *The Last Europeans*, July 1995.

55 *Ibid.*

56 Teer and Spence, *op. cit.*, 118.

57 Recalled by Sir Patrick Nairne, 'The 1975 British Referendum', *op. cit.*.

58 Butler and Kitzinger, *op. cit.*, 273.

59 Jenkins, *op. cit.*, 399.

60 Donoughue, *op. cit.*, 205.

61 Jenkins, *op. cit.*, 442.

62 See above, p. 48.

63 Jenkins, *op. cit.*, 470.

64 *Ibid*, 477, which is part of a naturally positive history of the episode. For the fullest first-hand sceptical account, see Edmund Dell, 'Britain and the Origins of the European Monetary System', *Contemporary European History* (March, 1994), 1–60. Also see Healey, *op. cit.*, 438–40.

65 Dell, *op. cit.*, 4–5.

66 Valéry Giscard d'Estaing, the Ditchley Lecture, 1985.

67 His book, *European Diary, 1977–1981* (Collins, 1989), attests to this for nearly 700 pages.

68 David Owen, *Time to Declare* (Michael Joseph, 1991), 66.
69 *Ibid.*, 248.

9. MARGARET THATCHER: DEUTSCHLAND ÜBER ALLES

 1 Interview, Lord Armstrong of Ilminster, 2 December 1993.
 2 Margaret Thatcher, *The Path to Power* (HarperCollins, 1995), 26.
 3 *Ibid.*, 31.
 4 *Ibid.*, 126.
 5 *Ibid.*, 127.
 6 *Ibid.*, 207–11.
 7 *Ibid.*, 330–3.
 8 Sir Nicholas Henderson. The text is reproduced in Henderson, *Channels and Tunnels* (Weidenfeld & Nicolson, 1987), 143.
 9 Simon Harris and Tim Josling, 'A Preliminary Look at the UK Food Industry and the CAP', paper delivered at Agra Europe Conference, 20 April 1977.
10 Sir Con O'Neill, 'Report on the Negotiations for Entry into the European Community, June 1970–July 1972' (Foreign Office, unpublished, 1972), ch. 33, para. 19.
11 Interview, Sir Michael Palliser, 3 September 1993.
12 Sir Michael Butler, *Europe: more than a continent* (William Heinemann, 1986), 93–4.
13 Interview, Sir David Hancock, 26 February 1993.
14 David Owen, *Time to Declare* (Michael Joseph, 1991), 245–8.
15 *Ibid.*, 281.
16 Interview, Lord Hunt of Tanworth, 13 January 1993.
17 Ian Gilmour, *Dancing with Dogma* (Simon & Schuster, 1992), 238–41, gives a full account of the scene. Another colourful version of the early Thatcher approach to Europe appears in Roy Jenkins, *A Life at the Centre* (Macmillan, 1991), 491–508.
18 Interview, Sir Michael Butler, 30 January 1993.
19 Nine million écus (the EEC unit of currency), against the forecast 700 million. See Butler, *op. cit.*, 100.
20 Interview, Helmut Schmidt, 6 February 1985.
21 Sir Charles Powell, interview for *The Last Europeans*, Channel Four TV, July 1995.
22 Witnessed by David Marsh: see his book, *Germany and Europe: the crisis of unity* (William Heinemann, 1994), 44.
23 *Ibid.*, 45.
24 Adam Gopnik, *New Yorker*, 3 June 1996.
25 Claude Cheysson, speaking on *The Last Europeans*, 11 December 1995.

26 Cited by Andrew Moravcsik, 'Negotiating the Single European Act: national interests and conventional statecraft in the European Community', *International Organisation* (Winter 1991).

27 Speech to the Netherlands Government, 7 February 1984.

28 *Daily Express*, 4 June 1984.

29 Sir Robin Renwick, interview for *The Last Europeans*, July 1995.

30 Butler, *op. cit.*, 108.

31 Speech in Avignon, 30 November 1984.

32 Interview, Emile Noël, 29 October 1993.

33 Sir Robin Renwick, interview for *The Last Europeans*, July 1995.

34 Lord Howe of Aberavon, speaking on *The Last Europeans*, 11 December 1995.

35 See Charles Grant, *Delors: inside the house that Jacques built* (Nicholas Brealey, 1994), 66.

36 *Ibid.*, 77.

37 Margaret Thatcher, *The Downing Street Years* (HarperCollins, 1993), 547.

38 Michel Petite, an intimate of both men, quoted in Grant, *op. cit.*, 68.

39 Thatcher, *The Downing Street Years*, 548.

40 Quoted in Geoffrey Howe, *Conflict of Loyalty* (Macmillan, 1994), 409.

41 *Ibid*, 407.

42 Thatcher, *The Downing Street Years*, 549.

43 Howe, *op. cit.*, 409.

44 Interview, Sir Michael Butler, 30 January 1993.

45 For a careful assessment, see Moravcsik, *op. cit.*

46 House of Commons, *Hansard*, 23 April 1986.

47 See Chapter 11.

48 David Williamson, speaking on *The Last Europeans*, 11 December 1995.

49 Sir Michael Butler, speaking on *The Last Europeans*, 11 December 1995.

50 Howe, *op. cit.*, 454.

51 *Ibid.*, 307.

52 Thatcher, *The Downing Street Years*, 314.

53 Interview, Emile Noël, 29 October 1993.

54 Howe, *op. cit.*, 448. Nigel Lawson, *The View from No. 11* (Bantam Press, 1992) supplies rivetingly detailed accounts of every significant meeting, including all Europe-connected ones, he attended from 1983 to 1989.

55 Alan Walters, *Britain's Economic Renaissance* (Oxford University Press, 1986).

56 Lawson, *op. cit.*, 499.

57 Howe, *op. cit.*, 450.

58 See Philip Stephens, *Politics and the Pound* (Macmillan, 1996), 77.

59 Thatcher, *The Downing Street Years*, 740.

60 Grant, *op. cit.*, 121.

61 Speech to the European Parliament, 6 July 1988.

62 *Jimmy Young Programme*, BBC Radio 2, 27 July 1988.

63 Thatcher, *The Downing Street Years*, 743.

64 *Ibid.*

65 *Ibid.*, 744.

66 *Ibid.*, 746.

67 Howe, *op. cit.*, 538.

68 Speech at Chatham House, 25 January 1989.

69 Lawson, *op. cit.*, 916.

70 The arguments surrounding this are more fully chronicled in my book, *One of Us* (Macmillan, 1989), 554 ff. Lawson, *op. cit.*, 898–936, Howe, *op. cit.*, 566–84, and Thatcher, *op. cit.*, 688–752 are indispensable sources for the phase.

71 Interview with David Frost, 24 November 1993.

72 Howe, *op. cit.*, 582.

73 Thatcher, *The Path to Power*, 347.

74 From Teltschik's own memoirs, cited by Alan Watson, 'Thatcher and Kohl – old rivalries explained', in Martyn Bond, Julie Smith and William Wallace (eds), *Eminent Europeans: personalities who shaped contemporary Europe* (Greycoat Press, 1996), 266.

75 Thatcher, *The Downing Street Years*, 791.

76 David Marsh, *Financial Times*, 30 September 1989.

77 Letter, *Daily Telegraph*, 6 September 1989.

78 Karl-Gunther von Hase, cited by Watson, *op. cit.*, 267.

79 The academics were Fritz Stern and Gordon Craig, both US-based, along with Timothy Garton Ash, Norman Stone. Hugh Trevor-Roper and George R. Urban.

80 The complete agenda is printed in George R. Urban, *Diplomacy and Disillusion at the Court of Margaret Thatcher* (I. B. Tauris, 1996), 147–9.

81 *Ibid.*, 128.

82 Printed in the *Independent on Sunday*, 15 July 1990.

83 Urban, *op. cit.*, 153.

84 *Spectator*, 12 July 1990.

85 Thatcher, *The Downing Street Years*, 722.

86 *Ibid.*, 723.

87 See Stephens, *op. cit.*, 140–67 for the best account of these.

88 Douglas Hurd, Scottish Conservative Conference, 11 May 1990.

89 House of Commons, *Hansard*, 27 October 1997

90 House of Commons, *Hansard*, 30 October 1990.

91 Anthony Meyer, *Stand Up and Be Counted* (William Heinemann, 1990), 162.

92 Michael Heseltine, *The Challenge of Europe: can Britain win?* (Weidenfeld & Nicolson, 1989).

93 Thatcher, *The Downing Street Years*, 842.
94 Speech, to the Konrad Adenauer Stiftung, Bonn, 11 March 1990.

10. WILLIAM CASH: EUROPE MADE ME

1 Peter Walker, *Staying Power; an autobiography* (Bloomsbury, 1991), 30.
2 Uwe Kitzinger, *Diplomacy and Persuasion* (Thames & Hudson, 1973), 177.
3 Charles de Gaulle, *Memoirs of Hope* (Weidenfeld & Nicholson, 1971), 194.
4 John Biffen, *Political Office or Political Power?: six speeches* (Centre for Policy Studies, 1977).
5 *Observer*, 18 August 1996.
6 Letter, *Daily Telegraph*, 21 January 1997.
7 Anthony Seldon and Stuart Ball (eds), *Conservative Century* (Oxford University Press, 1994), 273.
8 Interview, William Cash, 27 January 1998.
9 William Cash, *Against a Federal Europe* (Duckworth, 1991), 3.
10 House of Commons, *Hansard*, 23 April 1986.
11 House of Commons, *Hansard*, 27 June 1986.
12 House of Commons, *Hansard*, 10 July 1986.
13 Recounted by Body in 'The 1975 British Referendum on Europe: a witness seminar', 5 June 1995, *Contemporary British History* (Autumn 1996), 93.
14 House of Commons, *Hansard*, 23 April 1986.
15 *The Times*, 18 February 1965.
16 *The Times*, 7 May 1996.
17 Max Beloff, *The Future of British Foreign Policy* (London, 1969).
18 House of Lords, *Hansard*, 27 April 1994.
19 Lord Beloff, *Britain and European Union* (Macmillan, 1996).
20 'The 1975 British Referendum on Europe', *op. cit.*, 96.
21 For an account of the Maastricht negotiation, see Chapter 11.
22 Speech at the Bertelsman Forum, Petersburg Hotel, 3 April 1992.
23 Cash, *op. cit.*, 68–83.
24 Chris R. Tame, *The Euro-Sceptical Directory* (Bruges Group, 1997) lists both the bodies and the people considered to have contributed helpful work to the cause.
25 Michael Spicer, *A Treaty Too Far: a new policy for Europe* (Fourth Estate 1992).
26 Interview, William Cash, 27 January 1998.
27 See Chapter 11.
28 For the best account of the parliamentary trials of Maastricht, see David Baker, Andrew Gamble and Steve Ludlam, 'The Parliamentary Siege of Maastricht 1993: Conservative divisions and British ratification', *Parliamentary Affairs* (January 1994).

29 'Backbench Conservative Attitudes to European Integration', *Political Quarterly* (April–June 1995).

30 John Biffen, speaking on *The Last Europeans*, Channel Four TV, 11 December 1995.

31 Sir Geoffrey Howe, 'Sovereignty and Interdependence: Britain's place in the world', the London School of Economics Alumni Lecture, 8 June 1990, published in *International Affairs* (October, 1990).

32 Cash, *op. cit.*, 40.

33 Andrew Roberts, *The Aaachen Memorandum* (Orion, 1996).

34 Speech to the Royal Society of St George, 1964: cited in Kenneth Baker (ed.), *The Faber Book of Conservatism* (Faber, 1993), 205.

35 Alan Clark, *Diaries* (Weidenfeld & Nicolson, 1993), 14 April 1987.

36 House of Lords, *Hansard*, 8 March 1995.

37 House of Commons, *Hansard*, 23 April 1996.

38 Aidan O'Neill, *Decisions of the ECJ and their Constitutional Implications* (Butterworths, 1994), 17. O'Neill offers an admirable analysis and discussion of these questions.

39 Michael Howard, speech, 18 May 1996.

40 *The Times*, 4 July 1994.

41 Spicer, *op. cit.*, 193.

42 William Cash, *Democracy in the European Community: arguments against federalism* (Bow Group, 1991).

43 See Michael Mertes, *Frankfurter Allgemeine Zeitung*, 19 September 1989.

44 Spicer, *op. cit.*, 198–200.

45 Norman Lamont, interview for *The Last Europeans*, July 1995.

46 Speech to the Selsdon Group, 11 October 1994, reprinted in Norman Lamont, *Sovereign Britain* (Duckworth, 1995).

47 Interview, Sir James Goldsmith, *Guardian*, 12 October 1996.

48 *The Trap* (Macmillan, 1994); *The Response* (Macmillan, 1995).

49 Examined by Denis McShane, 'The Altered Ego', *Guardian*, 4 July 1996.

50 Interview, Sir James Goldsmith, *Guardian*, 12 October 1996.

51 See Alistair McAlpine, *The Times*, 7 October 1997, for a heavily Goldsmithite account of this transaction.

52 John Curtice and Michael Steed, Appendix 2, in David Butler and Dennis Kavanagh (eds), *The British General Election of 1997* (Macmillan, 1997), 308.

53 David Nicholson, MP for Taunton, who subsequently lost his seat. *Daily Telegraph*, 15 June 1996.

54 Bill Cash MP and Iain Duncan Smith MP, *A Response to Chancellor Kohl* (The European Foundation, 1996).

55 Helmut Kohl, speech to the University of Louvain, 2 February 1996.

56 House of Commons, *Hansard*, 3 December 1997.

11. John Major: At the Heart of Darkness

1 Conversation at the Guildhall, London, when Chancellor Kohl was made an Honorary Freeman of the City, 18 February 1998.

2 Anthony Seldon, *Major: a political life* (Weidenfeld & Nicolson, 1997), 46.

3 Recalled by William Rees-Mogg, *The Times*, 5 August 1996.

4 Seldon, *op. cit.*, 88.

5 *Ibid.*, 95.

6 See Chapter 9, pp. 340ff.

7 Seldon, *op. cit.*, 110.

8 See Philip Stephens, *Politics and the Pound* (Macmillan, 1996), 151–3.

9 Margaret Thatcher, *The Downing Street Years* (HarperCollins, 1993), 721.

10 *Ibid.*, 724.

11 Interview, Douglas Hurd, 28 October 1996.

12 Andrew Marr, *Independent*, 23 April 1997.

13 Interview, John Major, 1 November 1993.

14 Speech to the Konrad Adenauer Stiftung, 11 March 1991.

15 Interview, Sarah Hogg, 24 October 1996.

16 See Sarah Hogg and Jonathan Hill, *Too Close to Call* (Little, Brown, 1995), 78.

17 Seldon, *op. cit.*, 167.

18 *Daily Telegraph*, 22 November 1995.

19 The best account I came across of the preliminaries to Maastricht appears in Charles Grant, *Delors: inside the house that Jacques built* (Nicholas Brealey, 1994), 181–210.

20 Interview, Douglas Hurd, 28 October 1996.

21 Hugo Young, 'The Last Tory?', *New Yorker*, 3 February 1997.

22 Both Lamont and Major spoke on *The Poisoned Chalice*, BBC TV, 30 May 1996.

23 Seldon, *op. cit.*, 247.

24 Interview, Ruud Lubbers, 22 October 1996.

25 *Daily Mail*, 12 December 1991.

26 *Ibid.*

27 *Daily Telegraph*, 11 December 1991.

28 *Daily Telegraph*, 12 December 1991.

29 *The Times*, 12 December 1991.

30 Speech to the European Policy Forum, 10 July 1992.

31 The most accessible account of the ERM crisis appears in Stephens, *op. cit.*, 193–260.

32 Interview, John Major, 25 November 1996.

33 Private meeting, 2 July 1996.

34 *Panorama*, BBC TV, 9 June 1997.

35 Seldon, *op. cit.*, 321.
36 Graham Paterson and Andrew Pierce, 'Can Major Take the Strain?', *The Times*, 21 October 1992.
37 Andrew Neil, *Full Disclosure* (Macmillan, 1996), 9.
38 House of Commons, *Hansard*, 9 June 1993.
39 See his speeches, gathered in *Sovereign Britain* (Duckworth, 1995).
40 Off-the-record remarks to Michael Brunson, Independent Television News, 23 July 1993.
41 *Economist*, 25 September 1993.
42 Seldon, *op. cit.*, 350.
43 *Sunday Telegraph*, 17 December 1995.
44 Douglas Hurd, speech to the European Union of Women, London, 30 June 1992.
45 Seldon, *op. cit.*, 454.
46 House of Commons, *Hansard*, 22 March 1994.
47 The two were John Gummer, Environment Secretary, and Gillian Shephard, Minister for Agriculture.
48 House of Commons, *Hansard*, 29 March 1994.
49 *Guardian*, 25 March 1994.
50 Interview in *Der Spiegel*, 25 April 1994.
51 Speech at Ellesmere Port, 31 May 1994.
52 Speech at Leiden, 7 September 1994.
53 The exception was in January 1986, when she thought her resignation might be compelled by the Commons over the Westland affair. But Neil Kinnock, the Labour leader, missed his chance.
54 Seldon, *op. cit.*, 578.
55 See above, p. 331.
56 House of Commons, *Hansard*, 20 March 1996.
57 Seldon, *op. cit.*, 642.
58 House of Commons, *Hansard*, 21 May 1996.
59 *ABC* (newspaper), Madrid, 20 June 1996.
60 William Rees-Mogg, *The Times*, 23 May 1995.
61 Press conference, 3 April 1996.
62 Interview, John Major, 25 November 1996, preparatory to a *New Yorker* profile (*op. cit.*).
63 John Major, House of Commons, *Hansard*, 23 January 1997.

12. Tony Blair: Leading from the Edge

1 See Chapter 8.
2 Tony Benn, *The End of an Era: diaries, 1980–90* (Hutchinson, 1992), 1 October 1980.

3 Ivor Crewe and Anthony King, *SDP – The Birth, Life and Death of the Social Democratic Party* (Oxford University Press, 1995), 43.

4 A useful summary of the Labour history is to be found in Kevin Featherstone, *Socialist Parties and European Integration: a comparative history* (Manchester University Press, 1988).

5 David Butler and Dennis Kavanagh, *The British General Election of 1983* (Macmillan, 1984), 143.

6 'New Deal for Europe', in James Curran (ed.), *The Future of the Left* (Polity/New Socialist Press, 1984).

7 Cited in Featherstone, *op. cit.*, 66, from House of Commons, *Hansard*, 23 April 1986.

8 Giles Radice, *Offshore: Britain and the European Idea* (I. B. Tauris, 1992), 167.

9 Benn, *op. cit.*, 9 March 1989.

10 John Rentoul, *Tony Blair* (Little, Brown, 1995), 14.

11 *Ibid.*, 83.

12 *South Bucks Observer*, 16 April 1982.

13 *Guardian*, 10 May 1982, cited, as are some other quotes, by Rentoul, *op. cit.*.

14 For example, see Rentoul, *op. cit.*, 72.

15 *Ibid.*, 135.

16 Notably on 4 May 1993, 6 December 1993, 15 June 1994, 3 November 1994, 30 January 1995, 20 February 1995, 16 June 1995, 15 July 1996, 8 May 1996.

17 Speech at Chatham House, London, 5 April 1995.

18 Speech to the Friedrich-Ebert Stiftung, Bonn, 30 May 1995.

19 These quotes come, first, from BBC TV, 27 September 1992, and second, from House of Commons, *Hansard*, 1 February 1993, both cited by Rentoul, *op. cit.*, 438.

20 House of Commons, *Hansard*, 1 March 1995.

21 *Financial Times*, 17 June 1997.

22 Speech to the European Socialists Congress, Malmö, 6 June 1997.

23 Dinner at the Chancellor's Residence, Bonn, 29 October 1997.

24 As note 18.

25 See above, pp. 359–61.

26 Timothy Garton Ash, 'Europe's Endangered Liberal Order', *Foreign Affairs* March–April 1998.

27 Tony Judt, *A Grand Illusion?: an essay on Europe* (Penguin, 1996).

28 Tony Judt, *New York Review of Books*, 11 July 1996.

29 The most extensive and narratively revealing, if embittered, case against EMU was made by a former EU official, Bernard Connolly, in *The Rotten Heart of Europe: the dirty war for Europe's money* (Faber, 1995).

30 *Antenne 2*, 14 December 1990. William Cash, *Against a Federal Europe* (Duckworth, 1991), 58.

31 *Marche du Siècle*, French television, 26 February 1992.

32 *Daily Telegraph*, 7 August 1996.

33 Ann Leslie, 'What the Murder of These Girls Tells Us about Corruption at the Heart of Europe', *Daily Mail*, 21 October 1996.

34 Linda Colley, *Britons* (Yale University Press, 1992), 374.

35 Cash, *op. cit.*, 3.

36 William Waldegrave, 'Freedom v Empire', *Daily Telegraph*, 24 November 1997.

37 Michael Portillo, lecture to the Windsor Leadership Trust, 16 April 1998.

38 Norman Lamont, 'The People Will Kill the Euro,' *Daily Telegraph*, 30 March 1998.

39 The thesis brilliantly worked out in Alan S. Milward, *The European Rescue of the Nation State* (Routledge, 1992).

40 MORI series, inquiring into 'the most important issue' and 'other important issues', 1974–1991.

41 MORI, week of 22–26 July 1993, testing 'important issues': Unemployment 66 per cent, NHS 32 per cent, Economy 31 per cent, Law-and-Order 24 per cent, Europe 19 per cent.

42 European Commission, *Eurobarometer*, Nos 31 and 32, 1989; No. 36, 1991; No. 47, 1997.

43 *British Social Attitudes*, 12th report, 1995–6 edn (Dartmouth Publishing, 1996).

44 ICM poll, *Daily Mail*, 26 June 1991.

45 *Guardian*/ICM poll, *Guardian*, 8 April 1998.

46 MORI poll for the European Movement, published 16 February 1998.

47 Reported in the *Guardian*, 21 June 1996.

48 Interview, Ruud Lubbers, 22 October 1996.

49 *Financial Times*, 30 May 1975, in David Watt, *The Inquiring Eye* (Penguin, 1988), 62.

50 *Ibid.*

51 See above, page 29.

Bibliography

There is an immense literature bearing on the British relationship with Europe, and I make no pretence here to list it. Some of the academic papers and books I cite in the Notes contain several pages of references to other academic works, in several European languages. These are the works I have found helpful, or have in some way drawn on.

Noel Annan, *Our Age* (Fontana, 1990).

Timothy Bainbridge with Anthony Teasdale, *The Penguin Companion to European Union* (Penguin, 1996).

Kenneth Baker (ed.), *The Faber Book of Conservatism* (Faber, 1993).

George W. Ball, *The Past Has Another Pattern* (New York: W. W. Norton, 1982).

Elizabeth Barker, *Britain in a Divided Europe, 1945–70* (Weidenfeld & Nicolson, 1971).

Correlli Barnett, *The Audit of War* (Macmillan, 1986).

Lionel Bell, *The Throw that Failed* (Lionel Bell, 1995).

Lord Beloff, *Britain and European Union* (Macmillan, 1996).

Max Beloff, *The Future of British Foreign Policy* (London, 1969).

Nora Beloff, *The General Says No* (Penguin, 1963).

Tony Benn, *Out of the Wilderness: diaries, 1963–67* (Hutchinson, 1988).

Tony Benn, *Office without Power: diaries, 1968–72* (Hutchinson, 1988).

Tony Benn, *Against the Tide: diaries, 1973–76* (Hutchinson, 1989).

Tony Benn, *The End of an Era: diaries, 1980–90* (Hutchinson, 1992).

Martyn Bond, Julie Smith and William Wallace (eds), *Eminent Europeans: personalities who shaped contemporary Europe* (Greycoat Press, 1996).

Douglas Brinkley, *Dean Acheson: the Cold War years, 1953–71* (Yale University Press, 1992).

Leon Brittan, *Europe: the Europe we need* (Hamish Hamilton, 1994).

Brian Brivati and Harriet Jones (eds), *From Reconstruction to Integration: Britain and Europe since 1945* (Leicester University Press, 1993).

George Brown, *In my Way* (Victor Gollancz, 1971).

Tom Buchanan and Martin Conway (eds), *Political Catholicism in Europe, 1918–1965* (Oxford University Press, 1996).

Roger Bullen and M. E. Pelly (eds), *Documents on British Policy Overseas*, series ii, vol. i: *The Schuman Plan, the Council of Europe and Western European Integration, 1950–1952* (HMSO, 1986).

Alan Bullock, *Ernest Bevin*, 3 vols (Heinemann, 1960–83).

David Butler and Dennis Kavanagh (eds), *The British General Election of 1983* (Macmillan, 1984).

David Butler and Dennis Kavanagh (eds) *The British General Election of 1997* (Macmillan, 1997).

David Butler and Uwe Kitzinger, *The 1975 Referendum* (Macmillan, 2nd edn, 1996).

David Butler and Martin Westlake, *British Politics and European Elections, 1994* (Macmillan, St Martin's Press, 1995).

Sir Michael Butler, *Europe: more than a continent* (William Heinemann, 1986).

John Campbell, *Edward Heath* (Jonathan Cape, 1993).

Miriam Camps, *Britain and the European Community, 1955–63* (Oxford University Press, 1964).

William Cash, *Against a Federal Europe* (Duckworth, 1991).

Barbara Castle, *The Castle Diaries, 1964–70* (Weidenfeld & Nicolson, 1984).

Michael Charlton, *The Price of Victory* (BBC Publications, 1983).

Alan Clark, *Diaries* (Weidenfeld & Nicolson, 1993).

Lord Cockfield, *The European Union: creating the single market* (Wiley Chancery Law, 1994).

Linda Colley, *Britons* (Yale University Press, 1992).

John Colville, *The Fringes of Power: Downing Street Diaries, 1939–1955* (Hodder & Stoughton, 1985).

Bernard Connolly, *The Rotten Heart of Europe: the dirty war for Europe's money* (Faber, 1995).

Ivor Crewe and Anthony King, *SDP – The Birth, Life and Death of the Social Democratic Party* (Oxford University Press, 1995).

Richard Crossman, *The Diaries of a Cabinet Minister*, ed. Janet Morgan, vol. ii (Hamish Hamilton and Jonathan Cape, 1976).

James Curran (ed.), *The Future of the Left* (Polity/New Socialist Press, 1984).

Alex Danchev, *Oliver Franks, Founding Father* (Oxford University Press, 1993).

Edmund Dell, *The Schuman Plan and the British Abdication of Leadership in Europe* (Clarendon Press, 1995).

Roy Denman, *Missed Chances* (Cassell, 1996).

John Dickie, *Inside the Foreign Office* (Chapmans, 1992).

Bernard Donoughue and G. W. Jones, *Herbert Morrison: portrait of a politician* (Weidenfeld & Nicholson, 1973).

François Duchène, *Jean Monnet: the first statesman of interdependence* (W. W. Norton, 1994).

James Ellison, *Harold Macmillan's Fear of 'Little Europe'* (Leicester University Press, 1995).

Kevin Featherstone, *Socialist Parties and European Integration: a comparative history* (Manchester University Press, 1988).

Charles de Gaulle, *Memoirs of Hope* (Weidenfeld & Nicholson, 1971).

Stephen George, *Britain and European Co-operation since 1945* (Basil Blackwell, 1992).

Martin Gilbert, *Never Despair* (Minerva, 1988).

Ian Gilmour, *Dancing with Dogma* (Simon & Schuster, 1992).

Lord Gladwyn, *The Memoirs of Lord Gladwyn* (Weidenfeld & Nicholson, 1972).

James Goldsmith, *The Response* (Macmillan, 1995).

James Goldsmith, *The Trap* (Macmillan, 1994).

Margaret Gowing, *Independence and Deterrence: Britain and atomic energy, 1945–52*, vol. i (Macmillan, 1974).

Charles Grant, *Delors: inside the house that Jacques built* (Nicholas Brealey, 1994).

John Gunther, *Inside Europe* (Harper & Brothers, 1936).

Denis Healey, *The Time of my Life* (Michael Joseph, 1989).

Edward Heath, *Old World, New Horizons* (Oxford University Press, 1970).

Edward Heath, *Travels* (Sidgwick & Jackson, 1977).

Nicholas Henderson, *Channels and Tunnels* (Weidenfeld & Nicolson, 1987).

Peter Hennessy, *Never Again: Britain, 1945–1951* (Jonathan Cape, 1992).

Michael Heseltine, *The Challenge of Europe: can Britain win?* (Weidenfeld & Nicolson, 1989).

Sarah Hogg and Jonathan Hill, *Too Close to Call* (Little, Brown, 1995).

Martin Holmes (ed.), *The Eurosceptical Reader* (Macmillan, 1996).

Alistair Horne, *Macmillan, vol. i: 1894–1956* (Macmillan, 1988).

Alistair Horne, *Macmillan, vol. ii: 1957–1986* (Macmillan, 1989).

Geoffrey Howe, *Conflict of Loyalty* (Macmillan, 1994).

Douglas Hurd, *An End to Promises* (Collins, 1979).

Douglas Jay, *Change and Fortune* (Hutchinson, 1980).

Roy Jenkins, *European Diary, 1977–1981* (Collins, 1989).

Roy Jenkins, *A Life at the Centre* (Macmillan, 1991).

Roy Jenkins, *Nine Men of Power* (Hamish Hamilton, 1974).

Christopher Johnson, *In with the Euro, Out with the Pound: the single currency for Britain* (Penguin, 1996).

Tony Judt, *A Grand Illusion?: an essay on Europe* (Penguin, 1996).

Paul Kennedy, *The Rise and Fall of the Great Powers* (Vintage Books, 1989).

Cecil King, *The Cecil King Diary, 1965–70* (Jonathan Cape, 1972).

Henry Kissinger, *Years of Upheaval* (Weidenfeld & Nicolson, 1982).

Uwe Kitzinger, *Diplomacy and Persuasion* (Thames & Hudson, 1973).

Uwe Kitzinger, *The Second Try: Labour and the EEC* (Pergamon Press, 1968).

Keith Kyle, *Suez* (Weidenfeld & Nicolson, 1992).

Jean Lacouture, *De Gaulle: the ruler, 1945–1970* (Harvill, 1991).

Richard Lamb, *The Macmillan Years, 1957–1963* (John Murray, 1995).

Norman Lamont, *Sovereign Britain* (Duckworth, 1995).

Nigel Lawson, *The View from No. 11* (Bantam Press, 1992).

Bernard Ledwidge, *De Gaulle* (Weidenfeld & Nicholson, 1982).

Robert J. Lieber, *British Politics and European Unity* (Berkeley, 1970).

Harold Macmillan, *Tides of Fortune, 1945–1955* (Macmillan, 1969).

Donald Maitland, *Diverse Times, Sundry Places* (Alpha Press, 1996).

David Marsh, *Germany and Europe: the crisis of unity* (William Heinemann, 1994).

Richard Mayne and John Pinder, *Federal Union: the pioneers. A history of federal union* (Macmillan, 1990).

Anthony Meyer, *Stand Up and Be Counted* (William Heinemann, 1990).

Alan S. Milward, *The European Rescue of the Nation State* (Routledge, 1992).

Jean Monnet, *Memoirs* (Collins, 1978).

Kenneth O. Morgan, *Callaghan: a life* (Oxford University Press, 1997).

Kenneth O. Morgan, *The People's Peace: British History, 1945–1989* (Oxford University Press, 1990).

James Morris, *Farewell to Trumpets* (Penguin, 1979).

John Newhouse, *Europe Adrift* (Pantheon Books, 1997).

Jim Northcott, *The Future of Britain and Europe* (PSI Publishing, 1995).

Anthony Nutting, *Europe Will Not Wait* (Hollis & Carter, 1960).

Aidan O'Neill, *Decisions of the ECJ and their Constitutional Implications* (Butterworths, 1994).

George Orwell, *The English People* (London, 1994).

George Orwell, *Homage to Catalonia* (London, 1938).

George Orwell, *The Lion and the Unicorn* (London, 1941).

David Owen, *Time to Declare* (Michael Joseph, 1991).

Peter Paterson, *Tired and Emotional: the Life of Lord George Brown* (Chatto & Windus, 1993).

Ben Pimlott, *Harold Wilson* (HarperCollins, 1992).

Ben Pimlott, *Hugh Dalton* (Jonathan Cape, 1985).

Giles Radice, *Offshore: Britain and the European idea* (I. B. Tauris, 1992).

John Rentoul, *Tony Blair* (Little, Brown, 1995).

Nicholas Ridley, *My Style of Government* (Hutchinson, 1991).

Andrew Roth, *Enoch Powell* (Macdonald, 1970).

Anthony Sampson, *Anatomy of Britain* (Hodder & Stoughton, 1962).

Donald Sassoon, *One Hundred Years of Socialism* (I. B. Tauris, 1996).

Anthony Seldon, *Major: a political life* (Weidenfeld & Nicolson, 1997).

Anthony Seldon and Stuart Ball (eds), *Conservative Century* (Oxford University Press, 1994).

Jean-Jacques Servan-Schreiber, *Le Défi Américain* (Paris: Denoel, 1967).

Robert Shepherd, *Enoch Powell* (Hutchinson, 1996).

Robert Skidelsky and Vernon Bogdanor (eds), *The Age of Affluence* (Macmillan, 1970).

Paul-Henri Spaak, *The Continuing Battle* (Weidenfeld & Nicolson, 1971).

Michael Spicer, *A Treaty Too Far: a new policy for Europe* (Fourth Estate, 1992).

Dirk Spierenburg and Raymond Poiderin, *The History of the High Authority of the European Coal and Steel Community* (Weidenfeld & Nicolson, 1994).

Philip Stephens, *Politics and the Pound* (Macmillan, 1996).

F. Teer and J. D. Spence, *Political Opinion Polls* (Hutchinson, 1973).

Margaret Thatcher, *The Downing Street Years* (HarperCollins, 1993).

Margaret Thatcher, *The Path to Power* (HarperCollins, 1995).

Hugh Thomas, *Ever Closer Union: Britain's destiny in Europe* (Hutchinson, 1991).

Christopher Tugendhat, *Making Sense of Europe* (Viking, 1986).

George Urban, *Diplomacy and Disillusion at the Court of Margaret Thatcher* (I. B. Tauris, 1996).

Peter Walker, *Staying Power: an autobiography* (Bloomsbury, 1991).

Alan Walters, *Britain's Economic Renaissance* (Oxford University Press, 1986).

David Watt, *The Inquiring Eye* (Penguin, 1988).

George Wilkes (ed.), *Britain's Failure to Enter the European Community 1961–63* (Frank Cass, 1997).

Philip Williams, *Hugh Gaitskell* (Cape, 1979).

Harold Wilson, *The Labour Government, 1964–70: a personal record* (Weidenfeld & Nicolson, 1971).

Hugo Young, *One of Us* (Macmillan, 1989).

J. W. Young, *Britain and European Unity, 1945–1992* (Macmillan, 1993).

Philip Ziegler, *Wilson: the authorised life* (Weidenfeld & Nicolson, 1993).

Index